CANTONESE
Practical Dictionary

Cantonese-English
English-Cantonese

Hippocrene Books, Inc.
New York

Copyright © 2014 Hippocrene Books, Inc.

For information, address:
HIPPOCRENE BOOKS, INC.
171 Madison Ave.
New York, NY 10016
www.hippocrenebooks.com

FSC
www.fsc.org
MIX
Paper from
responsible sources
FSC® C011935

Library of Congress Cataloging-in-Publication Data

Cantonese-English/English-Cantonese practical dictionary /
  by Editors at Hippocrene Books.
     pages cm.
  ISBN 978-0-7818-1312-9 (pbk.) -- ISBN 0-7818-1312-3 (pbk.)
  1. Cantonese dialects--Dictionaries--English. 2. English
language--Dictionaries--Cantonese dialects. I. Hippocrene
Books (Firm)
  PL1736.C38 2013
  495.17'95127--dc23

                                              2013027066

Printed in the United States of America.

CONTENTS

ABBREVIATIONS

abbr.	abbreviation
adj.	adjective
adv.	adverb
aux.	auxiliary
comp.	computers
conj.	conjunction
det.	determiner
exclam.	exclamation
indef. art.	indefinite article
n.	noun
num.	number
phr.	phrase
pl.	plural
prep.	preposition
sing.	singular
smb.	somebody
smn.	someone
sth.	something
tech.	technical
v.	verb

INTRODUCTION

The Cantonese language, also known as Yue, can be dated back more than 2,000 years to the conquest of the native regions of southern China by northern armies, which led to a fusion of language and culture.

Today, Cantonese is one of the two official languages in Hong Kong and Macau and is also spoken in the southern area of Mainland China (Guangdong and Guangxi Province), and in Chinese communities in Indonesia, Vietnam, Malaysia, the United States, and the United Kingdom. Because of the different social systems of the countries and localities where Cantonese is spoken, it is common for its vocabulary and grammar to differ slightly from place to place.

Cantonese is unique among Chinese dialects in having its own writing system. Though written Cantonese shares many characters with written Mandarin Chinese, it follows rules of Cantonese grammar and makes use of many characters that are uncommon to, or completely alien to, written Mandarin Chinese. The widespread use of written Cantonese side-by-side with, or even in place of, written Mandarin is also unique to Cantonese-speaking regions——newspapers, signs, and even books of poetry written solely in Cantonese can be commonly found across Hong Kong and Macau. This dictionary adopts the standard Cantonese writing system found in Hong Kong for transcribing the words and phrases found within. Words in the Cantonese-English Dictionary section are listed in alphabetical order by the transliteration.

PRONUNCIATION GUIDE

Cantonese has five major Romanization systems, each with its own advantages and drawbacks. This book employs the most widely used system of the five—Yale Number Romanization. The sounds in the Yale system are meant to closely approximate English pronunciations: to make them, read the transcribed words much as you might in English.

The Cantonese **consonants** are:

b, p, m, f, d, t, n, l, g, k, h, ng, z, c, s, j, gw, kw

The Cantonese **vowels** are:

aa, aai, aau, aam, aan, aang, aap, aat, aak, ai, au, am, an, ang, ap, at, ak, e, ei, eng, ek, i, iu, im, in, ing, ip, it, ik, o, oi, ou, on, ong, ot, ok, u, ui, un, ung, ut, uk, oe, eoi, eon, oeng, eot, oek, yu, yun, yut, m, ng

Cantonese, like all Chinese dialects, is tonal. Under the Yale system, the tones are marked out by a number that immediately follows the Latin transcription of a character's pronunciation. Though Cantonese technically has only six tones, the Yale system uses tone numbers 7, 8, and 9 to distinguish three special tones that end in glottal stops (with a *-p*, *-t*, or *-k* sound). To make these tones, pronounce them much as you normally would, but cut the tone suddenly short, at the end.

The **tones** are as follows:

1, 7 is a high steady tone
2 is a high falling tone
3, 8 is a high rising tone
4 is a low falling tone
5 is a low rising tone
6, 9 is a low steady tone

PERSONAL PRONOUNS

The personal pronouns in Cantonese are:

Cantonese	English
我 [ngo5]	I
你 [neì5]	you
佢 [keuí5]	he/she
我哋 [ngo5 deì6]	we
你哋 [nei5 deì6]	you
佢哋 [keuí5 deì6]	they
我嘅 [ngo5 ge3]	mine
你嘅 [neì5 ge3]	yours
佢嘅 [keuí5 ge3]	his/hers
我哋嘅 [ngo5 deì6 ge3]	ours
你哋嘅 [neì5 deì6 ge3]	yours
佢哋嘅 [keuí5 deì6 ge3]	theirs

When the possessive pronouns are followed with nouns, 嘅 [ge3] should be omitted.

The structure of possessives with a noun should be:
        subject + quantifier + subject

我部電腦
[ngo5 bou6 din6 nou5]
my computer

佢媽咪
[keuì5 ma1 mi3]
his/her mother

你個女朋友
[keuì5 go5 neui5 pang4 yau5]
your girlfriend

QUANTIFIERS

The usage of distinct noun quantifiers can be difficult for non-Cantonese speakers, as pairing the appropriate quantifier (also called a "counting word") is often possible only with memorization. Fortunately, in Cantonese, the quantifiers 個 [go3] and 隻 [jek8] can be used for the majority of the objects and are easily understood by native Cantonese speakers, if you are uncertain of the right quantifier to use.

Some examples of different Cantonese quantifiers:

1. For humans, use 個 [go3]. When you emphasize the occupation of the person, use 名 [ming4].

一個人　　one person
[yat7 go3 yan4]

一名老師　one teacher
[yat7 ming4 lou5 si1]

2. For animals, use 隻 [jek8] or 條 [tiu4].

一隻蚊　　one mosquito
[yat7 jek8 man1]

一條魚　　one fish
[yat7 tiu4 yu4]

3. For plants, use 棵 [po1].

一棵樹　　one tree
[yat7 po1 syu6]

一棵草　　one grass
[yat7 po1 chou2]

4. For flowers and leaves, use 朵 [do2] or 塊 [faai3].

一朵花   one flower
[yat 7 do2 ta1]

一塊葉   one leaf
[yat7 faai3 yip9]

5. For books, use 本 [bun2].

一本書   one book
[yat7 bun2 syu1]

一本筆記   one notebook
[yat7 bun2 bat7 gei3]

6. For modes of transportation, use 架 [ga2].

一架單車   one bicycle
[yat7 ga2 daan1 che1]

一架飛機   one plane
[yat7 ga2 tei1 gei1]

7. For stationery and electronics, use 支 [ji1] or 部 [toi4].

一支筆   one pen
[yat7 ji1 bat7]

一部電腦   one computer
[yat7 bou6 din6 nou5]

8. For tools, use 把 [ba2].

一把刀   one knife
[yat7 ba2 dou1]

一把鉸剪   one pair of scissors
[yat7 ba2 gaau3 jin2]

A BRIEF GRAMMAR

1. Statements

Sentence structure: Subject + verb

我係一名老师。	I am a teacher.
我好開心。	I am very happy.
佢有個細佬。	He/She has a younger brother.
媽咪買蘋果。	Mom buys apples.

The English concept of *to be* in Cantonese is typically expressible with 係 [hai6]. When the verb is followed by an adjective, however, the 係 [hai6] can simply be dropped from the sentence.

2. Negative Statements

Sentence structure: Subject + negative word + verb

In Cantonese, negations are created by placing a negation word before the verb or idea the speaker wishes to negate. Some examples of negation words are 唔 [m4], 冇 [mou4], 未 [mei6].

我唔食辣。	I can't eat something spicy.
我冇瞓覺。	I didn't sleep.
我未食飯。	I haven't eaten yet.

3. Comparisons

Sentence Structure: A + adjective + 過 + B

我高過你。	I am taller than you.
月亮细過地球。	The moon is smaller than the earth.

4. Questions / Question Words

咩 [me1]	what
點解 [dim2 gaai2]	why
點樣 [dim2 yeung2]	how
幾多 [gei2 do1]	how much
幾時 [gei2 si4]	when
邊度 [bin1 dou6]	where
邊個 [bin1 go3]	which/who

For "yes" and "no" questions, the sentence structure is:
verb + 唔 + verb

你今晚嚟唔嚟呀？
Will you come tonight?

你係唔係警察呀？
Are you a policeman?

5. Passive sentences

Sentence structure: A + 俾 + B + verb

呢個蘋果俾老鼠咬過。
This apple was eaten by the rat.

佢俾人打咗一餐。
He/She was beaten (by someone).

Double objects:
Subject + verb + direct object + indirect object

我俾咗本書佢。
I gave him/her a book.

Tenses

Tense changes are expressed with the addition of time phrases or particles that express the appropriate tense. It is common in Cantonese to leave the tense of a phrase ambiguous, or unexpressed entirely, unless the speaker wants to emphasize this aspect of the action.

1. To form present continuous tense, add 緊 [gan2] after the verb.

佢睇緊報紙。　　He/She is reading a newspaper.
爸爸開緊會。　　Dad is having a meeting.

2. For simple past tense, add 咗 [jo2] after the verb.

我食咗雪糕。　　I ate the ice cream.
你測咗驗。　　You took the test.

3. For past perfect tense, add 過 [gwo3] after the verb.

我去過美國。　　I have been in the United States.
今日我出過去。　Today I have been out.

Particles

Particles are an important grammatical component in Cantonese, and are also critical to expressing emotions and subtleties in everyday speech. The following are a few useful ones to remember:

1. 㗎 [ga3]: expression of reservation and doubt

系唔系㗎?
[hai6 m4 hai6 ga3]
Are you sure? / Really?

考試成績幾時出來㗎?
[haau2 si3 sing4 jik7 gei2 si4 cheut7 lei4 ga3]
When will they announce the scores of the test?

2. 嘅 [ge3]: used in statements for emphasis on a particular part of a sentence.

原來系咁嘅。
[yun4 loi4 hai6 gam3 ge3]
This is the case. (*The emphasis is 'this.'*)

其實你同學唔系有心嘅。
[kei4 sat9 nei5 tung4 hok9 m4 hai6 yau5 sam1 ge3]
I don't think your classmate did it on purpose.
(*The emphasis is 'not on purpose.'*)

3. 呀 [a3]: used in conversation to soften the tone.

我好想去公園呀。
[ngo5 hou2 seung2 heui3 gung1 yun4 a3]
I really want to go to the park.

農民耕田好辛苦呀。
[nung4 man4 gaang1 tin4 hou2 san1 fu2 a3]
It's really tough work for the farmers to work in the fields.
(*showing sympathy for the farmers*)

4. 嘞 [laak8]: indicates something has already happened or a situation has changed

我食咗飯嘞。
[ngo5 sik9 jo2 faan6 laak8]
I have already eaten.

阿珍晨早畢咗業嘞!
[a3 jan1 san4 jou2 bat7 jo2 yip9 laak8]
A-Jan graduated a long time ago!

5. 未 [mei6]: used in a question to ask whether something has happened or not

你寫好作業未？

[nei5 se2 hou2 jok8 yip9 mei6]

Have you done your homework?

搵到工未？

[wan3 dou3 gung1 mei6]

Have you found a job yet?

6. 先 [sin1]: to indicate an action has to take place before something else happens, or a tone of impatience

你淋咗花先。

[nei5 lam4 jo2 fa1 sin1]

You water the flowers first.

你系米真系咁對我先？

[nei5 hai6 mai5 jan1 hai6 gam3 deui3 ngo5 sin1]

Are you really going to treat me this way?

7. 咩 [me1]: to express surprise or disbelief

達仔真系中咗獎咩？

[daat9 jai2 jan1 hai6 jung1 jo2 jeung2 me1]

Is it true that Little Daat has won a lottery?

(*The speaker finds it hard to believe that little Daat has won a lottery ... or he really hopes the opposite is true.*)

光叔唔系明年先出國咩？

[gwongq suk7 m4 hai6 ming4 nin4 sin1 cheut7 gwok8 me1]

Isn't it the case that Uncle Gwong will not leave the country until next year?

8. 啫 [je1]: to show a dismissive or disinterested attitude towards a situation

宜家讀博士都好普遍啫。

[yi4 ga1 duk9 bok8 si6 dou1 hou2 pou2 pin3 je1]

It's not so uncommon to be enrolled in a PhD program today.

(*Meaning, perhaps, that your mother really should not get so upset that her friends' child gets into a PhD program while you did not!*)

尼個人都唔系好差啫。

[nei4 go3 yan4 dou1 m4 hai6 hou2 cha1 je1]

I don't think this person is really that bad.

(*Please stop complaining about this person as I really don't care about him.*)

9. 啩 [gwa3]: used in a sentence where the speaker is not very sure

可能系啩。

[ho2 nang4 hai6 gwa3]

That may be true. (… but I am really not sure.)

梅姨聽日先過來啩。

[mui4 yi4 ting1 yat9 sin1 gwo3 lei4 gwa3]

Maybe Aunt Mui will not come over until tomorrow.

(*How about you just call her and ask?*)

10. 囉 [lo1]: to express a slightly impatient tone that someone doesn't see that something is so obvious

你飲完茶米去行街囉。

[nei5 yam2 yun4 cha4 mai5 heui3 hang4 gaai1 lo1]

You can go shopping after you have dim sum.

(*What else do you want me to say? I really want to get back to watching my soap opera.*)

廁紙米系沖涼房個櫃度囉。

[chi3 ji2 mai5 hai6 chung1 leung4 fong4 go3 gwai6 dok9 lo1]

The toilet paper is in the cabinet in the bathroom.

(*Are you blind or something?*)

POLITENESS

The loud and direct way in which Cantonese people conduct daily conversations often leaves foreigners with the impression that Cantonese is a "rude" language and culture. In reality, much the opposite is true: Cantonese people are incredibly friendly and interested in helping others—they just tend to be polite in a rude way. Despite all the loud and pointed talk, you'll often find that the Cantonese language makes an effort to be indirect and self- effacing, with regular uses of negations in everyday speech, such as '*not*' (唔), '*not very*' (唔係好), and '*not so*' (唔係咁). Here are some good examples:

This shirt looks horrible on you.
Cantonese: 呢件衫唔係好襯你。
     [ne1 gin6 saam1 m4 hai6 hou2 chan3 nei5]
The literal translation: *This shirt doesn't suit you very well.*

This fish tastes rotten.
Cantonese: 呢條魚唔係好新鮮。
     [ne1 tiu4 yu2 m4 hai6 hou2 san1 sin1]
The literal translation: *This fish doesn't taste very fresh.*

Your idea of walking there is a bad one.
Cantonese: 你行路去個度嘅提議唔係好好。
     [nei5 hang4 lou6 heui3 go3 dou6 ge3 tai4 yi5 m4 hai6 hou2 hou2]
The literal translation: *Your idea of walking there is not a very good one.*

Tom's girlfriend is overweight.
Cantonese: 阿Tom嘅女朋友唔係十分之苗條。
     [a3 Tom ge3 neui5 pang4 yau5 m4 hai6 sap9 fan1 ji1 miu4 tiu4]
The literal translation: *Tom's girlfriend is not very slim.*

NAMES

In Cantonese, acquaintances like to address their friends by adding 阿 [a3] before the last character of the person's name. For example, if someone's name is 王小明 [wong4 siu2 ming4], chances are high that he will be known as 阿明 [a3 ming4] by his friends.

Sometimes among families, seniors or older relatives of the same generation prefer to call their juniors or peers in a more intimate way, by adding 仔 [jai2] (*boy*) after the last character of the name of a male, or 女 [neui5] (*girl*) for a female. For example, if a boy's name is 張志豪 [jeung1 ji3 hou4], his parents, grandparents, uncles, aunts, and even older siblings and cousins usually call him 豪仔 [hou4 jai2]. If a girl's name is 陳可珠 [chan4 ho2 jyu1], she is very likely referred to as 珠女 [jyu1 neui5] among her family members. This practice usually stops when the junior family member in question reaches adulthood or gets married.

A similar rule also applies when addressing one's aunt or uncle. If you have an uncle who is a junior sibling to your parent named 張志豪 [jeung1 ji3 hou4], you will likely be asked to call him 豪叔 [hou4 suk7]. An aunt that is a junior sibling to your parent whose name is 陳可珠 [chan4 ho2 jyu1] would be called 珠姨 [jyu1 yi4].

Things are typically more formal in business settings, where English cultural mores persist from colonial times. In the office and in many shops, Cantonese refer to each other as Mr. (先生 [sin1 sang1], but often shortened to just 生 [sang1]), Mrs. (太太 [taai3 taai3], shortened to 太 [taai3]), and Miss (小姐 [siu2 je2]). For example, when 張志豪 [jeung1 ji3 hou4] meets 陳可珠 [chan4 ho2 jyu1] in the office, they will greet each as 張先生 [jeung1 sin1 sang1] (or just 張生 [jeung1 sang1] if they have met before, or 陳小姐 [chan4 siu2 je2]).

One particularly interesting naming convention that is typical of the Cantonese tendency to assimilate other cultures and languages is the standard of address between policemen and military and their superior officers: "阿sir" [a3 sir].

LUCK

The Cantonese culture places an unusually strong emphasis on luck. This creates some linguistic oddities you should be aware of.

For instance, when you search for an apartment, don't expect an empty flat to be advertised as "*vacant*" 空屋 [hung1 uk7]. Instead, look for a "*lucky apartment*" with 吉屋 [gat7 uk7] written on the door. This is because, in Cantonese, the pronunciation of 空屋 is the same as "*ominous house*" 凶屋 [hung1 uk7]. To avoid that unlucky linguistic association, Cantonese speakers "compensate" by interpolating a "lucky" antonym to replace the unlucky character in a word.

Some further examples of this tradition in action:

Sponge cucumber (aka Luffa):
Original Cantonese Name: 絲瓜 [si1 gwa1]
Too Similar To: 輸瓜 [syu1 gwa1] (*loser melon*)
Changed Name: 勝瓜 [sing3 gwa1] (*victory melon*)

Read books:
Original Cantonese: 讀書 [duk9 syu1]
Too Similar To: 讀輸 [duk9 syu1] (*reading loses*)
Changed Name: 讀贏 [duk9 yeng4] (*reading wins*)

Aunt (or mother of a friend/boyfriend/girlfriend):
Original Cantonese Name: 伯母 [baak8 mou5]
Too Similar To: 百冇 [baak8 mou5] (*have nothing*)
Changed Name: 伯有 [baak8 yau5] (*have everything*)

Alas, what is "lucky" for Cantonese speakers can often be frustrating for outsiders learning the language. Don't worry, though, even if these Cantonese habits are frustrating they are also, at least, always entertaining to learn.

CHINESE NEW YEAR GREETINGS

If luck weighs heavily on Cantonese speakers' minds in daily conversation, it becomes an outright obsession during important holidays, such as the Chinese New Year 新年 [san1 nin4]. During the New Year, which lasts from January 1st to 15th in the lunar calendar, you will notice that nearly all greetings, departures, and offerings of thanks or good wishes come in the form of lucky four-character phrases. Some common phrases include:

恭喜發財 [gung1 hei2 faat8 choi4]
You will be happy and rich!

身體健康 [san1 tai2 gin6 hong1]
You will have good health!

萬事如意 [maan6 si6 yu4 yi3]
Everything will go as you wish!

財源廣進 [choi4 yun4 gwong2 jeun3]
Wealth will find you from all directions!

龍馬精神 [lung4 ma5 jing1 san4]
You will have the vigor of the dragon and the horse!

心想事成 [sam1 seung2 si6 sing4]
All your wishes will come true!

一本萬利 [yat7 bun2 maan6 lei6]
Your business will make ten thousand dollars on a one-dollar investment!

如意吉祥 [yu4 yi3 gat7 cheung4]
Your life will be filled with fortune and happiness!

學業進步 [hok9 yip9 jeun3 bou6]
You will make great progress in your study!

LUCKY THINGS TO SAY ON OTHER OCCASIONS

It's important to correctly use these lucky phrases during important occasions, as many native speakers believe that the standard of "luck" set during these times (which is established through proper speech and action) will determine the luck of an individual for the entire year (or sometimes, entire lifetime). Important occasions where you should be sure to use appropriate (i.e., "lucky") speech include wedding banquets:

白頭偕老 [baak9 tau4 gaai1 lou5]
Live together until you two both have grey hair!

永結同心 [wing5 git8 tung4 sam1]
Join in one heart forever!

For traditional Cantonese, however, a long and happy marriage is not nearly as important as this wish, which you'll commonly hear at weddings from senior members of both families:

早生貴子 [jou2 sang1 gwai3 ji2]
Have a lovely son soon!

At birthday parties for younger people, you will usually hear the friends and families repeating this sentence:

祝你年年有咁日，歲歲有咁朝
[juk7 nei5 nin4 nin4 yau5 gam3 yat9, seui3 seui3 yau5 gam3 jiu1]
Wish you enjoy this day every year in the future!

If someone can enjoy his birthday every year in the future, he must live forever, right? What a simple but powerful wish!

You will need to adjust your speech patterns a bit if you are invited to a birthday party for older people. Elderly people tend to set their ambitions even higher than just being able to live forever. So in those situations you might say:

福如東海，壽比南山
[fu3 yu4 dung1 hoi2, sau6 bei2 naam4 saan1]
*May you have happiness as vast as the East China Sea
and live as long as the Southern Mountain.*

LUCKY NUMBERS

Luck doesn't stop with speech in the Cantonese language, it also extends into math, with "6" (陸 [luk9] or 六 [luk9]), "8" (捌 [baat8] or 八 [baat8]), and "9" (玖 [gau2] or 九 [gau2]) having the prestige as the luckiest numbers.

The meanings behind these lucky numbers are:

6   Everything will go towards success smoothly,
    without a hitch

8   The similar pronunciation to 發 [faat8] implies
    getting rich or making a fortune

9   Has the same sound as 久 [gau2] and implies
    endurance over many eons

While the "luckiness" of those three numbers is common across China, Cantonese have tried to further push the odds in their favor by determining that "2" (貳 [yi6] or 二 [yi6]) is also a lucky number, due to its similarity in pronunciation to both 易 [yi6] and the English word "easy." Who doesn't want life to be easy, after all?

Certain numbers containing these digits can also be considered lucky, or in some cases, make the numbers even luckier. Good examples include 12, 16, 18, and 19, since the "10" (拾 [sap9] or 十 [sap9]) pronounced in front of each of these lucky numbers sounds like 實 [sap9] or "*certain.*" That means that 12 is "*certainly easy,*" 16 is "*must go smoothly,*" 18 is "*assured wealth,*" and 19 is "*sure to last forever.*"

The Hong Kong government has also adeptly worked the Cantonese love of lucky numbers to maintain its world-famous low tax rate, by raising funds through auctioning license plates. Here's a few examples of such sales:

No. 2 was sold in 1993 for HKD$9.5 million.

No. 6 was sold in 1978 for HKD$330,000 to Sir Run Run Shaw, one of the richest men in Hong Kong.

No. 8 was sold in 1988 for HKD$5 million.

No. 10 was sold in 1994 for HKD$13 million.

Clearly, the Hong Kong government is convinced of the wealth these lucky numbers can really bring!

There are also unlucky numbers. The most avoided of these is 14. This is because it is a compound of the unlucky number "4" (肆 [sei3] or 四 [sei3]) which sounds similar to 死 [sei2] (*death*) and the number "10" (*certain*). The result? "Certain death." It is for this reason that many buildings in Hong Kong don't have fourth or fourteenth floors. It also explains why a lot of expensive real estate in south China sells for $3,999,999 (with lots of lucky nines) instead of simply $4 million.

TIME

Cantonese people tend to see an hour not as a collection of sixty minutes, but as a set of 12 five-minute intervals known as 字 [ji6] "*characters.*" Accordingly a Cantonese person will call the first five minutes of an hour 一個字 [yat7 go3 ji6], the next five minutes 兩個字 [leung5 go3 ji6], and so forth. If you want to tell your friend that you will meet at 2:20 pm on Thursday afternoon right in front of Statue Square, you would say:

禮拜四晏晝兩點四個字皇后像广场前面等。
[lai5 baai3 sei3 aan3 jau3 leung5 dim2 sei3 go3 ji6 wong4 hau6 jeung6 gwong2 cheung4 chin4 min6 dang2]

(NOTE: It would be best that you show up at 2:20 despite such an imprecise way of counting an hour, Cantonese people tend to be very punctual and impatient with delays!)

Sometimes, people will omit the 個字 [go3 ji6] and only say the number part. When you hear your friend ask to meet at 五點八 [ng5 dim2 baat8], he means 5:40, not 5:08.

One exception is a half-hour. 2:30 is expressed as two o'clock and a half:

兩點半 [leung5 dim2 bun3]

If you want to say "three o'clock sharp," use:

三點整 [saam1 dim2 jing2]

Some basic vocabulary related to time that is useful to know:

o'clock 點鐘 [dim2 jung1]
minute 分鐘 [fan1 jung1]
second 秒 [miu5]

day 日 [yat9]
today 咁日 [gam3 yat9]
yesterday 琴日 [kam4 yat9]
the day before yesterday 前日 [chin4 yat9]
three days ago 大前日 [daai6 chin4 yat9]
tomorrow 聽日 [teng1 yat9]
the day after tomorrow 後日 [hau6 yat9]
in three days 大後日 [daai6 hau6 yat9]

week 禮拜 [lai5 baai3]
this week 尼個禮拜 [nei4 go3 lai5 baai3]
last week 上個禮拜 [seung6 go3 lai5 baai3]
the week before last 上上個禮拜 [seung6 seung6 go3 lai5 baai3]
next week 下個禮拜 [ha6 go3 lai5 baai3]
the week after next 下下個禮拜 [ha6 ha6 go3 lai5 baai3]

month 月 [yut9]
(*For "this month," "next month," etc., use the same patterns as for weeks.*)

year 年 [nin4]
this year 咁年 [gam3 nin4]
last year 去年 [heui3 nin4]
the year before last year 前年 [chin4 nin4]
three years ago 大前年 [daai6 chin4 nin4]
next year 明年 [ming4 nin4]
the year after next 後年 [hau6 nin4]
in three years 大後年 [daai6 hau6 nin4]

CANTONESE–ENGLISH DICTIONARY

Note: The entries in the Cantonese-English section are listed in alphabetical order by the transliteration

A

鴉片 [a1 pin3] *n.* opium

啞 [a2] *adj.* mute

啞劇 [a2 kek9] *n.* pantomime, mime

啞劇演員 [a2 kek9 yin2 yun4] *n.* mime

阿布賈 [a3 bou3 ga2] *n.* Abuja (~, capital of Nigeria 尼日利亞 嘅首都)

阿布扎比 [a3 bou3 jaat8 bei2] *n.* Abu Dhabi (~, capital of United Arab Emirates 阿聯酋嘅首都)

阿塞拜疆 [a3 choi3 baai3 geung1] *n.* Azerbaijan; *adj.* Azerbaijani

亞松森 [a3 chung4 sam1] *n.* Asuncion (~, capital of Paraguay 巴拉圭嘅首都)

阿的斯阿貝巴 [a3 dik7 si1 a3 bui3 ba1] *n.* Addis Ababa (~, capital of Ethiopia 埃塞俄比亞嘅首都)

阿富汗 [a3 fu3 hon6] *n.* Afghanistan

阿富汗人 [a3 fu3 hon6 yan4] *n.* Afghan (*person from Afghanistan*)

阿根廷 [a3 gan1 ting4] *n.* Argentina; *adj.* Argentine

阿哥 [a3 go1] *n.* brother

阿克拉 [a3 hak7 laai1] *n.* Accra (~, capital of Ghana 加納嘅 首都)

阿什哈巴德 [a3 jaap9 ha1 ba1 dak7] *n.* Ashgabat (~, capital of Turkmenistan 土庫曼斯坦嘅 首都)

亞洲 [a3 jau1] *n.* Asia; *adj.* Asian

阿拉伯 [a3 laai1 baak8] *adj.* Arab

阿拉伯話 [a3 laai1 baak8 wa2] *n.* Arabic

阿聯酋 [a3 lyun4 yau4] *n.* United Arab Emirates (UAE)

亞麻 [a3 ma4] *n.* flax (~ seed 亞 麻籽, ~ powder 亞麻粉); linen

阿曼 [a3 maan6] *n.* Oman

阿美尼亞 [a3 mei5 nei4 a3] *n.* Armenia; *adj.* Armenian

阿姆斯特丹 [a3 mou5 si1 dak9 daan1] *n.* Amsterdam (~, capital of Netherlands 荷蘭嘅首都)

亞穆蘇克羅 [a3 muk9 sou1 hak7 lo4] *n.* Yamoussoukro (~, capital of Cote d'Ivoire 科特迪 瓦首都)

阿皮亞 [a3 pei4 a3] *n.* Apia (~, capital of Samoa 薩摩亞群島 嘅首都)

阿斯馬拉 [a3 si1 ma5 laai1] *n.* Asmara (~, capital of Eritrea 厄 立特里亞嘅首都)

阿斯塔納 [a3 si1 taap8 naap9] *n.* Astana (~, capital of Kazakhstan 哈薩克斯坦嘅首都)

阿士匹林 [a3 si6 pat7 lam4] *n.* aspirin

阿叔 [a3 suk7] *n.* uncle

阿姨 [a3 yi4] *n.* aunt

阿爾巴尼亞 [a3 yi5 ba1 nei4 a3] *n.* Albania

阿爾巴尼亞人 [a3 yi5 ba1 nei4 a3 yan4] *n.* Albanian

阿爾及利亞 [a3 yi5 kap9 lei6 a3] *n.* Algeria

阿爾及利亞人 [a3 yi5 kap9 lei6 a3 yan4] *n.* Algerian

阿爾及爾 [a3 yi5 kap9 yi5] *n.* Algiers (~, capital of Algeria 阿爾及利亞嘅首都)

埃塞俄比亞 [aai1 choi3 ngo4 bei2 a3] *n.* Ethiopia; *adj.* Ethiopian

嗌交 [aai3 gaau1] *n.* quarrel

罌粟 [aang1 suk7] *n.* poppy

罌粟籽 [aang1 suk7 ji2] *n.* poppy seed (~ cake 罌粟蛋糕)

鴨 [aap8] *n.* duck (wild ~ 野鴨; ~ in orange 鴨橙)

壓 [aat8] *v.* press; 壓好 *adj.* pressed

壓迫 [aat8 bik7] *v.* oppress; *n.* oppression

壓爛 [aat8 laan6] *adj.* crushed

壓力 [aat8 lik9] *n.* pressure, stress

壓碎 [aat8 seui3] *v.* crush, grate

壓碎咗嘅 [aat8 seui3 jo2 ge3] *adj.* grated (~ cheese 芝士碎, ~ pepper 辣椒粉, ~ nuts 乾果碎, ~ spice 辣椒粉)

押韻 [aat8 wan6] *n.* rhyme

壓抑 [aat8 yik7] *v.* restrain

厄瓜多爾 [ak7 gwa1 do1 yi5] *n.* Ecuador; *adj.* Ecuadorian

厄立特里亞 [ak7 laap9 dak9 lei5 a3] *n.* Eritrea

渥太華 [ak7 taai3 wa4] *n.* Ottawa (~, capital of Canada 加拿大首都)

鵪鶉 [am1 cheun1] *n.* partridge, quail

庵列 [am1 lit9] *n.* omelet (breakfast ~ 早餐庵列)

暗礁 [am3 jiu1] *n.* ledge

暗示 [am3 si6] *v.* imply

歐洲 [au1 jau1] *n.* Europe

歐洲人 [au1 jau1 yan4] *n.* European

歐盟 [au1 mang4] *n.* European Union (EU); 歐盟國家 EU country; 歐盟公民 EU citizen

歐美 [au1 mei5] *adj.* western

歐元 [au1 yun4] *n.* euro

B

巴巴多斯島 [ba1 ba1 do1 si1 dou2] *n.* Barbados

巴布亞新幾內亞 [ba1 bou3 a3 san1 gei1 noi6 a3] *n.* Papua New Guinea

巴庫 [ba1 fu3] *n.* Baku (~, capital of Azerbaijan 阿塞拜疆嘅首都)

巴格達 [ba1 gaak8 daat9] *n.* Baghdad (~, capital of Iraq 伊拉克嘅首都)

巴基斯坦 [ba1 gei1 si1 taan2] *n.* Pakistan; *adj.* Pakistani

巴哈馬 [ba1 ha1 ma5] *n.* Bahamas, The; *adj.* Bahamian

巴拉圭 [ba1 laai1 gwai1] *n.* Paraguay; *adj.* Paraguayan

巴黎 [ba1 lai4] *n.* Paris (~, capital of France 法國首都)

巴林 [ba1 lam4] *n.* Bahrain; *adj.* Bahraini

芭蕾舞 [ba1 leui5 mou5] *n.* ballet

巴洛克式 [ba1 lok8 hak7 sik7] *n.* baroque style

巴馬科 [ba1 ma5 fo1] *n.* Bamako (~, capital of Mali 馬里嘅首都)

巴拿馬 [ba1 na4 ma5] *n.* Panama; *adj.* Panamanian

巴拿馬城 [ba1 na4 ma5 sing4] *n.* Panama City (~, capital of Panama 巴拿馬首都)

巴西 [ba1 sai1] *n.* Brazil; *adj.* Brazilian

巴西利亞 [ba1 sai1 lei6 a3] *n.* Brasilia (~, capital of Brazil 巴西嘅首都)

巴斯特爾 [ba1 si1 dak9 yi5] *n.* Basseterre (~, capital of Saint Kitts and Nevis 聖克里斯托弗和尼維斯島嘅首都)

巴士 [ba1 si2] *n.* bus (city ~ 市內巴士, tourist ~ 旅遊巴士, ~ ride 搭巴士)

巴士站 [ba1 si2 jaam6] *n.* bus stop

巴士尾站 [ba1 si2 mei5 jaam6] *n.* bus terminal

巴士線 [ba1 si2 sin3] *n.* bus lane, bus route

巴氏消毒 [ba1 si6 siu1 duk9] *adj.* pasteurized (non-~ 冇巴氏消毒)

疤 [ba1] *n.* scar

巴馬臣芝士 [ba1 ma5 san4 ji1 si2] *n.* Parmesan cheese

巴西果仁 [ba1 sai1 gwo2 yan4] *n.* Brazil nut

罷工 [ba6 gung1] *n.* labor strike

罷免 [ba6 min5] *v.* oust

拜拜 [baai1 baai3] *phr.* goodbye!, bye!

擺甫士 [baai2 pou3 si2] *v.* pose (photography ~ *n.* 影相甫士)

擺脫 [baai2 tyut8] *v.* rid

敗家 [baai6 ga1] *adj.* prodigal

白蘭地 [baak6 laan4 dei6] *n.* akavit

百 [baak8] *n.* hundred

百分百 [baak8 fan6 baak8] *adv.* totally

百分比 [baak8 fan6 bei2] *n.* percentage

百分之 [baak8 fan6 ji1] *n.* per cent, percent

百貨公司 [baak8 fo3 gung1 si1] *n.* department store

百吉圈 [baak8 gat1 hyun1] *n.* bagel (half ~ 半個百吉圈)

百合花 [baak8 hap9 fa1] *n.* lily

百足 [baak8 juk7] *n.* centipede

百里香 [baak8 lei5 heung1] *n.* thyme

伯里茲 [baak8 lei5 ji1] *n.* Belize; *adj.* Belizean

百萬 [baak8 maan6] *num.* million

百萬富翁 [baak8 maan6 fu3 yung1] *n.* millionaire

百萬位元組 [baak8 maan6 wai2 yun4 jou2] *n.* megabyte (MB) (file size in ~ 文件大小系數百萬位元組)

伯爾尼 [baak8 yi5 nei4] *n.* Bern (~, capital of Switzerland 瑞士嘅首都)

百葉窗 [baak8 yip9 cheung1] *n.* shutter window, camera

白車 [baak9 che1] *n.* ambulance

白菜 [baak9 choi3] *n.* bok choy (baby ~ 白菜仔, Thai ~ 泰國白菜)

白金 [baak9 gam1] *n.* platinum; diamonds

白鴿 [baak9 gap8] *n.* pigeon

白汁 [baak9 jap7] *n.* white sauce

白酒 [baak9 jau2] *n.* liqueur

白鑞 [baak9 laap9] *n.* pewter

白領 [baak9 leng5] *n.* office worker

白麵包 [baak9 min6 baau1] *n.* white bread

白俄羅斯 [baak9 ngo5 lo4 si1] *n.* Belarus; *adj.* Belarusian

白色嘅 [baak9 sik7 ge3] *adj.* white (~ bread 白麵包, ~ cabbage 白菜, ~ sauce 白汁, ~ wine 葡萄白酒)

白頭髮 [baak9 tau4 faat8] *adj.* gray-haired

白日夢 [baak9 yat9 mung6] *n.* reverie

白羊座 [baak9 yeung4 jo6] *n.* Aries

白魚 [baak9 yu2] *n.* whitefish

白乳膠 [baak9 yu5 gaau1] *n.* gelatin

班 [baan1] *n.* class

斑點 [baan1 dim2] *n.* mottle

班吉 [baan1 gat7] *n.* Bangui (~, capital of Central African Republic 中非共和國嘅首都)

班戟 [baan1 gik7] *n.* pancake

班珠爾 [baan1 jyu1 yi5] *n.* Banjul (~, capital of The Gambia 岡比亞嘅首都)

斑馬 [baan1 ma5] *n.* zebra

板 [baan2] *n.* board

版本 [baan2 bun2] *n.* edition, version

版權 [baan2 kyun4] *n.* copyright

扮 [baan6] *v.* pretend

辦公時間 [baan6 gung1 si4 gaan3] *n.* business hours

扮嘢 [baan6 ye5] *n.* affectation, pretense, pretension

八 [baat8] *num* eight

八邊形 [baat8 bin1 ying4] *n.* octagon

八角 [baat8 gok8] *n.* aniseed

八卦 [baat8 gwa3] *adj.* nosy

八爪魚 [baat8 jaau2 yu2] *n.* octopus (~ legs 八爪魚腳, ~ soup 八爪魚湯)

八十 [baat8 sap9] *num.* eighty

八月份 [baat8 yut9 fan6] *n.* August (*abbr.* Aug.)

包 [baau1] *n.* bun (sesame seed ~ 芝麻包, poppy seed ~ 罌粟籽包, sweet ~ 甜包, meat filled ~ 肉包, wheat ~ 小麥包); package

包 [baau1] *n.* wrap (chicken ~ 雞肉卷)

包 [baau1] *v./n.* pack (~ a suitcase 打包行李; ~ of cigarettes 一包煙)

包袱 [baau1 fuk9] *n.* burden

包機 [baau1 gei1] *n.* charter flight

包裹 [baau1 gwo2] *n.* parcel

包含 [baau1 ham4] *v.* comprise, contain

包好 [baau1 hou2] *adj.* wrapped (was ~ 包咗起身)

包裝紙 [baau1 jong1 ji2] *n.* wrapping

包住 [baau1 jyu6] *v.* encase, muffle

包括 [baau1 kut8] *v.* include; *prep.* including

包括在內 [baau1 kut8 joi6 noi6] *adj.* included (is X ~? 包唔包埋X?); inclusive (be ~ 包埋)

包食宿 [baau1 sik9 suk7] *adv.* full board with all meals

包圍 [baau1 wai4] *v.* surround

鮑魚 [baau1 yu4] *n.* abalone

飽和度 [baau2 wo4 dou6] *n.* saturation

爆炒 [baau3 chaau2] *adj.* sautéed

爆發 [baau3 faat8] *n.* outbreak

爆谷 [baau3 guk1] *n.* popcorn

爆開 [baau3 hoi1] *v.* pop

爆炸 [baau3 ja3] *v.* burst, explode; *n.* explosion

爆竹 [baau3 juk7] *n.* crackers (graham ~ 全麥餅乾, salted ~ 鹹餅乾)

跛 [bai1] *adj.* lame

弊病 [bai6 beng6] *n.* malady

北極 [bak7 gik9] *n.* Arctic, North Pole

北極星 [bak7 gik9 sing1] *n.* lodestar

北京 [bak7 ging1] *n.* Beijing (~, capital of China 中國嘅首都)

北京烤鴨 [bak7 ging1 haau1 aap8] *n.* Peking duck

北韓 [bak7 hon4] *n.* North Korea

北美 [bak7 mei5] *adj.* North American

北面 [bak7 min6] *n.* north; *adj.* northern

北愛爾蘭 [bak7 oi3 yi5 laan4] *n.* Northern Ireland

泵 [bam1] *n.* pump

泵把 [bam1 ba2] *n.* bumper

賓館 [ban1 gun2] *n.* guesthouse

品牌 [ban2 paai4] *n.* brand

品脫 [ban2 tyut8] *n.* pint (*abbr.* pt.)

笨豬跳 [ban6 jyu1 tiu3] *n.* bungee-jumping

繃帶 [bang1 daai2] *n.* bandage

筆 [bat7] *n.* pen (ballpoint ~ 原

子筆)

不飽和 [bat7 baau2 wo4] *adj.*
unsaturated (~ fat 不飽和脂肪)

不切實際 [bat7 chit8 sat9 jai3]
adj. quixotic

不丹 [bat7 daan1] *n.* Bhutan; *adj.*
Bhutanese

不定式 [bat7 ding6 sik7] *n.*
infinitive

筆記 [bat7 gei3] *n.* note

筆記簿 [bat7 gei3 bou6] *n.*
notebook

不含乳製品 [bat7 ham4 yu5
jai3 ban2] *adj.* non-dairy

不可避免 [bat7 ho2 bei6 min5]
adj. inevitable; *adv.* inevitably

不可思議 [bat7 ho2 si1 yi5] *adj.*
mysterious; *n.* mystery

筆尖 [bat7 jim1] *n.* nib

不在場證據 [bat7 joi6 cheung4
jing3 geui3] *n.* alibi

筆名 [bat7 meng2] *n.* pseudonym

不滿 [bat7 mun5] *adj.* disapproving

不平等 [bat7 ping4 dang2] *n.*
inequality

不鏽鋼 [bat7 sau3 gong3] *adj.*
stainless steel

不孕不育 [bat7 yan6 bat7 yuk9]
adj. sterile, sterilized

啤酒 [be1 jau2] *n.* beer (canned ~
罐裝啤酒, bottled ~ 瓶裝啤
酒, pilsner ~ 淺色啤酒, ~ on
tap 散裝啤酒, draft ~ 生啤
酒, ale ~ 淡色啤酒, lager ~
儲藏啤酒, malted ~ 麥芽啤
酒, Guinness ~ 健力士啤酒,
wheat ~ 小麥啤酒, honey ale ~
蜜糖淺色啤酒, barley ~ 大麥
啤酒, oat ~ 燕麥啤酒)

啤酒廠 [be1 jau2 chong2] *n.*
brewery

悲觀 [bei1 gun1] *adj.* pessimistic

悲觀者 [bei1 gun1 je2] *n.*
pessimist

悲觀主義 [bei1 gun1 jyu2 yi6] *n.*
pessimism

悲劇 [bei1 kek9] *n.* tragedy

卑鄙 [bei1 pei2] *adj.* despicable

俾壓力 [bei2 aat8 lik9] *v.*
pressurize

彼此 [bei2 chi2] *adj.* mutual

俾錢 [bei2 chin2] *v.* pay

比賽 [bei2 choi3] *n.* contest,
match game; fire

比得包 [bei2 dak7 baau1] *n.* pita
bread

俾翻 [bei2 faan1] *v.* return, give
back

比較 [bei2 gaau3] *v.* compare; *n.*
comparison

比較鍾意 [bei2 gaau3 jung1 yi3]
v. prefer

比什凱克 [bei2 jaap9 hoi2
hak7] *n.* Bishkek (~, capital of
Kyrgyzstan 吉爾吉斯斯坦嘅
首都)

比例 [bei2 lai6] *n.* proportion,
ratio

比勒陀利亞 [bei2 lak9 to4 lei6
a3] *n.* Pretoria (~, administrative
capital of South Africa 南非行
政首都)

比利時 [bei2 lei6 si4] *adj.* Belgian;
n. Belgium

比率 [bei2 leut9] *n.* rate

比目魚 [bei2 muk9 yu2] *n.* plaice,
sole (fish)

俾你 [bei2 nei5] *phr.* here you are (help yourself 請自便)

比紹 [bei2 siu6] *n.* Bissau (~, capital of Guinea-Bissau 幾內亞比紹共和國嘅首都)

俾人搶劫 [bei2 yan4 cheung2 gip8] *adj.* robbed (I was ~! 我俾人搶劫!)

俾人偷咗 [bei2 yan4 tau1 jo2] *adj.* stolen

比喻 [bei2 yu6] *n.* analogy; *adj.* figurative; *n.* metaphor

俾 [bei2] *v.* let (~ me know 話俾我知, ~ me take your coat 遞你件褸俾我啦), grant, entitle, give

比 [bei2] *prep.* than

秘魯 [bei3 lou5] *n.* Peru; *adj.* Peruvian

秘密 [bei3 mat9] *adj.* secret; *adv.* secretly

秘書 [bei3 syu1] *n.* secretary

鼻 [bei6] *n.* nose

被撫養人 [bei6 fu2 yeung5 yan4] *n.* dependent

被告 [bei6 gou3] *n.* defendant; respondent

避開 [bei6 hoi1] *v.* avoid

被…襲擊 [bei6 … jaap9 gik7] *adj.* assaulted

被指控 [bei6 ji2 hung3] *phr.* charged with

被流放嘅人 [bei6 lau4 fong3 ge3 yan4] *n.* outcast

備忘錄 [bei6 mong4 luk9] *n.* memo, memorandum

避難 [bei6 naan6] *n.* refuge

被遺棄嘅 [bei6 wai4 hei3 ge3] *adj.* abandoned

避孕 [bei6 yan6] *n.* contraception

避孕嘅 [bei6 yan6 ge3] *adj.* contraceptive (~ pill 避孕藥)

避孕套 [bei6 yan6 tou3] *n.* condom

餅乾 [beng2 gon1] *n.* biscuit

病 [beng6] *n.* sickness, disease, illness

病毒 [beng6 duk9] *n.* virus (computer ~ 電腦病毒)

病房 [beng6 fong2] *n.* ward (at a hospital)

病咗 [beng6 jo2] *n.* ailing

病咗 [beng6 jo2] *adj.* ill, sick (I feel ~ 我病咗; ~ to one's stomach 作嘔; ~ in the head 有精神病)

病態 [beng6 taai3] *adj.* morbid; *n.* morbidity

病人 [beng6 yan4] *n.* patient (doctor's ~ 醫生嘅病人)

迫 [bik7] *adj.* crowded

迫切 [bik7 chit8] *adj.* desperate; *adv.* desperately

迫害 [bik7 hoi6] *v.* persecute; *n.* persecution

壁球比賽 [bik7 kau4 bei2 choi3] *n.* squash (*game*)

壁畫 [bik7 wa2] *n.* fresco, mural

邊 [bin1] *n.* side, rim

邊邊 [bin1 bin1] *n.* edge

鞭打 [bin1 da2] *v.* whip

邊度 [bin1 dou6] *adv.* where, anywhere, whither (where to 去邊度; where were you born? 你係邊度出世？)

邊度都得 [bin1 dou6 dou1 dak7] *conj.* wherever

邊個 [bin1 go3] *pron.* anyone, anybody, which, who, whom (Does anyone speak English? 有冇人識講英文？)

邊個都得 [bin1 go3 dou1 dak7] *pron.* whoever

邊個嘅 [bin1 go3 ge3] *det.* whose

邊一個 [bin1 yat7 go3] *det.* either

邊緣 [bin1 yun4] *n.* margin

扁蛋糕 [bin2 daan6 gou1] *n.* flat cake

扁豆 [bin2 dau2] *n.* lentil (~ soup 扁豆湯, black ~s 黑豆, green ~s 青豆, yellow ~s 黃豆)

貶值 [bin2 jik9] *n.* depreciation

扁南瓜 [bin2 naam4 gwa1] *n.* pattypan squash

扁桃腺 [bin2 tou4 sin3] *n.* tonsils

扁桃腺發炎 [bin2 tou4 sin3 faat8 yim4] *n.* tonsilitis

變速杆 [bin3 chuk7 gon1] *n.* gearshift lever

變速器 [bin3 chuk7 hei3] *n.* gearbox

變化 [bin3 fa3] *n.* variation; *v.* vary

變質 [bin3 jat7] *v.* rot; *adj.* spoiled (~ goods 變質嘅野)

變來變去 [bin3 loi4 bin3 heui3] *adj.* variable

變態 [bin3 taai3] *n.* perversion; *adj.* twisted

變幻莫測 [bin3 waan6 mok9 chak7] *adj.* capricious

變異 [bin3 yi6] *adj.* mutant, mutative; *n.* mutation

便秘 [bin6 bei3] *adj.* constipated; *n.* constipation

便服 [bin6 fok4] *n.* informal dress

便利設施 [bin6 lei6 chit8 si1] *n.* amenities

便利店 [bin6 lei6 dim3] *n.* convenience store

辯論 [bin6 leun6] *n.* debate, argument

辯護 [bin6 wu6] *v.* defend; plead

乒乓波 [bing1 bam1 bo1] *n.* ping-pong

冰川 [bing1 chyun1] *n.* glacier

冰袋 [bing1 doi2] *n.* cold pack

冰島 [bing1 dou2] *n.* Iceland; *adj.* Icelandic

冰凍 [bing1 dung3] *adj.* iced (~ tea 冰茶, ~ bun 冰皮包, ~ pastry 冰皮糕點)

冰凍果汁 [bing1 dung3 gwo2 jap7] *n.* sherbet (lemon ~ 檸檬冰凍果汁, orange ~ 冰凍橙汁)

冰沙 [bing1 sa1] *n.* smoothie, sorbet (fruit ~ 水果冰沙)

冰箱仔 [bing1 seung1 jai2] *n.* minibar

冰上曲棍球 [bing1 seung6 kuk7 gwan3 kau4] *n.* ice hockey

兵役 [bing1 yik9] *n.* military service

冰上曲棍球 [bing1 seung6 kuk7 gwan3 kau4] *n.* ice hockey

必需品 [bit7 seui1 ban2] *n.* requisite

必然 [bit7 yin4] *adv.* surely

必要 [bit7 yiu3] *adj.* imperative, essential

別墅 [bit9 seui5] *n.* mansion

標榜 [biu1 bong2] *v.* purport

標本 [biu1 bun2] *n.* specimen

標籤 [biu1 chim1] *n.* label, tag (price ~ 標價)

標點符號 [biu1 dim2 fu4 hou6] *n.* punctuation

標記 [biu1 gei3] *n.* marker, sign, notation

標準 [biu1 jeun2] *n.* criterion, norm, standard (~ charge 標準收費)

標誌 [biu1 ji3] *n.* symbol

標題 [biu1 tai4] *n.* heading

表達 [biu2 daat9] *n.* expression

表面 [biu2 min6] *n.* surface

表面上 [biu2 min6 seung6] *n.* prima facie

表明 [biu2 ming4] *v.* show (Can you ~ me? 你示範俾我睇，好唔好？)

表示 [biu2 si6] *v.* express

表兄弟姊妹 [biu2 hing1 dai6 ji2 mui6] *n.* cousin

表演 [biu2 yin2] *n.* performance, act; *v.* perform

表演嘅人 [biu2 yin2 ge3 yan4] *n.* performer

波 [bo1] *n.* ball (play ~ (*lit. and fig.*) 比賽開始); breast

菠菜 [bo1 choi3] *n.* spinach (~ leaves 菠菜葉, ~ dip 菠菜點醬)

波德戈里察 [bo1 dak7 gwo1 lei5 chaat8] *n.* Podgorica (~, capital of Montenegro 蒙特內格羅首都)

波多諾伏 [bo1 do1 nok9 fuk9] *n.* Porto-Novo (~, capital of Benin 貝寧彎首都)

坡度 [bo1 dou6] *n.* gradient

波動 [bo1 dung6] *v.* oscillate; *n.* oscillation

波哥大 [bo1 go1 daai6] *n.* Bogota (~, capital of Colombia 哥倫比亞嘅首都)

波黑 [bo1 hak7] *n.* Bosnia and Herzegovina

波蘭 [bo1 laan4] *n.* Poland; *adj.* Polish (~ food 波蘭菜)

玻璃 [bo1 lei1] *n.* glass material, container

玻璃器皿 [bo1 lei1 hei3 ming5] *n.* glassware

玻璃瓶 [bo1 lei1 ping4] *n.* decanter

玻利維亞 [bo1 lei6 wai4 a3] *n.* Bolivia; *adj.* Bolivian

菠蘿 [bo1 lo4] *n.* pineapple

菠蘿蜜 [bo1 lo4 mat9] *n.* jackfruit

波紋 [bo1 man4] *n.* ripple

波斯 [bo1 si1] *adj.* Persian (~ food 波斯菜)

波斯尼亞 [bo1 si1 nei4 a3] *adj.* Bosnian

波伊森莓 [bo1 yi1 sam1 mui4] *n.* boysenberry

播種 [bo3 jung2] *n.* sowing

博茨瓦納 [bok8 chi4 nga5 naap9] *n.* Botswana; person from Botswana

駁番 [bok8 faan1] *v.* rebut

駁嘴 [bok8 jeui2] *v.* retort

博物館 [bok8 mat9 gun2] *n.*
museum

膊頭 [bok8 tau4] *n.* shoulder

駁回 [bok8 wui4] *v.* overrule

薄餅 [bok9 beng2] *n.* flatbread,
pizza (cheese ~ 芝士薄餅,
vegetable ~ 青菜薄餅, meat ~
有肉薄餅)

薄餅店 [bok9 beng2 dim3] *n.*
pizzeria

薄荷 [bok9 ho4] *n.* peppermint,
mint (breath ~ 香口糖,
~ chocolate 薄荷朱古力, ~ tea
薄荷茶, ~ leaves 薄荷葉)

薄荷油 [bok9 ho4 yau4] *n.*
menthol

薄煎餅 [bok9 jin1 beng2] *n.*
blintze, crepe

薄膜 [bok9 mok9] *n.* membrane

薄片 [bok9 pin2] *n.* flakes (potato
~ 薯片, corn~ 粟米片)

薄片 [bok9 pin2] *adj.* flaky (~
pastry 千層餅)

邦邦 [bong1 bong1] *n.* bonbon

幫手 [bong1 sau2] *n.* assistance

幫手 [bong1 sau2] *v.* help (can
you ~ me? 你可以幫幫我嗎?,
I need ~ 我需要幫忙, ~! 救命
啊!, ~ line 求助熱線)

綁架 [bong2 ga3] *n.* abduction;
v. kidnap

綁緊 [bong2 gan2] *v.* truss

綁住 [bong2 jyu6] *adj.* bound
(~ to 同…綁住)

綁住繩滑落 [bong2 jyu6 sing4
waat9 lok9] *n.* rappeling

綁埋一齊 [bong2 maai4 yat7
chai4] *v.* tie sth. up

煲 [bou1] *n.* cooking pot

煲仔飯 [bou1 jai2 faan6] *n.* rice
pilaf

保持 [bou2 chi4] *v.* keep (~ the
change! 唔使找); sustain

補充 [bou2 chung1] *n.* supplement
(calcium ~ 補鈣, vitamin ~ 補
維他命, mineral ~ 補礦物質,
fiber ~ 補纖維素); auxiliary

補充說明 [bou2 chung1 syut8
ming4] *n.* postscript

補釘 [bou2 deng1] *n.* patch

保健品店 [bou2 gin6 ban2
dim3] *n.* health food store

保健食品 [bou2 gin6 sik9 ban2]
n. health food

保管 [bou2 gun2] *n.* escrow

保險 [bou2 him2] *n.* insurance

保險費 [bou2 him2 fai3] *n.*
insurance premium

保險公司 [bou2 him2 gung1
si1] *n.* insurance company

保險卡 [bou2 him2 kat1] *n.*
insurance card

保險絲 [bou2 him2 si1] *n.* fuse

保險絲盒 [bou2 him2 si1 haap2]
n. fuse box

保險索償 [bou2 him2 sok8
seung4] *n.* insurance claim

保質期 [bou2 jat7 kei4] *n.* sell-
by date

保證 [bou2 jing3] *n.* guarantee

保留 [bou2 lau4] *v.* conserve;
reserve; remain

堡壘 [bou2 leui5] *n.* rampart

保齡球 [bou2 ling4 kau4] *n.*
bowling ball

補牙 [bou2 nga4] *n.* dentures

保守 [bou2 sau2] *adj.* conservative

寶石 [bo2 sek9] *n.* gem, gemstone

保釋 [bou2 sik7] *n.* bail

保釋金 [bou2 sik7 gam1] *n.* bail bond

保鮮膜 [bou2 sin1 mok9] *n.* plastic wrap

寶塔 [bou2 taap8] *n.* pagoda

保溫瓶 [bou2 wan1 ping4] *n.* thermos

保護 [bou2 wu6] *v.* preserve, protect; *n.* protection

保護區 [bou2 wu6 keui1] *n.* conservation area

保佑 [bou2 yau6] *v.* bless (God ~ you! 願主保佑你！)

布 [bou3] *n.* cloth

報酬 [bou3 chau4] *n.* recompense, compensation

報答 [bou3 daap8] *n.* repayment

布達佩斯 [bou3 daat9 pui3 si1] *n.* Budapest (~, capital of Hungary 匈牙利嘅首都)

布甸 [bou3 din1] *n.* pudding

報到 [bou3 dou3] *n.* check-in

報道 [bou3 dou6] *v.* report

布加勒斯特 [bou3 ga1 lak9 si1 dak9] *n.* Bucharest (~, capital of Romania 羅馬尼亞嘅首都)

保加利亞 [bou3 ga1 lei6 a3] *n.* Bulgaria; *adj.* Bulgarian

布基納發索 [bou3 gei1 naap9 faat8 sok8] *n.* Burkina Faso

報紙 [bou3 ji2] *n.* newspaper

報紙攤 [bou3 ji2 taan1] *n.* newsstand

布瓊布拉 [bou3 king4 bou3 laai1] *n.* Bujumbura (~, capital of Burundi 布隆迪嘅首都)

布拉柴維爾 [bou3 laai1 chaai4 wai4 jyut6] *n.* Brazzaville (~, capital of Congo 剛果嘅首都)

布拉迪斯拉發 [bou3 laai1 dik9 si1 laai1 faat8] *n.* Bratislava (~, capital of Slovakia 斯洛伐克嘅首都)

布拉格 [bou3 laai1 gaak8] *n.* Prague (~, capital of Czech Republic 捷克共和國嘅首都)

布冧 [bou3 lam1] *n.* plum (~ brandy 布冧白蘭地, ~ pudding 布冧布甸, ~ jam 布冧果醬)

布里奇頓 [bou3 lei5 kei4 deun6] *n.* Bridgetown (~, capital of Barbados 巴巴多斯島嘅首都)

布料 [bou3 liu2] *n.* fabric

布魯塞爾 [bou3 lou5 choi3 yi5] *n.* Brussels (~, capital of Belgium 比利時嘅首都)

布隆迪 [bou3 lung4 dik9] *n.* Burundi

布隆方丹 [bou3 lung4 fong1 daan1] *n.* Bloemfontein (~, judiciary capital of South Africa 南非嘅司法首都)

報仇 [bou3 sau4] *n.* revenge

布宜諾斯艾利斯 [bou3 yi4 nok9 si1 ngaai6 lei6 si1] *n.* Buenos Aires (~, capital of Argentina 阿根廷嘅首都)

步 [bou6] *n.* step

步兵 [bou6 bing1] *n.* infantry

步槍 [bou6 cheung1] *n.* rifle

部份 [bou6 fan6] *n.* part, segment

暴風雪 [bou6 fung1 syut8] *n.* snowstorm

暴風雨 [bou6 fung1 yu5] *n.* storm

暴風雨警告 [bou6 fung1 yu5 ging2 gou3] *n.* storm warning

暴君 [bou6 gwan1] *n.* oppressor

部長 [bou6 jeung2] *n.* headwaiter

暴力 [bou6 lik9] *n.* violence; *adj.* violent; *adv.* violently

部落 [bou6 lok9] *n.* tribe

暴露 [bou6 lou6] *n.* revelation

部門 [bou6 mun4] *n.* branch, sector, ministry

哺乳動物 [bou6 yu5 dung6 mat9] *n.* mammal

杯 [bui1] *n.* mug, cup (coffee ~ 咖啡杯); mugging, robbery

杯托 [bui1 tok8] *n.* saucer

背景 [bui3 ging2] *n.* setting (place ~ 餐位餐具, dinner ~ 晚飯餐位)

貝殼 [bui3 hok8] *n.* shell

貝殼類動物 [bui3 hok8 leui6 dung6 mat9] *n.* shellfish

貝魯特 [bui3 lou5 dak9] *n.* Beirut (~, capital of Lebanon 黎巴嫩嘅首都)

貝寧灣 [bui3 ning4 waan1] *n.* Benin; *adj.* Beninese

背囊 [bui3 nong4] *n.* backpack, knapsack; backpackers; hostel

貝爾格萊德 [bui3 yi5 gaak8 loi4 dak7] *n.* Belgrade (~, capital of Serbia 塞爾維亞嘅首都)

貝爾莫潘 [bui3 yi5 mok9 pun1] *n.* Belmopan (~, capital of Belize 伯里茲嘅首都)

背 [bui3] *n.* back, at/in/to the back

背信棄義 [bui6 seun3 hei3 yi6] *v.* perfidy

瀑布 [buk9 bou3] *n.* waterfall

搬 [bun1] *v.* move (don't ~ him! 唔好郁佢！)

搬運公司 [bun1 wan6 gung1 si1] *v.* carrier

搬運工人 [bun1 wan6 gung1 yan4] *n.* mover, porter

本質 [bun2 jat7] *adj.* intrinsic

半島 [bun3 dou2] *n.* peninsula

半價 [bun3 ga3] *n.* half price

半徑 [bun3 ging3] *n.* radius

半公斤 [bun3 gung1 gan1] *quant.* half a kilo (1.1 lb.)

半公升 [bun3 gung1 sing1] *quant.* half a liter (0.5 qt.)

半木式 [bun3 muk9 sik7] *adj.* half-timbered

半瓶 [bun3 ping4] *n.* half bottle

半熟牛扒 [bun3 suk9 ngau4 pa4] *n.* rare steak

半甜 [bun3 tim4] *adj.* semi-sweet

半圓壁龕 [bun3 yun4 bik7 ham1] *n.* apse

叛變 [bun6 bin3] *adj.* mutinous; *n.* mutiny

叛亂 [bun6 lyun6] *n.* rebellion

伴娘 [bun6 neung1] *n.* bridesmaid

撥 [but9] *v.* dial

撥號音 [but9 hou6 yam1] *n.* dial tone

撥浪鼓 [but9 long6 gu2] *n.* rattle

C

叉 [cha1] *n.* fork

差啲 [cha1 di1] *adv.* nearly

叉住燒 [cha1 jyu6 siu1] *adj.* spit-roasted

差唔多 [cha1 m4 do1] *adv.* about

差異 [cha1 yi6] *n.* contrast

茶 [cha4] *n.* tea (a cup of ~ 一杯茶, green ~ 綠茶, black ~ 紅茶)

茶包 [cha4 baau1] *n.* teabag

茶煲 [cha4 bou1] *n.* teapot

茶餐廳 [cha4 chaan1 teng1] *n.* café

茶匙 [cha4 chi4] *n.* teaspoon

查詢服務 [cha4 seun1 fuk9 mou6] *n.* directory assistance

茶壺 [cha4 wu4] *n.* teakettle

差館 [chaai1 gun2] *n.* police station

踩單車 [chaai2 daan1 che1] *n.* cycling (~ path 單車徑, ~ enthusiast 單車發燒友)

踩單車嘅人 [chaai2 daan1 che1 ge3 yan4] *n.* bicyclist

柴 [chaai4] *n.* firewood

柴堆 [chaai4 deui1] *n.* pyre

柴油 [chaai4 yau4] *n.* diesel fuel

柴油發動機 [chaai4 yau4 faat8 dung6 gei1] *n.* diesel motor

冊 [chaak8] *n.* volume

拆開 [chaak8 hoi1] *v.* detach

賊仔 [chaak9 jai2] *n.* thief

參加 [chaam1 ga1] *v.* attend, participate

參觀 [chaam1 gun1] *v.* visit

參考 [chaam1 haau2] *n.* guidelines

參數 [chaam1 sou3] *n.* parameter

參議院 [chaam1 yi5 yun2] *n.* senate

參議員 [chaam1 yi5 yun4] *n.* senator

參與 [chaam1 yu5] *v.* involved in

參與者 [chaam1 yu5 je2] *n.* participant

慘敗 [chaam2 baai6] *n.* fiasco

懺悔 [chaam3 fui3] *v.* confess; *n.* confession

杉木 [chaam3 muk9] *n.* fir

蠶豆 [chaam4 dau2] *n.* broad beans

餐 [chaan1] *n.* meal

餐巾 [chaan1 gan1] *n.* napkin (paper ~ 紙巾)

餐具 [chaan1 geui6] *n.* utensils, tableware

餐館仔 [chaan1 gun2 jai2] *n.* diner

餐牌 [chaan1 paai2] *n.* menu (~ of the day 例牌)

餐廳 [chaan1 teng1] *n.* restaurant (formal ~ 高級餐廳, informal ~ 大排擋)

鏟 [chaan2] *n.* shovel, spade, spatula

產品 [chaan2 ban2] *n.* produce, product

鏟除 [chaan2 cheui4] *v.* eradicate

產物 [chaan2 mat9] *n.* creation

產生 [chaan2 sang1] *v.* generate

產業 [chaan2 yip9] *n.* industry

殘暴 [chaan4 bou6] *n.* cruelty (~ to animals 虐待動物)

殘渣 [chaan4 ja1] *n.* offal, residue

殘疾 [chaan4 jat9] *adj.* disabled, handicapped; *n.* handicap (*medical / golf*)

殘疾人士 [chaan4 jat9 yan4 si6] *n.* disabled person

殘忍 [chaan4 yan2] *adj.* cruel

殘餘 [chaan4 yu4] *n.* giblets (chicken ~ 雞雜碎, turkey ~ 火雞雜碎)

撐住 [chaang1 jyu6] *v.* bear; *n.* buttress

橙 [chaang2] *n.* orange

橙花 [chaang2 fa1] *n.* orange blossom

橙汁 [chaang2 jap7] *n.* orange juice

橙皮 [chaang2 pei4] *n.* orange peel

刷 [chaat8] *v.* brush (cooking ~ 廚具刷, to ~ with sauce 塗醬)

擦 [chaat8] *v.* expunge

插蘇 [chaap8 sou1] *n.* power points

插頭 [chaap8 tau4] *n.* socket (electric ~ 電插頭), electrical outlet, plug (pull the ~ 猛插頭)

插入 [chaap8 yap9] *v.* insert

察覺 [chaat8 gok8] *v.* perceive, detect; *n.* perception; *adj.* aware, perceptive

刷鞋 [chaat8 haai4] *v.* polish shoes

炒 [chaau2] *n.* stir-fry (~ chicken 炒雞)

炒蛋 [chaau2 daan6] *n.* scrambled eggs

吵雜聲 [chaau2 jaap9 seng1] *n.* clamor

炒魷魚 [chaau2 yau4 yu2] *v.* dismiss; *n.* dismissal

巢 [chaau4] *n.* nest

棲息地 [chai1 sik7 dei6] *n.* perch, habitat

砌圖 [chai3 tou4] *n.* puzzle

測光表 [chak7 gwong1 bui1] *n.* light meter

測量範圍 [chak7 leung4 faan6 wai4] *n.* gauge

測驗 [chak7 yim6] *n.* test

參考 [cham1 haau2] *v.* refer to; *n.* reference

侵權行為 [cham1 kyun4 hang4 wai4] *n.* tort

侵略 [cham1 leuk9] *n.* aggression

寢具 [cham2 geui6] *n.* bedding

沉澱 [cham4 din6] *n.* sediment

蕁麻 [cham4 ma4] *n.* nettle

沉默寡言 [cham4 mak9 gwa2 yin4] *n.* reticence

鱘魚 [cham4 yu2] *n.* sturgeon, zander

親戚 [chan1 chik7] *n.* relatives

親自 [chan1 ji6] *adv.* personally

親密 [chan1 mat9] *adv.* closely; *adj.* intimate; *n.* intimacy

親密關係 [chan1 mat9 gwaan1 hai6] *n.* affinity

親愛嘅 [chan1 oi3 ge3] *adj.* dear

親屬關係 [chan1 suk9 gwaan1 hai6] *n.* kinship

診斷 [chan2 dyun6] *v.* diagnose; *n.* diagnosis

診症室 [chan2 jing1 sat7] *n.* consultation room (doctor's)

診所 [chan2 so2] *n.* doctor's office, health center, clinic

襯 [chan3] *v.* fit

襯裙 [chan3 kwan4] *n.* petticoat

塵 [chan4] *n.* dirt

陳年 [chan4 nin4] *adj.* aged

陳述 [chan4 seut9] *n.* gift; presentation; allegation; time

層 [chang4] *n.* layer (~ed 分層, ~s 好多層)

層次 [chang4 chi3] *n.* level

七 [chat7] *num.* seven

七十 [chat7 sap9] *num.* seventy

七腮鰻 [chat7 soi1 maan4] *n.* lamprey

七月份 [chat7 yut9 fan6] *n.* July (*abbr.* Jul.)

抽筋 [chau1 gan1] *n.* cramp

抽象 [chau1 jeung6] *adj.* abstract

秋葵 [chau1 kwai4] *n.* okra

秋天 [chau1 tin1] *n.* autumn

醜聞 [chau2 man4] *n.* scandal

醜樣 [chau2 yeung6] *adj.* ugly

臭名 [chau3 ming4] *n.* notoriety

臭名遠播 [chau3 ming4 yun5 bo3] *adj.* notorious

臭脾氣 [chau3 pei4 hei3] *adj.* bad-tempered

臭氧 [chau3 yeung5] *n.* ozone

臭氧層 [chau3 yeung5 chang4] *n.* ozone layer

嗅鹽瓶 [chau3 yim4 ping4] *n.* vinaigrette

綢緞 [chau4 dyun6] *n.* satin

籌碼 [chau4 ma5] *n.* chip

奢侈 [che1 chi2] *n.* luxury

奢侈品 [che1 chi2 ban2] *n.* luxury goods

車 [che1] *n.* automobile (~ ferry 汽車渡輪, ~ insurance card 汽車保險卡)

車 [che1] *v.* sew

車房 [che1 fong4] *n.* car garage

車間 [che1 gaan1] *n.* workshop

車站 [che1 jaam6] *n.* station (police ~ 警察局, train ~ 火車站)

車軸 [che1 juk9] *n.* axle

車厘子 [che1 lei4 ji2] *n.* cherry (~ pie 車厘子批, ~ liqueur 車厘子酒, ~ sauce 車厘子醬)

車輛 [che1 leung6] *n.* vehicle

車尾燈 [che1 mei5 dang1] *n.* taillight

車牌 [che1 paai4] *n.* license plate

車牌號碼 [che1 paai4 hou6 ma5] *n.* license plate number

車衫 [che1 saam1] *n.* sewing

車位 [che1 wai6] *n.* parking space

斜 [che4] *adj.* oblique

斜坡 [che4 bo1] *n.* slope, ramp

斜埋一邊 [che4 maai4 yat7 bin1] *adj.* sideways

尺寸 [chek8 chyun3] *n.* dimension, measurement

赤道 [chek8 dou6] *n.* Equator

赤道幾內亞 [chek8 dou6 gei1 noi6 a3] *n.* Equatorial Guinea

赤字 [chek8 ji6] *n.* deficit

赤陶 [chek8 tou4] *adj.* terracotta

青豆 [cheng1 dau2] *n.* green beans; edamame

青香蕉 [cheng1 heung1 jiu1] *n.* green banana

青椒 [cheng1 jiu1] *n.* green pepper

青木瓜 [cheng1 muk9 gwa1] *n.* quince

青蘋果 [cheng1 ping4 gwo2] *n.* granny smith apple

青洋蔥 [cheng1 yeung4 chung1] *n.* spring onion

青魚 [cheng1 yu2] *n.* herring (pickled ~ 醃青魚)

請 [cheng2] *v.* hire, employ; *n.* guide, translator; teacher; driver; cook

請客 [cheng2 haak8] *n.* treat

請求 [cheng2 kau4] *n.* petition

吹 [cheui1] *v.* blow

吹風機 [cheui1 fung1 gei1] *n.* hairdryer

吹乾頭髮 [cheui1 gon1 tau4 faat8] *n.* blow-dry

催眠 [cheui1 min4] *n.* hypnotism; *v.* hypnotize

趨勢 [cheui1 sai3] *n.* tendency, trend

取模 [cheui2 mou4] *v.* un-mold

取捨 [cheui2 se2] *n.* alternative (~ lifestyle 另外嘅生活方式, ~ music 另類音樂)

取消 [cheui2 siu1] *v.* cancel

取消咗 [cheui2 siu1 jo2] *adj.* canceled

取消律師資格 [cheui2 siu1 leut9 si1 ji1 gaak8] *n.* disbarment (legal)

脆 [cheui3] *adj.* crisp

脆餅 [cheui3 beng2] *n.* shortcake (strawberry ~ 草莓脆餅)

脆口 [cheui3 hau2] *adj.* crunchy

脆麵包片 [cheui3 min6 baau1 pin2] *n.* melba (~ sauce 脆麵包碎醬, ~ toast 脆麵包多士)

脆粟米片 [cheui3 suk7 mai5 pin2] *n.* cornflakes

鎚 [cheui4] *n.* hammer

除 [cheui4] *v.* strip

隨便 [cheui4 bin2] *adj.* casual; *adv.* at random

除非 [cheui4 fei1] *conj.* unless; *prep.* until

隨機 [cheui4 gei1] *adj.* random

除夕 [cheui4 jik9] *n.* New Year's Eve

除咗 [cheui4 jo2] *prep.* beside, except, in addition (to); *adv.* aside from, apart from

除衫 [cheui4 saam1] *v.* undress

隨心所欲 [cheui4 sam1 so2 yuk9] *adv.* freely

隨身行李 [cheui4 san1 hang4 lei5] *n.* carry-on luggage

除油污 [cheui4 yau4 wu1] *v.* degrease

春天 [cheun1 tin1] *n.* spring (coil / season / water)

蠢 [cheun2] *adj.* dull, stupid

巡邏 [cheun4 lo4] *v.* patrol

馴鹿 [cheun4 luk9] *n.* reindeer

循環系統 [cheun4 waan4 hai6 tung2] *n.* circulatory system

巡迴演出 [cheun4 wui4 yin2 cheut7] *n.* tour (~ guide 導遊, ~ group 旅行團)

槍 [cheung1] *n.* gun

窗 [cheung1] *n.* window (~ shopping 隨便睇睇, ~ seat 窗口位, open the ~ 開窗, open a new ~ (*tech.*) 再開一個窗口)

窗框 [cheung1 kwaang1] *n.* pane

猖狂 [cheung1 kwong4] *adj.* rampant

窗簾 [cheung1 lim4] *n.* curtain (*window*)

搶 [cheung2] *v.* plunder; *n.* rip off (that's a ~ off 佔便宜)

搶救 [cheung2 gau3] *v.* salvage

搶劫 [cheung2 gip8] *v.* rob; *n.* robbery

搶劫犯 [cheung2 gip8 faan2] *n.* robber

唱 [cheung3] *v.* sing

唱碟機 [cheung3 dip9 gei1] *n.* CD-player; MP3 player

唱歌 [cheung3 go1] *n.* singing

唱片 [cheung3 pin2] *n.* disc, disk, CD

唱詩班 [cheung3 si1 baan1] *n.* choir

長 [cheung4] *adj.* long

長柄殼 [cheung4 beng3 hok8] *n.* ladle

長柄鍋 [cheung4 beng3 wo1] *n.* skillet

場地 [cheung4 dei6] *n.* site, compound; venue

長笛 [cheung4 dek9] *adj.* flute

長度 [cheung4 dou6] *n.* length

長方形 [cheung4 fong1 ying4] *n.* rectangle

長頸鹿 [cheung4 geng2 luk9] *n.* giraffe

長穀 [cheung4 guk7] *adj.* long-grain (~ rice 長穀米)

腸臟 [cheung4 jong6] *n.* bowel

長期 [cheung4 kei4] *adj.* long-term; *adv.* permanently

長期泊車 [cheung4 kei4 paak3 che1] *n.* long-term parking

長矛 [cheung4 maau4] *n.* lance

長命 [cheung4 meng6] *n.* longevity

長命過 [cheung4 meng6 gwo3] *v.* outlive

長篇大論 [cheung4 pin1 daai6 leun6] *n.* monologue

詳細 [cheung4 sai3] *adj.* detailed; *adv.* in detail

詳細講 [cheung4 sai3 gong2] *adj.* elaborate

詳細說明 [cheung4 sai3 syut8 ming4] *v.* specify

牆 [cheung4] *n.* wall (of a room/house/city)

長時間 [cheung4 si4 gaan3] *adv.* long-time

長途 [cheung4 tou4] *adj.* long-distance

長途巴士 [cheung4 tou4 ba1 si6] *n.* long-distance bus

長途跋涉 [cheung4 tou4 bat9 sip8] *n.* trek

長途特快車 [cheung4 tou4 dak9 faai3 che1] *n.* long-distance express train

長途電話 [cheung4 tou4 din6 wa2] *n.* long-distance call

長筒襪 [cheung4 tung2 mat9] *n.* stockings

腸胃炎 [cheung4 wai6 yim4] *n.* gastroenteritis

出版 [cheut7 baan2] *v.* publish; *n.* publication

出版商 [cheut7 baan2 seung1] *n.* publisher

出版業 [cheut7 baan2 yip9] *n.* publishing

出差 [cheut7 chaai1] *n.* business trip

出發 [cheut7 faat8] *v.* depart; *n.* departure

出價高過 [cheut7 ga3 gou1 gwo3] *v.* outbid

出口 [cheut7 hau2] *n.* exit (of a highway/truck/vehicles); *v.* export (~ a file *tech.* 輸出)

出去食 [cheut7 heui3 sik9] *v.* go out for a meal

出海 [cheut7 hoi2] *v.* sail; *n.* sailing (~ club 航海俱樂部, ~ instructor 風帆教練)

出汗 [cheut7 hon6] *v.* perspire

出咗問題 [cheut7 jo2 man6 tai4] *v.* go wrong

出租 [cheut7 jou1] *phr.* for rent

出奇 [cheut7 kei4] *adv.* unusually

出糧 [cheut7 leung4] *v.* remunerate

出面 [cheut7 min6] *adv.* out (of), way out; eat out

出名 [cheut7 meng2] *n.* fame; *adj.* famous

出生日期 [cheut7 sang1 yat9 kei4] *n.* date of birth

出世 [cheut7 sai3] *n.* birth

出世地方 [cheut7 sai3 dei6 fong1] *n.* place of birth

出世紙 [cheut7 sai3 ji2] *n.* birth certificate

出色 [cheut7 sik7] *adv.* beautifully; *adj.* outstanding

出人意料 [cheut7 yan4 yi3 liu6] *adj.* surprising

出讓 [cheut7 yeung6] *v.* relinquish

出現 [cheut7 yin6] *v.* arise, appear

黐 [chi1] *adj.* sticky

黐力 [chi1 lik9] *n.* adhesion

痴線 [chi1 sin3] *adj* crazy, nutty; *n.* nuts

齒輪 [chi2 leun4] *n.* gear

刺 [chi3] *n.* splinter

刺激 [chi3 gik7] *v.* excite, stimulate

刺客 [chi3 haak8] *n.* assassin

次序 [chi3 jeui6] *n.* order

廁紙 [chi3 ji2] *n.* toilet paper

刺殺 [chi3 saat8] *v.* assassinate; *n.* assassination

刺繡 [chi3 sau3] *n.* embroidery

廁所 [chi3 so2] *n.* restroom, washroom, lavatory

次要 [chi3 yiu3] *adj.* minor (he/she is a ~ 佢係未成年; it's a ~ problem 呢個係小問題)

遲 [chi4] *adj.* late; *n.* lateness

遲鈍 [chi4 deun6] *adj.* obtuse

遲啲 [chi4 di1] *adv.* later

遲到 [chi4 dou3] *v.* be late

匙羹 [chi4 gang1] *n.* spoon

匙羹連叉 [chi4 gang1 lin4 cha1] *n.* spork (spoon and fork)

瓷器 [chi4 hei3] *adj.* ceramic; *n.* ceramics, porcelain

辭職 [chi4 jik7] *v.* quit, resign; *n.* resignation

遲咗 [chi4 jo2] *adj.* delayed

持續時間 [chi4 juk9 si4 gaan3] *n.* continuance

瓷磚 [chi4 jyun1] *n.* tile

詞類 [chi4 leui6] *n.* part of speech

磁盤驅動器 [chi4 pun4 keui1 dung6 hei3] *n.* zip drive *comp.*

慈善 [chi4 sin6] *n.* charity; *adj.* philanthropic

慈善家 [chi4 sin6 ga1] *n.* philanthropist

慈善事業 [chi4 sin6 si6 yip9] *n.* philanthropy

磁石 [chi4 sek9] *n.* magnet

磁性 [chi4 sing3] *adj.* magnetic; *n.* magnetism

池塘 [chi4 tong4] *n.* pond

詞彙 [chi4 wui6] *n.* vocabulary

詞彙表 [chi4 wui6 biu2] *n.* glossary

持有人 [chi4 yau5 yan4] *n.* holder

似 [chi5] *v.* look like

柿 [chi5] *n.* persimmon

簽證 [chim1 jing3] *n.* visa

簽名 [chim1 meng2] *n.* signature

纖維 [chim1 wai4] *n.* fiber

纖維素 [chim1 wai4 sou3] *n.* cellulose

潛水 [chim4 seui2] *v.* dive; *n.* diving (no ~ 禁止潛水, ~ equipment 潛水設備)

潛水吸氣管 [chim4 seui2 kap7 hei3 gun2] *n.* snorkel

潛水衫 [chim4 seui2 saam1] *n.* wetsuit

千 [chin1] *num.* thousand

千層麵 [chin1 chang4 min6] *n.* lasagna

韆鞦 [chin1 chau1] *n.* swing

遷就 [chin1 jau6] *n.* concession

千位元組 [chin1 wai2 yun4 jou2] *n.* kilobyte (*abbr.* K) (file size in ~s 文件大小系數千字節)

淺 [chin2] *adj.* shallow (~ end 淺水區, a ~ person 膚淺嘅人)

錢 [chin2] *n.* money

前臂 [chin4 bei3] *n.* forearm

前輩 [chin4 bui3] *n.* precursor

前燈 [chin4 dang1] *n.* front light, headlight

前腳 [chin4 geuk8] *n.* foreleg

前景 [chin4 ging2] *n.* outlook, prospect

前奏 [chin4 jau3] *n.* prelude

前綴 [chin4 jeui3] *n.* prefix

前輪 [chin4 leun4] *n.* front wheel

前晚 [chin4 maan5] *n.* the day before yesterday

前面 [chin4 min6] *prep.* before; *n.* front (in ~ of 喺 … 前面)

前門 [chin4 mun4] *n.* front door

前哨 [chin4 saau3] *n.* outpost

前提 [chin4 tai4] *n.* hypothesis; prerequisite

前枱 [chin4 toi2] *n.* receptionist, front desk

前任 [chin4 yam6] *prefix* ex-; *n.* predecessor

前言 [chin4 yin4] *n.* preface, prologue; premises

青春 [ching1 cheun1] *n.* youth

青春期 [ching1 cheun1 kei4] *n.* puberty

清楚 [ching1 cho2] *v.* clear (~ the table 清枱, ~ through customs 清關); *adv.* clearly

清倉大減價 [ching1 chong1 daai6 gaam2 ga3] *n.* clearance sale, going-out-of-business sale

清單 [ching1 daan1] *n.* list

清風 [ching1 fung1] *n.* breeze

清教徒 [ching1 gaau3 tou4] *n.* puritan

清潔 [ching1 git8] *v.* clean; *n.* cleaning

清潔好 [ching1 git8 hou2] *v.* clean up

青年旅館 [chingq nin4 leui5 gun2] *n.* youth hostel

稱讚 [ching1 jaan3] *n.* praise

清真寺 [ching1 jan1 ji6] *n.* mosque

清盤 [ching1 pun4] v. liquidate; n. liquidation

清洗罪孽 [ching1 sai2 jeui6 yip9] v. sanctify

清新劑 [ching1 san1 jai1] n. deodorant

清醒 [ching1 sing2] adj conscious (be ~ 意識到)

清湯 [ching1 tong1] n. consommé

青銅 [ching1 tung4] n. bronze

請教 [ching2 gaau3] v. consult; n. consultation

請再講一次 [ching2 joi3 gong2 yat7 chi3] phr. pardon me?, excuse me?

請求 [ching2 kau4] n. request

請問我點去 [ching2 man6 ngo5 dim2 heui3] v. how do I get to

秤 [ching3] v. scale

秤重 [ching3 chung5] v. weigh (he ~ed the apples 佢秤咗啲蘋果, What do you ~? 你幾重？)

澄清 [ching4 ching1] adj. clarified; v. clarify (to ~ 去澄清)

程度 [ching4 dou6] n. extent

懲罰 [ching4 fat9] v. penalize; n. penalty, punishment

情況 [ching4 fong3] n. situation

程序 [ching4 jeui6] n. program, procedure

情節 [ching4 jit8] n. plot

情節提要 [ching4 jit8 tai4 yiu3] n. storyboard

情緒 [ching4 seui5] n. emotion, mood

情緒化 [ching4 seui5 fa3] adj. emotional, moody; adv. emotionally

情緒失控 [ching4 seui5 sat7 hung3] n. nervous breakdown

情態動詞 [ching4 taai3 dung6 chi4] n. modal

情願 [ching4 yun6] adv. rather,rather than

設備 [chit8 bei6] n. facility; fitting

徹底 [chit8 dai2] adj. thorough; adv. thoroughly, entirely

徹底打敗 [chit8 dai2 da2 baai6] v. rout

切丁 [chit8 ding1] diced

設定 [chit8 ding6] v. set

設計 [chit8 gai3] n. design

設計師 [chit8 gai3 si1] n. designer

切開 [chit8 hoi1] v. section (to ~ parts of meat 切一部分嘅肉)

設立 [chit8 laap9] n. setup

撤離 [chit8 lei4] n. withdrawal

切碎 [chit8 seui3] v. mince

切碎咗 [chit8 seui3 jo2] adj. minced

切碎嘅蔥 [chit8 seui3 ge3 chung1] n. chopped shallots

設施 [chit8 si1] n. facilities

切絲 [chit8 si1] adj./v. julienne

切成小塊 [chit8 sing4 siu2 faai3] v. cubed

撤消 [chit8 siu1] n. revocation; v. revoke

撤退 [chit8 teui3] v. retreat

超重 [chiu1 chung5] adj. overweight

超大 [chiu1 daai6] adj. huge, enormous

超過 [chiu1 gwo3] prep. beyond; v. exceed, outrun, overtake; adv. in excess of

超載 [chiu1 joi3] v. overload

超級 [chiu1 kap7] *n.* super (gas)

超細 [chiu1 sai3] *adj.* minuscule, tiny

超時 [chiu1 si4] *v.* overrun

超市 [chiu1 si5] *n.* supermarket

超聲波 [chiu1 sing1 bo1] *adj.* ultrasound

超人 [chiu1 yan4] *n.* superman

肖像 [chiu3 jeung6] *n.* image, portrait

朝代 [chiu4 doi6] *n.* dynasty

潮汐 [chiu4 jik9] *n.* tide

潮濕 [chiu4 sap7] *adj.* damp

朝聖者 [chiu4 sing3 je2] *n.* pilgrim

朝聖之旅 [chiu4 sing3 ji1 leui5] *n.* pilgrimage

搓 [cho1] *v.* knead

初步 [cho1 bou6] *adj.* preliminary, rudimentary

初中 [cho1 jung1] *n.* junior high school

初期 [cho1 kei4] *adj.* nascent

雛形 [cho1 ying4] *n.* rudiment

錯 [cho3] *adj.* wrong (~ number 打錯電話, there's something ~ 有啲唔妥, What's ~? 做乜嘢?)

錯綜複雜 [cho3 jung1 fuk7 jaap9] *n.* complexity

錯誤 [cho3 ng6] *n.* error, mistake

錯誤咁 [cho3 ng6 gam3] *adv.* wrongly

鋤頭 [cho4 tau4] *n.* pickaxe

鋤頭仔 [cho4 tau4 jai2] *n.* spuds

坐 [cho5] *v.* sit (~ down, please 請坐)

採購 [choi2 gau3] *n.* procurement

綵排 [choi2 paai4] *n.* rehearsal; *v.* rehearse

採石場 [choi2 sek9 cheung4] *n.* quarry

彩色 [choi2 sik7] *adj.* colored, multi-colored

彩色玻璃 [choi2 sik7 bo1 lei1] *n.* stained glass

彩色膠卷 [choi2 sik7 gaau1 gyun2] *n.* color film

採用 [choi2 yung6] *v.* adopt

菜 [choi3] *n.* dishes; cuisine

菜燉牛肉 [choi3 dan6 ngau4 yuk9] *n.* goulash (Hungarian ~ 奧地利菜燉牛肉, Polish ~ 波蘭菜燉牛肉)

塞拉利昂 [choi3 laai1 lei6 ngong4] *n.* Sierra Leone; *adj.* Sierra Leonean

賽馬 [choi3 ma5] *n.* racing

賽馬場 [choi3 ma5 cheung4] *n.* track race

塞內加爾 [choi3 noi6 ga1 yi5] *n.* Senegal; *adj.* Senegalese

塞浦路斯 [choi3 pou2 lou6 si1] *n.* Cyprus

塞浦路斯人 [choi3 pou2 lou6 si1 yan4] *n.* Cypriot

菜譜 [choi3 pou2] *n.* cookbook

塞舌爾 [choi3 sit6 yi5] *n.* Seychelles

菜油 [choi3 yau4] *n.* rapeseed oil, canola oil

塞爾維亞 [choi3 yi5 wai4 a3] *n.* Serbia; *adj.* Serbian

財產 [choi4 chaan2] *n.* property, estate, possession

裁定 [choi4 ding6] *n.* verdict

財富 [choi4 fu3] *n.* wealth

裁縫 [choi4 fung2] *n.* tailor

才智 [choi4 ji3] *n.* wit

財政 [choi4 jing3] *adj.* financial, fiscal

財政部 [choi4 jing3 bou6] *n.* treasury

材料 [choi4 liu2] *n.* material

才能 [choi4 nang4] *n.* capability

裁判 [choi4 pun3] *n.* referee

倉庫 [chong1 fu3] *n.* depot, repository, warehouse

倉鼠 [chong1 syu2] *n.* hamster

創始人 [chong3 chi2 yan4] *n.* originator

創造 [chong3 jou6] *v.* create

創新 [chong3 san1] *v.* innovate; *n.* innovation; *adj.* revolutionary

創意 [chong3 yi3] *n.* creativity

床 [chong4] *n.* bed

床單 [chong4 daan1] *n.* bed sheet, sheet of paper

床仔 [chong4 jai2] *n.* cot

床上用品 [chong4 seung6 yung6 ban2] *n.* household linen

床褥 [chong4 yuk9] *n.* mattress

操場 [chou1 cheung4] *n.* playground, playing field

粗口 [chou1 hau2] *n.* swear words

操作 [chou1 jok8] *v.* operate

操作員 [chou1 jok8 yun4] *n.* operator

粗俗 [chou1 juk9] *adj.* unrefined

粗麥麵包 [chou1 mak9 min6 baau1] *n.* pumpernickel

粗麵粉 [chou1 min6 fan2] *n.* grits

粗心 [chou1 sam1] *adj.* careless; *adv.* carelessly

粗糖[chou1 tong4] *n.* unrefined sugar

草 [chou2] *n.* grass

草本 [chou2 bun2] *adj.* herbaceous

草本植物 [chou2 bun2 jik9 mat9] *n.* herb

草叢 [chou2 chung4] *n.* bush

草地 [chou2 dei6] *n.* meadow

草稿 [chou2 gou2] *n.* draft

草菇 [chou2 gu1] *n.* button mushrooms

草藥 [chou2 yeuk9] *adj.* herbal (~ seasoning 香草調味料)

醋 [chou3] *n.* vinegar (white ~ 白醋, red ~ 紅醋, apple ~ 蘋果醋, ~ dressing 香醋沙律醬)

措詞 [chou3 chi4] *n.* phraseology

醋栗 [chou3 leut9] *n.* gooseberries

糙米 [chou3 mai5] *n.* brown rice

噪音 [chou3 yam1] *n.* noise

速度 [chuk7 dou6] *n.* speed, pace, velocity

速度計 [chuk7 dou6 gai3] *n.* speedometer

促進 [chuk7 jeun3] *v.* promote

沖 [chung1] *v.* rinse, bathe; flush; dash

蔥 [chung1] *n.* shallots

匆匆忙忙 [chung1 chung1 mong4 mong4] *adj.* in a hurry

衝突 [chung1 dat9] *n.* conflict

充電電線 [chung1 din6 din6 sin3] *n.* jumper cables

沖膠卷 [chung1 gaau1 gyun2] *v.* develop film

沖涼 [chung1 leung4] *n.* shower, bath

沖涼房 [chung1 leung4 fong2] *n.* bathroom

衝浪 [chung1 long6] *n.* surfing; *v.* surf (~ waves 滑浪)

衝浪板 [chung1 long6 baan2] *n.* surfboard

衝浪運動員 [chung1 long6 wan6 dung6 yun4] *n.* surfer

匆忙 [chung1 mong4] *v.* hurry, be in a hurry

充滿 [chung1 mun5] *adj.* replete

衷心 [chung1 sam1] *adv.* sincerely

沖淡 [chung1 taam5] *v.* dilute

衝入 [chung1 yap9] *v.* run into (crash)

寵物 [chung2 mat9] *n.* pet

寵壞 [chung2 waai6] *v.* spoil

蟲 [chung4] *n.* bug, insect, worm

重疊 [chung4 dip9] *v.* overlap

重複 [chung4 fuk7] *n.* repetition; *v.* repeat (please ~ that 請再講一次)

重複 [chung4 fuk7] *adj.* repeated; *adv.* repeatedly

松雞 [chung4 gai1] *n.* wood grouse

重建 [chung4 gin3] *v.* rebuild

重建嘅 [chung4 gin3 ge3] *adj.* rebuilt

重組 [chung4 jou2] *v.* restructure; *n.* restructuring

叢林 [chung4 lam4] *n.* jungle

從來 [chung4 loi4] *adv.* ever

從來都唔會 [chung4 loi4 dou1 m4 wui5] *adv.* never

從呢度 [chung4 ne1 dou6] *adv.* here, from here

蟲咬 [chung4 ngaau5] *n.* insect bite

重新加熱 [chung4 san1 ga1 yit9] *v.* re-heat

重新開始 [chung4 san1 hoi1 chi2] *v.* renew, resume; *n.* resumption

重新裝滿 [chung4 san1 jong1 mun5] *v.* replenish

重申 [chung4 san1] *v.* reiterate; *n.* reiteration

從事 [chung4 si6] *v.* engage

松鼠 [chung4 syu2] *n.* squirrel

松樹 [chung4 syu6] *n.* pine

重印 [chung4 yan3] *v.* reprint

松仁 [chung4 yan4] *n.* pine kernel

重現 [chung4 yin6] *v.* recur, reproduce; *n.* recurrence

從業人員 [chung4 yip9 yan4 yun4] *n.* practitioner

重 [chung5] *adv.* heavily; *adj.* heavy

重罪 [chung5 jeui6] *n.* felony

重量 [chung5 leung6] *n.* weight (My ~ is 112 kgs. 我重112公斤)

重力 [chung5 lik9] *n.* gravity; *adj.* gravitational

重生 [chung5 sang1] *n.* rebirth

處處 [chyu3 chyu3] *adv.* everywhere

廚房 [chyu4 fong2] *n.* kitchen (~ counter 廚房櫃枱)

櫥櫃 [chyu4 gwai6] *n.* cupboard, cabinet

廚具 [chyu4 geui6] *n.* cooker, kitchen set

廚師 [chyu4 si1] *n.* chef

柱 [chyu5] *n.* pillar

處方 [chyu5 fong1] *n.* prescription

處理 [chyu5 lei5] *n.* disposal; *v.* process, handle (to ~ food 加工食物) *v.* deal with something/ someone

處理不當 [chyu5 lei5 bat7 dong3] *n.* misconduct

處理器 [chyu5 lei5 hei3] *n. comp.* processor

柱廊 [chyu5 long4] *n.* portico

儲物櫃 [chyu5 mat9 gwai6] *n.* locker

處女 [chyu5 neui5] *n.* virgin

處女座 [chyu5 neui5 jo6] *n.* Virgo

村 [chyun1] *n.* village (~ inn 鄉村旅館)

穿窿 [chyun1 lung1] *n.* puncture

穿衣要求 [chyun1 yi1 yiu1 kau4] *n.* dress code

串 [chyun3] *n.* bunch; *v.* spell

串好 [chyun3 hou2] *adj.* skewered

串成一串 [chyun3 sing4 yat7 chyun3] *v.* skewer

傳播 [chyun4 bo3] *n.* transmission (auto ~ 自動排擋); propagation; *v.* transmit

存錢 [chyun4 chin2] *n.* saving (~s account 儲蓄存款賬號, life ~s 成世嘅積蓄); *v.* deposit money

傳達 [chyun4 daat9] *v.* convey

傳達室 [chyun4 daat9 sat7] *n.* delivery room

存款 [chyun4 fun2] *n.* deposit

存款單 [chyun4 fun2 daan1] *n.* certificate of deposit

傳教 [chyun4 gaau3] *v.* preach

傳教士 [chyun4 gaau3 si6] *n.* missionary

傳真 [chyun4 jan1] *n.* fax

傳真機 [chyun4 jan1 gei1] *n.* fax machine

存在 [chyun4 joi6] *v.* exist; *n.* existence

傳票 [chyun4 piu3] *n.* subpoena

傳統 [chyun4 tung2] *n.* tradition

傳統嘅 [chyun4 tung2 ge3] *adj.* traditional, conventional

傳統上 [chyun4 tung2 seung6] *adv.* traditionally

傳說 [chyun4 syut8] *n.* tale

傳染 [chyun4 yim5] *adj.* infectious

傳染性單核細胞增多症 [chyun4 yim5 sing3 daan1 hat9 sai3 baau1 jang1 do1 jing3] *n.* infectious mononucleosis

撮 [chyut8] *n.* pinch (~ of salt 一小撮鹽)

全部 [cyun4 bou6] *adj.* total

全景 [cyun4 ging2] *n.* panorama

全脂 [cyun4 ji1] *adj.* full-fat

全脂牛奶 [cyun4 ji1 ngau4 naai5] *n.* whole milk

全職 [cyun4 jik7] *n.* full-time work

全球 [cyun4 kau4] *adj.* global

全球化 [cyun4 kau4 fa3] *n.* globalization

全麥 [cyun4 mak9] *n.* whole wheat (~ flour 全麥麵粉, ~ bread 全麥麵包, ~ pasta 全麥意粉)

全民投票 [cyun4 man4 tau4 piu3] *n.* plebiscite, referendum

全面 [cyun4 min6] *adj.* extensive

全世界 [cyun4 sai3 gaai3] *adj.* worldwide

全新 [cyun4 san1] *adj.* brand-new

全神貫注 [cyun4 san4 gun3 jyu3] *v.* engross

全盛時期 [cyun4 sing6 si4 kei4] *n.* prime

全天候服務 [cyun4 tin 1 hau6 fuk9 mou6] *n.* twenty-four hour service

全屋人 [cyun4 uk7 yan4] *n.* household

D

打 [da2] *n./v.* punch; *v.* tie (~ a game 打成平手, ~ smth. up 綁埋一齊)

打扮好 [da2 baan6 hou2] *adj.* dressed (~ in formal attire 穿著正式)

打保齡球 [da2 bou2 ling4 kau4] *v.* bowling (to go ~ 打保齡球, ~ shoes 保齡球鞋)

打電話 [da2 din6 wa2] *v.* make a phone call

打嗝 [da2 gaak8] *n.* hiccup

打交 [da2 gaau1] *n.* fighting; *v.* fight

打攪 [da2 gaau2] *v.* interrupt; *n.* interruption (without ~ 順利)

打擊 [da2 gik7] *n.* shock

打官司 [da2 gun1 si1] *n.* litigation

打喊櫨 [da2 haam3 lou5] *v.* yawn

打開蓋 [da2 hoi1 goi3] *v.* uncap, uncork (~ed 打開咗蓋)

打開呢度 [da2 hoi1 ne4 dou6] open here

打折 [da2 jit8] *n.* discount (youth/children's ~ 兒童折扣, senior ~ 長者折扣, ~ store 打折店, percent ~ 幾折)

打爛 [da2 laan6] *v.* break

打冷震 [da2 laang5 jan3] *v.* quiver, shiver; *n.* shivers

打蠟 [da2 laap9] *v.* wax; *n.* waxing (skis, legs)

打獵 [da2 lip9] *v.* hunt; *n.* hunting

打牌 [da2 paai4] *v.* play cards

打成平手 [da2 sing4 ping4 sau2] *v.* tie a game

打吠 [da2 taai1] *v.* to knot a tie

打印 [da2 yan3] *v.* print

打印機 [da2 yan3 gei1] *n.* printer

打預防針 [da2 yu6 fong4 jam1] *n.* inoculation

歹徒 [daai2 tou4] *n.* ruffian

帶 [daai2] *n.* tape; [daai3] *v.* bring

帶領 [daai3 ling5] *v.* conduct

帶來 [daai3 loi4] *v.* to bring

帶頭人 [daai3 tau4 yan4] *n.* pacemaker

大 [daai6] *adj.* big, large

大比目魚 [daai6 bei2 muk9 yu2] *n.* turbot, halibut

大髀 [daai6 bei2] *n.* thigh (turkey ~ 火雞髀, chicken ~ 雞髀)

大餅 [daai6 beng2] *n.* Chinese pancake

大錘 [daai6 cheui4] *n.* mallet

大膽講 [daai6 daam2 gong2] *adj.* vocal

大啲 [daai6 di1] *adj.* bigger

大多數 [daai6 do1 sou3] *n.* majority

大道 [daai6 dou6] *n.* avenue

大塊肉 [daai6 faai3 yuk9] *n.* meatloaf

大方 [daai6 fong1] *n.* profusion; *adj.* generous, munificent; *adv.* generously

大風警報 [daai6 fung1 ging2 bou3] *n.* gale warning

大風雪 [daai6 fung1 syut8] *n.* blizzard

大街 [daai6 gaai1] *n.* main street

大減價 [daai6 gaam2 ga3] *n.* sale

大教堂 [daai6 gaau3 tong4] *n.* cathedral

大驚小怪 [daai6 geng1 siu2 gwaai3] *n.* fuss

大叫 [daai6 giu3] *n.* exclamation

大過 [daai6 gwo3] *adj.* larger

大蝦 [daai6 ha1] *n.* large prawn

大海 [daai6 hoi2] *n.* ocean

大學 [daai6 hok9] *n.* university

大學學位 [daai6 hok9 hok9 wai6] *n.* university degree

大學錄取 [daai6 hok9 luk9 cheui2] *v.* matriculate; *n.* matriculation

大雜燴 [daai6 jaap9 wui6] *n.* hash

大酒杯 [daai6 jau2 bui1] *n.* jeroboam

大自然 [daai6 ji6 yin4] *n.* nature

大蕉 [daai6 jiu1] *n.* plantain

大主教 [daai6 jyu2 gaau3] *n.* archbishop

大概 [daai6 koi3] *adj.* approximate; *adv.* approximately, roughly

大理石 [daai6 lei5 sek9] *n.* marble

大量 [daai6 leung6] *n.* mass, multitude, amount; *adj.* massive, substantial

大力撞 [daai6 lik9 jong6] *v.* pound (to ~ food in order to crush it)

大力咬 [daai6 lik9 ngaau5] *v.* munch

大陸 [daai6 luk9] *n.* continent; *adj.* continental (~ United States 美國大陸)

大麻 [daai6 ma4] *n.* hashish, marijuana

大馬士革 [daai6 ma5 si6 gaak8] *n.* Damascus (~, capital of Syria 敘利亞首都)

大麥 [daai6 mak9] *n.* barley

大排擋 [daai6 paai4 dong2] *n.* street food

大炮 [daai6 paau3] *n.* artillery

大陪審團 [daai6 pui4 sam2 tyun4] *n.* grand jury

大臣 [daai6 san4] *n.* minister

大寫鎖定 [daai6 se2 so2 ding6] *n. comp.* caps lock; ~ key 大寫鎖定鍵

大赦 [daai6 se3] *n.* amnesty

大聲 [daai6 seng1] *n.* loudness; *adj.* loud; *adv.* aloud

大使 [daai6 si3] *n.* ambassador

大使館 [daai6 si3 gun2] *n.* embassy

大食會 [daai6 sik9 wui2] *n.* feast

大城市 [daai6 sing4 si5] *adj.* metropolitan

大太陽 [daai6 taai3 yeung4] *adj.* sunny

大體上 [daai6 tai2 seung6] *adv.* broadly

大提琴 [daai6 tai4 kam4] *n.* cello

大頭菜 [daai6 tau4 choi3] *n.* kohlrabi; turnip

大頭針 [daai6 tau4 jam1] *n.* pin

大廳 [daai6 teng1] *n.* stateroom

大湯匙 [daai6 tong1 chi4] *n.* tablespoon

大堂 [daai6 tong4] *n.* hall, lobby

大屠殺 [daai6 tou4 saat8] *n.* holocaust, massacre

大話 [daai6 wa6] *n.* leasing

大話精 [daai6 wa6 jing1] *n.* liar

大黃 [daai6 wong4] *n.* rhubarb

大人 [daai6 yan4] *n.* adult

大耳窿 [daai6 yi5 lung1] *n.* usury

擔保 [daam1 bou2] *v.* ensure; *n.* warranty

擔架 [daam1 ga2] *n.* stretcher

擔心 [daam1 sam1] *v.* worry; *n.* misgiving; *adj.* worried

膽結石 [daam2 git8 sek9] *n.* grillstones

膽量 [daam2 leung6] *n.* courage

淡季 [daam6 gwai3] *adj.* off-peak

氮氣 [daam6 hei3] *n.* nitrogen

淡水 [daam6 seui2] *n.* fresh water

淡水鱈魚 [daam6 seui2 syut8 yu2] *n.* burbot (fish)

單 [daan1] *n.* bill (dollar) (~s 紙鈔, to pay the ~s 埋單)

單車 [daan1 che1] *n.* bicycle, bike,

單車道 [daan1 che1 dou6] *n.* bike lane

單車徑 [daan1 che1 ging3] *n.* biking path

單程票 [daan1 ching4 piu3] *n.* one-way ticket

單獨 [daan1 duk9] *adj.* individual, solo

單反相機 [daan1 faan2 seung1 gei1] *n.* SLR camera

單腳跳 [daan1 geuk8 tiu3] *n.* hops

單行道 [daan1 hang4 dou6] *adj.* one-way; *n.* one-way street

丹麥 [daan1 mak9] *n.* Denmark

丹麥酥皮餅 [daan1 mak9 sou1 pei4 beng2] *n.* Danish pastry

丹麥人 [daan1 mak9 yan4] *n.* Danish

單身 [daan1 san1] *adj.* single (*marital status*), unmarried

單數 [daan1 sou3] *adj.* singular

單位 [daan1 wai2] *n.* unit

單人床 [daan1 yan4 chong4] *n.* twin beds

單人房 [daan1 yan4 fong4] *n.* single room

蛋白杏仁餅 [daan2 baak9 hang6 yan4 beng2] *n.* macaroon (cocount ~ 椰子蛋白杏仁餅, nut ~ 蛋白杏仁餅, chocolate ~ 朱古力蛋白杏仁餅, vanilla ~ 香草蛋白杏仁餅)

蛋白酥 [daan2 baak9 sou1] *n.* meringue (lemon ~ 檸檬蛋白酥, lime ~ 青檸檬蛋白酥, ~ pie 蛋白酥派)

蛋羹 [daan2 gang1] *n.* custard (egg ~ 蛋羹, chocolate ~ 朱古力蛋羹, butter ~ 牛油蛋羹)

蛋糕 [daan6 gou1] *n.* cake (sponge ~ 海綿蛋糕, sugar ~ 甜蛋糕)

蛋糕店 [daan6 gou1 dim3] *n.* pastry shop

但係 [daan6 hai6] *conj.* but, whereas; *adv.* however

彈走 [daan6 jau2] *v.* flip

彈珠機 [daan6 jyu1 gei1] *n.* pinball machine

蛋奶酥 [daan6 naai5 sou1] *n.* soufflé

蛋撻仔 [daan6 taat3 jai2] *n.* tartlet

蛋黃 [daan6 wong4] *n.* yolk

蛋黃醬 [daan6 wong4 jeung3] *n.* mayonnaise

答 [daap8] *v.* respond

答辯人 [daap8 bin6 yan4] *n.*
pleader

答案 [daap8 on3] *n.* answer

搭順風車 [daap8 seun6 fung1 che1] *v.* hitchhike

搭郵輪 [daap8 yau4 leun4] *n.* cruise

達到 [daat9 dou3] *v.* achieve

達卡 [daat9 ka1] *n.* Dhaka (~, capital of Bangladesh 孟加拉首都)

達喀爾 [daat9 kak1 yi5] *n.* Dakar (~, capital of Senegal 塞內加爾嘅首都)

達累斯薩拉姆 [daat9 leui5 si1 saat8 laai1 mou5] *n.* Dar es Salaam (~, capital of Tanzania 坦桑尼亞首都)

低 [dai1] *adj.* low

低地 [dai1 dei6] *n.* lowland

低脂 [dai1 ji1] *adj.* low-fat

低卡路里 [dai1 ka1 lou6 lei5] *adj.* low-calorie

低醇度啤酒 [dai1 seun4 dou6 be1 jau2] *n.* low-alcohol beer

低音樂器 [dai1 yam1 ngok9 hei3] *n.* bass (electric ~ 電子低音吉他, ~ guitar 低音吉他, double string ~ 雙低音弦)

低於 [dai1 yu1] *prep.* below, under (~ control 處於控制之下)

抵 [dai2] *adj.* economic

底 [dai2] *n.* bottom

抵押權 [dai2 aat8 kyun4] *n.* pledge

底褲 [dai2 fu3] *n.* underpants, underwear

抵制 [dai2 jai3] *v.* boycott, resist

底座 [dai2 jo6] *n.* pedestal

抵抗 [dai2 kong3] *n.* resistance

抵消 [dai2 siu1] *v.* offset

帝國 [dai3 gwok8] *n.* empire

帝力 [dai3 lik9] *n.* Dili (~, capital of East Timor [Timor-Leste] 東帝汶首都)

帝王 [dai3 wong4] *adj.* regal

第八個 [dai6 baat8 go3] *adj.* eighth

第八十個 [dai6 baat8 sap9 go3] *adj.* eighteenth

第比利斯 [dai6 bei2 lei6 si1] *n.* Tbilisi (~, capital of Georgia 格魯吉亞首都)

第七個 [dai6 chat7 go3] *adj.* seventh

第七十個 [dai6 chat7 sap9 go3] *adj.* seventieth

第九個 [dai6 gau2 go3] *adj.* ninth

第九十個 [dai6 gau2 sap9 go3] *adj.* ninetieth

第六個 [dai6 luk9 go3] *adj.* sixth

第六十個 [dai6 luk9 sap9 go3] *adj.* sixtieth

第五個 [dai6 ng5 go3] *adj.* fifth

第五十個 [dai6 ng5 sap9 go3] *adj.* fiftieth

第三方 [dai6 saam1 fong1] *n.* third party

第三個 [dai6 saam1 go3] *adj.* third

第三十個 [dai6 saam1 sap9 go3] *adj.* thirtieth

第十八個 [dai6 sap9 baat8 go3] *adj.* eighteenth

第十七個 [dai6 sap9 chat7 go3] *adj.* seventeenth

第十九個 [dai6 sap9 gau2 go3] *adj.* nineteenth

第十個 [dai6 sap9 go3] *adj.* tenth

第十六個 [dai6 sap9 luk9 go3] *adj.* sixteenth

第十五個 [dai6 sap9 ng5 go3] *adj.* fifteenth

第十三個 [dai6 sap9 saam1 go3] *adj.* thirteenth

第十四個 [dai6 sap9 sei3 go3] *adj.* fourteenth

第十一個 [dai6 sap9 yat7 go3] *adj.* eleventh

第十二個 [dai6 sap9 yi6 go3] *adj.* twelfth

第四個 [dai6 sei3 go3] *adj.* fourth

第四十個 [dai6 sei3 sap9 go3] *adj.* fortieth

第一百個 [dai6 yat7 baak8 go3] *adj.* hundredth

第一次露面 [dai6 yat7 chi3 lou6 min6] *n.* debut (*also* début)

第一千個 [dai6 yat7 chin1 go3] *adj.* thousandth

第一 [dai6 yat7] *det.* ordinal num. first (~ course 頭道菜, ~ floor 一樓, ~ gear 一檔, ~ name 名)

第二十個 [dai6 yi6 sap9 go3] *adj.* twentieth

第二 [dai6 yi6] *n./adj.* second (*ordinal num. / unit of time*) (~ class 二等, ~ floor 二樓; ten ~s 好快)

第二意見 [dai6 yi6 yi3 gin3] *n.* second opinion

得 [dak7] *adj.* only

得到 [dak7 dou3] *v.* gain, get

德國 [dak7 gwok8] *adj.* German; *n.* Germany

德國鹹酸菜 [dak7 gwok8 haam4 syun1 choi3] *n.* sauerkraut

得閒 [dak7 haan4] *n.* free time, leisure

德黑蘭 [dak7 hak7 laan4] *n.* Tehran (~, capital of Iran 伊朗首都)

得罪 [dak7 jeui6] *v.* offend

得罪人 [dak7 jeui6 yan4] *adj.* offensive

得唔得 [dak7 m4 dak7] *n.* availability

得體 [dak7 tai2] *n.* propriety

得人驚 [dak7 yan4 geng1] *adj.* frightening, alarming, scary; horrible, terrible, shocking

得意 [dak7 yi3] *adj.* interesting; lovely, adorable

特別 [dak9 bit9] *adv.* especially, specially; *adj.* special (~ delivery 特別運送, ~ needs 特殊需要, today's ~ 今日特價)

特產 [dak9 chaan2] *n.* local speciality

特長 [dak9 cheung4] *n.* specialty (~ of the day 今日特色菜)

特定 [dak9 ding6] *adj.* particular, specific

特古西加爾巴 [dak9 gu2 sai1 ga1 yi5 ba1] *n.* Tegucigalpa (~, capital of Honduras 洪都拉斯首都)

特許經營 [dak9 heui2 ging1 ying4] *n.* franchise

特徵 [dak9 jing1] *n.* feature

特權 [dak9 kyun4] *n.* prerogative, privilege

特立尼達 [dak9 laap9 nei4 daat9] *adj.* Trinidadian

特立尼達和多巴哥 [dak9 laap9 nei4 daat9 wo4 do1 ba1 go1] *n.* Trinidad and Tobago

特使 [dak9 si3] *n.* emissary

燉 [dan6] *n.* stew (beef ~ 燉牛肉, vegetable ~ 燉青菜); *adj.* stewed

燉腎 [dan6 san5] *n.* kidney stew

燉肉 [dan6 yuk9] *n.* pot roast

燈 [dang1] *n.* lamp

燈膽 [dang1 daam2] *n.* lightbulb

登機證 [dang1 gei1 jing3] *n.* boarding pass

登記 [dang1 gei3] *v.* register; *n.* registration (~ form 登記表, vehicle ~ documents 車輛登記文件)

登記處 [dang1 gei3 chyu3] *n.* registry, check-in desk

燈籠椒 [dang1 lung4 jiu1] *n.* capsicums

登山家 [dang1 saan1 ga1] *n.* mountaineer

登山靴 [dang1 saan1 heu1] *n.* hiking boots

登山裝備 [dang1 saan1 jong1 bei6] *n.* hiking gear

登山路線 [dang1 saan1 lou6 sin3] *n.* hiking routes

燈塔 [dang1 taap8] *n.* beacon

登入 [dang1 yap9] *v. comp.* login; 登入用戶名 login ID, 登入你嘅帳戶 login to your account

等 [dang2] *n.* wait (~ time 等候時間); *v.* wait for (~ the tone 等待音)

等等！ [dang2 dang2] Wait!

等等 [dang2 dang2] etc. (*abbrev.* of et cetera); *adv.* such and such

等級 [dang2 kap7] *n.* rank, tier

等式 [dang2 sik7] *n.* equation

凳 [dang3] *n.* chair, bench

突發 [dat9 faat8] *n.* outburst

突擊搜查 [dat9 gik7 sau2 cha4] *n.* raid

突尼西亞 [dat9 nei4 sai1 a3] *n.* Tunisia

突尼斯 [dat9 nei4 si1] *n.* Tunis (~, capital of Tunisia 突尼亞嘅首都); *adj.* Tunisian

突然 [dat9 yin4] *adj.* sudden; *adv.* suddenly

突然跌低 [dat9 yin4 dit8 dai1] *v.* plump

豆 [dau2] *n.* bean

豆袋坐墊 [dau2 doi6 cho5 din2] *n.* bean bag

豆類 [dau2 leui6] *n.* legumes

豆類植物嘅種子 [dau2 leui6 jik9 mat9 ge3 jung2 ji2] *n.* leguminous seeds

豆腐 [dau6 fu6] *n.* bean curd, tofu

豆殼 [dau6 hok8] *n.* peapod, pod

逗號 [dau6 hou6] *n.* comma

豆仔 [dau6 jai2] *n.* string bean

豆煮粟米 [dau6 jyu2 suk7 mai5] *n.* succotash

豆芽 [dau6 nga4] *n.* sprouts (soy ~ 大豆芽, bean ~ 綠豆芽)

爹哋 [de1 di6] *n.* dad, father

地 [dei6] *n.* earth, soil

地板 [dei6 baan2] *n.* floor

地標 [dei6 biu1] *n.* landmark

地方 [dei6 fong1] *n.* spot, place

地方主義 [dei6 fong1 jyu2 yi6] *n.* provincialism

地方委員會 [dei6 fong1 wai2 yun4 wui2] *n.* local council

地下 [dei6 ha5] *adj.* ground (~ coffee 咖啡粉, ~ pepper 辣椒粉, ~ nuts 乾果粉); *n.* earth; reason; underground

地下室 [dei6 ha5 sat7] *n.* basement

地下通道 [dei6 ha5 tung1 dou6] *n.* underpass

地震 [dei6 jan3] *n.* earthquake

地質學 [dei6 jat7 hok9] *n.* geology

地質學家 [dei6 jat7 hok9 ga1] *n.* geologist

地址 [dei6 ji2] *n.* address (home ~ 屋企地址)

地氈 [dei6 jin1] *n.* carpet

地氈仔 [dei6 jin1 jai2] *n.* rug

地中海 [dei6 jung1 hoi2] *adj.* Mediterranean (~ food 地中海菜)

地中海海棗 [dei6 jung1 hoi2 hoi2 jou2] *n.* Mediterranean date

地球 [dei6 kau4] *n.* Earth

地區 [dei6 keui1] *n.* zone, region

地拉那 [dei6 laai1 na5] *n.* Tirane (~, capital of Albania 阿爾巴尼亞首都)

地理 [dei6 lei5] *n.* geography; *adj.* geographical

地牢 [dei6 lou4] *n.* crypt, vault

地頭 [dei6 tau4] *n.* territory

地鐵 [dei6 tit8] *n.* subway, metro

地鐵站 [dei6 tit8 jaam6] *n.* subway station, metro station

地圖 [dei6 tou4] *n.* map

地位 [dei6 wai6] *n.* standing, status

地形 [dei6 ying4] *n.* landscape

地獄 [dei6 yuk9] *n.* hell

釘埋一齊 [deng1 maai4 yat7 chai4] *v.* bind

頂 [deng2] *n.* top

訂 [deng6] *v.* subscribe

訂做 [deng6 jou6] *v.* customize

訂閱 [deng6 yut9] *n.* subscription

對比鮮明 [deui3 bei2 sin1 ming4] *adj.* contrasting

對齊 [deui3 chai4] *v.* align

對稱 [deui3 ching3] *n.* symmetry

對方付費電話 [deui3 fong1 fu6 fai3 din6 wa2] *n.* collect call

對付 [deui3 fu6] *v.* cope, cope with

對…好 [deui3 … hou2] *adj.* good for …

對著 [deui3 jyu3] *v.* orientate

對唔住 [deui3 m4 jyu6] *adj.* sorry (be ~ 覺得唔好意思, feel ~ 覺得唔好意思, I'm ~. 對唔住)

對面 [deui3 min6] *adj.* opposite; *adv.* across

對手 [deui3 sau2] *n.* adversary, competitor, opponent, rival

對話 [deui3 wa6] *n.* dialogue (memorize ~ 記住對話)

對應 [deui3 ying3] *adj.* corresponding

隊 [deui6] *n.* queue

隊列 [deui6 lit9] *n.* array

隊伍 [deui6 ng5] *n.* procession

噸 [deun1] *n.* ton

啲 [di1] *adj.* any; *det.* some (~ kind of 某種, You're ~ friend! 你真是好朋友!)

啲嘢 [di1 ye5] *pron.* something

的確 [dik7 kok8] *adv.* indeed

的黎波里 [dik7 lai4 bo1 lei5] *n.* Tripoli (~, capital of Libya 利比亞首都)

滴水 [dik7 seui2] *v.* drip

滴水獸 [dik7 seui2 sau3] *n.* gargoyle

的士 [dik7 si2] *n.* taxi, cab (~ stand 的士站, hail a ~ 截的士)

敵人 [dik9 yan4] *n.* enemy

敵意 [dik9 yi3] *n.* enmity

點半 [dim2 bun3] *quant.* half past

點都好 [dim2 dou1 hou2] *adv.* anyway

點火裝置 [dim2 fo2 jong1 ji3] *n.* ignition

點解 [dim2 gaai2] *adv.* why, why is that?

點擊量 [dim2 gik7 leung6] *n.* page view (website ~s 網站點擊量)

點綴 [dim2 jeui3] *v./n.* dot (to ~ 用小圓點標出; a ~ 一個小圓點))

點鐘 [dim2 jung1] *n.* o'clock (it's 5 ~ 宜家五點鐘啦)

點心 [dim2 sam1] *n.* dim sum

點樣 [dim2 yeung2] *conj.* how (~ are you? 最近點啊？)

店 [dim3] *n.* shop

店主 [dim3 jyu2] *n.* shopkeeper

顛倒 [din1 dou2] *n.* reversal

癲癇症患者 [din1 gaan4 jing3 waan6 je2] *adj.* epileptic

癲佬 [din1 lou2] *n.* lunatic

碘 [din2] *n.* iodine

典禮 [din2 lai5] *n.* ceremony (wedding ~ 結婚典禮, graduation ~ 畢業典禮)

典型 [din2 ying4] *adj.* typical

墊 [zin3] *n.* pad

電 [din6] *n.* electricity

電壓 [din6 aat8] *n.* voltage

電報 [din6 bou3] *n.* telegram

電池 [din6 chi4] *n.* battery

電池冇電 [din6 chi4 mou4 din6] *n.* dead battery

電單車 [din6 daan1 che1] *n.* motorcycle, motorbike

電動嘅 [din6 dung6 ge3] *adj.* electical, electric

電動牙刷 [din6 dung6 nga4 chaat8] *n.* electric toothbrush

電動鬚刨 [din6 dung6 sou1 paau4] *n.* electric razor/shaver

電動船 [din6 dung6 syun4] *n.* motorboat

電髮 [din6 faat8] *n.* perm

澱粉 [din6 fan2] *n.* starch

電解質 [din6 gaai2 jat7] *n.* electrolytes

奠基石 [din6 gei1 sek9] *n.* cornerstone

電子 [din6 ji2] *n.* electron; *adj.* electronic

電子表格 [din6 ji2 biu2 gaak8] *n.* spreadsheet

電子郵件 [din6 ji2 yau4 gin6] *n.* e-mail, email address

電子遊戲 [din6 ji2 yau4 hei3] *n.* arcade game

電子元件 [din6 ji2 yun4 gin6] *n.* electronics

電纜 [din6 laam6] *n.* cable

電路 [din6 lou6] *n.* circuit (short ~ 短路)

電腦 [din6 nou5] *n.* computer
電腦網絡 [din6 nou5 mong5 lok8] *n.* computer network
電腦遊戲 [din6 nou5 yau4 hei3] *n.* computer games
電訊 [din6 seun3] *n.* telecommunications
電視 [din6 si6] *n* TV, television; cable ~ 有線電視
電視劇 [din6 si6 kek9] *n.* soap opera
電線 [din6 sin3] *n.* wire
電話 [din6 wa2] *n.* (tele)phone call (make a ~ 打電話)
電話簿 [din6 wa2 bou6] *n.* (tele) phone directory, (tele)phone book (directory assistance 查號台）
電話號碼 [din6 wa2 hou6 ma5] *n.* (tele)phone number
電話卡 [din6 wa2 kat1] *n.* phone card
電話亭 [din6 wa2 ting4] *n.* phone booth
電話會議 [din6 wa2 wui6 yi5] *n.* conference call
電影 [din6 ying2] *n.* film, movie
電影院 [din6 ying2 yun2] *n.* movie theater
丁香 [ding1 heung1] *n.* clove; lilac
丁字骨牛扒 [ding1 ji6 gwat7 ngau4 pa2] *n.* T-bone steak
丁烷氣 [ding1 yun4 hei3] *n.* butane gas
鼎盛時期 [ding2 sing4 si4 kei4] *n.* heyday
定 [ding3] *conj.* or

訂婚 [ding3 fan1] *adj.* engaged to marry; *n.* engagement
定係 [ding3 hai6] *conj.* whether
訂枱 [ding3 toi4] *v.* reserve a table
定價 [ding6 ga3] *n.* fixed price
定期 [ding6 kei4] *adj.* periodical, regular
定期航班 [ding6 kei4 hong4 baan1] *n.* scheduled flight
定量 [ding6 leung6] *n.* ration
定位 [ding6 wai6] *v.* locate
定義 [ding6 yi6] *n.* definition; *v.* define
定型慕絲 [ding6 ying4 mou6 si1] *n.* hair mousse
疊 [dip9] *v.* fold
碟 [dip9] *n.* dish, plate
鰈類魚 [dip9 leui6 yu2] *n.* brill (*fish*)
跌 [dit8] *v.* go down
跌低 [dit8 dai1] *v.* slip
跌落嚟 [dit8 lok9 lai4] *v.* fall over/down; *n.* fall (*season*)
丟架 [diu1 ga2] *n.* shame
雕刻 [diu1 hak7] *v.* carve; *n.* engraving
雕刻品 [diu1 hak7 ban2] *n.* carving
雕刻刀 [diu1 hak7 dou1] *n.* carving knife
雕刻家 [diu1 hak7 ga1] *n.* sculptor
雕像 [diu1 jeung6] *n.* sculpture, statue; activity; artwork
雕像仔 [diu1 jeung6 jai2] *n.* figurines
吊床 [diu3 chong4] *n.* hammock

吊帶 [diu3 daai2] *n.* sling

吊橋 [diu3 kiu4] *n.* drawbridge

釣魚 [diu3 yu2] *n.* fishing (no ~ 嚴禁釣魚)

釣魚証 [diu3 yu2 jing3] *n.* fishing license

掉 [diu6] *v.* dump, cast, throw (~ sth. away 掉咗, ~ a party 舉辦排隊, ~ a fit 大發脾氣, ~ a ball 掟球)

調查 [diu6 cha4] *n.* inquiry, enquiry, investigation, survey; *v.* investigate

調查問卷 [diu6 cha4 man6 gyun2] *n.* questionnaire

調查庭 [diu6 cha4 ting4] *n.* preliminary hearing

掉咗 [diu6 jo2] *v.* get rid of

多邊 [do1 bin1] *adj.* multilateral

多半 [do1 bun3] *adv.* mostly

多產 [do1 chaan2] *adj.* prolific

多層蛋糕 [do1 chang4 daan6 gou1] *n.* multitiered cake

多啲 [do1 di1] *det.* more (some ~ 再多啲, no ~ 唔要啦, ~ slowly 慢啲)

多哥 [do1 go1] *n.* Togo

多個 [do1 go3] *adj.* multiple

多管閒事 [do1 gun2 haan4 si6] *adj.* officious

多功能電影院 [do1 gung1 nang4 din6 ying2 yun2] *n.* multiplex cinema

多過 [do1 gwo3] *v.* outnumber

多哈 [do1 ha1] *n.* Doha (~, capital of Qatar 卡塔爾首都)

多謝 [do1 je6] *v./n.* thank(s), thank you! (give ~s 轉達謝意)

多種多樣 [do1 jung2 do1 yeung6] *adj.* varied

多種形式 [do1 jung2 ying4 sik7] *adj.* multiform

多米尼加 [do1 mai5 nei4 ga1] *n.* Dominica; *adj.* Dominican

多米尼加共和國 [do1 mai5 nei4 ga1 gung6 wo4 gwok8] *n.* Dominican Republic

多米諾骨牌 [do1 mai5 nok9 gwat7 paai2] *n.* dominoes

多媒體 [do1 mui4 tai2] *n.* multimedia

多倍 [do1 pui5] *n.* multiped

多士 [do1 si2] *n.* toast (bread)

多士粒 [do1 si2 lap7] *n.* crouton

多士爐 [do1 si6 lou4] *n.* toaster

多山 [do1 saan1] *adj.* mountainous

多數 [do1 sou3] *adv.* probably

多胎 [do1 toi1] *adj.* multiparous

多雲 [do1 wan4] *adj.* cloudy, overcast

多樣性 [do1 yeung6 sing3] *n.* multiplicity

多餘 [do1 yu4] *adj.* spare (~ part 後備零件, ~ tire 後備胎); redundant

袋 [doi2] *n.* pocket; bag (plastic ~ 塑料袋, paper ~ 紙袋, tote ~ 大手提袋, canvas ~ 帆布袋)

代 [doi6] *n.* generation

代表 [doi6 biu2] *n.* delegate, representation, representative; *v.* represent

代表 [doi6 biu2] *adv.* on behalf of smb., on smb.'s behalf

代詞 [doi6 chi4] *n.* pronoun

代理行 [doi6 lei5 hong4] *n.* agency

代理人 [doi6 lei5 yan4] *n.* proxy, agent

代數 [doi6 sou3] *n.* algebra

代替 [doi6 tai3] *v.* replace; *n.* replacement (~ part 替換零件)

代替品 [doi6 tai3 ban2] *n./v.* substitute (Can I ~ X for Y? [*at a restaurant*] 我可唔可以用X換Y？)

度 [dok9] *v.* measure

度身訂做 [dok9 san1 ding6 jou6] *adj.* tailor-made

當地 [dong1 dei6] *adj.* local; *adv.* locally

當代 [dong1 doi6] *adj.* contemporary (~ style 現代風格, ~ art 現代藝術)

當季 [dong1 gwai3] *adj.* in season (fruit ~ 時令水果, produce ~ 時令蔬果)

當時 [dong1 si4] *adv.* then

當然 [dong1 yin4] *adv.* of course, certainly

擋風玻璃 [dong2 fung1 bo1 lei1] *n.* windshield

擋泥板 [dong2 nai4 baan2] *n.* fender

黨派政治 [dong2 paai3 jing3 ji6] *n.* party politics

檔案 [dong3 on3] *n.* archives

蕩失路 [dong6 sat7 lou6] *v.* get lost, lose one's way

刀叉 [dou1 cha1] *n.* cutlery

都得 [dou1 dak7] *adj.* acceptable

都夠 [dou1 gau3] *adj.* adequate; *adv.* adequately

都係 [dou1 hai6] *adv.* too (~ expensive 太貴, I'll have one ~ 我都想買一件, ~ much 太多)

刀仔 [dou1 jai2] *n.* knife

都柏林 [dou1 paak8 lam4] *n.* Dublin (~, capital of Ireland 愛爾蘭嘅首都)

刀片 [dou1 pin2] *n.* blade

島 [dou2] *n.* island

倒 [dou2] *v.* pour

賭 [dou2] *n.* betting

倒閉 [dou2 bai3] *v.* go out of business

賭博機 [dou2 bok8 gei1] *n.* gambling machine

賭場 [dou2 cheung4] *n.* casino

倒出來 [dou2 cheut7 loi4] *v.* decant

賭錢 [dou2 chin4] *v.* gamble; *n.* gambling

倒置蛋糕 [dou2 ji3 daan6 gou1] *n.* upside-down cake

倒晒 [dou2 saai3] *n.* emptying

到 [dou3] *v.* arrive (~ by plane 搭飛機, ~ by ship 搭船, ~ by vehicle 搭車)

到達 [dou3 daat9] *n.* arrival

到訪者 [dou3 fong2 je2] *n.* visitor

妒忌 [dou3 gei6] *adj.* jealous

到呢度 [dou3 ne1 dou6] *adv.* hither to here

到…上 [dou3 … seung6] *prep.* onto …

盜版 [dou6 baan2] *n.* piracy

杜松子 [dou6 chung4 ji2] *n.* juniper berries (~ liqueur 杜松子酒)

杜松子酒 [dou6 chung4 ji2 jau2] *n.* gin

導彈 [dou6 daan2] *n.* missile

道德 [dou6 dak7] *adj.* ethical (~ practices 道德實踐, ~

treatment 有道德的對待); *n.*
ethics; *adv.* morally

道德家 [dou6 dak7 ga1] *n.*
moralist

道德準則 [dou6 dak7 jeun2
jak7] *n.* moral compass

道德上 [dou6 dak7 seung6] *adj.*
moral

度度都冇 [dou6 dou6 dou1
mou5] *adv.* nowhere

度假區 [dou6 ga3 keui1] *n.*
holiday resort

度假勝地 [dou6 ga3 sing3 dei6]
n. resort

鍍金 [dou6 gam1] *adj.* gilded

道歉 [dou6 hip8] *v.* apologize
(I ~ 我道歉)

導航 [dou6 hong4] *v.* navigate

導航員 [dou6 hong4 yun4] *n.*
navigator

渡輪 [dou6 leun4] *n.* ferry

道路 [dou6 lou6] *n.* road (~
closed 前路不通, ~ conditions
道路狀況, ~ map 公路地圖,
~ work 整路)

導盲犬 [dou6 maang4 hyun2] *n.*
guidedog

杜尚別 [dou6 seung6 bit9]
n. Dushanbe (~, capital of
Tajikistan 塔吉克斯坦嘅首都)

導師 [dou6 si1] *n.* preceptor

導數 [dou6 sou3] *n.* derivative

導遊 [dou6 yau4] *n.* guide,tour
guide

篤 [duk7] *v.* poke

毒品 [duk9 ban2] *n.* narcotics,
drugs (take ~ 吸食毒品)

讀 [duk9] *n.* perusal; *v.* peruse

獨唱 [duk9 cheung3] *n.* solo

獨唱嘅人 [duk9 cheung3 ge3
yan4] *n.* soloist

毒刺 [duk9 chi3] *n.* sting

獨裁 [duk9 choi4] *n.* autocracy

獨裁者 [duk9 choi4 je2] *n.*
autocrat

獨特 [duk9 dak9] *adj.* unique,
characteristic

毒販 [duk9 faan3] *n.* drug dealer

獨家 [duk9 ga1] *adv.* exclusively

獨奏會 [duk9 jau3 wui2] *n.*
recital

讀者 [duk9 je2] *n.* reader

獨立 [duk9 laap9] *n.* independence;
adj. independent; *adv.*
independently

毒素 [duk9 sou3] *n.* toxin

讀書 [duk9 syu1] *n.* reading

毒藥 [duk9 yeuk9] *n.* poison

東北 [dung1 bak7] *adj.* northeast

東帝汶 [dung1 dai3 man6] *n.*
East Timor (Timor-Leste)

東方 [dung1 fong1] *adj.* oriental

東京 [dung1 ging1] *n.* Tokyo (~,
capital of Japan 日本嘅首都)

冬菇 [dung1 gu1] *n.* black
mushroom

冬甩 [dung1 lat7] *n.* doughnut
(sprinkled ~ 糖粉冬甩, glazed
~ 糖衣冬甩, chocolate ~ 朱古
力冬甩, frosted ~ 糖霜冬甩,
plain ~ 原味冬甩)

冬眠 [dung1 min4] *n.* hibernation

東面 [dung1 min6] *n.* east; *adj.*
eastern

東南面 [dung1 naam4 min6] *n.*
southeast

冬天 [dung1 tin1] *n.* winter

董事 [dung2 si6] *n.* director (~ of a company/university/film 公司董事 / 大學主任 / 電影導演)

凍 [dung3] *v.* chill; *adj.* icy, cold (feel ~ 覺得凍, ~ drink 冷飲, ~ meal 凍肉, ~ soup 凍湯)

棟篤笑 [dung3 duk7 siu3] *n.* stand-up comic

凍乾 [dung3 gon1] *adj.* freeze-dried

凍朱古力 [dung3 jyu1 gu1 lik7] *n.* cold chocolate drink

凍奶糕 [dung3 naai5 gou1] *n.* parfait

動詞 [dung6 chi4] *n.* verb

動詞詞組 [dung6 chi4 chi4 jou2] *n.* phrasal verb

動機 [dung6 gei1] *n.* motivation, motive

動力 [dung6 lik9] *n.* momentum

動亂 [dung6 lyun6] *n.* riot

動脈 [dung6 mak9] *n.* artery

動物 [dung6 mat9] *n.* animal; 動物飼料 animal feed; 動物權利 animal rights

動物園 [dung6 mat9 yun4] *n.* zoo

動名詞 [dung6 ming4 chi4] *n.* gerund

動腦筋 [dung6 nou5 gan1] *v.* brainstorm

動畫 [dung6 wa2] *n.* animation; *adj.* animated

動畫片 [dung6 wa2 pin2] *n.* cartoon (animated), animated film

短 [dyun2] *adj.* short

短褲 [dyun2 fu3] *n.* shorts

短距光 [dyun2 keui5 gwong1] *adj.* low-beam

短路 [dyun2 lou6] *n.* short circuit

短篇小說 [dyun2 pin1 siu2 seui3] *n.* short story

短視 [dyun2 si6] *adj.* short-sighted

短語 [dyun2 yu5] *n.* phrase

鍛鍊 [dyun3 lin6] *n.* workout

斷頭台 [dyun6 tau4 toi4] *n.* guillotine

F

花 [fa1] *n.* flower

花邊 [fa1 bin1] *n.* lace

花店 [fa1 dim3] *n.* florist

花瓣 [fa1 faan6] *n.* petal

花粉 [fa1 fan2] *n.* pollen

花粉過敏 [fa1 fan2 gwo3 man5] *n.* hay fever

花粉量 [fa1 fan2 leung6] *n.* pollen count

花紋 [fa1 man4] *n.* pattern

花蜜 [fa1 mat9] *n.* nectar

花名 [fa1 meng2] *n.* nickname

花瓶 [fa1 ping4] *n.* vase

花盆 [fa1 pun4] *n.* flowerpot

花生 [fa1 sang1] *n.* peanut (~ butter 花生醬, ~ oil 花生油)

花生醬 [fa1 sang1 jeung3] *n.* peanut butter

花言巧語 [fa1 yin4 haau2 yu5] *n.* rhetoric

花園 [fa1 yun2] *n.* garden

化學 [fa3 hok9] *n.* chemistry

化學家 [fa3 hok9 ga1] *n.* chemist

化學嘅 [fa3 hok9 ge3] *adj.* chemical

化妝 [fa3 jong1] *n.* make-up, cosmetics

化妝品 [fa3 jong1 ban2] *adj.* cosmetics

化妝品部 [fa3 jong1 ban2 bou6] *n.* cosmetics department

化妝品專櫃 [fa3 jong1 ban2 jyun1 gwai6] *n.* cosmetics counter

化石 [fa3 sek9] *n.* fossil

化油器 [fa3 yau4 hei3] *n.* carburetor

塊 [faai3] *n.* pieces

快 [faai3] *adj.* fast, quick, rapid

快餐 [faai3 chaan1] *n.* fast food

快車 [faai3 che1] *n.* express train

快速退房 [faai3 chuk7 teui3 fong4] *n.* express checkout

快件 [faai3 gin6] *n.* express mail

筷子 [faai3 ji2] *n.* chopsticks

快樂 [faai3 lok9] *n.* pleasure

快門 [faai3 mun4] *n.* diaphragm

快線 [faai3 sin3] *n.* shuttle, shuttle service

番梘 [faan1 gaan2] *n.* soap

返工 [faan1 gung1] *v./n.* function, labor, work (it doesn't ~ 唔得, I'm late for ~ 我返工遲到, I hope this ~s out 我希望今次得啦); *adj.* working

番去 [faan1 heui3] *v.* go back

蕃茄 [faan1 ke2] *n.* tomato (green ~ 青蕃茄, ~ sauce 茄汁, ~ paste 蕃茄醬, ~ juice 蕃茄汁, ~ puree 茄膏)

蕃茄仔 [faan1 ke2 jai2] *n.* cherry tomatoes

蕃茄汁 [faan1 ke2 jap7] *n.* tomato juice

蕃茄醬 [faan1 ke2 jeung3] *n.* tomato paste

返嚟 [faan1 lai4] *v.* come back

翻新 [faan1 san1] *v.* renovate, retread; *n.* renovation

番石榴 [faan1 sek9 lau2] *n.* guava (~ nectar 番石榴果茶)

蕃薯 [faan1 syu5] *n.* yam
(candied ~ 甜薯）

翻譯 [faan1 yik9] *v.* interpret,
translate; *n.* interpretation,
translation; interpreter

反一 [faan2 -] *prefix* anti-

反駁 [faan2 bok8] *n.* refutation,
rejoinder; *v.* refute

反叛 [faan2 bun6] *adj.* rebellious

反彈 [faan2 daan6] *v.* rebound

反對 [faan2 deui3] *n.* objection;
v. oppose; *prep.* against

反對黨 [faan2 deui3 dong2] *n.*
opposition

反動派 [faan2 dung6 paai3] *n.*
reactionary

反感 [faan2 gam2] *n.* antipathy,
odium, repugnance, repulsion;
v. disgust

反擊 [faan2 gik7] *v.* retaliate; *n.*
retaliation

反核 [faan2 hat9] *adj.* antinuclear

反政府 [faan2 jing3 fu2] *adj.*
anti-government

返老還童 [faan2 lou5 waan4
tung4] *n.* rejuvenation

反手 [faan2 sau2] *n.* backhand

反射 [faan2 se6] *n.* reflection
(*thought / mirror*)

反射器 [faan2 se6 hei3] *n.*
reflector

反射作用 [faan2 se6 jok8
yung6] *n.* reflex

反射性 [faan2 se6 sing3] *adj.*
reflexive

反思 [faan2 si1] *v.* reflect

反省 [faan2 sing2] *v.* introspect;
n. introspection

反應 [faan2 ying3] *v.* react; *n.*
reaction

反應堆 [faan2 ying3 deui1] *n.*
reactor

販毒 [faan3 duk9] *n.* drug
trafficking

煩 [faan4] *adj.* disturbing

帆布 [faan4 bou3] *n.* canvas

帆布包 [faan4 bou3 baau1] *n.*
rucksack

繁衍 [faan4 hin2] *v.* breed

繁殖 [faan4 jik9] *v.* propagate

繁重 [faan4 jung6] *adj.* onerous

煩惱 [faan4 nou5] *n.* bother

繁榮 [faan4 wing4] *n.* boom,
prosperity; *v.* prosper, flourish;
adj. prosperous

梵蒂岡 [faan6 dai3 gong1] *n.*
Holy See (Vatican City); Vatican
City (~, capital of Vatican City
(Holy See) 梵蒂岡首都）

犯法 [faan6 faat8] *adj.* illegal (it
is ~ 呢個係犯法, is it ~? 咁樣
犯唔犯法？); *adv.* illegally; *v.*
commit a crime

飯盒 [faan6 haap2] *n.* lunch box

犯罪 [faan6 jeui6] *n.* crime,
offense

犯罪 [faan6 jeui6] *adj.* criminal
(~ investigation 刑事偵察）

犯規 [faan6 kwai1] *n.* foul (*in
sports*)

飯廳 [faan6 teng1] *n.* dining room

飯堂 [faan6 tong4] *n.* cafeteria

範圍 [faan6 wai4] *n.* boundary,
range, scope, spectrum

發情期 [faat8 ching4 kei4] *n.* rut

發癲 [faat8 din1] *adj.* frantic

發顛咁 [faat8 din1 gam3] *adv.* wildly

發電機 [faat8 din6 gei1] *n.* generator

法定 [faat8 ding6] *adj.* statutory

法定假日 [faat8 ding6 ga3 yat9] *n.* national holiday

法定訴訟程序 [faat8 ding6 sou3 jung6 ching4 jeui6] *n.* due process

法定人數 [faat8 ding6 yan4 sou3] *n.* quorum

發動機 [faat8 dung6 gei1] *n.* engine

法官 [faat8 gun1] *n.* judge

法國 [faat8 gwok8] *n.* France

法國 [faat8 gwok8] *adj.* French (~ food 法國菜)

發光 [faat8 gwong1] *adj.* lucent, luminous, shiny

發光 [faat8 gwong1] *n.* radiance; *v.* shine

發酵 [faat8 haau1] *v.* ferment

發粉 [faat8 fan2] *n.* baking powder

發震 [faat8 jan3] *v.* quake

發脹 [faat8 jeung3] *adj.* bloated

發展 [faat8 jin2] *n.* development

法規 [faat8 kwai1] *n.* statute

發狂 [faat8 kwong4] *n.* rampage

法拉非 [faat8 laai1 fei1] *n.* falafel

法蘭克福香腸 [faat8 laan4 hak7 fuk7 heung1 cheung2] *n.* frankfurter, hot dog

法理學 [faat8 lei5 hok9] *n.* jurisprudence

法律 [faat8 leut9] *n.* law

法律顧問 [faat8 leut9 gu3 man6] *n.* counsel, counselor (*legal*)

法令 [faat8 ling6] *n.* decree

髮廊 [faat8 long4] *n.* hairdresser salon

琺琅質 [faat8 long4 jat7] *n.* enamel

發明 [faat8 ming4] *v.* invent; *n.* invention

發霉 [faat8 mui4] *adj.* moldy, musty

發牌 [faat8 paai4] *v.* deal

發票 [faat8 piu3] *n.* invoice

發誓 [faat8 sai6] *v.* swear

發神經 [faat8 san4 ging1] *adj.* mad

發生 [faat8 sang1] *v.* happen, occur; *n.* incidence, occurrence

發生乜嘢事？ [faat8 sang1 mat7 ye5 si6] *phr.* What happened?

發射 [faat8 se6] *v.* launch

法式多士 [faat8 sik7 do1 si6] *n.* French toast

發燒 [faat8 siu1] *n.* fever

法庭 [faat8 ting4] *n.* court (*legal / tennis*)

發音 [faat8 yam1] *v.* pronounce; *n.* pronunciation

法人 [faat8 yan4] *adj.* corporate

發炎 [faat8 yim4] *n.* inflammation; *adj.* inflammatory

發現 [faat8 yin6] *v.* discover; *n.* discovery

髮型 [faat8 ying4] *n.* hairdo

髮型師 [faat8 ying4 si1] *n.* hairdresser

髮型屋 [faat8 ying4 uk7] *n.* hair salon

法院 [faat8 yun2] *n.* courthouse

法院拘票 [faat8 yun2 keui1 piu3] *n.* bench warrant (*legal*)

輝煌 [fai1 wong4] *n.* refulgence; *adj.* refulgent

肺 [fai3] *n.* lungs

費 [fai3] *n.* fee

廢物回收 [fai3 mat9 wui4 sau1] *n.* recycling (~ bin 廢物回收站)

肺炎 [fai3 yim4] *n.* pneumonia

費用 [fai3 yung6] *n.* expenditure, expense

分 [fan1] *v.* divide, split

分別 [fan1 bit9] *n.* difference

分佈 [fan1 bou3] *n.* distribution

分詞 [fan1 chi4] *n.* participle

分發 [fan1 faat8] *v.* distribute

分機 [fan1 gei1] *n.* extension (~ cord 延長電線)

分居 [fan1 geui1] *adj.* separated

燻香腸 [fan1 heung1 cheung4] *n.* mortadella

分享 [fan1 heung2] *v.* share

分開 [fan1 hoi1] *n.* separation

分開咗 [fan1 hoi1 jo2] *adj.* separate

分開洗 [fan1 hoi1 sai2] *phr.* wash separately

分號 [fan1 hou6] *n.* semicolon

分紅 [fan1 hung4] *n.* bonus

分鐘 [fan1 jung1] *n.* minute (just a ~ 好快, one ~ 好快)

分區 [fan1 keui1] *adj.* zoning (~ laws 城市區劃法)

芬蘭 [fan1 laan4] *n.* Finland; *adj.* Finnish

婚禮 [fan1 lai5] *n.* wedding (~ anniversary 結婚週年紀念, ~ cake 結婚蛋糕, ~ present 結婚禮物, ~ ring 結婚戒指)

分類 [fan1 leui6] *n.* classification; *v.* classify

昏迷 [fan1 mai4] *n.* coma; *adj.* unconscious

昏迷狀態 [fan1 mai4 jong6 taai3] *n.* narcosis

分派 [fan1 paai3] *n.* allocation

分配 [fan1 pui3] *v.* allocate

分散 [fan1 saan3] *adj.* scattered

分析 [fan1 sik7] *n.* analysis; *v.* analyze

分析師 [fan1 sik7 si1] *n.* analyst

分數 [fan1 sou3] *n.* score (~board 記分牌)

婚姻 [fan1 yan1] *n.* marriage

婚姻狀況 [fan1 yan1 jong6 fong3] *n.* marital status

薰衣草 [fan1 yi1 chou2] *n.* lavender

粉 [fan2] *n.* powder

粉刺 [fan2 chi3] *n.* acne

粉刺膏 [fan2 chi3 gou1] *n.* acne cream/medicine

粉紅色 [fan2 hung4 sik7] *adj.* pink

粉狀 [fan2 jong6] *adj.* powdery

粉末 [fan2 mut9] *n.* powder

粉撲 [fan2 pok8] *n.* puff

瞓 [fan3] *v.* sleep

瞓低 [fan3 dai1] *v.* lie down

瞓著咗 [fan3 jeuk8 jo2] *adj.* asleep

訓練 [fan3 lin6] *n.* training (sports ~ 體育訓練)

墳墓 [fan4 mou6] *n.* grave

墳場 [fan4 cheung4] *n.* cemetery

憤怒 [fan5 nou6] *n.* outrage, rage

份工 [fan6 gung1] *n.* employment (~ office 職業介紹所)

分子 [fan6 ji2] *n.* molecule, numerator

份量 [fan6 leung6] *n.* portion

分數 [fan6 sou3] *n.* fraction (*math term*)

弗里敦 [fat7 lei5 deun1] *n.* Freetown (~, capital of Sierra Leone 塞拉利昂嘅首都)

忽略 [fat7 leuk9] *v.* overlook

罰 [fat9] *v.* punish

佛得角 [fat9 dak7 gok8] *n.* Cape Verde

佛手瓜 [fat9 sau2 gwai1] *n.* chayote

否認 [fau2 ying6] *v.* deny

浮 [fau4] *v.* float

啡色 [fe1 sik7] *adj.* brown

飛 [fei1] *v.* fly

非歐盟公民 [fei1 au1 mang4 gung1 man4] *n.* non-EU citizens

非前綴 [fei1 chin4 jeui3] *n.* non-prefix

非凡嘅成就 [fei1 faan4 ge3 sing4 jau6] *n.* triumph

非法入侵 [fei1 faat8 yap9 cham1] *v.* trespass; *n.* trespassing (No ~ 非請勿入)

非法入境 [fei1 faat8 yap9 ging2] *n.* illegal entry

飛機 [fei1 gei1] *n.* aircraft, airplane

飛機師 [fei1 gei1 si1] *n.* pilot

非洲 [fei1 jau1] *n.* Africa

非洲人 [fei1 jau1 yan4] *adj.* African

非吸煙 [fei1 kap7 yin1] *adj.* non-smoking

非吸煙人士 [fei1 kap7 yin1 yau4 si6] *n.* non-smoker

菲律賓 [fei1 leut9 ban1] *n.* Philippines

菲律賓人 [fei1 leut9 ban1 yan4] *n.* Filipino

菲力牛扒 [fei1 lik9 ngau4 pa2] *n.* filet mignon

飛蛾 [fei1 ngo4] *n.* moth

非常 [fei1 seung4] *adv.* very much

非線性 [fei1 sin3 sing3] *adj.* nonlinear

非小說類 [fei1 siu2 syut8 leui6] *n.* non-fiction

翡翠 [fei2 cheui3] *n.* emerald

斐濟 [fei2 jai3] *n.* Fiji; *adj.* Fijian

誹謗 [fei2 pong3] *n.* libel; *v.* malign

記得 [gei3 dak7] *v.* recall, recollect

肥 [fei4] *adj.* fat (non-~ 脫脂, ~ content 脂肪含量, percent body ~ 身體脂肪百分比)

肥矮 [fei4 ai2] *adj.* chunky (~ pieces 好大塊)

肥胖 [fei4 bun6] *adj.* obese

肥胖症 [fei4 bun6 jing3] *n.* obesity

肥料 [fei4 liu2] *n.* compost, manure

科特迪瓦 [fo1 dak9 dik9 nga5] *n.* Cote d'Ivoire

科學 [fo1 hok9] *n.* science; *adj.* scientific

科學家 [fo1 hok9 ga1] *n.* scientist

科倫坡 [fo1 leun4 bo1] *n.* Colombo (~, capital of Sri Lanka 斯里蘭卡嘅首都)

科摩羅 [fo1 mo1 lo4] *n.* Comoros

科納克里 [fo1 naap9 hak7 lei5] *n.* Conakry (~, capital of Guinea 幾內亞嘅首都)

科索沃 [fo1 sok8 yuk7] *adj.* Kosovar; *n.* Kosovo

科幻小說 [fo1 waan6 siu2 seui3] *n.* science fiction

科威特 [fo1 wai1 dak9] *n.* Kuwait; *adj.* Kuwaiti

科威特城 [fo1 wai1 dak9 sing4] *n.* Kuwait City (~, capital of Kuwait 科威特嘅首都)

火 [fo2] *n.* fire (~ escape 走火通道, ~ truck 消防車, ~ pit 火堆)

火柴 [fo2 chaai4] *n.* matches

火車 [fo2 che1] *n.* train

火車站 [fo2 che1 jaam6] *n.* train station

火車頭 [fo2 che1 tau4] *n.* locomotive

火槍 [fo2 cheung1] *n.* musket

火槍手 [fo2 cheung1 sau2] *n.* musketeer

火堆 [fo2 deui1] *n.* fire pit

火雞 [fo2 gai1] *n.* turkey (roasted ~ 烤火雞, honey-glazed ~ 蜜烤火雞, smoked ~ 煙燻火雞)

火機 [fo2 gei1] *n.* lighter

火警 [fo2 ging2] *n.* fire alarm

火警鐘 [fo2 ging2 jung1] *n.* fire alarm

火氣 [fo2 hei3] *n.* anger

火箭 [fo2 jin3] *n.* rocket

火爐 [fo2 lou4] *n.* furnace, stove

火龍果 [fo2 lung4 gwo2] *n.* dragonfruit

火山 [fo2 saan1] *n.* volcano

火星 [fo2 sing1] *n.* Mars

火腿 [fo2 teui2] *n.* ham

火腿三文治 [fo2 teui2 saam1 man4 ji6] *n.* ham sandwich

火焰 [fo2 yim6] *n.* flame

貨幣 [fo3 bai6] *adj.* monetary; *n.* currency, money

貨車 [fo3 che1] *n.* lorry, truck

課程 [fo3 ching4] *n.* course (in a meal); direction; classes

貨架 [fo3 ga2] *n.* gondola lift

課室 [fo3 sat7] *n.* classroom

霍尼亞拉 [fok8 nei4 a3 laai1] *n.* Honiara (~, capital of Solomon Islands 所羅門群島嘅首都)

方便 [fong1 bin6] *adj.* convenient

方便攜帶 [fong1 bin6 kwai4 daai3] *adj.* portable

方法 [fong1 faat8] *n.* method; way (it's on the ~ to … 嚟緊, I've lost my ~ 盪失路,which ~? 點行?, that ~ 嗰邊)

荒廢 [fong1 fai3] *adj.* ruined

方向 [fong1 heung3] *n.* direction (in the ~ of 沿著...方向)

方舟 [fong1 jau1] *n.* ark

荒謬 [fong1 mau6] *adj.* absurd, ridiculous

慌失失 [fong1 sat7 sat7] *adj.* alarmed

方位 [fong1 wai2] *n.* directions

荒野 [fong1 ye5] *n.* moor

方言 [fong1 yin4] *n.* dialect

房 [fong2] *n.* room

房間號碼 [fong2 gaan1 hou4 ma5] *n.* room number (at hotel)

房價 [fong2 ga3] *n.* room rate

紡織品 [fong2 jik7 ban2] *n.* textiles

放 [fong3] *v.* put (~ in 放入, ~ out 攞出, ~ sth. on 著, ~ sth. out 放出去)

放出去 [fong3 cheut7 heui3] *v.* put sth. out

放大 [fong3 daai6] *n.* amplification; *v.* amplify, enlarge; *adj.* enhanced

放低 [fong3 dai1] *v.* lower

放火 [fong3 fo2] *v.* set fire to

放棄 [fong3 hei3] *v.* give (sth) up, renounce

放褸處 [fong3 leui5 chyu3] *n.* coat check

放鬆 [fong3 sung1] *v.* relax; *n.* relaxation; *adj.* relaxed

放入 [fong3 yap9] *v.* put in

放羊 [fong3 yeung4] *v.* graze

防潮布 [fong4 chiu4 bou3] *n.* groundcloth

防彈 [fong4 daan2] *adj.* bullet-proof

房地產 [fong4 dei6 chaan2] *n.* real estate

房地產經紀 [fong4 dei6 chaan2 ging1 gei2] *n.* real estate agent

房東 [fong4 dung1] *n.* landlord

防凍劑 [fong4 dung3 jai1] *n.* antifreeze

防腐嘅 [fong4 fu6 ge3] *adj.* antiseptic

防腐劑 [fong4 fu6 jai1] *n.* preservatives

防風草 [fong4 fung1 chou2] *n.* parsnip

防風衣 [fong4 fung1 yi1] *n.* windbreaker

房間服務 [fong4 gaan1 fuk9 mou6] *n.* room service

防曬霜 [fong4 saai3 seung1] *n.* suntan lotion, sunblock, sunscreen lotion

防水 [fong4 seui2] *adj.* waterproof (~ shoes 水鞋)

防水鏡 [fong4 seui2 geng3] *n.* goggles

防疫 [fong4 yik9] *v.* be vaccinated against

呼吸 [fu1 kap7] *n.* respiration; *v.* respire

呼吸系統 [fu1 kap7 hai6 tung2] *n.* respiratory system

孵 [fu1] *v.* incubate

俘虜 [fu1 lou5] *n.* captive

苦 [fu2] *adj.* bitter

俯衝 [fu2 chung1] *v.* plunge

苦苣 [fu2 geui6] *n.* endive

苦杏酒 [fu2 hang6 jau2] *n.* amaretti; absinthe

斧頭 [fu2 tau4] *n.* axe

褲 [fu3] *n.* trousers, pants

副本 [fu3 bun2] *n.* photocopy

副產品 [fu3 chaan2 ban2] *n.* by-product

副詞 [fu3 chi4] *n.* adverb

副作用 [fu3 jok8 yung6] *n.* side effects

符合邏輯 [fu4 hap9 lo4 chap7] *adj.* logical

符合猶太教規嘅 [fu4 hap9 yau4 taai3 gaau3 kwai1 ge3] *adj.* kosher (non-~ 唔符合猶太教規嘅, ~ meal 符合猶太教規嘅食物)

扶手電梯 [fu4 sau2 din6 tai1] *n.* escalator

婦科醫生 [fu5 fo1 yi1 sang1] *n.* gynecologist

腐敗 [fu6 baai6] *adj.* corrupt, corrupted; *n.* corruption

付費電話 [fu6 fai3 din6 wa2] *n.* pay phone

付款 [fu6 fun2] *n.* payment

附近 [fu6 gan6] *adj.* near, nearby

負責 [fu6 jaak8] *phr.* in charge of

負責任 [fu6 jaak8 yam6] *adj.* responsible

腐爛 [fu6 laan6] *n.* decay; *v.* rot

腐爛咗 [fu6 laan6 jo2] *adj.* rotten

附錄 [fu6 luk9] *n.* appendix

訃聞 [fu6 man4] *n.* obituary

負面 [fu6 min6] *adj.* negative

父母 [fu6 mou5] *n.* parent

附屬 [fu6 suk9] *adj.* subsidiary

輔音 [fu6 yam1] *n.* consonant

恢復 [fui1 fuk9] *v.* revert

恢復青春 [fui1 fuk9 ching1 cheun1] *v.* rejuvenate

灰 [fui1] *n.* ash

灰泥 [fui1 nai4] *n.* plaster

灰色 [fui1 sik7] *adj.* grey

悔恨 [fui3 han6] *n.* remorse

晦氣 [fui3 hei3] *n.* mishap

腹腔鏡 [fuk7 hong1 geng3] *n.* laparoscope

複習 [fuk7 jaap9] *n.* review

複雜 [fuk7 jaap9] *adj.* complex, complicated

複製品 [fuk7 jai3 ban2] *n.* replica, reproduction

複製再貼上 [fuk7 jai3 joi3 tip8 seung5] *v. comp.* copy and paste

腹足動物 [fuk7 juk7 dung6 mat9] *n.* gastropod

福納省 [fuk7 naap9 saang2] *n.* Funafuti (~ province, capital of Tuvalu 圖瓦盧嘅首都)

輻射 [fuk7 se6] *v.* radiate; *n.* radiation

複數形式 [fuk7 sou3 ying4 sik7] *n.* plural

福音 [fuk7 yam1] *n.* gospel

服從 [fuk9 chung4] *v.* submit

伏特加 [fuk9 dak9 ga1] *n.* vodka

復發 [fuk9 faat8] *v.* relapse

復興 [fuk9 hing1] *adj.* resurgent

復職 [fuk9 jik7] *v.* reinstate; *n.* reinstatement

服務 [fuk9 mou6] *v.* serve

服務 [fuk9 mou6] *n.* service (church/restaurant/car ~ 接送服務, ~ charge 服務費)

服務器 [fuk9 mou6 hei3] *n.* server (*tech.*)

服務台 [fuk9 mou6 toi4] *n.* information desk/counter/office

復活 [fuk9 wut9] *n.* resurgence, revival; *v.* revive

復活節 [fuk9 wut9 jit8] *n.* Easter

復活節快樂 [fuk9 wut9 jit8 faai3 lok9] *phr.* Happy Easter!

復原 [fuk9 yun4] *n.* restoration; *v.* restore

復原咗 [fuk9 yun4 jo2] *adj.* restored

寬 [fun1] *adj.* broad

寬頻 [fun1 pan4] *n.* broadband

寬頻連接 [fun1 pan4 lin4 jip8] broadband connection/internet

寬恕 [fun1 syu3] *v.* pardon

歡迎 [fun1 ying4] *v.* welcome (~ to … 歡迎來到, ~! 熱烈歡迎！)

寬容 [fun1 yung4] *n.* leniency; *adj.* lenient

風 [fung1] *n.* wind

蜂巢 [fung1 chau4] *n.* beehive, honeycomb

風車 [fung1 che1] *n.* windmill

風趣 [fung1 cheui3] *adj.* humorous

蜂房 [fung1 fong4] *n.* apiary

風格 [fung1 gaak8] *n.* style

風格上 [fung1 gaak8 seung6] *adj.* stylistic

風紀 [fung1 gei2] *n.* prefect

封建 [fung1 gin3] *adj.* feudal

風景 [fung1 ging2] *n.* scenery

風險 [fung1 him2] *n.* risk

風流嘢 [fung1 lau4 ye5] *n.* romp

蜂蜜芥末 [fung1 mat9 gaai3 mut9] *n.* honey mustard

蜂蜜酒 [fung1 mat9 jau2] *n.* mead

風濕 [fung1 sap7] *adj.* rheumatic; *n.* rheumatism

豐收 [fung1 sau1] *n.* harvest

風扇皮帶 [fung1 sin3 pei4 daai3] *n.* fan belt

諷刺 [fung3 chi3] *adj.* ironic; *n.* irony, sarcasm, satire

鳳尾魚 [fung6 mei5 yu4] *n.* anchovy

奉承 [fung6 sing4] *n.* adulation, flattery; *v.* flatter

闊 [fut8] *adj.* wide

闊度 [fut8 dou6] *n.* width

G

家常菜 [ga1 seung4 choi3] *n.* comfort food

加 [ga1] *prep.* plus; *v.* add

痂 [ga1] *n.* scab

加速 [ga1 chuk7] *n.* speeding

加速器 [ga1 chuk7 hei3] *n.* accelerator

加德滿都 [ga1 dak7 mun5 dou1] *n.* Kathmandu (~, capital of Nepal 尼泊爾嘅首都)

加法 [ga1 faat8] *n.* addition

家教 [ga1 gaau3] *n.* tutor

家居裝修 [ga1 geui1 jong1 sau1] *n.* home furnishings

加固 [ga1 gu3] *v.* reinforce

加工過 [ga1 gung1 gwo3] *adj.* processed (~ food 加工食品, un-~ food 新鮮食品)

家禽 [ga1 kam4] *n.* fowl, poultry

加強 [ga1 keung4] *adj.* fortified

加拉加斯 [ga1 laai1 ga1 si1] *n.* Caracas (~, capital of Venezuela 委內瑞拉嘅首都)

加侖 [ga1 leun4] *n.* gallon

加埋 [ga1 maai4] *v.* combine

加味 [ga1 mei6] *adj.* flavored (~ water 風味水, chocolate-~ 朱古力味, vanilla-~ 香草味, strawberry-~ 草莓味)

家務 [ga1 mou6] *n.* housekeeping, housework

加拿大 [ga1 na4 daai6] *n.* Canada; *adj.* Canadian

加納 [ga1 naap9] *n.* Ghana; *adj.* Ghanaian

嘉年華 [ga1 nin4 wa6] *n.* carnival

加蓬 [ga1 pung4] *n.* Gabon

家常菜 [ga1 seung4 choi3] *n.* home-style cooking, comfort food

傢俬 [ga1 si1] *n.* furniture

家庭 [ga1 ting4] *n.* family

家庭主婦 [ga1 ting4 jyu2 fu5] *n.* housewife

加入 [ga1 yap9] *n.* involvement; *v.* join

加油站 [ga1 yau4 jaam6] *n.* gas station

加鉛 [ga1 yun4] *adj.* leaded

假 [ga2] *adj.* artificial (~ sweetener 人工甜味劑, ~ flavoring 人工香精, ~ coloring 人工色素); *adv.* artificially (~ flavored 加咗香精)

架 [ga2] *n.* frame (*picture / glasses*)

假設 [ga2 chit8] *v.* assume, presume, presuppose; *n.* assumption, presumption, presupposition

假嘅 [ga2 ge3] *adj.* false

假名 [ga2 meng2] *n.* alias

假釋 [ga2 sik7] *n.* parole

假羊皮紙 [ga2 yeung4 pei4 ji2] *n.* parchment paper

假如 [ga2 yu4] *conj.* provided, providing

架罉 [ga3 chang1] *n.* tool

價錢 [ga3 chin4] *n.* price

咖啡 [ga3 fe1] *n.* coffee (~ with

milk 加牛奶咖啡, sugared ~ 甜咖啡, dark ~ 黑咖啡, mocca ~ 莫卡咖啡, vanilla ~ 香草味咖啡, cappucino ~ 卡布奇諾)

咖啡杯 [ga3 fe1 bui1] *n.* coffee mug

咖啡店 [ga3 fe1 dim3] *n.* coffee shop

咖啡粉 [ga3 fe1 fan2] *n.* ground coffee

咖啡罐 [ga3 fe1 gun3] *n.* coffeepot

咖啡色頭髮嘅女人 [ga3 fe1 sik7 tau4 faat8 ge3 neui5 yan4] *n.* brunette

咖啡因 [ga3 fe1 yan1] *n.* caffeine

價值 [ga3 jik9] *n.* value

嫁妝 [ga3 jong1] *n.* dowry

假期 [ga3 kei4] *n.* holiday, vacation (on ~ 休假)

咖哩 [ga3 lei1] *n.* curry (Indian ~ 印度咖哩, chicken ~ 咖哩雞, ~ powder 咖哩粉, ~ sauce 咖哩汁)

駕駛執照 [ga3 sai2 jap7 jiu3] *n.* driver's license, driver's permit

街 [gaai1] *n.* street (~ children 乞兒仔, ~ food 大排檔)

街燈 [gaai1 dang1] *n.* streetlight

階段 [gaai1 dyun6] *n.* phase

街口 [gaai1 hau2] *n.* corner

街區 [gaai1 keui1] *n.* block

解凍 [gaai2 dung3] *v.* defrost

解放 [gaai2 fong3] *n.* emancipation

解開 [gaai2 hoi1] *v.* undo

解決 [gaai2 kyut8] *v.* resolve, settle

解決方法 [gaai2 kyut8 fong1 faat8] *n.* solution

解剖學 [gaai2 pau2 hok9] *n.* anatomy

解釋 [gaai2 sik7] *v.* explain; *n.* explanation

解藥 [gaai2 yeuk9] *n.* antidote

介詞 [gaai3 chi4] *n.* preposition

芥菜 [gaai3 choi3] *n.* mustard greens

戒酒 [gaai3 jau2] *v.* rehabilitate

戒指 [gaai3 ji2] *n.* ring *(jewelry)*

芥辣 [gaai3 laat9] *n.* mustard, wasabi

芥末蛋 [gaai3 mut9 daan6] *n.* deviled eggs

介紹 [gaai3 siu6] *v.* introduce (may I ~ X? 不如我介紹X俾你識啊？); *n.* introduction

介入 [gaai3 yap9] *n.* interference with other drugs

隔牆 [gaak8 cheung4] *n.* partition

隔開 [gaak8 hoi1] *n.* division

格仔餅 [gaak8 jai2 beng2] *n.* waffle

格拉那達 [gaak8 laai1 na5 daat9] *n.* Grenada; *adj.* Grenadian

隔離 [gaak8 lei4] *adj.* adjacent, adjoining; *v.* Sequester

隔离 [gaak8 lei4] *v.* to single out

隔離鄰舍 [gaak8 lei4 leun4 se3] *n.* neighbor

格魯吉亞 [gaak8 lou5 gat7 a3] *n.* Georgia; *adj.* Georgian

革命 [gaak8 ming6] *n.* revolution

格式 [gaak8 sik7] *n.* format (~ a document 文件統一格式)

格言 [gaak8 yin4] *n.* motto

監倉 [gaam1 chong1] *n.* cells (spreadsheet ~ 數據表嘅格)

監督 [gaam1 duk7] *n.* supervision

監犯 [gaam1 faan2] *n.* prisoner

監禁 [gaam1 gam3] *n.* captivity

監管機構 [gaam1 gun2 gei1 kau3] *n.* regulator

監考 [gaam1 haau2] *v.* invigilate, monitor, supervise

監考員 [gaam1 haau2 yun4] *n.* invigilator, proctor, monitor

監視 [gaam1 si6] *n.* surveillance

監護 [gaam1 wu6] *n.* custody, guardianship

監護人 [gaam1 wu6 yan4] *n.* curator, guardian (legal ~ 法定 監護人)

監獄 [gaam1 yuk9] *n.* jail, prison

減 [gaam2] *v.* deduct

減肥 [gaam2 fei4] *v.* lose weight

減肥嘅人 [gaam2 fei4 ge3 yan4] *n.* dieter

減輕 [gaam2 heng1] *n.* alleviation, remission; *v.* relieve

減少 [gaam2 siu2] *n.* reduction; *v.* reduce, decrease ~ weight 減 肥, ~ prices 減價

減少 [gaam2 siu2] *adj.* reduced

尷尬 [gaam3 gaai3] *adj* awkward; *adv.* awkwardly; *n.* embarrassment

奸商 [gaan1 seung1] *n.* profiteer

揀 [gaan2] *v.* choose, select

柬埔寨 [gaan2 bou3 jaai6] *n.* Cambodia; *adj.* Cambodian

簡單 [gaan2 daan1] *adj.* simple

揀定 [gaan2 ding6] *v.* choose (~ a side 揀定立場)

簡短 [gaan2 dyun2] *adj.* brief

簡介 [gaan2 gaai3] *n.* profile

簡歷 [gaan2 lik9] *n.* resumé

間接 [gaan3 jip8] *adj.* indirect; *adv.* indirectly

間接引語 [gaan3 jip8 yan5 yu5] *n.* indirect speech

耕種 [gaang1 jung3] *adj.* cultivated

耕田 [gaang1 tin4] *n.* farming; *v.* plow

甲板 [gaap8 baan2] *n.* deck (ship ~ 輪船甲板, ~ of cards 一疊牌)

甲蟲 [gaap8 chung4] *n.* beetle

甲殼類動物 [gaap8 hok8 leui6 dung6 mat9] *n.* crustacean

甲魚湯 [gaap8 yu4 tong1] *n.* turtle soup

甲由 [gaat9 jaat9] *n.* cockroach

交叉點 [gaau1 cha1 dim2] *n.* intersection

交叉路口 [gaau1 cha1 lou6 hau2] *n.* level crossing

膠袋 [gaau1 doi2] *n.* plastic bag

交罰款 [gaau1 fat9 fun2] *v.* pay a fine

交響樂 [gaau1 heung2 ngok9] *n.* symphony

郊區 [gaau1 keui1] *n.* environs, outskirts, suburb

交流 [gaau1 lau4] *v.* communicate; *n.* communication

交流發電機 [gaau1 lau4 faat8 din6 gei1] *n.* alternator

膠囊 [gaau1 nong4] *n.* capsule

交朋友 [gaau1 pang4 yau5] *v.* make friends (with)

膠水 [gaau1 seui2] *n.* glue

交通 [gaau1 tung1] *n.* traffic (~ circle 交通環島, ~ jam 交

通堵塞, ~ accident 交通意外, ~ light 紅綠燈, ~ police 交警, ~ ticket 交通罰單)

交換 [gaau1 wun6] *v.* exchange (~ a purchase 替換)

郊遊 [gaau1 yau4] *n.* outing

攪 [gaau2] *v.* mix, stir

搞錯咗 [gaau2 cho3 jo2] *adj.* mistaken

攪打 [gaau2 da2] *adj.* whipped (~ cream 生忌廉, ~ eggs 打蛋, ~ milk 生奶, ~ cheese 忌廉芝士)

搞掂 [gaau2 dim1] *v.* accomplish

搞掂咗 [gaau2 dim1 jo2] *adj.* accomplished

搞複雜 [gaau2 fuk7 jaap9] *v.* complicate (~ matters 複雜嘅野)

搞鬼 [gaau2 gwai2] *n.* mischief; *adj.* mischievous

餃子 [gaau2 ji2] *n.* dumpling (Chinese) (meat ~ 肉餃, vegetable ~ 素餃, cheese ~ 芝士餃)

攪爛 [gaau2 laan6] *v.* mash; *adj.* mashed (~ potatoes 薯蓉)

搞唔清楚 [gaau2 m4 ching1 cho2] *v.* confuse

攪埋一齊 [gaau2 maai4 yat7 chai4] *v.* blend; *n.* stirring, mixing

攪拌機 [gaau2 pun6 gei1] *n.* blender

搞神祕 [gaau2 san4 bei3] *v.* mystify

搞笑 [gaau2 siu3] *adj.* comic, amusing, hilarious, funny

狡猾 [gaau2 waat9] *adj.* cunning

教 [gaau3] *v.* teach

教程 [gaau3 ching4] *n.* tutorial (online ~ 網上教程)

教訓 [gaau3 fan3] *n.* lesson

教學 [gaau3 hok9] *n.* teaching

教學法 [gaau3 hok9 faat8] *n.* pedagogy

校正 [gaau3 jeng3] *v.* adjust; *n.* alignment (margin ~ 頁邊對齊, tire ~ 校輪胎)

鉸剪 [gaau3 jin2] *n.* scissors

教區 [gaau3 keui1] *n.* parish

教練 [gaau3 lin6] *n.* coach, trainer

教授 [gaau3 sau6] *n.* professor

教堂 [gaau3 tong4] *n.* church (~ service 禮拜)

教堂仔 [gaau3 tong4 jai2] *n.* chapel

教堂中殿 [gaau3 tong4 jung1 din6] *n.* nave

教育 [gaau3 yuk9] *v.* educate; *n.* education

雞蛋 [gai1 daan6] *n.* egg (~ white 蛋白, ~ yolk 蛋黃, ~ beater 打蛋器)

雞蛋餅 [gai1 daan6 beng2] *n.* quiche

雞蛋花 [gai1 daan6 fa1] *n.* frangipane

雞蛋果 [gai1 daan6 gwo2] *n.* passionfruit

雞尾酒 [gai1 mei5 jau2] *n.* cocktail

雞碎 [gai1 seui3] *n.* pittance

雞湯 [gai1 tong1] *n.* chicken stock

雞肉 [gai1 yuk9] *n.* chicken (~ breast 雞胸肉, ~ soup 雞湯, ~ wings 雞翼, ~ wrap 雞肉卷, ~ salad 雞肉沙律)

計仔 [gai2 jai2] *n.* idea

計 [gai3] *v.* compute

計程錶 [gai3 ching4 biu1] *n.* odometer

計錯 [gai3 cho3] *v.* miscalculate

繼續 [gai3 juk9] *adj.* continuous; *adv.* continuously

繼續 [gai3 juk9] *v.* continue, go on, be going on

計時器 [gai3 si4 hei3] *n.* timer (oven ~ 焗爐計時器)

計數 [gai3 sou3] *n.* calculation, counting; *v.* calculate, count

計算 [gai3 syun3] *n.* computing

計算機 [gai3 syun3 gei1] *n.* calculator (graphing ~ 繪圖計算機)

計劃 [gai3 waak9] *n.* plan, planning

計人數 [gai3 yan4 sou3] *n.* head count

柑 [gam1] *n.* citrus (~ flavored 柑味, ~ fruit 柑果, ~ juice 柑汁)

甘比亞 [gam1 bei2 a3] *n.* The Gambia

金邊 [gam1 bin1] *n.* Phnom Penh (~, capital of Cambodia 柬埔寨嘅首都)

甘草精 [gam1 chou2 jing1] *n.* licorice (red ~ 紅甘草精, black ~ 黑甘草精)

金髮碧眼 [gam1 faat8 bik7 ngaan5] *adj.* blond(e)

金桔 [gam1 gat7] *n.* kumquat

甘菊 [gam1 guk7] *n.* chamomile

金器 [gam1 hei3] *n.* gold plate

甘蔗糖漿 [gam1 je3 tong4 jeung1] *n.* cane syrup

金字塔 [gam1 ji6 taap8] *n.* pyramid

甘藍 [gam1 laam4] *n.* rutabaga

甘藍菜 [gam1 laam4 choi3] *n.* kale

今晚 [gam1 maan5] *adv.* tonight

金牛座 [gam1 ngau4 jo6] *n.* Taurus

金沙薩 [gam1 sa1 saat8] *n.* Kinshasa (~, capital of Congo 剛果嘅首都)

金斯敦 [gam1 si1 deun1] *n.* Kingston (~, capital of Jamaica 牙買加嘅首都); Kingstown (~, capital of Saint Vincent and the Grenadines 聖文森特和格林納丁斯嘅首都)

金色 [gam1 sik7] *adj.* golden

金屬 [gam1 suk9] *n.* metal

金湯力 [gam1 tong1lik9] *n.* gin and tonic

今日 [gam1 yat9] *adv.* today

今日特價 [gam1 yat9 dak9 ga3] *n.* today's special

甘油 [gam1 yau4] *n.* glycerin

金融 [gam1 yung4] *n.* finance

敢 [gam2] *v.* dare

錦標賽 [gam2 biu1 choi3] *n.* championship

感情 [gam2 ching4] *n.* affection

感動 [gam2 dung6] *adj.* impressed

感化院 [gam2 fa3 yun2] *n.* reformatory

感激 [gam2 gik7] *adj.* grateful

感興趣 [gam2 hing3 cheui3] *adj.* taken (seat)

橄欖 [gam2 laam5] *n.* olive

橄欖油 [gam2 laam5 yau4] *n.*
olive oil

感冒 [gam2 mou6] *v.* have a cold

感受 [gam2 sau6] *n.* feeling

感人 [gam2 yan4] *adj.* moving

感染 [gam2 yim5] *v.* infect; *n.*
infection

感染咗 [gam2 yim5 jo2] *adj.*
infected

咁 [gam3] *adv.* so (~ that 所以,
~-called 所謂)

咁 [gam3] *det.* such (~ as 例如,
~ and ~ 等等, ~ a shame! 真係
可惜!)

禁閉 [gam3 bai3] *n.* incarceration

禁忌 [gam3 gei6] *adj.* taboo

咁好 [gam3 hou2] *phr.* so good;
adj. providential

禁制令 [gam3 jai3 ling6] *n.*
injunction

禁止 [gam3 ji2] *adj.* prohibited,
banned; *n.* prohibition; *v.* prohibit,
ban

橄欖 [gam3 laam5] *n.* olive
(black ~ 黑橄欖, green ~ 青
橄欖, pitted ~ 去核橄欖,
unpitted ~ 有核橄欖, Greek ~
希臘橄欖)

橄欖油 [gam3 laam5 yau4] *n.*
olive oil

咁啱 [gam3 ngaam1] *v.* coincide

感歎號 [gam3 taan3 hou6] *n.*
exclamation point

禁慾 [gam3 yuk9] *n.* ascetic

筋 [gan1] *n.* tendon

根 [gan1] *n.* root

跟班 [gan1 baan1] *n.* retinue

根本 [gan1 bun2] *adj.* fundamental

根本上 [gan1 bun2 seung6] *adv.*
essentially

根據 [gan1 geui3] *prep.* according
to, subject to

跟蹤 [gan1 jung1] *v.* track

跟住 [gan1 jyu6] *prep.* along,
alongside (get ~ with … 同…
相處)

跟住 [gan1 jyu6] *adj.* following;
adv. subsequently; *v.* follow

跟住嘅 [gan1 jyu6 ge3] *adj.*
accompanying

緊 [gan2] *adj.* tight; *adv.* tightly

緊急 [gan2 gap7] *adj.* urgent

緊急避孕藥 [gan2 gap7 bei6
yan6 yeuk9] *n.* morning-after
pill

緊急情況 [gan2 gap7 ching4
fong3] *n.* emergency (~ medical
services 緊急醫療服務, ~
brake 緊急煞制, ~ exit 逃生
出口)

緊張 [gan2 jeung1] *n.* tension;
adj. nervous, stressed; *adv.*
nervously

僅致問候! [gan2 ji3 man6
hau6] *phr.* Best wishes!

緊鄰著 [gan2 leun4 jyu3] *prep.*
next to

緊身褲 [gan2 san1 fu3] *n.*
leggings, tights

謹慎 [gan2 san6] *n.* caution,
prudence; *adj.* cautious, prudent

緊縮 [gan2 suk7] *v.* retrench; *n.*
retrenchment

僅獲許可證者停放 [gan2
wok9 heui2 ho2 jing3 je2 ting4
fong3] *phr.* permit-holders only

緊要 [gan2 yiu3] *adj.* crucial

近排 [gan6 paai4] *adj.* recent; *adv.* recently

近排先 [gan6 paai4 sin1] *adv.* freshly

近視 [gan6 si6] *n.* myopia; *adj.* near-sighted

更改 [gang1 goi2] *v.* alter; *n.* alteration

更年期 [gang1 nin4 kei4] *n.* menopause

更新咗 [gang1 san1 jo2] *adj.* updated

更衣室 [gang1 yi1 sat7] *n.* changing room, fitting room

急 [gap7] *adv.* sharply

急救 [gap7 gau3] *n.* first aid

急救箱 [gap7 gau3 seung1] *n.* first-aid kit

急症室 [gap7 jing3 sat7] *n.* emergency room

急流 [gap7 lau4] *n.* rapids

急性 [gap7 sing3] *adj.* acute (~ pain 急性疼痛, ~ angle 尖銳嘅意見)

鴿 [gap8] *n.* dove

拮 [gat1] *v.* prick

吉布提 [gat7 bou3 tai4] *n.* Djibouti (~, capital of Djibouti 吉布提嘅首都)

吉祥物 [gat7 cheung4 mat9] *n.* mascot

吉利 [gat7 lei6] *adj.* auspicious

吉隆坡 [gat7 lung4 bo1] *n.* Kuala Lumpur (~, capital of Malaysia 馬來西亞嘅首都)

吉普 [gat7 pou2] *n.* jeep

吉爾吉斯斯坦 [gat7 yi5 gat7 si1 si1 taan2] *n.* Kyrgyzstan; *adj.* Kyrgyzstani, *also* Kyrgyz

狗 [gau2] *n.* dog

九 [gau2] *num.* nine

久巴 [gau2 ba1] *n.* Juba (~, capital of South Sudan 南蘇丹嘅首都)

韭菜 [gau2 choi3] *n.* leek (~ soup 韭菜湯)

狗仔 [gau2 jai2] *n.* puppy

糾正 [gau2 jing3] *n.* rectification; *v.* rectify, redress

狗鯊 [gau2 sa1] *n.* dogfish

九十 [gau2 sap9] *num.* ninety

狗虱 [gau2 sat7] *n.* flea

狗屋 [gau2 uk7] *n.* kennel

韭黃 [gau2 wong4] *n.* chives

九月份 [gau2 yut9 fan6] *n.* September

夠 [gau3] *adj.* ample; *det.* enough of

救 [gau3] *v.* save

救濟品 [gau3 jai3 ban2] *n.* alms

購買 [gau3 maai5] *n.* purchase

購物券 [gau3 mat9 gyun3] *n.* token

購物中心 [gau3 mat9 jung1 sam1] *n.* mall, shopping center

購物籃 [gau3 mat9 laam4] *n.* shopping basket

救命啊！ [gau3 meng6 a1] *exclam.* Help!

救世主 [gau3 sai3 jyu2] *n.* salvation

救生圈 [gau3 sang1 hyun1] *n.* life preserver

救生艇 [gau3 sang1 teng5] *n.* lifeboat

救生衣 [gau3 sang1 yi1] *n.* life jacket

救生員 [gau3 sang1 yun4] *n.* lifeguard

救星 [gau3 sing1] *n.* saviour

救贖 [gau3 suk9] *n.* redemption

救援 [gau3 wun4] *v.* rescue

嘞 [gau6] *n.* lump

舊 [gau6] *adj.* used (~ to sth 習慣, ~ to do sth. 以前成日做)

舊年 [gau6 nin2] *adv.* last year

嘅 [ge3] *prep.* of

基本 [gei1 bun2] *adj.* basic

基本上 [gei1 bun2 seung6] *adv.* basically

機場 [gei1 cheung4] *n.* airport

機場保安 [gei1 cheung4 bou2 on1] *n.* airport security

機場候機樓 [gei1 cheung4 hau6 gei1 lau4] *n.* airport terminal

機場稅 [gei1 cheung4 seui3] *n.* airport tax

基礎 [gei1 cho2] *n.* foundation, basis

基礎設施 [gei1 cho2 chit8 si1] *n.* infrastructure

基地 [gei1 dei6] *n.* base (sauce ~ 原料, based on 基於)

基多 [gei1 do1] *n.* Quito (~, capital of Ecuador 厄瓜多爾嘅首都)

基督徒 [gei1 duk7 tou4] *adj.* Christian

機動車道 [gei1 dung6 che1 dou6] *n.* motorway

幾乎冇 [gei1 fu4 mou5] *adv.* hardly

基輔 [gei1 fu6] *n.* Kyiv (~, capital of Ukraine 烏克蘭嘅首都)

基加利 [gei1 ga1 lei6] *n.* Kigali (~, capital of Rwanda 盧旺達嘅首都)

基金 [gei1 gam1] *n.* fund

機械 [gei1 haai6] *n.* machine; *adj.* mechanical

機械裝置 [gei1 haai6 jong1 ji3] *n.* mechanism

基希那烏 [gei1 hei1 na5 wu1] *n.* Chisinau (~, capital of Moldova 摩爾多瓦嘅首都)

機器 [gei1 hei3] *n.* machinery

機器人 [gei1 hei3 yan4] *n.* robot

機構 [gei1 kau3] *n.* institution; *adj.* institutional

基里巴斯 [gei1 lei5 ba1 si1] *n.* Kiribati

幾內亞 [gei1 noi6 a3] *n.* Guinea

幾內亞比紹共和國 [gei1 noi6 a3 bei2 siu6 gung6 wo4 gwok8] *n.* Guinea-Bissau

機洗 [gei1 sai2] *adj.* machine washable

機會 [gei1 wui6] *n.* chance, occasion, opportunity

機會主義 [gei1 wui6 jyu2 yi6] *n.* opportunism

基因 [gei1 yan1] *n.* DNA (gene deoxyribonucleic acid), double helix

基因改良食品 [gei1 yan1 goi2 leung4 sik9 ban2] *n.* genetically modified food

機油 [gei1 yau2] *n.* petrol, oil

機油濾清器 [gei1 yau2 leui6 ching1 hei3] *n.* oil filter

基於 [gei1 yu1] *adj.* based on

肌肉 [gei1 yuk9] *n.* muscle

肌肉發達 [gei1 yuk9 faat8 daat9] *adj.* muscular

肌肉痛 [gei1 yuk9 tung3] *n.* myalgia

幾 [gei2] *adv.* fairly, pretty, quite

幾多次 [gei2 do1 chi3] *phr.* how many times?

幾多錢 [gei2 do1 chin4] *phr.* how much?

幾多歲 [gei2 do1 seui3] *phr.* how old?

紀律 [gei2 leut9] *n.* discipline

紀錄片 [gei2 luk9 pin2] *n.* documentary film

幾時 [gei2 si4] *adv.* when

幾時都得 [gei2 si4 dou1 dak7] *conj.* whenever

寄 [gei3] *v.* send

記分牌 [gei3 fan1 paai4] *n.* scoreboard

記號 [gei3 hou6] *n.* mark

記者 [gei3 je2] *n.* reporter

記住 [gei3 jyu6] *v.* remember (~ me 記住我)

記錄 [gei3 luk9] *n.* record

紀念 [gei3 nim6] *n.* remembrance in honor of

紀念品 [gei3 nim6 ban2] *n.* souvenir

紀念品店 [gei3 nim6 ban2 dim3] *n.* souvenir shop

紀念碑 [gei3 nim6 bei1] *n.* memorial, monument

紀念儀式 [gei3 nim6 yi4 sik7] *n.* commemoration

寄生蟲 [gei3 sang1 chung4] *n.* parasite

寄信人 [gei3 seun3 yan4] *n.* sender

記事表 [gei3 si6 biu2] *n.* docket

寄宿 [gei3 suk7] *n.* boarding

寄宿證 [gei3 suk7 jing3] *n.* boarding pass

技工 [gei6 gung1] *n.* mechanic

技巧 [gei6 haau2] *n.* technique

忌廉 [gei6 lim1] *n.* cream (~ sauce 忌廉汁, ~ soup 忌廉湯, ~ cheese 忌廉芝士, ~ cake 忌廉蛋糕, ~ of chicken 忌廉雞, ~ of wheat 忌廉小麥, ~ of tomato 忌廉番茄)

忌廉 [gei6 lim1] *adj.* creamed (~ corn 忌廉粟米, ~ green beans 忌廉青豆)

技能 [gei6 nang4] *n.* skill

妓女 [gei6 neui5] *n.* prostitute

技術 [gei6 seut9] *n.* technology (cutting-edge ~ 尖端技術)

技術上 [gei6 seut9 seung6] *adj.* technical

驚 [geng1] *adj.* frightened, afraid, scared

頸 [geng2] *n.* neck

頸巾 [geng2 gan1] *n.* scarf

頸渴 [geng2 hot8] *n.* thirst; *adj.* thirsty

頸鏈 [geng2 lin2] *n.* necklace

鏡 [geng3] *n.* mirror

鏡片 [geng3 pin3] *n.* camera lens; eyeglasses

鏡頭蓋 [geng3 tau4 goi3] *n.* lens cap

居民 [geui1 man4] *n.* resident

居心不良 [geui1 sam1 bat7 leung4] *adj.* malicious

矩陣 [geui2 jan6] *n.* matrix

鋸 [geui3] *n.* saw

句號 [geui3 hou6] *n.* full stop

句子 [geui3 ji2] *n.* sentence (*legal / grammar*)

巨大 [geui6 daai6] *adj.* monumental, tremendous

具體 [geui6 tai2] *adj.* concrete

巨人 [geui6 yan4] *n.* giant

腳 [geuk8] *n.* foot (on ~ 行路); leg

腳踏 [geuk8 daap9] *n.* pedal

腳瓜囊 [geuk8 gwa1 nong1] *n.* shank; top of leg

腳踭 [geuk8 jaang1] *n.* heel

腳趾 [geuk8 ji2] *n.* toe

腳眼 [geuk8 ngaan5] *n.* ankle

薑 [geung1] *n.* ginger (~ powder 薑粉, ~ ale 薑汁無酒精飲料, ~ beer 薑啤, ~bread 薑包, ~bread house 薑餅屋, ~snap 薑汁小食, ~ cake 薑餅蛋糕)

僵硬 [geung1 ngaang6] *adj.* stiff (~ neck 瞓捩頸)

擊敗 [gik7 baai6] *v.* defeat

激動 [gik7 dung6] *n.* thrill; *adj.* thrilled

劍擊 [gim3 gik7] *n.* fencing (*sport*)

激光 [gik7 gwong1] *n.* laser

激氣 [gik7 hei3] *adj.* upsetting

激增 [gik7 jang1] *v.* proliferate; *n.* proliferation

激進 [gik7 jeun3] *adj.* radical

激進分子 [gik7 jeun3 fan6 ji2] *n.* activist

激勵 [gik7 lai6] *n.* incentive, stimulus; *v.* motivate

激流 [gik7 lau4] *n.* torrent

激烈 [gik7 lit9] *adj.* intense, stormy

激烈程度 [gik7 lit9 ching4 dou6] *n.* intensity

激嬲 [gik7 nau1] *n.* provocation, aggravation; *v.* upset, provoke, aggravate, irritate

激嬲咗 [gik7 nau1 jo2] *adj.* irritated

擊退 [gik7 teui3] *v.* repel, repulse

擊暈 [gik7 wan4] *v.* stun

結盟 [gik8 mang4] *adj.* allied

極點 [gik9 dim2] *n.* pole

極度開心 [gik9 dou6 hoi1 sam1] *n.* rapture

極端 [gik9 dyun1] *adj.* extreme; *adv.* extremely

極光 [gik9 gwong1] *n.* aurora

極之 [gik9 ji1] *adv.* highly; badly

兼職 [gim1 jik7] *n.* part-time job/work

檢查 [gim2 cha4] *v.* check

檢察官 [gim2 chaat8 gun1] *n.* prosecutor

檢查站 [gim2 cha4 jaam6] *n.* checkpoint

檢舉 [gim2 geui2] *v.* prosecute; *n.* prosecution

檢疫 [gim2 yik9] *n.* quarantine

劍 [gim3] *n.* sword

劍魚 [gim3 yu2] *n.* swordfish

堅持 [gin1 chi4] *v.* insist (on), persevere, persist

堅強 [gin1 keung4] *adj.* tough

堅決 [gin1 kyut8] *adj.* determined, resolute; *adv.* firmly

堅決拒絕 [gin1 kyut8 keui5 jyut9] *n.* rebuff

見 [gin3] *v.* see, meet (pleased to ~ you 好高興認識你)

建造 [gin3 jou6] *n.* construction (under ~ 整緊)

建築學 [gin3 juk7 hok9] *n.* architecture

建築學嘅 [gin3 juk7 hok9 ge3] *adj.* architectural

建築物 [gin3 juk7 mat9] *n.* building

建築商 [gin3 juk7 seung1] *n.* builder

建築師 [gin3 juk7 si1] *n.* architect

建立 [gin3 laap9] *v.* establish, found; *n.* establishment

見面地方 [gin3 min6 dei6 fong1] *n.* meeting place

建議 [gin3 yi5] *v.* propose; *n.* advice (ask for ~ 請教意見), proposal, proposition

健康 [gin6 hong1] *adj.* healthy; *n.* fitness, health

鍵盤 [gin6 pun4] *n.* keyboard (piano/computer)

健身房 [gin6 san1 fong2] *n.* gym

件事 [gin6 si6] *n.* incident

經度 [ging1 dou6] *n.* longitude

經紀 [ging1 gei2] *n.* broker

經過 [ging1 gwo3] *v.* go by; *prep.* via, through

驚喜 [ging1 hei2] *n.* surprise

經濟 [ging1 jai3] *n.* economy

經濟艙 [ging1 jai3 chong1] *n.* economy class

經濟學 [ging1 jai3 hok9] *n.* economics

經濟學家 [ging1 jai3 hok9 ga1] *n.* economist

經濟衰退 [ging1 jai3 seui1 teui3] *n.* recession

經痛 [ging1 tung3] *n.* period, menstruation

經理 [ging1 lei5] *n.* manager

驚訝 [ging1 nga6] *n.* astonishment; *adj.* surprised

冰山 [ging1 saan1] *n.* iceberg

經銷商 [ging1 siu1 seung1] *n.* dealer (drug ~ 毒販, car ~ 汽車代理)

經已 [ging1 yi5] *adv.* already

經驗 [ging1 yim6] *n.* experience

經營 [ging1 ying4] *v.* manage

經營上嘅 [ging1 ying4 seung6 ge3] *adj.* managerial

警察 [ging2 chaat8] *n.* police

警笛聲 [ging2 dek9 seng1] *n.* siren

警告 [ging2 gou3] *v.* warn; *n.* warning (~ light 警告信號燈, health ~ 健康警告)

警長 [ging2 jeung2] *n.* sheriff

警訊 [ging2 seun3] *n.* police report

景色 [ging2 sik7] *n.* scene

莖 [ging3] *n.* stem

敬禮 [ging3 lai5] *v.* salute

敬佩 [ging3 pui3] *n.* admiration; *v.* admire

敬畏 [ging3 wai3] *n.* awe

競爭 [ging6 jaang1] *v.* compete; *n.* competition, rivalry

競選 [ging6 syun2] *n.* campaign

結 [git8] *n.* node, knot

結腸 [git8 cheung4] *n.* colon

結束 [git8 chuk7] *v.* cease

結塊 [git8 faai3] *n.* clot (blood ~ 血塊)

結婚 [git8 fan1] *v.* marry

結婚蛋糕 [git8 fan1 daan6 gou1] *n.* wedding cake

結婚戒指 [git8 fan1 gaai3 ji2] *n.* wedding ring

結婚週年紀念 [git8 fan1 jau1 nin4 gei2 nim6] *n.* wedding anniversary

結婚禮物 [git8 fan1 lai5 mat9] *n.* wedding present

結局 [git8 guk9] *n.* ending

結果 [git8 gwo2] *adv.* consequently; *n.* result

結晶 [git8 jing1] *adj.* crystallized (~ sugar 結晶糖, ~ caramel 結晶焦糖)

結咗婚嘅 [git8 jo2 fan1 ge3] *adj.* married

結構 [git8 kau3] *n.* structure

結構上 [git8 kau3 seung6] *adv.* structurally

結構上嘅 [git8 kau3 seung6 ge3] *adj.* structural

結論 [git8 leun6] *n.* conclusion

結他 [git8 ta1] *n.* guitar

結他手 [git8 ta1 sau2] *n.* guitarist

傑出 [git9 cheut7] *n.* preeminence; *adj.* prominent

傑作 [git9 jok8] *n.* masterpiece

驕傲 [giu1 ngou6] *n.* pride; *adv.* proudly

驕傲嘅 [giu1 ngou6 ge3] *adj.* proud

轎 [giu2] *n.* palanquin

叫 [giu3] *v.* call (for), shout, yell

叫醒 [giu3 seng2] *v.* wake (~ up 叫醒, ~ someone 叫醒某人, ~-up call 叫醒服務)

歌 [go1] *n.* song

哥本哈根 [go1 bun2 ha1 gan1] *n.* Copenhagen (~, capital of Denmark 丹麥嘅首都)

哥特式 [go1 dak9 sik7] *n.* Gothic-style

哥根蘇拿芝士 [go1 gan1 sou1 na4 ji1 si2] *n.* gorgonzola cheese

歌劇 [go1 kek9] *n.* opera

歌劇院 [go1 kek9 yun2] *n.* opera house

哥倫比亞 [go1 leun4 bei2 a3] *n.* Colombia; *adj.* Colombian

哥斯達黎加 [go1 si1 daat9 lai4 ga1] *n.* Costa Rica; *adj.* Costa Rican

歌星 [go1 sing1] *n.* singer

嗰度 [go2 dou6] *adv.* over there, there (~ are/is 有, please go ~ 請去嗰度)

嗰個 [go2 go3] *det.* that (~'s all 係咁多, ~'s fine 冇問題, ~'s true! 冇錯, Did you see ~? 你有冇睇到?), that one, the

個啲 [go3 di1] *adj.* those

個個 [go3 go3] *adj.* every (~ day 每日, ~ hour 每個鐘, ~ week 每個星期, ~ year 每年)

個個星期 [go3 go3 sing1 kei4] *adv.* weekly

個個人 [go3 go3 yan4] *pron.* everyone, everybody

個性 [go3 sing3] *n.* personality

個人 [go3 yan4] *adj.* personal

個人電腦 [go3 yan4 din6 nou5] *n.* personal computer (*abbr.* PC)

改 [goi2] *v.* change (~ trains 換車, ~ a baby 換尿片)

改革 [goi2 gaak8] *v.* reform; *n.* reformation

改革者 [goi2 gaak8 je2] *n.* reformer

改革論者 [goi2 gaak8 leun6 je2] *n.* progressive

改寄 [goi2 gei3] *v.* redirect

改進 [goi2 jeun3] *v.* improve

改進咗 [goi2 jeun3 jo2] *n.* improved

改造 [goi2 jou6] *v.* transform; *n.* transformation

蓋 [goi3] *n.* lid

角 [gok8] *n.* horned animal; instrument; car

覺得 [gok8 dak7] *v.* feel (~ sick 病咗, ~ hot 覺得熱, ~ cold 覺得凍)

覺得醜 [gok8 dak7 chau2] *adj.* ashamed

覺得反感 [gok8 dak7 faan2 gam2] *adj.* disgusted

覺得煩 [gok8 dak7 faan4] *adj.* annoyed

覺得尷尬 [gok8 dak7 gaam3 gaai3] *adj.* embarrassed

覺得可疑 [gok8 dak7 ho2 yi4] *adj.* suspicious

覺得悶 [gok8 dak7 mun6] *adj.* bored

角度 [gok8 dou6] *n.* angle (obtuse/acute/right ~ 銳角, what's your ~? 你點睇？)

各自 [gok8 ji6] *adj.* respective; *adv.* respectively

各種各樣 [gok8 jung2 gok8 yeung6] *adj.* various

閣樓 [gok8 lau4] *n.* turret

角色 [gok8 sik7] *n.* role

杆 [gon1] *n.* rod

乾 [gon1] *adj.* dry

肝 [gon1] *n.* liver

乾杯 [gon1 bui1] *v.* Cheers!

乾腸 [gon1 cheung4] *n.* dried sausage

乾果 [gon1 gwo2] *n.* dried fruit

乾果粉 [gon1 gwo2 fan2] *n.* ground nuts

乾旱 [gon1 hon5] *n.* drought

干紅辣椒 [gon1 hung4 laat9 jiu1] *n.* chipotle

肝泥香腸 [gon1 nai4 heung1 cheung2] *n.* liverwurst

乾洗 [gon1 sai2] *n.* dry cleaning

乾洗店 [gon1 sai2 dim3] *n.* dry cleaner, dry-cleaning

干涉 [gon1 sip8] *v.* intervene; *n.* intervention

乾衣機 [gon1 yi1 gei1] *n.* dryer

趕 [gon2] *v.* rush

趕出屋企 [gon2 cheut7 uk7 kei2] *v.* lock out, lock oneself out

趕走 [gon2 jau2] *v.* evict; *n.* eviction

剛果共和國 [gong1 gwo2 gung6 wo4 gwok8] *n.* Congo, Republic of the

剛果民主共和國 [gong1 gwo2 man4 jyu2 gung6 wo4 gwok8] *n.* Congo, Democratic Republic of the

剛果人 [gong1 gwo2 yan4] *adj.* Congolese

講 [gong2] *v.* say (Can you ~ it again? 你可唔可以再講一次?, How do you ~ ...? 你話

點?, Can you ~ it in English? 請你用英文再講一次好嗎?)

講粗口 [gong2 chou1 hau2] *n.* swearing

講大話 [gong2 daai6 wa6] *v.* lie (~ on a bed 瞓喺張床度); lie, tell falsehoods

港口 [gong2 hau2] *n.* port, harbor (~ area 港口區)

講明 [gong2 ming4] *v.* illustrate

講師 [gong2 si1] *n.* lecturer

講笑 [gong2 siu3] *n.* railery, mockery; *v.* joke (are you joking? 你講笑呀?)

講數 [gong2 sou3] *v.* negotiate; *n.* negotiation

講話 [gong2 wa2] *n.* utterance

港灣 [gong2 waan1] *n.* bay (to keep at ~ 牽制)

講嘢唔清唔楚 [gong2 ye5 m4 ching1 m4 cho2] *v.* mumble

講英文 [gong2 ying1 man2] *adj.* English-speaking

鋼琴 [gong3 kam4] *n.* piano

降落傘 [gong3 lok9 saan3] *n.* parachute

葛縷子籽 [got8 leui5 ji2 ji2] *n.* caraway seed

割 [got8] *v.* cut

高 [gou1] *adj.* high, tall

高壓線 [gou1 aat8 sin3] *n.* high-voltage line

高層住宅 [gou1 chang4 jyu6 jaak9] *n.* high-rise apartment building

高潮 [gou1 chiu4] *n.* climax

高速公路 [gou1 chuk7 gung1 lou6] *n.* highway

高速公路交匯處 [gou1 chuk7 gung1 lou6 gaau1 wui6 chyu3] *n.* highway interchange

高速路警察 [gou1 chuk7 lou6 ging2 chaat8] *n.* highway police

高速路入口 [gou1 chuk7 lou6 yap9 hau2] *n.* expressway entrance

高達芝士 [gou1 daat9 ji1 si2] *n.* gouda cheese

高凳 [gou1 dang3] *n.* stool (chair / feces sample)

高竇 [gou1 dau6] *adj.* superior

糕點 [gou1 dim2] *n.* pastry

高度 [gou1 dou6] *n.* height

高度計 [gou1 dou6 gai3] *n.* altimeter

高科技 [gou1 fo1 gei6] *adj.* high-tech (*also* hi-tech)

高峰期 [gou1 fung1 kei4] *n.* rush hour

高腳酒杯 [gou1 geuk8 jau2 bui1] *n.* goblet

高貴 [gou1 gwai3] *adj.* noble

高脂濃忌廉 [gou1 ji1 nung4 gei6 lim4] *n.* heavy cream

高中 [gou1 jung1] *n.* high school

高級教士 [gou1 kap7 gaau3 si6] *n.* prelate

高級汽油 [gou1 kap7 hei3 yau4] *n.* premium gas

高粱 [gou1 leung4] *n.* sorghum

高粱酒 [gou1 leung4 jau2] *n.* sorghum alcohol

高雅 [gou1 nga5] *adj.* refined

高山滑雪 [gou1 saan1 waat9 syut8] *n.* downhill skiing

高溫 [gou1 wan1] *n./v.* heat (pre~ 預先加熱, ~ stove 加熱爐頭, ~ oven 加熱焗爐, to ~ 加熱)

高爾夫球 [gou1 yi5 fu1 kau4] *n.* golf

高爾夫球場 [gou1 yi5 fu1 kau4 cheung4] *n.* golf course

睪丸 [gou1 yun2] *n.* testicles

高原 [gou1 yun4] *n.* plateau

孤獨 [gu1 duk9] *adj.* lonely, lonesome

孤立 [gu1 laap9] *v.* isolate; *adj.* isolated

孤兒 [gu1 yi4] *n.* orphan

孤兒院 [gu1 yi4 yun2] *n.* orphanage

鼓 [gu2] *n.* drum (play the ~s 打鼓)

估 [gu2] *v.* guess

古巴 [gu2 ba1] *n.* Cuba; *adj.* Cuban

古典 [gu2 din2] *adj.* classic, classical

古典主義 [gu2 din2 jyu2 yi6] *n.* Classicism

古典音樂 [gu2 din2 yam1 ngok9] *n.* classical music

估到 [gu2 dou2] *adj.* expected

股東 [gu2 dung1] *n.* shareholder

古董 [gu2 dung2] *adj.* vintage (~ wine 佳釀)

古董 [gu2 dung2] *n.* antique (~ store 古董店)

股份 [gu2 fan2] *n.* stake

估價 [gu2 ga3] *v.* assess; *n.* assessment, valuation

古建築 [gu2 gin3 juk7] *n.* historic building

古怪 [gu2 gwaai3] *adj.* outlandish

鼓掌 [gu2 jeung2] *v.* clap

古跡 [gu2 jik7] *n.* historic site

鼓勵 [gu2 lai6] *v.* encourage; *n.* encouragement

古老 [gu2 lou5] *adj.* ancient

古老也芝士 [gu2 lou5 ya5 ji1 si2] *n.* gruyere cheese

估唔到 [gu2 m4 dou3] *adv.* surprisingly

股票 [gu2 piu3] *n.* stock (chicken ~ 雞肉, fish ~ 魚肉, ~ exchange 股票交易所, ~ option 期權, Do you have it in ~? 你有存貨嗎？)

股票交易所 [gu2 piu3 gaau1 yik9 so2] *n.* stock exchange

古色古香 [gu2 sik7 gu2 heung1] *adj.* quaint

古銅色 [gu2 tung4 sik7] *adj.* tan

固定 [gu3 ding6] *adj.* fixed

固定劑 [gu3 ding6 jai1] *n.* fixative (spray with a ~ 定型噴慕)

顧客 [gu3 haak8] *n.* client, customer (~ information/service 顧客資訊/服務, ~ parking 顧客專用停車場)

故仔 [gu3 jai2] *n.* story (*narrative / building level*)

顧問 [gu3 man6] *n.* adviser, advisor, consultant

故意 [gu3 yi3] *adj.* deliberate; *adv.* deliberately

故意 [gu3 yi3] *adv.* on purpose

故意刁難 [gu3 yi3 diu1 naan4] *adj.* obstructive

故意破壞 [gu3 yi3 po3 waai6] *n.* sabotage

菊苣 [guk7 geui6] *n.* radicchio

焗 [guk9] *v.* bake; *adj.* oven-baked

焗過 [guk9 gwo3] *adj.* baked (~ casserole 砂鍋菜, ~ potato 焗薯仔)

局限 [guk9 haan6] *n.* limitation

焗爐 [guk9 lou4] *n.* oven (~ browned 焗爐 ~ roasted 焗爐焗)

焗爐手套 [guk9 lou4 sau2 tou3] *n.* oven mitt

局外人 [guk9 ngoi6 yan4] *n.* outsider

焗燶 [guk9 nung1] *adj.* oven-browned

焗盤 [guk9 pun4] *n.* baking pan, baking sheet

焗薯仔 [guk9 syu4 jai2] *n.* potatoes au gratin

觀察 [gun1 chaat8] *v.* observe; *n.* observation

觀察敏銳 [gun1 chaat8 man5 yeui6] *adj.* perceptive

觀察員 [gun1 chaat8 yun4] *n.* observer

觀點 [gun1 dim2] *n.* point, viewpoint

官方 [gun1 fong1] *adj.* official

觀景小路 [gun1 ging2 siu2 lou6] *n.* nature trail

觀光 [gun1 gwong1] *n.* sightseeing (go ~ 旅遊)

觀眾 [gun1 jung3] *n.* audience

官僚 [gun1 liu4] *n.* bureaucrat

官僚體制 [gun1 liu4 tai2 jai3] *n.* bureaucracy

官司 [gun1 si1] *n.* lawsuit

管 [gun2] *n.* pipe (smoking ~ 排煙管)

管制 [gun2 jai3] *v.* regulate; *n.* regulation; *adj.* regulatory

管制藥 [gun2 jai3 yeuk9] *n.* controlled substance

管理 [gun2 lei5] *v.* govern

管理部門 [gun2 lei5 bou6 mun4] *n.* administration

管理層 [gun2 lei5 chang4] *n.* management

管弦樂 [gun2 yin4 ngok9] *adj.* orchestral

管弦樂隊 [gun2 yin4 ngok9 deui6] *n.* orchestra

鸛 [gun3] *n.* stork

罐 [gun3] *n.* jar

罐裝 [gun3 jong1] *adj.* canned (~ vegetables 罐裝蔬菜, ~ meat 罐裝肉, ~ goods 罐裝食物)

半食宿 [gun3 sik9 suk7] *n.* half board room with some meals

灌輸 [gun3 syu1] *n.* infusion

罐頭 [gun3 tau4] *n.* tin

罐頭水果 [gun3 tau4 seui2 gwo2] *n.* fermented fruits

工 [gung1] *n.* job (what's your ~? 你做乜野架?)

供品 [gung1 ban2] *n.* offering

公廁 [gung1 chi3] *n.* public toilet

工程 [gung1 ching4] *n.* project

工程師 [gung1 ching4 si1] *n.* engineer

工廠 [gung1 chong2] *n.* factory

工廠直銷店 [gung1 chong2 jik9 siu1 dim3] *n.* outlet, factory outlet

功課 [gung1 fo3] *n.* homework

公雞 [gung1 gai1] *n.* rooster

公斤 [gung1 gan1] *n.* kilogram (2.2 lbs.)

工具 [gung1 geui6] *n.* instrument

工具欄 [gung1 geui6 laan4] *n.* toolbar (computer program ~ 電腦工具欄)

工具箱 [gung1 geui6 seung1] *n.* kit

攻擊 [gung1 gik7] *v.* strike (hit); *n.* attack (heart ~ 心臟病)

恭敬 [gung1 ging3] *adj.* reverential

公告欄 [gung1 gou3 laan4] *n.* bulletin board

公共電話 [gung1 gung6 din6 wa2] *n.* public telephone

公共交通工具 [gung1 gung6 gaau1 tung1 gung1 geui6] *n.* public transportation

公共有限公司 [gung1 gung6 yau5 haan6 gung1 si1] *n.* Public Limited Company *(abbr.* plc, *also* PLC)

恭喜 [gung1 hei2] *v.* congratulate; *n.* congratulations

恭喜晒！ [gung1 hei2 saai3] *phr., exclam.* Congratulations!

公開 [gung1 hoi1] *v.* expose; *n.* exposure; *adv.* publicly

工匠 [gung1 jeung6] *n.* artisan

工資 [gung1 ji1] *n.* wage

公證員 [gung1 jing3 yun4] *n.* notary

公正 [gung1 jing3] *n.* justice

工作簡介 [gung1 jok8 gaan2 gaai3] *n.* job description

工作證 [gung1 jok8 jing3] *n.* work permit

工作室 [gung1 jok8 sat7] *n.* studio

工作人員 [gung1 jok8 yan4 yun4] *n.* crew

工作日 [gung1 jok8 yat9] *n.* weekday

公眾 [gung1 jung3] *adj.* public

公眾地方 [gung1 jung3 dei6 fong1] *n.* public building

公用電話 [gung1 yung6 din6 wa2] *n.* public telephone

公主 [gung1 jyu2] *n.* princess

公里 [gung1 lei5] *n.* kilometer *(abbrev.* K / 0.6 miles)

功勞 [gung1 lou4] *n.* exploit (~s of smn. 事跡)

公民 [gung1 man4] *n.* citizenship

公民權利 [gung1 man4 kyun4 lei6] *n.* civil rights

功能 [gung1 nang4] *n.* function

工藝品 [gung1 ngai6 ban2] *n.* folk handicrafts

工藝店 [gung1 ngai6 dim3] *n.* craft store

公牛 [gung1 ngau4] *n.* bull

公平 [gung1 ping4] *adj.* fair; *n.* equity

公司 [gung1 si1] *n.* company

公式 [gung1 sik7] *n.* formula (spreadsheet ~ 數據表公式)

工頭 [gung1 tau4] *n.* foreman

工人 [gung1 yan4] *n.* worker

供應 [gung1 ying3] *n.* supply

供應商 [gung1 ying3 seung1] *n.* supplier

工業 [gung1 yip9] *adj.* industrial

工業區 [gung1 yip9 keui1] *n.* industrial district

公園 [gung1 yun2] *n.* park (city ~ 城市公園, car ~ 停車場)

拱門 [gung2 mun4] *n.* arch

貢獻 [gung3 hin3] *v.* contribute; *n.* contribution

共產主義 [gung6 chaan2 jyu2 yi6] *adj.* communist

共同 [gung6 tung4] *adj.* joint

共同 [gung6 tung4] *adv.* in common

共和黨 [gung6 wo4 dong2] *n.* republican

共和國 [gung6 wo4 gwok8] *n.* republic

瓜 [gwa1] *n.* melon

寡婦 [gwa2 fu5] *n.* widow

寡佬 [gwa2 lou2] *n.* widower

寡佬派對 [gwa2 lou2 paai3 deui3] *n.* bachelor party

寡頭政治 [gwa2 tau4 jing3 ji6] *n.* oligarchy

掛 [gwa3] *v.* hang

掛號信 [gwa3 hou4 seun3] *n.* registered mail

掛氈 [gwa3 jin1] *n.* tapestry

掛住 [gwa3 jyu6] *v.* miss (*feel absence*); *adj.* overhanging

掛鎖 [gwa3 so2] *n.* padlock

拐杖 [gwaai2 jeung2] *n.* crutches

拐杖糖 [gwaai2 jeung6 tong2] *n.* candy cane

關 [gwaan1] *v.* shut; switch smth. off

關鍵 [gwaan1 gin6] *adj.* critical

關鍵字 [gwaan1 gin6 ji6] *n.* keyword (~ search 關鍵字搜索)

關係 [gwaan1 hai6] *n.* affiliation, relations, relationship

關係 [gwaan1 hai6] *v.* regard (Give my ~s to … 請幫我問候)

關係 [gwaan1 hai6] *prep.* regarding

關係到 [gwaan1 hai6 dou3] *v.* concern

關節 [gwaan1 jit8] *n.* joints

關節炎 [gwaan1 jit8 yim4] *n.* arthritis (have ~ 有關節炎)

關聯 [gwaan1 lyun4] *n.* link (website ~ 網站連結)

關心 [gwaan1 sam1] *adj.* concerned

關於 [gwaan1 yu1] *v.* pertain; *prep.* concerning, pertaining to

慣例 [gwaan3 lai6] *n.* convention (~ hall 會議廳)

刮 [gwaat8] *v.* scrape

刮痕 [gwaat8 han4] *n.* scrape

圭亞那 [gwai1 a3 na5] *n.* Guyana; *adj.* Guyananese

歸根究底 [gwai1 gan1 gau3 dai2] *adv.* ultimately

皈依 [gwai1 yi1] *v.* convert

詭計 [gwai2 gai3] *n.* trick

貴 [gwai3] *adj.* expensive

季節 [gwai3 jit8] *v.* season (~ed 調咗味, ~ing 調味料)

季節性 [gwai3 jit8 sing3] *adj.* seasonal

貴族 [gwai3 juk9] *n.* aristocracy

貴族階級 [gwai3 juk9 gaai1 kap7] *n.* nobility

貴重物品 [gwai3 jung6 mat9 ban2] *n.* valuables

櫃枱 [gwai6 toi2] *n.* counter

櫃桶 [gwai6 tung2] *n.* drawer

軍隊 [gwan1 deui6] *n.* army

軍火 [gwan1 fo2] *n.* munitions

軍火庫 [gwan1 fo2 fu3] *n.* arsenal

軍官 [gwan1 gun1] *n.* officer

軍工廠 [gwan1 gung1 chong2] *n.* armory

均衡 [gwan1 hang4] *n.* equilibrium

君主 [gwan1 jyu2] *n.* monarch

君主制 [gwan1 jyu2 jai3] *n.* monarchy

軍團 [gwan1 tyun4] *n.* regiment

均勻 [gwan1 wan4] *adj.* homogenized

軍人 [gwan1 yan4] *n.* soldier

郡 [gwan6] *n.* county

轟炸 [gwang1 ja3] *v.* bombard; *n.* bombardment

骨 [gwat7] *n.* bone

骨架 [gwat7 ga3] *n.* skeleton

骨折 [gwat7 jit8] *n.* fracture

骨髓 [gwat7 seui5] *n.* bone marrow

掘 [gwat9] *v.* dig

倔頭路 [gwat9 tau4 lou6] *n.* dead end

果汁 [gwo2 jap7] *n.* juice (grape ~ 葡萄汁, grapefruit ~ 柚子汁, lemon ~ 檸檬汁, orange ~ 橙汁, cherry ~ 車厘子汁, apple ~ 蘋果汁, pear ~ 梨汁, tomato ~ 番茄汁)

果汁飲料 [gwo2 jap7 yam2 liu6] *n.* ade (lemon~ 檸檬水, lime~ 青檸檬水)

果醬 [gwo2 jeung3] *n.* jam

果盤 [gwo2 pun4] *n.* compote (fruit ~ 水果盤, apple ~ 蘋果盤)

果糖 [gwo2 tong4] *n.* fructose

果仁 [gwo2 yan4] *n.* nut

果仁蛋糕 [gwo2 yan4 daan6 gou1] *n.* torte

果仁糖 [gwo2 yan4 tong2] *n.* praline

果仁燕麥 [gwo2 yan4 yin3 mak9] *n.* muesli

果肉 [gwo2 yuk9] *n.* pulp (fruit)

果園 [gwo2 yun4] *n.* orchard

過多 [gwo3 do1] *adj.* profuse

過去 [gwo3 heui3] *adj.* past

過咗時 [gwo3 jo2 si4] *adj.* obsolete

過期 [gwo3 kei4] *v.* expire; *adj.* overdue

過濾 [gwo3 leui6] *v./n.* filter (coffee ~ 咖啡過濾紙, without ~ 冇過濾)

過濾咗 [gwo3 leui6 jo2] *adj.* filtered (~ water 過濾咗嘅水)

過量 [gwo3 leung6] *n.* excess (~ baggage 行李過重)

過敏 [gwo3 man5] *adj.* allergic (I'm ~ to 我對... 敏感)

過敏 [gwo3 man5] *n.* allergy (food ~ 食物過敏, medicine ~ 藥物過敏)

過敏原 [gwo3 man5 yun4] *n.* allergen

過時 [gwo3 si4] *adj.* outdated

過夜 [gwo3 ye6] *n.* overnight

國防 [gwok8 fong4] *n.* defense

國家 [gwok8 ga1] *n.* country (~ inn 鄉村旅館, ~ music 鄉村音樂)

國家區號 [gwok8 ga1 keui1 hou6] *n.* country code

國界 [gwok8 gaai3] *n.* border

國歌 [gwok8 go1] *n.* anthem

國際 [gwok8 jai3] *adj.* international

國際長途 [gwok8 jai3 cheung4 tou4] *n.* international call

國際學生證 [gwok8 jai3 hok9 saang1 jing3] *n.* international student card

國籍 [gwok8 jik9] *n.* nationality

國民生產總值 [gwok8 man4 sang1 chaan2 jung2 jik9] *n.* GDP (Gross Domestic Product)

國外 [gwok8 ngoi6] *adj.* overseas; *adv.* abroad

國內 [gwok8 noi6] *adj.* domestic

國內醫療服務 [gwok8 noi6 yi1 liu4 fuk9 mou6] *phr.* national health service

國王 [gwok8 wong4] *n.* king

國會 [gwok8 wui2] *n.* parliament

國會大廈 [gwok8 wui2 daai6 ha6] *n.* parliament building

國有 [gwok8 yau5] *adj.* national

國有化 [gwok8 yau5 fa3] *n.* nationalization; *v.* nationalize

光標 [gwong1 biu1] *n.* cursor (on computer screen)

光輝 [gwong1 fai1] *n.* blaze

光澤 [gwong1 jaak9] *n.* gloss, polish

光猛 [gwong1 maang5] *adj.* bright; *adv.* brightly

光盤 [gwong1 pun4] *n.* compact disc, CD, DVD

廣播員 [gwong2 bo3 yun4] *n.* announcer

廣場 [gwong2 cheung4] *n.* main square

廣泛 [gwong2 faan3] *adv.* widely

廣告 [gwong2 gou3] *n.* advertising (~ agency 廣告公司, ~ executive 廣告經理)

捐 [gyun1] *v.* donate (~d by 由... 捐贈, ~ blood 捐血, ~ bone marrow 捐骨髓 ~ organ 捐贈器官)

捐 [gyun1] *n.* donation

卷 [gyun2] *v.* curl; *adj.* curly; *n.* roll ~ bread 麵包卷, ~ call 點名

卷髮 [gyun2 faat8] *n.* ringlet

卷軸 [gyun2 juk9] *n.* reel

捲心菜絲 [gyun2 sam1 choi3 si1] *n.* slaw (cole~ 捲心菜絲沙律, apple ~ 蘋果絲沙律, cabbage ~ 大白菜絲沙律)

卷薯條 [gyun2 syu4 tiu4] *n.* curly fries

H

蝦 [ha1] *n.* prawn, shrimp
(butterfly ~ 蝴蝶蝦)

哈博羅內 [ha1 bok8 lo4 noi6]
n. Gaborone (~, capital of
Botswana 博茨瓦納嘅首都)

哈拉雷 [ha1 laai1 leui4] *n.*
Harare (~, capital of Zimbabwe
津巴布韋嘅首都)

哈密瓜 [ha1 mat9 gwa1] *n.*
cantaloupe

蛤蟆 [ha1 mo1] *n.* toad

哈瓦那 [ha1 nga5 na5] *n.* Havana
(~, capital of Cuba 古巴嘅首都)

哈薩克斯坦 [ha1 saat8 hak7
si1 taan2] *n.* Kazakhstan; *adj.*
Kazakhstani

哈爾瓦糕 [ha1 yi5 nga5 gou1]
n. halva

下定決心 [ha6 ding6 kyut8 sam1]
v. determine

下個星期 [ha6 go3 sing1 kei4]
adv. next week

下個站有落！[ha6 go3 jaam6
yau5 lok9] *phr.* next stop!

下個月 [ha6 go3 yut9] *adv.* next
month

下降 [ha6 gong3] *n.* decline

下晝 [ha6 jau3] *adv.* PM

夏至 [ha6 ji3] *n.* summer solstice

下載 [ha6 joi3] *v. comp.* download
(free ~ 免費下載, ~ a file
下載文件)

下流 [ha6 lau4] *adj.* obscene; *n.*
obscenity

下面 [ha6 min6] *adv.* down

下年 [ha6 nin2] *n.* next year

下扒 [ha6 pa4] *n.* chin, jaw

下鋪 [ha6 pou1] *n.* lower berth

下身癱瘓 [ha6 san1 taan1 wun6]
adj. paraplegic

夏天 [ha6 tin1] *n.* summer (~
schedule 夏令時間, ~ solstice
夏至, ~ vacation 暑假)

夏威夷 [ha6 wai1 yi4] *adj.*
Hawaiian (~ food 夏威夷菜)

下一個 [ha6 yat7 go3] *adj.* next

嘥 [haai4] *adj.* coarse, rough

鞋 [haai4] *n.* shoe (~ repair shop 修
鞋鋪, ~ store 鞋店, ~ polisher
刷鞋佬)

蟹 [haai5] *n.* crab (~ cakes 蟹餅,
~ meat 蟹肉, artificial ~ 素蟹)

喀布爾 [haak3 bou3 yi5] *n* Kabul
(~, capital of Afghanistan 阿富
汗嘅首都)

喀麥隆 [haak3 mak9 lung4] *n.*
Cameroon; *adj.* Cameroonian

喀土穆 [haak3 tou2 muk9] *n.*
Khartoum (~, capital of Sudan
蘇丹嘅首都)

赫爾辛基 [haak7 yi5 san1 gei1]
n. Helsinki (~, capital of Finland
芬蘭嘅首都)

嚇 [haak8] *v.* frighten

客艙 [haak8 chong1] *n.* cabin

客艙板 [haak8 chong1 baan2] *n.*
cabin deck

客房送餐服務 [haak8 fong2
sung3 chaan1 fuk9 mou6] *n.*
room service (*at a hotel*)

客氣說話 [haak8 hei3 syut3
wa6] *n.* pleasantry

客廳 [haak8 teng1] *n.* living room

嚇壞 [haak8 waai6] *v.* astonish

餡 [haam2] *n.* stuffing (turkey ~ 火雞餡)

餡餅 [haam2 beng2] *n.* flan

喊 [haam3] *v.* cry

鹹 [haam4] *adj.* salty

鹹牛肉 [haam4 ngau4 yuk9] *n.* corned beef

鹹濕 [haam4 sap7] *n.* lust

慳 [han1] *adj.* provident

慳錢 [haan1 chin2] *adj.* frugal

限速 [haan6 chuk7] *n.* speed limit

限制 [haan6 jai3] *n.* restraint; *v.* restrict

限載 [haan6 joi3] *n.* load limit

行差踏錯 [haang4 cha1 daap9 cho3] *adv.* astray; *v.* go astray

行得好艱難 [haang4 dak7 hou2 gan1 naan4] *v.* plod

行到 [haang4 dou3] *v.* reach

行街 [haang4 gaai1] *v.* shop, go shopping

行開! [haang4 hoi1] *phr., exclam.* Go away!

行雷 [haang4 leui4] *n.* thunder

行路 [haang4 lou6] on foot

行人道 [haang4 yan4 dou6] *n.* pedestrian crossing

行人區 [haang4 yan4 keui1] *n.* pedestrian zone

盒 [haap2] *n.* box

峽谷 [haap9 guk7] *n.* ravine

烤 [haau1] *v.* broil

敲 [haau1] *v.* knock

酵 [haau1] *n.* enzymes

烤 [haau1] *adj.* roast (~ beef 烤牛肉)

哮喘 [haau1 chyun2] *n.* asthma (have ~ 有哮喘)

烤咗 [haau1 jo2] *v.* roast

酵母 [haau1 mou5] *v.* leaven

酵母菌 [haau1 mou5 kwan2] *n.* yeast

烤羊肉串 [haau1 yeung4 yuk9 chyun3] *n.* kebab (chicken/lamb)

烤肉架 [haau1 yuk9 ga2] *adj.* rotisserie

考古 [haau2 gu2] *adj.* archeological

考古學 [haau2 gu2 hok9] *n.* archeology

考慮 [haau2 leui6] *v.* consider; *n.* consideration

巧妙嘅應答 [haau2 miu6 ge3 ying3 daap8] *n.* repartee

烤硬咗 [haau2 ngaang6 jo2] *n.* hard-baked (~ crust 烤硬咗麵包皮)

考試 [haau2 si3] *n.* exam

考試合格 [haau2 si3 hap9 gaak8] *v.* pass an exam

效果 [haau6 gwo2] *n.* effect

效率 [haau6 leut9] *n.* efficiency

喺 [hai6] *prep.* at (~ first 開始, ~ last 最後, ~ least 至少, ~ random 隨便, ~ stake 處於成敗關頭)

係 [hai6] *v.* be; *exclam.* yes

喺…前面 [hai6 … chin4 min6] *prep.* in front (of)

喺…範圍內 [hai6 … faan6 wai4 noi6] *prep.* within

喺…嘅 [hai6 … ge3] *v.* belong

喺…嘅基礎 [hai6 … ge3 gei1 cho2] *v.* underlie

喉嗰度 [hai6 go2 dou6] *adv.* over there

喺公眾場合 [hai6 gung1 jung3 cheung4 hap9] *prep.* in public

喺…下面 [hai6 … ha6 min6] *prep.* underneath

喺…後面 [hai6 … hau6 min6] *prep.* behind

喺…之前 [hai6 … ji1 chin4] *adj.* prior to

喺…之間 [hai6 … ji1 gaan1] *prep.* between

喺…期間 [hai6 … kei4 gaan1] *conj.* while (~ you wait 系你等 嘅期間)

喺其他地方 [hai6 kei4 ta1 dei6 fong1] *adv.* elsewhere

喺呢度 [hai6 ne4 dou6] *adv.* over here

喺…上 [hai6 … seung6] *prep.* on

喺…上面 [hai6 … seung6 min6] *prep.* above

喺船上 [hai6 syun4 seung6] *adv.* on board

系統 [hai6 tung2] *n.* system

喺屋企 [hai6 uk7 kei5] *adv.* in time, in place

喺…入面 [hai6 … yap9 min6] *prep.* inside

刻 [hak7] *v.* incise

克 [hak7] *n.* gram (*abbr.* g.)

黑白 [hak7 baak9] *adj.* black and white

黑醋 [hak7 chou3] *n.* balsamic vinaigrette

黑豆 [hak7 dau2] *n.* black beans

克服 [hak7 fuk9] *v.* overcome

黑咖啡 [hak7 ga3 fe1] *n.* black coffee

克制 [hak7 jai3] *v.* refrain

黑椒 [hak7 jiu1] *n.* black pepper

黑椒牛扒 [hak7 jiu1 ngau4 pa2] *n.* pepper steak

克羅地亞 [hak7 lo4 dei6 a3] *n.* Croatia; *adj.* Croatian

克隆 [hak7 lung4] *v.* clone; *n.* cloning

黑米 [hak7 mai5] *n.* black rice

黑麥 [hak7 mak9] *n.* rye (~ bread 黑麥麵包)

黑莓 [hak7 mui4] *n.* blackberry

黑眼豆 [hak7 ngaan5 dau2] *n.* black-eyed peas

黑色 [hak7 sik7] *adj.* black

龕 [ham1] *n.* alcove

坎培拉 [ham2 pui4 laai1] *n.* Canberra (~, capital of Australia 澳洲嘅首都)

砍伐森林 [ham2 fat9 sam1 lam4] *n.* deforestation

坎帕拉 [ham2 paak8 laai1] *n.* Kampala (~, capital of Uganda 烏干達嘅首都)

含蓄 [ham4 chuk7] *adj.* reticent

含酒精飲品 [ham4 jau2 jing1 yam2 ban2] *n.* liquor, hard liquor

含磷 [ham4 leun4] *n.* phosphorous

含糊 [ham4 wu4] *n.* ambiguity

含二氧化碳 [ham4 yi6 yeung5 fa3 taan3] *adj.* carbonated

含鉛汽油 [ham4 yun4 hei3 yau4] *n.* leaded gasoline

狠心 [han2 sam1] *adj.* relentless

痕 [han4] *v.* itch (have an ~ 好痕)

肯定 [hang2 ding6] *adj.* sure (Are you ~? 你肯唔肯定架?)

肯雅 [hang2 nga5] *n.* Kenya; *adj.* Kenyan

行程表 [hang4 ching4 biu2] *n.* itinerary

行動 [hang4 dung6] *n.* action

行街 [haang4 gaai1] *v.* go shopping; *n.* shopping (~ basket 購物籃, ~ cart 購物車, ~ center 購物中心, ~ mall 購物中心)

行軍 [hang4 gwan1] *v.* march

行政管理 [hang4 jing3 gun2 lei5] *adj.* administrative

行政區 [hang4 jing3 keui1] *n.* district (administrative)

行李 [hang4 lei5] *n.* baggage (~ cart 行李車, ~ check 行李托管, ~ check office/room 行李寄存處, ~ locker 行李櫃, ~ claim 取行李, ~ reclaim area 取行李處)

行李架 [hang4 lei5 ga2] *n.* rack (~ of lamb 羊架, ~ of ribs 排骨架)

行李櫃 [hang4 lei5 gwai6] *n.* baggage locker

行李限額 [hang4 lei5 haan6 ngaak2] *n.* luggage allowance

行李箱 [hang4 lei5 seung1] *n.* suitcase

行李托管 [hang4 lei5 tok8 gun2] *n.* baggage check

行銷 [hang4 siu1] *n.* marketing

行為 [hang4 wai4] *n.* behavior

行人路 [hang4 yan4 lou6] *n.* pavement, footpath

杏樹 [hang6 syu6] *n.* apricot (~ jam/preserves 杏醬)

杏仁 [hang6 yan4] *n.* almond (~ butter 杏仁膏, ~ oil 杏仁油)

杏仁蛋白軟糖 [hang6 yan4 daan2 baak9 yun5 tong2] *n.* marzipan

杏仁碎 [hang6 yan4 seui3] *n.* crushed almonds

瞌眼瞓 [hap7 ngaan5 fan3] *v.* doze

合併 [hap9 bing3] *v.* merge

合唱隊 [hap9 cheung3 deui6] *n.* chorus

合得來 [hap9 dak7 loi4] *v.* click

合得人 [hap9 dak7 yan4] *adj.* sociable

合法化 [hap9 faat8 fa3] *n.* legalization

合法 [hap9 faat8] *adj.* legal (is it ~? 合唔合法架?); *adv.* legally

合夥公司 [hap9 fo2 gung1 si1] *n.* partnership

合作 [hap9 jok8] *n.* cooperation; *adj.* cooperative

合理 [hap9 lei5] *adj.* reasonable (~ doubt 合理疑點); *adv.* reasonably

合理化 [hap9 lei5 fa3] *v.* rationalize

合理性 [hap9 lei5 sing3] *n.* rationality

合成 [hap9 sing4] *adj.* synthetic (~ material 合成材料)

合桃 [hap9 tou4] *n.* walnut, pecan (~ pie 合桃批)

合同 [hap9 tung4] *n.* contract

乞人憎 [hat7 yan4 jang1] *adj.* awful

乞兒 [hat7 yi1] *n.* beggar

乞兒仔 [hat7 yi4 jai2] *n.* street children

核測試 [hat9 chak7 si3] *n.* nuclear tests

核彈 [hat9 daan2] *n.* nuclear bomb

核電站 [hat9 din6 jaam6] *n.* nuclear power station

核物理 [hat9 mat9 lei5] *n.* nuclear physics

核武 [hat9 mou5] *n.* nuclear weapons

核能 [hat9 nang4] *n.* nuclear energy

核心 [hat9 sam1] *n.* core

口 [hau2] *n.* mouth

口才 [hau2 choi4] *n.* eloquence

口氣 [hau2 hei3] *n.* breath

口哨 [hau2 saau3] *n.* whistle

口水 [hau2 seui2] *n.* saliva

口水肩 [hau2 seui2 gin1] *n.* bib

口信 [hau2 seun3] *n.* message

口述 [hau2 seut9] *adj.* oral

口頭 [hau2 tau4] *adj.* spoken; *adv.* orally

口套 [hau2 tou3] *n.* muzzle

口音 [hau2 yam1] *n.* accent

吼住 [hau3 jyu6] *v.* stare

喉嚨 [hau4 lung4] *n.* throat

喉嚨發炎 [hau4 lung4 faat8 yim4] *n.* laryngitis

厚 [hau5] *adj.* thick

厚度 [hau5 dou6] *n.* thickness

後備燈 [hau6 bei6 dang1] *n.* backup lights

後備零件 [hau6 bei6 ling4 gin6] *n.* spare part

後備胎 [hau6 bei6 toi1] *n.* spare tire

候補票 [hau6 bou2 piu3] *n.* standby ticket

候診室 [hau6 chan2 sat7] *n.* waiting room

後燈 [hau6 dang1] *n.* rear light

後代 [hau6 doi6] *n.* posterity

後悔 [hau6 fui3] *v.* regret; *n.* repentance; *adj.* rueful

後果 [hau6 gwo2] *n.* consequence

後者 [hau6 je2] *adj.* latter

後綴 [hau6 jeui3] *n.* suffix

後輪 [hau6 leun4] *n.* back wheel

後來 [hau6 loi4] *adj.* subsequent; *adv.* afterwards

後面 [hau6 min6] *n.* rear, backside

後門 [hau6 mun4] *n.* rear door, back door

後生 [hau6 saang1] *adj.* young

候選人 [hau6 syun2 yan4] *n.* candidate

後退 [hau6 teui3] *v.* recede

後院 [hau6 yun2] *n.* yard

希臘 [hei1 laap9] *n.* Greece; *adj.* Greek

希望 [hei1 mong6] *adj.* hopefully; *v.* wish

稀釋咗 [hei1 sik7 jo2] *adj.* diluted

起 [hei2] *v.* build

起波紋 [hei2 bo1 man4] *adj.* rippled

喜鵲 [hei2 cheuk8] *n.* magpie

起好 [hei2 hou2] *adj.* built

起帳篷 [hei2 jeung3 pung4] *v.* pitch a tent

喜劇 [hei2 kek9] *n.* comedy

起源 [hei2 yun4] *n.* origin

氣壓計 [hei3 aat8 gai3] *n.* barometer

氣泵 [hei3 bam1] *n.* air pump

汽車 [hei3 che1] *n.* car (by ~ 開車, ~ deck 汽車甲板, ~ garage 車房, ~ park 停車場, ~ rental 租車)

汽車車體修理廠 [hei3 che1 che1 tai2 sau2 lei5 chong2] *n.* body shop

汽車代理 [hei3 che1 doi6 lei5] *n.* car dealer

汽車甲板 [hei3 che1 gaap8 baan2] *n.* car deck

汽車旅館 [hei3 che1 leui5 gun2] *n.* motel

器材 [hei3 choi4] *n.* equipment

氣墊 [hei3 din2] *n.* air mattress

氣氛 [hei3 fan1] *n.* atmosphere

戲服 [hei3 fuk9] *n.* costume

器官 [hei3 gun1] *n.* organ (*anat.*)

氣候 [hei3 hau6] *n.* climate

汽酒 [hei3 jau2] *n.* sparkling wine

氣象學 [hei3 jeung6 hok9] *n.* meteorology

氣象學家 [hei3 jeung6 hok9 ga1] *n.* meteorologist

氣球 [hei3 kau4] *n.* balloon

戲劇 [hei3 kek9] *n.* drama (~ class 戲劇課, ~ teacher 戲劇老師)

棄權證書 [hei3 kyun4 jing3 syu1] *n.* waiver

氣瓶 [hei3 ping4] *n.* gas cylinder

汽水 [hei3 seui2] *n.* soft drink, soda (flavored ~ 有味汽水, ~ water 蘇打水)

汽油 [hei3 yau4] *n.* gas (gasoline/ methane)

戲院 [hei3 yun2] *n.* theater

吃驚 [hek8 ging1] *v.* amaze; *adj.* amazed

輕輕 [heng1 heng1] *adv.* softly

輕拍 [heng1 paak8] *v.* tap

靴 [heu1] *n.* boot

虛張聲勢 [heui1 jeung1 sing1 sai3] *v.* bluff

虛構 [heui1 kau3] *n.* figment; *adj.* fictional

虛無主義 [heui1 mou4 jyu2 yi6] *n.* nihilism

許可 [heui2 ho2] *v.* permit

許可證 [heui2 ho2 jing3] *n.* warrant

去 [heui3] *v.* get to; *prep.* to

去除 [heui3 cheui4] *n.* removal

去咗殼 [heui3 jo2 hok8] *v.* husked (~ corn 去咗殼粟米)

去鱗 [heui3 leun4] *v.* de-scale a fish

去攞 [heui3 lo2] *v.* get, go get

去核 [heui3 wat9] *adj.* pitted (~ cherries 去核車厘子, ~ prunes 去核西梅, ~ olives 去核橄欖, ~ dates 去核海棗)

向 [heung3] *prep.* toward(s)

香檳 [heung1 ban1] *n.* champagne

香腸 [heung1 cheung2] *n.* sausage

香草 [heung1 chou2] *n.* vanilla (~ pod 香草豆莢, ~ bean 香草豆, ~ extract 香草濃縮, ~ essence 香草精華, ~ milk 香草味牛奶)

鄉村 [heung1 chyun1] *n.* countryside

鄉村旅館 [heung1 chyun1 leui5 gun2] *n.* country inn

鄉村音樂 [heung1 chyun1 yam1 ngok9] *n.* country music

香菇 [heung1 gu1] *n.* shiitake mushroom

鄉下 [heung1 ha5] *adj.* rustic

鄉下佬 [heung1 ha5 lou2] *n.* rustic

香口膠 [heung1 hau2 gaau1] *n.* gum, chewing gum

香蕉 [heung1 jiu1] *n.* banana (~ leaves 蕉葉)

香料 [heung1 liu6] *n.* spice (~ blend 混合香料)

香味 [heung1 mei6] *n.* aroma (~tic 有香味)

香水 [heung1 seui2] *n.* perfume

香芋 [heung1 wu6] *n.* taro

香油 [heung1 yau4] *n.* balm

香櫞 [heung1 yun4] *n.* citron

響緊 [heung2 gan2] *v.* ring; *n.* ringing

響喇叭 [heung2 la1 ba1] *v.* honk

享受 [heung2 sau6] *v.* enjoy (~ oneself 開心)

響...入面 [heung2 ... yap9 min6] *prep.* among, amongst

向前 [heung3 chin4] *adj.* forward (move ~ 前進)

向下 [heung3 ha6] *adj.* downward

向後退 [heung3 hau6 teui3] *v.* reverse (please ~ the charges 請撤回控訴, drive in ~ 倒車)

向中心 [heung3 jung1 sam1] *adv.* inwards

向量 [heung3 leung6] *n.* vector

向上 [heung3 seung6] *adj.* upward; *adv.* upwards

向日葵 [heung3 yat9 kwai4] *n.* sunflower

謙虛 [him1 heui1] *adj.* humble; *n.* humility

欠 [him3] *v.* owe (how much do I ~? 我爭幾多錢?)

牽制 [hin1 jai3] *v.* to keep at bay

牽連 [hin1 lin4] *v.* incriminate

蜆 [hin2] *n.* clam (~ bisque 蜆肉濃湯, ~ chowder 蜆肉雜燴)

遣返 [hin2 faan2] *v.* repatriate; *n.* repatriation

譴責 [hin2 jaak8] *v.* reprimand

顯著 [hin2 jyu3] *adj.* notable; *adv.* significantly

顯露 [hin2 lou6] *v.* emerge

顯示 [hin2 si6] *v.* display

顯示屏 [hin2 si6 ping4] *n.* monitor (computer ~ 電腦顯示屏)

顯然 [hin2 yin4] *adj.* apparent; *adv.* apparently

獻俾 [hin3 bei2] *v.* dedicate

憲法 [hin3 faat8] *n.* constitution, constitutional law; *adj.* constitutional

氫 [hing1] *n.* hydrogen

輕 [hing1] *adj.* light (*color / weight*); *v.* light (a cigarette/fire)

輕便 [hing1 bin4] *adj.* compact

輕便嬰兒床 [hing1 bin6 ying1 yi chong4] *n.* portable crib

兄弟姊妹 [hing1 dai6 ji2 mui6] *n.* siblings

氫化 [hing1 fa3] *v.* hydrogenize

興奮 [hing1 fan5] *adj.* excited; *n.* excitement

興高采烈 [hing1 gou1 choi2 lit9]
adj. cheerful; *adv.* cheerfully
輕拍 [hing1 paak8] *n.* pat
輕罪 [hing1 jeui6] *n.* misdemeanor
輕易 [hing1 yi6] *adv.* lightly
興趣 [hing3 cheui3] *n.* interest
興致 [hing3 ji3] *n.* spirits
慶祝 [hing3 juk7] *v.* celebrate; *n.*
celebration
協奏曲 [hip8 jau3 kuk7] *n.*
concerto
協調 [hip8 tiu4] *v.* coordinate
協會 [hip8 wui5] *n.* institute
協議 [hip8 yi5] *n.* settlement
歇斯底里 [hit8 si1 dai2 lei5] *n.*
hysteria; *adj.* hysterical
可持續 [ho2 chi4 juk9] *adj.*
sustainable
可行 [ho2 hang4] *adj.* feasible
可可 [ho2 ho2] *n.* cocoa (~
powder 可可粉, ~ milk 可可
奶, ~ cream 可可忌廉)
可可牛油 [ho2 ho2 ngau4 yau4]
n. cocoa butter
可卡因 [ho2 ka1 yan1] *n.* cocaine
可靠 [ho2 kaau3] *adj.* reliable
可憐 [ho2 lin4] *adj.* pathetic
可樂 [ho2 lok9] *n.* coke
可能 [ho2 nang4] *adj.* likely; *v.*
modal might; *adv.* possibly
可能性 [ho2 nang4 sing3] *n.*
odds, possibility
可能性唔大 [ho2 nang4 sing3
m4 daai6] *adj.* unlikely
可惜 [ho2 sik7] *adv.* unfortunately
可數 [ho2 sou2] *adj.* countable
可回收 [ho2 wui4 sau1] *adj.*
recyclable

可撤消 [ho2 chit8 siu1] *adj.*
revocable
可以 [ho2 yi5] *v.* could (*vs.* can);
modal may; *adj.* available
可以下載 [ho2 yi5 ha6 joi3] *adj.*
tech. downloadable (~ content
可下載內容)
可以整番好 [ho2 yi5 jing2 faan1
hou2] *n.* reparable
可以種野 [ho2 yi5 jung3 ye5]
adj. arable
可以攞到 [ho2 yi5 lo2 dou2]
adj. obtainable
可以手洗 [ho2 yi5 sau2 sai2]
adj. hand washable
可以生物分解 [ho2 yi5
sang1 mat9 fan1 gaai2] *adj.*
biodegradable
河 [ho4] *n.* river (~ cruise 游船河)
河邊 [ho4 bin1] *n.* riverbank
荷蘭 [ho4 laan1] *adj* Dutch; *n.*
Netherlands, The (*aka* Holland)
河內 [ho4 noi6] *n.* Hanoi (~,
capital of Vietnam 越南嘅首都)
河船 [ho4 syun4] *n.* riverboat
河豚 [ho4 tyun4] *n.* blowfish
開 [hoi1] *v.* activate, steer, unlock;
adj. open
開波 [hoi1 bo1] *n.* kick-off
開槍 [hoi1 cheung1] *v.* shoot
開場白 [hoi1 cheung4 baak9] *n.*
preamble
開始 [hoi1 chi2] *n.* outset; *v.* start
(~ a car 開車)
開始 [hoi1 chi2] *adv.* at first
開處方 [hoi1 chyu3 fong1] *v.*
prescribe
開發 [hoi1 faat8] *v.* develop

開荒 [hoi1 fong1] *v.* reclaim; *n.* reclamation

開公司 [hoi1 gung1 si1] *n.* start-up company

開關 [hoi1 gwaan1] *n.* switch

開羅 [hoi1 lo4] *n.* Cairo (~, capital of Egypt 埃及嘅首都)

開幕 [hoi1 mok9] *n.* opening

開普敦 [hoi1 pou2 deun1] *n.* Cape Town (~, legislative capital of South Africa)

開塞鑽 [hoi1 sak7 jyun3] *n.* corkscrew

開心 [hoi1 sam1] *v.* rejoice, enjoy oneself; *n.* happiness; *adj.* happy; *adv.* happily

開心見誠 [hoi1 sam1 gin3 sing4] *adv.* openly

開心果 [hoi1 sam1 gwo2] *n.* pistachios

開頭 [hoi1 tau4] *n.* beginning

開庭 [hoi1 ting4] *n.* session

開胃 [hoi1 wai6] *adj.* piquant

開胃菜 [hoi1 wai6 choi3] *n.* appetizer

開胃酒 [hoi1 wai6 jau2] *n.* aperitif

開胃水 [hoi1 wai6 seui2] *n.* tonic water

開會 [hoi1 wui2] *n.* meeting

開玩笑 [hoi1 wun6 siu3] *n.* prank

海 [hoi2] *n.* sea

海拔高度 [hoi2 bat9 gou1 dou6] *n.* height above sea level

海邊 [hoi2 bin1] *n.* seashore

海報 [hoi2 bou3] *n.* poster

海膽 [hoi2 daam2] *n.* sea urchin

海地 [hoi2 dei6] *n.* Haiti; *adj.* Haitian

海鯛 [hoi2 diu1] *n.* bream (~ fish 海鯛魚)

海盜 [hoi2 dou6] *n.* pirate

海甘藍 [hoi2 gam1 laam4] *n.* sea kale

海關 [hoi2 gwaan1] *n.* customs

海關官員 [hoi2 gwaan1 gun1 yun4] *n.* customs official

海關申報表 [hoi2 gwaan1 san1 bou3 biu2] *n.* customs declaration/forms

海龜 [hoi2 gwai1] *n.* turtle (~ soup 海龜湯)

海軍 [hoi2 gwan1] *n.* navy; *adj.* marine

海峽 [hoi2 haap9] *n.* channel

海螺 [hoi2 lo4] *n.* sea snails

海洛英 [hoi2 lok8 ying1] *n.* heroin

海鱸 [hoi2 lou4] *n.* sea bass

海鱸魚 [hoi2 lou4 yu4] *n.* sea perch

海綿 [hoi2 min4] *n.* sponge

海綿蛋糕 [hoi2 min4 daan6 gou1] *n.* sponge cake

海牙 [hoi2 nga4] *n.* The Hague (~, seat of government of Netherlands)

海岸 [hoi2 ngon6] *n.* coast

海平面 [hoi2 ping4 min6] *n.* sea level

凱撒沙律 [hoi2 saat3 sa1 leut2] *n.* caesar salad

海水 [hoi2 seui2] *n.* seawater

海鮮 [hoi2 sin1] *n.* seafood

海扇殼 [hoi2 sin3 hok8] *n.* cockles

海鱔 [hoi2 sin5] *n.* moray eel

海星 [hoi2 sing1] *n.* starfish

海王星 [hoi2 wong4 sing1] *n.* Neptune

害蟲 [hoi6 chung4] *n.* pest

害人 [hoi6 yan4] *adj.* pernicious

殼 [hok8] *n.* husk (corn~ 粟米殼); shell (oyster ~ 龍蝦殼, clam ~ 蜆殼)

學 [hok9] *v.* learn

學校 [hok9 haau6] *n.* school

學者 [hok9 je2] *n.* scholar

學生 [hok9 saang1] *n.* student (~ card 學生證, ~ discount 學生折扣)

學術 [hok9 seut9] *adj.* academic

學士 [hok9 si6] *n.* bachelor (~ party 寡佬派對)

學位 [hok9 wai2] *n.* degree

學院 [hok9 yun6] *n.* college

看更 [hon1 gaang1] *n.* guard, night porter

罕見 [hon2 gin3] *adj.* unique, rare

罕有 [hon2 yau5] *adv.* rarely

漢堡包 [hon3 bou2 baau1] *n.* burger (veggie ~ 素漢堡包, ostrich ~ 鴕鳥肉漢堡包, cheese~ 芝士漢堡包)

韓國 [hon4 gwok8] *adj.* Korean

汗 [hon6] *n.* sweat

糠 [hong1] *n.* bran

康復 [hong1 fuk9] *v.* recover; *n.* recovery (health)

行 [hong4] *n.* row (spreadsheet ~ 數據表橫行)

航班 [hong4 baan1] *n.* flight (~ attendant 空姐, ~ of stairs 樓梯級)

航班編號 [hong4 baan1 pin1 hou6] *n.* flight number

航海 [hong4 hoi2] *n.* navigation

航空 [hong4 hung1] *n.* aviation

航空公司 [hong4 hung1 gung1 si1] *n.* airline

航空郵件 [hong4 hung1 yau4 gin6] *n.* airmail (by ~ 空郵)

巷仔 [hong6 jai2] *n.* alley

項目 [hong6 muk9] *n.* item

喝彩 [hot8 choi2] *v.* cheer

渴望 [hot8 mong6] *n.* desire

好 [hou2] *adj.* good; *adv.* very (~ good 十分之好, ~ much 非常)

好啊 [hou2 a1] *adv.* why not?

好呀 [hou2 a3] *exclam.* OK!; *adv.* okay

好斜 [hou2 che4] *adv.* steeply

好似 [hou2 chi5] *prep.* like; *v.* seem

好彩 [hou2 choi2] *adv.* fortunately

好彩 [hou2 choi2] *adj.* lucky

好處 [hou2 chyu3] *n.* benefit

好大風 [hou2 daai6 fung1] *adj.* windy

好大聲 [hou2 daai6 seng1] *adv.* loudly

好大浸味 [hou2 daai6 jam3 mei6] *adj.* tangy

好抵 [hou2 dai2] *n.* a good value

好啲 [hou2 di1] *adj.* better, best

好多 [hou2 do1] *pron.* lots (of); a lot (of); *det.* much; *adj.* numerous

好多 [hou2 do1] *det.* many

好快 [hou2 faai3] *adv.* shortly; *phr.* just a minute

好幾個 [hou2 gei2 go3] *det.* several

好記性 [hou2 gei3 sing3] *adj.* retentive

好劾 [hou2 gui6] *adj.* exhausted

好開胃 [hou2 hoi1 wai6] *adj.* appetizing

好好食 [hou2 hou2 sik9] *adj.* palatable

好辣 [hou2 laat9] *n.* pungency; *adj.* pungent, hot, spicy

好靚 [hou2 leng3] *adj.* attractive; *adv.* nicely

好亂 [hou2 lyun6] *adj.* confused, confusing

好味 [hou2 mei6] *adj.* delicious, tasty

好難理解 [hou2 naan4 lei5 gaai2] *adj.* incomprehensible

好炳 [hou2 naat8] *adj.* scalding

好嬲咁 [hou2 nau1 gam3] *adv.* angrily

好犀利 [hou2 sai1 lei6] *adj.* amazing

好心 [hou2 sam1] *n.* kindness; *adj.* benevolent *adv.* kindly

好食 [hou2 sik9] *adj.* savory

好少 [hou2 siu2] *det.* few

好討厭 [hou2 tou2 yim3] *adj.* annoying

好玩 [hou2 waan2] *adj.* entertaining

好運 [hou2 wan6] *n.* luck

好運！ [hou2 wan6] *phr., exclam.* Good luck!

好人 [hou2 yan4] *adj.* benign

好有想像力 [hou2 yau5 seung2 jeung6 lik9] *adj.* imaginative

好嘢 [hou2 ye5] *exclam.* hooray!, yeah!

好遠 [hou2 yun5] *adj.* distant

好客 [hou3 haak8] *n.* hospitality

耗盡 [hou3 jeun6] *v.* exhaust

好奇 [hou3 kei4] *adj.* curious; *adv.* curiously

蠔 [hou4] *n.* oyster (~ soup 生蠔湯, ~ shell 蠔殼)

毫克 [hou4 hak7] *n.* milligram (*abbr.* mg.)

毫米 [hou4 mai5] *n.* millimeter (*abbr.* mm.)

毫無疑問 [hou4 mou4 yi4 man6] *adv.* undoubtedly

豪華 [hou4 wa4] *n.* opulence; *adj.* lush

豪華房車 [hou4 wa4 fong2 che1] *n.* limousine

後台 [hou6 toi4] *n.* background

胸 [hung1] *n.* brisket (*meat*)

空 [hung1] *adj.* vacant

空白 [hung1 baak9] *adj.* blank

空白鍵 [hung1 baak9 gin6] *n. comp.* spacebar

胸部 [hung1 bou6] *n.* bosom

兇殘 [hung1 chaan4] *adj.* murderous

空出 [hung1 cheut7] *v.* vacate

空地 [hung1 dei6] *n.* open air

空間 [hung1 gaan1] *n.* space, outer space

空嘅 [hung1 ge3] *adj.* empty

空氣 [hung1 hei3] *n.* air (~ conditioning 空調, ~ filter 空氣濾清器, ~ mattress 氣墊, ~ pump 氣泵, ~ sickness 暈機)

空氣濾清器 [hung1 hei3 leui6 ching1 hei3] *n.* air filter

空姐 [hung1 je2] *n.* flight attendant

空中 [hung1 jung3] *adj.* aerial

空缺 [hung1 kyut8] *n.* vacancy (no ~ 唔請人)

匈牙利 [hung1 nga4 lei6] *n.*
Hungary; *adj.* Hungarian

空心 [hung1 sam1] *adj.* hollow

空調 [hung1 tiu4] *n.* air conditioning

胸圍 [hung1 wai4] *n.* bra

恐怖 [hung2 bou3] *n.* horror

恐怖分子 [hung2 bou3 fan6 ji2]
n. terrorist

恐怖片 [hung2 bou3 pin2] *n.*
horror film

恐懼 [hung2 geui6] *n.* fear

孔雀 [hung2 jeuk8] *n.* peacock

控告 [hung3 gou3] *v.* indict; *n.*
indictment

控制 [hung3 jai3] *n.* control

控制住 [hung3 jai3 jyu6] *adj.*
controlled (~ substance 管制藥)

烘爐 [hung3 lou4] *n.* toaster oven

烘培粉 [hung3 pui4 fan2] *n.*
baking mix

紅寶石 [hung4 bou2 sek9] *n.*
ruby

紅橙 [hung4 chaang4] *n.* blood
orange

紅醋粟 [hung4 chou3 suk7] *n.*
black currant

洪都拉斯 [hung4 dou1 laai1 si1]
n. Honduras; *adj.* Honduran

紅花油 [hung4 fa1 yau4] *n.*
safflower oil

紅酒 [hung4 jau2] *n.* wine (~
cellar 酒窖, ~ list 酒單, dry
champagne ~ 乾性香檳酒,
rose ~ 淡紅葡萄酒, merlot ~
梅洛葡萄酒, sparkling ~ 汽
酒, vintage ~ 佳釀, sweet ~ 甜
酒, medium dry ~ 半乾葡萄
酒, medium sweet ~ 半甜葡

萄酒, frothy ~ 汽酒, table ~
餐酒)

紅椒 [hung4 jiu1] *n.* cayenne
pepper, red pepper

紅辣椒 [hung4 laat9 jiu1] *n.* chili
(~ pepper 紅辣椒, ~ powder 紅
辣椒粉, ~ sauce 紅辣椒醬, ~
soup 紅辣椒湯)

紅利 [hung4 lei6] *n.* dividend

紅蘿蔔 [hung4 lo4 baak9] *n.*
carrot (~ cake 紅蘿蔔蛋糕)

紅莓 [hung4 mui2] *n.* cranberry
(~ juice 紅莓汁, ~ sauce 紅
莓醬)

洪水 [hung4 seui2] *n.* flood

紅色 [hung4 sik7] *adj.* red

紅燒 [hung4 siu1] *n.* teriyaki (~
sauce 紅燒醬, ~ paste 紅燒醬,
~ chicken 紅燒雞肉)

紅桑子 [hung4 song1 ji2] *n.*
bilberry, raspberry

圈套 [hyun1 tou3] *n.* trap

勸 [hyun3] *v.* advise

勸說 [hyun3 syut8] *n.* persuasion

血 [hyut8] *n.* blood (donate ~
捐血)

血壓 [hyut8 aat8] *n.* blood pressure

血清 [hyut8 ching1] *n.* serum

血塊 [hyut8 faai3] *n.* blood clot

血漿 [hyut8 jeung1] *n.* plasma

血拴塞 [hyut8 saan1 sak7] *n.*
thrombosis

血統 [hyut8 tung2] *n.* lineage

血液循環 [hyut8 yik9 cheun4
waan4] *n.* circulation

血型 [hyut8 ying4] *n.* blood type

I

X光 [ik7 si4 gwong1] *n.* X-ray (~
  examination X光檢查)

J

揸 [ja1] *v.* squeeze

揸車 [ja1] *n.* driving

炸彈 [ja3 daan2] *n.* bomb (~ threat 炸彈威脅)

乍得 [ja3 dak7] *n.* Chad; *adj.* Chadian

詐騙 [ja3 pin3] *n.* fraud

炸魷魚圈 [ja3 yau4 yu4 hyun1] *n.* fried calamari

炸藥 [ja3 yeuk9] *n.* dynamite

炸肉排 [ja3 yuk9 paai4] *n.* schnitzel

炸肉丸 [ja3 yuk9 yun4] *n.* croquettes

債 [jaai3] *n.* debt

債券 [jaai3 gyun3] *n.* bond

債主 [jaai3 jyu2] *n.* creditor

窄 [jaak8] *adj.* narrow

窄路 [jaak8 lou6] *n.* narrow road

責任 [jaak8 yam6] *n.* responsibility (take ~ 負責任)

摘 [jaak9] *v.* pluck, pick

斬 [jaam2] *v.* chop

斬好 [jaam2 hau2] *adj.* chopped

暫住 [jaam6 jyu6] *n.* sojourn

暫時 [jaam6 si4] *adv.* temporarily

暫時 [jaam6 si4] *adj.* temporary (~ exhibit 臨時展覽, ~ worker 臨時工, ~ situation 暫時嘅情況)

暫時性 [jaam6 si4 sing3] *n.* provisionality

暫時停車 [jaam6 si4 ting4 che1] *n.* short-term parking

贊比亞 [jaan3 bei2 a3] *n.* Zambia

贊助 [jaan3 jo6] *n.* patronage; *v.* patronize

贊助商 [jaan3 jo6 seung1] *n.* sponsor

贊助人 [jaan3 jo6 yan4] *n.* patron

賺 [jaan6] *v.* earn

賺大錢 [jaan6 daai6 chin4] *adj.* lucrative

眨眼 [jaap8 ngaan5] *v.* blink

集幣 [jaap9 bai6] *n.* coin collection

雜草藥 [jaap9 chou2 yeuk9] *n.* mixed herbs

雜貨 [jaap9 fo3] *n.* groceries

雜貨店 [jaap9 fo3 dim3] *n.* grocery store

雜貨鋪 [jaap9 fo3 pou3] *n.* general store

襲擊 [jaap9 gik7] *v.* assault

習慣 [jaap9 gwaan3] *n.* habit

雜果賓治 [jaap9 gwo2 ban1 ji6] *n.* fruit punch

雜果仁 [jaap9 gwo2 yan4] *n.* mixed nuts

集合 [jaap9 hap9] *n.* rally

雜誌 [jaap9 ji3] *n.* magazine

集中 [jaap9 jung1] *v.* focus

雜種 [jaap9 jung2] *n.* hybrid

雜米 [jaap9 mai5] *n.* mixed rice

雜沙律 [jaap9 sa1 leut9] *n.* mixed salad

雜食動物 [jaap9 sik9 dung6 mat9] *n.* omnivore

集體登山 / 遊行 [jaap9 tai2 dang1 saan1/yau4 hang4] *n.* organized hike/walk

嘲笑 [jaau1 siu3] *v.* ridicule

爪 [jaau2] *n.* paw

罩 [jaau3] *n.* casing

劑量 [jai1 leung4] *n.* dose (recommended ~ 建議用量)

仔 [jai2] *n.* son

仔女 [jai2 neui5] *n.* offspring

祭品 [jai3 ban2] *n.* oblation

制服 [jai3 fuk9] *n.* uniform

制止 [jai3 ji2] *v.* prevent

製造商 [jai3 jou6 seung1] *n.* maker

製陶工人 [jai3 tou4 gung1 yan4] *n.* potter

製圖學 [jai3 tou4 hok9] *n.* graphics (computer ~ 電腦製圖, ~ card 顯卡)

側鏡 [jak7 geng3] *n.* side mirror

側面 [jak7 min6] *n.* flank

針 [jam1] *n.* needle

針灸 [jam1 gau3] *n.* acupuncture

針眼 [jam1 ngaan5] *n.* eyelet

針筒 [jam1 tung2] *n.* syringe

枕頭 [jam2 tau4] *n.* pillow

枕頭袋 [jam2 tau4 doi2] *n.* pillowcase

浸 [jam3] *v.* dip

浸喺燒著嘅酒裡面嘅嘢 [jam3 hai6 siu1 joi6 ge3 jau2 leui5 min6 ge3 ye5] *n.* flambé

浸腍 [jam3 nam4] *v.* macerate

浸死 [jam3 sei2] *v.* drown (be drowning 沉緊)

真 [jan1] *adj.* true (that's not ~ 唔係真嘅, ~ or false 真定假, be ~ 真嘅)

真定假 [jan1 ding6 ga2] *adj.* true or false

真嘅 [jan1 ge3] *v.* be true

珍寶 [jan1 bou2] *n.* treasure

珍貴 [jan1 gwai3] *adj.* precious

真係 [jan1 hai6] *adv.* really

珍珠 [jan1 jyu1] *n.* pearl

珍珠雞 [jan1 jyu1 gai1] *n.* guinea fowl

真菌 [jan1 kwan2] *n.* fungus

真實性 [jan1 sat9 sing3] *n.* authenticity

真相 [jan1 seung3] *n.* truth

真誠 [jan1 sing4] *adj.* sincere

真係好 [jan1 hai6 hou2] *adj.* considerable (~ odds 可能性好大)

真係好 [jan1 hai6 hou2] *adv.* considerably

鎮 [jan3] *n.* town (~ hall 市政廳)

鎮壓 [jan3 aat8] *v.* quell; *n.* repression

鎮定 [jan3 ding6] *adj.* composed; *n.* composure

鎮定劑 [jan3 ding6 jai1] *n.* sedative

震驚 [jan3 ging1] *adj.* shocked

震級 [jan3 kap7] *n.* magnitude

陣雨 [jan6 yu5] *n.* rainshower

憎 [jang1] *v.* hate

增加 [jang1 ga1] *v.* increase

憎恨 [jang1 han6] *n.* hatred

增值稅 [jang1 jik9 seui3] *n.* VAT (value-added tax) (~ receipt 增值稅發票)

爭強好勝 [jang1 keung6 hou3 sing1] *adj.* competitive

爭論 [jang1 leun6] *v.* argue

僧鯊 [jang1 sa1] *n.* monkfish

贈品 [jang6 ban2] *n.* free gift

汁 [jap7] *n.* sauce

執法官 [jap7 faat8 gun1] *n.* marshal

執著 [jap7 jeuk9] *adj.* persistent; *n.* preoccupation

執照 [jap7 jiu3] *n.* license

質地 [jat7 dei2] *n.* texture

質地差 [jat7 dei2 cha1] *adj.* flimsy

質子 [jat7 ji2] *n.* proton

質量 [jat7 leung6] *n.* quality

質量好 [jat7 leung4 hou2] *adj.* high quality

質問 [jat7 man6] *v.* confront

侄仔 [jat9 jai2] *n.* nephew

侄女 [jat9 neui5] *n.* niece

窒息 [jat9 sik7] *n.* choke

州 [jau1] *n.* state

周不時 [jau1 bat1 si4] *adv.* often

州長 [jau1 jeung2] *n.* governor

週期性 [jau1 kei4 sing3] *adj.* recurrent

週期 [jau1 kei4] *n.* cycle; *adj.* periodic

周末 [jau1 mut9] *n.* weekend

周年紀念 [jau1 nin4 gei2 nim6] *n.* anniversary (happy ~ 週年快樂!, ~ present 週年紀念禮物)

周圍行吓 [jau1 wai4 haang4 ha5] *v.* wander

周圍 [jau1 wai4] *adv.* around; *adj.* environmental

酒 [jau2] *n.* alcohol

走 [jau2] *v.* go

酒吧 [jau2 ba1] *n.* bar (wine ~ 酒吧, ~ service 酒吧服務)

酒杯 [jau2 bui1] *n.* wineglass

走地 [jau2 dei6] *adj.* cage-free (~ chicken 走地雞, ~ eggs 走地雞蛋, ~ beef 走地牛)

酒店 [jau2 dim3] *n.* hotel

走火通道 [jau2 fo2 tung1 dou6] *n.* fire escape

酒鬼 [jau2 gwai2] *n.* reveller

酒浸車厘子 [jau2 jam3 che1 lei4 ji2] *n.* maraschino cherry

酒精中毒 [jau2 jing1 jung1 duk9] *adj.* alcoholic (~ beverage 酒精飲品)

走咗 [jau2 jo2] *adj.* gone, all gone; *adv.* away

酒庄 [jau2 jong1] *n.* winery

走甩 [jau2 lat7] *v.* escape

走囉 [jau2 lo1] *phr.* let's go

走佬 [jau2 lou2] *v.* abscond

酒米 [jau2 mai5] *n.* pimple

酒瓶 [jau2 ping4] *n.* carafe (water ~ 水瓶, wine ~ 酒瓶)

酒舖 [jau2 pou3] *n.* liquor store

就快 [jau6 faai3] *adv.* almost; *v.* shall

就快唔掂 [jau6 faai3 m4 dim1] *adv.* on the rocks

就快死 [jau6 faai3 sei2] *adj.* dying

就算 [jau6 syun3] *conj.* although; *prep.* despite; *adv.* nevertheless

就業中心 [jau6 yip9 jung1 sam1] *n.* job center

遮 [je1] *n.* umbrella

遮住 [je1 jyu6] *v.* cover; *adj.* covered

遮住嘅嘢 [je1 jyu6 ge3 ye5] *n.* covering

啫喱 [je3 lei2] *n.* jello (~ mix 啫喱粉, ~ powder 啫喱粉, ~ mold 啫喱模)

啫喱糖 [je1 lei2 tong2] *n.* jellybeans

借 [je3] *v.* lend (could you ~ me X? 你可唔可以借X俾我？)

借錢嘅人 [je3 chin2 ge3 yan4] *n.* debtor

蓆 [jek6] *n.* mat

追 [jeui1] *v.* chase

追擊炮 [jeui1 gik7 paau3] *n.* mortar

追蹤 [jeui1 jung1] *v.* trace

追求 [jeui1 kau4] *v.* pursue; *n.* pursuit

嘴唇 [jeui2 seun4] *n.* lip

最 [jeui3] *det.* most

最差 [jeui3 cha1] *adj.* worst

最初 [jeui3 cho1] *adj.* initial; *adv.* initially

最大化 [jeui3 daai6 fa3] *v.* maximize profit

最低收費 [jeui3 dai1 sau1 fai3] *n.* minimum charge

最多 [jeui3 do1] *adj.* maximum

最快 [jeui3 faai3] *adj.* quickest

最近 [jeui3 gan6] *adj.* latest

最近點啊 [jeui3 gan6 dim2 a1] *phr.* how are things?

最近點樣？ [jeui3 gan6 dim2 yeung6] *phr.* how is it going?

最後 [jeui3 hau6] *adj.* final; *prep.* in the end; *adv.* at last

最好 [jeui3 hou2] *adj.* best

醉咗 [jeui3 jo2] *adj.* drunk

最終 [jeui3 jung1] *adj.* ultimate

最鍾意 [jeui3 jung1 yi3] *adj.* favorite (*tech.* add to ~s 加入收藏夾)

最重要 [jeui3 jung6 yiu1] *adj.* foremost

最近 [jeui3 kan5] *adj.* nearest

最平 [jeui3 ping4] *adj.* cheapest

最上層 [jeui3 seung6 chang4] *n.* topside

最少 [jeui3 siu2] *adj.* minimum; *det.* least, at least

最小化 [jeui3 siu2 fa3] *v.* minimize (*comp.* ~ screen 屏幕最小化)

聚集 [jeui6 jaap9] *v.* muster

聚酯嘅 [jeui6 ji2 gei3] *adj.* polyester

敘利亞 [jeui6 lei6 a3] *n.* Syria; *adj.* Syrian

罪惡 [jeui6 ok8] *adj.* evil

敘事 [jeui6 si6] *adj.* narrative

序數 [jeui6 sou3] *n.* ordinal

聚會 [jeui6 wui6] *n.* party (social ~ 社交聚會, political ~ 政黨)

聚會地方 [jeui6 wui6 dei6 fong1] *n.* gathering place

罪孽 [jeui6 yit9] *n.* sin

著 [jeuk8] *v.* wear, put smth. on

著火開關 [jeuk8 fo2 hoi1 gwaan1] *n.* ignition key

雀仔 [jeuk8 jai2] *n.* bird

爵士 [jeuk8 si6] *n.* jazz

津巴布韋 [jeun1 ba1 bou3 wai5] *n.* Zimbabwe

榛子 [jeun1 ji2] *n.* hazelnut

樽裝 [jeun1 jong1] *adj.* bottled (~ water 樽裝水)

遵守 [jeun1 sau2] *v.* obey; *n.* observance

準 [jeun2] *adj.* accurate; *adv.* accurately

準備 [jeun2 bei6] *n.* preparation; *v.* prepare

準確 [jeun2 kok8] *adj.* exact (~

---

amount 準確用量, ~ change 準確找錢)

準備好 [jeun2 bei6 hou2] *adj.* ready

進步 [jeun3 bou6] *n.* improvement

進化 [jeun3 fa3] *n.* evolution; *v.* evolve; *adj.* evolutionary

進攻 [jeun3 gung1] *n.* offense

進貢 [jeun3 gung3] *n.* tribute

進行 [jeun3 hang4] *v.* proceed; *n.* proceeding

進行中 [jeun3 hang6 jung3] *adv.* in progress

進口 [jeun3 hau2] *n.* import

進展 [jeun3 jin2] *n.* progress

進入 [jeun3 yap9] *n.* entry (~ visa 入境簽證)

進一步 [jeun3 yat7 bou6] *adj.* further

盡快 [jeun6 faai3] *phr.* as soon as possible

章 [jeung1] *n.* chapter

樟腦草 [jeung1 nou5 chou2] *n.* catmint, catnip

漿糊 [jeung1 wu4] *n.* paste

掌握 [jeung2 ak7] *v.* possess

獎品 [jeung2 ban2] *n.* award

長大 [jeung2 daai6] *v.* grow up

獎金 [jeung2 gam1] *n.* prize

長者 [jeung2 je2] *n.* senior citizen

長者折扣 [jeung2 je2 jit8 kau3] *n.* senior discount

獎勵 [jeung2 lai6] *n.* reward

獎牌 [jeung2 paai4] *n.* medal

脹 [jeung3] *v.* swell

障礙 [jeung3 ngoi6] *n.* barrier

帳篷 [jeung3 pung4] *n.* tent (~ peg 帳篷樁, ~ pole 帳篷柱, pitch a ~ 起帳篷)

賬戶 [jeung3 wu6] *n.* account

橡膠 [jeung6 gaau1] *n.* rubber

象棋 [jeung6 kei2] *n.* chess

橡木 [jeung6 muk9] *n.* oak

象牙海岸 [jeung6 nga4 hoi2 ngon6] *adj.* Ivoirian

橡皮糖 [jeung6 pei4 tong2] *n.* gumdrop

知 [ji1] *v.* know (~ something/ someone 知道 / 知識, how to ~ 點知)

資產 [ji1 chaan2] *n.* asset

資產階級 [ji1 chaan2 gaai1 kap7] *adj.* bourgeois

支持 [ji1 chi4] *n.* support

支持者 [ji1 chi4 je2] *n.* supporter

之前 [ji1 chin4] *adj.* previous; *adv.* previously

資格 [ji1 gaak8] *n.* qualification

之後 [ji1 hau6] *prep.* after

支氣管炎 [ji1 hei3 gun2 yim4] *n.* bronchitis

蜘蛛 [ji1 jyu1] *n.* spider

蜘蛛網 [ji1 jyu1 mong5] *n.* web

資歷淺 [ji1 lik9 chin2] *adj.* junior

資料 [ji1 liu2] *n.* information

支路 [ji1 lou6] *n.* bypass, road

芝麻 [ji1 ma4] *n.* sesame seed (~ powder 芝麻粉, ~ bun 芝麻包)

芝麻菜 [ji1 ma4 choi3] *n.* arugula

芝麻油 [ji1 ma4 yau4] *n.* sesame oil

支票簿 [ji1 piu3 bou6] *n.* checkbook

支票抬頭 [ji1 piu3 toi4 tau4] *adj.* payable to

姿勢 [ji1 sai3] *v.* gesture; *n.* posture

芝士 [ji1 si2] *n.* cheese (goat ~ 羊奶芝士, cow ~ 牛奶芝士, blue ~ 藍紋芝士, muenster ~ 明斯特芝士, cheddar ~ 車打芝士, yellow ~ 黃色芝士, american ~ 美式芝士, monterey jack ~ 蒙特雷傑克芝士, swiss ~ 瑞士芝士, brie ~ 法國芝士)

芝士蛋糕 [ji1 si2 daan6 gou1] *n.* cheesecake

芝士火鍋 [ji1 si2 fo2 wo1] *n.* cheese fondue

芝士餃 [ji1 si2 gaau2] *n.* cheese dumpling

芝士醬 [ji1 si2 jeung3] *n.* cheese sauce

知識 [ji1 sik7] *n.* knowledge

姿態 [ji1 taai6] *n.* poise

孜然 [ji1 yin4] *n.* cumin (~ powder 孜然粉, ~ seeds 孜然籽)

資源 [ji1 yun4] *n.* resource

紙 [ji2] *n.* paper

紙板 [ji2 baan2] *n.* cardboard

只不過 [ji2 bat7 gwo3] *adj.* mere

紙杯蛋糕 [ji2 bui1 daan6 gou1] *n.* cupcake

紫菜 [ji2 choi3] *n.* seaweed (~ wrap 紫菜卷)

子彈 [ji2 daan2] *n.* bullet

指定 [ji2 ding6] *v.* dictate; *adv.* specifically

紙袋 [ji2 doi2] *n.* paper or plastic shopping bag

指導 [ji2 dou6] *n.* guidance

指揮 [ji2 fai1] *v.* command

指甲 [ji2 gaap8] *n.* nail

紙巾 [ji2 gan1] *n.* tissue

子句 [ji2 geui3] *n.* clause

紙盒 [ji2 hap9] *n.* carton (milk ~ 盒裝牛奶)

指向 [ji2 heung3] *v.* point to

指控 [ji2 hung3] *v.* accuse (~[d] of 指控...做了)

紫紅色 [ji2 hung4 sik7] *n.* amaranth

止血貼 [ji2 hyut8 tip8] *n.* band-aid

指責 [ji2 jaak8] *v.* rebuke; *n.* reproof

指令 [ji2 ling4] *n.* directive

姊妹 [ji2 mui6] *n.* sister

指南針 [ji2 naam4 jam1] *n.* compass (moral ~ 道德準則)

子午線 [ji2 ng5 sin3] *n.* meridian

仔細 [ji2 sai3] *adj.* careful; *adv.* carefully

仔細檢查 [ji2 sai3 gim2 cha4] *v.* examine

指示 [ji2 si6] *n.* instruction

指示燈 [ji2 si6 dang1] *n.* pilot light

紫色 [ji2 sik7] *adj.* purple

紫色苦白菜 [ji2 sik7 fu2 baak9 choi3] *n.* chicory

止痛藥 [ji2 tung3 yeuk9] *n.* painkiller

至高無上 [ji3 gou1 mou4 seung6] *adj.* supreme

至關重要 [ji3 gwaan1 jung6 yiu3] *adj.* vital

志向 [ji3 heung3] *n.* aim

智利 [ji3 lei6] *n.* Chile; *adj.* Chilean

智力 [ji3 lik9] *adj.* intellectual

致癌 [ji3 ngaam4] *adj.* cancerous

致癌物 [ji3 ngaam4 mat9] *n.* carcinogen

智商 [ji3 seung1] *n.* intelligence

至少 [ji3 siu2] *adv.* at least

智慧 [ji3 wai6] *n.* wisdom

致意 [ji3 yi3] *n.* salutation

字 [ji6] *n.* word

自備午飯 [ji6 bei6 ng5 faan6] *n.* packed lunch

自稱 [ji6 ching1] *v.* profess

痔瘡 [ji6 chong1] *n.* hemorrhoids

自從 [ji6 chung4] *prep.* since

字典 [ji6 din2] *n.* dictionary

自動 [ji6 dung6] *adj.* automatic

自動 [ji6 dung6] *adv.* automatically

自動駕駛 [ji6 dung6 ga3 sai2] *n.* automatic transmission

自動洗衣店 [ji6 dung6 sai2 yi1 dim3] *n.* launderette

自動提款機 [ji6 dung6 tai4 fun2 gei1] *n.* ATM (automated teller machine)

自負 [ji6 fu6] *n.* egotism; *adj.* pretentious

自己整嘅 [ji6 gei2 jing2 ge3] *adj.* homemade (~ meal 自己煮菜, ~ pie 自製批)

自己一個 [ji6 gei2 yat7 go3] *adj.* alone (leave me ~ 唔好理我)

自己郁手 [ji6 gei2 yuk7 sau2] *n.* do-it-yourself (*abbr.* DIY)

自己 [ji6 gei2] *adj.* own (on one's ~ 自己一個人)

自己 [ji6 gei2] *n.* self

自僱人士 [ji6 gu3 yan4 si6] *adj.* self-employed

自治區 [ji6 ji6 keui1] *n.* municipality

自助 [ji6 jo6] *n.* self-service

治療 [ji6 liu4] *n.* treatment (~ room 治療室, alternative ~ 替代治療)

治療方法 [ji6 liu4 fong1 faat8] *n.* remedy

飼料 [ji6 liu6] *n.* feed (chicken ~ 雞飼料, pig ~ 豬飼料)

自戀 [ji6 lyun2] *n.* narcissism

字面上 [ji6 min6 seung6] *adj.* literal

字幕 [ji6 mok6] *n.* subtitles (a film with ~ 一部有字幕嘅電影)

字母表 [ji6 mou5 biu2] *n.* alphabet

自我 [ji6 ngo5] *n.* ego

自我介紹 [ji6 ngo5 gaai3 siu6] *v.* introduce oneself

自信 [ji6 seun3] *n.* confidence; *adj.* confident; *adv.* confidently

自相矛盾 [ji6 seung1 maau4 teun5] *n.* paradox

自私 [ji6 si1] *adj.* selfish

字體 [ji6 tai2] *n.* font (large/small ~ 大 / 細字體)

自慰 [ji6 wai3] *v.* masturbate

自衛 [ji6 wai6] *n.* self-defense

自由 [ji6 yau4] *adj.* free

自由 [ji6 yau4] *n.* freedom

自由自在 [ji6 yau4 ji6 joi6] *n.* ease

自然 [ji6 yin4] *adj.* natural (~ flavors 自然風味, ~ ingredients 天然原料); *adv.* naturally

自然保護區 [ji6 yin4 bou2 wu6 keui1] *n.* nature reserve

自然科學 [ji6 yin4 fo1 hok9] *n.* natural sciences

寺院 [ji6 yun2] *n.* monastery

自願 [ji6 yun6] *adv.* voluntarily; *adj.* voluntary

即刻 [jik1 hak7] *adj.* instant (~ coffee 即沖咖啡, ~ rice 即食米飯, ~ meal 微波爐餐)

織 [jik7] *v.* knit

積極 [jik7 gik9] *adj.* active; *adv.* actively

即管 [jik7 gun2] *conj.* though

即係 [jik7 hai6] *abbr.* i.e.

即刻 [jik7 hak7] *adj.* prompt; *adv.* immediately, as soon as

跡象 [jik7 jeung6] *n.* indication

即決審判 [jik7 kyut8 sam2 pun3] *n.* summary judgment

職業 [jik7 yip9] *n.* occupation

職業介紹所 [jik7 yip9 gaai3 siu6 so2] *n.* employment office

脊骨 [jik8 gwat7] *n.* spinal column

值 [jik9] *adj.* worth (~ seeing 好值得一睇, What is this ~? 呢個值幾多錢？)

直 [jik9] *adv.* straight (~ ahead 直行)

直腸 [jik9 cheung4] *n.* rectum

直腸直肚 [jik9 cheung4 jik9 tou5] *adj.* outspoken

值錢 [jik9 chin2] *adj.* valuable (~ article 貴重物品)

直情 [jik9 ching4] *adv.* simply

直達 [jik9 daat9] *adv.* nonstop

值得 [jik9 dak7] *adj.* worthy

值得嘉獎 [jik9 dak7 ga1 jeung2] *adj.* laudable

值得讚 [jik9 dak7 jaan3] *adj.* praiseworthy

直到 [jik9 dou3] *conj.* until, till

直飛 [jik9 fei1] *n.* direct flight/train

直徑 [jik9 ging3] *n.* diameter

直覺 [jik9 gok8] *n.* instinct

直角 [jik9 gok8] *n.* square (*geometric*)

直行 [jik9 haang4] *adv.* straight ahead

藉口 [jik9 hau2] *n.* pretext

直接 [jik9 hip8] *adj.* direct; *adv.* directly

植物 [jik9 mat9] *n.* plant; *adj.* botanical

植物牛油 [jik9 mat9 ngau4 yau4] *n.* margarine

植物園 [jik9 mat9 yun4] *n.* botanical garden

直線 [jik9 sin3] *adj.* linear

直升機 [jik9 sing1 gei1] *n.* helicopter

尖叫 [jim1 giu3] *v.* scream

占星術 [jim1 sing1 seut9] *n.* astrology

尖塔 [jim1 taap8] *n.* pinnacle

尖銳 [jim1 yeui6] *adj.* pointed

佔據 [jim3 geui3] *v.* preoccupy

佔領 [jim3 ling5] *v.* occupy

佔優勢 [jim3 yau1 sai3] *v.* predominate

佔用 [jim3 yung6] *n.* occupancy

佔優勢嘅 [jim4 yau1 sai3 ge3] *adj.* dominant

氈 [jin1] *n.* blanket

展覽 [jin2 laam5] *v.* exhibit; *n.* exhibition

展覽箱 [jin2 laam5 seung1] *n.* display case

剪頭髮 [jin2 tau4 faat8] *n.* haircut (have a ~ 剪頭髮)

箭 [jin3] *n.* arrow (*comp.* mouse ~ 鼠標)

戰鬥 [jin3 dau3] *n.* battle (historic ~ 歷史上有名嘅戰鬥, ~ site 戰場)

戰爭 [jin3 jang1] *n.* war (~ memorial 戰爭紀念碑, ~ movies 戰爭片, World W~ II 二次大戰)

戰略 [jin3 leuk9] *n.* strategy

戰略上 [jin3 leuk9 seung6] *adv.* strategically

戰略性 [jin3 leuk9 sing3] *adj.* strategic

徵兵 [jing1 bing1] *v.* get drafted

精彩 [jing1 choi2] *adj.* wonderful

蒸粗麥粉 [jing1 chou1 mak9 fan2] *n.* couscous

蒸發 [jing1 faat8] *adj.* evaporated (~ milk 煉奶); *v.* vaporize

蒸氣 [jing1 hei3] *n.* steam

精緻 [jing1 ji3] *n.* delicacies; *adj.* delicate

正中 [jing1 jung1] *adj.* central

精確 [jing1 kok8] *adj.* precise

精確度 [jing1 kok8 dou6] *adj.* precision

蒸餾 [jing1 lau6] *v.* distill; *n.* distillation

蒸餾 [jing1 lau6] *adj.* distilled (~ water 蒸餾水, ~ vinegar 蒸醋)

精靈 [jing1 ling4] *n.* elf

精美 [jing1 mei5] *adv.* finely

精明 [jing1 ming4] *n.* sagacity; *adj.* sophisticated

精神 [jing1 san4] *n.* mind

精神 [jing1 san4] *adj.* mental

精神病學 [jing1 san4 beng6 hok9] *n.* psychiatry

精神病患者 [jing1 san4 beng6 waan6 je3] *n.* psychopath

精神病院 [jing1 san4 beng6 yun6] *n.* asylum

精神科醫生 [jing1 san4 fo1 yi1 sang1] *n.* psychiatrist

精神上 [jing1 san4 seung6] *adj.* spiritual; *adv.* mentally

精神混亂 [jing1 san4 wan6 lyun6] *adj.* delirious

偵探 [jing1 taam3] *n.* detective (~ novels 偵探小說), private investigator

精糖 [jing1 tong4] *n.* refined sugar

正統 [jing1 tung2] *adj.* orthodox

精華 [jing1 wa4] *n.* essence (almond ~ 杏仁精華素, tomato ~ 番茄精華素, vanilla ~ 香草精華素, citrus ~ 西柚精華素)

蒸熱 [jing1 yit9] *adj.* steamed (~ vegetables 蒸熱青菜)

徵用 [jing1 yung6] *n.* requisition

整 [jing2] *v.* repair (~ shop 修理鋪)

整白 [jing2 baak9] *v.* blanched

整巢 [jing2 chaau4] *v.* ruffle

整齊 [jing2 chai4] *n.* orderly

整凍 [jing2 dung3] *v.* chilled

整緊 [jing2 gan2] *adj.* under construction

整乾 [jing2 gon1] *v.* dried (~ sausage 乾腸, ~ fruit 乾果, ~ meat 肉乾)

整好 [jing2 hou2] *adj.* ready-made

整企里 [jing2 kei5 lei5] *v.* tidy up

整邋遢 [jing2 laat9 taat8] *v.* stain (*n.* a ~ 一個邋遢, ~ remover 除污劑, tea ~ 茶漬, food ~ 菜漬)

整亂 [jing2 lyun6] *v.* muddle

整模 [jing2 mou2] *v.* to mold

整濕 [jing2 sap7] *v.* saturate

整成粉狀 [jing2 seng4 fan2 jong6] *adj.* powdered

整成麥芽 [jing2 seng4 mak9 nga4] *adj.* malted (~ beer 麥芽啤酒, ~ liquor 麥芽酒)

整成碎 [jing2 seng4 seui3] *v.* crumble

整傷 [jing2 seung1] *v.* injure

整彎 [jing2 waan1] *v.* bend

整入 [jing2 yap9] *v.* embed

整瘀 [jing2 yu2] *v.* bruise

政策 [jing3 chaak8] *n.* policy

正餐 [jing3 chaan1] *n.* dinner (~ plate 大盤, ~ set 晚餐套餐)

政黨 [jing3 dong2] *n.* political party

政府 [jing3 fu2] *n.* government

證據 [jing3 geui3] *n.* evidence

證供 [jing3 gung1] *n.* testimony

政客 [jing3 haak8] *n.* politician

政治 [jing3 ji6] *n.* politics

政治上 [jing3 ji6 seung6] *adj.* political; *adv.* politically

正直 [jing3 jik9] *adj.* righteous

正正 [jing3 jing3] *adv.* precisely

症狀 [jing3 jong6] *n.* symptom (*of illness*)

政權 [jing3 kyun4] *n.* regime

正面 [jing3 min6] *adj.* positive

證明 [jing3 ming4] *v.* prove

證明有理 [jing3 ming4 yau5 lei5] *v.* justify

正門 [jing3 mun4] *n.* portal

證實 [jing3 sat9] *n.* affirmation; *v.* affirm, confirm

正常 [jing3 seung4] *adj.* normal

正常化 [jing3 seung4 fa3] *v.* normalize

正常來講 [jing3 seung4 loi4 gong2] *adv.* normally

正常皮膚 [jing3 seung4 pei4 fu1] *n.* normal skin

正式 [jing3 sik7] *adj.* formal; *adv.* officially

證書 [jing3 syu1] *n.* certificate (birth ~ 出生紙, ~ of deposit 存款單)

證人 [jing3 yan4] *n.* witness

淨重 [jing6 chung5] *n.* net weight

淨低嘅 [jing6 dai1 ge3] *adj.* remaining

淨低嘅嘢 [jing6 dai1 ge3 ye5] *n.* remainder

靜啲 [jing6 di1] *adj.* quieter

淨化 [jing6 fa3] *v.* purify; *n.* purification

淨係 [jing6 hai6] *adv.* just

静脈 [jing6 mak9] *n.* vein

接 [jip8] *v.* fetch

接待處 [jip8 doi6 chyu3] *n.* reception (~ desk 接待處)

接近 [jip8 gan6] *v.* approach; *n.* proximity; *prep.* close to

接管 [jip8 gun2] *n.* takeover (hostile ~ 惡意收購)

接骨木 [jip8 gwat7 muk9] *n.* elderberry

接種疫苗 [jip8 jung2 yik9 miu4] *n.* vaccination

接力 [jip8 lik9] *n.* relay

接埋 [jip8 maai4] *v.* pick smb. up

接生婆 [jip8 sang1 po4] *n.* midwife

接收器 [jip8 sau1 hei3] *n.* receiver, receptor

接受 [jip8 sau6] *v.* accept

接人 [jip8 yan4] *n.* pick-up

結冰 [jit8 bing1] *v.* freeze

折疊式小刀 [jit8 dip9 sik7 siu2 dou1] *n.* penknife

哲學 [jit8 hok9] *n.* philosophy

哲學家 [jit8 hok9 ga1] *n.* philosopher

節奏 [jit8 jau3] *n.* rhythm

折磨 [jit8 mo4] *v.* torture

節日 [jit8 yat9] *n.* festival

節日折扣 [jit8 yat9 jip8 kau3] *n.* holiday discount

節日安排 [jit8 yat9 on1 paai4] *n.* holiday schedule

捷克共和國 [jit9 hak7 gung6 wo4 gwok8] *n.* Czech Republic

捷克人 [jit9 hak7 yan4] *n.* Czech

截止日期 [jit9 ji2 yat9 kei4] *n.* deadline

截氣閥 [jit9 hei3 fat9] *n.* shutoff valve

睫毛膏 [jit9 mou4 gou1] *n.* mascara, cosmetics

招待 [jiu1 doi6] *v.* entertain

朝早 [jiu1 jou2] *adv.* a.m., this morning

招牌菜 [jiu1 paai4 choi3] *n.* house specialty

招牌酒 [jiu1 paai4 jau2] *n.* house wine

招聘 [jiu1 ping3] *v.* recruit; *n.* recruitment

招聘廣告 [jiu1 ping3 gwong2 gou3] *n.* want ad (*for job*)

焦糖 [jiu1 tong4] *n.* caramel (~ sauce 焦糖汁, ~ cream 焦糖忌廉, dark ~ 黑焦糖)

焦糖燉蛋 [jiu1 tong4 dun2 daan5] *n.* caramel custard

焦糖汁 [jiu1 tong4 jap7] *n.* caramel sauce

蕉葉 [jiu1 yip9] *n.* banana leaves

沼澤 [jiu2 jaak9] *n.* marsh

照顧 [jiu3 gu3] *n.* care; *v.* take care of, look after

照光 [jiu3 gwong1] *v.* illuminate

照明 [jiu3 ming4] *n.* illumination

嚼 [jiu6] *v.* chew

嚼得好大聲 [jiu6 dak7 hou2 daai6 seng1] *v.* crunch

召集 [jiu6 jaap9] *v.* summon

左邊 [jo2 bin1] *adj.* left (to the ~ 系左邊), on the left

阻止 [jo2 ji2] *v.* prohibit

阻撓 [jo2 naau4] *v.* obstruct

阻礙 [jo2 ngoi6] *v.* retard, block; *n.* obstacle

阻塞 [jo2 sak7] *n.* blockage

左右為難 [jo2 yau6 wai4 naan4] *n.* quandary

左翼 [jo2 yik9] *adj.* left-wing

左翼分子 [jo2 yik9 fan6 ji2] *n.* leftist

佐治敦 [jo3 ji6 deun1] *n.* Georgetown (~, capital of Guyana 圭亞那嘅首都)

助攻 [jo6 gung1] *v.* assist (*sports term*)

坐骨神經痛 [jo6 gwat7 san4 ging1 tung3] *n.* sciatica

助手 [jo6 sau2] *n.* assistant

助聽器 [jo6 ting1 hei3] *n.* hearing aid

座位編號 [jo6 wai2 pin1 hou6] *n.* seat number

座右銘 [jo6 yau6 ming5] *n.* maxim

災難 [joi1 naan6] *n.* disaster

再 [joi3] *prefix* re- (~use 再用)

再三保證 [joi3 saam1 bou2 jing3] *v.* reassure

再生 [joi3 sang1] *n.* regeneration

在場 [joi6 cheung4] *n.* presence

在生 [joi6 sang1] *adj.* alive

再用 [joi3 yung6] *v.* re-use

作 [jok8] *v.* make up; do over

作嘔 [jok8 au2] *n.* nausea

作詞人 [jok8 chi4 yan4] *n.* songwriter

作家 [jok8 ga1] *n.* novelist, writer

作者 [jok8 je2] *n.* author

作曲 [jok8 kuk7] *v.* compose; *n.* composition

作曲家 [jok8 kuk7 ga1] *n.* composer

作為 [jok8 wai4] *prep.* as (~ soon ~ 即刻, ~ well ~ 一樣)

作為回報 [jok8 wai4 wui4 bou3] *adv.* in return

作嘢 [jok8 ye5] make sth. up

裝 [jong1] *v.* case

裝貨 [jong1 fo3] *n.* load

裝滿 [jong1 mun5] *v.* fill

裝修 [jong1 sau1] *v.* decorate; *n.* decoration

裝飾 [jong1 sik7] *n.* garnish; *adj.* decorative

裝飾物 [jong1 sik7 mat9] *n.* ornament

葬禮 [jong3 lai5] *n.* funeral

撞 [jong6] *v.* hit

撞車 [jong6 che1] *n.* crash (~ helmet 頭盔, ~ test dummy 碰撞測試假人)

狀況 [jong6 fong3] *n.* condition

撞見 [jong6 gin3] *v.* encounter; *adj.* discovered

藏紅花 [jong6 hung4 fa1] *n.* saffron

撞爛 [jong6 laan6] *v.* smash

撞傷 [jong6 seung1] *n.* contusion

狀態 [jong6 taai3] *n.* mode

租 [jou1] *adj.* rental (~ car 租嘅車), rented; *v.* rent (for ~ 出租, ~ out 租出)

租車 [jou1 che1] *n.* car rental

租出 [jou1 cheut7] *v.* rent out

租金 [jou1 gam1] *n.* rent

租客 [jou1 haak8] *n.* tenant

租約 [jou1 yeuk8] *n.* lease

棗 [jou2] *n.* jujube

早 [jou2] *adj.* early (too ~ 太早)

組 [jou2] *n.* group

祖輩 [jou2 bui3] *n.* grandparent

早餐 [jou2 chaan1] *n.* breakfast (~ cereal 早餐麥片, ~ bar 早餐吧)

早產 [jou2 chaan2] *adj.* premature

早啲 [jou2 di1] *adj.* earlier

祖國 [jou2 gwok8] *n.* homeland

組織 [jou2 jik7] *v.* organize; *n.* organization

組織上 [jou2 jik7 seung6] *adj.* organizational

祖籍 [jou2 jik9] *n.* roots

早午餐 [jou2 ng5 chaan1] *n.* brunch

早晨 [jou2 san4] *n.* morning; *phr.* good morning

早上 [jou2 seung6] *adv.* morning, in the morning

祖先 [jou2 sin1] *n.* ancestor

組成公司 [jou2 sing4 gung1 si1] *v.* incorporate

做 [jou6] *aux. v.* do

造反 [jou6 faan2] *v.* rebel

做結論 [jou6 git8 leun6] *v.* conclude

做唔到決定嘅陪審團 [jou6 m4 dou3 kyut8 ding6 ge3 pui4 sam2 tyun4] hung jury

做唔好 [jou6 m4 hou2] *adj.* incompetent

做完[jou6 yun4] *v.* complete, finish

做完咗 [jou6 yun4 jo2] *adj.* complete (~ meal 一個大餐)

竹 [juk7] *n.* bamboo (~ shoots 竹筍)

捉 [juk7] *v.* capture

粥 [juk7] *n.* gruel (rice)

足夠 [juk7 gau3] *adj.* sufficient; *adv.* sufficiently

祝酒 [juk7 jau2] *v.* to make a toast (with a drink)

足迹 [juk7 jik7] *n.* trail

捉咗 [juk7 jo2] *adj.* arrested

足球 [juk7 kau4] *n.* soccer (~ game 足球比賽)

燭台 [juk7 toi4] *n.* candlestick

續隨子 [juk9 cheui4 ji2] *n.* capers

逐啲 [juk9 di1] *adj.* gradual; *adv.* gradually

續約 [juk9 yeuk8] *n.* renewal

俗語 [juk9 yu5] *n.* slang

鐘擺 [jung1 baai2] *n.* pendulum

鐘錶商 [jung1 biu1 seung1] *n.* watchmaker

中場休息 [jung1 cheung4 yau1 sik7] *n.* intermission

中等 [jung1 dang2] *adj.* medium

中等偏熟 [jung1 dang2 pin1 suk9] *adj.* medium well done (~ steak 中等偏熟牛扒)

終點站 [jung1 dim2 jaam6] *n.* terminal

終端機 [jung1 dyun1 gei1] *n.* computer terminal

中東 [jung1 dung1] *adj.* Middle Eastern (~ food 中東菜)

中非共和國 [jung1 fei1 gung6 wo4 gwok8] *n.* Central African Republic

縱火 [jung1 fo2] *n.* arson

中間 [jung1 gaan1] *adj.* middle, intermediate

宗教 [jung1 gaau3] *n.* religion

宗教儀式 [jung1 gaau3 yi4 sik7] *n.* religious service

中筋麵粉 [jung1 gan1 min6 fan2] *n.* all-purpose flour

中國 [jung1 gwok8] *n.* China; *adj.* Chinese

中國菜 [jung1 gwok8 choi3] *n.* Chinese food

鐘 [jung1] *n.* clock, bell

中止 [jung1 ji2] *v.* abort (*military / medical*)

中子 [jung1 ji2] *n.* neutron

中軸 [jung1 juk9] *n.* axis

中立 [jung1 laap9] *adj.* neutral

棕櫚主日 [jung1 leui2 jyu2 yat9] *n.* Palm Sunday

棕櫚心 [jung1 leui4 sam1] *n.* heart of palm

棕櫚油 [jung1 leui4 yau4] *n.* palm oil

中美洲 [jung1 mei5 jau1] *adj.* Central American (~ food 中美洲菜)

中世紀 [jung1 sai3 gei3] *adj.* medieval

中心 [jung1 sam1] *n.* center

忠心 [jung1 sam1] *n.* royalty

忠臣 [jung1 san4] *n.* loyal

忠誠 [jung1 sing4] *n.* allegiance; *adj.* devoted; *adv.* faithfully

中提琴 [jung1 tai4 kam4] *n.* viola

鐘頭 [jung1 tau4] *n.* hour

中和 [jung1 wo4] *v.* neutralize

中央處理器 [jung1 yeung1 chyu3 lei5 hei3] *n.* CPU (computer)

中央暖氣系統 [jung1 yeung1 nyun5 hei3 hai6 tung2] *n.* central heating

鍾意 [jung1 yi3] *v.* adore

終於 [jung1 yu1] *adv.* finally

總 [jung2] *adj.* gross

腫 [jung2] *n.* swelling

總經理 [jung2 ging1 lei5] *n.* executive

總結 [jung2 git8] *n.* summary

總共 [jung2 gung6] *adv.* altogether

種子 [jung2 ji2] *n.* seeds

腫咗 [jung2 jo2] *adj.* swollen

種族 [jung2 juk9] *n.* race (*sport / descent*); *adj.* racial

種族歧視 [jung2 juk9 kei4 si6] *n.* racism

總理 [jung2 lei5] *n.* prime minister

種類 [jung2 leui6] *n.* kind (what ~ of 乜嘢種類)

總數 [jung2 sou3] *n.* sum

總體嘅 [jung2 tai2 ge3] *adj.* general

總體來講 [jung2 tai2 loi4 gong2] *adj.* overall

總统 [jung2 tung2] *n.* president

種 [jung3] *v.* grow; *n.* planting

中風 [jung3 fung1] *n.* stroke

綜合 [jung3 hap9] *n.* synthesis

綜合保險 [jung3 hap9 bou2 him2] *n.* comprehensive insurance

綜合症 [jung3 hap9 jing3] *n.* syndrome

種植園 [jung3 jik9 yun4] *n.* plantation

中傷 [jung3 seung1] *v.* snipe

中暑 [jung3 syu2] *n.* sunstroke

縱容 [jung3 yung4] *v.* pamper

仲差 [jung6 cha1] *adj.* worse

仲長 [jung6 cheung4] *adj.* longer

仲裁 [jung6 choi4] *n.* arbitration

仲大聲 [jung6 daai6 seng1] *adv.* louder

重點 [jung6 dim2] *n.* emphasis

頌歌 [jung6 go1] *n.* ode

仲係 [jung6 hai6] *adv.* still (I'm ~ waiting 仲等緊架)

頌文 [jung6 man4] *n.* panegyric

仲未 [jung6 mei6] *adv.* yet (not ~ 未啊)

仲平 [jung6 ping4] *adj.* cheaper

仲生 [jung6 saang1] *adj.* living

仲有 [jung6 yau5] *adj.* furthermore; *adv.* moreover

重要 [jung6 yiu1] *adj.* important

重要嘅係 [jung6 yiu1 ge3 hai6] *adv.* importantly

重要性 [jung6 yiu1 sing3] *n.* importance

豬 [jyu1] *n.* pig (~ ears 豬耳, ~ feet 豬腳, ~ knuckles 豬肘)

珠寶 [jyu1 bou2] *n.* jewelry

珠寶商 [jyu1 bou2 seung1] *n.* jeweler

朱古力 [jyu1 gu1 lik7] *n.* chocolate (box of ~s 一箱朱古力, ~ ice cream 朱古力雪糕, ~ cake 朱古力蛋糕, ~ filling 朱古力餡, milk ~ 牛奶朱古力, dark ~ 黑朱古力, white ~ 白朱古力)

朱古力餅 [jyu1 gu2 lik7 beng2] *n.* brownie

朱古力粉 [jyu1 gu2 lik7 fan2] *n.* jimmies

朱古力漿 [jyu1 gu2 lik7 jeung2] *n.* chocolate syrup

朱古力條 [jyu1 gu2 lik7 tiu4] *n.* chocolate bar

豬柳肉 [jyu1 lau5 yuk9] *n.* pork loin

豬扒 [jyu1 pa2] *n.* pork chop

豬手 [jyu1 sau2] *n.* pork knuckle

豬頭 [jyu1 tau4] *n.* boar's head

豬頭肉凍 [jyu1 tau4 yuk9 dung3] *n.* head cheese

豬油 [jyu1 yau4] *n.* lard

豬肉 [jyu1 yuk9] *n.* pork (~ chops 豬扒, ~ fat 豬油, ~ stew 燉豬肉)

豬肉豆 [jyu1 yuk9 dau6] *n.* pork and beans (canned ~ 罐裝豬肉豆)

豬肉腸 [jyu1 yuk9 cheung4] *n.* pork sausage

煮 [jyu2] *v.* cook (~ed *v./adj.* 煮熟)

主菜 [jyu2 choi3] *n.* main course

煮得太熟 [jyu2 dak7 taai3 suk9] *adj.* overdone

主動 [jyu2 dung6] *n.* initiative

主教 [jyu2 gaau3] *n.* bishop

主公 [jyu2 gung1] *n.* lord

煮滾 [jyu2 gwan2] *adj.* boiled

主張 [jyu2 jeung1] *v.* urge

主席 [jyu2 jik9] *n.* chairman, chairwoman

主流 [jyu2 lau4] *n.* mainstream

主題 [jyu2 tai4] *n.* theme

主人 [jyu2 yan4] *n.* host

主人翁 [jyu2 yan4 yung1] *n.* protagonist

煮嘢 [jyu2 ye5] *n.* cooking (~ facilities 廚具, ~ instructions 烹飪方法)

主頁 [jyu2 yip9] *n., comp.* homepage (Internet ~ 互聯網主頁, set ~ to 設置主頁)

主要 [jyu2 yiu3] *adj.* primary; *adv.* mainly

主要道路[jyu2 yiu3 dou6 lou6] *n.* main road

注定 [jyu3 ding6] *v.* predetermine

蛀牙 [jyu3 nga4] *n.* cavity

住 [jyu6] *v.* reside

注射 [jyu3 se6] *v.* inject; *n.* injection

注射器針頭 [jyu3 se6 hei3 jam1 tau4] *n.* hypodermic needle

注射疫苗 [jyu3 se6 yik9 miu4] *v.* vaccinate (be ~d against 防疫)

注意 [jyu3 yi3] *n.* attention; *v.* pay attention to

住客 [jyu6 haak8] *n.* occupant

住宅 [jyu6 jaak9] *n.* housing

住宅區 [jyu6 jaak9 keui1] *n.* housing district

住宿 [jyu6 suk7] *n.* accommodation(s)

住宿加早餐 [jyu6 suk7 ga1 jou2 chaan1] *n.* bed and breakfast

專科 [jyun1 fo1] *adj.* specialized

專科學校 [jyun1 fo1 hok9 haau6] *n.* academy

專家 [jyun1 ga1] *n.* expert

尊敬 [jyun1 ging3] *v.* revere; *n.* reverence

專攻 [jyun1 gung1] *v.* specialize

尊重 [jyun1 jung6] *n.* respect

專利 [jyun1 lei6] *n.* patent; *adj.* proprietary

專心 [jyun1 sam1] *adj.* rapt; *n.* concentration

專心做 [jyun1 sam1 jou6] *n.* concentrate

磚頭 [jyun1 tau4] *n.* brick

專業 [jyun1 yip9] *adj.* professional

專業技能 [jyun1 yip9 gei6 nang4] *n.* expertise

鱒魚 [jyun1 yu2] *n.* trout

專用 [jyun1 yung6] *adj.* exclusive

轉 [jyun2] *v.* turn (~ down 拒絕, ~ left! 左轉, ~ on 開, ~ up the volume 大聲啲, Where do I ~? 我要喺邊度轉彎？)

傳記 [jyun2 gei3] *n.* biography

轉換器 [jyun2 wun6 hei3] *n.* adapter

轉讓 [jyun2 yeung6] *v.* transfer

轉型 [jyun2 ying4] *n.* transition

鑽石 [jyun3 sek9] *n.* diamond

絕對 [jyut9 deui3] *adj.* absolute; *adv.* absolutely

絕密 [jyut9 mat9] *adj.* confidential

K

卡路里 [ka1 lou6 lei5] *n.* calorie

卡斯特里 [ka1 si1 dak9 lei5] *n.* Castries (~, capital of Saint Lucia 聖盧西亞島嘅首都)

卡塔爾 [ka1 taap8 yi5] *n.* Qatar; *adj.* Qatari

靠 [kaau3] *prep.* by (~ means of 通過)

靠山 [kaau3 saan1] *n.* prop

啓動摩打 [kai2 dung6 mo1 da2] *n.* starter motor

啓發 [kai2 faat8] *v.* inspire

琴晚 [kam4 maan5] *adv.* last night

琴日 [kam4 yat9] *adv.* yesterday (the day before ~ 前晚)

芹菜 [kan4 choi3] *n.* celery (Chinese ~ 香芹, ~ root 芹菜根, ~ sticks 芹菜條)

吸 [kap7] *v.* suck

吸收 [kap7 sau1] *v.* absorb

吸引 [kap7 yan5] *v.* attract; *adj.* enticing

吸引力 [kap7 yan5 lik9] *n.* attraction

吸引人 [kap7 yan5 yan4] *adj.* fascinating

咳 [kat7] *v.* cough (~ syrup 止咳糖漿, ~ medicine 藥水)

卡片 [kat7 pin2] *n.* card (play ~s 打牌)

臼齒 [kau3 chi2] *n.* molar

扣好 [kau3 hou2] *v.* fasten

扣留 [kau3 lau4] *n.* retention

購物 [kau3 mat9] *n.* shopping; *v.* shop

購物籃 [kau3 mat9 laam4] *n.* shopping basket

購物車 [kau3 mat9 che1] *n.* shopping cart

購物中心 [kau3 mat9 jung1 sam1] *n.* shopping center, shopping mall

構思好 [kau3 si1 hou2] *adj.* formulated, devoloped

構成 [kau3 sing4] *v.* constitute

球賽 [kau4 choi3] *n.* ball game

球莖 [kau4 ging3] *n.* tuber

球狀 [kau4 jong6] *adj.* spherical

求其睇睇 [kau4 kei4 tai2 tai2] *v.* browse

球拍 [kau4 paak8] *n.* racket (*sports*)

球棒 [kau4 paang5] *n.* bat (*sports*)

騎 [ke4] *v.* ride (~ a horse 騎馬, ~ a bike 騎車; *n.* take a ~ 搭順風車, give a ~ to smb. 搭某人一程)

茄膏 [ke2 gou1] *n.* tomato puree

茄瓜 [ke2 gwa1] *n.* aubergine

茄汁 [ke2 jap7] *n.* ketchup, tomato sauce

茄子 [ke2 ji2] *n.* eggplant

騎兵 [ke4 bing1] *n.* cavalry

騎馬 [ke4 ma5] *n.* horseback riding

騎師 [ke4 si1] *n.* jockey, rider

旗 [kei4] *n.* flag

期間 [kei4 gaan1] *prep.* during

奇怪 [kei4 gwaai3] *adj.* odd, peculiar, strange; *adv.* oddly, strangely

期權 [kei4 kyun4] *n.* stock option

期望 [kei4 mong6] *n.* expectation

棋盤 [kei4 pun4] *n.* chessboard

歧視 [kei4 si6] *n.* discrimination

其他 [kei4 ta1] *adj.* other; *adv.* else, something else

祈禱 [kei4 tou2] *v.* pray; *n.* prayer

奇異果 [kei4 yi6 gwo2] *n.* kiwi

奇遇 [kei4 yu6] *n.* adventure

企 [kei5] *v.* stand (~ in line 排隊, ~ up 企起身)

企起身 [kei5 hei2 san1] *adv.* up (~ there 上面嗰度, ~ to 由...決定, ~ till now 直到宜家, going ~ 上緊去, look ~ 抬頭); *v.* stand up

企里 [kei5 lei5] *adv.* neatly

企里 [kei5 lei5] *adj.* tidy (~ up 整企里)

企業 [kei5 yip9] *n.* enterprise

劇本 [kek9 bun2] *n.* script

劇烈 [kek9 lit9] *adj.* dramatic; *adv.* dramatically

區 [keui1] *n.* neighborhood

拘捕 [keui1 bou2] *v.* arrest

驅蟲劑 [keui1 chung4 jai1] *n.* repellent

區分 [keui1 fan1] *v.* distinguish

區間 [keui1 gaan1] *n.* interval

區號 [keui1 hou6] *n.* area code

俱樂部 [keui1 lok9 bou6] *n.* clubhouse

區域性 [keui1 wik9 sing3] *adj.* regional (~ cooking 地方菜, ~ dish 地方菜, ~ recipe 地方菜)

佢 [keui5] *pron.* he, him, it, she

佢哋 [keui5 dei6] *pron.* they

佢哋嘅 [keui5 dei6 ge3] *adj.* their; *pron.* theirs

佢哋自己 [keui5 dei6 ji6 gei2] *pron.* themselves

佢嘅 [keui5 ge3] *pron.* her, his, its

佢自己 [keui5 ji6 gei2] *pron.* herself, himself, itself

拒絕 [keui5 jyut9] *v.* reject; *n.* rejection

距離 [keui5 lei4] *n.* distance (keep your ~ 唔好再行近)

強大 [keung4 daai6] *adj.* powerful

強調 [keung4 diu6] *v.* emphasize

強姦 [keung4 gaan1] *n.* rape; *adj.* raped

強制 [keung4 jai3] *adj.* mandatory

強烈 [keung4 lit9] *adv.* strongly

強烈抗議 [keung4 lit9 kong3 yi5] *n.* outcry

強加 [keung5 ga1] *v.* impose

強制 [keung5 jai3] *v.* oblige

鉗仔 [kim4 jai2] *n.* tweezers

虔誠 [kin4 sing4] *adj.* religious (~ service 宗教儀式)

傾斜 [king1 che4] *n.* incline

傾偈 [king1 gai2] *n.* conservation; *v.* talk (~ to 同...講話, ~ it over 接手)

蠍子 [kit8 ji2] *n.* scorpion

橋 [kiu4] *n.* bridge

蕎麥 [kiu4 mak9] *n.* buckwheat

橋牌 [kiu4 paai4] *n.* bridge (*card game*)

鈣 [koi3] *n.* calcium

概念 [koi3 nim6] *n.* conception; *adj.* conceptual

蓋印 [koi3 yan3] *v.* stamp a passport

確定 [kok8 ding6] *adj.* definite; *adv.* definitely

確定 [kok8 ding6] *v.* make sure

礦工 [kong3 gung1] *n.* pitman

抗震 [kong3 jan3] *adj.* shockproof

擴展 [kong3 jin2] *v.* expand

抗生素 [kong3 sang1 sou3] *n.* antibiotic (prescribe ~s 開抗生素)

抗體 [kong3 tai2] *n.* antibody

抗菌膏 [kong3 kwan2 gou1] *n.* antiseptic cream

抗議 [kong3 yi5] *n.* protest

潰瘍 [kui2 yeung4] *n.* ulcer

曲棍球 [kuk7 gwan3 kau4] *n.* hockey (ice ~ 冰上曲棍球)

曲奇 [kuk7 kei4] *n.* cookie (*tech.* Internet ~s 訪問網站數據)

曲線 [kuk7 sin3] *n.* curve

窮 [kung4] *adj.* poor

窮鬼 [kung4 gwai2] *n.* pauper

括弧 [kut8 wu4] *n.* bracket

誇大 [kwa1 daai6] *v.* exaggerate

誇張 [kwa1 jeung1] *adj.* rhetorical

跨國 [kwa3 gwok8] *adj.* multi-national

框架 [kwaang1 ga2] *n.* framework

規定 [kwai1 ding6] *n.* rules

規範 [kwai1 faan6] *n.* precept

規格 [kwai1 gaak8] *n.* specification

盔甲 [kwai1 gaap8] *n.* armor

葵花籽 [kwai4 fa1 ji2] *n.* sunflower seeds

葵花油 [kwai4 fa1 yau4] *n.* sunflower oil

昆蟲學 [kwan1 chung4 hok9] *n.* entomology

困境 [kwan3 ging2] *n.* adversity

困住 [kwan3 jyu6] *v.* confine; *adj.* confined

困難 [kwan3 naan4] *n.* difficulty

困擾 [kwan3 yiu2] *v.* perplex; *n.* perplexity

群 [kwan4] *n.* cluster

裙 [kwan4] *n.* skirt

裙帶關係 [kwan4 daai3 gwaan1 hai6] *n.* nepotism

群眾 [kwan4 jung3] *n.* crowd

礦泉水 [kwong3 chyun4 seui2] *n.* mineral water

礦物 [kwong3 mat9] *n.* minerals

礦物質 [kwong3 mat9 jat7] *n.* mineral

礦石 [kwong3 sek9] *n.* ore

狂歡 [kwong4 fun1] *n.* revelry

狂笑 [kwong4 siu3] *v.* roar

狂熱 [kwong4 yit9] *n.* mania; *adj.* fervent

拳擊 [kyun4 gik7] *n.* boxing (~ ring 拳擊台)

權利平等 [kyun4 lei6 ping4 dang2] *n.* equal rights

權勢 [kyun4 sai3] *n.* potency

拳頭 [kyun4 tau4] *n.* fist

權威 [kyun4 wai1] *n.* authority

缺點 [kyut8 dim2] *n.* shortage

決定 [kyut8 ding6] *v.* decide; *n.* decision (~ making 做決定)

缺陷 [kyut8 haam6] *n.* deficiency

決心 [kyut8 sam1] *n.* determination

缺少 [kyut8 siu2] *n./v.* lack

L

喇嘛 [la1 ma3] *n.* llama

罅 [la3] *n.* crack

喇叭 [la3 ba1] *n.* amplifier

拉 [laai1] *v.* pull

拉巴特 [laai1 ba1 dak9] *n.* Rabat (~, capital of Morocco 摩洛哥嘅首都)

拉巴斯 [laai1 ba1 si1] *n.* La Paz (~, administrative capital of Bolivia 玻利维亚的行政首都)

拉開 [laai1 hoi1] *v.* unzip (~ clothing 拉鍊, ~ a computer file 解壓縮文件) ; pull out (sign on a door)

拉鏈 [laai1 lin4] *n.* zipper

拉鍊 [laai1 lin6] *v.* zip (~ a computer file 壓縮文件)

拉傷 [laai1 seung1] *v.* strain

拉傷肌肉 [laai1 seung1 gei1 yuk9] *v.* strain a muscle

拉脫維亞 [laai1 tyut8 wai4 a3] *n.* Latvia; *adj.* Latvian

肋骨 [laak9 gwat7] *n.* rib

籃 [laam4] *n.* basket (muffin ~ 鬆餅籃, fruit ~ 水果籃, ~ of ... 一籃...)

藍寶石 [laam4 bou2 sek9] *n.* sapphire

藍調 [laam4 diu6] *n.* blues (~ music 藍調音樂, to have the ~ 難過)

籃球 [laam4 kau4] *n.* basketball

藍莓 [laam4 mui4] *n.* blueberries

藍色 [laam4 sik7] *adj.* blue

欖球 [laam5 kau4] *n.* rugby

纜車 [laam6 che1] *n.* cable car

纜車吊椅 [laam6 che1 diu3 yi2] *n.* chairlift

纜索 [laam6 sok8] *n.* guy rope

濫用 [laam6 yung6] *n.* abuse

欄杆 [laan4 gon1] *n.* railing

懶 [laan5] *adj.* lazy

爛布 [laan6 bou3] *n.* rag

爛咗 [laan6 jo2] *adj.* damaged; *v.* breakdown

爛咗嘅 [laan6 jo2 ge3] *adj.* broken (~ bone 骨骼斷裂)

冷衫 [laang1 saam1] *n.* sweater

冷藏 [laang5 chong4] *adj.* frozen (~ food 冷藏食品, ~ ice 結冰, ~ vegetables 冷藏蔬菜, ~ meat 冷藏肉, ~ pastry 冷藏糕點)

冷藏櫃 [laang5 chong4 gwai6] *n.* freezer

冷淡 [laang5 daam6] *n.* nonchalance; *adj.* lukewarm

冷凍 [laang5 dung3] *n.* refrigeration

冷氣 [laang5 hei3] *n.* air conditioning

冷靜 [laang5 jing6] *adj.* calm; *adv.* calmly

冷漠 [laang5 mok9] *adv.* coldly

冷盤 [laang5 pun2] *n.* cold cuts (bologne ~ 冷盤大紅腸, ham ~ 冷盤火腿, turkey ~ 冷盤火雞)

蠟筆 [laap9 bat7] *n.* pastel, pale color

瀝青 [laap9 cheng1] *n.* pitch

立法 [laap9 faat8] *n.* legislation

立法機關 [laap9 faat8 gei1 gwaan1] *n.* legislature

立方體 [laap9 fong1 tai2] *n.* cube

蠟像 [laap9 jeung6] *n.* waxwork

蠟燭 [laap9 juk7] *n.* candle

垃圾 [laap9 saap8] *n.* trash, garbage

垃圾袋 [laap9 saap8 doi2] *n.* trash/garbage bags

垃圾桶 [laap9 saap8 tung2] *n.* trash/garbage can

立陶宛 [laap9 tou4 yun2] *n.* Lithuania; *adj.* Lithuanian

臘肉 [laap9 yuk9] *n.* cured meat

辣 [laat9] *adj.* spicy (~ pepper 辣椒, ~ sauce 辣醬, ~ taste 辣味)

辣蕃茄醬 [laat9 faan1 ke2 jeung3] *n.* salsa (hot ~ 特辣蕃茄醬, mild ~ 中辣蕃茄醬, spicy ~ 辣蕃茄醬)

辣雞翼 [laat9 gai1 yik9] *n.* buffalo wings

辣醬油 [laat9 jeung3 yau4] *n.* Worcestershire sauce

辣椒 [laat9 jiu1] *n.* pimiento

辣椒粉 [laat9 jiu1 fan2] *n.* paprika, ground pepper

辣椒醬 [laat9 jiu1 jeung3] *n.* hot sauce, pepper sauce

辣椒油 [laat9 jiu1 yau4] *n.* tabasco sauce

邋遢 [laat9 taat8] *adj.* dirty

邋遢嘢 [laat9 taat8 ye5] *n.* filth

黎巴嫩 [lai4 ba1 nyun6] *n.* Lebanon; *adj.* Lebanese

藜麥 [lai4 mak9] *n.* quinoa

黎明 [lai4 ming4] *n.* dawn

嚟呢度 [lai4 nei4 dou6] *adv* here, to here

禮拜 [lai5 baai3] *n.* week (this ~ 呢個禮拜); church service

禮拜六 [lai5 baai3 luk9] *n.* Saturday

禮拜五 [lai5 baai3 ng5] *n.* Friday

禮拜三 [lai5 baai3 saam1] *n.* Wednesday

禮拜四 [lai5 baai3 sei3] *n.* Thursday

禮拜一 [lai5 baai3 yat7] *n.* Monday

禮拜日 [lai5 baai3 yat9] *n.* Sunday

禮拜二 [lai5 baai3 yi6] *n.* Tuesday

禮品店 [lai5 ban2 dim3] *n.* gift shop

禮服 [lai5 fuk9] *n.* formal dress

禮貌 [lai5 maau6] *n.* courtesy

禮物 [lai5 mat9] *n.* gift

禮數 [lai5 sou3] *n.* etiquette

禮儀 [lai5 yi4] *n.* protocol

厲害 [lai6 hoi6] *n.* prowess; *adj.* excellent

荔枝 [lai6 ji1] *n.* lychee

例子 [lai6 ji2] *n.* example (for ~ 例如)

例外 [lai6 ngoi6] *n.* exception

例湯 [lai6 tong1] *n.* soup of the day

例如 [lai6 yu4] *abbr.* e.g. (for example); *adv.* for example, such as

勒索 [lak9 sok8] *v.* blackmail

冧 [lam3] *v.* collapse

臨床 [lam4 chong4] *adj.* clinical

臨時 [lam4 si4] *adj.* interim

臨時保母 [lam4 si4 bou2 mou5] *n.* babysitter

臨時滯留 [lam4 si4 jai6 lau4] *n.* layover

林業 [lam4 yip9] *n.* forestry

粒子 [lap7 ji2] *n.* particle

笠頭衫 [lap7 tau4 saam1] *n.* pullover

甩皮 [lat7 pei4] *v.* molt

甩頭髮 [lat7 tau4 faat8] *adj.* balding

褸 [lau1] *n.* coat (~ check 放褸處, ~ hanger 掛褸衣架)

流 [lau4] *v.* flow

瘤 [lau4] *n.* tumor (benign ~ 良性腫瘤, malignant ~ 惡性腫瘤)

流鼻水 [lau4 bei6 seui2] *n.* runny nose

流產 [lau4 chaan2] *n.* miscarriage

留低 [lau4 dai1] *v.* stay

留低印象 [lau4 dai1 yan3 jeung6] *v.* impress

流動資金 [lau4 dung6 ji1 gam1] *n.* liquidity

流動性 [lau4 dung6 sing3] *n.* mobility

流放 [lau4 fong3] *v.* ostracize

流感 [lau4 gam2] *n.* flu

流行 [lau4 hang4] *v.* prevail

流行病 [lau4 hang4 beng6] *n.* epidemic

流行性感冒 [lau4 hang4 sing3 gam2 mou6] *n.* influenza

流行音樂 [lau4 hang4 yam1 ngok9] *n.* pop music

流血 [lau4 hyut8] *v.* bleed, be bleeding

留級 [lau4 kap7] *n.* retardation

瀏覽器 [lau4 laam5 hei3] *n.* browser (internet ~ 互聯網瀏覽器)

流利 [lau4 lei6] *adj.* fluent

榴槤 [lau4 lin4] *n.* durian

流浪 [lau4 long6] *v.* rove

流沙 [lau4 sa1] *n.* quicksand

流星 [lau4 sing1] *n.* meteor

樓梯 [lau4 tai1] *n.* stair

樓梯井 [lau4 tai1 jing2] *n.* stairwell

樓梯級 [lau4 tai1 kap7] *n.* flight of stairs

留有 [lau4 yau5] *v.* retain

留言板 [lau4 yin4 baan2] *n.* message board

溜冰 [lau6 bing1] *n.* ice skate

溜冰鞋 [lau6 bing1 haai4] *n.* roller skates

漏氣嘅車軚 [lau6 hei3 ge3 che1 taai1] *n.* flat tire

漏咗 [lau6 jo2] *v.* leave out

梨 [lei4] *n.* pear

嚟 [lei4] *v.* come

離婚 [lei4 fan1] *n.* divorce; *adj.* divorced

離合器 [lei4 hap9 hei3] *n.* clutch

離合器踏板 [lei4 hap9 hei3 daap9 baan2] *n.* clutch pedal

離開 [lei4 hoi1] *v.* place, leave smth. (leave in peace 和平分手, leave me alone 唔好理我)

離子 [lei4 ji2] *n.* ion

離奇 [lei4 kei4] *adj.* bizarre

厘米 [lei4 mai5] *n.* centimeter (*abbr.* cm.)

離心 [lei4 sam1] *adj.* acentric

離線 [lei4 sin3] *adj. comp.* offline (webpage is ~ 呢個網頁離咗線)

里程 [lei5 ching4] *n.* mileage

里程碑 [lei5 ching4 bei1] *n.*
milestone

理髮師 [lei5 faat8 si1] *n.* barber

里加 [lei5 ga1] *n.* Riga (~, capital
of Latvia 拉脫維亞嘅首都)

理解 [lei5 gaai2] *v.* understand (I
don't ~ 我唔明白)

理解 [lei5 gaai2] *n.* understanding
(to reach an ~ 達成共識)

理論 [lei5 leun6] *n.* theory

理論基礎 [lei5 leun6 gei1 cho2]
n. rationale

理論上 [lei5 leun6 seung6] *adj.*
theoretical

理想 [lei5 seung2] *adj.* ideal;
adv. ideally

理想主義 [lei5 seung2 jyu2 yi6]
n. idealism

理想主義者 [lei5 seung2 jyu2
yi6 je2] *n.* idealist

里斯本 [lei5 si1 bun2] *n.* Lisbon
(~, capital of Portugal 葡萄牙
嘅首都)

理性 [lei5 sing3] *n.* sense; *adj.*
rational

理所當然 [lei5 so2 dong1 yin4]
adv. rightly

理由 [lei5 yau4] *n.* reason (~ for
travel 旅遊嘅理由)

鯉魚 [lei5 yu2] *n.* cyprinoid

脷 [lei6] *n.* tongue (pig ~ 豬脷,
cow ~ 牛脷)

利 [lei6] *adj.* sharp, sharp-edged

利伯維爾 [lei6 baak8 wai4
yi5] *n.* Libreville (~, capital of
Gabon 加蓬嘅首都)

利比亞 [lei6 bei2 a3] *n.* Libya;
adj. Libyian

利比里亞 [lei6 bei2 lei5 a3] *n.*
Liberia

利隆圭 [lei6 lung4 gwai1] *n.*
Lilongwe (~, capital of Malawi
馬拉維嘅首都)

利馬 [lei6 ma5] *n.* Lima (~,
capital of Peru 秘魯嘅首都)

利馬豆 [lei6 ma5 dau6] *n.* lima
beans

利雅得 [lei6 nga5 dak7] *n.*
Riyadh (~, capital of Saudi
Arabia 沙特阿拉伯嘅首都)

利尿 [lei6 niu6] *n.* diuretic

利潤 [lei6 yeun6] *n.* profit

利益 [lei6 yik7] *n.* behalf (on ~ of
smb. / on smb.'s ~ 代表)

叻 [lek7] *adj.* good at

叻過 [lek7 gwo3] *v.* outdo,
outshine; preponderate

靚 [leng3] *adj.* beautiful

靚仔 [leng3 jai2] *adj.* handsome

靚排骨 [leng3 paai4 gwat7] *n.*
baby back ribs

雷克雅末克 [leui4 hak7 nga5
mut9 hak7] *n.* Reykjavik (~,
capital of Iceland 冰島嘅首都)

驢 [leui4] *n.* donkey

騾仔 [leui4 jai2] *n.* mule

雷魚 [leui4 yu4] *n.* ray (fish)

鋁 [leui5] *n.* aluminum (~ foil 錫
紙, ~ pan 鋁盤, ~ pot 鋁鍋)

旅館 [leui5 gun2] *n.* hostel

旅行 [leui5 hang4] *n.* trip

旅行支票 [leui5 hang4 ji1 piu3]
n. traveler's check

旅行社 [leui5 hang4 se5] *n.*
travel agency

旅行團 [leui5 hang4 tyun4] *n.* tour group

累積 [leui5 jik7] *v.* accumulate; *n.* accumulation

旅遊 [leui5 yau4] *n.* traveling; *v.* travel, go sightseeing

旅遊指南 [leui5 yau4 ji2 naam4] *n.* guidebook

類 [leui6] *n.* sort

類似 [leui6 chi5] *v.* resemble

類型 [leui6 ying4] *n.* type (What ~ of …? 乜嘢種類, She is not my ~ 我唔鍾意佢)

略略 [leuk9 leuk9] *adv.* briefly

略略 [leuk9 leuk9] *adv.* slightly

卵巢 [leun2 chaau4] *n.* ovary

輪班 [leun4 baan1] *n.* rotation

倫特 [leun4 dak9] *n.* Lent

倫敦 [leun4 deun1] *n.* London (~, capital of United Kingdom 英國嘅首都)

輪輻 [leun4 fuk7] *n.* spoke (of a wheel)

輪蓋 [leun4 goi3] *n.* hubcap

輪流 [leun4 lau4] *adj.* alternate (~ route 另外一條路)

輪船 [leun4 syun4] *n.* steamer

輪椅 [leun4 yi2] *n.* wheelchair

論壇 [leun6 taan4] *n.* forum

兩個都 [leung2 go3 dou1] *adj.* both

量杯 [leung4 bui1] *n.* measuring cup

涼茶 [leung4 cha4] *n.* herbal tea

涼鞋 [leung4 haai4] *n.* sandal

糧食 [leung4 sik9] *n.* grain

良性腫瘤 [leung4 sing3 jung2 lau4] *n.* benign tumor

兩次 [leung5 chi3] *adv.* twice (~ a day 一日兩次)

兩夫婦 [leung5 fu1 fu5] *n.* couple

兩極 [leung5 gik9] *adj.* polar

兩個星期 [leung5 go3 sing1 kei4] *n.* fortnight

兩倍 [leung5 pui5] *adj.* double (~ bed 雙人床, ~ room 雙人房)

栗子 [leut9 ji2] *n.* chestnut

律師 [leut9 si1] *n.* lawyer

律師資格考試 [leut9 si1 ji1 gaak8 haau2 si3] bar exam (*legal*)

律師助手 [leut9 si1 jo6 sau2] *n.* paralegal

栗色 [leut9 sik7] *n.* sorrel

力 [lik9] *n.* force

力學 [lik9 hok9] *n.* mechanics

力量 [lik9 leung6] *n.* strength

歷史 [lik9 si2] *n.* history

歷史學家 [lik9 si2 hok9 ga1] *n.* historian

歷史上 [lik9 si2 seung6] *adj.* historical

連花園嘅公寓 [lin4 fa1 yun2 ge3 gung1 yu6] *n.* garden apartment

連傢俬嘅 [lin4 ga1 si1 ge3] *adj.* furnished

連號 [lin4 hou6] *n.* hyphen

蓮子 [lin4 ji2] *n.* lotus seeds

連接 [lin4 jip8] *v.* connect; *n.* connection; *adj.* connected

連接詞 [lin4 jip8 chi4] *n.* conjunction

連續 [lin4 juk9] *adj.* uninterrupted

連身裙 [lin4 san1 kwan4] *n.* dress (~ code 穿衣要求)

鍊金術 [lin6 gam1 seut9] *n.* alchemy

練習 [lin6 jaap9] *n.* practice

鍊罩 [lin6 jaau3] *n.* chain guard

煉奶 [lin6 naai5] *n.* evaporated milk

煉獄 [lin6 yuk9] *n.* purgatory

拎起 [ling1 hei2] *v.* lift

零 [ling4] *num.* zero

靈丹妙藥 [ling4 daan1 miu6 yeuk9] *n.* nostrum

令尷尬 [ling4 gaam1 gaai3] *v.* embarrass

靈感 [ling4 gam2] *n.* inspiration

零件 [ling4 gin6] *n.* spare part

菱角 [ling4 gok8] *n.* water chestnut

令... 覺得好煩 [ling4 … gok8 dak7 hou2 faan4] *v.* annoy

令...可以 [ling4 … ho2 yi5] *v.* enable

令...好悶 [ling4 … hou2 mun6] *v.* bore

陵墓 [ling4 mou6] *n.* mausoleum

靈媒 [ling4 mui4] *n.* psychic

令...滿意 [ling4 … mun5 yi3] *v.* satisfy (to ~ 取悅)

令...失望 [ling4 … sat7 mong6] *v.* disappoint

零售 [ling4 sau6] *n.* retail

零售價 [ling4 sau6 ga3] *n.* retail price

零售商 [ling4 sau6 seung1] *n.* retailer

零售業 [ling4 sau6 yip9] *n.* retailing

零食 [ling4 sik9] *n.* snack (~ bar 小食吧, ~ food 零食)

令...癱瘓 [ling4 … tann2 wun6] *v.* paralyse

靈魂 [ling4 wan4] *n.* soul (~ music 靈魂音樂, ~ food 美國 南方黑人傳統食物)

靈活 [ling4 wut9] *adj.* flexible

靈活性 [ling4 wut9 sing3] *n.* flexibility

令人擔心 [ling4 yan4 daam1 sam1] *adj.* worrying

令人反感 [ling4 yan4 faan2 gam2] *adj.* disgusting

令人放鬆 [ling4 yan4 fong3 sung1] *adj.* relaxing

令人尷尬 [ling4 yan4 gaam1 gaai3] *adj.* embarrassing

令人抑鬱 [ling4 yan4 yik7 wat7] *adj.* depressing

令人興奮 [ling4 yan4 hing1 fan5] *adj.* exciting

令人好悶 [ling4 yan4 hou2 mun6] *adj.* boring

令人作嘔 [ling4 yan4 jok8 au2] *adj.* revolting

令人唔開心 [ling4 yan4 m4 hoi1 sam1] *adj.* unpleasant

令人滿意 [ling4 yan4 mun5 yi3] *adj.* satisfying

令人失望 [ling4 yan4 sat7 mong6] *adj.* disappointing

令人印象深刻 [ling4 yan4 yan3 jeung6 sam1 hak7] *adj.* impressive

令人愉快 [ling4 yan4 yu4 faai3] *adj.* pleasing

羚羊 [ling4 yeung4] *n.* antelope

令...抑鬱 [ling4 … yik7 wat7] *v.* depress

零用錢 [ling4 yng6 chin2] *n.*
allowance

領導 [ling5 dou6] *n.* lead (metal);
v. lead (guide)

領導能力 [ling5 dou6 nang4
lik9] *n.* leadership

領導人 [ling5 dou6 yan4] *n.*
leader

領獎台 [ling5 jeung2 toi4] *n.*
rostrum

領悟 [ling5 ng6] *n.* realization

領事館 [ling5 si6 gun2] *n.*
consulate

領先 [ling5 sin1] *n.* precedence

領退休金嘅人 [ling5 teui3 yau1
gam1 ge3 yan4] *n.* pensioner

領土 [ling5 tou2] *n.* domain

領域 [ling5 wik9] *n.* realm

另外 [ling6 ngoi6] *adj.* another

獵人 [lip9 yan4] *n.* hunter

獵鷹 [lip9 ying1] *n.* falcon

列清單 [lit9 ching1 daan1] *adj.*
itemized

烈酒 [lit9 jau2] *n.* hard liquor

列支敦士登 [lit9 ji1 deun1 si6
dang1] *n.* Liechtenstein; *adj.*
Liechtensteiner

烈士 [lit9 si6] *n.* martyr

療養院 [liu4 yeung5 yun6] *n.*
sanatorium

攞出來 [lo2 cheut7 lei4] *v.*
withdraw (~ money 取錢)

攞 [lo2] *v.* carry

攞出 [lo2 cheut7] *v.* put out

攞到 [lo2 dou2] *v.* obtain

攞番 [lo2 faan1] *v.* retrieve

攞起 [lo2 hei2] *v.* pick sth. up

攞走 [lo2 jau2] *v.* take (~ a taxi

坐的士, ~ time 慢慢, ~ a
nap 瞓一陣, ~ action 行動, ~
advantage of 佔便宜, ~ away
攞走, ~ care (of) 照顧, ~ in 吸
收, ~ me to 帶我去, ~ off 除
衫, ~ out 攞出去, ~ part (in)
參加, ~ photographs 影相, ~
place 發生, ~ smth. off 除衫, ~
offense 俾激嬲)

攞住 [lo2 jyu6] *v.* hold

裸體 [lo2 tai2] *adj.* naked

蘿蔔 [lo4 baak9] *n.* radish

蘿蔔蓉 [lo4 baak9 yung4] *n.*
mashed turnips

邏輯 [lo4 chap7] *n.* logic

羅非魚 [lo4 fei1 yu4] *n.* tilapia

羅勒 [lo4 lak9] *n.* basil

羅馬 [lo4 ma5] *n.* Rome

羅馬教皇 [lo4 ma5 gaau3 wong4]
n. pope

羅馬尼亞 [lo4 ma5 nei4 a3] *n.*
Romania; *adj.* Romanian

羅馬式建築風格 [lo4 ma5
sik7 gin3 juk7 fung1 gaak8] *n.*
Romanesque style

羅望子 [lo4 mong6 ji2] *n.*
tamarind

羅安達 [lo4 on1 daat9] *n.*
Luanda (~, capital of Angola 安
哥拉首都)

螺絲 [lo4 si1] *n.* screw

螺絲批 [lo4 si1 pai1] *n.*
screwdriver

羅索 [lo4 sok8] *n.* Roseau (~,
capital of Dominica 多米尼加
首都)

羅宋湯 [lo4 sung3 tong1] *n.*
borsch (red ~ 紅羅宋湯, white

~ 白羅宋湯, Polish ~ 波蘭 羅宋湯, Russian ~ 俄羅斯羅 宋湯)

螺旋 [lo4 syun4] *n.* spire

來自 [loi4 ji6] *v.* derive

萊索托 [loi4 sok8 tok8] *n.* Lesotho

來回旅程嘅 [loi4 wui4 leui5 ching4 ge3] *adj.* round-trip

來回票 [loi4 wui4 piu3] *n.* round-trip ticket

來源 [loi4 yun4] *n.* source

落後 [lok6 hau6] *adj.* backward (move ~s 向後退)

洛美 [lok8 mei5] *n.* Lome (~, capital of Togo 多哥嘅首都)

落 [lok9] *v.* drop (~ someone off 放低)

落車 [lok9 che1] *v.* get off

樂趣 [lok9 cheui3] *n.* fun (for ~ 玩玩, have ~ 玩得開心)

落貨 [lok9 fo3] *v.* unload

樂觀 [lok9 gun1] *n.* optimism; *adj.* optimistic

落後 [lok9 hau6] *v.* lag

落後嘅人 [lok9 hau6 ge3 yan4] *n.* laggard

落可可風格 [lok9 ho2 ho2 fung1 gaak8] *n.* Rococo style

落樓 [lok9 lau4] *adv.* downstairs

落毛毛雨 [lok9 mou4 mou4 yu5] *v.* drizzle

樂天派 [lok9 tin1 paai3] *n.* optimist

樂意 [lok9 yi3] *adv.* readily

狼吞虎嚥 [long4 tan1 fu2 yin3] *v.* devour

朗誦 [long5 jung6] *n.* recitation

朗誦 [long5 jung6] *v.* recite

朗姆酒 [long5 mou5 jau2] *n.* rum

浪 [long6] *n.* wave

浪費 [long6 fai3] *v.* waste; *n.* profligacy

浪漫 [long6 maan6] *adj.* romantic

浪漫主義 [long6 maan6 jyu2 yi6] *n.* Romanticism

盧布爾雅那 [lou4 bou3 yi5 nga5 na5] *n.* Ljubljana (~, capital of Slovenia 斯洛文尼 亞嘅首都)

勞動 [lou4 dung6] *n.* labor

勞動節 [lou4 dung6 jit8] *n.* May Day (May 1); Labor Day

勞動力 [lou4 dung6 lik9] *n.* workforce

盧薩卡 [lou4 saat8 ka1] *n.* Lusaka (~, capital of Zambia 贊 比亞嘅首都)

盧森堡 [lou4 sam1 bou2] *n.* Luxembourg

蘆筍 [lou4 seun2] *n.* asparagus (~ soup 蘆筍湯, ~ tips 蘆筍尖)

牢騷 [lou4 sou1] *n.* grievance

盧旺達 [lou4 wong6 daat9] *n.* Rwanda; *adj.* Rwandan

蘆薈 [lou4 wui6] *n.* aloe (~ juice 蘆薈汁, ~ cream 蘆薈乳液)

鱸魚 [lou4 yu2] *n.* picarel (fish)

老 [lou5] *adj.* old

老化 [lou5 fa3] *v.* aging (~ meat 爛咗嘅肉)

老公 [lou5 gung1] *n.* husband

老鎮 [lou5 jan3] *n.* old town

老婆 [lou5 po4] *n.* wife

老細 [lou5 sai3] *n.* employer (equal opportunity ~ 平等機 會僱主)

老實 [lou5 sat9] *adj.* honest; *adv.* honestly

滷水 [lou5 seui2] *n.* brine

老師 [lou5 si1] *n.* teacher

老式 [lou5 sik7] *adj.* old-fashioned

老鼠 [lou5 syu2] *n.* mouse (animal)

老撾 [lou5 wo1] *n.* Laos; *adj.* Laotian

老友 [lou5 yau5] *n.* fellow

路 [lou6] *n.* lane

路標 [lou6 biu1] *n.* signpost

路費 [lou6 fai3] *n.* toll

露餡三文治 [lou6 ham6 saam1 man4 ji6] *n.* open-faced sandwiches

路線 [lou6 sin3] *n.* route

路線圖 [lou6 sin3 tou4] *n.* road map

露天市場 [lou6 tin1 si5 cheung4] *n.* fairground

露天泳池 [lou6 tin1 wing6 chi4] *n.* outdoor pool

路人 [lou6 yan4] *n.* pedestrian (~ crossing 行人道, ~ zone 行人區)

路易港 [lou6 yik9 gong2] *n.* Port Louis (~, capital of Mauritius 毛里裘斯嘅首都)

露營場地 [lou6 ying4 cheung4 dei6] *n.* campground

露營嘅人 [lou6 ying4 ge3 yan4] *n.* camper; vehicle

轆 [luk7] *n.* wheel

鹿 [luk9] *n.* deer

六 [luk9] *num.* six

綠茶 [luk9 cha4] *n.* green tea

錄取 [luk9 cheui2] *n.* admittance

綠豆 [luk9 dau6] *n.* mung beans

陸軍中尉 [luk9 gwan1 jung1 wai3] *n.* lieutenant

六合彩 [luk9 hap9 choi2] *n.* lottery

錄起 [luk9 hei2] *adv.* on tap

氯氣 [luk9 hei3] *n.* chlorine

綠洲 [luk9 jau1] *n.* oasis

六十 [luk9 sap9] *num.* sixty

陸上運輸 [luk9 seung6 wan6 syu1] *n.* portage

綠色 [luk9 sik7] *adj.* green

綠色蔬菜 [luk9 sik7 so1 choi3] *n.* greens (mixed ~ 雜菜, assorted ~ 雜菜)

錄音 [luk9 yam1] *n.* recording

錄音帶 [luk9 yam1 daai3] *n.* cassette

錄音機 [luk9 yam1 gei1] *n.* recorder

錄影帶 [luk9 ying2 daai3] *n.* video (~ camera 錄影機, ~ card 視頻卡, ~ game 電子遊戲, ~ recorder 錄像機, ~ cassette 錄像帶)

鹿腰畫廊 [luk9 yiu1 wa2 long4] *n.* haunch of venison

鹿肉 [luk9 yuk9] *n.* venison

鹿茸 [luk9 yung4] *n.* antler

六月份 [luk9 yut9 fan6] *n.* June

窿 [lung1] *n.* hole, potholes

籠 [lung4] *n.* cage

聾 [lung4] *adj.* deaf

龍蒿 [lung4 gou1] *n.* tarragon

龍蝦 [lung4 ha1] *n.* lobster

龍蝦湯 [lung4 ha1 tong1] *n.* lobster bisque

龍葵 [lung4 kwai4] *n.* morels

龍舌蘭 [lung4 sit8 laan4] *n.* agave

壟斷 [lung5 dyun6] *n.* monopoly

聯邦 [lyun4 bong1] *adj.* federal

聯邦調查局 [lyun4 bong1 diu6 cha4 guk9] *n.* FBI (U.S. Federal Bureau of Investigation)

聯繫 [lyun4 hai6] *v.* relate; *n.* contact; *v.* be in contact with

聯合 [lyun4 hap9] *v.* unite

聯合護照 [lyun4 hap9 wu6 jiu3] *n.* joint passport

聯絡船 [lyun4 lok8 syun4] *n.* tender (boat)

聯盟 [lyun4 mang4] *n.* union

聯想 [lyun4 seung2] *v.* associate (~d with … 同…有關係)

亂 [lyun6] *n.* mess

亂七八糟 [lyun6 chat7 baat8 jou1] *adj.* untidy

亂講野 [lyun6 gong2 ye5] *v.* rave

亂摸 [lyun6 mo2] *v.* fumble

亂噏 [lyun6 ngap7] *n.* nonsense

亂劈 [lyun6 pek8] *n.* slash

M

唔 [m4] *adv.* not

唔俾入嚟 [m4 bei2 yap9 lai4] *v.* keep out

唔出聲 [m4 cheut7 seng1] *n.* silence; *adj.* silent

唔黐 [m4 chi1] *adj.* non-stick (~ pan 不黏鍋, ~ cooking utensil 不黏廚具)

唔似 [m4 chi5] *prep.* unlike

唔清楚 [m4 ching1 cho2] *n.* illegibility; *adj.* blurred (~ vision 睇得唔清楚)

唔清唔楚 [m4 ching1 m4 cho2] *adj.* ambiguous

唔請人 [m4 ching2 yan4] *n.* no vacancy

唔情願 [m4 ching4 yun6] *adj.* loath

唔錯 [m4 cho3] *adv.* not bad

唔道德 [m4 dou6 dak7] *adj.* immoral

唔緊要 [m4 gan2 yiu3] *phrase* never mind

唔吉利 [m4 gat7 lei6] *adj.* ominous

唔夠 [m4 gau3] *adj.* insufficient

唔見咗 [m4 gin3 jo2] *v.* disappear; *adj.* missing

唔該 [m4 goi1] *exclam.* please!

唔該晒 [m4 goi1 saai3] thank you

唔公平 [m4 gung1 ping4] *adj.* unfair; *adv.* unfairly

唔貴 [m4 gwai3] *adj.* inexpensive

唔係幾好 [m4 hai6 gei2 hou2] *n.* not very good

唔係 [m4 hai6] *adv.* no

唔肯定 [m4 hang2 ding6] *adj.* uncertain

唔可以進入 [m4 ho2 yi5 jeun3 yap9] *adj.* inaccessible

唔開心 [m4 hoi1 sam1] *n.* unhappiness; *adj.* unhappy

唔好 [m4 hou2] *n.* disadvantage

唔好彩 [m4 hou2 choi2] *adj.* unlucky

唔好嘅 [m4 hou2 ge3] *adj.* bad

唔好亂扰垃圾 [m4 hou2 lyun6 dam2 laap9 saap8] *phr.* no littering

唔准 [m4 jeun2] *adj.* forbidden

唔知點解 [m4 ji1 dim2 gaai2] *adv.* somehow

唔重要 [m4 jung6 yiu3] *adj.* unimportant

唔確定 [m4 kok8 ding6] *n.* uncertainty

唔甩色 [m4 lat7 sik7] *adj.* colorfast

唔老實 [m4 lou5 sat9] *adj.* dishonest; *adv.* dishonestly

唔啱 [m4 ngaam1] *n.* fault; *adj.* incorrect

唔耐煩 [m4 noi6 faan4] *adj.* impatient; *adv.* impatiently

唔安全 [m4 on1 cyun4] *adj.* unsafe

唔批准 [m4 pai1 jeun2] *v.* disapprove (of)

唔平均 [m4 ping4 gwan1] *adj* uneven (~ road surface 路面 唔平)

唔平穩 [m4 ping4 wan2] *adj.* unsteady

唔使客氣 [m4 sai2 haak8 hei3] *phr*. You're welcome!

唔使諗 [m4 sai2 nam2] *phr*. no way!

唔新鮮 [m4 san1 sin1] *adj*. stale

唔食得 [m4 sik9 dak7] *adj*. non-edible, inedible

唔舒服 [m4 syu1 fuk9] *adj*. uncomfortable

唔透明 [m4 tau3 ming4] *n*. opacity; *adj*. opaque

唔停 [m4 ting4] *adj* constant; *adv*. constantly

唔停咁俾 [m4 ting4 gam3 bei2] *v*. ply

唔同 [m4 tung4] *v*. differ; *adj*. different; *adv*. differently

唔同意 [m4 tung4 yi3] *v*. disagree

唔衛生 [m4 wai6 sang1] *adj*. unsanitary

唔穩定 [m4 wan2 ding6] *adj*. unstable

唔友好 [m4 yau5 hou2] *adj*. unfriendly

唔友善 [m4 yau5 sin6] *adj*. hostile

唔認同 [m4 ying6 tung4] *n*. disagreement

唔願意 [m4 yun6 yi3] *adj*. reluctant, unwilling

孖 [ma1] *n*. pair

嗎啡 [ma1 fe1] *n*. morphia

媽咪 [ma1 mi3] *n*. mom, mother

孖生 [ma1 saang1] *n*. twin (~ beds 單人床)

孖胎 [ma1 toi1] *n*. twins

麻包袋 [ma4 baau1 doi2] *n*. sack

麻花 [ma4 fa1] *n*. twist bun

麻煩 [ma4 faan4] *n*. trouble

麻煩嘢 [ma4 faan4 ye5] *n*. nuisance

麻疹 [ma4 jan2] *n*. measles

麻醉 [ma4 jeui3] *n*. anesthesia

麻醉嘅 [ma4 jeui3 ge3] *adj*. anesthetic

麻醉劑 [ma4 jeui3 jai1] *n*. narcotic

麻麻地 [ma4 ma4 dei2] *adj*. average

麻麻/婆婆 [ma4 ma2/po2 po2] *n*. grandmother

馬 [ma5] *n*. horse

碼 [ma5] *n*. size

馬賽克 [ma5 choi3 hak7] *n*. mosaic

馬達 [ma5 daat9] *n*. motor

馬達加斯加 [ma5 daat9 ga1 si1 ga1] *n*. Madagascar

馬德里 [ma5 dak7 lei5] *n*. Madrid (~, capital of Spain 西班牙嘅首都)

馬鮫魚 [ma5 gaau1 yu2] *n*. mackerel

馬仔 [ma5 jai2] *n*. pony

馬朱羅 [ma5 jyu1 lo4] *n*. Majuro (~, capital of Marshall Islands 馬紹爾群島嘅首都)

馬球 [ma5 kau4] *n*. polo

馬其頓 [ma5 kei4 deun6] *adj*. Macedonian

馬其頓王國 [ma5 kei4 deun6 wong4 gwok8] *n*. Macedonia

馬拉博 [ma5 laai1 bok8] *n*. Malabo (~, capital of Equatorial Guinea 赤道幾內亞嘅首都)

馬拉松 [ma5 laai1 chung4] *n*. marathon

馬拉維 [ma5 laai1 wai4] *n*. Malawi

馬騮 [ma5 lau1] *n.* monkey

馬里恩莓 [ma5 lei5 yan1 mui4] *n.* marionberry

馬里 [ma5 lei5] *n.* Mali

馬累 [ma5 leui5] *n* Male (~, capital of Maldives 馬爾代夫嘅首都)

馬來西亞 [ma5 loi4 sai1 a3] *n.* Malaysia; *adj.* Malaysian

馬那瓜湖 [ma5 na5 gwa1 wu4] *n.* Managua (~, capital of Nicaragua 尼加拉瓜嘅首都)

馬尼拉 [ma5 nei4 laai1] *n.* Manila (~, capital of Philippines 菲律賓嘅首都)

螞蟻 [ma5 ngai5] *n.* ant

馬鞍 [ma5 on1] *n.* saddle

馬棚 [ma5 paang4] *n.* stables

馬普托 [ma5 pou2 tok8] *n.* Maputo (~, capital of Mozambique 莫桑比克嘅首都)

馬塞盧 [ma5 sak7 lou4] *n.* Maseru (~, capital of Lesotho 萊索托嘅首都)

馬術學校 [ma5 seut9 hok9 haau6] *n.* horse-riding school

馬斯喀特 [ma5 si1 ka1 dak9] *n.* Muscat (~, capital of Oman 阿曼嘅首都)

馬繩 [ma5 sing4] *n.* harness

馬紹爾群島 [ma5 siu6 yi5 kwan4 dou2] *n.* Marshall Islands

馬蘇里拉芝士 [ma5 sou1 lei5 laai1 ji1 si6] *n.* mozzarella (~ sticks 馬蘇里拉芝士條)

馬蹄蟹 [ma5 tai4 haai5] *n.* horseshoe crab

碼頭 [ma5 tau4] *n.* pier

馬桶 [ma5 tung2] *n.* toilet (~ paper 廁紙, public ~ 公廁)

馬鬱蘭 [ma5 wat7 laan4] *n.* marjoram

螞蟥 [ma5 wong4] *n.* leech

馬爾代夫 [ma5 yi5 doi6 fu1] *n.* Maldives

馬耳他 [ma5 yi5 ta1] *n.* Malta

埋 [maai4] *v.* bury

埋伏 [maai4 fuk9] *v.* ambush

買 [maai5] *v.* buy

買得起 [maai5 dak7 hei2] *v.* afford

買家 [maai5 ga1] *n.* buyer

買賣 [maai5 maai6] *n.* dealings

賣 [maai6] *v.* sell

賣菜嘅 [maai6 choi3 ge3] *n.* greengrocer

賣家 [maai6 ga1] *n.* seller

賣咗 [maai6 jo2] *adj.* sold (~ out 賣晒)

賣晒 [maai6 saai3] *adj.* fully booked, sold out

賣淫 [maai6 yam4] *n.* prostitution

鰻魚 [maan4 yu4] *n.* eel (smoked ~ 煙薰鰻魚, live ~ 生鰻魚)

晚飯 [maan5 faan6] *n.* supper

晚安 [maan5 on1] *phr.* good night, good evening

慢 [maan6] *adj.* slow (~ down! 慢啲!, ~ traffic 車輛前進緩慢); *adv.* slowly

漫步 [maan6 bou6] *v.* roam; *n.* ramble

慢車 [maan6 che1] *n.* local train

曼谷 [maan6 guk7] *n.* Bangkok (~, capital of Thailand 泰國嘅首都)

萬象 [maan6 jeung6] *n.* Vientiane (~, capital of Laos 老撾嘅首都)

慢慢行 [maan6 maan1 haang4] *v.* amble

慢慢咬 [maan6 maan6 ngaau5] *n.* nibble

萬能 [maan6 nang4] *n.* omnipotence; *adj.* omnipotent

萬能之計 [maan6 nang4 ji1 gai3] *n.* panacea

慢跑 [maan6 paau2] *n.* jogging

慢性 [maan6 sing3] *adj.* chronic

漫畫 [maan6 wa2] *n.* comics

漫畫書 [maan6 wa2 syu1] *n.* comic book

萬一 [maan6 yat7] *adv.* in case (of)

萬用箱 [maan6 yung6 seung1] *n.* multipack

盲 [maang4] *adj.* blind

盲字 [maang4 ji6] *n.* braille

盲腸炎 [maang5 cheung4 yim4] *n.* appendicitis

猛打 [maang5 da2] *v.* lambaste

猛撲 [maang5 pok8] *v.* pounce

孟加拉 [maang6 ga1 laai1] *n.* Bangladesh; *adj.* Bangladeshi

抹 [maat8] *v.* wipe

抹塵 [maat8 chan4] *v.* dust (~ing 掃塵, ~ed 掃過塵)

貓 [maau1] *n.* cat

貓仔 [maau1 jai2] *n.* kitten

貓眼石 [maau1 ngaan5 sek9] *n.* opal

貓頭鷹 [maau1 tau4 ying1] *n.* owl

錨 [maau4] *n.* anchor

矛 [maau4] *n.* pike

茅屋芝士 [maau4 uk7 ji1 si6] *n.* cottage cheese

咪錶 [mai1 biu1] *n.* parking meter

迷 [mai4] *n.* myth

迷迭香 [mai4 dit9 heung1] *n.* rosemary

迷宮 [mai4 gung1] *n.* maze

迷戀 [mai4 lyun2] *v.* obsess; *n.* obsession

謎語 [mai4 yu5] *n.* riddle

米 [mai5] *n.* rice (~ pudding 米飯布甸, ~ pilaf 米肉飯, ~ cake 年糕)

米諾魚 [mai5 nok9 yu4] *n.* minnow

米碎 [mai5 seui3] *n.* crushed ice

米黃色 [mai5 wong4 sik7] *n.* beige

脈搏 [mak9 bok8] *n.* pulse

墨鏡 [mak9 geng3] *n.* sunglasses

麥粥 [mak9 juk7] *n.* kasha

默默無聞 [mak9 mak9 mou4 man4] *n.* obscurity

麥納麥 [mak9 naap9 mak9] *n.* Manama (~, capital of Bahrain 巴林嘅首都)

麥芽 [mak9 nga4] *n.* wheat germ

麥芽啤酒 [mak9 nga4 be1 jau2] *n.* ale

麥片 [mak9 pin3] *n.* cereal (whole grain ~ 全糧麥片, sweet ~ 甜麥片, oat ~ 燕麥麥片, morning ~ 早餐麥片)

墨西哥 [mak9 sai1 go1] *n.* Mexico; *adj.* Mexican

墨西哥辣番茄沙律 [mak9 sai1 go1 faan1 ke2 sa1 leut9] *n.* pico de gallo

墨西哥城 [mak9 sai1 go1 sing4] *n.* Mexico City (~, capital of Mexico 墨西哥嘅首都)

墨西哥粟米薄餅 [mak9 sai1 go1 suk7 mai5 bok9 beng2] *n.* tortilla (flour ~ 麵粉墨西哥粟米薄餅, yellow ~ 黃墨西哥粟米薄餅, soft ~ 軟墨西哥粟米薄餅, hard ~ 硬墨西哥粟米薄餅, corn ~ 墨西哥粟米薄餅, ~ shell 墨西哥粟米薄餅皮, ~ chips 墨西哥粟米薄餅薯條)

墨西哥粟米煎餅 [mak9 sai1 go1 suk7 mai5 jin1 beng2] *n.* burrito (bean and cheese ~ 芝士加豆墨西哥粟米煎餅)

墨西哥胡椒 [mak9 sai1 go1 wu4 jiu1] *n.* jalapeno peppers

陌生 [mak9 sang1] *adj.* unfamiliar

陌生人 [mak9 sang1 yan4] *n.* stranger

墨水 [mak9 seui2] *n.* ink

墨魚 [mak9 yu4] *n.* cuttlefish

蚊 [man1] *n.* mosquito

蚊叮 [man1 deng1] *n.* mosquito bite

蚊叮蟲咬 [man1 deng1 chung4 ngaau5] *n.* insect bite

蚊香 [man1 heung1] *n.* mosquito coil

蚊帳 [man1 jeung3] *n.* mosquito net

聞 [man4] *v.* smell (What's that ~? 咩味？)

文化 [man4 fa3] *adj.* cultural

文化 [man4 fa3] *n.* culture

文化復興 [man4 fa3 fuk9 hing1] *n.* (the) Renaissance

文科 [man4 fo1] *n.* liberal arts

民間 [man4 gaan1] *n.* folk

民間藝術 [man4 gaan1 ngai6 seut9] *n.* folk art

文件 [man4 gin2] *n.* document

文學名著 [man4 hok9 ming4 jyu3] *n.* classics

文學 [man4 hok9] *n.* literature

文章 [man4 jeung1] *n.* article

文字 [man4 ji6] *n.* text

文字處理 [man4 ji6 chyu2 lei5] *n.* word processing

文職 [man4 jik7] *n.* office work

民族 [man4 juk9] *n.* nation

民族嘅 [man4 juk9 ge3] *adj.* ethnic

民俗音樂 [man4 juk9 yam1 ngok9] *n.* folk music

民主 [man4 jyu2] *n.* democracy

文萊 [man4 loi4] *n.* Brunei

文盲 [man4 maang4] *n.* illiteracy

文明 [man4 ming4] *adj.* civil

文書 [man4 syu1] *n.* writ

文選 [man4 syun2] *n.* anthology

民意調查 [man4 yi3 tiu4 cha4] *n.* polls

敏感 [man5 gam2] *n.* sensitivity; *adj.* sensitive

問 [man6] *v.* ask (~ a question 問問題, ~ about 關心, ~ for 要)

問候 [man6 hau6] *v.* greet; *n.* greeting

問號 [man6 hou6] *n.* question mark

問題 [man6 tai4] *n.* question

盟友 [mang4 yau5] *n.* ally

乜 [mat7] *pron.* what (~ is that? 乜嘢嚟㗎, ~ time is it? 宜家幾點鐘？)

乜都得 [mat7 dou1 dak7] *det.* whatever

密 [mat9] *adv.* thickly

襪 [mat9] *n.* sock

密度 [mat9 dou6] *n.* density

密封 [mat9 fung1] *v.* seal (to ~ closed 黏好)

蜜蜂 [mat9 fung1] *n.* bee

蜜柑 [mat9 gam1] *n.* mandarin orange

密克羅尼西亞聯邦 [mat9 hak7 lo4 nei4 sai1 a3 lyun4 bong1] *n.* Micronesia, Federated States of

蜜汁 [mat9 jap7] *n.* honeydew

蜜餞 [mat9 jin3] *adj.* candied (~ fruit 蜜餞水果); *n.* preserves (fruit ~ 水果蜜餞)

蜜餞淮山 [mat9 jin3 waai4 saan1] *n.* candied yams

物種 [mat9 jung2] *n.* species

物理 [mat9 lei5] *n.* physics

物理學家 [mat9 lei5 hok9 ga1] *n.* physicist

物理治療 [mat9 lei5 ji6 liu4] *n.* physical therapy

密碼 [mat9 ma5] *n.* password (account ~ 帳戶密碼, login with ~ 登入帳戶)

物體 [mat9 tai2] *n.* object

蜜糖 [mat9 tong4] *n.* honey

蜜柚 [mat9 yau2] *n.* tangelo

蜜月 [mat9 yut9] *n.* honeymoon (on a ~ 度蜜月)

謀殺 [mau4 saat8] *v.* murder; *n.* murder, homicide

某個地方 [mau5 go3 dei6 fong1] *adv.* somewhere

謬論 [mau6 leun6] *n.* fallacy

貿易 [mau6 yik9] *n.* trade (~ union 工會, international ~ 國際貿易, a fair ~ 公平交易)

微波爐 [mei4 bo1 lou4] *n.* microwave

麋鹿 [mei4 luk9] *n.* moose

微妙 [mei4 miu6] *adj.* subtle

微小 [mei4 siu2] *adj.* slight

微型 [mei4 ying4] *n.* miniature

微笑 [mei4 siu3] *v.* smile

鎂 [mei5] *n.* magnesium

尾 [mei5] *n.* tail (ox ~ 牛尾, pig ~ 豬尾)

美德 [mei5 dak7] *n.* virtue

美金 [mei5 gam1] *n.* dollar

美國 [mei5 gwok8] *n.* United States of America (*abbrev.* U.S.A.)

美國西南部印第安人 [mei5 gwok8 sai1 naam4 bou6 yan3 dai6 on1 yan4] *adj.* Southwest American (~ food 美國西南部印地安人菜, ~ spice 美國西南部印地安人香料)

美酒佳餚 [mei5 jau2 gaai1 ngaau4] *n.* ambrosia

美貌 [mei5 maau6] *n.* beauty

美食家 [mei5 sik9 ga1] *n.* epicure

美食節 [mei5 sik9 jit8] *n.* food festival

味 [mei6] *n.* flavor (what ~s do you have? 你點吔咩味)

未啊 [mei6 a1] *adv.* not yet

未定 [mei6 ding6] *adj.* pending

味道 [mei6 dou6] *n.* taste

未發酵 [mei6 faat8 haau1] *adj.* unleavened (~ bread 未發酵麵包)

未婚妻 [mei6 fan1 chai1] *n.* fiancée

未婚夫 [mei6 fan1 fu1] *n.* fiancé

未知 [mei6 ji1] *adj.* unknown

未裝修 [mei6 jong1 sau1] *adj.* unfurnished

魅力 [mei6 lik9] *n.* charm

未來 [mei6 loi4] *n.* future

未成年人 [mei6 sing4 nin4 yan4] *n.* minor

未熟 [mei6 suk9] *adj.* unripe (~ fruit 未熟嘅水果, ~ vegetable 未熟嘅菜)

未熟晒 [mei6 suk9 saai3] *adj.* underdone, rare

名 [meng2] *n.* (first) name (what's your ~? 你叫咩名?, my ~ is 我叫)

命 [meng6] *n.* fate

面 [min2] *n.* face

棉簽 [min4 chim1] *n.* swab

棉花 [min4 fa1] *n.* cotton (~seed oil 棉花籽油, ~ plant 棉花廠)

棉花糖 [min4 fa1 tong2] *n.* marshmallow

綿羊 [min4 yeung2] *n.* sheep (~'s milk cheese 羊奶芝士)

免除 [min5 cheui4] *n.* exemption

緬甸 [min5 din6] *adj.* Myanma (Burmese); *n.* Myanmar (Burma)

免費 [min5 fai3] *n.* free admission; *adj.* free of charge, on the house

勉強 [min5 keung5] *n.* reluctance; *adv.* unwillingly

免稅 [min5 seui3] *adj.* duty-free (~ goods 免稅品, ~ shop 免稅店)

免疫 [min5 yik9] *n.* immunization

免疫系統 [min5 yik9 hai6 tung2] *n.* immune system

免疫力 [min5 yik9 lik9] *n.* immunity

麵 [min6] *n.* noodles

麵包 [min6 baau1] *n.* bread (naan ~ 印度麵包, oat ~ 燕麥麵包, white ~ 白麵包, wheat ~ 小麥麵包, whole wheat ~ 全麥麵包, whole grain ~ 全麥麵包, rye ~ 黑麥麵包, pumpkin ~ 南瓜餅, potato ~ 薯仔餅, banana ~ 香蕉餅, sweet ~ 甜麵包)

麵包車 [min6 baau1 che1] *n.* van

麵包店 [min6 baau1 dim3] *n.* bakery

麵包棍 [min6 baau1 gwan3] *n.* bread stick

麵包皮 [min6 baau1 pei4] *n.* crust (pie ~ 批邊)

麵包糠 [min6 baau1 hong1] *n.* breadcrumbs

麵包師傅 [min6 baau1 si1 fu6] *n.* baker

面部 [min6 bou6] *adj.* facial (~ features 面部特徵); *n.* facial, beauty treatment

面青青 [min6 cheng1 cheng1] *adj.* pale

麵粉 [min6 fan2] *n.* flour

麵筋 [min6 gan1] *n.* gluten (~ free 冇麵筋, ~ extract 麵筋濃縮物)

面具 [min6 geui6] *n.* mask (diving ~ 潛水面罩)

麵棍 [min6 gwan3] *n.* rolling pin

面紅 [min6 hung4] *n.* blush, rouge

面罩 [min6 jaau3] *n.* visor

面積 [min6 jik7] *n.* area

面珠 [min6 jyu1] *n.* cheek

面無表情 [min6 mou4 biu2 ching4] *adv.* blankly

面紗 [min6 sa1] *n.* veil

面相 [min6 seung3] *n.* physiognomy

面試 [min6 si3] *n.* interview

面色 [min6 sik7] *n.* complexion

麵團 [min6 tyun4] *n.* dough (cookie ~ 曲奇麵團)

名詞 [ming4 chi4] *n.* noun

名氣 [ming4 hei3] *n.* popularity

明顯 [ming4 hin2] *adj.* distinct, evident, obvious; *adv.* obviously

明智 [ming4 ji3] *adj.* sensible

名片 [ming4 pin2] *n.* business card

明信片 [ming4 seun3 pin2] *n.* postcard

冥想 [ming4 seung2] *n.* meditation

明斯克 [ming4 si1 hak7] *n.* Minsk (~, capital of Belarus 白俄羅斯嘅首都)

名勝 [ming4 sing3] *n.* point of interest

名人 [ming4 yan4] *n.* notability

名義上 [ming4 yi6 seung6] *adj.* nominal

搣爛 [mit7 laan6] *v.* rip

滅火器 [mit9 fo2 hei3] *n.* fire extinguisher

苗條 [miu2 tiu5] *adj.* slim

描寫 [miu4 se2] *v.* portray

描述 [miu4 seut9] *v.* describe; *n.* description

廟 [miu6] *n.* temple

摩加迪沙 [mo1 ga1 dik9 sa1] *n.* Mogadishu (~, capital of Somalia 索馬里嘅首都)

蘑菇汁 [mo1 gu1 jap7] *n.* mushroom sauce

魔鬼 [mo1 gwai2] *n.* devil

魔蝎座 [mo1 hit8 jo6] *n.* Capricorn

摩洛哥 [mo1 lok8 go1] *n.* Morocco; *adj.* Moroccan

摩納哥 [mo1 naap9 go1] *n.* Monaco (~, capital of Monaco 摩納哥嘅首都)

摩納哥人 [mo1 naap9 go1 yan4] *adj./n.* Monegasque (person from Monaco)

魔術 [mo1 seut9] *n.* magic

魔術師 [mo1 seut9 si1] *n.* magician

摩爾多瓦 [mo1 yi5 do1 nga5] *n.* Moldova

摸 [mo2] *v.* touch (keep in ~ 保持聯繫)

磨 [mo4] *v.* rub

磨咖啡機 [mo4 ga3 fe1 gei1] *n.* coffeemaker

蘑菇 [mo4 gu1] *n.* mushroom

磨難 [mo4 naan6] *n.* ordeal

磨碎 [mo4 seui3] *v.* grind

剝殼 [mok7 hok8] *v.* shell

剝咗皮 [mok7 jo2 pei4] *adj.* skinned (~ meat 去咗皮嘅肉, ~ almonds 去皮杏仁)

剝皮 [mok7 pei4] *v.* peel

剝削 [mok7 seuk8] *n.* exploitation; *v.* exploit

幕布 [mok9 bou3] *n.* theater curtain

莫羅尼 [mok9 lo4 nei4] *n.* Moroni (~, capital of Comoros 科摩羅嘅首都)

莫斯科 [mok9 si1 fo1] *n.* Moscow (~, capital of Russia 俄羅斯嘅首都)

莫桑比克 [mok9 song1 bei2 hak7] *n./adj.* Mozambique

莫爾茲比港 [mok9 yi5 ji1 bei2 gong2] *n.* Port Moresby (~, capital of Papua New Guinea 巴布亞新幾内亞嘅首都)

忙 [mong4] *n.* favor; *adj.* busy

忘記 [mong4 gei3] *v.* forget (don't ~ to 記得, ~ it 算啦)

芒果 [mong4 gwo2] *n.* mango (~ jam 芒果醬, ~ chutney 芒果酸辣醬, ~ pickle 酸芒果, ~ juice 芒果汁)

網 [mong5] *n.* net

網吧 [mong5 ba1] *n.* Internet café

網站 [mong5 jaam6] *n.* website

網站夾書籤 [mong5 jaam6 gaap8 syu1 chim1] *v.* bookmark a website

網址 [mong5 ji2] *n. comp.* URL

網球 [mong5 kau4] *n.* tennis

網球場 [mong5 kau4 cheung4] *n.* tennis court

網絡 [mong5 lok8] *n.* network (computer ~ 電腦網絡, ~ through contacts 關係網絡)

網絡公司 [mong5 lok8 gung1 si1] *n.* dot-com

蟒蛇 [mong5 se4] *n.* python

網上 [mong5 seung6] *adj.* online (to go ~ 上網, search ~ 網上查詢)

網頁 [mong5 yip9] *n.* web page

望一眼 [mong6 yat7 ngaan5] *n.* glimpse

望遠鏡 [mong6 yun5 geng3] *n.* telescope

帽 [mou2] *n.* hat, cap

模 [mou2] *n.* mold (*v.* to ~ 整模)

無情 [mou4 ching4] *adj.* pitiless

無處不在 [mou4 chyu3 bat7 joi6] *n.* omnipresence; *adj.* omnipresent

無花果 [mou4 fa1 gwo2] *n.* fig

模範 [mou4 faan6] *n.* model (*profession / setting an example / a miniature representation*)

模仿 [mou4 fong2] *v.* impersonate; *n.* imitation

無家可歸 [mou4 ga1 ho2 gwai1] *adj.* homeless

無辜 [mou4 gu1] *adj.* innocent

毛骨悚然 [mou4 gwat7 sung2 yin4] *adj.* thrilling

無光飾面 [mou4 gwong1 sik7 min6] *n.* matte finish (*not glossy*)

無限 [mou4 haan6] *adj.* unlimited (~ mileage 冇里程限制)

無效審判 [mou4 haau6 sam2 pun3] *n.* (*legal*) mistrial

毛孔 [mou4 hung2] *n.* pore

無罪釋放 [mou4 jeui6 sik7 fong3] *v.* (*legal*) acquit; *n.* acquittal

毛象 [mou4 jeung6] *n.* mammoth

無知 [mou4 ji1] *n.* ignorance; *adj.* ignorant

無政府主義者 [mou4 jing3 fu2 jyu2 yi6 je2] *n.* anarchist

無賴 [mou4 laai6] *n.* rogue

無禮 [mou4 lai5] *adj.* outrageous

無理 [mou4 lei5] *adj.* unreasonable

毛里裘斯 [mou4 lei5 kau4 si1] *n.* Mauritius

毛利塔尼亞 [mou4 lei6 taap8 nei4 a3] *n.* Mauritania

無聊 [mou4 liu4] *adj.* prosaic

毛皮 [mou4 pei4] *n.* fur

無神論者 [mou4 san4 leun6 je2] *n.* atheist

無實際意義 [mou4 sat9 jai3 yi3 yi6] *adj.* moot

無視 [mou4 si6] *v.* ignore

無線上網 [mou4 sin3 seung5 mong5] *n.* wireless internet

無所不知 [mou4 so2 bat7 ji1] *n.* omniscience; *adj.* omniscient

無糖 [mou4 tong4] *adj.* sugar-free

模糊 [mou4 wu4] *adj.* faint (feel ~ 暈)

無意中聽到 [mou4 yi3 jung1 teng1 dou3] *v.* overhear

模型 [mou4 ying4] *n.* mold

無鉛 [mou4 yun4] *adj.* unleaded, lead-free (~ gasoline 無鉛汽油)

姆巴巴納 [mou5 ba1 ba1 naap9] *n.* Mbabane (~, capital of Swaziland 斯威士蘭嘅首都)

冇必要 [mou5 bit7 yiu3] *adj.* unnecessary

冇察覺到 [mou5 chaat8 gok8 dou3] *adj.* oblivious

冇膽匪類 [mou5 daam2 fei2 leui6] *n.* coward

冇得退 [mou5 dak7 teui3] *adj.* non-returnable

冇到 [mou5 dou3] *n.* absence; *adj.* absent

舞蹈家 [mou5 dou6 ga1] *n.* dancer

冇加甜 [mou5 ga1 tim4] *adj.* unsweetened

冇咖啡因 [mou5 ga3 fe1 yan1] *adj.* caffeine-free

母雞 [mou5 gai1] *n.* hen

冇骨 [mou5 gwat7] *adj.* boneless (~ chicken 去骨雞肉)

武器 [mou5 hei3] *n.* arms, weapon

冇可能 [mou5 ho2 nang4] *adj.* impossible

冇可能接受 [mou5 ho2 nang4 jip8 sau6] *adj.* unacceptable, unbearable

冇害 [mou5 hoi6] *adj.* harmless

冇酒精 [mou5 jau2 jing1] *adj.* non-alcoholic (~ beverage 無酒精飲料, ~ beer 無酒精啤酒)

冇酒精啤酒 [mou5 jau2 jing1 be1 jau2] *n.* non-alcoholic beer

冇酒精飲料 [mou5 jau2 jing1 yam2 liu6] *n.* non-alcoholic beverage

冇精神 [mou5 jing1 san4] *n.* lethargy

冇咗 [mou5 jo2] *prep.* without

武裝嘅 [mou5 jong1 ge3] *adj.* armed

冇其他嘢 [mou5 kei4 ta1 ye5] *pron.* nothing else

冇規律 [mou5 kwai1 leut9] *adj.* irregular

冇禮貌 [mou5 lai5 maau6] *adj.* rude; *adv.* rudely

冇能力 [mou5 nang4 lik9] *n.* inability; *adj.* unable

冇事 [mou5 si6] *adj.* all right

母性 [mou5 sing3] *n.* motherhood

冇所謂 [mou5 so2 wai6] *adv.* not at all

舞廳 [mou5 teng1] *n.* discotheque, disco

舞台 [mou5 toi4] *n.* stage

舞台造型 [mou5 toi4 jou6 ying4] *n.* tableau

冇人 [mou5 yan4] *pron.* no one; *n.* no one, nobody

冇一個 [mou5 yat7 go3] *det.* neither

冇油 [mou5 yau4] *v.* run out of fuel

冇嘢 [mou5 ye5] *pron.* nothing

冇嘢做嘅 [mou5 ye5 jou6 ge3] *adj.* idle

冇嘢啦 [mou5 ye2 la1] *conj.* never mind

冇意識 [mou5 yi3 sik7] *n.* oblivion

侮辱 [mou5 yuk9] *v.* insult; *n.* humiliation

冇用 [mou5 yung6] *adj.* useless

霧 [mou6] *n.* fog

墓碑 [mou6 bei1] *n.* gravestone

霧燈 [mou6 dang1] *n.* fog light

冒險 [mou6 him2] *n.* venture

務實 [mou6 sat9] *adj.* pragmatic

慕絲 [mou6 si1] *n.* mousse (chocolate ~ 朱古力慕絲)

莓 [mui4] *n.* berry

玫瑰 [mui4 gwai3] *n.* rose

梅萊凱奧克 [mui4 loi4 hoi2 ngou3 hak7] *n.* Melekeok (~, capital of Palau 帕勞群島嘅首都)

媒體 [mui4 tai2] *n.* media

煤油 [mui4 yau4] *n.* kerosene

煤油爐 [mui4 yau4 lou4] *n.* kerosene stove

每場 [mui5 cheung4] *adv.* per round

每個 [mui5 go3] *det.* each

每個鐘 [mui5 go3 jung1] *n.* every hour

每個月 [mui5 go3 yut9] *adj.* monthly

每公升嘅價錢 [mui5 gung1 sing1 ge3 ga3 chin4] *n.* price per liter

每年 [mui5 nin4] *n.* every year

每日 [mui5 yat9] *adv.* per day; *n.* every day

木 [muk9] *n.* wood (~ carving 木雕刻)

木板 [muk9 baan2] *n.* plank

目標 [muk9 biu1] *n.* goal (*objective/sports*)

牧場 [muk9 cheung4] *n.* pasture

目的 [muk9 dik7] *n.* purpose (~ of visit 訪問嘅目的)

目的地 [muk9 dik7 dei6] *n.* destination

木羹 [muk9 gang1] *n.* wooden spoon

木瓜 [muk9 gwa1] *n.* papaya

木製 [muk9 jai3] *adj.* wooden

目錄 [muk9 luk9] *n.* catalog

木乃伊 [muk9 naai5 yi1] *n.* mummy

木偶 [muk9 ngau5] *n.* puppet

木偶表演 [muk9 ngau5 biu2 yin2] *n.* puppet show

木塞 [muk9 sak7] *n.* cork

牧師 [muk9 si1] *n.* preacher

苜蓿芽 [muk9 suk7 nga4] *n.* alfalfa sprouts

木薯 [muk9 syu4] *n.* cassava

木炭 [muk9 taan3] *n.* charcoal (~ grilled 炭燒)

牧羊人批 [muk9 yeung4 yan4 pai1] *n.* shepherd's pie

門 [mun4] *n.* gate (*fence/airport*)

門診部 [mun4 chan2 bou6] *n.* out-patient department

門口 [mun4 hau2] *n.* doorway

門鈴 [mun4 ling4] *n.* night bell

門廊 [mun4 long4] *n.* porch

滿 [mun5] *adj.* full (be ~ 食飽, ~ flavor 味道十足, ~ amount 足量)

滿意 [mun5 yi3] *n.* satisfaction

滿意 [mun5 yi3] *adj.* satisfied (I'm not ~ with this 我唔滿意)

燜 [mun6] *v.* braised (~ pork 燜豬肉)

燜雞 [mun6 gai1] *n.* stewing fowl

悶悶不樂 [mun6 mun6 bat7 lok9] *v.* mope

蒙得維的亞 [mung4 dak7 wai4 dik7 a3] *n.* Montevideo (~, capital of Uruguay 烏拉圭嘅首都)

蒙特內格羅 [mung4 dak9 noi6 gaak8 lo4] *n.* Montenegro

檬鰈 [mung4 dip9] *n.* lemon sole

蒙古 [mung4 gu2] *n.* Mongolia; *adj.* Mongolian

蒙羅維亞 [mung4 lo4 wai4 a3] *n.* Monrovia (~, capital of Liberia 利比亞嘅首都)

夢 [mung6] *n.* dream

茉莉 [mut9 lei6] *n.* jasmine (~ tea 茉莉花茶, ~ flower 茉莉花, ~ extract 茉莉花濃縮)

抹片試驗 [mut9 pin2 si3 yim6] *n.* pap smear

沒收 [mut9 sau1] *n.* seizure

沒藥 [mut9 yeuk9] *n.* myrrh

N

拿騷 [na4 sou1] *n.* Nassau (~, capital of The Bahamas 巴哈馬嘅首都)

奶嘴 [naai5 jeui2] *n.* pacifier

奶樽 [naai5 jeun1] *n.* feeding bottle

奶類製品 [naai5 leui6 jai3 ban2] *n.* dairy (~ product 奶製品, ~ cream 牛奶忌廉, non-~ 不含乳製品)

奶昔 [naai5 sik7] *n.* milkshake (strawberry ~ 士多啤梨奶昔, chocolate ~ 朱古力奶昔, vanilla ~ 雲呢拿奶昔)

男僕人 [naam4 buk9 yan4] *n.* valet (~ service 男僕人服伺)

男廁 [naam4 chi3] *n.* men's restroom/toilet

南非 [naam4 fei1] *n.* South Africa; *adj.* South African

男夥計 [naam4 fo2 gai3] *n.* clerk, waiter

南方 [naam4 fong1] *adj.* southern

南極 [naam4 gik9] *n.* South Pole

南瓜 [naam4 gwa1] *n.* pumpkin (~ pie 南瓜批, ~ bread 南瓜餅, ~ seeds 南瓜籽)

南韓 [naam4 hon4] *n.* South Korea

男仔 [naam4 jai2] *n.* boy

男子漢 [naam4 ji2 hon3] *adj.* masculine

男裝 [naam4 jong1] *n.* menswear

南美 [naam4 mei5] *adj.* South American (~ food 南美菜)

南面 [naam4 min6] *n.* south

男朋友 [naam4 pang4 yau5] *n.* boyfriend

男性 [naam4 sing3] *adj.* male

南蘇丹 [naam4 sou1 daan1] *n.* South Sudan

男人 [naam4 yan2] *n.* man

難 [naan4] *adj.* difficult

難過 [naan4 gwo3] *n.* sadness; *adj.* sad; *adv.* sadly

難民 [naan6 man4] *n.* refugee

鈉 [naap9] *n.* sodium

納米比亞 [naap9 mai5 bei2 a3] *n.* Namibia; *adj.* Namibian

納稅人 [naap9 seui3 yan4] *n.* taxpayer

燶親 [naat8 chan1] *v.* scald

鬧鐘 [naau6 jung1] *n.* alarm (~ clock 鬧鐘, fire ~ 火警鐘)

鬧市 [naau6 si5] *adv.* downtown

泥 [nai4] *n.* soil

諗 [nam2] *v.* think, think about

諗番 [nam2 faan1] *v.* retrospect

諗法 [nam2 faat8] *n.* concept

能力 [nang4 lik9] *n.* ability

嬲 [nau1] *adj.* angry

扭 [nau2] *v.* twist (~ an ankle 扭傷腳)

鈕 [nau2] *n.* button

扭開 [nau2 hoi1] *v.* unscrew

扭傷 [nau2 seung1] *n.* sprain

扭傷咗 [nau2 seung1 jo2] *adj.* sprained (~ ankle 扭傷腳)

尼亞美 [nei4 a3 mei5] *n.* Niamey (~, capital of Niger 尼日爾嘅首都)

尼泊爾 [nei4 bok9 yi5] *n.* Nepal; *adj.* Nepali

尼科西亞 [nei4 fo1 sai1 a3] *n.* Nicosia (~, capital of Cyprus 塞浦路斯嘅首都)

尼加拉瓜 [nei4 ga1 laai1 gwa1] *n.* Nicaragua; *adj.* Nicaraguan

尼姑庵 [nei4 gu1 am1] *n.* nunnery

尼古丁 [nei4 gu2 ding1] *n.* nicotine

尼龍 [nei4 lung4] *adj.* nylon

尼日利亞 [nei4 yat9 lei6 a3] *n.* Nigeria; *adj.* Nigerian

尼日爾 [nei4 yat9 yi5] *n.* Niger

你 [nei5] *pron.* you (*sing./pl.*)

你嘅 [nei5 ge3] *pron.* yours (~ truly 僅致問候, Is this ~? 係唔係真架)

你自己 [nei5 ji6 gei2] *pron.* yourself

女 [neui5] *n.* daughter

女廁 [neui5 chi3] *n.* ladies'/women's restroom/toilet

女夥計 [neui5 fo2 gai3] *n.* waitress

女仔 [neui5 jai2] *n.* girl

女裝 [neui5 jong1] *n.* ladieswear, women's clothing

女權主義 [neui5 kyun4 jyu2 yi6] *n.* feminism

女權主義者 [neui5 kyun4 jyu2 yi6 je2] *n.* feminist

女朋友 [neui5 pang4 yau5] *n.* girlfriend

女士 [neui5 si6] *n.* madam, lady

女性 [neui5 sing3] *adj.* female, feminine

女同性戀 [neui5 tung4 sing3 lyun2] *adj.* lesbian

女護士長 [neui5 wu6 si6 jeung2] *n.* matron

女人 [neui5 yan2] *n.* women

娘家姓 [neung4 ga1 sing3] *n.* maiden name

五 [ng5] *num.* five

午餐肉 [ng5 chaan1 yuk9] *n.* lunchmeat

五花八門 [ng5 fa1 baat8 mun4] *adj.* assorted (~ cheeses 雜芝士, ~ flavors 雜味, ~ vegetables 雜菜, ~ meats 雜肉)

午飯 [ng5 faan6] *n.* lunch

五金鋪 [ng5 gam1 pou2] *n.* hardware store

五角大樓 [ng5 gok8 daai6 lau4] *n.* pentagon

午安 [ng5 on1] *phr.* good afternoon

五十 [ng5 sap9] *num.* fifty

午夜 [ng5 ye6] *n.* midnight

五月 [ng5 yut9] *n.* May

誤差範圍 [ng6 cha1 faan6 wai4] *n.* margin of error

誤解 [ng6 gaai2] *n.* misconception

牙 [nga4] *n.* tooth

牙刷 [nga4 chaat8] *n.* toothbrush

牙籤 [nga4 chim1] *n.* toothpick

牙科 [nga4 fo1] *n.* dental

牙甘藍 [nga4 gam1 laam4] *n.* Brussels sprouts

牙膏 [nga4 gou1] *n.* toothpaste

牙箍 [nga4 ku1] *n.* braces

牙買加 [nga4 maai5 ga1] *n.* Jamaica; *adj.* Jamaican

牙買加丑橘 [nga4 maai5 ga1 chau2 gwat7] *n.* ugli fruit

牙線 [nga4 sin3] *n.* dental floss

牙痛 [nga4 tung3] *n.* toothache

牙醫 [nga4 yi1] *n.* dentist

牙醫助手 [nga4 yi1 jo6 sau2] *n.* hygienist

雅典 [nga5 din2] *n.* Athens (~, capital of Greece 希臘嘅首都)

瓦杜茲 [nga5 dou6 ji1] *n.* Vaduz (~, capital of Liechtenstein 列支敦士登嘅首都)

雅加達 [nga5 ga1 daat9] *n.* Jakarta (~, capital of Indonesia 印度尼西亞嘅首都)

瓦加杜古 [nga5 ga1 dou6 gu2] *n.* Ouagadougou (~, capital of Burkina Faso 布基納發索嘅首都)

瓦萊塔 [nga5 loi4 taap8] *n.* Valletta (~, capital of Malta 馬耳他嘅首都)

瓦努阿圖 [nga5 nou5 a3 tou4] *n.* Vanuatu

雅溫得 [nga5 wan1 dak7] *n.* Yaounde (~, capital of Cameroon 喀麥隆嘅首都)

艾草 [ngaai6 chou2] *n.* wormwood

呃 [ngaak7] *v.* cheat

呃人嘅 [ngaak7 yan4 ge3] *adj.* fraudulent

額外 [ngaak9 ngoi6] *adj.* extra, additional

額頭 [ngaak9 tau4] *n.* forehead

啱 [ngaam1] *adj.* correct; *adv.* correctly

啱啱好 [ngaam1 ngaam1 hou2] *v.* happen to (do)

啱身嘅 [ngaam1 san1 ge3] *adj.* shaped

癌症 [ngaam4 jing3] *n.* cancer

岩石 [ngaam4 sek9] *n.* rock

(*geological/musical*) (~ band 搖滾樂團, ~ and roll 搖滾, ~ climbing 攀岩)

晏晝 [ngaan3 jau3] *n.* afternoon (in the ~ 喺下晝, this ~ 今日下午)

顏料 [ngaan4 liu6] *n.* paint

顏色 [ngaan4 sik7] *n.* color

眼 [ngaan5] *n.* eye (~ test 視力測試)

眼瞓 [ngaan5 fan3] *adj.* sleepy

眼科醫生 [ngaan5 fo1 yi1 sang1] *n.* opthalmologist

眼甘甘 [ngaan5 gam1 gam1] *v.* ogle

眼嘅 [ngaan5 ge3] *adj.* ocular

眼鏡 [ngaan5 geng3] *n.* eyeglasses

眼鏡店 [ngaan5 geng3 dim3] *n.* optician

眼光 [ngaan5 gwong1] *n.* insight

眼睫毛 [ngaan5 jit9 mou4] *n.* eyelash

眼球 [ngaan5 kau4] *n.* eyeball

眼淚 [ngaan5 leui6] *n.* tear (*weeping/rip*)

贋品 [ngaan6 ban2] *n.* forgery

硬 [ngaang6] *adj.* hard (*firm/difficult*)

硬化 [ngaang6 fa3] *v.* ossify

硬頸 [ngaang6 geng2] *n.* obstinacy; *adj.* headstrong; *adv.* stiffly

押後 [ngaap8 hau6] *v.* postpone; *n.* postponement

咬 [ngaau5] *v.* bite

危地馬拉 [ngai4 dei6 ma5 laai1] *n.* Guatemala; *adj.* Guatemalan

危地馬拉城 [ngai4 dei6 ma5 laai1 sing4] *n.* Guatemala City

(~, capital of Guatemala 危地
馬拉首都)

危機 [ngai4 gei1] *n.* crisis

危險 [ngai4 him2] *n.* danger; *adj.*
dangerous

偽證 [ngai6 jing3] *n.* perjury

偽造 [ngai6 jou6] *v.* fabricate

毅力 [ngai6 lik9] *n.* persistence

藝術 [ngai6 seut9] *n.* art (~ gallery
畫廊); *adj.* artistic

藝術品 [ngai6 seut9 ban2] *n.*
fine arts

藝術家 [ngai6 seut9 ga1] *n.* artist

藝術作品 [ngai6 seut9 jok8
ban2] *n.* artwork

藝人 [ngai6 yan4] *n.* entertainer

銀 [ngan4] *n.* silver (~plate 銀碟,
~ware 銀器)

銀包 [ngan4 baau1] *n.* purse

銀仔 [ngan4 jai2] *n.* coin (~
collection 集幣)

銀杏樹 [ngan4 hang6 syu6]
n. ginkgo (~ bilobo 銀杏, ~
powder 銀杏粉, ~ seeds 銀
杏籽)

銀河系 [ngan4 ho4 hai6] *n.*
galaxy

銀行 [ngan4 hong4] *n.* bank (~
card 銀行卡, ~ charges 銀行
收費)

銀行家 [ngan4 hong4 ga1] *n.*
banker

銀行戶口 [ngan4 hong4 wu6
hau2] *n.* bank account

銀魚 [ngan4 yu4] *n.* whitebait fish

鉤 [ngau1] *n.* hook

勾引 [ngau1 yan5] *v.* allure

嘔吐物 [ngau2 tou3 mat9] *n.* vomit

牛 [ngau4] *n.* cow

牛百葉 [ngau4 baak8 yip9] *n.*
tripe

牛肩扒 [ngau4 gin1 pa2] *n.*
chuck steak

牛後髀肉扒 [ngau4 hau6 bei2
yuk9 pa2] *n.* rumpsteak

牛後腹牛扒 [ngau4 hau6 fuk7
ngau4 pa4] *n.* flank steak

牛仔布 [ngau4 jai2 bou3] *n.*
denim

牛仔褲 [ngau4 jai2 fu3] *n.* jeans

牛仔肉 [ngau4 jai2 yuk9] *n.* veal
(~ stew 燉牛仔肉)

牛至 [ngau4 ji3] *n.* oregano

牛尾 [ngau4 mei5] *n.* oxtail

牛尾湯 [ngau4 mei5 tong1] *n.*
oxtail soup

牛奶 [ngau4 naai5] *n.* milk (~
subsitute 牛奶替代品, nonfat
~ 脫脂牛奶, skim ~ 低脂牛
奶, whole ~ 全脂牛奶, soy ~
豆漿, chocolate ~ 朱古力奶,
light ~ 淡奶, vanilla ~ 雲呢拿
味奶)

牛奶點心 [ngau4 naai5 dim2
sam1] *n.* milk bar

牛奶忌廉 [ngau4 naai5 gei6
lim4] *n.* dairy cream

牛扒 [ngau4 pa2] *n.* steak (T'bone
~ 丁骨牛扒, ~ tartare 生肉糕)

牛扒海鮮套餐 [ngau4 pa2 hoi2
sin1 tou3 chaan1] *n.* surf and
turf

牛皮菜 [ngau4 pei4 choi3] *n.*
Swiss chard

牛肚 [ngau4 tou5] *n.* tripe (cow
stomach)

牛油 [ngau4 yau4] *n.* butter (cocoa ~ 可可牛油, apple ~ 蘋果牛油, peanut ~ 花生醬)

牛油果 [ngau4 yau4 gwo2] *n.* avocado

牛油糖果 [ngau4 yau4 tong4 gwo2] *n.* butterscotch

牛肉 [ngau4 yuk9] *n.* beef (~ tongue 牛脷, ~ meatball 牛肉丸, ~ stock 牛肉湯, ~ burger 牛肉漢堡包, ~ stew 燉牛肉, ~ marrow 牛骨髓, ~ stomach 牛肚, ~ chuck 牛肉)

牛肉乾 [ngau4 yuk9 gon1] *n.* beef jerky

牛肉漢堡包 [ngau4 yuk9 hon3 bou2 baau1] *n.* hamburger steak

偶然 [ngau5 yin4] *adj.* accidental; *adv.* accidentally

鵝 [ngo2] *n.* goose

哦 [ngo4] *v.* prattle

鵝肝 [ngo4 gon1] *n.* goose liver paté

鵝肝醬 [ngo4 gon1 jeung3] *n.* foie gras

鵝卵石 [ngo4 leun2 sek9] *n.* pebble

俄羅斯 [ngo4 lo4 si1] *n.* Russia; *adj.* Russian

俄羅斯聯邦 [ngo4 lo4 si1 lyun4 bong1] *n.* Russian Federation

我 [ngo5] *pron.* I, me

我哋 [ngo5 dei6] *pron.* we, us

我哋嘅 [ngo5 dei6 ge3] *adj.* our, ours

我哋自己 [ngo5 dei6 ji6 gei2] *pron.* ourselves

我嘅 [ngo5 ge3] my, mine (that's ~ 我嘎)

我自己 [ngo5 ji6 gei2] *pron.* myself (I'll do it ~ 我自己嚟啦)

臥鋪 [ngo6 pou1] *n.* sleeper

外幣 [ngoi6 bai6] *n.* foreign currency

外科醫生 [ngoi6 fo1 yi1 sang1] *n.* surgeon

外父 [ngoi6 fu2] *n.* father-in-law

外交官 [ngoi6 gaau1 gun1] *n.* diplomat

外國 [ngoi6 gwok8] *adj.* foreign

外國人 [ngoi6 gwok8 yan4] *n.* foreigner

外向 [ngoi6 heung3] *adj.* outgoing

外來 [ngoi6 loi4] *adj.* exotic

外賣 [ngoi6 maai6] *n.* take-out food (Chinese ~ 中餐外賣)

外面 [ngoi6 min6] *n.* outside; *adj.* outer, external

外母 [ngoi6 mou5] *n.* mother-in-law

外門 [ngoi6 mun4] *n.* outer door

外匯兌換處 [ngoi6 wui6 deui6 wun6 chyu3] *n.* currency exchange office

外匯局 [ngoi6 wui6 guk9] *n.* exchange office

外形 [ngoi6 ying4] *n.* form

外語 [ngoi6 yu5] *n.* foreign languages

外遇 [ngoi6 yu6] *n.* affair

樂隊 [ngok9 deui6] *n.* band (*musical*)

樂器 [ngok9 hei3] *n.* musical instrument

鱷梨醬 [ngok9 lei4 jeung3] *n.* guacamole

昂菜 [ngong4 choi3] *n.* watercress (~ soup 昂菜湯)

奧地利 [ngou3 dei6 lei6] *n.* Austria; *adj.* Austrian

澳洲 [ngou3 jau1] *n.* Australia; *adj.* Australian

奧斯陸 [ngou3 si1 luk9] *n.* Oslo (~, capital of Norway 挪威嘅首都)

奧運會 [ngou3 wan6 wui5] *n.* Olympic Games

屋企 [uk7 kei2] *n.* home (at ~ 喺屋企, go ~ 返屋企)

呢啲 [ni1 di1] *adj./pron.* these

呢度 [ni1 dou6] *adv.* here

呢個 [ni1 go3] *adj.* this (~ afternoon 今日晏晝, ~ one 呢個, ~ is impossible! 冇可能, ~ time 呢次, I want ~ 我想要呢個)

匿埋 [nik7 maai4] *v.* hide

匿名 [nik7 ming4] *n.* anonymity; *adj.* anonymous

黏土 [nim1 tou2] *n.* clay

黏液 [nim1 yik9] *n.* mucus

年 [nin4] *n* year (Happy New ~! 新年快樂!, this ~ 今年, twenty-seven ~s old 廿七歲)

年紀 [nin4 gei2] *n.* age

年輕人 [nin4 heng1 yan4] *n.* lad

年長嘅 [nin4 jeung2 ge3] *adj.* senior (~ citizen 長者, ~ discount 長者折扣)

年級 [nin4 kap7] *n.* grade

年年 [nin4 nin4] *adj.* annual; *adv.* annually

檸檬 [ning4 mung4] *n.* lemon (~grass 檸檬草, ~ extract 檸檬濃縮, ~ blossom 檸檬花, ~ peel 檸檬皮, ~ zest 檸檬香味)

檸檬水 [ning4 mung4 seui2] *n.* lemonade

鳥結糖 [niu5 git8 tong4] *n.* nougat

尿 [niu6] *n.* urine

尿片 [niu6 pin2] *n.* diaper (~ rash 尿布疹, change a ~ 換尿片)

挪威 [no4 wai1] *n.* Norway; *adj.* Norwegian

內比都 [noi6 bei2 dou1] *n.* Naypyidaw (*also* Nay Pyi Taw) (~, administrative capital of Myanmar [Burma])

內部 [noi6 bou6] *n.* interior; *adj.* internal

奈洛比 [noi6 lok8 bei2] *n.* Nairobi (~, capital of Kenya 肯雅嘅首都)

耐性 [noi6 sing3] *n.* patience (have ~ 有耐性)

內胎 [noi6 tai1] *n.* inner tube

內容 [noi6 yung4] *n.* content (dietary ~ 飲食結構, protein ~ 蛋白質含量, fat ~ 脂肪含量, fiber ~ 纖維含量, sugar ~ 糖含量)

囊腫 [nong4 jung2] *n.* cyst

腦 [nou5] *n.* brain

努庫阿洛法 [nou5 fu3 a3 lok8 faat8] *n.* Nuku'alofa (~, capital of Tonga 湯加嘅首都)

腦震盪 [nou5 jan3 dong6] *n.* concussion (he has a ~ 佢有腦震盪)

努力 [nou5 lik9] *v.* struggle; *n.* effort, struggle

瑙魯島 [nou5 lou5 dou2] *n.* Nauru

腦膜炎 [nou5 mok9 yim4] *n.* meningitis

努瓦克肖特 [nou5 nga5 hak7 chiu3 dak9] *n.* Nouakchott (~, capital of Mauritania 毛利塔尼亞嘅首都)

農產品市場 [nung4 chaan2 ban2 si5 cheung4] *n.* produce market

農場 [nung4 cheung4] *n.* farm

農場大嘅 [nung4 cheung4 daai6 ge3] *adj.* farm-grown

農村 [nung4 chyun1] *adj.* rural

農學 [nung4 hok9] *n.* agronomy

農作物 [nung4 jok8 mat9] *n.* crop

膿腫 [nung4 jung2] *n.* abscess

農民 [nung4 man4] *n.* farmer

濃味魚肉湯 [nung4 mei6 yu4 yuk9 tong1] *n.* bouillabaisse

濃縮 [nung4 suk7] *n.* concentrate (juice ~ 濃縮果汁, fruit ~ 濃縮果汁)

濃縮 [nung4 suk7] *adj.* condensed (~ milk 煉奶, ~ juice 濃縮果汁, ~ soup 濃湯)

濃縮咖啡 [nung4 suk7 ga3 fe1] *n.* espresso

濃縮果汁 [nung4 suk7 gwo2 jap7] *n.* squash (vegetable) (summer ~ 西葫蘆)

濃湯 [nung4 tong1] *n.* puree (pea ~ 青豆濃湯, corn ~ 粟米濃湯)

濃豌豆湯 [nung4 wun2 dau6 tong1] *n.* pea soup (split ~ with ham 濃火腿豌豆湯)

農藥 [nung4 yeuk9] *n.* pesticide

農業 [nung4 yip9] *n.* agriculture; *adj.* agricultural

暖 [nyun5] *adj.* warm (~ weather 溫暖氣候, It's too ~ in here 尼度太熱啦)

暖啲 [nyun5 di1] *adj.* warmer

暖氣 [nyun5 hei3] *n.* heating

暖氣裝置 [nyun5 hei3 jong1 ji3] *n.* radiator (*in a car/room*)

暖爐 [nyun5 lou4] *n.* heater

O

噢 [o1] *exclam.* oh!

哀悼 [oi1 dou6] *v.* mourn; *n.* condolence

哀悼者 [oi1 dou6 je2] *n.* mourner

埃及 [oi1 kap9] *n.* Egypt; *adj.* Egyptian

哀嘆 [oi1 taan3] *v.* lament; *n.* lamentation

愛 [oi3] *n.* love

愛情小說 [oi3 ching4 siu2 syut8] *n.* romance

愛國 [oi3 gwok8] *n.* patriotic

愛國者 [oi3 gwok8 je2] *n.* patriot

愛國主義 [oi3 gwok8 jyu2 yi6] *n.* patriotism

愛好 [oi3 hou3] *n.* hobby

愛滋病 [oi3 ji1 beng6] *n.* AIDS

愛滋病病毒 [oi3 ji1 beng6 beng6 duk9] *n.* HIV

愛沙尼亞 [oi3 sa1 nei4 a3] *n.* Estonia; *adj.* Estonian

愛人 [oi3 yan4] *n.* lover

愛爾蘭 [oi3 yi5 laan4] *n.* Ireland

愛爾蘭人 [oi3 yi5 laan4 yan4] *n.* Irish

惡 [ok8] *adj.* unkind

惡搞 [ok8 gaau2] *n.* parody

惡夢 [ok8 mung6] *n.* nightmare

惡死 [ok8 sei2] *adj.* aggressive

惡性腫瘤 [ok8 sing3 jung2 lau4] *n.* malignant tumor

惡意 [ok8 yi3] *n.* malice

安全 [on1 cyun4] *n.* safety; *adj.* secure

安全帶 [on1 cyun4 daai2] *n.* seat belt

安全嘅 [on1 cyun4 ge3] *adj.* safe (~ sex 安全性交, feel ~ 覺得安全)

安多拉 [on1 do1 laai1] *n.* Andorra

安多拉城 [on1 do1 laai1 sing4] *n.* Andorra la Vella (~, capital of Andorra 安多拉嘅首都)

安撫 [on1 fu2] *v.* soothe

氨基酸 [on1 gei1 syun1] *n.* amino acids

安哥拉 [on1 go1 laai1] *n.* Angola

安康魚 [on1 hong1 yu2] *n.* angler (fisherman)

安靜 [on1 jing6] *adv.* quietly

安靜嘅 [on1 jing6 ge3] *adj.* quiet

安裝 [on1 jong1] *v.* install; *n.* installation

安卡拉 [on1 ka2 laai1] *n.* Ankara (~, capital of Turkey 土耳其嘅首都)

安曼 [on1 maan6] *n.* Amman (~, capital of Jordan 約旦嘅首都)

安眠藥 [on1 min4 yeuk9] *n.* sleeping pills

按摩師 [on1 mo1 si1] *n.* chiropractor

安排 [on1 paai4] *v.* arrange; *n.* arrangement

安培 [on1 pui4] *n.* amperes, amps

安心 [on1 sam1] *n.* relief

安士 [on1 si2] *n.* ounce

安息日 [on1 sik7 yat9] *n.* Sabbath

安提瓜同巴布達 [on1 tai4 gwa1 tung4 ba1 bou3 daat9] *n.* Antigua and Barbuda

安慰劑 [on1 wai3 jai1] *n.* placebo

按揭 [on3 kit8] *n.* mortgage
按摩 [on3 mo1] *n.* massage
按摩師 [on3 mo1 si1] *n.* masseur
按順序 [on3 seun6 jeui6] *adj.*
  sequential, linear
按回車鍵 [on3 wui4 che1 gin6] *v.*
  hit enter [key] (*on a computer*)

P

趴低 [pa1 dai1] v. prostrate

怕醜 [pa3 chau2] adj. shy

爬 [pa4] n. climb

爬蟲類動物 [pa4 chung4 leui6 dung6 mat9] n. reptile

爬山 [pa4 saan1] n. mountain climbing

爬山單車 [pa4 saan1 daan1 che1] n. mountain bike

牌 [paai4] n. tablet

排 [paai4] n. platoon

排除 [paai4 cheui4] v. exclude; prep. excluding

排出嘅野 [paai4 cheut7 ge3 ye5] n. discharge

排隊 [paai4 deui6] v. stand in line

排放 [paai4 fong3] n. emission

排骨 [paai4 gwat7] n. spareribs

排氣管 [paai4 hei3 gun2] n. exhaust pipe

排字母 [paai4 ji6 mou5] adj. alphabetical; adv. alphabetically

排球 [paai4 kau4] n. volleyball

排列 [paai4 lit9] n. permutation

排舞 [paai4 mou5] n. choreography

排舞師 [paai4 mou5 si1] n. choreographer

排水 [paai4 seui2] v. drain

泊車 [paak8 che1] n. parking (~ fines/ticket 停車罰單, ~ lot 停車場, ~ space 車位)

拍檔 [paak8 dong3] n. partner

帕拉馬里博 [paak8 laai1 ma5 lei5 bok8] n. Paramaribo (~, capital of Suriname 蘇里南嘅首都)

柏拉圖式 [paak8 laai1 tou4 sik7] adj. platonic

柏林 [paak8 lam4] n. Berlin (~, capital of Germany 德國嘅首都)

帕利基爾 [paak8 lei6 gei1 yi5] n. Palikir (~, capital of Micronesia 密克羅尼西亞聯邦首都)

帕勞群島 [paak8 lou6 kwan4 dou2] n. Palau

拍賣 [paak8 maai6] n. auction

盼著 [paan3 jyu3] v. look forward to

烹調 [paang1 diu6] n. gastronomy

烹飪 [paang1 yam6] n. culinary

棚 [paang4] n. hut

膨脹 [paang4 jeung3] n. expansion

棒球 [paang5 kau4] n. baseball

棒球棒 [paang5 kau4 paang5] n. baseball pitcher

泡芙 [paau1 fu4] n. profiteroles

拋光 [paau1 gwong1] n. glossy finish photos

拋棄咗 [paau1 hei3 jo2] adj. deserted

拋射物 [paau1 se6 mat9] n. projectile

跑 [paau2] v. run (in sports / operate something)

跑步 [paau2 bou6] n. running (~ shoes 跑鞋, ~ water 自來水)

跑步嘅人 [paau2 bou6 ge3 yan4] n. runner

跑道 [paau2 dou6] n. track (for running)

跑馬 [paau2 ma5] n. horse racing

豹 [paau3] *n.* leopard

刨木 [paau4 muk9] *v.* polish wood

刨絲器 [paau4 si1 hei4] *n.* grater (cheese ~ 芝士刨絲器)

批 [pai1] *n.* strudel, pie (apple ~ 蘋果批, blueberry ~ 藍莓批, cherry ~ 車厘子批)

批發 [pai1 faat8] *n.* wholesale

批發商 [pai1 faat8 seung1] *n.* distributor

批准 [pai1 jeun2] *v.* approve (of); *n.* permission, approval

批准嘅 [pai1 jeun2 ge3] *adj.* allowed (be ~ to ... 批准做..., not ~ to ... 唔批准做...)

批評 [pai1 ping4] *v.* criticize; *n.* criticism

批評家 [pai1 ping4 ga1] *n.* critic (film ~ 影評家, literary ~ 文學評論家)

噴髮膠 [pan3 faat8 gaau1] *n.* hair spray

噴霧 [pan3 mou6] *n.* spray

噴水池 [pan3 seui2 chi4] *n.* fountain

頻繁 [pan4 faan4] *adj.* frequent; *adv.* frequently

貧乏 [pan4 fat9] *adj.* meager

貧血 [pan4 hyut8] *n.* anemia; *adj.* anemic

貧困 [pan4 kwan3] *n.* privation

瀕臨滅絕物種 [pan4 lam4 mit9 jyut9 mat9 jung2] *n.* endangered species (~ list 瀕臨滅絕物種列表, ~ rank 瀕臨滅絕物種種類)

頻率 [pan4 leut9] *n.* frequency

朋友 [pang4 yau5] *n.* friend (*f./m.*)

匹配 [pat7 pui3] *adj.* matching

皮 [pei4] *n.* peel (orange ~ 橙皮)

皮褸 [pei1 lau1] *n.* jacket

披露 [pei1 lou6] *v.* disclose; *n.* disclosure

砒霜 [pei1 seung1] *n.* arsenic

屁股 [pei3 gu2] *n.* hip

譬如 [pei3 yu4] *adv.* for instance

皮 [pei4] *n.* leather

皮帶 [pei4 daai3] *n.* belt (below the ~ 肚臍下, Bible ~ 聖經地帶)

皮膚 [pei4 fu1] *n.* skin

皮革製品 [pei4 gaak8 jai3 ban2] *n.* leather goods

皮疹 [pei4 jan2] *n.* rash

脾臟 [pei4 jong6] *n.* spleen

枇杷 [pei4 pa4] *n.* loquat

平 [peng4] *adj.* cheap; *adv.* cheaply

編輯 [pin1 chap7] *v.* edit; *n.* editor

偏見 [pin1 gin3] *n.* bias

偏愛 [pin1 oi3] *n.* preference

偏袒 [pin1 taan2] *adv.* partially

偏頭痛 [pin1 tau4 tung3] *n.* migraine

騙子 [pin3 ji2] *n.* impostor

拼寫 [ping1 se2] *n.* spelling

屏幕 [ping2 mok9] *n.* screen (~ door 紗門, computer ~ 電腦屏幕)

瓶 [ping4] *n.* bottle (~ opener 開瓶器, ~ of sth. 一瓶)

平 [ping4] *adj.* flat (~ tire 爆胎)

平底鑊 [ping4 dai2 wok9] *n.* pan

平等 [ping4 dang2] *n.* equality; *adv.* equally

平方 [ping4 fong1] *v.* square

平房 [ping4 fong4] *n.* one-story house

評估 [ping4 gu2] *v.* appraise; *n.* appraisal

蘋果 [ping4 gwo2] *n.* apple (~ juice 蘋果汁, ~ tart 蘋果撻, ~sauce 蘋果醬, ~ pie 蘋果批, ~ brandy 蘋果白蘭地)

蘋果酒 [ping4 gwo2 jau2] *n.* apple cider

蘋果牛油 [ping4 gwo2 ngau4 yau4] *n.* apple butter

平衡 [ping4 hang4] *n.* balance

平行 [ping4 hang4] *adj.* parallel

評論 [ping4 leun6] *n.* comment

平民 [ping4 man4] *n.* civilian

平紋細布 [ping4 man4 sai3 bou3] *n.* muslin

平面設計 [ping4 min6 chit8 gai3] *n.* graphic design

平面視覺藝術 [ping4 min6 si6 gok8 ngai6 seut9] *n.* graphic art

平面視覺藝術家 [ping4 min6 si6 gok8 ngai6 seut9 ga1] *n.* graphic artist

平安夜 [ping4 on1 ye6] *n.* Christmas Eve

瓶塞 [ping4 sak7] *n.* stopper

平息 [ping4 sik7] *v.* pacify

平台 [ping4 toi4] *n.* platform

平穩 [ping4 wan2] *adj.* steady; *adv.* steadily

平和 [ping4 wo4] *adj.* bland

平壤 [ping4 yeung6] *n.* Pyongyang (~, capital of Korea 北韓嘅首都)

漂白 [piu1 baak9] *n.* bleach

票 [piu3] *n.* ticket (~ agency 售票代理處, ~ holder 持票人, ~ collector 收票員, ~ machine 售票機, ~ office 售票處, one-way ~ 單程票)

票價 [piu3 ga3] *n.* fare

破產 [po3 chaan2] *v.* bankrupt; *n.* bankruptcy

破傷風 [po3 seung1 fung1] *n.* tetanus

破壞 [po3 waai6] *v.* destroy; *n.* destruction

破壞咗 [po3 waai6 jo2] *adj.* destroyed

扑嚇扑嚇 [pok8 haak8 pok8 haak8] *n.* flounder

撲克 [pok8 hak7] *n.* poker (~ game 撲克牌)

撲滅 [pok8 mit9] *v.* quench

撲撲跳 [pok8 pok8 tiu3] *v.* palpitate

樸素 [pok8 sou3] *adj.* plain (~ yogurt 原味乳酪, ~ flavor 原味)

旁白 [pong4 baak9] *n.* narrator

旁邊 [pong4 bin1] *adv.* aside (~ from 除咗)

膀胱 [pong4 gwong1] *n.* bladder

膀胱炎 [pong4 gwong1 yim4] *n.* cystitis

旁證 [pong4 jing3] *n.* circumstantial evidence

鋪大理石 [pou1 daai6 lei5 sek9] *adj.* marbled (~ meat 五花肉)

鋪路石 [pou1 lou6 sek9] *n.* paving stone

普拉亞 [pou2 laai1 a3] *n.* Praia (~, capital of Cape Verde 佛得角嘅首都)

普拉提 [pou2 laai1 tai4] *n.* Pilates

普里什蒂纳 [pou2 lei5 sam6 dai3 naap9] *n.* Pristina (~, capital of Kosovo 科索沃嘅首都)

普遍 [pou2 pin3] *n.* prevalence; *adj.* prevalent, widespread

普通 [pou2 tung1] *n.* mediocrity; *adj.* ordinary

蒲公英 [pou4 gung1 ying1] *n.* dandelion (~ greens 蒲公英嫩葉, ~ leaves 蒲公英葉)

菩提樹 [pou4 tai4 syu6] *n.* linden tree

葡萄白酒 [pou4 tou4 baak9 jau2] *n.* white wine

葡萄牙 [pou4 tou4 nga4] *n.* Portugal; *adj.* Portuguese

葡萄糖 [pou4 tou4 tong4] *n.* glucose

葡萄園 [pou4 tou4 yun4] *n.* vineyard

胚胎 [pui1 toi1] *n.* embryo

配菜 [pui3 choi3] *n.* side dish, side order

配合 [pui3 hap9] *n.* combination

配額 [pui3 ngaak9] *n.* quota

配偶 [pui3 ngau5] *n.* spouse (*m./f.*)

配音 [pui3 yam1] *adj.* dubbed

陪審團 [pui4 sam2 tyun4] *n.* jury

賠償 [pui4 seung4] *v.* reimburse; *n.* reimbursement

判斷 [pun3 dyun6] *n.* judgement

判例法 [pun3 lai6 faat8] *n.* case law

盆 [pun4] *n.* basin

盤問 [pun4 man6] *n.* cross-examination

陪 [puui4] *v.* accompany

S

沙 [sa1] *n.* sand

紗布 [sa1 bou3] *n.* gauze

沙特阿拉伯 [sa1 dak9 a3 laai1 baak8] *n.* Saudi Arabia

沙甸魚 [sa1 din1 yu2] *n.* sardine

沙葛 [sa1 got8] *n.* jicama

沙律 [sa1 leut2] *n.* salad (~ bar 沙律吧)

沙樂美腸 [sa1 lok9 mei5 cheung4] *n.* salami

沙漠 [sa1 mok9] *n.* desert

沙灘 [sa1 taan1] *n.* beach

沙田柚 [sa1 tin4 yau2] *n.* pomelo

砂糖桔 [sa1 tong4 gat7] *n.* tangerine

沙鍋 [sa1 wo1] *n.* casserole (tuna ~ 吞拿魚砂鍋)

鯊魚 [sa1 yu4] *n.* shark (~ steak 鯊魚扒, ~ fin 魚翅, ~ tail 鯊魚尾)

灑 [sa2] *v.* sprinkle

曬 [saai3] *det.* all (~ day 成日, ~ night 成晚, ~-night pharmacy 24小時藥店)

曬黑 [saai3 hak7] *adj.* browned

曬後潤膚露 [saai3 hau6 yeun6 fu1 lou6] *n.* after-sun lotion

曬傷 [saai3 seung1] *n.* sunburn; *adj.* sunburned

三 [saam1] *num.* three

衫 [saam1] *n.* clothes

三分之一 [saam1 fan1 ji1 yat7] *n.* one-third

衫夾 [saam1 gaap8] *n.* clothespin

三角褲 [saam1 gok8 fu3] *n.* briefs

三角形 [saam1 gok8 ying4] *n.* triangle

三文治 [saam1 man4 ji6] *n.* sandwich (ham and cheese ~ 火腿芝士三文治, veggie ~ 素菜三文治, turkey ~ 火雞三文治)

三文魚 [saam1 man4 yu2] *n.* salmon

三文魚慕斯 [saam1 man4 yu2 mou6 si1] *n.* salmon mousse

三十 [saam1 sap9] *num.* thirty

三人組合 [saam1 yan4 jou2 hap9] *n.* trio

三葉草 [saam1 yip9 chou2] *n.* clover

三月 [saam1 yut9] *n.* March

閂 [saan1] *v.* close

山 [saan1] *n.* hill

山背 [saan1 bui3] *n.* ridge

刪除 [saan1 cheui4] *v.* delete (*comp.* ~ key 消除鍵, ~ a file 刪除文件)

山頂 [saan1 deng2] *n.* peak

山間小路 [saan1 gaan1 siu2 lou6] *n.* mountain path

山谷 [saan1 guk7] *n.* valley

山口 [saan1 hau2] *n.* mountain pass

閂咗 [saan1 jo2] *adj.* closed (~ for renovations 裝修停業, ~ for vacation 假期停業, ~ to traffic 唔准通行)

山葵 [saan1 kwai4] *n.* horseradish

山蘿蔔 [saan1 lo4 baak9] *n.* chervil

山窿 [saan1 lung1] *n.* cave

山脈 [saan1 mak9] *n.* mountain chain, mountain range

山羊 [saan1 yeung4] *n.* goat (kid ~ 山羊仔, ~ cheese 羊奶芝士, ~ meat 山羊肉)

散咗 [saan2 jo2] *v.* fall apart

散文 [saan2 man4] *n.* prose

散播 [saan3 bo3] *v.* spread (~ing 散播緊)

散步 [saan3 bou6] *v.* walk (~ on 繼續行)

疝氣 [saan3 hei3] *n.* hernia

散開 [saan3 hoi1] *v.* scatter

蛋白質 [saan6 baak9 jat7] *n.* protein

生 [saang1] *adj.* raw; *phr.* give birth (to)

生菜 [saang1 choi3] *n.* lettuce

生咗鏽 [saang1 jo2 sau3] *adj.* rusty

生手 [saang1 sau2] *n.* amateur

生鮮 [saang1 sin1] *adj.* farm-fresh

生鐵 [saang1 tit8] *n.* cast iron (~ stove 生鐵爐)

生日 [saang1 yat9] *n.* birthday

生日快樂 [saang1 yat9 faai3 lok9] *phr.* Happy birthday!

生日派對 [saang1 yat9 paai3 deui3] *n.* birthday party

生意 [saang1 yi3] *n.* business (~ card 名片, ~ class 商業課程, ~ hours 辦公時間, ~ trip 出差, go out of ~ 倒閉)

生意人 [saang1 yi3 yan4] *n.* business person

省 [saang2] *n.* province

省略 [saang2 leuk9] *n.* omission

省略號 [saang2 leuk9 hou6] *n.* apostrophe

殺 [saat8] *v.* kill

殺蟲水 [saat8 chung4 seui2] *n.* insect repellant

撒旦 [saat8 daan3] *n.* Satan

薩格勒布 [saat8 gaak8 lak9 bou3] *n.* Zagreb (~, capital of Croatia 克羅地亞嘅首都)

煞掣 [saat8 jai3] *n.* brake (~ pads 煞掣腳踏, ~light 煞掣燈)

薩拉熱窩 [saat8 laai1 yit9 wo1] *n.* Sarajevo (~, capital of Bosnia and Herzegovina 波黑嘅首都)

薩摩亞 [saat8 mo1 a3] *adj.* Samoan

薩摩亞群島 [saat8 mo1 a3 kwan4 dou2] *n.* Samoa

薩那 [saat8 na5] *n.* Sanaa (~, capital of Yemen 也門嘅首都)

殺人 [saat8 yan4] *n.* manslaughter

殺人兇手 [saat8 yan4 hung1 sau2] *n.* murderer

薩爾瓦多 [saat8 yi5 nga5 do1] *n.* El Salvador

稍為醃一下 [saau2 wai4 yip8 yat7 ha6] *adj.* lightly salted

哨兵 [saau3 bing1] *n.* picket

篩 [sai1] *v.* sift; *n.* sieve

西班牙 [sai1 baan1 nga4] *n.* Spain; *adj.* Spanish

西班牙凍湯 [sai1 baan1 nga4 dung3 tong1] *n.* gazpacho

西班牙港 [sai1 baan1 nga4 gong2] *n.* Port-of-Spain (~, capital of Trinidad and Tobago 特立尼達和多巴哥嘅首都)

西班牙香腸 [sai1 baan1 nga4 heung1 cheung4] *n.* chorizo

西班牙海鮮飯 [sai1 baan1 nga4 hoi2 sin1 faan6] *n.* paella

西北 [sai1 bak7] *adj.* northwest

西瓜 [sai1 gwa1] *n.* watermelon

西裝外套 [sai1 jong1 ngoi6 tou3] *n.* blouse

西芹 [sai1 kan4] *n.* parsley (~ flakes 西芹碎, ~ seasoning 西芹調味料)

西蘭花 [sai1 laan4 fa1] *n.* broccoli

西冷 [sai1 laang1] *n.* sirloin (~ steak 西冷牛扒)

西冷牛扒 [sai1 laang1 ngau4 pa2] *n.* strip loin

西米 [sai1 mai5] *n.* tapioca (~ pudding 西米布丁)

西面 [sai1 min6] *n.* west

西梅乾 [sai1 mui2 gon1] *n.* prune (~ juice 西梅汁)

犀牛 [sai1 ngau4] *n.* rhinoceros

西葫蘆 [sai1 wu4 lou4] *n.* zucchini (fried ~ 炒西葫蘆, ~ chips 西葫蘆薯條)

西柚 [sai1 yau2] *n.* grapefruit

西洋跳棋 [sai1 yeung4 tiu3 kei4] *n.* checkers

洗衣店 [sai1 yi1 dim3] *n.* laundry (place/clothes), laundromat

洗 [sai2] *n.* washing (~ machine 洗衣機, ~ powder 洗衣粉)

洗 [sai2] *v.* wash (~ dishes 洗碗, hand ~ 手洗)

使到 [sai2 dou3] *v.* render

洗劫 [sai2 gip8] *v.* ransack

洗禮 [sai2 lai5] *n.* baptism

洗面盆 [sai2 min6 pun4] *n.* washbasin

洗眼水 [sai2 ngaan5 seui2] *n.* eyewash

洗衫設備 [sai2 saam1 chit8 bei6] *n.* laundry facilities

洗衫服務 [sai2 saam1 fuk9 mou6] *n.* laundry service

洗頭水 [sai2 tau4 seui2] *n.* shampoo

洗碗布 [sai2 wun2 bou3] *n.* dish towel

洗碗機 [sai2 wun2 gei1] *n.* dishwasher (~ proof 可放入洗碗機, dishwashing liquid/soap 洗碗機用洗碗液)

洗碗液 [sai2 wun2 yik9] *n.* detergent

洗衣機 [sai2 yi1 gei1] *n.* washing machine

使用 [sai2 yung6] *n.* usage

使用說明 [sai2 yung6 syut8 ming4] *n.* instructions (~ for use 使用說明)

細 [sai3] *adj.* small

細胞 [sai3 baau1] *n.* cell

細包仔 [sai3 baau1 jai2] *n.* packet

細啲 [sai3 di1] *adj.* smaller

細袋 [sai3 doi2] *n.* pouch

世界 [sai3 gaai3] *n.* world (W~ Cup 世界杯, the New W~ 新大陸)

世紀 [sai3 gei2] *n.* century

細賬 [sai3 jeung3] *n.* itemized bill

細節 [sai3 jit8] *n.* detail

世俗 [sai3 juk9] *adj.* secular

細菌 [sai3 kwan2] *n.* bacteria; *adj.* bacterial

勢力 [sai3 lik9] *n.* power

細佬 [sai3 lou2] *n.* younger brother

細路 [sai3 lou6] *n.* child (~'s seat 細路凳, ~'s bed 細路床)

細路仔 [sai3 lou6 jai2] *n.* children (~'s discount 小童折扣, ~'s menu 兒童餐牌, ~'s pool 小童泳池, ~'s game 細路哥遊戲)

細路仔份量 [sai3 lou6 jai2 fan6 leung6] *n.* children's portions

細路女 [sai3 lou6 neui5] *n.* girl, little girl

細木屋 [sai3 muk9 uk7] *n.* chalet

細粒 [sai3 nap7] *n.* granules

細細啖 [sai3 sai3 daam6] *adj.* bite-size

細細聲講 [sai3 sai3 seng1 gong2] *v.* whisper

世仇 [sai3 sau4] *n.* feud

細聲講 [sai3 seng1 gong2] *v.* murmur

細聲投訴 [sai3 seng1 tau4 sou3] *v.* mutter

細提子乾 [sai3 tai4 ji2 gon1] *n.* currants (red ~ 紅細提子乾, black ~ 黑細提子乾)

誓言 [sai6 yin4] *n.* oath

塞 [sak7] *n.* clog

塞咗 [sak7 jo2] *adj.* blocked

塞滿 [sak7 mun5] *adj.* stuffed (I'm ~ 食飽喇, ~ eggs 釀蛋, ~ bell peppers 釀燈籠椒, ~ tomatoes 釀番茄)

深 [sam1] *adj.* deep (~ end of pool 泳池深水區)

深層 [sam1 chang4] *adj.* underlying

深切治療 [sam1 chit8 ji6 liu4] *n.* intensive care

心地好 [sam1 dei2 hou2] *adj.* nice

深度 [sam1 dou6] *n.* depth

心絞痛 [sam1 gaau2 tung3] *n.* angina

心悸 [sam1 gwai3] *n.* palpitations

深刻 [sam1 hak7] *adj.* profound

心口 [sam1 hau2] *n.* chest

心口針 [sam1 hau2 jam1] *n.* brooch

心臟 [sam1 jong6] *n.* heart

心臟病 [sam1 jong6 beng6] *n.* heart condition, heart attack

心臟病發作 [sam1 jong6 beng6 faat8 jok8] *n.* heart attack

心臟搭橋 [sam1 jong6 daap8 kiu4] *n.* heart bypass

森林 [sam1 lam4] *n.* forest

心理學 [sam1 lei5 hok9] *adj.* psychological

心理學家 [sam1 lei5 hok9 ga1] *n.* psychologist

心理治療 [sam1 lei5 ji6 liu4] *n.* therapy

心靈 [sam1 ling4] *n.* psyche

深奧 [sam1 ngou3] *n.* profundity

深仇 [sam1 sau4] *n.* rancor

深思熟慮 [sam1 si1 suk9 leui6] *v.* mull

深色嘅 [sam1 sik7 ge3] *adj.* dark (grow ~ 天黑)

心跳 [sam1 tiu3] *n.* heartbeat

心軟 [sam1 yun5] *v.* relent

審查 [sam2 cha4] *v.* inspect; *n.* inspection

審計 [sam2 gai3] *n.* audit

審計員 [sam2 gai3 yun4] *n.*
auditor

審美 [sam2 mei5] *adj.* aesthetic
(*also* esthetic); *n.* aesthetics

審判 [sam2 pun3] *n.* trial

滲透 [sam3 tau3] *v.* pervade

滲入 [sam3 yap9] *v.* penetrate; *n.*
penetration

甚至 [sam6 ji3] *adv.* even

伸 [san1] *v.* stretch

新版本 [san1 baan2 bun2] *n.*
new releases

新陳代謝 [san1 chan4 doi6 je6]
n. metabolism; *adj.* metabolic

申請 [san1 ching2] *v.* apply; *n.*
application

伸出 [san1 cheut7] *v.* stick out

新德里 [san1 dak7 lei5] *n.* New
Delhi (~, capital of India 印度
嘅首都)

新地 [san1 dei2] *n.* sundae

身份 [san1 fan2] *n.* identification

身分證 [san1 fan2 jing3] *n.*
identity card

身分證明文件 [san1 fan2 jing3
ming4 man4 gin2] *n.* identity
document

辛苦 [san1 fu2] *adj.* painstaking

呻苦 [san1 fu2] *v.* complain

新加坡 [san1 ga1 bo1] *n.*
Singapore (~, capital of
Singapore 新加坡嘅首都)

新加坡 [san1 ga1 bo1] *adj.*
Singaporean

新教徒 [san1 gaau3 tou4] *n.*
Protestant

新近 [san1 gan6] *adv.* newly

新嘅 [san1 ge3] *adj.* new

新郎 [san1 long4] *n.* bridegroom

新聞 [san1 man4] *n.* news

新聞記者 [san1 man4 gei3 je2]
n. journalist

新聞業 [san1 man4 yip9] *n.*
journalism

新娘 [san1 neung1] *n.* bride; *adj.*
bridal (~ party 新娘派對, ~
store 新娘服店)

新年 [san1 nin4] *n.* New Year

新年快樂 [san1 nin4 faai3 lok9]
phr. Happy New Year!

新西蘭 [san1 sai1 laan4] *n.* New
Zealand; *adj.* New Zealander

身手靈活 [san1 sau2 ling4
wut9] *adj.* agile

新手 [san1 sau2] *n.* beginner

新石器時代 [san1 sek9 hei3 si4
doi6] *adj.* neolithic

紳士 [san1 si2] *n.* gentleman

新鮮 [san1 sin1] *adj.* fresh (~
fish 鮮魚, ~ fruit 新鮮水果,
~ produce 新鮮蔬果, ~ meat
鮮肉)

新鮮薯仔 [san1 sin1 syu4 jai2] *n.*
new potatoes

申訴 [san1 sou3] *n.* plea

辛酸 [san1 syun1] *n.* poignancy;
adj. poignant

身體 [san1 tai2] *adj.* physical; *n.*
body

身體健康 [san1 tai2 gin6
hong1] *phr.* Good health!

身體上 [san1 tai2 seung6] *adv.*
physically

新穎 [san1 wing6] *n.* novelty

身形 [san1 ying4] *n.* figures

神 [san4] *n.* deity

神祕 [san4 bei3] *adj.* mystic

神秘主義 [san4 bei3 jyu2 yi6] *n.* mysticism

神父 [san4 fu6] *n.* priest

神經 [san4 ging1] *n.* nerve

神經病學 [san4 ging1 beng6 hok9] *n.* neurology

神經科專家 [san4 ging1 fo1 jyun1 ga1] *n.* neurologist

神經系統 [san4 ging1 hai6 tung2] *n.* nervous system

神經衰弱 [san4 ging1 seui1 yeuk9] *n.* neurosis

神龕 [san4 ham1] *n.* shrine

神智 [san4 ji3] *n.* consciousness

神聖 [san4 sing3] *adj.* holy

神聖化 [san4 sing3 fa3] *n.* sanctification

神壇 [san4 taan4] *n.* pulpit

神檯 [san4 toi4] *n.* altar (~ piece 神檯裝飾)

神話故事 [san4 wa2 gu3 si6] *n.* mythology

神魂顛倒 [san4 wan4 din1 dou2] *v.* fascinate; *n.* fascination; *adj.* fascinated

腎 [san5] *n.* kidney

生啤酒 [sang1 be1 jau2] *n.* draft beer

生產 [sang1 chaan2] *v.* manufacture; *n.* manufacturing

生產力 [sang1 chaan2 lik9] *n.* productivity

生產商 [sang1 chaan2 seung1] *n.* producer

生存 [sang1 chyun4] *v.* live; *n.* survival

生長 [sang1 jeung2] *n.* growth

生殖 [sang1 jik9] *adj.* reproductive

生殖器 [sang1 jik9 hei3] *n.* genitals

生物 [sang1 mat9] *n.* biology; creature

生物多樣性 [sang1 mat9 do1 yeung6 sing3] *n.* biodiversity

生物技術 [sang1 mat9 gei6 seut9] *n.* biotechnology, biotech, bio fuels

生命 [sang1 meng6] *n.* life

生態系統 [sang1 taai3 hai6 tung2] *n.* ecosystem

生活水平 [sang1 wut9 seui2 ping4] *n.* living standard

生肉 [sang1 yuk9] *n.* rare meat

濕 [sap7] *adj.* wet

濕地 [sap7 dei6] *n.* swamp

濕度 [sap7 dou6] *n.* humidity

濕晒 [sap7 saai3] *v.* saturate (~d fat 飽和脂肪)

十 [sap9] *num.* ten

十八 [sap9 baat8] *num.* eighteen

十七 [sap9 chat7] *num.* seventeen

十分 [sap9 fan1] *adv.* greatly

十分之好 [sap9 fan1 ji1 hou2] *adj.* fantastic, very good

十分嚴重 [sap9 fan1 yim4 jung6] *adj.* severe; *adv.* severely

十九 [sap9 gau2] *num.* nineteen

十字架 [sap9 ji6 ga2] *n.* cross

十六 [sap9 luk9] *num.* sixteen

十五 [sap9 ng5] *num.* fifteen

十五十六 [sap9 ng5 sap9 luk9] *v.* hesitate

十年 [sap9 nin4] *n.* decade

十三 [sap9 saam1] *num.* thirteen

十四 [sap9 sei3] *num.* fourteen

十一 [sap9 yat7] *num.* eleven
十一月份 [sap9 yat7 yut9 fan6]
n. November (*abbr.* Nov.)
十二 [sap9 yi6] *num.* twelve
十二宮圖 [sap9 yi6 gung1 tou4]
n. zodiac
十二月份 [sap9 yi6 yut9 fan6] *n.*
December (*abbr.* Dec.)
十億 [sap9 yik7] *num.* billion
十月份 [sap9 yut9 fan6] *n.*
October (*abbr.* Oct.)
虱 [sat7] *n.* lice
失敗 [sat7 baai6] *n.* failure
失敗咗 [sat7 baai6 jo2] *adj.*
unsuccessful
失控 [sat7 hung3] *adj.* uncontrolled
失血 [sat7 hyut8] *v.* lose blood
失物認領處 [sat7 mat9 ying6
ling5 chyu3] *n.* lost and found
office
失眠 [sat7 min4] *n.* insomnia
失望 [sat7 mong6] *adj.* disappointed;
n. disappointment
室外 [sat7 ngoi6] *adj.* outdoor(s)
室外泳池 [sat7 ngoi6 wing6
chi4] *n.* outdoor swimming pool
室內 [sat7 noi6] *adj.* indoor
室內泳池 [sat7 noi6 wing6 chi4]
n. indoor pool
膝頭 [sat7 tau4] *n.* knee
室友 [sat7 yau5] *n.* roommate
失憶 [sat7 yik7] *n.* amnesia
失業 [sat7 yip9] *adj.* unemployed;
n. unemployment (~ compensation
失業救濟金)
實習生 [sat9 jaap9 sang1] *n.*
probationer

實際 [sat9 jai3] *adj.* practical;
adv. practically
實際嘅 [sat9 jai3 ge3] *adj.* actual
實際上 [sat9 jai3 seung6] *adv.*
actually
實質 [sat9 jat7] *n.* substance
實質上 [sat9 jat7 seung6] *adv.*
substantially
實心 [sat9 sam1] *adj.* solid
實施 [sat9 si1] *v.* implement; *n.*
implementation
實驗品 [sat9 yim6 ban2] *n.*
guinea pig
實驗室 [sat9 yim6 sat7] *n.*
laboratory, lab
實用主義 [sat9 yung6 jyu2 yi6]
n. pragmatism
實用性 [sat9 yung6 sing3] *n.*
practicability
搜查 [sau1 cha4] *n.* search
收藏 [sau1 chong4] *n.* collection
收藏家 [sau1 chong4 ga1] *n.*
collector
收多咗錢 [sau1 do1 jo2 chin4] *v.*
overcharge
收到 [sau1 dou2] *v.* receive
修道院 [sau1 dou6 yun6] *n.*
convent
收費 [sau1 fai3] *n.* charge (to
bring ~s against 起訴)
收據 [sau1 geui3] *n.* receipt
收件人 [sau1 gin6 yan4] *n.*
recipient
修改 [sau1 goi2] *v.* revise; *n.*
modification, revision
收割 [sau1 got8] *v.* reap
收割機 [sau1 got8 gei1] *n.* reaper
收集 [sau1 jaap9] *v.* collect

修甲 [sau1 gaap8] *n.* manicure

修剪 [sau1 jin2] *v.* trim; *n.* trimming

收購 [sau1 kau3] *n.* acquisition

修理鋪 [sau1 lei5 pou3] *n.* repair shop

收買 [sau1 maai5] *v.* bribe

修女 [sau1 neui5] *n.* nun

收銀機 [sau1 ngan2 gei1] *n.* cash register

收銀員 [sau1 ngan2 yun4] *n.* cashier

收稅 [sau1 seui3] *v.* levy

收信人 [sau1 seun3 yan4] *n.* addressee

收市價 [sau1 si5 ga3] *n.* last call

修飾 [sau1 sik7] *v.* retouch

收縮 [sau1 suk7] *n.* contraction

收音機 [sau1 yam1 gei1] *n.* radio

收入 [sau1 yap9] *n.* earnings (YTD ~ 今年到現在為止收入, quarterly ~ 季度收入)

收養 [sau1 yeung5] *v.* foster

收容所 [sau1 yung4 so2] *n.* shelter

手 [sau2] *n.* hand

手把 [sau2 ba2] *n.* handlebars

手板 [sau2 baan2] *n.* palm

手臂 [sau2 bei3] *n.* arm (*anat.*)

手冊 [sau2 chaak8] *n.* brochure

手槍 [sau2 cheung1] *n.* pistol

手電筒 [sau2 din6 tung2] *n.* flashlight

手檔變速箱 [sau2 dong3 bin3 chuk7 seung1] *n.* manual transmission (*car*)

手動 [sau2 dung6] *n.* handbrake (*manual*)

手段 [sau2 dyun6] *n.* means

首府 [sau2 fu2] *n.* capital

手縫 [sau2 fung4] *adj.* handsewn

手巾 [sau2 gan1] *n.* towel

手巾仔 [sau2 gan1 jai2] *n.* handkerchief

手機 [sau2 gei1] *n.* cell/cellular/mobile phone

手稿 [sau2 gou2] *n.* manuscript

手工 [sau2 gung1] *n.* craft; *adj.* handmade

手工藝品 [sau2 gung1 ngai6 ban2] *n.* handicrafts

手踭 [sau2 jaang1] *n.* elbow

手袖 [sau2 jau6] *n.* sleeve

手指 [sau2 ji2] *n.* finger

手指公 [sau2 ji2 gung1] *n.* thumb

首席 [sau2 jik9] *adj.* chief

手足情 [sau2 juk7 ching4] *n.* brotherhood

手銬 [sau2 kau3] *n.* handcuff

守規矩 [sau2 kwai1 geui2] *v.* behave

手鏈 [sau2 lin6] *n.* bracelet

守門員 [sau2 mun4 yun4] *n.* goalkeeper

首相 [sau2 seung3] *n.* premier

手相術 [sau2 seung3 seut9] *n.* palmistry

手術 [sau2 seut9] *n.* surgery

手術刀 [sau2 seut9 dou1] *n.* scalpel

守時 [sau2 si4] *n.* punctuality; *adj.* punctual

搜查令 [sau2 sok8 ling6] *n.* search warrant

搜索引擎 [sau2 sok8 yan5 king4] *n. comp.* search engine

手提包 [sau2 tai4 baau1] *n.* handbag

手提電腦 [sau2 tai4 din6 nou5] *n.* laptop computer

手提行李 [sau2 tai4 hang4 lei5] *n.* hand baggage

手推車 [sau2 teui1 che1] *n.* trolley

手套 [sau2 tou3] *n.* glove

手腕 [sau2 wun2] *n.* wrist

首爾 [sau2 yi5] *n.* Seoul (~, capital of South Korea 南韓嘅首都)

首映 [sau2 ying2] *n.* premiere

瘦 [sau3] *adj.* thin, lean (~ meat 瘦肉, ~ cuisine 清淡飲食)

鏽 [sau3] *n.* rust

仇恨 [sau4 han6] *n.* animosity

受保護 [sau6 bou2 wu6] *adj.* protected (~ species 受保護動物)

受保護建築 [sau6 bou2 wu6 gin3 juk7] *n.* listed building

受苦 [sau6 fu2] *v.* suffer

受歡迎 [sau6 fun1 ying4] *adj.* popular

受過訓練 [sau6 gwo3 fan3 lin6] *adj.* trained

受害者 [sau6 hoi6 je2] *n.* victim

受咗傷 [sau6 jo2 seung1] *adj.* wounded, injured

授權 [sau6 kyun4] *v.* authorize

授權書 [sau6 kyun4 syu1] power of attorney

受難周 [sau6 naan6 jau1] *n.* Holy Week

售票廳 [sau6 piu3 teng1] *n.* box office

售票員 [sau6 piu3 yun4] *n.* conductor (*of train/orchestra/ electricity*)

受傷 [sau6 seung1] *v.* hurt, be hurt (where does it ~? 整親邊度?)

受傷 [sau6 seung1] *n.* injury

壽司 [sau6 si1] *n.* sushi (~ roll 壽司卷)

受託人 [sau6 tok8 yan4] *n.* fiduciary

受約束 [sau6 yeuk8 chuk7] *adj.* restricted

寫 [se2] *v.* write

寫低 [se2 dai1] *v.* write down

捨棄 [se2 hei3] *v.* forsake

寫字樓 [se2 ji6 lau4] *n.* office

瀉出 [se3 cheut7] *v.* spill

卸貨 [se3 fo3] *adj.* discharged

瀉藥 [se3 yeuk9] *n.* laxative

蛇 [se4] *n.* snake

社區 [se5 keui1] *n.* community

社團 [se5 tyun4] *n.* club

社會 [se5 wui5] *adj.* social (~ sciences 社會科學, ~ security 社會福利, ~ welfare 社會福利, ~ democratic 社會民主黨)

社會 [se5 wui5] *n.* society

社會主義者 [se5 wui5 jyu2 yi6 je2] *adj.* socialist

社會上 [se5 wui5 seung6] *adv.* socially

射擊 [se6 gik7] *n.* shot gun; injection

麝香 [se6 heung1] *n.* musk

射手座 [se6 sau2 jo6] *n.* Sagittarius

射線 [se6 sin3] *n.* ray

死 [sei2] *v.* die; *n.* death

死板 [sei2 baan2] *adj.* rigid

死火 [sei2 fo2] *n.* anchorage

死罪 [sei2 jeui6] *n.* capital crime

死咗 [sei2 jo2] *adj.* dead

死亡率 [sei2 mong4 leut9] *n.* mortality

四 [sei3] *num.* four

四分之一 [sei3 fan6 ji1 yat7] *quant.* quarter (~ past eight / 8:15 八點三, ~ to one / 12:45 十二點九, ~ tank of gas 四分一油箱油)

四合院 [sei3 hap9 yun6] *n.* quadrangle

四開 [sei3 hoi1] *adj.* quartered

四輪驅動 [sei3 leun4 keui1 dung6] *n.* four-wheel drive

四門汽車 [sei3 mun4 hei3 che1] *n.* four-door car

四倍 [sei3 pui5] *n.* quadruple

四十 [sei3 sap9] *num.* forty

四圍望 [sei3 wai4 mong6] *v.* look around

四月份 [sei3 yut9 fan6] *n.* April (*abbr.* Apr.)

錫 [sek8] *v.* kiss

錫紙 [sek8 ji2] *n.* aluminum foil

石灰 [sek9 fui1] *n.* lime (~ extract 青檸檬濃縮, ~ juice 青檸檬汁)

石蠟 [sek9 laap9] *n.* paraffin

石榴色 [sek9 lau2 sik7] *n.* garnet

石榴 [sek9 lau2] *n.* pomegranate (~ seeds 石榴籽)

碩士 [sek9 si6] *n.* master

石頭 [sek9 tau4] *n.* stone

聲 [seng1] *n.* sound

醒咗 [seng2 jo2] *adj.* awake

成個 [seng4 go3] *adj.* whole (~ wheat 全麥, ~ milk 全脂牛奶)

成口 [seng4 hau2] *adj.* mouthful

成日 [seng4 yat9] *adv.* always

成日變 [seng4 yat9 bin3] *adj.* dynamic

成日見 [seng4 yat9 gin3] *adj.* common

成日落雨 [seng4 yat9 lok9 yu5] *adj.* rainy

衰格 [seui1 gaak8] *adj.* nasty

衰咗 [seui1 jo2] *v.* fail

衰竭 [seui1 kit8] *n.* prostration

衰人 [seui1 yan4] *n.* jerk

需要 [seui1 yiu3] *v. modal* need

需要許可證 [seui1 yiu1 heui2 ho2 jing3] *phr.* permit required

水 [seui2] *n./adj.* water (~ bottle 水樽, ~ faucet 水喉, ~ heater 熱水器, ~ skis 滑水, ~ supply 水供應, mineral ~ 礦泉水, spring ~ 山泉水, sparkling ~ 汽水, soda ~ 汽水)

水獺 [seui2 chaat8] *n.* otter

水池 [seui2 chi4] *n.* pool (swimming ~ 游泳池)

水彩 [seui2 choi2] *n.* watercolor

水底 [seui2 dai2] *adj.* underwater

水庫 [seui2 fu3] *n.* reservoir

水罐 [seui2 gun3] *n.* pitcher (~ of water 一罐水)

水果 [seui2 gwo2] *n.* fruit (~ syrup 水果糖漿, ~ juice 果汁, ~ salad 水果沙律, ~ picking 摘水果)

水果白蘭地 [seui2 gwo2 baak9 laan4 dei6] *n.* fruit brandy

水果撻 [seui2 gwo2 taat8] *n.* fruit tart

水鞋 [seui2 haai4] *n.* waterproof shoes

水坑 [seui2 haang1] *n.* puddle

水喉 [seui2 hau4] *n.* faucet

水喉工 [seui2 hau4 gung1] *n.* plumber

水晶 [seui2 jing1] *n.* crystal

水蒸氣 [seui2 jing1 hei3] *n.* vapor

水族館 [seui2 juk9 gun2] *n.* aquarium

水煮 [seui2 jyu2] *adj.* poached (~ egg 水煮蛋, ~ bone marrow 煲骨髓)

水煮蛋 [seui2 jyu2 daan6] *n.* hard-boiled egg, soft-boiled egg

水渠 [seui2 keui4] *n.* aqueduct

水利 [seui2 lei6] *n.* irrigation

水陸路信件 [seui2 luk9 lou6 seun3 gin6] *n.* surface mail

水母 [seui2 mou5] *n.* jellyfish

水泥 [seui2 nai4] *n.* cement

水銀 [seui2 ngan4] *n.* mercury

水泡 [seui2 paau1] *n.* bubble

水疱 [seui2 paau3] *n.* blister

水瓶座 [seui2 ping4 jo6] *n.* Aquarius

水平 [seui2 ping4] *adj.* horizontal

水平面積 [seui2 ping4 min6 jik7] *n.* level area

水手 [seui2 sau2] *n.* sailor

水上摩托 [seui2 seung6 mo1 tok8] *n.* jet-ski

水仙 [seui2 sin1] *n.* narcissus

水田 [seui2 tin4] *n.* paddy

水壺 [seui2 wu2] *n.* kettle

水煙袋 [seui2 yin1 doi2] *n.* hookah

稅 [seui3] *n.* tax

碎 [seui3] *n.* crumb (bread ~ 麵包碎)

碎片 [seui3 pin2] *n.* fragment

說服 [seui3 fuk9] *v.* persuade, convince

稅收 [seui3 sau1] *n.* taxation

碎石 [seui3 sek9] *n.* rubble

垂直 [seui4 jik9] *adj.* vertical

瑞典 [seui6 din2] *n.* Sweden; *adj.* Swedish

睡袋 [seui6 doi2] *n.* sleeping bag

隧道 [seui6 dou6] *n.* tunnel

睡房 [seui6 fong2] *n.* bedroom

睡褲 [seui6 fu3] *n.* pajamas

睡袍 [seui6 pou4] *n.* robe

瑞士 [seui6 si6] *n.* Switzerland; *adj.* Swiss

瑞士卷 [seui6 si6 gyun2] *n.* jelly roll

瑞士芝士 [seui6 si6 ji1 si6] *n.* Swiss cheese

睡衣 [seui6 yi1] *n.* lingerie

詢問處 [seun1 man6 chyu3] *n.* information counter/office

筍野 [seun2 ye5] *n.* bargain

信 [seun3] *n.* letter

信封 [seun3 fung1] *n.* envelope

瞬間 [seun3 gaan1] *n.* moment

信號 [seun3 hou6] *n.* signal

信念 [seun3 nim6] *n.* faith (*religious*)

信箱 [seun3 seung1] *n.* mailbox

信任 [seun3 yam6] *n.* trust

信仰 [seun3 yeung5] *n.* beliefs

信用 [seun3 yung6] *n.* credit

信用卡 [seun3 yung6 kat7] *n.* credit card (~ number 信用卡號碼)

純 [seun4] *adj.* pure

純潔 [seun4 git8] *n.* purity

唇膏 [seun4 gou1] *n.* lipstick

純粹 [seun4 seui6] *adj.* sheer; *adv.* purely

純粹主義者 [seun4 seui6 jyu2 yi6 je2] *n.* purist

純素食者 [seun4 sou3 sik9 je2] *adj.* vegan

順利 [seun6 lei6] *adv.* smoothly

順勢療法 [seun6 sai3 liu4 faat8] *n.* homeopathy

箱 [seung1] *n.* bin

霜 [seung1] *n.* frost

商品 [seung1 ban2] *n.* commodity

相似 [seung1 chi5] *adj.* similar; *adv.* similarly

相處融洽 [seung1 chyu3 yung4 hap7] *v.* get on well

相等 [seung1 dang2] *adj.* equivalent

相對 [seung1 deui3] *adj.* relative; *adv.* relatively

相對而言 [seung1 deui3 yi4 yin4] *adj.* comparative

商店 [seung1 dim3] *n.* store (~ directory 商店目錄, ~ window 商店櫥窗)

霜凍 [seung1 dung3] *adj.* frosted

傷感 [seung1 gam2] *n.* pathos

相關 [seung1 gwaan1] *n.* correlation; *adj.* relevant

相關性 [seung1 gwaan1 sing3] *n.* relevance

雙關語 [seung1 gwaan1 yu5] *n.* pun

傷口 [seung1 hau2] *n.* wound

傷害 [seung1 hoi6] *n.* harm

雙子座 [seung1 ji2 jo6] *n.* Gemini

傷心 [seung1 sam1] *n.* grief; *adj.* mournful

相信 [seung1 seun3] *n.* believe

商人 [seung1 yan4] *n.* merchant

雙人床 [seung1 yan4 chong4] *n.* double bed

雙人房 [seung1 yan4 fong4] *n.* double room

商業 [seung1 yip9] *adj.* commercial

商業課程 [seung1 yip9 fo3 ching4] *n.* business class

商業區 [seung1 yip9 keui1] *n.* commercial zone

雙魚座 [seung1 yu4 jo6] *n.* Pisces

雙語 [seung1 yu5] *adj.* bilingual

想 [seung2] *v.* expect

相 [seung2] *n.* photograph, photo (take a ~ 影相)

相機 [seung2 gei1] *n.* camera (~ case 相機袋, ~ shop/store 相機銷)

想像 [seung2 jeung6] *v.* imagine; *n.* imagination

想知道 [seung2 ji1 dou6] *v.* wonder

相簿 [seung2 bou6] *n.* photo album

常青樹 [seung4 ching1 syu6] *n.* evergreen

常規 [seung4 kwai1] *n.* routine

嘗試 [seung4 si3] *n.* attempt

常用語手冊 [seung4 yung6 yu5 sau2 chaak8] *n.* phrase book

上坡 [seung5 bo1] *adj.* uphill

上車 [seung5 che1] *v.* get on

上發條 [seung5 faat8 tiu4] *v.* wind sth. up

上咗年紀 [seung5 jo2 nin4 gei3] *adj.* elderly

上樓 [seung5 lau4] *adv.* upstairs

上網 [seung5 mong5] *v.* surf the Internet

上癮 [seung5 yan2] *adj.* addicted

上油 [seung5 yau4] *v.* lubricate

上釉 [seung5 yau6] *n.* glaze (barbecue ~ 燒烤糖汁, sweet ~ 甜霜, sugar ~ 糖霜, honey ~ 蜜糖霜)

上帝 [seung6 dai3] *n.* God

上等 [seung6 dang2] *adj.* fine (~ cut 細切煙草, ~ powder 細粉, ~ food 美食)

上等牛扒 [seung6 dang2 ngau4 pa4] *n.* prime rib

上個星期 [seung6 go3 sing1 kei4] *adv.* last week

上個月 [seung6 go3 yut9] *adv.* last month

上下顛倒 [seung6 ha6 din1 dou2] *adv.* upside down

上下文 [seung6 ha6 man4] *n.* context

上好 [seung6 hou2] *adj.* superlative

上面 [seung6 min6] *adj.* upper

上面一層 [seung6 min6 yat7 chang4] *n.* topping (salad ~ 沙律配料, meat ~ 肉餡)

上網 [seung6 mong5] *v.* to go online

上鋪 [seung6 pou1] *n.* upper berth

上身 [seung6 san1] *n.* upper body

上訴 [seung6 sou3] *n.* appeal

恤衫 [seut7 saam1] *n.* shirt

術語 [seut9 yu5] *n.* parlance

促進 [shuk7 jeun3] *n.* boost

詩 [si1] *n.* poem

絲綢 [si1 chau4] *n.* silk

蓍草 [si1 chou2] *n.* yarrow

絲帶 [si1 daai3] *n.* ribbon

私底下 [si1 dai2 ha6] *adv.* privately

斯德哥爾摩 [si1 dak7 go1 yi5 mo1] *n.* Stockholm (~, capital of Sweden 瑞典嘅首都)

司法部 [si1 faat8 bou6] *n.* judiciary

司法權 [si1 faat8 kyun4] *n.* jurisdiction

施肥 [si1 fei4] *v.* nourish

斯科普里 [si1 fo1 pou2 lei5] *n.* Skopje (~, capital of Macedonia 馬其頓王國嘅首都)

司機 [si1 gei1] *n.* driver

詩歌 [si1 go1] *n.* poverty

思考 [si1 haau2] *v.* think; *n.* thinking

詩學 [si1 hok9] *n.* poetics

獅子 [si1 ji2] *n.* lion

獅子座 [si1 ji2 jo6] *n.* Leo

撕爛 [si1 laan6] *v.* shred; *adj.* torn (muscle)

斯里巴加灣市 [si1 lei5 ba1 ga1 waan1 si5] *n.* Bandar Seri Begawan (~, capital of Brunei 文萊嘅首都)

斯里蘭卡 [si1 lei5 laan4 ka1] *n.* Sri Lanka; *adj.* Sri Lankan

斯洛伐克 [si1 lok8 fat9 hak7] *n.* Slovakia; *adj.* Slovakian, Slovak

斯洛文尼亞 [si1 lok8 man4 nei4 a3] *n.* Slovenia; *adj.* Slovenian

思路 [si1 lou6] *n.* train of thought

絲襪 [si1 mat9] *n.* pantyhose

斯佩爾特麵粉 [si1 pui3 yi5 dak9 min6 fan2] *n.* spelt flour

私生 [si1 sang1] *adj.* illegitimate

私生子 [si1 sang1 ji2] *n.* bastard

斯威士蘭 [si1 wai1 si6 laan4] *n.* Swaziland

私隱 [si1 yan2] *n.* privacy

詩人 [si1 yan4] *n.* poet

私人 [si1 yan4] *adj.* private

私人房間 [si1 yan4 fong4 gaan1] *n.* private room

私人醫院 [si1 yan4 yi1 yun2] *n.* private hospital

私有財產 [si1 yau5 choi4 chaan2] *n.* private property

私有化 [si1 yau5 fa3] *n.* privatization

詩意 [si1 yi3] *adj.* poetic

史前 [si2 chin4] *adj.* prehistoric

史前藝術 [si2 chin4 ngai6 seut9] *n.* prehistoric art

史官 [si2 gun1] *n.* annalist, chronicler

試 [si3] *v.* try (~ hard 好努力, ~ on 試衫)

弒君 [si3 gwan1] *n.* regicide

嗜好 [si3 hou3] *n.* proclivity

試驗 [si3 yim6] *n.* experiment

試驗性 [si3 yim6 sing6] *adj.* experimental

試用期 [si3 yung6 kei4] *n.* probation

時差 [si4 cha1] *n.* jet lag (be ~ged 有時差)

時代 [si4 doi6] *n.* era

時間 [si4 gaan3] *n.* time (*hour/ repetition*) (free ~ 得閒, on ~ 準時, What ~ is it? 宜家幾 點? , short on ~ 唔夠時間)

時間表 [si4 gaan1 biu2] *n.* schedule

時期 [si4 kei4] *n.* period

時尚 [si4 seung6] *n.* fashion; *adj.* fashionable

時事 [si4 si6] *n.* current affairs

時態 [si4 taai3] *n.* tense

市場 [si5 cheung4] *n.* market

市場價 [si5 cheung4 ga3] *n.* market price

市長 [si5 jeung2] *n.* mayor

市政 [si5 jing3] *adv.* municipal

市政廳 [si5 jing3 ting1] *n.* town hall

市中心 [si5 jung1 sam1] *n.* center of town

市民 [si5 man4] *n.* citizen

事 [si6] *n.* matter (what's the ~? 乜嘢事?)

事前 [si6 chin4] *n.* beforehand

士多啤梨 [si6 do1 be1 lei4] *n.* strawberry

視覺 [si6 gok8] *adj.* visual

事例 [si6 lai6] *n.* case

視力 [si6 lik9] *n.* vision

視網膜 [si6 mong5 mok9] *n.* retina

事實 [si6 sat9] *n.* fact

事實上 [si6 sat9 seung6] *adv.* virtually

事先 [si6 sin1] *adv.* in advance

示威 [si6 wai1] *n.* demonstration

事業 [si6 yip9] *n.* career

骰 [sik7] *n.* dice (roll the ~ 摘骰仔)

色情 [sik7 ching4] *adj.* erotic

適當 [sik7 dong3] *adj.* appropriate; *adv.* properly

釋放 [sik7 fong3] *v.* release

適合 [sik7 hap9] *adj.* suitable (~ for 適合, ~ with lunch 適合當 午飯, ~ with dinner 適合當

晚飯，~ with dessert 適合當
甜品)

識好多語言嘅人 [sik7 hou2
do1 yu5 yin4 ge3 yan4] *n.*
polyglot

色狼 [sik7 long4] *n.* pervert

蟋蟀 [sik7 seut7] *n.* crickets

蜥蜴 [sik7 yik9] *n.* lizard

適應 [sik7 ying3] *v.* adapt

食 [sik9] *v.* eat

食晏時間 [sik9 aan3 si4 gaan3]
n. lunchtime

食品櫃 [sik9 ban2 gwai6] *n.*
pantry

食品防腐劑 [sik9 ban2 fong4
fu6 jai1] *n.* food preservatives

食草動物 [sik9 chou2 dung6
mat9] *n.* herbivore

食得 [sik9 dak7] *adj.* edible (non-
~ 唔食得)

食得開心啲！ [sik9 dak7 hoi1
sam1 di1] *phr.* Enjoy your meal!

食得開胃啲 [sik9 dak7 hoi1
wai6 di1] *phr.* Bon appetit!

食飯 [sik9 faan6] *n.* dining (~ car
餐車，~ out 出去食飯); *v.* dine
to ~ 食飯

蝕刻版畫 [sik9 hak7 baan2 wa2]
n. etching

食指 [sik9 ji2] *n.* forefinger

食物 [sik9 mat9] *n.* food

食物金字塔 [sik9 mat9 gam1 ji6
taap8] *n.* food pyramid

食物中毒 [sik9 mat9 jung3
duk9] *n.* food poisoning

食物添加劑 [sik9 mat9 tim1 ga1
jai1] *n.* food additives

食譜 [sik9 pou2] *n.* recipe

食人魚 [sik9 yan4 yu2] *n.* piranha

食煙 [sik9 yin1] *n.* smoking (No ~
禁止吸煙)

食肉動物 [sik9 yuk9 dung6 mat9]
n. predator

食用香草 [sik9 yung6 heung1
chou2] *n.* champignons, button
mushrooms

食用色素 [sik9 yung6 seik7
sou3] *n.* food coloring

食用水 [sik9 yung6 seui2] *n.*
drinkable water; *adj.* potable

閃 [sim2] *v.* flare; *n.* flicker

閃電 [sim2 din6] *n.* lightning

閃光 [sim2 gwong1] *v.* flash

閃光燈攝影 [sim2 gwong1 dang1
sip8 ying2] *n.* flash photography

閃閃發光 [sim2 sim2 faat8
gwong1] *adj.* sparkling

仙丹 [sin1 daan1] *n.* elixer

先見之明 [sin1 gin3 ji1 ming4]
n. foresight

先進 [sin1 jeun3] *adj.* advanced

先知 [sin1 ji1] *n.* oracle

先驅 [sin1 keui1] *n.* pioneer

先例 [sin1 lai6] *n.* precedent

先唔講 [sin1 m4 gong2] *prep.*
apart from

先生 [sin1 saang1] *n.* sir

仙人掌 [sin1 yan4 jeung2] *n.*
cactus

癬 [sin2] *n.* ringworm

腺 [sin3] *n.* gland

線 [sin3] *n.* line (*geometry*/*subway*),
queue

扇貝 [sin3 bui3] *n.* scallops

煽動 [sin3 dung6] *v.* agitate; *n.*
instigation

擅闖 [sin6 chong2] *v.* intrude

擅闖者 [sin6 chong2 je2] *n.* intruder

贍養費 [sin6 yeung5 fai3] *n.* alimony

升 [sing1] *v.* go up; *n.* liter

聲稱 [sing1 ching1] *v.* claim

升降機 [sing1 gong3 gei1] *n.* elevator

升起 [sing1 hei2] *v.* rise

星號 [sing1 hou6] *n.* asterisk

星象 [sing1 jeung6] *n.* stars

升職 [sing1 jik7] *n.* promotion; *v.* promote

升值 [sing1 jik9] *v.* appreciate in value

星座 [sing1 jo6] *n.* constellation

星球 [sing1 kau4] *n.* planet

勝利 [sing1 lei6] *n.* laurel (~ leaves 月桂葉)

聲明 [sing1 ming4] *n.* statement (make a ~ [*to police*] 落證供)

聲望 [sing1 mong6] *n.* prominence

星星 [sing1 sing1] *n.* star

星星形狀 [sing1 sing1 ying4 jong6] *adj.* star-shaped (~ pastry / ~ vegetables)

星雲 [sing1 wan4] *n.* nebula

聲譽 [sing1 yu6] *n.* reputation

繩 [sing2] *n.* rope, string

醒目 [sing2 muk9] *adj.* clever, brilliant

姓 [sing3] *n.* last name

性別 [sing3 bit9] *n.* gender

性別上 [sing3 bit9 seung6] *adv.* sexually

性別歧視 [sing3 bit9 kei4 si6] *n.* sexism

聖餐 [sing3 chaan1] *n.* communion

性取向 [sing3 cheui2 heung3] *n.* sexuality

性傳染 [sing3 chyun4 yim5] *adj.* venereal (~ disease 性傳染病)

聖誕節 [sing3 daan3 jit8] *n.* Christmas

聖誕節當日 [sing3 daan3 jit8 dong3 yat9] *n.* Christmas Day

聖誕節快樂 [sing3 daan3 jit8 faai3 lok9] *phr.* Merry Christmas

聖誕節裝飾 [sing3 daan3 jit8 jong1 sik7] *n.* Christmas decorations

聖地 [sing3 dei6] *n.* sanctuary

聖地牙哥 [sing3 dei6 nga4 go1] *n.* Santiago (~, capital of Chile 智利嘅首都)

聖多美 [sing3 do1 mei5] *n.* Sao Tome (~, capital of Sao Tome and Principe 聖多美和普林西比嘅首都)

聖多美和普林西比 [sing3 do1 mei5 wo4 pou2 lam4 sai1 bei2] *n.* Sao Tome and Principe

聖多明各 [sing3 do1 ming4 gok8] *n.* Santo Domingo (~, capital of Dominican Republic 多米尼加共和國嘅首都)

性感 [sing3 gam2] *adj.* sexy

聖經 [sing3 ging1] *n.* Bible

性高潮 [sing3 gou1 chiu4] *n.* orgasm

聖克里斯托弗和尼維斯島 [sing3 hak7 lei5 si1 tok8 fat7 wo4 nei4 wai4 si1 dou2] *n.* Saint Kitts and Nevis

聖荷西 [sing3 ho4 sai1] *n.* San

Jose (~, capital of Costa Rica 哥斯達黎加嘅首都)

聖佐治 [sing3 jo3 ji6] *n.* Saint George's (~, capital of Grenada 格拉那達嘅首都)

聖禮 [sing3 lai5] *n.* sacrament

勝利 [sing3 lei6] *n.* victory

聖盧西亞島 [sing3 lou4 sai1 a3 dou2] *n.* Saint Lucia

聖馬力諾 [sing3 ma5 lik9 nok9] *n.* San Marino

聖文森特和格林納丁斯 [sing3 man4 sam1 dak9 wo4 gaak8 lam4 naap9 ding1 si1] *n.* Saint Vincent and the Grenadines

聖薩爾瓦多 [sing3 saat8 yi5 nga5 do1] *n.* San Salvador (~, capital of El Salvador 薩爾瓦多嘅首都)

聖詩 [sing3 si1] *n.* psalm

性騷擾 [sing3 sou1 yiu2] *v.* molest; *n.* molestation

聖人 [sing3 yan4] *n.* sage

聖約翰 [sing3 yeuk8 hon6] *n.* Saint John's (~, capital of Antigua and Barbuda 安提瓜同巴布達嘅首都)

姓 [sing3] *n.* last name

乘 [sing4] *v.* multiply

承辦酒席 [sing4 baan6 jau2 jik9] *n.* catering (~ service 餐飲服務)

承包人 [sing4 baau1 yan4] *n.* contractor

成比例 [sing4 bei2 lai6] *adj.* proportional

城堡 [sing4 bou2] *n.* castle

成本 [sing4 bun2] *n.* cost

承擔 [sing4 daam1] *v.* undertake

城垛 [sing4 do2] *n.* battlement

乘法 [sing4 faat8] *n.* multiplication

成見 [sing4 gin3] *n.* prejudice

成功 [sing4 gung1] *v.* succeed

乘客 [sing4 haak8] *n.* passenger

城際列車 [sing4 jai3 lit9 che1] *n.* intercity train

成就 [sing4 jau6] *n.* achievement

成績單 [sing4 jik7 daan1] *n.* transcript

承諾 [sing4 nok9] *n.* commitment

承受 [sing4 sau6] *v.* undergo

城市 [sing4 si5] *n.* city (~ center 市中心, ~ wall 城牆, ~ limits 城市邊緣)

成熟 [sing4 suk9] *n.* maturity

成為 [sing4 wai4] *v.* become

承認 [sing4 ying6] *v.* acknowledge

成語 [sing4 yu5] *n.* idiom

剩菜 [sing6 choi3] *adj.* leftover

盛況 [sing6 fong3] *n.* pageantry

剩女 [sing6 neui5] *n.* bachelorette (~ party 剩女派對)

剩餘 [sing6 yu4] *n.* rest (~ area 休息區, allow to ~ 可以休息)

攝氏 [sip8 si6] *n.* celsius

攝影 [sip8 ying2] *n.* photography

攝影師 [sip8 ying2 si1] *n.* photographer

褻瀆 [sit8 duk9] *v.* profane: *n.* sacrilege

泄露 [sit8 lou6] *n.* leak

消除 [siu1 cheui4] *v.* purge

消除鍵 [siu1 cheui4 gin6] *n. comp.* delete key

消毒 [siu1 duk9] *n.* disinfect

消毒水 [siu1 duk9 seui2] *n.* germicide

消化 [siu1 fa3] *v.* digest

消化不良 [siu1 fa3 bat7 leung4] *n.* indigestion

消化系統 [siu1 fa3 hai6 tung2] *n.* digestive system

消費 [siu1 fai3] *n.* consumption

消費者 [siu1 fai3 je2] *n.* consumer

消防 [siu1 fong4] *n.* fire department

消防車 [siu1 fong4 che1] *n.* fire truck

宵禁 [siu1 gam3] *n.* curfew

消極 [siu1 gik9] *adj.* passive

燒烤 [siu1 haau1] *n.* barbecue (~ sauce 燒烤汁, ~ flavor 燒烤味, ~ chips 燒烤味薯片, ~ grill 燒烤爐)

燒烤油 [siu1 haau1 yau4] *n.* grilling oil

燒香腸 [siu1 heung1 cheung1] *n.* grilled sausage

燒著 [siu1 jeuk9] *v.* flame

燒芝士 [siu1 ji1 si2] *n.* grilled cheese

燒豬肉 [siu1 jyu1 yuk9] *n.* pork roast

銷路 [siu1 lou6] *n.* sales (~ clerk 推銷員, ~ department 銷售部, ~ receipt 銷售發票, ~ tax 銷售稅)

消滅 [siu1 mit9] *v.* annihilate; *n.* annihilation

燒爐 [siu1 nung1] *v.* char

燒爐魚 [siu1 nung1 yu4] *n.* char (fish)

銷售稅 [siu1 sau6 seui3] *n.* sales tax

小茴香 [siu1 wui4 heung1] *n.* dill (~ pickles 小茴香酸果, ~ seasoning 小茴香調味品)

消音器 [siu1 yam1 hei3] *n.* muffler

燒魚 [siu1 yu2] *n.* grilled fish

燒肉 [siu1 yuk9] *n.* broiled meat

小矮人 [siu2 ai2 yan4] *n.* pigmy

小斑點 [siu2 baan1 dim2] *n.* moat

小本經營 [siu2 bun2 ging1 ying4] *adj.* shoestring

小冊子 [siu2 chaak8 ji2] *n.* booklet; bus tickets

小測驗 [siu2 chak7 yim6] *n.* quiz

小丑 [siu2 chau2] *n.* clown

少啲 [siu2 di1] *det.* less

小販 [siu2 faan2] *n.* vendor

小費 [siu2 fai3] *n.* tip (*gratuity*)

小腹 [siu2 fuk7] *n.* lower abdomen

小行星 [siu2 hang4 sing1] *n.* asteroid

小姐 [siu2 je2] *n.* Miss

小組 [siu2 jou2] *n.* panel

小溪 [siu2 kai1] *n.* stream

小路 [siu2 lou6] *n.* side street

小龍蝦 [siu2 lung4 ha1] *n.* crayfish

小賣部 [siu2 maai6 bou6] *n.* grocery store

小米 [siu2 mai5] *n.* millet

小麥 [siu2 mak9] *n.* wheat (~ bread 小麥麵包, ~ pasta 小麥糊)

小麥布甸 [siu2 mak9 bou3 din6] *n.* semolina pudding

小問題 [siu2 man6 tai4] *n.* ailment

小母牛 [siu2 mou5 ngau4] *n.* heifer

小食店 [siu2 sik9 dim3] *n.* snack bar

少數民族 [siu2 sou3 man4 juk9] *n.* minority

小說 [siu2 syut8] *n.* novel

小題大做 [siu2 tai4 daai6 jou6] *n.* petulance

小提琴 [siu2 tai4 kam4] *n.* violin

小童池 [siu2 tong3 chi4] *n.* kiddie pool

笑柄 [siu3 beng3] *n.* mockery

笑 [siu3] *v.* laugh

笑聲 [siu3 sing1] *n.* laugh(ter)

兆頭 [siu6 tau4] *n.* omen

梳 [so1] *n.* comb

蔬菜 [so1 choi3] *n.* vegetable (~ stew 燉青菜, ~ broth 菜湯)

蔬菜燉肉 [so1 choi3 dan6 yuk9] *n.* ragout

梳打水 [so1 da2 seui2] *n.* carbonated water

疏忽 [so1 fat7] *v.* neglect; *n.* oversight

疏縫工 [so1 fung4 gung1] *n.* baster

疏散 [so1 saan3] *v.* evacuate

鎖 [so2] *v.* lock

鎖鏈 [so2 lin4] *n.* chain

所羅門群島 [so2 lo4 mun4 kwan4 dou2] *n.* Solomon Islands

鎖匙 [so2 si4] *n.* key

鎖匙扣 [so2 si4 kau3] *n.* key ring

所屬 [so2 suk9] *adj.* possessive

所謂 [so2 wai6] *adj.* so-called

所有 [so2 yau5] *pron.* everything

所有財產 [so2 yau5 choi4 chaan2] *n.* holding

所有權 [so2 yau5 kyun4] *n.* ownership

所以 [so2 yi5] *adv.* therefore

傻 [so4] *adj.* silly

傻瓜 [so4 gwa1] *n.* fool

傻佬 [so4 lou2] *n.* rover

腮腺炎 [soi1 sin3 yim4] *n.* mumps

索非亞 [sok8 fei1 a3] *n.* Sofia (~, capital of Bulgaria 保加利亞嘅首都)

塑膠 [sok8 gaau1] *n.* plastic; *adj.* acrylic

唦氣 [sok8 hei3] *v.* pant; *n.* wheezing

索馬里 [sok8 ma5 lei5] *n.* Somalia; *adj.* Somalian

索引 [sok8 yan5] *n.* index

桑莓 [song1 mui4] *n.* mulberry (wild ~ 野桑莓)

桑拿 [song1 na4] *n.* sauna

爽口 [song2 hau2] *adj.* chewable (~ tablet 可以咬嘅藥, ~ supplements 可以咬嘅補品)

酥餅 [sou1 beng2] *n.* popovers

蘇打水 [sou1 da2 seui2] *n.* baking soda

蘇丹 [sou1 daan1] *n.* Sudan; *adj.* Sudanese

蘇格蘭 [sou1 gaak8 laan4] *n.* Scotland; *adj.* Scottish

蘇克雷 [sou1 hak7 leui4] *n.* Sucre (~, judicial capital of Bolivia 玻利維亞司法首都)

鬚後水 [sou1 hau6 seui2] *n.* aftershave lotion

蘇里南 [sou1 lei5 naam4] *n.* Suriname

蘇瓦 [sou1 nga5] *n.* Suva (~, capital of Fiji 斐濟嘅首都)

鬚刨 [sou1 paau2] *n.* razor (~ blade 鬚刨刀片)

酥皮水果餡餅 [sou1 pei4 seui2 gwo2 haam6 beng2] *n.* cobbler (peach ~ 酥皮桃仔餡餅, cherry ~ 酥皮車厘子餡餅, apple ~ 酥皮蘋果餡餅)

騷擾 [sou1 yiu2] *v.* disturb (do not ~ 請勿打擾, ~ the peace 破壞平靜); *n.* harassment

數字 [sou2 ji6] *n.* figure

數字順序 [sou2 ji6 seun6 jeui6] *n.* numerical order

數唔晒 [sou2 m4 saai3] *adj.* uncountable

掃 [sou3] *v.* whisk

素菜 [sou3 choi3] *n.* meatless dishes

素餃 [sou3 gaau2] *n.* vegetable dumpling

數據 [sou3 geui3] *n.* data

數據庫 [sou3 geui3 fu3] *n. comp.* database (computer ~ 電腦數據庫)

數據機 [sou3 geui3 gei1] *n. comp.* modem (Internet ~ 上網數據機)

數學 [sou3 hok9] *n.* mathematics

數字 [sou3 ji6] *n.* number

塑造 [sou3 jou6] *v.* shape

訴訟當事人 [sou3 jung6 dong1 si6 yan4] *n.* litigant

數量 [sou3 leung6] *n.* amount

數碼 [sou3 ma5] *adj.* digital

掃描 [sou3 miu4] *v.* scan

掃描器 [sou3 miu4 hei3] *n.* scanner

素描 [sou3 miu4] *n.* sketch

素食者 [sou3 sik9 je2] *adj.* vegetarian (~ dish 素菜, ~ soup 素湯, ~ menu 素菜菜單)

燒爛 [sui1 laan6] *adj.* burned

燒傷 [sui1 seung1] *n.* burn; *adj.* burnt (~ toast 燒燶多士)

宿醉 [suk7 jeui3] *n.* hangover

粟米 [suk7 mai5] *n.* corn (~flakes 粟米片, ~ oil 粟米油, ~meal 粟米餐, ~ syrup 粟米糖漿, creamed ~ 牛油粟米)

粟米薄餅卷 [suk7 mai5 bok9 beng2 gyun2] *n.* taco (fish ~ 魚肉粟米薄餅卷, ~ sauce 粟米薄餅卷醬, ~ shell 粟米薄餅卷皮, ~ meat 肉粟米薄餅卷)

粟米熱狗 [suk1 mai5 yit6 gau2] *n.* corn dog

粟粉 [suk7 fan2] *n.* cornstarch

粟米餡卷 [suk7 mai5 haam6 gyun2] *n.* tamale

粟米粥 [suk7 mai5 juk7] *n.* polenta

粟米麵包 [suk7 mai5 min6 baau1] *n.* cornbread

粟米片 [suk7 mai5 pin2] *n.* nachos

宿命論 [suk7 ming6 leun6] *n.* predestination

縮寫 [suk7 se2] *n.* abbreviation

宿舍 [suk7 se3] *n.* dormitory

熟 [suk9] *adj.* ripe (~ fruit 熟生果, ~ vegetables 食得嘅青菜)

贖番 [suk9 faan1] *v.* redeem

贖金 [suk9 gam1] *n.* ransom

贖罪 [suk9 jeui6] *n.* atonement

熟練 [suk9 lin6] *adj.* skilled

熟食店 [suk9 sik9 dim3] *n.* deli

屬性 [suk9 sing3] *n.* attribute

熟人 [suk9 yan4] *n.* acquaintance

屬於 [suk9 yu1] *v.* belong to

鬆 [sung1] *adj.* loose

鬆餅 [sung1 beng2] *n.* muffin (bran ~ 麩皮鬆餅, blueberry ~ 藍莓鬆餅, cherry ~ 車厘子鬆餅, banana nut ~ 香蕉果仁鬆餅, whole grain ~ 全麥鬆餅)

鬆餅 [sung1 beng2] *n.* puff pastry

松露 [sung1 lou6] *n.* truffle (chocolate ~ 朱古力松露)

鬆身 [sung1 san1] *adj.* loose-fitting

送貨 [sung3 fo3] *v.* deliver

送貨上門 [sung3 fo3 seung5 mun4] *n.* delivery

送走 [sung3 jau2] *v.* give smth. away

崇拜 [sung4 baai3] *n.* worship

書 [syu1] *n.* book

輸 [syu1] *v.* lose (*not win*)

輸出 [syu1 cheut7] *n. tech.* output

書籤 [syu1 chim1] *n.* bookmark

抒情 [syu1 ching4] *adj.* lyric

書呆子 [syu1 daai1 ji2] *n.* pedant

書店 [syu1 dim3] *n.* bookstore

賭 [dou2] *v.* bet

書法 [syu1 faat8] *n.* calligraphy

書房 [syu1 fong4] *n.* study

舒服 [syu1 fuk9] *adj.* comfortable

輸家 [syu1 ga1] *n.* loser

輸血 [syu1 hyut8] *n.* transfusion

書面 [syu1 min6] *adj.* literary

書枱 [syu1 toi2] *n.* desk

輸入 [syu1 yap9] *n.* input

輸入文件 [syu1 yap9 man4 gin6] *v. comp.* import files

鼠標 [syu2 biu1] *n. comp.* mouse, mouse arrow

暑假 [syu2 ga3] *n.* summer vacation

薯餅 [syu4 beng2] *n.* hash browns

薯仔 [syu4 jai2] *n.* potato (baked ~ 焗薯仔, roasted ~ 烤薯仔, red ~ 紅薯)

薯仔湯 [syu4 jai2 tong1] *n.* potato soup

薯條 [syu4 tiu4] *n.* chips (potato ~ 薯條, tortilla ~ 粟米片)

薯蓉 [syu4 yung4] *n.* mashed potatoes

樹 [syu6] *n.* tree

豎起 [syu6 hei2] *adj.* erected

豎行 [syu6 hong4] *n.* column (spreadsheet ~ 數據表嘅豎行)

樹仔 [syu6 jai2] *n.* sapling

豎琴 [syu6 kam4] *n.* harp

豎框 [syu6 kwaang1] *n.* mullion

樹林 [syu6 lam4] *n.* woods

樹皮 [syu6 pei4] *n.* bark

樹身 [syu6 san1] *n.* trunk (of car)

樹葉 [syu6 yip9] *n.* foliage

酸 [syun1] *adj.* sour (~ cream 酸忌廉, ~ milk 酸奶) ; tart (~ taste 酸味)

孫 [syun1] *n.* grandchild

宣佈 [syun1 bou3] *v.* declare

宣佈無罪 [syun1 bou3 mou4 jeui6] *v.* exonerate

宣佈斷絕關係 [syun1 bou3 tyun5 jyut9 gwaan1 hai6] *n.* renunciation

酸車厘子 [syun1 che1 lei4 ji2] *n.* morello cherries

宣傳 [syun1 chyun4] *v.* advertise

宣傳人員 [syun1 chyun4 yan4 yun4] *n.* propagandist

酸化 [syun1 fa3] *v.* acidify

酸鹼值 [syun1 gaan2 jik9] *n.* pH

酸忌廉 [syun1 gei6 lim1] *n.* sour cream

孫仔 [syun1 jai2] *n.* grandson

宣紙 [syun1 ji2] *n.* rice paper

酸辣醬 [syun1 laat9 jeung3] *n.* chutney (pineapple ~ 菠蘿醬, apple ~ 蘋果醬, date ~ 海棗醬, spicy ~ 辣醬, mango ~ 芒果醬)

酸奶酒 [syun1 naai5 jau2] *n.* kefir (strawberry ~ 草莓酸奶酒, vanilla ~ 香草酸奶酒)

孫女 [syun1 neui5] *n.* granddaughter

宣誓 [syun1 sai6] *n.* affidavit (*legal*)

酸性 [syun1 sing3] *n.* acidity

酸痛 [syun1 tung3] *adj.* sore (have a ~ throat 喉嚨痛, be ~ 覺得痛)

酸黃瓜 [syun1 wong4 gwa1] *n.* gherkins

宣言 [syun1 yin4] *n.* manifesto

選 [syun2] *v.* elect

選舉團 [syun2 geui2 tyun4] *n.* electoral college

選擇 [syun2 jaak9] *n.* choice

選民 [syun2 man4] *n.* electorate

選美比賽 [syun2 mei5 bei2 choi3] *n.* pageant

損失 [syun2 sat7] *n.* loss

選修 [syun2 sau1] *adj.* elective

損壞 [syun2 waai6] *n.* damage

蒜 [syun3] *n.* garlic (~ sauce 蒜茸醬, ~ powder 蒜粉)

算命佬 [syun3 meng6 lou2] *n.* fortuneteller

蒜茸蛋黃醬 [syun3 yung4 daan6 wong4 jeung3] *n.* garlic mayonnaise, aioli

蒜蓉忌廉大蝦 [syun3 yung4 gei6 lim1 daai6 ha1] *n.* shrimp scampi

船 [syun4] *n.* ship

船長 [syun4 jeung2] *n.* captain

船槳 [syun4 jeung2] *n.* paddle

旋轉 [syun4 jyun2] *v.* spin; *n.* rotary

旋律 [syun4 leut9] *n.* melody

船上面 [syun4 seung5 min6] *adv.* aboard

雪 [syut8] *n.* snow (~ tires 雪地防滑輪胎, powder ~ 粉狀雪, fresh ~ 初雪, wet ~ 雪水, ~storm 暴風雪)

雪崩 [syut8 bang1] *n.* avalanche

雪茄 [syut8 ga1] *n.* cigars

雪糕 [syut8 gou1] *n.* ice cream (~ cake 雪糕蛋糕, low-fat ~ 低脂雪糕, non-fat ~ 脫脂雪糕, non-dairy ~ 脫脂雪糕)

雪糕店 [syut8 gou1 dim3] *n.* ice cream parlor

雪櫃 [syut8 gwai6] *n.* refrigerator, fridge

雪梨酒 [syut8 lei4 jau2] *n.* sherry (~ glass 高腳酒杯)

說明書 [syut8 ming4 syu1] *n.* prospectus

雪條 [syut8 tiu4] *n.* ice pops

鱈魚 [syut8 yu2] *n.* whiting, haddock

T

他他醬 [ta1 ta1 jeung3] *n.* tartar sauce

軚 [taai1] *n.* tire

泰迪熊 [taai3 dik9 hung4] *n.* teddy bear

太多 [taai3 do1] *n.* redundancy; *adv.* too much

態度 [taai3 dou6] *n.* attitude

貸款 [taai3 fun2] *n.* loan

太監 [taai3 gaam3] *n.* eunuch

太貴 [taai3 gwai3] *adv.* too expensive

泰國 [taai3 gwok8] *n.* Thailand; *adj.* Thai

太好 [taai3 hou2] *adj.* great

太好啦! [taai3 hou2 la1] *phr.* Great!

太空人 [taai3 hung1 yan4] *n.* astronaut

太子港 [taai3 ji2 gong2] *n.* Port-au-Prince (~, capital of Haiti 海地嘅首都)

太靚 [taai3 leng3] *adj.* magnificent

太太 [taai3 taai2] *n.* Mrs.

太陽 [taai3 yeung4] *n.* sun

太陽遮 [taai3 yeung4 je1] *n.* parasol

太熱 [taai3 yit9] *v.* overheat

軚盤 [taai5 pun4] *n.* steering wheel

探病時間 [taam3 beng6 si4 gaan1] *n.* visiting hours

探測 [taam3 chak7] *v.* probe

探出 [taam3 cheut7] *v.* lean out

探險 [taam3 him2] *n.* exploration

探索 [taam3 sok8] *v.* explore

坦克 [taan2 hak7] *n.* tank

坦誠 [taan2 sing4] *adj.* genuine

坦桑尼亞 [taan2 song1 nei4 a3] *n.* Tanzania; *adj.* Tanzanian

碳 [taan3] *n.* carbon (~ copy 副本)

炭 [taan3] *n.* coal

碳水化合物 [taan3 seui2 fa3 hap9 mat9] *n.* carbohydrate (complex ~ 複合碳水化合物, simple ~ 簡單碳水化合物)

塔 [taap8] *n.* tower

塔吉克斯坦 [taap8 gat7 hak7 si1 taan2] *adj.* Tajikistan

塔拉瓦環礁 [taap8 laai1 nga5 waan4 jiu1] *n.* Tarawa Atoll (~, capital of Kiribati 基里巴斯嘅首都)

塔林 [taap8 lam4] *n.* Tallinn (~, capital of Estonia 愛沙尼亞嘅首都)

塔那那利佛 [taap8 na5 na5 lei6 fat7] *n.* Antananarivo (~, capital of Madagascar 馬達加斯加嘅首都)

塔什干 [taap8 sam6 gon1] *n.* Tashkent (~, capital of Uzbekistan 烏茲別克斯坦嘅首都)

梯 [tai1] *n.* ladder

睇 [tai2] *v.* look

體操 [tai2 chou1] *n.* gymnastics

睇得出 [tai2 dak7 cheut7] *adj.* perceptible

睇得見 [tai2 dak7 gin3] *adj.* noticeable

睇法 [tai2 faat8] *n.* perspective

睇唔清楚 [tai2 m4 ching1 cho2] *adj.* illegible

睇手相嘅人 [tai2 sau2 seung1 ge3 yan4] *n.* palmist

睇睇 [tai2 tai2] *v.* look

體育場 [tai2 yuk9 cheung4] *n.* stadium

體育用品 [tai2 yuk9 yung6 ban2] *n.* sporting goods (~ store 體育用品店)

替代治療 [tai3 doi6 ji6 liu4] *n.* alternative treatment

剃刀 [tai3 dou1] *n.* shaver

替死鬼 [tai3 jeui6 yeung4] *n.* scapegoat

剃鬚 [tai3 sou1] *v.* shave (one's face)

剃鬚刷 [tai3 sou1 chaat8] *n.* shaving brush

剃鬚膏 [tai3 sou1 gou1] *n.* shaving cream

替換 [tai3 wun6] *v.* exchange a purchase

提倡 [tai4 cheung3] *n.* advocacy

提倡者 [tai4 cheung3 je2] *n.* advocate

提出 [tai4 cheut7] *v.* offer

提到 [tai4 dou3] *v.* mention (don't ~ it 唔好客氣)

提高 [tai4 gou1] *v.* raise

提供證據嘅責任 [tai4 gung1 jing3 geui3 ge3 jaak8 yam4] burden of proof

提供 [tai4 gung1] *v.* provide

提子 [tai4 ji2] *n.* grape

提子乾 [tai4 ji2 gon1] *n.* raisin

提子汁 [tai4 ji2 jap7] *n.* grape juice

提子蒸餾酒 [tai4 ji2 jing1 lau6 jau2] *n.* grape spirit

提子油 [tai4 ji2 yau4] *n.* grapeseed oil

提煉 [tai4 lin6] *v.* refine

提煉廠 [tai4 lin6 chong2] *n.* refinery

提名 [tai4 ming4] *n.* nomination

題目 [tai4 muk9] *n.* topic

提神 [tai4 san4] *v.* refresh, to be refreshing (*comp.* refresh a webpage 刷新網頁)

提醒 [tai4 sing2] *v.* remind

提議 [tai4 yi5] *v.* suggest

冰...開心 [tam3 ... hoi1 sam1] *v.* amuse

吞 [tan1] *v.* swallow

吞沒 [tan1 mut9] *v.* engulf

吞拿魚 [tan1 na4 yu2] *n.* tuna (~ salad 吞拿魚沙律)

藤蔓 [tang4 maan6] *n.* vine

偷 [tau1] *v.* steal

偷睇 [tau1 tai2] *v.* peep

偷嘢 [tau1 ye5] *n.* shoplifting

透氣 [tau2 hei3] *v.* breathe

透支 [tau3 ji1] *v.* overdraw

透明 [tau3 ming4] *adj.* transparent

頭 [tau4] *n.* head

投標 [tau4 biu1] *v.* bid

頭道菜 [tau4 dou6 choi3] *n.* first course

頭髮 [tau4 faat8] *n.* hair

頭巾 [tau4 gan1] *n.* hood (*of a car*)

頭骨 [tau4 gwat7] *n.* skull

頭銜 [tau4 haam4] *n.* title

投降 [tau4 hong4] *v.* surrender

投資 [tau4 ji1] *v.* invest; *n.* investment

投資者 [tau4 ji1 je2] *n.* investor

投資組合 [tau4 ji1 jou2 hap9] *n.* portfolio

頭盔 [tau4 kwai1] *n.* helmet

頭皮 [tau4 pei4] *n.* scalp

投票 [tau4 piu3] *n.* ballot (~ box 投票箱, ~ paper 選票)

頭盤 [tau4 pun4] *n.* first course

投訴 [tau4 sou3] *n.* complaint; *v.* file a complaint

頭痛 [tau4 tung3] *n.* headache; *v.* have a headache

頭暈 [tau4 wan4] *adj.* dizzy (feel ~ 覺得好暈)

投入 [tau4 yap9] *adj.* dedicated

投影機 [tau4 ying2 gei1] *n.* projector

踢 [tek8] *v.* kick

聽 [teng1] *v.* hear, listen

聽講 [teng1 gong2] *v.* hear about/of

聽力 [teng1 lik9] *n.* hearing

聽力測試 [teng1 lik9 chak7 si3] *n.* hearing test

推 [teui1] *v.* push (sign on a door)

推動 [teui1 dung6] *v.* propel

推薦 [teui1 jin3] *v.* recommend

退出 [teui3 cheut7] *v. comp.* log out/off

退錢 [teui3 chin2] *n.* refund

退房 [teui3 fong2] *n.* check out

退格鍵 [teui3 gaak8 gin6] *n. comp.* backspace, backspace key

退咗休 [teui3 jo2 yau1] *adj.* retired

退休 [teui3 yau1] *v.* retire

退休金 [teui3 yau1 gam1] *n.* pension

盾 [teun5] *n.* shield

T恤 [ti1 seut7] *n.* T-shirt

甜 [tim4] *adj.* sweet (~ and sour sauce 甜酸醬, ~ bread, 甜麵包 ~ pepper 甜椒, ~ potato 番薯)

甜品 [tim4 ban2] *n.* dessert

甜菜 [tim4 choi3] *n.* beet

甜菜根 [tim4 choi3 gan1] *n.* beetroot

甜椒 [tim4 jiu1] *n.* bell pepper (red ~ 紅甜椒, yellow ~ 黃甜椒, orange ~ 橙色甜椒, green ~ 青甜椒)

甜味劑 [tim4 mei6 jai1] *n.* sweetener (no calorie ~ 無熱量甜味劑, artificial ~ 人工甜味劑)

甜麵包乾 [tim4 min6 baau1 gon1] *n.* rusk

甜牛奶 [tim4 ngau4 naai5] *n.* dulce de leche

甜筒 [tim4 tung2] *n.* ice cream cone

天 [tin1] *n.* sky

天窗 [tin1 cheung1] *n.* sunroof

天才 [tin1 choi4] *n.* genius

天花板 [tin1 fa1 baan2] *n.* ceiling

天份 [tin1 fan6] *n.* talent

天黑 [tin1 haak7] *n.* night (at ~ 晚黑, good~ 晚安, spend the ~ 過夜)

天氣 [tin1 hei3] *n.* weather (~ forecast 天氣預報, ~ report 氣象報告)

天蠍座 [tin1 hit8 jo6] *n.* Scorpio

天井 [tin1 jeng2] *n.* courtyard

天主教 [tin1 jyu2 gaau3] *adj.* Catholic

天文學 [tin1 man4 hok9] *n.* astronomy

天文學家 [tin1 man4 hok9 ga1] *n.* astronomer

天文台 [tin1 man4 toi4] *n.* observatory

天棚 [tin1 paang4] *n.* sunshade

天秤座 [tin1 ping3 jo6] *n.* Libra

天生 [tin1 sang1] *adj.* innate

天使 [tin1 si2] *n.* angel

天線 [tin1 sin3] *n.* antenna

天體沙灘 [tin1 tai2 sa1 taan1] *n.* nudist beach

天堂 [tin1 tong4] *n.* paradise, heaven

田 [tin4] *n.* field (soccer/football/rugby ~足球場, ~ hockey 草地曲棍球)

填充物 [tin4 chung1 mat9] *n.* filling (fruit ~ 水果餡, pastry ~ 糕點餡, meat ~ 肉餡, jam ~ 醬, dental ~ 補牙)

田雞 [tin4 gai1] *n.* frog

田雞腳 [tin4 gai1 geuk8] *n.* frog's legs

田園沙律 [tin4 yun4 sa1 leut9] *n.* garden salad

田園生活 [tin4 yun4 sang1 wut9] *n.* rusticity

聽日 [ting1 yat9] *adv.* tomorrow (~ morning 聽日晏晝, day after ~ 後日, See you ~! 聽日見！)

聽覺 [ting3 gok8] *adj.* auditory

聽眾 [ting3 jung3] *n.* listener

亭 [ting4] *n.* pavilion

停 [ting4] *phr.* Halt!

廷布 [ting4 bou3] *n.* Thimphu (~, capital of Bhutan 不丹嘅首都)

停車場 [ting4 che1 cheung4] *n.* parking garage, car park, parking lot

停車罰單 [ting4 che1 fat9 daan1] *n.* parking fine/ticket

停頓 [ting4 deun6] *v.* pause

停電 [ting4 din6] *n.* power outage

庭警 [ting4 ging2] *n.* bailiff

停止 [ting4 ji2] *v.* stop (~ sign 停止指示牌, ~ at … 停喺, ~!, 唔好郁!)

貼 [tip8] *v.* stick (~ out 伸出)

貼喺 [tip8 hai2] *v.* attach

貼住 [tip8 jyu6] *adj.* attached

貼士 [tip8 si2] *n.* gratuity

鐵 [tit8] *n.* iron

鐵軌 [tit8 gwai2] *n.* rail

鐵製品 [tit8 jai3 ban2] *n.* ironwork

鐵路 [tit8 lou6] *n.* railroad (~ crossing 鐵路道口)

鐵路軌道 [tit8 lou6 gwai2 dou6] *n.* railroad track

挑釁性 [tiu1 yan6 sing3] *adj.* provocative

挑染 [tiu1 yim5] *v.* highlight (*hair*)

跳 [tiu3] *v.* jump

跳板 [tiu3 baan2] *n.* diving board

跳動 [tiu3 dung6] *n.* pulsation

跳高運動員 [tiu3 gou1 wan6 dung6 yun4] *n.* jumper

跳蚤市場 [tiu3 jou2 si5 cheung4] *n.* flea market

跳舞 [tiu3 mou5] *n.* dance

條 [tiu4] *n.* strips (bacon ~ 煙肉條)

條款 [tiu4 fun2] *n.* provision

調解 [tiu4 gaai2] *v.* mediate

調解員 [tiu4 gaai2 yun4] *n.* mediator

調好味嘅肉碎 [tiu4 hou2 mei6 ge3 yuk9 seui3] *n.* forcemeat

調整 [tiu4 jing2] *n.* adjustment (flavor ~ 調味, temperature ~ 調整溫度)

調節器 [tiu4 jit8 hei3] *n.* conditioner (hair ~ 護髮素)

調咗味 [tiu4 jo2 mei6] *adj.* seasoned

條例 [tiu4 lai6] *n.* ordinance

條紋 [tiu4 man4] *n.* stripe

調味料 [tiu4 mei6 liu6] *n.* seasoning, condiments, relish (sweet ~ 甜調味料, spicy ~ 辣調味料)

調色板 [tiu4 sik7 baan2] *n.* palette

挑戰 [tiu1 jin3] *n.* challenge

拖 [to1] *v.* drag

拖車 [to1 che1] *n.* trailer

拖肥糖 [to1 fei2 tong4] *n.* toffee

拖鞋 [to1 haai2] *n.* sandals

拖延 [to1 yin4] *n.* procrastination

橢圓形 [to2 yun4 ying4] *adj.* oval shape

陀螺 [to4 lo2] *n.* gyro

鴕鳥 [to4 niu5] *n.* ostrich

妥協 [to5 hip8] *v.* compromise

枱 [toi2] *n.* table (~ tennis 乒乓球, dinner ~ 餐台, ~ cover 枱布)

枱波 [toi2 bo1] *n.* billiards

枱布 [toi2 bou3] *n.* tablecloth

台北 [toi4 bak7] *n.* Taipei (~, capital of Taiwan 台灣首都)

苔蘚 [toi4 sin2] *n.* moss

台灣 [toi4 waan1] *n.* Taiwan; *adj.* Taiwanese

託管人 [tok8 gun2 yan4] *n.* trustee

托盤 [tok8 pun4] *n.* serving tray

托兒所 [tok8 yi4 so2] *n.* daycare

湯 [tong1] *n.* soup (chicken ~ 雞湯, vegetable ~ 菜湯, cream ~ 忌廉湯, cabbage ~ 大白菜湯, fish ~ 魚湯, tomato ~ 番茄湯)

湯加 [tong1 ga1] *n.* Tonga

湯碗 [tong1 wun2] *n.* soup bowl

湯丸 [tong1 yun2] *n.* gnocchi

燙傷 [tong3 seung1] *v.* singe

糖 [tong4] *n.* sugar (~cane 蔗糖, brown ~ 紅糖)

唐突 [tong4 dat9] *adj.* abrupt

糖粉 [tong4 fan2] *n.* powdered sugar

堂兄弟姊妹 [tong4 hing1 dai6 ji2 mui6] *n.* cousin (father's side)

糖漿 [tong4 jeung1] *n.* syrup (maple ~ 楓葉糖漿, fruit ~ 水果糖漿)

糖精 [tong4 jing1] *n.* saccharin

糖粒 [tong4 nap7] *n.* granulated sugar

糖尿病 [tong4 niu6 beng6] *n.* diabetes

糖霜 [tong4 seung1] *n.* frosting

糖衣 [tong4 yi1] *n.* icing (flavored ~ 加味糖衣, chocolate ~ 朱古力糖衣, sweet ~ 糖衣, sugar ~ 糖衣)

土地 [tou2 dei6] *n.* land

土堆 [tou2 deui1] *n.* mound

土匪 [tou2 fei2] *n.* bandit

土庫曼斯坦 [tou2 fu3 maan6 si1 taan2] *n.* Turkmenistan

土著 [tou2 jyu3] *adj.* aboriginal

討論 [tou2 leun6] *v.* discuss

土木工程 [tou2 muk9 gung1 ching4] *n.* engineering

土生土長 [tou2 sang1 tou2 jeung2] *adj.* native

土耳其 [tou2 yi5 kei4] *n.* Turkey; *adj.* Turkish (~ bath 土耳其浴)

套 [tou3] *n.* suite

套房 [tou3 fong2] *n.* apartment (~ building 一棟公寓)

兔仔 [tou3 jai2] *n.* rabbit

圖 [tou4] *n.* chart

桃 [tou4] *n.* peach

圖表 [tou4 biu2] *n.* diagram

陶瓷品 [tou4 chi4 ban2] *n.* pottery

徒弟 [tou4 dai2] *n.* apprentice

逃犯 [tou4 faan2] *n.* outlaw

屠夫 [tou4 fu1] *n.* butcher

圖解 [tou4 gaai2] *adj.* graphic (~ design 平面設計)

塗咗麵包碎 [tou4 jo2 min6 baau1 seui3] *adj.* breaded

塗咗麵粉 [tou4 jo2 min6 fan2] *v.* floured

塗咗牛油 [tou4 jo2 ngau4 yau4] *adj.* buttered

途中 [tou4 jung1] *adv.* in transit

圖瓦盧 [tou4 nga5 lou4] *n.* Tuvalu

逃生出口 [tou4 sang1 cheut7 hau2] *n.* emergency exit

塗色 [tou4 sik7] *n.* painting (*activity*/*hobby*)

圖書館 [tou4 syu1 gun2] *n.* library

圖書管理員 [tou4 syu1 gun2 lei5 yun4] *n.* librarian

淘汰 [tou4 taai3] *v.* eliminate

塗一層 [tou4 yat7 chang4] *adj.* coated (sugar ~ 塗一層糖, glaze ~ 上一層釉)

塗油 [tou4 yau4] *v.* baste

肚腩 [tou5 naam5] *n.* belly

肚屙 [tou5 ngo1] *n.* diarrhea; *v.* have diarrhea

肚餓 [tou5 ngo6] *adj.* hungry

調酒師 [tui4 jau2 si1] *n.* bartender

通道 [tung1 dou6] *n.* access (~ computer file 訪問電腦文件)

通貨膨脹 [tung1 fo3 paang4 jeung3] *n.* inflation

通風設備 [tung1 fung1 chit8 bei6] *n.* ventilator

通告 [tung1 gou3] *n.* notice

通過 [tung1 gwo3] *adv.* by means of

通行高度 [tung1 haang4 gou1 dou6] *n.* headroom (*height restriction*)

通行證 [tung1 hang4 jing3] *n.* pass

通知 [tung1 ji1] *v.* inform

通勤 [tung1 kan4] *v.* commute

通勤車 [tung1 kan4 che1] *v.* commuter train

通心粉 [tung1 sam1 fan2] *n.* macaroni (~ salad 通心粉沙律, ~ and cheese 芝士通心粉)

通信 [tung1 seun3] *v.* correspond

通常 [tung1 seung4] *adv.* usually

桶 [tung2] *n.* bucket (~ list 最後心願)

統治 [tung2 ji6] *n.* reign

統治者 [tung2 ji6 je2] *n.* ruler

統一 [tung2 yat7] *adj.* united

痛 [tung3] *n.* ache

痛苦 [tung3 fu2] *n.* pain; *v.* be in pain

銅 [tung4] *n.* copper

同 [tung4] *prep.* with

同…保證 [tung4 … bou2 jing3] *v.* assure

同輩 [tung4 bui3] *n.* peer

同伴 [tung4 bun6] *n.* companion

同情 [tung4 ching4] *n.* sympathy

銅管樂器 [tung4 gun2 ngok9 hei3] *n.* brass

童子雞 [tung4 ji2 gai1] *n.* spring chicken

童裝衫 [tung4 jong1 saam1] *n.* children's wear

同盟 [tung4 mang4] *n.* league

同謀 [tung4 mau4] *v.* aid and abet (*legal*)

同某人見面 [tung4 mau5 yan4 gin3 min6] *v.* join someone (may I ~ you? 我同你一齊好唔好?)

童年 [tung4 nin4] *n.* childhood

同時 [tung4 si4] *adv.* meanwhile

同事 [tung4 si6] *n.* colleague

同性戀 [tung4 sing3 lyun2] *adj.* homosexual

同性戀酒吧 [tung4 sing3 lyun2 jau2 ba1] *n.* gay club

同意 [tung4 yi3] *v.* agree

團隊 [tyun4 deui6] *n.* team

斷絕關係 [tyun5 jyut9 gwaan1 hai6] *n.* repudiation

脫脂 [tyut8 ji1] *n.* fat-free; *adj.* non-fat

脫脂奶 [tyut8 ji1 naai5] *n.* skim milk

脫位 [tyut8 wai6] *adj.* dislocated

U

屋 [uk7] *n.* house
屋頂 [uk7 ding2] *n.* roof
屋架 [uk7 ga2] *n.* roof rack
屋仔 [uk7 jai2] *n.* cottage

W

畫 [wa2] *n.* picture
畫家 [wa2 ga1] *n.* painter
畫廊 [wa2 long4] *n.* gallery
划獨木舟 [wa4 duk9 muk9 jau1] *n.* canoeing
華氏 [wa4 si6] *n.* fahrenheit
划艇 [wa4 teng5] *n.* rowing
划船 [wa4 syun4] *v.* row a boat
話 [wa6] *n.* saying
話俾…知 [wa6 bei2 … ji1] *v.* tell …
話俾人知 [wa6 bei2 yan4 ji1] *v.* reveal
華沙 [wa6 sa1] *n.* Warsaw (~, capital of Poland 波蘭嘅首都)
話事 [wa6 si6] *v.* dominate
華盛頓特區 [wa6 sing4 deun6 dak9 keui1] *n.* Washington, D.C. (~, capital of United States of America 美國嘅首都)
話題 [wa6 tai4] *n.* subject (*school/topic*) (change the ~ 轉話題)
懷舊 [waai4 gau6] *n.* nostalgia
懷念 [waai4 nim6] *phr.* in memory of
懷孕 [waai4 yan6] *n.* pregnancy (~ test 驗孕)
懷疑 [waai4 yi4] *v.* suspect
壞咗 [waai6 jo2] *v.* go bad; *adj.* out of order
壞影響 [waai6 ying2 heung2] *n.* repercussion
挖泥 [waait8 nai4] *v.* dredge; *n.* dredging
畫 [waak9] *n.* painting (*art*)

或者 [waak9 je2] *adv.* maybe
畫輪廓 [waak9 leun4 gwok8] *v.* outline
畫畫 [waak9 wa2] *v.* draw (~ an object 畫靜物, ~ a crowd 引起圍觀)
彎咗 [waan1 jo2] *adj.* bent
玩 [waan2] *v.* play (*an instrument / a game*)
玩得開心 [waan2 dak7 hoi1 sam1] *adj.* enjoyable
玩啤牌 [waan2 pe1 paai2] *v.* play cards
玩水池 [waan2 seui2 chi4] *n.* paddling pool
還 [waan4] *v.* repay
還押候審 [waan4 aat8 hau6 sam2] *v.* remand
環境 [waan4 ging2] *n.* environment
幻燈片 [waan6 dang1 pin2] *n.* slides (*images*)
幻想 [waan6 seung2] *n.* fantasy
橫樑 [waang4 leung4] *n.* beam (wood ~ 木樑, high ~ / low ~ 高橫樑 / 低橫樑)
滑 [waat9] *adj.* smooth
滑翔機 [waat9 cheung4 gei1] *n.* glider
滑輪 [waat9 leun4] *n.* pulley
滑浪風帆 [waat9 long6 fung1 faan4] *v.* windsurf
滑水 [waat9 seui2] *n.* water-skiing
滑雪 [waat9 syut8] *v.* ski (~ boots 雪靴, ~ lifts 滑雪纜車, ~ poles 滑雪杆, ~ school 滑雪

學校, ~ trail 滑雪道, ~ing 滑雪, ~er 滑雪者

滑雪纜車票 [waat9 syut8 laam6 che1 piu3] *n.* lift pass (*skiing*)

滑雪衫 [waat9 syut8 saam1] *n.* anorak

威化餅 [wai1 fa3 beng2] *n.* wafer

威脅 [wai1 hip8] *n.* threat

威望 [wai1 mong6] *n.* prestige

委內瑞拉 [wai1 noi6 seui6 laai1] *n.* Venezuela; *adj.* Venezuelan

威士忌 [wai1 si6 gei6] *n.* whiskey

委託 [wai1 tok8] *adj.* commissioned by

威爾斯 [wai1 yi5 si1] *n.* Wales; *adj.* Welsh

毀滅 [wai2 mit9] *v.* obliterate

委員會 [wai2 yun4 wui5] *n.* council, committee

喂 [wai3] *exclam./slang* hey! (~ there 喂, 你啊!)

餵 [wai3] *v.* feed

違背 [wai4 bui3] *n.* infraction

遺產 [wai4 chaan2] *n.* heritage

維持 [wai4 chi4] *v.* maintain

遺傳 [wai4 chyun4] *adj.* genetic

遺傳學 [wai4 chyun4 hok9] *n.* genetics

維多利亞 [wai4 do1 lei6 a3] *n.* Victoria (~, capital of Seychelles 塞舌爾嘅首都)

違反 [wai4 faan2] *v.* breach

遺棄 [wai4 hei3] *v.* abandon

遺址 [wai4 ji2] *n.* ruins

遺跡 [wai4 jik7] *n.* relic

遺囑認證 [wai4 juk7 ying3 jing3] *v.* probate

圍住...轉 [wai4 jyu3 ... jyun3] *v.* orbit ...

圍裙 [wai4 kwan2] *n.* apron

維拉港 [wai4 laai1 gong2] *n.* Port-Vila (~, capital of Vanuatu 瓦努阿圖嘅首都)

圍欄 [wai4 laan4] *n.* fence

唯心 [wai4 sam1] *adj.* idealistic

維修 [wai4 sau1] *n.* maintenance

維他命 [wai4 ta1 ming6] *n.* vitamin (~ tablet 維他命丸, ~ supplement 維他命補品)

維也納 [wai4 ya5 naap9] *n.* Vienna (~, capital of Austria 奧地利嘅首都)

唯一 [wai4 yat7] *n.* sole shoes

維爾紐斯 [wai4 yi5 nau2 si1] *n.* Vilnius (~, capital of Lithuania 立陶宛嘅首都)

緯度 [wai5 dou6] *n.* latitude

位 [wai2] *n.* seat (*in theater / on train*) (~ belt 安全帶, ~ number 座位編號, ~ reservation 訂座, Excuse me, you're in my ~ 唔好意思, 你坐咗我個位)

胃 [wai6] *n.* stomach

胃口 [wai6 hau2] *n.* appetite

位置 [wai6 ji3] *n.* location

為咗 [wai6 jo2] in order to

惠靈頓 [wai6 ling4 deun6] *n.* Wellington (~, capital of New Zealand 新西蘭嘅首都)

胃唔舒服 [wai6 m4 syu1 fuk9] *n.* upset stomach

衛生巾 [wai6 saang1 gan1] *n.* sanitary napkin

衛生棉條 [wai6 saang1 min4 tiu2] *n.* tampon

衛星 [wai6 sing1] n. satellite (~ dish 碟形衛星電視天線, ~ TV 衛星電視)

胃痛 [wai6 tung3] n. stomachache; v. have a stomachache

胃炎 [wai6 yim4] n. gastritis

溫泉 [wan1 chyun4] n. hot spring

溫得和克 [wan1 dak7 wo4 hak7] n. Windhoek (~, capital of Namibia 納米比亞嘅首都)

溫度 [wan1 dou6] n. temperature

溫度計 [wan1 dou6 gai3] n. thermometer

溫暖 [wan1 nyun5] n. warmth

溫和 [wan1 wo4] adj. placid

溫柔 [wan1 yau4] adj. gentle

瘟疫 [wan1 yik9] n. pestilence, plague

穩定 [wan2 ding6] adj. stable

搵 [wan2] v. find (~ out sth 搵到)

搵翻 [wan2 faan1] v. retrieve (~ a file 檢索文件)

搵到 [wan3 dou3] adj. located

搵食 [wan3 sik9] n. livelihood

雲 [wan4] n. cloud

暈 [wan4] v. feel faint

暈車浪 [wan4 che1 long6] adj. carsick

雲豆 [wan4 dau6] n. kidney beans

暈機 [wan4 gei1] n. air sickness

雲雀 [wan4 jeuk8] n. lark

暈浪 [wan4 long6] n. motion sickness

暈船浪 [wan4 syun4 long6] adj. seasick

允許 [wan5 heui2] v. allow

允許釣魚 [wan5 heui2 diu3 yu4] phr. fishing permitted

運動 [wan6 dung6] n. sport, sports (~ club 健身房, ~ field 運動場)

運動場 [wan6 dung6 cheung4] n. sporting ground

運動鞋 [wan6 dung6 haai4] n. sneakers

運動衫 [wan6 dung6 saam1] n. sweatshirt

運動員 [wan6 dung6 yun4] n. athletics

運費 [wan6 fai3] n. shipping charge

混合 [wan6 hap9] n. mixture

運氣 [wan6 hei3] n. fortune

運河 [wan6 ho4] n. canal

運作 [wan6 jok8] n. operation

運作上 [wan6 jok8 seung6] adj. operational

韻律學 [wan6 leut9 hok9] n. prosody

混亂 [wan6 lyun6] adj. scrambled (~ eggs 炒蛋)

運送 [wan6 sung3] v. transport

運輸 [wan6 syu1] n. transit (in ~ 途中)

宏偉 [wang4 wai5] adj. grand

榮譽 [wing4 yu6] n. honor

永久 [wing5 gau2] adj. perpetual

永久收藏 [wing5 gau2 sau1 chong4] n. permanent collection

永恆 [wing5 hang4] adj. everlasting

永遠 [wing5 yun5] adv. forever

泳衣 [wing6 yi1] n. bikini

鍋爐 [wo1 lou4] n. boiler

蝸牛 [wo1 ngau4] n. snail

和解 [wo4 gaai2] n. reconciliation

禾杆草 [wo4 gon1 chou2] *n.* straw

和諧 [wo4 haai4] *n.* harmony

和睦 [wo4 muk9] *n.* amity; *adj.* amicable

和平 [wo4 ping4] *n.* peace

和善 [wo4 sin6] *adj.* amiable

鑊 [wok9] *n.* wok

獲獎者 [wok9 jeung2 je2] *n.* laureate

黃包車 [wong4 baau1 che1] *n.* rickshaw

蝗蟲 [wong4 chung4] *n.* locust

黃豆 [wong4 dau6] *n.* soy (~ sauce 黃豆醬, ~beans 黃豆, ~ milk 豆漿)

黃昏 [wong4 fan1] *n.* evening (good ~ 晚安, this ~ 今晚, ~ service 晚上禮拜服務)

黃蜂 [wong4 fung1] *n.* wasp

黃金 [wong4 gam1] *n.* gold

黃薑粉 [wong4 geung1 fan2] *n.* turmeric

王冠 [wong4 gun1] *n.* crown

皇宮 [wong4 gung1] *n.* palace

黃瓜 [wong4 gwa1] *n.* cucumber (~ soup 黃瓜湯)

皇后 [wong4 hau6] *n.* empress

王后 [wong4 hau6] *n.* queen (*royal/chess*)

王子 [wong4 ji2] *n.* prince

黃綠醫生 [wong4 luk9 yi1 sang1] *n.* quack (*fake doctor*)

王室 [wong4 sat7] *adj.* royal

黃色 [wong4 sik7] *adj.* yellow (~ pages 黃頁)

黃色牛油 [wong4 sik7 ngau4 yau4] *n.* browned butter

黃疸 [wong4 taan2] *n.* jaundice

烏干達 [wu1 gon1 daat9] *n.* Uganda; *adj.* Ugandan

烏龜 [wu1 gwai1] *n.* tortoise

烏克蘭 [wu1 hak7 laan4] *n.* Ukraine; *adj.* Ukrainian

烏黑 [wu1 hak7] *adj.* raven

烏茲別克斯坦人 [wu1 ji1 bit9 hak7 si1 taan2 yan4] *n.* Uzbek (*person from Uzbekistan*)

烏茲別克斯坦 [wu1 ji1 bit9 hak7 si1 taan2] *n.* Uzbekistan

烏拉圭人 [wu1 laai1 gwai1 yan4] *n.* Uruguay; Uruguayan

烏蘭巴托 [wu1 laan4 ba1 tok8] *n.* Ulaanbaatar (~, capital of Mongolia 蒙古嘅首都)

污染 [wu1 yim5] *n.* pollution

糊 [wu2] *n.* batter (pancake ~ 班戟粉, pastry ~ 糕點粉)

壺 [wu2] *n.* jug

蝴蝶 [wu4 dip9] *n.* butterfly

蝴蝶結 [wu4 dip9 git8] *n.* bowtie

胡椒粉 [wu4 jiu1 fan2] *n.* pepper (green ~ 青胡椒粉, red ~ 紅胡椒粉, yellow ~ 黃胡椒粉, orange ~ 橙色胡椒粉)

葫蘆 [wu4 lou4] *n.* gourd (vegetable ~ 菜葫蘆)

葫蘆巴 [wu4 lou4 ba1] *n.* fenugreek

鬍鬚 [wu4 sou1] *n.* moustache

胡言亂語 [wu4 yin4 lyun6 yu5] *v.* babble

弧形 [wu4 ying4] *adj.* curved

湖 [wu4] *n.* lake

互動 [wu6 dung6] *adj.* interactive (~ program 互動遊戲)

護髮產品 [wu6 faat8 chaan2 ban2] *n.* haircare product

護髮素 [wu6 faat8 sou3] *n.* hair conditioner

護照 [wu6 jiu3] *n.* passport (~ control 護照管理, ~ number 護照號碼)

護照相 [wu6 jiu3 seung3] *n.* passport-size photo

護林員 [wu6 lam4 yun4] *n.* ranger

互聯網 [wu6 lyun4 mong5] *n.* Internet

護身符 [wu6 san1 fu4] *n.* amulet

互相 [wu6 seung1] *pron.* each other, one another

護士 [wu6 si6] *n.* nurse

護城河 [wu6 sing4 ho4] *n.* moat

互惠互利 [wu6 wai6 wu6 lei6] *adj.* reciprocal

會員 [wui2 yun4] *n.* member in/ of a group

會員身分 [wui2 yun4 san1 fan6] *n.* membership

回報 [wui4 bou3] *v.* reciprocate

回程票 [wui4 ching4 piu3] *n.* return ticket

回答 [wui4 daap8] *n.* response

回覆 [wui4 fuk7] *n.* reply

回教徒 [wui4 gaau3 tou4] *adj.* Muslim

茴香 [wui4 heung1] *n.* fennel; caraway

茴香籽 [wui4 heung1 ji2] *n.* caraway seeds

回響 [wui4 heung2] *v.* resound

茴芹 [wui4 kan4] *n.* anise

回扣 [wui4 kau3] *n.* rebate

回收 [wui4 sau1] *v.* recycle

回音 [wui4 yam1] *n.* echo

回憶 [wui4 yik7] *n.* memory

回憶錄 [wui4 yik7 luk9] *n.* memoir

回形針 [wui4 ying4 jam1] *n.* safety pins

會 [wui5] *v.* will

會傳染嘅 [wui5 chyun4 yim5 ge3] *adj.* contagious

會飛嘅 [wui5 fei1 ge3] *adj.* flying

會死嘅 [wui5 sei2 ge3] *adj.* mortal

會議廳 [wui5 yi5 ting1] *n.* convention hall

匯錢 [wui6 chin2] *n.* remittance

會錯意 [wui6 cho3 yi3] *n.* misunderstanding (there's been a ~ 有誤會)

會計 [wui6 gai3] *n.* accountant

匯率 [wui6 leut9] *n.* exchange rate

匯票 [wui6 piu3] *n.* money order

會議 [wui6 yi5] *n.* conference (~ call 電話會議)

會議室 [wui6 yi5 sat7] *n.* conference room

碗 [wun2] *n.* bowl

豌豆 [wun2 dau6] *n.* pea (~ soup 豌豆湯)

碗架 [wun2 ga2] *n.* dishrack

援軍 [wun4 gwan1] *n.* reinforcement

援助 [wun4 jo6] *n.* aid

換 [wun6] *v.* shift (~ gears 換檔, ~ key 換檔鍵)

換車 [wun6 che1] *v.* change trains

換錢 [wun6 chin2] *n.* currency exchange (~ office 外匯兌換處, ~ rate 匯率)

緩衝器 [wun6 chung1 hei3] *n.* shock absorber

玩具 [wun6 geui6] *n.* toy

玩具店 [wun6 geui6 dim3] *n.*
　toy store

活動 [wut9 dung6] *n.* activity

活力 [wut9 lik9] *n.* energy

活潑 [wut9 put8] *adj.* lively

活塞 [wut9 sak7] *n.* stopcock

活體檢視 [wut9 tai2 gim2 si6] *n.*
　biopsy (skin ~ 皮膚活體檢視,
　bone ~ 骨頭活體檢視)

Y-Z

也門 [ya5 mun4] *n.* Yemen; *adj.*
Yemeni

曳 [yai6] *adj.* naughty

陰道 [yam1 dou6] *n.* vagina

陰道感染 [yam1 dou6 gam2
yim5] *n.* vaginal infection

音節 [yam1 jit8] *n.* syllable

陰涼 [yam1 leung4] *adj.* shady

陰謀 [yam1 mau4] *n.* scheme

音樂 [yam1 ngok9] *n.* music

音樂家 [yam1 ngok9 ga1] *n.*
musician

音樂商店 [yam1 ngok9 seung1
dim3] *n.* music store

音樂會 [yam1 ngok9 wui2] *n.*
concert (~ hall 音樂廳, live ~
現場演奏)

陰魂不散 [yam1 wan4 bat7
saan3] *v.* haunt

飲 [yam2] *v.* drink

飲醉 [yam2 jeui3] *v.* be drunk

飲料 [yam2 liu6] *n.* beverage,
drink

飲食 [yam2 sik9] *adj.* dietary (~
fiber 食用纖維, ~ supplements
飲食補品, ~ restrictions 飲食
限制)

任期 [yam4 kei4] *n.* term (*political*)

任務 [yam4 mou6] *n.* task

任性 [yam6 sing3] *adj.* perverse

恩賈梅納 [yan1 ga2 mui4 naap9]
n. N'Djamena (~, capital of
Chad 乍得嘅首都)

因住 [yan1 jyu6] *v.* beware (~ of
dog! 因住！入面有狗)

欣賞 [yan1 seung2] *v.* appreciate
(~ in value 升值)

因素 [yan1 sou3] *n.* factor (*SPF/
sunblock*)

因為 [yan1 wai6] *conj.* because;
adj. due to

隱藏 [yan2 chong4] *v.* conceal

隱士 [yan2 si6] *n.* recluse

隱形眼鏡 [yan2 ying4 ngaan5
geng3] *n.* contact lens (eye
drops for ~ 隱形眼鏡液)

印刷術 [yan3 chaat8 seut9] *n.*
printing

印度 [yan3 dou6] *n.* India; *adj.*
Indian (~ food 印度菜, ~ tea
印度茶葉, ~ seasoning 印度
菜調味料)

印度香米 [yan3 dok9 heung1
mai5] *n.* basmati rice

印度尼西亞 [yan3 dou6 nei4
sai1 a3] *n.* Indonesia; *adj.*
Indonesian

印象 [yan3 jeung6] *n.* impression

仁 [yan4] *n.* kernel (corn ~ 粟米
粒, grain ~ 糧粒)

人 [yan4] *n.* people

人格化 [yan4 gaak8 fa3] *n.*
personification

人工 [yan4 gung1] *n.* salary,
remuneration

人工香精 [yan4 gung1 heung1
jing1] *n.* artificial flavoring

人工色素 [yan4 gung1 sik7
sou3] *n.* artificial coloring

人工甜味劑 [yan4 gung1 tim4 mei6 jai1] *n.* artificial sweetener

人客 [yan4 haak8] *n.* guest (dinner ~ 晚飯客人)

人行道 [yan4 hang4 dou6] *n.* walkway, crossing (~ guard 交通協助員)

人口 [yan4 hau2] *n.* population

人口多 [yan4 hau2 do1] *adj.* populous

人口普查 [yan4 hau2 pou2 cha4] *n.* census

人質 [yan4 ji3] *n.* hostage

人字拖 [yan4 ji6 to1] *n.* flip-flops

人權 [yan4 kyun4] *n.* human rights

人物 [yan4 mat9] *n.* character

人物肖像畫家 [yan4 mat9 chiu3 jeung6 wa2 ga1] *n.* portrait artist

人身保護令 [yan4 san1 bou2 wu6 ling4] (writ of) habeas corpus (*legal*)

人體模型 [yan4 tai2 mou4 ying4] *n.* mannequin

引起 [yan5 hei2] *v.* incur

引號 [yan5 hou6] *n.* quotation marks

引用 [yan5 yung6] *n.* quotation

入 [yap9] *v.* enter

入場費 [yap9 cheung4 fai3] *n.* admission, admission fee (~ ticket 入場票)

入境簽證 [yap9 ging2 chim1 jing3] *n.* entry visa

入口 [yap9 hau2] *n.* entrance

入去 [yap9 heui3] *prep.* into

入籍 [yap9 jik9] *v.* naturalize

入住 [yap9 jyu6] check-in

入面 [yap9 min6] *adj.* inner

入息稅 [yap9 sik7 seui3] *n.* income tax

一 [yat7] *num.* one

一百週年 [yat7 baak8 jau1 nin4] *n.* centenary

一部分 [yat7 bou6 fan6] *n.* section

一般 [yat7 bun1] *adv.* commonly, in general

一半 [yat7 bun3] *n.* half

一切照實陳述 [yat7 chai3 jiu3 sat9 chan4 seut9] voir dire

一齊 [yat7 chai4] *adv.* together (~ with … 同…一齊)

一齊住 [yat7 chai4 jyu6] *v.* live together

一次 [yat7 chi3] *adv.* once

一次性 [yat7 chi3 sing3] *adj.* disposable)

一次性尿片 [yat7 chi3 sing3 niu6 pin2] *n.* disposable diapers

一次性相機 [yat7 chi3 sing3 seung3 gei1] *n.* disposable camera

一次用量嘅針劑 [yat7 chi3 yung6 leung4 ge3 jam1 jai1] *n.* ampule

一匙羹 [yat7 chi4 gang1] *n.* spoonful

一打 [yat7 da2] *n.* dozen

一大片荒地 [yat7 daai6 pin3 fong1 dei6] *n.* fava bans

一啖 [yat7 daam6] *n.* morsel

一堆 [yat7 deui1] *n.* pile (fish ~ 一堆魚)

一啲 [yat7 di1] *n.* bit (in a ~ 好快, a little ~ 一啲啲)

一定 [yat7 ding6] *v. modal* must

一疊牌 [yat7 dip9 paai4] *n.* deck of cards

一檔 [yat7 dong3] *n.* first gear

一塊 [yat7 faai3] *n.* slice (~s 一塊塊, to ~ 切成一塊塊, ~d 切塊)

一塊地 [yat7 faai3 dei6] *n.* piece of land

一塊肉 [yat7 faai3 yuk9] *n.* cut of meat

一瓣蒜 [yat7 faan6 syun3] *n.* clove of garlic

一分錢 [yat7 fan1 chin4] *n.* cent (*abbr.* c., ct.)

一夫多妻 [yat7 fu1 do1 chai1] *n.* polygamy

一夫一妻 [yat7 fu1 yat7 chai1] *n.* monogamy

一副象棋 [yat7 fu3 jeung6 kei4] *n.* chess set

一嚿番梘 [yat7 gau4 faan1 gan2] *n.* bar of soap

一個 [yat7 go3] *indef. art.* a, an

一個都冇 [yat7 go3 dou1 mou5] *pron.* none

一個個 [yat7 go3 go3] *adv.* separately (wash ~ 分開洗)

一個號碼 [yat7 go3 hou6 ma5] *num.* one

一集 [yat7 jaap9] *n.* episode

一陣間 [yat7 jan6 gaan1] *n.* momentary

一張票 [yat7 jeung1 piu3] *n.* single ticket,

一致 [yat7 ji3] *n.* accordance, in accordance with; *adj.* consistent

一粒粒 [yat7 lap7 lap7] *adj.* granulated (~ sugar 糖粒)

一樓 [yat7 lau2] *n.* ground floor

一流 [yat7 lau4] *n.* first class

一樓 [yat7 lau4] *n.* first floor

一連串 [yat7 lin4 chyun3] *n.* series

一路順風 [yat7 lou6 seun6 fung1] *phr.* Bon voyage!

一條麵包 [yat7 tiu4 min6 baau1] *n.* loaf of bread

一套衫 [yat7 tou3 saam1] *n.* suit (*men's/women's*)

一樣 [yat7 yeung6] *adj.* same (If it's the ~ to you 如果你情況都一樣, the ~ thing 同一樣嘢, I'll have the ~ 我都要同一樣嘢); *adv.* as well as

一月份 [yat7 yut9 fan6] *n.* January (*abbr.* Jan.)

日 [yat9] *n.* day (~ after tomorrow 後日, ~ trip 一日遊, ~ pass/ticket 日票)

日報 [yat9 bou3] *n.* journal

日本 [yat9 bun2] *n.* Japan; *adj.* Japanese (~ tea 日本茶)

日場 [yat9 cheung4] *n.* matinée

日出 [yat9 cheut7] *n.* sunrise

日記 [yat9 gei3] *n.* diary

日光 [yat9 gwong1] *adj.* solar

日光浴 [yat9 gwong1 yuk9] *v.* sunbathe

日期 [yat9 kei4] *n.* date (~ of birth 出生日期)

日曆 [yat9 lik9] *n.* calendar

日落 [yat9 lok9] *n.* sunset

日常 [yat9 seung4] *adj.* daily

日常飲食 [yat9 seung4 yam2 sik9] *n.* diet (be on a ~ 減肥, ~ menu 減肥餐)

日常用品 [yat9 seung4 yung6 ban2] *n.* supplies

日蝕 [yat9 sik9] *n.* eclipse

日頭 [yat9 tau2] *n.* daytime

日用品 [yat9 yung6 ban2] *n.* household goods

丘比特 [yau1 bei2 dak9] *n.* Cupid

優點 [yau1 dim2] *n.* advantage

憂慮 [yau1 leui6] *n.* anxiety

幽靈 [yau1 ling4] *n.* phantom

優雅 [yau1 nga5] *adj.* elegant

優勢 [yau1 sai3] *n.* predominance

憂傷 [yau1 seung1] *n.* melancholy

休息 [yau1 sik7] *n.* repose

休息室 [yau1 sik7 sat7] *n.* lounge

優先 [yau1 sin1] *n.* priority

優先權 [yau1 sin1 kyun4] *n.* lien

休庭 [yau1 ting4] *v.* recess

優惠券 [yau1 wai6 gyun3] *n.* coupon

休會 [yau1 wui2] *v.* postpone

郵費 [yau3 fai3] *n.* postage

幼稚 [yau3 ji6] *adj.* naive

幼稚園 [yau3 ji6 yun2] *n.* kindergarten

疣 [yau4] *n.* wart

油 [yau4] *n.* oil (sesame ~ 芝麻油, olive ~ 橄欖油, canola ~ 油菜籽油)

油錶 [yau4 biu1] *n.* oil gauge

郵差 [yau4 chaai1] *n.* postman

油漆 [yau4 chat7] *v.* lacquered

由始至終 [yau4 chi2 ji3 jung1] *prep.* throughout

油菜籽油 [yau4 choi3 ji2 yau4] *n.* canola oil

油滴盤 [yau4 dik7 pun4] *n.* drip pan

由分子組成 [yau4 fan1 ji2 jou2 sing4] *adj.* molecular

游擊隊員 [yau4 gik7 deui6 yun4] *n.* partisan

郵件 [yau4 gin6] *n.* mail

郵件待領 [yau4 gin6 doi6 ling5] *n.* general delivery

郵局 [yau4 guk9] *n.* post office

遊客 [yau4 haak8] *n.* traveler (~'s check 旅行支票)

遊行 [yau4 hang4] *n.* parade

遊戲 [yau4 hei3] *n.* game (*sport / wild animals*)

遊戲節目 [yau4 hei3 jit8 muk9] *n.* game show

遊戲室 [yau4 hei3 sat7] *n.* game room

遊戲小組 [yau4 hei3 siu2 jou2] *n.* play group

油炸 [yau4 ja3] *v.* deep-fry; *adj.* deep-fried

油炸餡餅 [yau4 ja3 haam6 beng2] *n.* fritter

油炸面圈 [yau4 ja3 min6 hyun1] *n.* pretzel (salted ~ 加鹽油炸面圈, unsalted ~ 無鹽油炸面圈)

油汁 [yau4 jap7] *n.* drippings

油脂 [yau4 ji1] *n.* grease (cooking ~ 食用油脂, ~ pan 滑脂盤)

郵政局長 [yau4 jing3 guk9 jeung2] *n.* postmaster

郵政編碼 [yau4 jing3 pin1 ma5] *n.* postal code

由...組成 [yau4 ... jou2 sing4] *v.* consist of ...

尤其 [yau4 kei4] *adv.* notably

遊樂園 [yau4 lok9 yun4] *n.* amusement park

油麥菜 [yau4 mak9 choi3] *n.* romaine lettuce

郵票 [yau4 piu3] *n.* stamp, postage stamp

游水 [yau4 seui2] *n.* swim; *v.* go for a swim

油箱 [yau4 seung1] *n.* gas tank

油性 [yau4 sing3] *adj.* oily

油性皮膚 [yau4 sing3 pei4 fu1] *n.* oily skin

油性頭髮 [yau4 sing3 tau4 faat8] *n.* greasy hair

猶太教教士 [yau4 taai3 gaau3 gaau3 si6] *n.* rabbi

猶太人 [yau4 taai3 yan4] *n.* Jew

猶太人教堂 [yau4 taai3 yan4 gaau3 tong4] *n.* synagogue

遊艇 [yau4 teng5] *n.* yacht

油桃 [yau4 tou4] *n.* nectarine

油畫 [yau4 wa2] *n.* oil painting

游泳池 [yau4 wing6 chi4] *n.* swimming pool (indoor/outdoor ~ 室內 / 室外泳池)

由於 [yau4 yu1] *adv.* on account of

魷魚 [yau4 yu2] *n.* squid

有 [yau5] *v. aux.* have; must; *phr.* there are/is

有必要 [yau5 bit7 yiu3] *adj.* necessary

有幫助 [yau5 bong1 jo6] *adj.* instrumental

有部份 [yau5 bou6 fan6] *adv.* partly

誘捕 [yau5 bou6] *n.* entrapment

有錢 [yau5 chin2] *adj.* rich (~ flavor 濃味, ~ texture 肉質細膩)

有才能 [yau5 choi4 nang4] *adj.* capable (of)

有創意 [yau5 chong1 yi3] *adj.* creative

有充分細節卻無法證實 [yau5 chung1 fan6 sai3 jit8 keuk8 mou4 faat8 jing3 sat9] *adj.* circumstantial (~ evidence 旁證)

有彈力 [yau5 daan4 lik9] *adj.* elastic

有得退嘅 [yau5 dak7 teui3 ge3] *n.* returnable

有啲 [yau5 di1] *adv.* somewhat

有導遊嘅遊覽 [yau5 dou6 yau4 ge3 yau4 laam5] *n.* guided tour (museum ~ 博物館有導遊嘅遊覽, ~ walk 有導遊嘅步行遊覽)

有毒 [yau5 duk9] *adj.* toxic

有毒廢物 [yau5 duk9 fai3 mat9] *n.* toxic waste

有計劃 [yau5 gai3 waak9] *adj.* designed

有筋 [yau5 gan1] *adj.* stringy

有機 [yau5 gei1] *adj.* organic (~ milk 有機牛奶, ~ chicken 有機雞肉, ~ produce 有機蔬果, ~ grown 有機種植)

有機體 [yau5 gei1 tai2] *n.* organism

有幾多 [yau5 gei2 do1] *phr.* how many?

有幾經常 [yau5 gei2 ging1 seung4] *phr.* how often?

有記號 [yau5 gei3 hou6] *adj.* marked

有技巧 [yau5 gei6 haau2] *adv.* skillfully

有技能 [yau5 gei6 nang4] *adj.* skillful

有經驗 [yau5 ging1 yim6] *adj.* experienced

有角 [yau5 gok8] *adj.* angular

有關 [yau5 gwaan1] *adj.* related (to)

有軌電車 [yau5 gwai2 din6 che1] *n.* streetcar, tramway

有限 [yau5 haan6] *adj.* limited

有限公司 [yau5 haan6 gung1 si1] *n.* Ltd. (*abbr. of* Limited)

有哮喘 [yau5 haau1 chyun2] *n.* asthmatic

有效 [yau5 haau6] *adj.* valid

有效率 [yau5 haau6 leut9] *adj.* efficient

有效日期 [yau5 haau6 yat9 kei4] *n.* expiration date

有口才 [yau5 hau2 choi4] *adj.* eloquent

有希望 [yau5 hei1 mong6] *adj.* promising

有香味 [yau5 heung1 mei6] *adj.* aromatic

有興趣 [yau5 hing1 cheui3] *adj.* interested in

有可能 [yau5 ho2 nang4] *adj.* potential

有害 [yau5 hoi6] *adj.* harmful

有好多鵝卵石 [yau5 hou2 do1 ngo4 leun2 sek9] *adj.* pebbly

友好 [yau5 hou2] *adj.* friendly

有罪 [yau5 jeui6] *adj.* guilty

有資格 [yau5 ji1 gaak8] *adj.* qualified

有節奏 [yau5 jit8 jau3] *adj.* rhythmic

有焦糖 [yau5 jiu1 tong4] *adj.* caramelized (~ onion 焦糖洋蔥)

有咗 [yau5 jo2] *adj.* pregnant

有傾向 [yau5 king1 heung3] *adj.* prone

有規律 [yau5 kwai1 leut9] *adv.* regularly

有冷氣 [yau5 laang5 hei3] *adj.* air-conditioned (*abbr.* A/C)

有禮貌 [yau5 lai5 maau6] *adj.* polite

有良好教育 [yau5 leung4 hou2 gaau3 yuk9] *adj.* educated

有歷史價值 [yau5 lik9 si2 ga3 jik9] *adj.* historic

有問題 [yau5 man6 tai4] *adj.* problematic

有魅力 [yau5 mei6 lik9] *adj.* charming

有味 [yau5 mei6] *adj.* odorous

有名 [yau5 meng4] *adj.* renowned

有霧 [yau5 mou6] *adj.* foggy

有能力 [yau5 nang4 lik9] *v.* able, be able to

有硬殼 [yau5 ngaang6 hok8] *adj.* encrusted

有愛滋病 [yau5 oi3 ji1 beng6] *adj.* HIV-positive

有沙 [yau5 sa1] *adj.* sandy (~ beach 沙灘)

有授權 [yau5 sau6 kyun4] *adj.* authorized

有時 [yau5 si4] *adv.* sometimes

有線電視 [yau5 sin3 din6 si6] *n.* cable TV

有酸味 [yau5 syun1 mei6] *adj.* acidulated

有天份 [yau5 tin1 fan6] *adj.* talented

有條件 [yau5 tiu4 gin6] *adj.* conditional

有條罅 [yau5 tiu4 la3] *adj.* cracked

有條紋 [yau5 tiu4 man4] *adj.* striped

有同情心 [yau5 tung4 ching4 sam1] *adj.* sympathetic

有屋出租 [yau5 uk7 cheut7 jou1] *n.* house for rent

誘惑 [yau5 waak9] *n.* allurement

有威望 [yau5 wai1 mong6] *adj.* prestigious

有人 [yau5 yan4] *pron.* somebody

有人工 [yau5 yan4 gung1] *adj.* paid

有人性 [yau5 yan4 sing3] *adj.* human

有氧運動 [yau5 yeung5 wan6 dung6] *n.* aerobics

友誼 [yau5 yi4] *n.* friendship

有營養 [yau5 ying4 yeung5] *adj.* nutritious

有型 [yau5 ying4] *adj.* *slang* cool

有遠見 [yau5 yun5 gin3] *adj.* far-sighted

有用 [yau5 yung6] *adj.* useful

又 [yau6] *adv.* again

又悶又熱 [yau6 mun6 yau6 yit9] *adj.* muggy

椰菜 [ye4 choi3] *n.* cabbage (red ~ 紅椰菜, green ~ 青椰菜, ~ soup 椰菜湯, ~ wrap 椰菜卷)

椰菜花 [ye4 choi3 fa1] *n.* cauliflower

椰子 [ye4 ji2] *n.* coconut (~ powder 椰子粉, ~ milk 椰子奶, ~ cream 椰子忌廉)

耶烈萬 [ye4 lit9 maan6] *n.* Yerevan (~, capital of Armenia 亞美尼亞嘅首都)

耶路撒冷 [ye4 lou6 saat8 laang5] *n.* Jerusalem (~, capital of Israel 以色列嘅首都)

耶穌受難日 [ye4 sou1 sau6 naan6 yat9] *n.* Good Friday

爺爺/公公 [ye4 ye4/gung1 gung1] *n.* grandfather

野餐 [ye5 chaan1] *n.* picnic, picnic lunch

野餐地方 [ye5 chaan1 dei6 fong1] *n.* picnic area

野餐籃 [ye5 chaan1 laam4] *n.* picnic basket

嘢 [ye5] *n.* thing, stuff

野雞 [ye5 gai1] *n.* pheasant

野豬 [ye5 jyu1] *n.* wild boar

野牛 [ye5 ngau4] *n.* bison

野生車厘子 [ye5 saang1 che1 lei4 ji2] *n.* wild cherry

野心 [ye5 sam1] *n.* ambition

野生 [ye5 sang1] *adj.* wild (~ animal 野生動物, ~ duck 野鴨, ~ berries 野莓)

野生動物 [ye5 sang1 dung6 mat9] *n.* wildlife

野生黃莓 [ye5 sang1 wong4 mui4] *n.* cloudberry, knotberry, bake apple

野兔 [ye5 tou3] *n.* hare

夜總會 [ye6 jung2 wui2] *n.* night club

夜生活 [ye6 sang1 wut9] *n.* nightlife

贏 [yeng4] *v.* win

贏家 [yeng4 ga1] *n.* winner

贏咗 [yeng4 jo2] *adj.* winning

銳角 [yeui6 gok8] *n.* obtuse/ acute/right angle

約束 [yeuk8 chuk7] *n.* constraint

約旦 [yeuk8 daan3] *n.* Jordan; *adj.* Jordanian

約旦杏 [yeuk8 daan3 hang6] *n.* Jordan almonds

約旦棗 [yeuk8 daan3 jou2] *n.* Jordan dates

約好 [yeuk8 hou2] *adj.* promissory

約會 [yeuk8 wui6] *n.* rendezvous

藥 [yeuk9] *n.* medicine (*drug*), pharmaceutical drug

藥店 [yeuk9 dim3] *n.* drugstore

虐待狂 [yeuk9 doi6 kwong4] *n.* sadism

藥房 [yeuk9 fong4] *n.* pharmacy

藥膏 [yeuk9 gou1] *n.* ointment

瘧疾 [yeuk9 jat9] *n.* malaria

藥物 [yeuk9 mat9] *n.* medication

藥拴 [yeuk9 saan1] *n.* suppository

藥水 [yeuk9 seui2] *n.* cough medicine

藥丸 [yeuk9 yun2] *n.* pill (*medication*)

潤膚霜 [yeun6 fu1 seung1] *n.* moisturizing cream, skin moisturizer

潤喉糖 [yeun6 hau4 tong4] *n.* lozenge (*cough / throat*)

潤滑 [yeun6 waat9] *n.* lubrication

潤滑油 [yeun6 waat9 yau4] *n.* lubricant

羊 [yeung4] *n.* lamb (breast of ~ 羊胸, leg of ~ 羊腿, loin of ~ 羊腰, saddle of ~ 羊鞍)

洋蔥 [yeung4 chung1] *n.* onion (red ~ 紅洋蔥, green ~ 青洋蔥, white ~ 白洋蔥, sweet ~ 甜洋蔥)

洋蔥圈 [yeung4 chung1 hyun1] *n.* onion rings

洋蔥湯 [yeung4 chung1 tong1] *n.* onion soup

洋薊 [yeung4 gai3] *n.* artichoke (~ hearts 洋薊心)

陽具 [yeung4 geui6] *n.* penis

洋姜 [yeung4 geung1] *n.* Jerusalem artichoke

陽光 [yeung4 gwong1] *n.* sunlight

羊雜碎 [yeung4 jaap9 seui3] *n.* haggis

羊毛 [yeung4 mou4] *n.* wool

羊奶芝士 [yeung4 naai5 ji1 si6] *n.* sheep's milk cheese

羊鞍 [yeung4 on1] *n.* saddle of lamb

揚聲器 [yeung4 sing1 hei3] *n.* speaker

羊蹄 [yeung4 tai4] *n.* lamb trotter

陽台 [yeung4 toi4] *n.* balcony, sundeck

羊肚菇 [yeung4 tou5 gu1] *n.* morel mushroom

羊肉 [yeung4 yuk9] *n.* mutton

羊肉串 [yeung4 yuk9 chyun3] *n.* shish kebab (chicken ~ 雞肉串, lamb ~ 羊肉串)

羊肉泡饃 [yeung4 yuk9 paau1 mo4] *n.* bread soup

氧化 [yeung5 fa3] *adj.* oxidized

養肥 [yeung5 fei4] *v.* fattened (~ chicken 肥雞, ~ pig 肥豬, ~ goose 肥鵝, ~ duck 肥鴨)

仰光 [yeung5 gwong1] *n.* Rangoon (Yangon) (~, capital of

Myanmar (Burma) 緬甸首都)

氧氣 [yeung5 hei3] *n.* oxygen

養料 [yeung5 liu6] *n.* nutrient

樣板 [yeung6 baan2] *n.* sample

樣品 [yeung6 ban2] *n.* prototype

衣車 [yi1 che1] *n.* sewing machine

伊頓芝士 [yi1 deun6 ji1 si2] *n.* Edam cheese

衣架 [yi1 ga2] *n.* hanger

衣櫃 [yi1 gwai6] *n.* closet

醫好 [yi1 hou2] *v.* cure

醫好咗 [yi1 hou2 jo2] *adj.* cured

衣著打扮 [yi1 jeuk8 da2 baan6] *n.* appearance

依照 [yi1 jiu3] *prep.* per (~ hour/ night/week 每個鐘 / 每晚 / 每個星期)

伊拉克 [yi1 laai1 hak7] *n.* Iraq; *adj.* Iraqi

依賴 [yi1 laai6] *v.* depend on

醫療不當 [yi1 liu4 bat7 dong3] *n.* malpractice

醫療保險 [yi1 liu4 bou2 him2] *n.* health insurance

伊朗 [yi1 long5] *n.* Iran; *adj.* Iranian

衣帽間 [yi1 mou6 gaan1] *n.* cloakroom

醫生 [yi1 sang1] *n.* doctor (*abbr.* Dr.)

伊斯蘭堡 [yi1 si1 laan4 bou2] *n.* Islamabad (~, capital of Pakistan 巴基斯坦首都)

伊斯蘭嘅 [yi1 si1 laan4 ge3] *adj.* Islamic

醫師 [yi1 si1] *n.* physician

醫藥 [yi1 yeuk9] *adj.* medical

醫院 [yi1 yun2] *n.* hospital

意大利 [yi3 daai6 lei6] *n.* Italy; *adj.* Italian

意大利闊條麵 [yi3 daai6 lei6 fut8 tiu2 min6] *n.* fettuccini

意大利辣香腸 [yi3 daai6 lei6 laat9 heung1 cheung4] *n.* pepperoni

意大利牛奶芝士 [yi3 daai6 lei6 ngau4 naai5 ji1 si2] *n.* ricotta cheese

意大利餛飩 [yi3 daai6 lei6 wan4 tan1] *n.* ravioli

意大利肉汁燴飯 [yi3 daai6 lei6 yuk9 jap7 wui6 faan6] *n.* risotto

意粉 [yi3 fan2] *n.* spaghetti, pasta (angel hair ~ 天使麵)

意見 [yi3 gin3] *n.* opinion

意料之外 [yi3 liu6 ji1 ngoi6] *adj.* unexpected

意外 [yi3 ngoi6] *n.* accident

意思 [yi3 si1] *n.* meaning; *v.* mean (what does this ~? 呢個係乜嘢意思？)

意識形態 [yi3 sik7 ying4 taai3] *adj.* ideological

意識 [yi3 sik7] *n.* awareness (to raise ~ 增加人們嘅認識)

意圖 [yi3 tou4] *n.* intention

意圖未遂 [yi3 tou4 mei6 seui6] *adj.* attempted

意願 [yi3 yun6] *n.* willingness

胰島素 [yi4 dou2 sou3] *n.* insulin

移動 [yi4 dung6] *adj.* mobile

兒科醫生 [yi4 fo1 yi1 sang1] *n.* pediatrician

而家 [yi4 ga1] *adv.* now

儀器 [yi4 hei3] *n.* device

移開 [yi4 hoi1] *v.* remove

移植 [yi4 jik9] *v.* transplant

而唔係 [yi4 m4 hai6] *prep.* instead of

移民 [yi4 man4] *n.* immigration, emigration

疑問 [yi4 man6] *n.* query

疑心 [yi4 sam1] *n.* suspicion

儀式 [yi4 sik7] *n.* ritual

兒童保護 [yi4 tung4 bou2 wu6] *n.* childproof cap

兒童保育 [yi4 tung4 bou2 yuk9] *n.* childcare

議程 [yi5 ching4] *n.* agenda

已付郵資 [yi5 fu6 yau4 ji1] *adv.* postage paid

耳仔 [yi5 jai2] *n.* ear

耳仔痛 [yi5 jai2 tung3] *n.* earache; *v.* have an earache

議事廳 [yi5 si6 teng1] *n.* chamber (judge's ~s 法官辦公室)

以色列 [yi5 sik7 lit9] *n.* Israel; *adj.* Israeli

耳環 [yi5 waan4] *n.* earring

以...為生 [yi5 ... wai6 sang1] *n.* living: do for a living

耳藥水 [yi5 yeuk9 seui2] *n.* ear drops

二 [yi6] *num.* two (~-door car 兩門車, ~-lane highway; 雙行高速公路)

易變質 [yi6 bin3 jat7] *adj.* perishable

二等 [yi6 dang2] *adj.* second class

義工 [yi6 gung1] *n.* volunteer

二進制 [yi6 jeun3 jai3] *adj.* binary

二樓 [yi6 lau4] *n.* second floor

義務 [yi6 mou6] *n.* obligation

二奶 [yi6 naai1] *n.* mistress

二十四小時營業 [yi6 sap9 sei3 siu2 si4 ying4 yip9] *adj., phr.* open all night

二十 [yi6 sap9] *num.* twenty

二手 [yi6 sau2] *n.* secondhand (~ bookstore 二手書店, ~ goods 二手嘢)

二手店 [yi6 sau2 dim3] *n.* secondhand store

異性戀 [yi6 sing3 lyun2] *adj.* heterosexual

二月份 [yi6 yut9 fan6] *n.* February (*abbr.* Feb.)

抑鬱 [yik7 wat7] *n.* depression

抑鬱症 [yik7 wat7 jing3] *n.* melancholia

翼 [yik9] *n.* wing (*of a bird/building*)

液化 [yik9 fa3] *v.* liquefy

亦唔係 [yik9 m4 hai6] *conj.* nor

疫苗 [yik9 miu4] *n.* vaccine

液態氧氣 [yik9 taai3 yeung5 hei3] *n.* lox

液體 [yik9 tai2] *n.* liquid

閹割 [yim1 got8] *n.* neuter

醃好 [yim1 hou2] *adj.* marinated

醃製 [yim1 jai3] *adj.* preserved

醃汁 [yim1 jap7] *n.* marinade

醃尖 [yim1 jim1] *n.* carp

醃三文魚 [yim1 saam1 man4 yu2] *n.* marinated salmon

嚴格 [yim4 gaak8] *adj.* strict

嚴重 [yim4 jung6] *adj.* serious

嚴重毀壞 [yim4 jung6 wai2 waai6] *v.* mutilate

嚴厲 [yim4 lai6] *adj.* rigorous

鹽 [yim4] *n.* salt

鹽瓶 [yim4 ping4] *n.* salt container

鹽醃 [yim4 yip8] *adj.* salted

染 [yim5] *v.* dye

染色體 [yim5 sik7 tai2] *n.* chromosome; chromosomal abnormalities

驗光師 [yim6 gwong1 si1] *n.* optometrist

驗血 [yim6 hyut8] *n.* blood test

驗證 [yim6 jing3] *v.* validate (~ tickets 車票生效)

驗票 [yim6 piu3] *v.* stamp a ticket

驗孕 [yim6 yan6] *n.* pregnancy test

煙 [yin1] *n.* cigarette (~ paper 煙紙)

煙草 [yin1 chou2] *n.* tobacco (~ shop 煙草店, chewing ~ 咬煙草, ~ plant 煙草廠)

煙花 [yin1 fa1] *n.* fireworks

煙薰 [yin1 fan1] *adj.* smoked (~ meat 煙肉, ~ bacon 煙肉, ~ salmon 煙三文魚)

煙灰缸 [yin1 fui1 gong1] *n.* ashtray

胭脂蟲籽 [yin1 ji1 chung4 ji2] *n.* cochineal seeds

胭脂魚 [yin1 ji1 yu2] *n.* mullet

煙民 [yin1 man4] *n.* smoker

煙筒 [yin1 tung2] *n.* chimney

煙肉 [yin1 yuk9] *n.* bacon (~ and eggs 煙肉煎蛋, ~ strips 煙肉條)

演唱會 [yin2 cheung3 wui2] *n.* gig

演講家 [yin2 gong2 ga1] *n.* orator

演講 [yin2 gong2] *n.* lecture

演講術 [yin2 gong2 seut9] *n.* oratory

鼴鼠 [yin2 syu2] *n.* mole

演員 [yin2 yun4] *n.* actor, actress

燕麥 [yin3 mak9] *n.* oatmeal

弦 [yin4] *n.* chord

延長 [yin4 cheung4] *v.* prolong

延長電線 [yin4 cheung4 din6 sin3] *n.* extension cord

延遲 [yin4 chi4] *n.* delay

研究 [yin4 gau3] *n.* research

研究結果 [yin4 gau3 git8 gwo2] *n.* finding

研究生 [yin4 gau3 sang1] *n.* graduate

研究員 [yin4 gau3 yun4] *n.* researcher

延續 [yin4 juk9] *v.* perpetuate

燃料 [yin4 liu6] *n.* fuel

言外之意 [yin4 ngoi6 ji1 yi3] *n.* implication

延伸 [yin4 san1] *v.* extend

研討會 [yin4 tou2 wui2] *n.* seminar

現代 [yin6 doi6] *adj.* modern

現金 [yin6 gam1] *n.* cash (~ register 收銀機, ~ deposit 存現金)

現象 [yin6 jeung6] *n.* phenomenon

現在 [yin6 joi6] *adj.* present

現實主義 [yin6 sat9 jyu2 yi6] *n.* realism

現實主義者 [yin6 sat9 jyu2 yi6 je2] *n.* realist

現實 [yin6 sat9] *n.* reality

現時 [yin6 si4] *adj.* current

現任 [yin6 yam4] *n.* incumbent

諺語 [yin6 yu5] *n.* proverb

英鎊 [ying1 bong2] *n.* sterling

英吋 [ying1 chyun3] *n.* inch

應得 [ying1 dak7] *v.* deserve

應該 [ying1 goi1] *v. modal* should, ought to

英國 [ying1 gwok8] *n.* Britain; *adj.* British (~ food 英國菜)

英雄 [ying1 hung4] *n.* hero

鷹嘴豆 [ying1 jeui2 dau2] *n.* chickpea, garbanzo bean

鷹嘴豆蓉 [ying1 jeui2 dau6 yung4] *n.* hummus (spicy ~ 辣鷹嘴豆蓉)

英里 [ying1 lei5] *n.* mile

英文 [ying1 man2] *adj.* English

英畝 [ying1 mau5] *n.* acre

英明 [ying1 ming4] *adj.* wise

鸚鵡 [ying1 mou5] *n.* parrot

英式鬆餅 [ying1 sik7 sung1 beng2] *n.* scone

應承 [ying1 sing4] *v.* promise

嬰兒 [ying1 yi4] *n.* baby, infant (~ carriage/stroller 嬰兒車, ~ food 嬰兒食物, ~ clothes 嬰兒衫, ~ powder 嬰兒奶粉, ~ wipes 嬰兒濕紙巾)

嬰兒床 [ying1 yi4 chong4] *n.* crib

嬰兒房 [ying1 yi4 fong2] *n.* nursery room

嬰兒配方奶粉 [ying1 yi4 pui3 fong1 naai5 fan2] *n.* infant formula

嬰兒衫 [ying1 yi4 saam1] *n.* babywear

嬰兒濕紙巾 [ying1 yi4 sap7 ji2 gan1] *n.* baby wipes

影 [ying2] *n.* shadow (cast a ~ 蒙上陰影)

影響 [ying2 heung2] *n.* impact

影響力 [ying2 heung2 lik9] *n.* influence

影射 [ying2 se6] *n.* allusion

影相 [ying2 seung2] *v.* take a photo(graph)

影印 [ying2 yan3] *n.* copy; *v.* make a copy

影印機 [ying2 yan3 gei1] *n.* photocopier

營地 [ying4 dei6] *n.* camp, campground, campsite

凝結 [ying4 git8] *adj.* congealed (~ fat 凝固脂, ~ sauce 凝結醬, ~ liquid 冷凝液)

凝結咗 [ying4 git8 jo2] *adj.* clotted (~ cream 濃縮忌廉, ~ sauce 凝結咗嘅醬)

迎合 [ying4 hap9] *v.* cater

形象 [ying4 jeung6] *n.* imagery

盈利 [ying4 lei6] *adj.* profitable

盈利能力 [ying4 lei6 nang4 lik9] *n.* profitability

刑事偵察 [ying4 si6 jing1 chaat8] *n.* criminal investigation

形成 [ying4 sing4] *n.* formation

營養 [ying4 yeung5] *n.* nourishment

營養不良 [ying4 yeung5 bat7 leung4] *n.* malnutrition

迎嬰派對 / 新娘送禮會 [ying4 ying1 paai3 deui3/san1 neung4 sung3 lai5 wui5] *n.* baby/bridal shower

營業額 [ying4 yip9 ngaak9] *n.* turnover

營業時間 [ying4 yip9 si4 gaan3] *n.* opening hours

盈餘 [ying4 yu4] *n.* surplus

凝乳 [ying4 yu5] *n.* curds

形容詞 [ying4 yung4 chi4] *n.* adjective

認 [ying6] *v.* admit

認出 [ying6 cheut7] *v.* recognize

認可 [ying6 ho2] *n.* recognition

認真 [ying6 jan1] *adv.* seriously

認罪協議 [ying6 jeui6 hip8 yi5] *n.* plea bargain

認為 [ying6 wai4] *v.* reckon

醃 [yip8] *adj.* pickled (~ vegetables 鹹菜, ~ meat 醃肉)

醃牛肉 [yip8 ngau4 yuk9] *n.* jerk seasoning

葉 [yip9] *n.* leaf

頁 [yip9] *n.* page

頁尾 [yip9 mei5] *n.* footer (add ~ to document 文件加頁尾)

業主 [yip9 jyu2] *n.* proprietor

頁首 [yip9 sau2] *n.* header (add ~ to a document 文件加頁首)

業務 [yip9 mou6] *n.* business

熱 [yit9] *adj.* hot (~ temperature 氣溫高, ~ spicy 好辣)

熱茶 [yit9 cha4] *n.* hot tea

熱情 [yit9 ching4] *n.* enthusiasm

熱衷 [yit9 chung1] *adj.* keen on

熱帶 [yit9 daai3] *adj.* tropical (~ flavor 熱帶風味, ~ fruit 熱帶水果, ~ juice 熱帶水果汁)

熱狗 [yit9 gau2] *n.* hot dog

熱狗攤檔 [yit9 gau2 taan1 dong3] *n.* hot-dog stand

熱朱古力 [yit9 jyu1 gu1 lik7] *n.* hot chocolate

熱烈歡迎 [yit9 lit9 fun1 ying4] *n.* ovation

熱葡萄酒 [yit9 pou4 tou4 jau2] *n.* mulled wine

熱心 [yit9 sam1] *adj.* keen

熱水 [yit9 seui2] *n.* hot water

腰 [yiu1] *n.* waist

腰部嫩肉 [yiu1 bou6 nyun6 yuk9] *n.* tenderloin (beef ~ 牛嘅腰部嫩肉)

邀請 [yiu1 ching2] *n.* invitation

邀請來 [yiu1 ching2 loi4] *v.* invite for

腰骨 [yiu1 gwat7] *n.* spine, backbone

腰果 [yiu1 gwo2] *n.* cashew

要求 [yiu1 kau4] *n.* requirement

繞路 [yiu2 lou6] *n.* detour

腰痛 [yiu1 tung3] *n.* backache

要 [yiu3] *v.* ask for

要俾錢嘅 [yiu3 bei2 chin2 ge3] *adj.* payable

要負責任 [yiu3 fu6 jaak8 yam6] *adj.* liable

要交 [yiu3 gaau1] *adj.* due (~ to 因為)

要幾耐? [yiu3 gei2 noi6] *phr.* how long?

搖 [yiu4] *v.* shake

搖滾 [yiu4 gwan2] *n.* rock and roll

遙控器 [yiu4 hung3 hei3] *n.* remote control

搖籃曲 [yiu4 laam4 kuk7] *n.* lullaby

謠言 [yiu4 yin4] *n.* rumor

遙遠 [yiu4 yun5] *adj.* remote

迂腐 [yu1 fu6] *adj.* pedantic

魚 [yu2] *n.* fish (~ sauce 魚露, ~ stall 魚檔, ~ sticks 魚串, ~ allergy 對魚敏感)

瘀 [yu2] *n.* bruise
魚蛋 [yu4 daan2] *n.* fishballs
魚店 [yu4 dim3] *n.* fish store
瑜珈 [yu4 ga1] *n.* yoga
魚竿 [yu4 gon1] *n.* fishing rod
如果唔係 [yu4 gwo2 m4 hai6] *adv.* otherwise
如果 [yu4 gwo2] *conj.* if
魚子醬 [yu4 ji2 jeung3] *n.* caviar
魚籽 [yu4 ji2] *n.* roe
魚群 [yu4 kwan4] *n.* fish stock
魚鱗 [yu4 leun4] *n.* scales
娛樂 [yu4 lok9] *n.* amusement (~ arcade 遊樂場, ~ park 遊樂園)
漁民 [yu4 man4] *n.* fisherman
魚片 [yu4 pin2] *n.* fillet (chicken ~ 雞片, fish ~ 魚片)
魚肉 [yu4 yuk9] *n.* fish stock
魚肉凍 [yu4 yuk9 dung3] *n.* fish jelly
雨 [yu5] *n.* rain (it's ~ing 落緊雨)
乳清 [yu5 ching1] *n.* whey
語法 [yu5 faat8] *n.* grammar
乳鴿 [yu5 gap8] *n.* squab, fowl
雨刮 [yu5 gwaat8] *n.* windshield wiper
雨季 [yu5 gwai3] *n.* monsoon
語氣 [yu5 hei3] *n.* tone
宇宙 [yu5 jau6] *n.* universe
與眾不同 [yu5 jung3 bat7 tung4] *adj.* distinctive
乳豬 [yu5 jyu1] *n.* suckling pig
雨褸 [yu5 lau1] *n.* raincoat
乳酪 [yu5 lok3] *n.* yogurt (low-fat ~ 低脂乳酪)
羽毛 [yu5 mou4] *n.* feather

羽毛球 [yu5 mou4 kau4] *n.* badminton
乳糖 [yu5 tong4] *n.* lactose (~ intolerant 可以消化乳糖)
雨雲 [yu5 wan4] *n.* nimbus
語音 [yu5 yam1] *n.* phonetics
語音導遊 [yu5 yam1 dou6 yau4] *n.* audio-guide
羽衣甘藍葉 [yu5 yi1 gam1 laam4 yip9] *n.* collard greens
乳液 [yu5 yik9] *n.* emulsion, lotion
語言 [yu5 yin4] *n.* language
語言課程 [yu5 yin4 fo3 ching4] *n.* language course
語言學 [yu5 yin4 hok9] *n.* linguistics
語言學家 [yu5 yin4 hok9 ga1] *n.* linguist
羽絨被 [yu5 yung4 pei5] *n.* duvet
愈 [yu6] *adv.* increasingly
預報 [yu6 bou3] *n.* forecast
預測 [yu6 chak7] *v.* predict
預訂 [yu6 deng6] *n.* reservation; *v.* make/have an appointment
預訂處 [yu6 ding3 chyu3] *n.* reservation desk
愉快 [yu6 faai3] *adj.* pleasant
預防 [yu6 fong4] *n.* precaution
預計 [yu6 gai3] *n.* projection
預感 [yu6 gam2] *n.* premonition
預知 [yu6 ji1] *n.* prescience
預早 [yu6 jou2] *adj.* advance (~ booking 預訂, ~ sale 預售)
預料 [yu6 liu6] *v.* anticipate
預謀 [yu6 mau4] *n.* premeditation
預示 [yu6 si6] *v.* portend
預先煮好 [yu6 sin1 jyu2 hou2] *v.* precook

預兆 [yu6 siu6] *n.* auspice

預算 [yu6 syun3] *n.* budget

預約 [yu6 yeuk8] *n.* appointment

寓言 [yu6 yin4] *n.* parable

預言 [yu6 yin4] *n.* prophecy

預言家 [yu6 yin4 ga1] *n.* prophet

郁得 [yuk7 dak7] *adj.* movable

郁唔到 [yuk7 m4 dou3] *adj.* stuck

肉 [yuk9] *n.* meat

肉餅 [yuk9 beng2] *n.* cutlet
(lamb ~ 羊肉餅, mutton ~ 羊
肉餅, chicken ~ 雞肉餅)

肉餅仔 [yuk9 beng2 jai2] *n.*
patty (chicken ~ 雞肉餅仔,
fish ~ 魚肉餅仔)

肉串 [yuk9 chyun3] *n.* skewered
kebab

肉豆蔻 [yuk9 dau6 kau3] *n.*
nutmeg

肉凍 [yuk9 dung3] *n.* aspic (~
sauce 肉凍醬)

肉餃 [yuk9 gaau2] *n.* meat dumpling

浴巾 [yuk9 gan1] *n.* bath towel

肉羹 [yuk9 gang1] *n.* bouillon

肉乾 [yuk9 gon1] *n.* dried meat

浴缸 [yuk9 gong1] *n.* bidet

肉桂 [yuk9 gwai3 pei4] *n.*
cinnamon (~ roll 肉桂卷, ~
stick 肉桂條, ~ powder 肉桂
粉, ~ doughnut 肉桂冬甩, ~
cake 肉桂蛋糕)

肉餡粟米卷 [yuk9 haam6 suk7
mai5 gyun2] *n.* enchilada

肉汁 [yuk9 jap7] *n.* meat stock,
gravy (turkey ~ 火雞汁, beef ~
牛肉汁)

肉泥 [yuk9 nai4] *n.* paté

肉眼牛扒 [yuk9 ngaan5 ngau4
pa2] *n.* rib-eye steak

肉片 [yuk9 pin2] *n.* sliced meats

肉碎 [yuk9 seui3] *n.* minced meat

肉丸 [yuk9 yun2] *n.* meatballs

怨 [yun3] *v.* blame

怨恨 [yun3 han6] *n.* spite

原版 [yun4 baan2] *n.* original
version

鉛筆 [yun4 bat7] *n.* pencil

原始 [yun4 chi2] *adj.* primitive

圓柱 [yun4 chyu5] *adj.* cylindrical

完全 [yun4 cyun4] *adv.* fully;
adv. completely

完全一樣 [yun4 cyun4 yat7
yeung6] *adj.* identical

元旦 [yun4 daan3] *n.* New Year's
Day

圓頂 [yun4 deng2] *n.* dome

原告 [yun4 gou3] *n.* plaintiff

完工 [yun4 gung1] *n.* completion

員工 [yun4 gung1] *n.* staff

懸掛式滑翔機 [yun4 gwa3 sik7
waat9 cheung4 gei1] *n.* hangglider

圓圈 [yun4 hyun1] *n.* circle

原則 [yun4 jak7] *n.* principle

原子 [yun4 ji2] *n.* atom

原子筆 [yun4 ji2 bat7] *n.* ballpoint
pen

原子核 [yun4 ji2 hat9] *n.* nucleus

原子能 [yun4 ji2 nang4] *adj.*
atomic

圓括號 [yun4 kut8 hou6] *n.*
parenthesis

原諒 [yun4 leung6] *v.* forgive

原料 [yun4 liu2] *n.* ingredient;
sauce base

原來 [yun4 loi4] *adj.* original

原路行番 [yun4 lou6 hang4 faan1] *v.* retrace

完美 [yun4 mei5] *adj.* perfect

玄妙 [yun4 miu6] *n.* oracular

懸崖 [yun4 ngaai4] *n.* cliff

園藝 [yun4 ngai6] *n.* gardening

園藝中心 [yun4 ngai6 jung1 sam1] *n.* garden center

芫茜 [yun4 sai1] *n.* cilantro (~ flakes 芫茜碎, ~ sauce 芫茜醬)

完成 [yun4 sing4] *v.* finish

元素 [yun4 sou3] *n.* element

元音 [yun4 yam1] *n.* vowel

原因 [yun4 yan1] *n.* cause

圓形 [yun4 ying4] *adj.* round

遠 [yun5] *adv.* far (how ~ 有幾遠)

遠啲 [yun5 di1] *adv.* further, furthest

軟件 [yun5 gin6] *n.* software

遠古 [yun5 gu2] *adj.* primeval

軟骨 [yun5 gwat7] *n.* cartilage

遠光燈 [yun5 gwong1 dang1] *n.* high-beam lights

軟芝士 [yun5 ji1 si6] *n.* soft cheese

遠足 [yun5 juk7] *v.* hike

遠視 [yun5 si6] *n.* far-sighted

軟熟 [yun5 suk9] *adj.* soft

軟糖 [yun5 tong2] *n.* fudge (~ pops 軟糖汽水, ~ brownie 軟糖朱古力布朗尼)

軟弱 [yun5 yeuk9] *adj.* weak (~ flavor 冇乜味, ~ taste 冇乜味, to be ~ 軟弱)

願意 [yun6 yi3] *adj.* amenable

統計 [yung2 gai3] *adj.* statistical

統計學 [yung2 gai3 hok9] *n.* statistics

統計上 [yung2 gai3 seung6] *n.* statistic

佣金 [yung2 gam1] *n.* commission

擁抱 [yung2 pou5] *n.* hug; *v.* give a hug

冗員 [yung2 yun4] *n.* redundance

溶 [yung4] *v.* melt

熔咗 [yung4 jo2] *adj.* molten

溶解 [yung4 gaai2] *v.* dissolve (~ in water 可水中溶解)

容光煥發 [yung4 gwong1 wun6 faat8] *adj.* radiant

融合 [yung4 hap9] *v.* meld

容器 [yung4 hei3] *n.* container

溶劑 [yung4 jai1] *n.* solvent

溶咗 [yung4 jo2] *v.* melted (~ cheese 芝士泥, ~ butter 牛油水, ~ chocolate 朱古力泥)

容量 [yung4 leung6] *n.* capacity

熔岩 [yung4 ngaam4] *n.* lava

傭人 [yung4 yan4] *n.* servant

容易 [yung4 yi6] *adj.* easy

容易起火 [yung4 yi6 hei2 fo2] *adj.* fiery

勇 [yung5] *adj.* brave

用 [yung6] *v.* use (~ before 保質期係, for my personal ~ 私用)

用得 [yung6 dak7] *adj.* functional

用緊嘅 [yung6 gan2 ge3] *adj.* occupied

用公式表達 [yung6 gung1 sik7 biu2 daat9] *v.* formulate

用炭燒 [yung6 taan3 siu1] *v.* char-broiled

用炭燒 [yung6 taan3 siu1] *adj.* charcoal-grilled

用戶 [yung6 wu6] *n.* subscriber

用戶名 [yung6 wu6 meng2] *n.* username (website ~ 網站用戶名稱)

用藥過量 [yung6 yeuk9 gwo3 leung6] *n.* overdose

月 [yut9] *n.* month (this ~ 尼個月)

月經 [yut9 ging1] *n.* menstruation

月經前緊張 [yut9 ging1 chin4 gan2 jeung1] *n.* premenstrual tension

月桂樹葉 [yut9 gwai3 syu6 yip9] *n.* bay leaf

月亮 [yut9 leung6] *n.* moon

越南 [yut9 naam4] *n.* Vietnam; *adj.* Vietnamese

越位 [yut9 wai6] *adj.* offside

越野 [yut9 ye5] *n.* cross-country (~ running/team 越野賽跑, ~ skiing 越野滑雪, ~ skis 越野滑雪)

傳奇 [zyun6 kei4] *n.* legend

ENGLISH–CANTONESE
DICTIONARY

A

a / an *indef. art.* 一個 [yat7 go3]

a.m. *adv.* 朝早 [jiu1 jou2]

abalone *n.* 鮑魚 [baau1 yu4]

abandon *v.* 遺棄 [wai4 hei3]

abandoned *adj.* 被遺棄嘅 [bei6 wai4 hei3 ge3]

abbey *n.* 修道院 [sau1 dou6 yun6]

abbreviation *n.* 縮寫 [suk7 se2]

abdomen *n.* 肚腩 [tou5 naam5]

abduction *n.* 綁架 [bong2 ga3]

ability *n.* 能力 [nang4 lik9]

able *v.* 有能力 [yau5 nang4 lik9]; *adj.* 有能力嘅 [yau5 nang4 lik9 ge3]; **be ~ to** 有能力

aboard *adv.* 船上面 [syun4 seung6 min6]; *prep.* 上船 [seung2 syun4]

aboriginal *adj.* 土著 [tou2 jyu3]

abort (*military / medical*) *v.* 中止 [jung1 ji2]

abortion *n.* 流產 [lau4 chaan2]

about *adv.* 差唔多 [cha1 m4 do1]; *prep.* 關於 [gwaan1 yu1]

above *prep.* 喺…上面 [hai6 … seung5 min6]; *adv.* 高於 [gou1 yu1]

abroad *adv.* 國外 [gwok8 ngoi6]

abrupt *adj.* 唐突 [tong4 dat9]

abscess *n.* 膿腫 [nung4 jung2]

abscond *v.* 走佬 [jau2 lou2]

absence *n.* 冇到 [mou5 dou3]

absent *adj.* 冇到 [mou5 dou3]

absinthe *n.* 苦艾酒 [fu2 ngaai6 jau2]

absolute *adj.* 絕對 [jyut9 deui3]

absolutely *adv.* 絕對 [jyut9 deui3]

absorb *v.* 吸收 [kap7 sau1]

abstract *adj.* 抽象 [chau1 jeung6]

absurd *adj.* 荒謬 [fong1 mau6]

Abu Dhabi *n.* 阿布扎比 [a3 bou3 jaat8 bei2]; **~, capital of United Arab Emirates** 阿聯酋嘅首都

Abuja *n.* 阿布賈 [a3 bou3 ga2]; **~, capital of Nigeria** 尼日利亞嘅首都

abuse *n.* 濫用 [laam6 yung6]; *v.* 濫用 [laam6 yung6]

academic *adj.* 學術 [hok9 seut9]

academy *n.* 專科學校 [jyun1 fo1 hok9 haau6]

accelerator *n.* 加速器 [ga1 chuk7 hei3]

accent *n.* 口音 [hau2 yam1]

accept *v.* 接受 [jip8 sau6]

acceptable *adj.* 都得 [dou1 dak7]

access *n.* 通道 [tung1 dou6]; *v.* 進入 [jeun3 yap9]; **~ a computer file** 訪問電腦文件

accident *n.* 意外 [yi3 ngoi6]

accidental *adj.* 偶然 [ngau5 yin4]

accidentally *adv.* 偶然 [ngau5 yin4]

accommodation(s) *n.* 住宿 [jyu6 suk7]

accompany *v.* 陪 [puui4]

accompanying *adj.* 跟住嘅 [gan1 jyu6 ge3]

accomplish *v.* 搞掂 [gaau2 dim1]

accomplished *adj.* 搞掂咗 [gaau2 dim1 jo2]

accomplishment *n.* 成就 [sing4 jau6]

accordance: in ~ with *n.* 一致 [yat7 ji3]

according to *prep.* 根據 [gan1 geui3]

account *n.* 賬戶 [jeung3 wu6]; *v.* 導致 [dou6 ji3]; **on ~ of** 由於

accountant *n.* 會計 [wui6 gai3]

Accra *n.* 阿克拉 [a3 hak7 laai1]; **~, capital of Ghana** 加納嘅首都

accumulate *v.* 累積 [leui5 jik7]

accumulation *n.* 累積 [leui5 jik7]

accurate *adj.* 準 [jeun2]

accurately *adv.* 準 [jeun2]

accuse *v.* 指控 [ji2 hung3]; **~(d) of** 指控…做了

acentric *adj.* 離心 [lei4 sam1]

acre *n.* 英畝 [ying1 mau5]

ache *n.* 痛 [tung3]

achieve *v.* 達到 [daat9 dou3]

achievement *n.* 成就 [sing4 jau6]

acid *n.* 酸 [syun1]

acidify *v.* 酸化 [syun1 fa3]

acidity *n.* 酸性 [syun1 sing3]

acidulated *adj.* 有酸味 [yau5 syun1 mei6]

acknowledge *v.* 承認 [sing4 ying6]

acne *n.* 粉刺 [fan2 chi3]; **~ cream/medicine** 粉刺膏

acorn *n.* 橡實 [jeung6 sat9]

acorn squash *n.* 南瓜 [naam4 gwa1]; **~ soup** 南瓜羹

acquaintance *n.* 熟人 [suk9 yan4]

acquainted *adj.* 熟 [suk9]; **become ~** 熟絡起來

acquire *v.* 攞到 [lo2 dou2]

acquisition *n.* 收購 [sau1 kau3]

acquit *v.* 無罪釋放 [mou4 jeui6 sik7 fong3]

acquittal *n.* 無罪釋放 [mou4 jeui6 sik7 fong3]

across *adv.* 對面 [deui3 min6]; *prep.* 對面 [deui3 min6]

acrylic *adj.* 塑膠 [sou3 gaau1]

act *n.* 表演 [biu2 yin2]; *v.* 行動 [hang4 dung6]

action *n.* 行動 [hang4 dung6]

activate *v.* 開 [hoi1]

active *adj.* 積極 [jik7 gik9]

actively *adv.* 積極 [jik7 gik9]

activist *n.* 激進分子 [gik7 jeun3 fan6 ji2]

activity *n.* 活動 [wut9 dung6]

actor/actress *n.* 演員 [yin2 yun4]

actual *adj.* 實際嘅 [sat9 jai3 ge3]

actually *adv.* 實際上 [sat9 jai3 seung5]

acupuncture *n.* 針灸 [jam1 gau3]

acute *adj.* 急性 [gap7 sing3]; **~ pain** 急性疼痛; **~ angle** 尖銳嘅意見

ad (advertisement) 廣告 [gwong2 gou3]

adapt *v.* 適應 [sik7 ying3]

adapter *n.* 轉換器 [jyun2 wun6 hei3]

add *v.* 加 [ga1]

addicted *adj.* 上癮 [seung5 yan2]

addiction *n.* 癮 [seung5]

Addis Ababa *n.* 亞的斯貝巴 [a3 dik7 si1 bui3 ba1]; **~, capital of Ethiopia** 埃塞俄比亞嘅首都

addition *n.* 加法 [ga1 faat8]

additional *adj.* 額外 [ngaak9 ngoi6]

address *n.* 地址 [dei6 ji2]; *v.* 強調 [keung4 diu6]; **home ~** 屋企地址

addressee *n.* 收信人 [sau1 seun3 yan4]

ade *n.* 果汁飲品 [gwo2 jap7 yam2 ban2]; **lemon~** 檸檬水; **lime~** 青檸檬水

adept *adj.* 厲害 [lai6 hoi6]

adequate *adj.* 都夠 [dou1 gau3]

adequately *adv.* 都夠 [dou1 gau3]

adhere *v.* 遵守 [jeun1 sau2]

adherence *n.* 遵守 [jeun1 sau2]

adhesion *n.* 黐力 [chi1 lik9]

adhesive *adj.* 膠水 [gaau1 seui2]

adjacent *adj.* 隔籬 [gaak8 lei4]

adjective *n.* 形容詞 [ying4 yung4 chi4]

adjoining *adj.* 隔籬 [gaak8 lei4]

adjust *v.* 校正 [gaau3 jing1]

adjustment *n.* 調整 [tiu4 jing2]; **flavor ~** 調味; **temperature ~** 調整溫度

administration *n.* 管理部門 [gun2 lei5 bou6 mun4]

administrative *adj.* 行政管理 [hang4 jing3 gun2 lei5]; **~ district** 行政區

admiration *n.* 敬佩 [ging3 pui3]

admire *v.* 敬佩 [ging3 pui3]

admission *n.* 入場費 [yap9 cheung4 fai3]; **~ fee** 入場費; **~ ticket** 入場票

admit *v.* 認 [ying6]

admittance *n.* 錄取 [luk9 cheui2]

adopt *v.* 採用 [choi2 yung6]

adorable *adj.* 得意 [dak7 yi3]

adore *v.* 鍾意 [jung1 yi3]

adult *n.* 大人 [daai6 yan4]; *adj.* 成年嘅 [sing4 nin4 ge3]

adulation *n.* 奉承 [fung6 sing4]

advance *adj.* 預早 [yu6 jou2], **~ booking** 預訂, **~ sale** 預售; *n.* 預付款 [yu6 fu6 fun2]; *v.* 推進 [teui1 jeun3]

advanced *adj.* 先進 [sin1 jeun3]

advantage *n.* 優點 [yau1 dim2]

adventure *n.* 奇遇 [kei4 yu6]

adverb *n.* 副詞 [fu3 chi4]

adversary *n.* 對手 [deui3 sau2]

adversity *n.* 困境 [kwan3 ging2]

advertise *v.* 宣傳 [syun1 chyun4]

advertisement *n.* 廣告 [gwong2 gou3]

advertising *n.* 廣告 [gwong2 gou3]; **~ agency** 廣告公司; **~ executive** 廣告經理

advice *n.* 建議 [gin3 yi5]; **ask for ~** 請教意見

advise *v.* 勸 [hyun3]

adviser (*also* **advisor**) *n.* 顧問 [gu3 man6]

advocacy *n.* 提倡 [tai4 cheung1]

advocate *n.* 提倡者 [tai4 cheung1 je2]

aerial *adj.* 空中 [hung1 jung1]

aerobics *n.* 有氧運動 [yau5 yeung5 wan6 dung6]

aesthetic (*also* **esthetic**, **~s**) *adj.* 審美 [sam2 mei5]; *n.* 審美 [sam2 mei5]

affair *n.* 外遇 [ngoi6 yu6]

affect *v.* 影響 [ying2 heung2]

affectation *n.* 扮野 [baan3 ye5]

affection *n.* 感情 [gam2 ching4]

affidavit *n.* 宣誓 [syun1 sai6] law

affiliation *n.* 關係 [gwaan1 hai6]

affinity *n.* 親密關係 [chan1 mat9 gwaan1 hai6]

affirm *v.* 證實 [jing3 sat9]

affirmation *n.* 證實 [jing3 sat9]

afflict *v.* 折磨 [jit8 mo4]

affliction *n.* 痛苦 [tung3 fu2]

affluence *n.* 有錢 [yau5 chin2]

afford *v.* 買得起 [maai5 dak7 hei2]

Afghan (*person from Afghanistan*) *adj./n.* 阿富汗人 [a3 fu3 hon4 yan4]

Afghanistan *n.* 阿富汗 [a3 fu3 hon4]

afraid *adj.* 驚 [geng1]

Africa *n.* 非洲 [fei1 jau1]

African *n.* 非洲人 [fei1 jau1 yan4]

after *prep.* 之後 [ji1 hau6]; *conj.* 之後 [ji1 hau6]; *adv.* 之後 [ji1 hau6]

afternoon *n.* 晏晝 [ngaan3 jau3]; **in the ~** 晏晝; **this ~** 今日晏晝

aftershave lotion *n.* 鬚後水 [sou1 hau6 seui2]

after-sun lotion *n.* 曬後乳液 [saai3 hau6 yu5 yik9]

afterwards *adv.* 後來 [hau6 loi4]

again *adv.* 又 [yau6]

against *prep.* 反對 [faan2 deui3]

agave *n.* 龍舌蘭 [lung4 sit8 laan4]

age *n.* 年紀 [nin4 gei2]

aged *adj.* 陳年 [chan4 nin4]

agency *n.* 代理行 [doi6 lei5 hong4]

agenda *n.* 議程 [yi5 ching4]

agent *n.* 代理人 [doi6 lei5 yan4]

aggravate *v.* 激嬲 [gik7 nau1]

aggravation *n.* 激嬲 [gik7 nau1]

aggression *n.* 侵略 [cham1 leuk9]

aggressive *adj.* 惡死 [ok8 sei2]

aging *v.* 老化 [lou5 fa3]; **~ meat** 爛咗嘅肉

agile *adj.* 身手靈活 [san1 sau2 ling4 wut9]

agitate *v.* 煽動 [sin3 dung6]

agitation *n.* 煽動 [sin3 dung6]

ago *adv.* 之前 [ji1 chin4]

agony *n.* 痛苦 [tung3 fu2]

agonize *v.* 折磨 [jit8 mo4]

agrarian *adj.* 農業 [nung4 yip9]

agree *v.* 同意 [tung4 yi3]

agreement *n.* 同意 [tung4 yi3]

agricultural *adj.* 農業 [nung4 yip9]

agriculture *n.* 農業 [nung4 yip9]

agronomy *n.* 農學 [nung4 hok9]

ahead *adv.* 預早 [yu6 jou2]

ahead of *prep.* 喺…之前 [hai2 … ji1 chin4]

aid *n.* 援助 [wun4 jo6]; *v.* 援助 [wun4 jo6]

aid and abet *v.* 同謀 [tung4 mau4]; **~ a criminal** 同謀

AIDS *n.* 愛滋病 [oi3 ji1 beng6]

ailing *n.* 病咗 [beng6 jo2]

ailment *n.* 小問題 [siu2 man6 tai4]

aim *n.* 志向 [ji3 heung3]; *v.* 瞄準 [miu4 jeun2]

air *n.* 空氣 [hung1 hei3]; **~ filter** 空氣清新機; **~ mattress** 氣墊; **~ pump** 氣泵; **~ sickness** 暈機浪

air-conditioned *adj.* 有冷氣 [yau5 laang5 hei3]

air conditioning (A/C) *n.* 冷氣 [laang5 hei3]

aircraft *n.* 飛機 [fei1 gei1]

airline *n.* 航空公司 [hong4 hung1 gung1 si1]

airmail *n.* 空郵 [hung1 yau4]; **by ~** 用空郵寄

airplane *n.* 飛機 [fei1 gei1]

airport *n.* 機場 [gei1 cheung4]; ~ **terminal** 機場大樓; ~ **tax** 機場稅; ~ **security** 機場保安

aisle *n.* 通道 [tung1 dou6]; ~ **seat** 靠通道嘅位

akavit *n.* 白蘭地 [baak9 laan1 dei2]

alarm *n.* 鬧鐘 [naau6 jung1]; *v.* 警告 [ging2 gou3]; ~ **clock** 鬧鐘; **fire** ~ 火警

alarmed *adj.* 慌失失 [fong1 sat7 sat7]

alarming *adj.* 得人驚 [dak7 yan4 geng1]

Albania *n.* 阿爾巴尼亞 [a3 yi5 ba1 nei4 a3]

Albanian *adj.* 阿爾巴尼亞人 [a3 yi5 ba1 nei4 a3 yan4]

albeit *conj.* 就算 [jau6 syun3]

album (photo ~) *n.* 相簿 [seung2 bou6]

alchemy *n.* 煉金術 [lin6 gam1 seut9]

alcohol *n.* 酒 [jau2]

alcoholic *adj.* 酒精中毒 [jau2 jing1 jung3 duk9], ~ **beverage** 酒精飲品; *n.* 酒鬼 [jau2 gwai2]

alcove *n.* 龕 [ham1]

ale *n.* 麥芽啤酒 [mak9 nga4 be1 jau2]

alfalfa sprouts *n.* 苜蓿芽 [muk9 suk7 nga4]

algebra *n.* 代數 [doi6 sou3]

Algeria *n.* 阿爾及利亞 [a3 yi5 kap9 lei6 a3]

Algerian *adj.* 阿爾及利亞人 [a3 yi5 kap9 lei6 a3 yan4]

Algiers *n.* 阿爾及爾 [a3 yi5 kap9 yi5]; ~, **capital of Algeria** 阿爾及利亞嘅首都

alias *n.* 假名 [ga2 meng2]

alibi *n.* 不在場證據 [bat7 joi6 cheung4 jing3 geui3]

alien *adj.* 外國 [ngoi6 gwok8]; *n.* 外星人 [ngoi6 sing1 yan4]

align *v.* 對齊 [deui3 chai4]

alignment *n.* 校正 [gaau3 jeng1], **margin** ~ 頁邊對齊, **tire** ~ 校輪胎

alimony *n.* 贍養費 [sin6 yeung5 fai3]

alive *adj.* 在生 [joi6 saang1]

all *det.* 全部[chyun4 bou6]; *pron.* 全部[chyun4 bou6]; *adv.* 全部[chyun4 bou6]; *adj.* 全部 [chyun4 bou6]; ~ **day** 成日; ~ **night** 成晚, ~ **night pharmacy** 24小時藥店

all right *adj.* 冇事 [mou5 si6] *adv.* 冇事 [mou5 si6]; *exclam.* 好啊 [hou2 a3]

allegation *n.* 陳述 [chan4 seut9]

allergen *n.* 過敏原 [gwo3 man5 yun4]

allegiance *n.* 忠誠 [jung1 sing4]

allergic *adj.* 過敏 [gwo3 man5], **I'm ~ to** 我對…敏感

allergy *n.* 過敏 [gwo3 man5], **food ~** 食物過敏, **medicine ~** 藥物過敏

alleviation *n.* 減輕 [gaam2 heng1]

alley *n.* 巷仔 [hong6 jai2]

allied *adj.* 結盟 [git8 mang4]

allocate *v.* 派 [paai3]

allocation *n.* 分派 [fan1 paai3]

allow *v.* 允許 [wan5 heui2]

allowance *n.* 零用錢 [ling4 yung6 chin2]

allowed *adj.* 批准嘅 [pai1 jeun2 ge3] **be ~ to** 批准做..., **not ~ to** 唔准做...

all-purpose flour *n.* 中筋麵粉 [jung1 gan1 min6 fan2]

allure *v.* 勾引 [ngau1 yan5]

allurement *n.* 誘惑 [yau5 waak9]

allusion *n.* 影射 [ying2 se6]

allusive *adj.* 影射 [ying2 se6]

ally *n.* 盟友 [mang4 yau5]; *v.* 結盟 [gik8 mang4]

almond *n.* 杏仁 [hang6 yan4]; **~ butter** 杏仁醬; **~ oil** 杏仁油

almost *adv.* 就快 [jau6 faai3]

alms *n.* 救濟品 [gau3 jai3 ban2]

aloe *n.* 蘆薈 [lou4 wui6]; **~ juice** 蘆薈汁; **~ cream** 蘆薈乳液

alone *adj.* 自己一個 [ji6 gei2 yat7 go3]; *adv.* 自己一個 [ji6 gei2 yat7 go3]; **leave me ~** 唔好理我

along *prep.* 跟住 [gan1 jyu6]; *adv.* 一齊 [yat7 chai4]; **get ~ with** 同...相處

alongside *prep.* 跟住 [gan1 jyu6]; *adv.* 一齊 [yat7 chai4]

aloud *adv.* 大聲 [daai6 seng1]

alphabet *n.* 字母表 [ji6 mou5 biu2]

alphabetical *adj.* 排字母 [paai4 ji6 mou5]

alphabetically *adv.* 排字母 [paai4 ji6 mou5]

already *adv.* 經已 [ging1 yi5]

also *adv.* 又 [yau6]

altar *n.* 神檯 [san4 toi2]; **~piece** 神檯裝飾

alter *v.* 更改 [gang1 goi2]

alteration *n.* 更改 [gang1 goi2]

alternate *adj.* 輪流 [leun4 lau2], **~ route** 另外一條路

alternative *n.* 取捨 [cheui2 se2]; *adj.* 可以選擇嘅 [ho2 yi5 syun2 jaak9 ge3], **~ lifestyle** 另外嘅生活方式, **~ music** 另外嘅音樂, **~ treatment** 替代治療 [tai3 doi6 ji6 liu4]

alternatively *adv.* 如果唔係 [yu4 gwo2 m4 hai6]

alternator *n.* 交流發電機 [gaau1 lau4 faat8 din6 gei1]

although *conj.* 就算 [jau6 syun3]

altimeter *n.* 高度計 [gou1 dou6 gai3]

altitude *n.* 態度 [taai3 dou6]

altogether *adv.* 總共 [jung2 gung6]

aluminum *n.* 鋁 [leui5]; **~ pan** 鋁盤; **~ pot** 鋁鍋

aluminum foil *n.* 鋁箔 [leui5 bok9]

always *adv.* 成日 [seng4 yat9]

amaranth *n.* 紫紅色 [ji2 hung4 sik7]

amaretti *n.* 苦杏酒 [fu2 hang6 jau2]

amateur *n.* 生手 [saang1 sau2]; *adj.* 業餘 [yip9 yu4]

amaze *v.* 吃驚 [hek8 ging1]

amazed *adj.* 吃驚 [hek8 ging1]

amazing *adj.* 好犀利 [hou2 sai1 lei6]

ambassador *n.* 大使 [daai6 si3]

ambiguity *n.* 含糊 [ham4 wu4]

ambiguous *adj.* 唔清唔楚 [m4 ching1 m4 cho2]

ambition *n.* 野心 [ye5 sam1]

amble *v.* 慢慢行 [maan6 maan1 haang4]

ambrosia *n.* 美酒佳餚 [mei5 jau2 gaai1 ngaau4]

ambulance *n.* 白車 [baak9 che1]

ambush *v.* 埋伏 [maai4 fuk9]

amenable *adj.* 願意 [yun6 yi3]

amenities *n.* 便利設施 [bin6 lei6 chit8 si1]

American *adj.* 美國 [mei5 gwok8]

amiable *adj.* 和善 [wo4 sin6]

amicable *adj.* 和睦 [wo4 muk9]

amino acids *n.* 氨基酸 [on1 gei1 syun1]

amity *n.* 和睦 [wo4 muk9]

Amman *n.* 安曼 [on1 maan6]; **~, capital of Jordan** 約旦嘅首都

amnesia *n.* 失憶 [sat7 yik7]

amnesty *n.* 大赦 [daai6 se3]

among *prep.* 響…入面 [heung2 … yap9 min6]

amount *n.* 數量 [sou3 leung6]; *v.* 等於 [dang2 yu1]

amperes / amps *n.* 安培 [on1 pui4]

ample *adj.* 夠 [gau3]

amplification *n.* 放大 [fong3 daai6]

amplifier *n.* 喇叭 [la1 ba1]

amplify *v.* 放大 [fong3 daai6]

amulet *n.* 護身符 [wu6 san1 fu4]

ampule *n.* 一次用量嘅針劑 [yat7 chi3 yung6 leung6 ge3 jam1 jai1]

Amsterdam *n.* 阿姆斯特丹 [a3 mou5 si1 dak9 daan1]; **~, capital of Netherlands** 荷蘭嘅首都

amuse *v.* 氹…開心 [tam3 … hoi1 sam1]

amused *adj.* 開心 [hoi1 sam1]

amusement *n.* 娛樂 [yu4 lok9]; **~ arcade** 遊樂場; **~ park** 遊樂園

amusing *adj.* 搞笑 [gaau2 siu3]

an *art.* 一個 [yat7 go3]

analogy *n.* 比喻 [bei2 yu6]

analysis *n.* 分析 [fan1 sik7]

analyst *n.* 分析師 [fan1 sik7 si1]

analyze *v.* 分析 [fan1 sik7]

anarchist *n.* 無政府主義者 [mou4 jing3 fu2 jyu2 yi6 je2]

anatomy *n.* 解剖學 [gaai2 fau2 hok9]

ancestor *n.* 祖先 [jou2 sin1]

anchor *n.* 錨 [maau4]

anchorage *n.* 死火 [sei2 fo2]; **no ~** 唔准停車

anchovies *n.* 鳳尾魚 [fung6 mei5 yu2]

anchovy *n.* 鳳尾魚 [fung6 mei5 yu2]

ancient *adj.* 古老 [gu2 lou5]

and *conj.* 同 [tung4]

Andorra *n.* 安多拉 [on1 do1 laai1]

Andorra la Vella *n.* 安多拉城 [on1 do1 laai1 sing4]; **~, capital of Andorra** 安多拉嘅首都

anemia *n.* 貧血 [pan4 hyut8]

anemic *adj.* 貧血 [pan4 hyut8]

anesthetic *adj.* 麻醉藥 [ma4 jeui3 yeuk9]

angel *n.* 天使 [tin1 si2]

anger *n.* 火氣 [fo2 hei3]

angina *n.* 心絞痛 [sam1 gaau2 tung3]

angle *n.* 角度 [gok8 dou6], **obtuse/acute/right ~** 鈍角/銳角/直角, **what's your ~?** 你點睇?

angler (*fisherman*) n. 安康魚 [on1 hong1 yu2]

Angola n. 安哥拉 [on1 go1 laai1]

angrily adv. 好嬲咁 [hou2 nau1 gam3]

angry adj. 嬲 [nau1]

angular adj. 有角 [yau5 gok8]

animal n. 動物 [dung6 mat9]; ~ **feed** 動物飼料; ~ **rights** 動物權利

animated adj. 動畫 [dung6 wa2], ~ **films** 動畫片

animation n. 動畫 [dung6 wa2]

animosity n. 仇恨 [sau4 han6]

anise n. 茴芹 [wui4 kan4]

aniseed n. 八角 [baat8 gok8]

Ankara n. 安卡拉 [on1 ka2 laai1]; ~, **capital of Turkey** 土耳其嘅首都

ankle n. 腳眼 [geuk8 ngaan5]

annalist n. 史官 [si2 gun1]

annihilate v. 消滅 [siu1 mit9]

annihilation n. 消滅 [siu1 mit9]

anniversary n. 週年紀念 [jau1 nin4 gei2 nim6]; **happy ~!** 週年快樂!; ~ **present** 週年紀念禮物

announce v. 宣佈 [syun1 bou3]

announcement n. 通知 [tung1 ji1]

announcer n. 廣播員 [gwong2 bo3 yun4]

annoy v. 令...覺得好討厭 [ling4 ... gok8 dak7 hou2 tou2 yim3]

annoyed adj. 覺得好討厭 [gok8 dak7 hou2 tou2 yim3]

annoying adj. 好討厭 [hou2 tou2 yim3]

annual adj. 年年 [nin4 nin4]

annually adv. 年年 [nin4 nin4]

anonymity n. 匿名 [nik7 ming4]

anonymous adj. 匿名 [nik7 ming4]

anorak n. 滑雪衫 [waat9 syut8 saam1]

another adj. 另外 [ling6 ngoi6]; det. 另外 [ling6 ngoi6]; pron. 另外一個 [ling6 ngoi6 yat7 go3]

answer n. 答案 [daap8 on3]; v. 答 [daap8]

ant n. 螞蟻 [ma5 ngai5]

Antananarivo n. 塔那那利佛 [taap8 na5 na5 lei6 fat7]; ~, **capital of Madagascar** 馬達加斯加嘅首都

antelope n. 羚羊 [ling4 yeung4]

antenna n. 天線 [tin1 sin3]

anthem n. 國歌 [gwok8 go1]

anthology n. 文選 [man4 syun2]

anti- 反[faan2]

antibiotics n. 抗生素 [kong3 sang1 sou3], **prescribe ~** 開抗生素

antibody n. 抗體 [kong3 tai2]

anticipate v. 預料 [yu6 liu6]

antidote n. 解藥 [gaai2 yeuk9]

antifreeze n. 防凍劑 [fong4 dung3 jai1]

anti-government adj. 反政府 [faan2 jing3 fu2]

Antigua and Barbuda n. 安提瓜同巴布達 [on1 tai4 gwa1 tung4 ba1 bou3 daat9]

antinuclear adj. 反核 [faan2 hat9]

antipathy n. 反感 [faan2 gam2]

antique n. 古董 [gu2 dung2]; ~ **store** 古董店

antiseptic *adj.* 防腐嘅 [fong4 fu6 ge3]; ~ **cream** 抗菌膏; *n.* 防腐劑 [fong4 fu6 jai1]

antler *n.* 鹿茸 [luk9 yung4]

anxiety *n.* 憂慮 [yau1 leui6]

anxious *adj.* 憂慮 [yau1 leui6]

anxiously *adv.* 憂慮 [yau1 leui6]

any *adj.* 啲 [di1]; *det.* 啲 [di1]; *pron.* 啲 [di1]; *adv.* 啲 [di1]

anybody *pron.* 邊個 [bin1 go3]

anyone *pron.* 邊個 [bin1 go3]; **does ~ speak English?** 有冇人識講英文？

anything *pron.* 乜 [mat7]; ~ **else?** 仲有冇嘢？

anyway *adv.* 點都好 [dim2 dou1 hou2]

anywhere *adv.* 邊度 [bin1 dou6]

apart *adv.* 分開 [fan1 hoi1]

apart from *prep.* 先唔講 [sin1 m4 gong2]

apartment *n.* 套房 [tou3 fong2]; ~ **building** 一棟公寓

aperitif *n.* 開胃酒 [hoi1 wai6 jau2]

Apia *n.* 阿皮亞 [a3 pei4 a3]; ~, **capital of Samoa** 薩摩亞群島嘅首都

apiary *n.* 蜂房 [fung1 fong4]

apologize *v.* 道歉 [dou6 hip8]

apostrophe *n.* 省略號 [saang2 leuk9 hou6]

apparent *adj.* 顯然 [hin2 yin4]

apparently *adv.* 顯然 [hin2 yin4]

appeal *n.* 上訴 [seung6 sou3]; *v.* 上訴 [seung6 sou3]

appear *v.* 出現 [cheut7 yin6]

appearance *n.* 衣著打扮 [yi1 jeuk8 da2 baan6]

appendicitis *n.* 盲腸炎 [maang5 cheung4 yim4]

appendix *n.* 附錄 [fu6 luk9]

appetite *n.* 胃口 [wai6 hau2]

appetizer *n.* 開胃菜 [hoi1 wai6 choi3]

appetizing *adj.* 好開胃 [hou2 hoi1 wai6]

apple *n.* 蘋果 [ping4 gwo2]; ~ **juice** 蘋果汁; ~ **tart** 蘋果撻; ~ **sauce** 蘋果醬; ~ **pie** 蘋果批; ~ **brandy** 蘋果白蘭地

application *n.* 申請 [san1 ching2]

apply *v.* 申請 [san1 ching2]

appoint *v.* 派 [paai3]

appointment *n.* 預約 [yu6 yeuk8], **make an ~** 預訂, **have an ~** 預訂

appraise *v.* 評估 [ping4 gu2]

appraisal *n.* 評估 [ping4 gu2]

appreciate *v.* 欣賞 [yan1 seung2]; ~ **in value** 升值

apprentice *n.* 徒弟 [tou4 dai6]

approach *v.* 接近 [jip8 gan6]; *n.* 辦法 [baan6 faat8]

appropriate *adj.* 適當 [sik7 dong3]

approval *n.* 批准 [pai1 jeun2]

approve (of) *v.* 批准 [pai1 jeun2]

approving *adj.* 滿意 [mun5 yi3]

approximate *adj.* 大概 [daai6 koi3]

approximately *adv.* 大概 [daai6 koi3]

apricot *n.* 杏樹 [hang6 syu6]; ~ **jam/preserves** 杏醬

April (*abbr.* **Apr.)** *n.* 四月份 [sei3 yut9 fan6]

apron *n.* 圍裙 [wai4 kwan2]

apse *n.* 半圓壁龕 [bun3 yun4 bik7 ham1]

aquarium *n.* 水族館 [seui2 juk9 gun2]

Aquarius *n.* 水瓶座 [seui2 ping4 jo6]

aqueduct *n.* 水渠 [seui2 keui4]

Arab *adj.* 阿拉伯 [a3 laai1 baak8]

Arabic (language) *n.* 阿拉伯話 [a3 laai1 baak8 wa2]

arable *adj.* 可以種野 [ho2 yi5 jung3 ye5]

arbitration *n.* 仲裁 [jung6 choi4]

arcade game *n.* 電子遊戲 [din6 ji2 yau4 hei3]

arch *n.* 拱門 [gung2 mun4] *v.* 拱起 [gung2 hei2]

archbishop *n.* 大主教 [daai6 jyu2 gaau3]

archeological *adj.* 考古 [haau2 gu2]

archeology *n.* 考古學 [haau2 gu2 hok9]

architect *n.* 建築師 [gin3 juk7 si1]

architectural *adj.* 建築上 [gin3 juk7 seung6]

architecture *n.* 建築學 [gin3 juk7 hok9]

archives *n.* 檔案 [dong3 on3]

Arctic *n.* 北極 [bak7 gik9]

area *n.* 面積 [min6 jik7]

area code *n.* 區號 [keui1 hou6]

Argentina *n.* 阿根廷 [a3 gan1 ting4]

Argentine *adj.* 阿根廷 [a3 gan1 ting4]

argue *v.* 辯論 [bin6 leun6]

argument *n.* 辯論 [bin6 leun6]

Aries *n.* 白羊座 [baak9 yeung4 jo6]

arise *v.* 出現 [cheut7 yin6]

aristocracy *n.* 貴族 [gwai3 juk9]

aristocrat *n.* 貴族 [gwai3 juk9]

ark *n.* 方舟 [fong1 jau1]

arm *n.* *(anat.)* 手臂 [sau2 bei3]; *v.* 武裝 [mou5 jong1] (**weapon** 武器）

armed *adj.* 武裝嘅 [mou5 jong1 ge3]

Armenia *n.* 亞美尼亞 [a3 mei5 nei4 a3]

Armenian *adj.* 亞美尼亞 [a3 mei5 nei4 a3]

armory *n.* 軍工廠 [gwan1 gung1 chong2]

armor *n.* 盔甲 [kwai1 gaap8]

arms *n.* 武器 [mou5 hei3]

army *n.* 軍隊 [gwan1 deui2]

aroma *n.* 香味 [heung1 mei6]

aromatic *adj.* 有香味 [yau5 heung1 mei6]

around *adv.* 周圍 [jau1 wai4]; *prep.* 周圍 [jau1 wai4]

arrange *v.* 安排 [on1 paai4]

arrangement *n.* 安排 [on1 paai4]

array *n.* 隊列 [deui6 lit9]

arrest *v.* 拘捕 [keui1 bou2]; *n.* 拘捕 [keui1 bou2]

arrested *adj.* 捉咗 [juk7 jo2]

arrival *n.* 到達 [dou3 daat9]

arrive *v.* 到 [dou3], ~ **by plane** 搭飛機, ~ **by ship** 搭船, ~ **by vehicle** 搭車

arrow *n.* 箭 [jin3]; **mouse** ~ *(tech.)* 鼠標

arrowroot *n.* 木薯 [muk9 syu4]

arsenal *n.* 軍火庫 [gwan1 fo2 fu3]

arsenic *n.* 砒霜 [pei1 seung1]

arson *n.* 縱火 [jung3 fo2]

art *n.* 藝術 [ngai6 seut9]; ~
  gallery 畫廊

artery *n.* 動脈 [dung6 mak9]

arthritis *n.* 關節炎 [gwaan1 jit8
  yim4]; **have ~** 有關節炎

artichoke *n.* 洋薊 [yeung4 gai3];
  ~ hearts 洋薊心

article *n.* 文章 [man4 jeung1]

artificial *adj.* 假 [ga2];
  ~ sweetener 人工甜味劑;
  ~ flavoring 人工香精;
  ~ coloring 人工色素

artificially *adv.* 假 [ga2]; ~
  flavored 加咗香精

artillery *n.* 大炮 [daai6 paau3]

artisan *n.* 工匠 [gung1 jeung6]

artist *n.* 藝術家 [ngai6 seut9
  ga1]

artistic *adj.* 藝術 [ngai6 seut9]

artwork *n.* 藝術作品 [ngai6
  seut9 jok8 ban2]

arugula *n.* 芝麻菜 [ji1 ma4
  choi3]

as *prep.* 作為 [jok8 wai4]; *adv.*
  一樣 [yat7 yeung6]; *conj.* 由於
  [yau4 yu1]; **~ soon** ~ 即刻;
  ~ well ~ 一樣

ascetic *n.* 禁慾 [gam3 yuk9]

ashamed *adj.* 覺得醜 [gok8 dak7
  chau2]

Ashgabat *n.* 阿什哈巴德 [a3
  jaap9 ha1 ba1 dak7]; **~, capital
  of Turkmenistan** 土庫曼斯坦
  嘅首都

ash *n.* 灰 [fui1]

ashtray *n.* 煙灰缸 [yin1 fui1
  gong1]

Asia *n.* 亞洲 [a3 jau1]

Asian *adj.* 亞洲 [a3 jau1]

aside *adv.* 旁邊 [pong4 bin1];
  prep. 喺…旁邊 [hai2 … pong4
  bin1]; **~ from** 除咗

ask *v.* 問 [man6], **~ a question** 問
  問題, **~ about** 關心, **~ for** 要

asleep *adj.* 瞓着咗 [fan3 jeuk8
  jo2]

Asmara *n.* 阿斯馬拉 [a3 si1
  ma5 laai1]; **~, capital of Eritrea**
  厄立特里亞嘅首都

asparagus *n.* 蘆筍 [lou4 seun2];
  ~ soup 蘆筍湯; **~ tips** 蘆筍尖

aspartame *n.* 甜味劑 [tim4 mei6
  jai1]

aspect *n.* 方位 [fong1 wai6]

aspic *n.* 肉凍 [yuk9 dung3]

aspirin *n.* 阿士匹靈 [a3 si6 pat7
  ling4]

assassin *n.* 刺客 [chi3 haak8]

assassinate *v.* 刺殺 [chi3 saat8]

assassination *n.* 刺殺 [chi3 saat8]

assault *n.* 襲擊 [jaap9 gik7]

assaulted *adj.* 被…襲擊 [bei6 …
  jaap9 gik7]

assess *v.* 估價 [gu2 ga3]

assessment *n.* 估價 [gu2 ga3]

asset *n.* 資產 [ji1 chaan2]

assist *(sports term)* *v.* 幫助 [bong1
  jo6]

assistance *n.* 幫手 [bong1 sau2]

assistant *n.* 助手 [jo6 sau2]; *adj.*
  輔助 [fu6 jo6]

associate *v.* 聯想 [lyun4 seung2];
  n. 同事 [tung4 si6]; **~d with**
  同…有關係

association *n.* 社團 [se5 tyun4]

assorted *adj.* 五花八門 [ng5
  fa1 baat8 mun4], **~ cheeses**
  雜芝士, **~ flavors** 雜味, **~
  vegetables** 雜菜, **~ meats** 雜肉

assume *v.* 假設 [ga2 chit8]

assumption *n.* 假設 [ga2 chit8]

assure *v.* 同…保證 [tung4 … bou2 jing3]

Astana *n.* 阿斯塔納 [a3 si1 taap8 naap9]; ~, **capital of Kazakhstan** 哈薩克斯坦嘅首都

asterisk *n.* 星號 [sing1 hou6]

asteroid *n.* 小行星 [siu2 haang4 sing1]

astonish *v.* 嚇壞 [haak8 waai6]

astonishment *n.* 驚訝 [ging1 nga5]

asthma *n.* 哮喘 [haau1 chyun2]; **have ~** 有哮喘

asthmatic *n.* 有哮喘 [yau5 haau1 chyun2]

astray *adv.* 行差踏錯 [haang4 cha1 daap9 cho3]; **go ~** 蕩失路

astronaut *n.* 太空人 [taai3 hung1 yan4]

astronomer *n.* 天文學家 [tin1 man4 hok9 ga1]

astronomy *n.* 天文學 [tin1 man4 hok9]

astrology *n.* 占星術 [jim1 sing1 seut9]

Asuncion *n.* 亞松森 [a3 sung1 sam1]; ~, **capital of Paraguay** 巴拉圭嘅首都

asylum *n.* 精神病院 [jing1 san4 beng6 yun2]

at *prep.* 喺 [hai2], **~ first** 開始, **~ last** 最後, **~ least** 至少, **~ random** 隨便, **~ stake** 處於成敗關頭

atheist *n.* 無神論者 [mou4 san4 leun6 je2]

Athens *n.* 雅典 [nga5 din2]; ~, **capital of Greece** 希臘嘅首都

athletics *n.* 運動員 [wan6 dung6 yun4]

ATM (automated teller machine) *n.* 自動提款機 [ji6 dung6 tai4 fun2 gei1]

atmosphere *n.* 氣氛 [hei3 fan1]

atom *n.* 原子 [yun4 ji2]

atomic *adj.* 原子能 [yun4 ji2 nang4]

atonement *n.* 贖罪 [suk9 jeui6]

attach *v.* 貼喺 [tip8 hai2]

attached *adj.* 貼住 [tip8 jyu6]

attack *n.* 攻擊 [gung1 gik7], **heart ~** 心臟病; *v.* 攻擊 [gung1 gik7]

attempt *n.* 嘗試 [seung4 si3]; *v.* 嘗試 [seung4 si3]

attempted *adj.* 意圖 [yi3 tou4]

attend *v.* 參加 [chaam1 ga1]

attention *n.* 注意 [jyu3 yi3]

attitude *n.* 態度 [taai3 dou6]

attorney *n.* 律師 [leut9 si1]

attract *v.* 吸引 [kap7 yan5]

attraction *n.* 吸引力 [kap7 yan5 lik9]

attractive *adj.* 好靚 [hou2 leng3]

attribute *n.* 屬性 [suk9 sing3]; *v.* 歸咎於 [gwai1 gau3 yu1]

aubergine *n.* 茄瓜 [ke2 gwa1]

auction *n.* 拍賣 [paak8 maai6]; *v.* 拍賣 [paak8 maai6]

audience *n.* 觀眾 [gun1 jung3]

audio-guide *n.* 語音導遊 [yu5 yam1 dou6 yau4]

audit *n.* 審計 [sam2 gai3]; *v.* 審計 [sam2 gai3]

auditor *n.* 審計員 [sam2 gai3 yun4]

auditory *adj.* 聽覺 [ting3 gok8]

August (*abbr.* **Aug.)** *n.* 八月份 [baat8 yut9 fan6]

aunt *n.* 阿姨 [a3 yi4]

aurora *n.* 極光 [gik9 gwong1]

auspice *n.* 預兆 [yu6 siu6]

auspicious *adj.* 吉利 [gat7 lei6]

austere *adj.* 樸素 [pok8 sou3]

Australia *n.* 澳洲 [ngou3 jau1]

Australian *adj.* 澳洲 [ngou3 jau1]

Austria *n.* 奧地利 [ngou3 dei6 lei6]

Austrian *adj.* 奧地利 [ngou3 dei6 lei6]

authentic *adj.* 真 [jan1]

authenticity *n.* 真實性 [jan1 sat9 sing3]

author *n.* 作者 [jok8 je2]

authority *n.* 權威 [kyun4 wai1]

authorize *v.* 授權 [sau6 kyun4]

authorized *adj.* 有授權 [yau5 sau6 kyun4]

autocracy *n.* 獨裁 [duk9 choi4]

autocrat *n.* 獨裁者 [duk9 choi4 je2]

automatic *adj.* 自動 [ji6 dung6] (~ car transmission 汽車自動變速器)

automatically *adv.* 自動 [ji6 dung6]

automatic transmission *n.* 自動駕駛 [ji6 dung6 ga3 sai2]

automobile *n.* 車 [che1]; ~ ferry 汽車渡輪; ~ insurance card 汽車保險卡

autumn *n.* 秋天 [chau1 tin1]

auxiliary (~ verb) *n.* 補充 [bou2 chung1]

availability *n.* 得唔得 [dak7 m4 dak7]

available *adj.* 可以 [ho2 yi5]

avalanche *n.* 雪崩 [syut8 bang1]

avenue *n.* 大道 [daai6 dou6]

average *adj.* 麻麻地 [ma4 ma4 dei2]; *n.* 平均水平 [ping4 gwan1 seui2 ping4]

aviation *n.* 航空 [hong4 hung1]

avocado *n.* 牛油果 [ngau4 yau4 gwo2]

avoid *v.* 避開 [bei6 hoi1]

awake *adj.* 醒咗 [seng2 jo2]

award *n.* 獎品 [jeung2 ban2]; *v.* 獎勵 [jeung2 lai6]

aware *adj.* 察覺 [chaat8 gok8]

awareness *n.* 意識 [yi3 sik7]; **to raise ~** 增加人們嘅認識

away *adv.* 走咗 [jau2 jo2]

awe *n.* 敬畏 [ging3 wai3]

awful *adj.* 乞人憎 [hat7 yan4 jang1]

awfully *adv.* 乞人憎 [hat7 yan4 jang1]

awkward *adj.* 尷尬 [gaam1 gaai3]

awkwardly *adv.* 尷尬 [gaam1 gaai3]

axe *n.* 斧頭 [fu2 tau2]

axis *n.* 中軸 [jung1 juk9]

axle *n.* 車軸 [che1 juk9]

Azerbaijan *n.* 阿塞拜疆 [a3 sak7 baai3 geung1]

Azerbaijani *adj.* 阿塞拜疆 [a3 sak7 baai3 geung1]

B

babble *v.* 胡言亂語 [wu4 yin4 lyun6 yu5]

baby *n.* 嬰兒 [bi4 bi1]; ~ **carriage/ stroller** 嬰兒車; ~ **food** 嬰兒食物; ~ **clothes** 嬰兒衫; ~ **powder** 嬰兒奶粉; ~ **wipes** 嬰兒濕紙巾

baby backribs *n.* 靚排骨 [leng3 paai4 gwat7]

babysitter *n.* 臨時保母 [lam4 si4 bou2 mou5]

babywear *n.* 嬰兒衫 [be1 be1 saam1]

bachelor *n.* 學士 [hok9 si6]; ~ **party** 寡佬派對

bachelorette *n.* 剩女 [sing6 neui5]; ~ **party** 剩女派對

back *n.* 背 [bui3]; *adj.* 背面嘅 [bui3 min6 ge3], ~ **door** 後門, ~ **wheel** 後輪; *adv.* **at/in/to the** ~ 從背面 [chung4 bui3 min6]; **go** ~ 番去

backache *n.* 腰痛 [yiu1 tung3]

backbone *n.* 腰骨 [yiu1 gwat7]

background *n.* 後台 [hou6 toi4]

backhand *n.* 反手 [faan2 sau2]

backpack *n.* 背囊 [bui3 nong4]

backspace *(computer)* *n.* 退格鍵 [teui3 gaak8 gin6]; ~ **key** 退格鍵

backup lights *n.* 後備燈 [hau6 bei6 dang1]

backward *adj.* 落後 [lok6 hau6]; *adv.* 向後 [heung3 hau6]; **move ~s** 向後退

bacon *n.* 煙肉 [yin1 yuk9]; ~ **and eggs** 煙肉煎蛋; ~ **strips** 煙肉條

bacteria *n.* 細菌 [sai3 kwan2]

bacterial *adj.* 細菌 [sai3 kwan2]

bad *adj.* 唔好嘅 [m4 hou2 ge3]

badly *adv.* 極之 [gik9 ji1]

badminton *n.* 羽毛球 [yu5 mou4 kau4]

bad-tempered *adj.* 臭脾氣 [chau3 pei4 hei3]

bag *n.* 袋 [doi2], **plastic** ~ 膠袋, **paper** ~ 紙袋, **tote** ~ 大手提袋, **canvas** ~ 帆布袋

bagel *n.* 麵包圈 [min6 baau1 hyun1]; **half** ~ 半個麵包圈

baggage *n.* 行李 [hang4 lei5]; ~ **cart** 行李車; ~ **locker** 行李櫃; ~ **check** 行李托管, ~ **check office** 行李寄存處, ~ **check room** 行李寄存處; ~ **claim** 取行李, ~ **reclaim area** 取行李處

Baghdad *n.* 巴格達 [ba1 gaak8 daat9]; ~, **capital of Iraq** 伊拉克嘅首都

Bahamas, The *n.* 巴哈馬 [ba1 ha1 ma5]

Bahamian *adj.* 巴哈馬 [ba1 ha1 ma5]

Bahrain *n.* 巴林 [ba1 lam4]

Bahraini *adj.* 巴林 [ba1 lam4]

bail *n.* 保釋 [bou2 sik7]

bail bond *n.* 保釋金 [bou2 sik7 gam1]

bailiff *n.* 庭警 [ting4 ging2]

bake *v.* 焗 [guk9]

baked *adj.* 焗過 [guk9 gwo3], ~ **casserole** 砂鍋菜, ~ **potato** 焗薯仔

baker *n.* 麵包師傅 [min6 baau1 si1 fu2]

bakery *n.* 麵包店 [min6 baau1 dim3]

baking pan *n.* 焗盤 [guk9 pun2]

baking powder *n.* 發酵粉 [faat8 haau1 fan2]

baking soda *n.* 蘇打水 [sou1 da2 seui2]

baking sheet *n.* 焗盤 [guk9 pun2]

Baku *n.* 巴庫 [ba1 fu3]; ~, **capital of Azerbaijan** 阿塞拜疆嘅首都

balance *n.* 平衡 [ping4 hang4]; *v.* 平衡 [ping4 hang4]

balcony *n.* 陽台 [yeung4 toi4]

balding *adj.* 甩頭髮 [lat7 tau4 faat8]

ball *n.* 波 [bo1]; **play** ~ (*lit. and fig.*) 比賽開始

ballet *n.* 芭蕾舞 [ba1 leui5 mou5]

ballgame *n.* 球賽

balloon *n.* 氣球 [hei3 kau4]

ballot *n.* 投票 [tau4 piu3]; ~ **box** 投票箱; ~ **paper** 選票

ballpoint pen *n.* 圓珠筆

balm *n.* 香油 [heung1 yau4]

balsamic vinaigrette *n.* 黑醋汁 [hak7 chou3 jap7]

Bamako *n.* 巴馬科 [ba1 ma5 fo1]; ~, **capital of Mali** 馬里嘅首都

bamboo *n.* 竹 [juk7]; ~ **shoots** 竹筍

ban *v.* 禁止 [gam1 ji2]; *n.* 禁令 [gam1 ling4]

banana *n.* 香蕉 [heung1 jiu1]; ~ **leaves** 蕉葉

band *n.* 樂隊 [ngok9 deui2]

bandage *n.* 繃帶 [baang6 daai2]; *v.* 包紮 [baau1 jaat8]

band-aid *n.* 止血貼 [ji2 hyut8 tip8]

Bandar Seri Begawan *n.* 斯里巴加灣市 [si1 lei5 ba1 ga1 waan1 si5]; ~, **capital of Brunei** 文萊嘅首都

bandit *n.* 土匪 [tou2 fei2]

Bangkok *n.* 曼谷 [maan6 guk7]; ~, **capital of Thailand** 泰國嘅首都

Bangladesh *n.* 孟加拉 [maang6 ga1 laai1]

Bangladeshi *adj.* 孟加拉 [maang6 ga1 laai1]

Bangui *n.* 班吉 [baan1 gat7]; ~, **capital of Central African Republic** 中非共和國嘅首都

Banjul *n.* 班珠爾 [baan1 jyu1 yi5]; ~, **capital of The Gambia** 岡比亞嘅首都

bank *n.* 銀行 [ngan4 hong4]; ~ **card** 銀行卡; ~ **charges** 銀行收費

bank account *n.* 銀行戶口 [ngan4 hong4 wu6 hau2]

banker *n.* 銀行家 [ngan4 hong4 ga1]

bankrupt *adj.* 破產 [po3 chaan2]

bankruptcy *n.* 破產 [po3 chaan2]

baptism *n.* 洗禮 [sai2 lai5]

bar *(tavern)* n. 酒吧 [jau2 ba1]; **wine ~** 酒吧; **~ service** 酒吧服務; **~ of soap** 一嚿梘

bar exam *(legal)* 律師資格考試 [leut9 si1 ji1 gaak8 haau2 si3]

Barbados n. 巴巴多斯島 [ba1 ba1 do1 si1 dou2]

barbecue n. 燒烤 [siu1 haau1]; v. 燒烤 [siu1 haau1]; **~ sauce** 燒烤汁, **~ flavor** 燒烤味, **~ chips** 燒烤味薯片, **~ grill** 燒烤爐

barber n. 理髮師 [lei5 faat8 si1]

barding v. 馬嘅裝飾 [ma5 ge3 jong1 sik7]

bargain n. 筍野 [seun2 ye5]; v. 講價 [gong2 ga3]

barley n. 大麥 [daai6 mak9]

bark n. 樹皮 [syu6 pei4]

barometer n. 氣壓計 [hei3 aat8 gai3]

Baroque style n. 巴洛克式 [ba1 lok8 hak7 sik7]

barrel n. 桶 [tung2]

barrier n. 障礙 [jeung3 ngoi6]

bartender n. 調酒師 [tiu4 jau2 si1]

base n. 基地 [gei1 dei6], **sauce ~** 原料; v. 基於 [gei1 yu1]; **~d on** 基於

basement n. 地下室 [dei6 ha6 sat7]

basic *adj.* 基本 [gei1 bun2]

basically *adv.* 基本上 [gei1 bun2 seung6]

basil n. 羅勒 [lo4 lak9]

basin n. 盆 [pun4]

basis n. 基礎 [gei1 cho2]

basket n. 籃 [laam…2], **muffin ~** 鬆餅籃, **fruit ~** 水果籃, **~ of … ** 一籃…

basketball n. 籃球 [laam4 kau4]

basmati rice n. 印度香米 [yan3 dok9 heung1 mai5]

bass *(music)* n. 低音樂器 [dai1 yam1 ngok9 hei3]; *adj.* 低音 [dai1 yam1]; **electric ~** 電子低音吉他, **~ guitar** 低音吉他, **double string ~** 雙低音弦

Basseterre n. 巴斯特爾 [ba1 si1 dak9 yi5]; **~, capital of Saint Kitts and Nevis** 聖克里斯托弗和尼維斯島嘅首都

bastard n. 私生子 [si1 sang1 ji2]

baste v. 塗油 [tou4 yau4]

baster n. 疏縫工 [so1 fung4 gung1]

bat n. 球棒 [kau4 paang5]; 蝙蝠 [pin1 fuk7]

bath n. 沖涼 [chung1 leung4]

bathe v. 沖 [chung1]

bathing cap n. 浴帽 [yuk9 mou6]

bathing suit n. 泳衣 [wing6 yi1]

bathroom n. 沖涼房 [chung1 leung4 fong2]

bath towel n. 浴巾 [yuk9 gan1]

batter n. 糊 [wu2], **pancake ~** 班戟粉, **pastry ~** 糕點粉

battery n. 電池 [din6 chi4]

battle n. 戰鬥 [jin3 dau3], **historic ~** 歷史上有名嘅戰鬥, **~ site** 戰場

battlement n. 城垛 [sing4 do2]

bay n. 港灣 [gong2 waan1]; **to keep at ~** 牽制

bay leaf n. 月桂樹葉 [yut9 gwai3 syu6 yip9]

be *aux. v.* 係 [hai6]; **~ sick** 病咗

beach n. 沙灘 [sa1 taan1]

beacon n. 燈塔 [dang1 taap8]

beak *n.* 嘴 [jeui2]

beam *(of light)* *n.* 大樑 [daai3 leung4]; **high/low ~** *(light)* 高 / 低大樑; **wood ~** 木樑

bean *n.* 豆 [dau2]

beanbag *n.* 豆袋坐墊 [dau2 doi6 cho5 din3]

bean curd *n.* 豆腐 [dau6 fu6]

bean sprouts *n.* 豆芽 [dau2 nga4]

bear *v.* 撐住 [chaang1 jyu6]; *n.* 熊 [hung4]

beard *n.* 鬍鬚 [wu4 sou1]

beat *n.* 心跳 [sam1 tiu3]; *v.* 打 [da2]

beautiful *adj.* 靚 [leng3]

beautifully *adv.* 出色 [cheut7 sik7]

beauty *n.* 美貌 [mei5 maau6]

because *conj.* 因為 [yan1 wai6]; **~ of** *prep.* 因為 [yan1 wai6]

become *v.* 成為 [sing4 wai4]

bed *n.* 床 [chong4]; **~ linen/sheet** 床單

bed and breakfast *n.* 住宿加早餐 [jyu6 suk7 ga1 jou2 chaan1]

bedding *n.* 寢具 [cham2 geui6]

bedroom *n.* 睡房 [seui6 fong2]

bee *n.* 蜜蜂 [mat9 fung1]

beef *n.* 牛肉 [ngau4 yuk9]; **~ tongue** 牛脷, **~ meatball** 牛肉丸, **~ stock** 牛肉湯, **~ burger** 牛肉漢堡包, **~ stew** 燉牛肉, **~ marrow** 牛骨髓, **~ stomach** 牛肚, **~ chuck** 牛肉

beef jerky *n.* 牛肉乾 [ngau4 yuk9 gon1]

beehive *n.* 蜂竇 [fung1 dau6]

beer *n.* 啤酒 [be1 jau2]; **canned ~** 罐裝啤酒, **bottled ~** 瓶裝啤酒, **pilsner ~** 淺色啤酒, **~ on tap** 散裝啤酒, **draft ~** 生啤酒, **ale ~** 淡色啤酒, **lager ~** 儲藏啤酒, **malted ~** 麥芽啤酒, **Guinness ~** 健力士啤酒, **wheat ~** 小麥啤酒, **honey ale ~** 蜜糖淺色啤酒, **barley ~** 大麥啤酒, **oat ~** 燕麥啤酒

beet *n.* 甜菜 [tim4 choi3]

beetle *n.* 甲蟲 [gaap8 chung4]

beetroot *n.* 甜菜根 [tim4 choi3 gan1]

before *prep.* 前面 [chin4 min6]; *conj.* 喺. . . 前面 [hai2 ... chin4 min6]; *adv.* 前面 [chin4 min6]

beforehand *n.* 事前 [si6 chin4]

beggar *n.* 乞兒 [hat7 yi1]

begin *v.* 開始 [hoi1 chi2]

beginner *n.* 新手 [san1 sau2]

beginning *n.* 開頭 [hoi1 tau4]

behalf *n.* 利益 [lei6 yik7]; **on ~ of smb.** 代表, **on smb.'s ~** 代表

behave *v.* 守規矩 [sau2 kwai1 geui2]

behavior *n.* 行為 [hang4 wai4]

behind *prep.* 喺...後面 [hai2 ... hau6 min6]; *adv.* 後面 [hau6 min6]

beige *n.* 米黃色 [mai5 wong4 sik7]

Beijing *n.* 北京 [bak7 ging1]; **~, capital of China** 中國嘅首都

Beirut *n.* 貝魯特 [bui3 lou5 dak9]; **~, capital of Lebanon** 黎巴嫩嘅首都

Belarus *n.* 白俄羅斯 [baak9 ngo4 lo4 si1]

Belarusian *adj.* 白俄羅斯 [baak9 ngo4 lo4 si1]

Belgian *adj.* 比利時 [bei2 lei6 si4]

Belgium *n.* 比利時 [bei2 lei6 si4]

Belgrade *n.* 貝爾格萊德 [bui3 yi5 gaak8 lou4 dak7]; ~, **capital of Serbia** 塞爾維亞嘅首都

belief *n.* 睇法 [tai2 faat8]

beliefs *n.* 信仰 [seun3 yeung5]

believe *v.* 相信 [seung1 seun3]

Belize *n.* 伯里茲 [baak8 lei5 ji1]

Belizean *adj.* 伯里茲 [baak8 lei5 ji1]

bell *n.* 鐘 [jung1]

bell pepper *n.* 甜椒 [tim4 jiu1], **red** ~ 紅甜椒, **yellow** ~ 黃甜椒, **orange** ~ 橙色甜椒, **green** ~ 青甜椒

belly *n.* 肚腩 [tou5 naam5]

Belmopan *n.* 貝爾莫潘 [bui3 yi5 mok9 pun1]; ~, **capital of Belize** 伯里茲嘅首都

belong *v.* 係…嘅 [hai6 … ge3]; ~ **to** 屬於

below *prep.* 低於 [dai1 yu1]; *adv.* 低於 [dai1 yu1]

belt *n.* 皮帶 [pei4 daai2]; **below the** ~ 肚臍下; **Bible** ~ 聖經地帶

bench *n.* 凳 [dang3]

bench warrant *(legal) n.* 法院拘票 [faat8 yun2 geui1 piu3]

bend *v.* 整彎 [jing2 waan1]; *n.* 彎 [waan1]

beneath *prep.* 喺…下面 [hai2 … ha6 min6]; *adv.* 下面 [ha6 min6]

benefit *n.* 好處 [hou2 chyu3]; *v.* 得到好處 [dak7 dou3 hou2 chyu3]

benevolence *n.* 好心 [hou2 sam1]

benevolent *adj.* 好心 [hou2 sam1]

benign *adj.* 好人 [hou2 yan4]

Benin *n.* 貝寧彎 [bui3 ning4 waan1]

Beninese *adj.* 貝寧彎 [bui3 ning4 waan1]

bent *adj.* 彎咗 [wwan1 jo2]

Berlin *n.* 柏林 [paak8 lam4]; ~, **capital of Germany** 德國嘅首都

Bern *n.* 伯爾尼 [baak8 yi5 nei4]; ~, **capital of Switzerland** 瑞士嘅首都

berry *n.* 莓 [mui2]

berth *n.* 臥鋪 [ngo6 pou1]

beside *prep.* 除咗 [cheui4 jo2]

best *adj.* 最好 [jeui3 hou2]; *adv.* 最好 [jeui3 hou2]; **Best wishes!** 僅致問候!

bet *v.* 輸賭 [syu1 dou2]; *n.* 賭 [dou2]

better *adj.* 好啲 [hou2 di1]; *adv.* 好啲 [hou2 di1]

betting *n.* 賭 [dou2]

between *prep.* 喺…之間 [hai2 … ji1 gaan1]; *adv.* 之間 [ji1 gaan1]

beverage *n.* 飲品 [yam2 ban2]

beware *v.* 因住 [yan1 jyu6]; ~ **of dog** 因住! 入面有狗

beyond *prep.* 超過 [chiu1 gwo3]; *adv.* 更加遠嗰度 [gang3 ga1 yun5 go2 duk9]

Bhutan *n.* 不丹 [bat7 daan1]

Bhutanese *adj.* 不丹 [bat7 daan1]

bias *n.* 偏見 [pin1 gin3]

bib *n.* 口水兜 [hau2 seui2 dau1]

Bible *n.* 聖經 [sing3 ging1]

bicycle *n.* 單車 [daan1 che1]; ~ **path/lane** 單車道

bicyclist *n.* 踩單車嘅人 [chaai2 daan1 che1 ge3 yan4]

bid *v./n.* 投標 [tau4 biu1]

bidet *n.* 浴缸 [yuk9 gong1]

big *adj.* 大 [daai6]

bigger *adj.* 大啲 [daai6 di1]

bike *n.* 單車 [daan1 che1]

biking path *n.* 單車道 [daan1 che1 dou6]

bikini *n.* 泳衣 [wing6 yi1]

bilberry *n.* 紅桑子 [hung4 song1 ji2]

bilingual *adj.* 雙語 [seung1 yu5]

bill *n. (dollar)* 單 [daan1]; ~**s** 紙鈔, **to pay the** ~**s** 買單

billiards *n.* 枱球 [toi2 kau4]

billion *n.* 十憶 [sap9 yik7]

bin *n.* 箱 [seung1]

binary *adj.* 二進制 [yi6 jeun3 jai3]

bind *v.* 綁埋一齊 [bong2 maai4 yat7 chai4]

binoculars *n.* 望遠鏡 [mong6 yun5 geng3]

biodegradable *adj.* 可以生物降解 [ho2 yi5 sang1 mat9 gong3 gaai2]

biodiversity *n.* 生物多樣性 [sang1 mat9 do1 yeung6 sing3]

biography *n.* 傳記 [jyun2 gei3]

biological *adj.* 生物 [sang1 mat9]

biology *n.* 生物 [sang1 mat9]

biopsy *n.* 活體檢視 [wut9 tai2 gim2 si6], **skin** ~ 皮膚活體檢視, **bone** ~ 骨頭活體檢視

biotechnology *n.* 生物技術 [sang1 mat9 gei6 seut9]

bird *n.* 雀仔 [jeuk8 jai2]

birth *n.* 出世 [cheut7 sai3]

birth certificate *n.* 出世紙 [cheut7 sai3 ji2]

birthday *n.* 生日 [saang1 yat9]

birthday party *n.* 生日派對 [saang1 yat9 paai3 deui3]

biscuit *n.* 餅仔 [beng2 jai2]

Bishkek *n.* 比什凱克 [bei2 jaap9 hoi2 hak7]; ~, **capital of Kyrgyzstan** 吉爾吉斯斯坦嘅首都

bishop *n.* 主教 [jyu2 gaau3]

bison *n.* 野牛 [ye5 ngau4]

Bissau *n.* 比紹 [bei2 siu6]; ~, **capital of Guinea-Bissau** 幾內亞比紹共和國嘅首都

bit (a little ~) *n.* 一啲啲 [yat7 di1 di1]; **in a** ~ 好快

bite *v./n.* 咬 [ngaau5]; **insect** ~ 蟲咬

bite-size *adj.* 細細啖 [sai3 sai3 daam6]

bits *n.* 一啲啲 [yat7 di1 di1]

bitter *adj.* 苦 [fu2]

bitterly *adv.* 痛苦 [tung3 fu2]

bizarre *adj.* 離奇 [lei4 kei4]

black *adj./n.* 黑色 [hak7 sik7], ~ **coffee** 黑咖啡, ~ **and white** 黑白, ~ **pepper** 黑椒

black currant *n.* 紅醋粟 [hung4 chou3 suk7]

blackmail *v.* 勒索 [lak9 sok8]

black mushroom *n.* 冬菇 [dung1 gu1]

black rice *n.* 黑米 [hak7 mai5]

blackbeans *n.* 黑豆 [hak7 dau2]

blackberry *n.* 黑莓 [hak7 mui2]

blackened *adj.* 煙燻 [yin1 fan1]; ~ **meat** 燻肉

black-eyed peas *n.* 黑眼豆 [hak7 ngaan5 dau2]

bladder *n.* 膀胱 [pong4 gwong1]

blade *n.* 刀片 [dou1 pin2]

blame *v.* 怨 [yun3]; *n.* 埋怨 [maai4 yun3]

blanched *v.* 整白 [jing2 baak9]

bland *adj.* 平和 [ping4 wo4]

blank *adj.* 空白 [hung1 baak9]; *n.* 空白地方 [hung1 baak9 dei6 fong1]

blanket *n.* 氈 [jin1]

blankly *adv.* 面無表情 [min6 mou4 biu2 ching4]

blaze *n.* 光輝 [gwong1 fai1]

bleach *n.* 漂白 [piu1 baak9]

bleed *v.* 流血 [lau4 hyut8]

blend *v.* 攪埋一齊 [gaau2 maai4 yat7 chai4]

blended *adj.* 攪埋一齊 [gaau2 maai4 yat7 chai4]

blender *n.* 攪拌機 [gaau2 bun6 gei1]

bless *v.* 保佑 [bou2 yau6]; **God ~ you!** 願主保佑你！

blind *adj.* 盲 [maang4]; *v.* 整盲 [jing2 maang4]

blink *v.* 眨眼 [jaap8 ngaan5]

blintzes *n.* 薄煎餅 [bok9 jin1 beng2], **Polish~** 波蘭薄煎餅, **German ~** 德國薄煎餅

blister *n.* 水泡 [seui2 paau1]

blizzard *n.* 大風雪 [daai6 fung1 syut8]

bloated *adj.* 發脹 [faat8 jeung3]

block *n.* 街區 [gaai1 keui1], **~ of ice** 一嚿冰

blockage *n.* 阻塞 [jo2 sak7]

blocked *adj.* 塞咗 [sak7 jo2]

Bloemfontein *n.* 布隆方丹 [bou3 lung4 fong1 daan1]; **~, judiciary capital of South Africa** 南非嘅司法首都

blond/blonde *adj./n.* 金髮碧眼 [gam1 faat8 bik7 ngaan5]

blood *n.* 血 [hyut8]; **donate ~** 捐血

blood orange *n.* 紅橙 [hung4 chaang4]

blood pressure *n.* 血壓 [hyut8 aat8]

blood test *n.* 驗血 [yim1 hyut8]

blood type *n.* 血型 [hyut8 ying4]

blouse *n.* 西裝外套 [sai1 jong1 ngoi6 tou3]

blow *v.* 吹 [cheui1]; *n.* 打擊 [da2 gik7]

blow-dry *n.* 吹乾頭髮 [cheui1 gon1 tau4 faat8]; *v.* 吹乾 [cheui1 gon1]

blowfish *n.* 河豚 [ho4 tyun4]

blue *adj./n.* 藍色 [laam4 sik7]

blueberries *n.* 藍莓 [laam4 mui2]

blues *n.* 藍調 [laam4 diu6]; **~ music** 藍調音樂; **to have the ~** 難過

bluff *v.* 虛張聲勢 [heui1 jeung1 sing1 sai3]

blurred *adj.* 唔清楚 [m4 ching1 cho2]; **~ vision** 睇得唔清楚

blush *n./v.* 面紅 [min6 hung4]

board *n.* 板 [baan2]; *v.* 上車 [seung5 che1], **~ a ship/train/ plane** 上船／上火車／上飛機

boarding *n.* 寄宿 [gei3 suk7]

boarding pass *n.* 登機證 [dang1 gei1 jing3]

boar's head *n.* 豬頭 [jyu1 tau4]

boat *n.* 船 [syun4]

body *n.* 身體 [san1 tai2]; **wine ~** 酒體; **full ~** 全身

body shop *n.* 汽車車體修理廠 [hei3 che1 che1 tai2 sau2 lei5 chong2]

Bogota *n.* 波哥大 [bo1 go1 daai6]; **~, capital of Colombia** 哥倫比亞嘅首都

boil *n.* *(on skin)* 膿腫 [nung4 jung2]; *v.* 煮滾 [jyu2 gwan2]

boiled *adj.* 煮滾 [jyu2 gwan2]

boiler *n.* 鍋爐 [wo1 lou4]

bok choy *n.* 白菜 [baak9 choi3], **baby ~** 白菜仔, **Thai ~** 泰國白菜

Bolivia *n.* 玻利維亞 [bo1 lei6 wai4 a3]

Bolivian *adj.* 玻利維亞 [bo1 lei6 wai4 a3]

bomb *n.* 炸彈 [ja3 daan2]; *v.* 放炸彈 [fong3 ja3 daan2]; **~ threat** 炸彈威脅

bombard *v.* 轟炸 [gwang1 ja3]

bombardment *n.* 轟炸 [gwang1 ja3]

Bon appetit! *phr.* 食得開胃啲 [sik9 dak7 hoi1 wai6 di1]

bonbon *n.* 邦邦 [bong1 bong1]

Bon voyage! *phr.* 一路順風 [yat7 lou6 seun6 fung1]

bond *n.* 債券 [jaai3 gyun3]; *v.* 團結 [tyun4 git8]

bone *n.* 骨 [gwat7]

boneless *adj.* 冇骨 [mou5 gwat7]; **~ chicken** 冇骨雞肉

bonus *n.* 分紅 [fan1 hung4]

book *n.* 書 [syu1]; *v.* 預訂 [yu6 deng6]

booking *n.* 預訂 [yu6 deng6]

booklet *n.* 小冊子 [siu2 chaak8 ji2]

bookmark *n.* 書籤 [syu1 chim1]; *v.* 標記 [biu1 gei3]; **~ website** 俾網站夾書籤

bookstore *n.* 書店 [syu1 dim3]

boom *n./v.* 繁榮 [faan4 wing4]]

boost *n.v.* 促進 [chuk7 jeun3]

boot *n.* 靴 [heu1]

border *n.* 國界 [gwok8 gaai3] *v.* 同...接壤 [tung4 ... jip8 yeung6]

bore *v.* 令...好煩 [ling4 ... hou2 faan4]

bored *adj.* 覺得煩 [gok8 dak7 faan4]

boring *adj.* 令人好煩 [ling4 yan4 hou2 faan4]

born *adj.* 天生 [tin1 saang1]; *v.* 支持 [ji1 chi4]

borrow *v.* 借 [je3]

borrower *n.* 借錢嘅人 [je3 chin4 ge3 yan4]

borsch *n.* 羅宋湯 [lo4 sung3 tong1], **red ~** 紅羅宋湯, **white ~** 白羅宋湯, **Polish ~** 波蘭羅宋湯, **Russian ~** 俄羅斯羅宋湯

Bosnia and Herzegovina *n.* 波黑 [bo1 hak7]

Bosnian *adj.* 波斯尼亞 [bo1 si1 nei4 a3]

bosom *n.* 胸部 hung1 bou6[]

boss *n.* 老細 [lou5 sai3]; *v.* 指揮 [ji2 fai1]

botanical *adj.* 植物 [jik9 mat9]

botanical garden *n.* 植物園 [jik9 mat9 yun4]

both *adj./det.* 兩個都 [leung2 go3 dou1]; *pron.* 兩個 [leung2 go3]

bother *n.* 煩惱 [faan4 nou5]; *v.* 煩住 [faan4 jyu6]

Botswana *n.* 博茨瓦納 [bok8 chi4 nga5 naap9]

bottle *n.* 瓶 [ping4]; ~ **opener** 開瓶器

bottled *adj.* 瓶裝 [ping4 jong1]; ~ **water** 瓶裝水

bottom *n.* 底 [dai2]; *adj.* 底部 [dai2 bou6]

bouillabaisse *n.* 濃味魚肉湯 [nung4 mei6 yu4 yuk9 tong1]

bouillon *n.* 肉羹 [yuk9 gang1]

bound *adj.* 綁住 [bong2 jyu6]; ~ **to** … 同…綁住

boundary *n.* 範圍 [faan6 wai4]

bourgeois *adj.* 資產階級 [ji1 chaan2 gaai1 kap7]

bowel *n.* 腸臟 [cheung4 jong6]

bowl *n.* 碗 [wun2]

bowling (*to go* ~) *v.* 打保齡球 [da2 bou2 ling4 kau4]

bowling ball *n.* 保齡球 [bou2 ling4 kau4]

bowling shoes *n.* 保齡球鞋 [bou2 ling4 kau4 haai4]

box *n.* 盒 [hap9]; *v.* 裝入個盒度 [jong1 yap9 go3 hap9 dok6]

box office *n.* 售票廳 [sau6 piu3 teng1]

boxing *n.* 拳擊 [kyun4 gik7]; ~ **ring** 拳擊台

boy *n.* 男仔 [naam4 jai2]

boycott *v.* 抵制 [dai2 jai3]

boyfriend *n.* 男朋友 [naam4 pang4 yau5]

boysenberry *n.* 波伊森莓 [bo1 yi1 sam1 mui2]

bra *n.* 胸圍 [hung1 wai4]

bracelet *n.* 手鍊 [sau2 lin2]

braces *n.* 牙箍 [nga4 ku1]

bracket *n.* 括弧 [kut8 wu4]

braille *n.* 盲字 [maang4 ji6]

brain *n.* 腦 [nou5]

braise *v.* 燜 [man1]

braised *adj.* 煲熟 [bou1 suk9]; ~ **pork** 燜豬肉

brake *n.* 煞掣 [saat8 jai3]; ~ **pads** 煞掣腳踏; ~**light** 煞掣燈

bran *n.* 糠 [hong1]

branch *n.* 部門 [bou6 mun4]

brand *n.* 品牌 [ban2 paai4]

brand-new *adj.* 全新 [cyun4 san1]

Brasilia *n.* 巴西利亞 [ba1 sai1 lei6 a3]; ~, **capital of Brazil** 巴西嘅首都

brass *n.* 銅管樂器 [tung4 gun2 ngok9 hei3]

brassiere (bra) *n.* 胸圍 [hung1 wai4]

Bratislava *n.* 布拉迪斯拉發 [bou3 laai1 dik9 si1 laai1 faat8]; ~, **capital of Slovakia** 斯洛伐克嘅首都

brave *adj.* 勇 [yung5]

Brazil *n.* 巴西 [ba1 sai1]

Brazil nut *n.* 鮑魚果 [baau1 yu4 gwo2]

Brazilian *adj.* 巴西 [ba1 sai1]

Brazzaville *n.* 布拉紮維 [bou3 laai1 jaat8 wai4]; ~, **capital of Congo** 剛果嘅首都

breach *v./n.* 違反 [wai4 faan2]

bread *n.* 麵包 [min6 baau1]; **nan** ~ 印度麵包, **oat** ~ 燕麥麵包, **white** ~ 白麵包, **wheat** ~ 小麥麵包, **whole wheat** ~ 全麥麵包, **whole grain** ~ 全糧麵包, **rye** ~ 黑麥麵包, **pumpkin** ~ 南瓜餅, **potato** ~ 薯仔餅, **banana** ~ 香蕉餅, **sweet** ~ 甜麵包

bread soup *n.* 羊肉泡饃 [yeung4 yuk9 paau1 mo4]

breadcrumbs *n.* 麵包碎 [min6 baau1 seui3]

breaded *adj.* 塗咗麵包碎 [tou4 jo2 min6 baau1 seui3]

breading *n.* 食物 [sik9 mat9]

breadstick *n.* 麵包棍 [min6 baau1 gwan3]

break *v.* 打爛 [da2 laan6]; *n.* 間斷 [gaan1 dyun6]; ~ **down** 爛咗

breakdown *n.* 情緒失控 [ching4 seui5 sat7 hung3]; **nervous** ~ 情緒失控

breakfast *n.* 早餐 [jou2 chaan1]; ~ **cereal** 早餐麥片; ~ **bar** 早餐吧

bream *n.* 海鯛 [hoi2 diu1]

breast *n.* 波 [bo1]

breath *n.* 口氣 [hau2 hei3]

breathe *v.* 透氣 [tau2 hei3]

breathing *n.* 逼真 [bik7 jan1]

breed *v.* 繁衍 [faan4 hin2]; *n.* 血統 [hyut8 tung2]

breeze *n.* 清風 [ching1 fung1]

brewery *n.* 啤酒廠 [be1 jau2 chong2]

bribe *v.* 收買 [sau1 maai5]

brick *n.* 磚頭 [jyun1 tau4]

bridal *adj.* 新娘 [san1 neung1], ~ **party** 新娘派對, ~ **store** 新娘服店

bride *n.* 新娘 [san1 neung1]

bridegroom *n.* 新郎 [san1 long4]

bridesmaid *n.* 伴娘 [bun6 neung1]

bridge *n.* 橋 [kiu4]

Bridgetown *n.* 布里奇頓 [bou3 lei5 kei4 deun6]; ~, **capital of Barbados** 巴巴多斯島嘅首都

brief *adj.* 簡短 [gaan2 dyun2]; *v.* 簡要介紹 [gaan2 yiu1 gaai3 siu6]

briefly *adv.* 略略 [leuk9 leuk9]

briefs *n.* 三角褲 [saam1 gok8 fu3]

bright *adj.* 光猛 [gwong1 maang5]

brightly *adv.* 光猛 [gwong1 maang5]

brill *n.* 鰈類魚 [dip9 leui6 yu2]

brilliant *adj.* 醒目 [sing1 muk9]

brine *n.* 滷水 [lou5 seui2]

bring *v.* 帶 [daai3]; **to** ~ 帶來

brisket (beef/veal/lamb) *n.* 胸 [hung1]

Britain *n.* 英國 [ying1 gwok8]

British *adj.* 英國 [ying1 gwok8]; ~ **food** 英國菜

broad *adj.* 寬 [fun1]

broad beans *n.* 蠶豆 [chaam4 dau2]

broadband *n.* 寬頻 [fun1 pan4]; ~ **connection/Internet** 寬頻連接

broadcast *v.* 放 [fong3]; *n.* 廣播 [gwong2 bo3]

broadly *adv.* 大體上 [daai6 tai2 seung6]

broccoli *n.* 西蘭花 [sai1 laan4 fa1]

brochure *n.* 手冊 [sau2 chaak8]

broil *v.* 烤 [haau1]

broiled meat *n.* 燒肉 [siu1 yuk9]

broken *adj.* 爛咗嘅 [laan6 jo2 ge3]; **~ bone** 骨骼斷裂

broker *n.* 經紀 [ging1 gei2]

bronchitis *n.* 支氣管炎 [ji1 hei3 gun2 yim4]

bronze *n.* 青銅 [ching1 tung4]

brooch *n.* 心口針 [sam1 hau2 jam1]

broth *n.* 湯 [tong1], **chicken ~** 雞湯, **cooking ~** 煮湯, **fish ~** 魚湯, **vegetable ~** 青菜湯, **fish ~** 海鮮湯

brother *n.* 阿哥 [a3 go1]

brotherhood *n.* 手足情 [sau2 juk7 ching4]

brown *adj./n.* 棕色 [jung1 sik7]

brown rice *n.* 糙米 [chou3 mai5]

browned *adj.* 曬黑 [saai3 hak7]

browned butter *n.* 黃色牛油 [wong4 sik7 ngau4 yau4]

brownie *n.* 朱古力餅 [jyu1 gu1 lik7 beng2]

browse *v.* 求其睇睇 [kau4 kei4 tai2 tai2]

browser *n.* 瀏覽器 [lau4 laam5 hei3]; **Internet ~** 互聯網瀏覽器

bruise *v.* 整瘀 [jing2 yu2]; *n.* 瘀 [yu2]

brunch *n.* 早午餐 [jou2 ng5 chaan1]

Brunei *n.* 文萊 [man4 loi4]

brunette *n.* 咖啡色頭髮嘅女人 [ga3 fe1 sik7 tau4 faat8 ge3 neui5 yan4]; *adj.* 咖啡色 [ga3 fe1 sik7]

brush *v.* 刷 [chaat8], **to ~ with sauce** 塗醬; *n.* 刷 [chaat2], **cooking ~** 廚具刷

Brussels *n.* 布魯塞爾 [bou3 lou5 choi3 yi5]; **~, capital of Belgium** 比利時嘅首都

Brussels sprouts *n.* 牙甘藍 [nga4 gam1 laam4]

bubble *n.* 水泡 [seui2 paau1]

Bucharest *n.* 布加勒斯特 [bou3 ga1 lak9 si1 dak9]; **~, capital of Romania** 羅馬尼亞嘅首都

bucket *n.* 桶 [tung2]

buckwheat *n.* 蕎麥 [kiu4 mak9]

Budapest *n.* 布達佩斯 [bou3 daat9 pui3 si1]; **~, capital of Hungary** 匈牙利嘅首都

budget *n.* 預算 [yu6 syun3]

Buenos Aires *n.* 布宜諾斯艾利斯 [bou3 yi4 nok9 si1 ngaai6 lei6 si1]; **~, capital of Argentina** 阿根廷嘅首都

buffalo wings *n.* 辣雞翼 [laat9 gai1 yik9]

bug *n.* 蟲 [chung4]

build *v.* 起 [hei2]

builder *n.* 建築商 [gin3 juk7 seung1]

building *n.* 建築物 [gin3 juk7 mat9]

built *adj.* 起好 [hei2 hau2]

Bujumbura *n.* 布瓊布拉 [bou3 king4 bou3 laai1]; **~, capital of Burundi** 布隆迪嘅首都

Bulgaria *n.* 保加利亞 [bou3 ga1 lei6 a3]

Bulgarian *adj.* 保加利亞 [bou3 ga1 lei6 a3]

bull *n.* 公牛 [gung1 ngau4]

bullet *n.* 子彈 [ji2 daan2]

bulletin board *n.* 公告欄 [gung1 gou3 laan4]

bullet-proof *adj.* 防彈 [fong4 daan2]

bumper *n.* 保險槓 [bou2 him2 gong3]

bun *n.* 包 [baau1], **sesame seed ~** 芝麻包, **poppy seed ~** 罌粟籽 包, **sweet ~** 甜包, **meat-filled ~** 肉包, **wheat ~** 小麥包

bunch *n.* 串 [chyun3]

bungalow *n.* 平房 [ping4 fong4]

bungee-jumping *n.* 笨豬跳 [bun2 jyu1 tiu3]

bureaucracy *n.* 官僚體制 [gun1 liu4 tai2 jai3]

bureaucrat *n.* 官僚 [gun1 liu4]

burbot *n.* 淡水鱈魚 [daam6 seui2 syut8 yu2]

burden *n.* 包袱 [baau1 fuk9]; *v.* 煩 [faan4]

burden of proof 提供證據嘅責 任 [tai4 gung1 jing3 geui3 ge3 jaak8 yam4]

burger *n.* 漢堡包 [hon3 bou2 baau1], **veggie ~** 素漢堡包, **ostrich ~** 鴕鳥肉漢堡包, **cheese ~** 芝士漢堡包

Burkina Faso *n.* 布基納發索 [bou3 gei1 naap9 faat8 sok8]

Burma (Myanmar) *n.* 緬甸 [min5 din6]

Burmese *adj.* 緬甸 [min5 din6]

burn *n.* 燒傷 [siu1 seung1]; *v.* 燒 [siu1]

burned *adj.* 燒爛 [siu1 laan6]; **sun~** 晒傷

burnt *adj.* 燒傷 [siu1 seung1], **~ toast** 燒燶嘅土司

burrito *n.* 墨西哥粟米煎餅 [mak9 sai1 go1 suk7 mai5 jin1 beng2], **bean and cheese ~** 芝 士加豆墨西哥粟米煎餅

burst *v.* 爆炸 [baau3 ja3]

Burundi *n.* 布隆迪 [bou3 lung4 dik9]

bury *v.* 埋 [maai4]

bus *n.* 巴士 [ba1 si2], **city ~** 市內 巴士, **tourist ~** 旅遊巴士, **~ lane** 巴士道, **~ route** 巴士道, **~ stop** 巴士站, **~ terminal** 巴 士終點站, **~ ride** 搭巴士

bush *n.* 草叢 [chou2 chung4]

business *n.* 生意 [saang1 yi3], **~ card** 名片, **~ class** 商業課程, **~ hours** 辦公時間, **~ trip** 出 差, **go out of ~** 倒閉

business person *n.* 生意人 [saang1 yi3 yan4]

busy *adj.* 忙 [mong4]

but *conj.* 但係 [daan6 hai6]

butane gas *n.* 丁烷氣 [ding1 yun2 hei3]

butcher *n.* 屠夫 [tou4 fu1]

butter *n.* 牛油 [ngau4 yau4], **cocoa ~** 可可牛油, **apple ~** 蘋 果牛油, **peanut ~** 花生牛油

buttered *adj.* 塗咗牛油 [tou4 jo2 ngau4 yau4]

butterfly *n.* 蝴蝶 [wu4 dip2]

buttermilk *n.* 脫脂奶 [tyut8 ji1 naai5]

butterscotch *n.* 牛油糖果 [ngau4 yau4 tong4 gwo2]

button *n.* 鈕 [nau2]

button mushrooms *n.* 草菇

buttress *n.* 撐住 [chaang1 jyu6]

buy *v.* 買 [maai5]

buyer *n.* 買家 [maai5 ga1]

by *prep.* 靠 [kaau3]; *adv.* 隔籬 [gaak8 lei4]; **~ means of** 通過

bye! *phr.* 拜拜 [baai3 baai3]

bypass *n.* 支路 [ji1 lou6]; **heart ~** 心臟搭橋

by-product *n.* 副產品 [fu3 chaan2 ban2]

C

cab *n.* 的士 [dik7 si2]

cabaret *n.* 夜總會 [ye6 jung2 wui2]

cabbage *n.* 椰菜 [ye4 choi3], **red ~** 紅椰菜, **green ~** 青椰菜, **~ soup** 椰菜湯, **~ wrap** 椰菜卷

cabin *n.* 客艙 [haak8 chong1]; **~ deck** 客艙板

cabinet *n.* 櫥櫃 [chyu4 gwai6]

cable *n.* 電纜 [din6 laam6]

cable car *n.* 纜車 [laam6 che1]

cable TV *n.* 有線電視 [yau5 sin3 din6 si6]

cactus *n.* 仙人掌 [sin1 yan4 jeung2]

Caesar salad *n.* 古羅馬式沙律 [gu2 lo4 ma5 sik7 sa1 leut9]

café *n.* 茶餐廳 [cha4 chaan1 teng1]

cafeteria *n.* 飯堂 [faan6 tong4]

caffeine *n.* 咖啡因 [ga3 fe1 yan1]

caffeine-free *adj.* 有咖啡因 [mou5 ga3 fe1 yan1]

cage *n.* 籠 [lung4]

cage-free *adj.* 走地 [jau2 dei6], **~ chicken** 走地雞, **~ eggs** 走地雞蛋, **~ beef** 走地牛

Cairo *n.* 開羅 [hoi1 lo4]; **~, capital of Egypt** 埃及嘅首都

cajole *v.* 勾引 [ngau1 yan5]

cake *n.* 蛋糕 [daan6 gou1], **sponge ~** 海綿蛋糕, **sugar ~** 甜蛋糕

calamari *n.* 魷魚 [yau4 yu2]

calamity *n.* 災難 [joi1 naan6]

calcium *n.* 鈣 [koi3]

calculate *v.* 計數 [gai3 sou3]

calculation *n.* 計數 [gai3 sou3]

calculator *n.* 計算機 [gai3 syun3 gei1]; **graphing ~** 繪圖計算機

calendar *n.* 日曆 [yat9 lik9]

call *v.* 叫 [giu3], **~ for** 叫, **~ collect** 對方付費電話; *n.* 電話 [din6 wa2]

calligraphy *n.* 書法 [syu1 faat8]

calm *adj.* 冷靜 [laang5 jing6]; *v.* 叫...冷靜 [giu3 ... laang5 jing6]

calmly *adv.* 冷靜 [laang5 jing6]

calorie *n.* 卡路里 [ka1 lou6 lei5]

Cambodia *n.* 柬埔寨 [gaan2 bou3 jaai6]

Cambodian *adj.* 柬埔寨 [gaan2 bou3 jaai6]

camera *n.* 相機 [seung2 gei1]; **~ case** 相機套, **~ shop/store** 相機店

Cameroon *n.* 喀麥隆 [haak8 mak9 lung4]

Cameroonian *adj.* 喀麥隆 [haak8 mak9 lung4]

camomile *n.* 甘菊 [gam1 guk7]

camp *n.* 營地 [ying4 dei6]; *v.* 露營 [lou6 ying4]

campaign *n.* 競選 [ging6 syun2]

camper *n.* 露營嘅人 [lou6 ying4 ge3 yan4]

campground *n.* 露營場地 [lou6 ying4 cheung4 dei6]

can v. 可以 [ho2 yi5]; n. 罐頭 [gun3 tau2]; **~ned goods** 罐頭食物, **~ opener** 開罐器

Canada n. 加拿大 [ga1 na4 daai6]

Canadian adj. 加拿大 [ga1 na4 daai6]

canal n. 運河 [wan6 ho4]

Canberra n. 坎培拉 [ham2 pui4 laai1]; **~, capital of Australia** 澳洲嘅首都

cancel v. 取消 [cheui2 siu1]

canceled adj. 取消咗 [cheui2 siu1 jo2]

cancer n. 癌症 [ngaam4 jing3]

cancerous adj. 致癌 [ji3 ngaam4]

carcinogen n. 致癌物 [ji3 ngaam4 mat9]

candidate n. 候選人 [hau6 syun2 yan4]

candied adj. 蜜餞 [mat9 jin3], **~ fruit** 蜜餞生果

candied yams n. 蜜餞淮山 [mat9 jin3 waai4 saan1]

candle n. 蠟燭 [laap9 juk7]

candlestick n. 燭台 [juk7 toi4]

candy n. 糖 [tong2], **hard ~** 硬糖, **soft ~** 軟糖, **gummy ~** 軟糖

candy cane n. 棒棒糖 [paang5 paang5 tong2]

cane syrup n. 甘蔗糖漿 [gam1 je3 tong4 jeung1]

canned adj. 罐裝 [gun3 jong1], **~ vegetables** 罐裝蔬菜, **~ meat** 罐裝肉, **~ goods** 罐裝食物

canoeing n. 划獨木舟 [wa1 duk9 muk9 jau1]

cantaloupe n. 哈密瓜 [ha1 mat9 gwa1]

canvas n. 帆布 [faan4 bou3]

cap n. 帽 [mou6]

capability n. 才能 [choi4 nang4]

capable (of) adj. 有才能 [yau5 choi4 nang4]

capacity n. 容量 [yung4 leung6]

Cape Town n. 開普敦 [hoi1 pou2 deun1]; **~, legislative capital of South Africa** 南非嘅立法首都

Cape Verde n. 佛得角 [fat9 dak7 gok8]

capers n. 續隨子 [juk9 cheui4 ji2]

capital n. 首府 [sau2 fu2]; adj. 超級好 [chiu1 kap7 hou2], **~ crime** 死罪

Capricorn n. 魔蠍座 [mo1 kit8 jo6]

capricious adj. 變幻莫測 [bin3 waan6 mok9 chak7]

cap lock comp. n. 大寫鎖定 [daai6 se2 so2 ding6]; **~ key** 大寫鎖定鍵

capsicums n. 燈籠椒 [dang1 lung4 jiu1]

capsule n. 膠囊 [gaau1 nong4]

captain n. 船長 [syun4 jeung2]

captive n. 俘虜 [fu1 lou5]

captivity n. 監禁 [gaam1 gam3]

capture v. 捉 [juk7]; n. 佔領 [jim3 ling5]

car n. 汽車 [hei3 che1], **by ~** 開車, **~ deck** 汽車甲板, **~ garage** 車房, **~ park** 停車場, **~ rental** 租車

Caracas n. 加拉加斯 [ga1 laai1 ga1 si1]; **~, capital of Venezuela** 委內瑞拉嘅首都

carafe *n.* 酒瓶 [jau2 ping4], **water ~** 水瓶, **wine ~** 酒瓶

caramel *n.* 焦糖 [jiu1 tong4]; **dark ~** 黑焦糖

caramel custard *n.* 焦糖燉蛋 [jiu1 tong4 dun2 daan2]

caramel sauce *n.* 焦糖汁 [jiu1 tong4 jap7]

caramelized *adj.* 有焦糖 [yau5 jiu1 tong4], **~ onion** 焦糖洋蔥

caraway *n.* 芷茴香 [ji2 wui4 heung1]

caraway seeds *n.* 芷茴香籽 [ji2 wui4 heung1 ji2]

carbohydrate *n.* 碳水化合物 [taan3 seui2 fa3 hap9 mat9], **complex ~** 複合碳水化合物, **simple ~** 簡單碳水化合物

carbon *n.* 碳 [taan3]; **~ copy** 副本

carbonated *adj.* 含二氧化碳 [ham4 yi6 yeung5 fa3 taan3]; **~ water** 蘇打水

carburetor *n.* 化油器 [fa3 yau4 hei3]

card *n.* 卡片 [kat7 pin2]; *v.* 記 係卡片度 [gei3 hai6 kat7 pin2 dok9]; **play ~s** 打牌

cardboard *n.* 紙板 [ji2 baan2]

care *n.* 照顧 [jiu3 gu3]; *v.* 關心 [gwaan1 sam1]; **take ~ of** 照 顧; **don't ~ for** 唔鍾意

career *n.* 事業 [si6 yip9]

careful *adj.* 仔細 [ji2 sai3]

carefully *adv.* 仔細 [ji2 sai3]

careless *adj.* 粗心 [chou1 sam1]

carelessly *adv.* 粗心 [chou1 sam1]

caring *adj.* 有同情心 [yau5 tung4 ching4 sam1]

caricature *n.* 漫畫 [maan6 wa2]

carnival *n.* 嘉年華 [ga1 nin4 wa6]

carp *n.* 醃尖 [yim1 jim1]

carpet *n.* 地氈 [dei6 jin1]

carrier *n.* 搬運公司 [bun1 wan6 gung1 si1]

carrier bag *n.* 紙袋 [ji2 doi2]

carrot *n.* 紅蘿蔔 [hung4 lo4 baak9]; **~ cake** 紅蘿蔔蛋糕

carry *v.* 攞 [lo2]

carry-on luggage *n.* 隨身行李 [cheui4 san1 hang4 lei5]

cart *n.* 手推車 [sau2 teui1 che1]

cartilage *n.* 軟骨 [yun5 gwat7]

carton *n.* 紙盒 [ji2 hap9], **milk ~** 盒裝牛奶

cartoon *n.* 動畫片 [dung6 wa2 pin2]

carve *v.* 雕刻 [diu1 haak7]

carving *n.* 雕刻品 [diu1 haak7 ban2], **~ knife** 雕刻刀

case *n.* 事例 [si6 lai6]; *v.* 裝 [jong1]

case law *n.* 判例法 [pun3 lai6 faat8]

cash *n.* 現金 [yin6 gam1], **~ deposit** 存現金; *v.* 套現 [tou3 yin2]

cash register *n.* 收銀機 [sau1 ngan4 gei1]

cashew *n.* 腰果 [yiu1 gwo2]

cashier *n.* 收銀員 [sau1 ngan4 yun4]

casing *n.* 罩 [jaau3]

casino *n.* 賭場 [dou2 cheung4]

cassava *n.* 木薯 [muk9 syu4]

casserole *n.* 沙鍋 [sa1 wo1], **tuna ~** 吞拿魚砂鍋

cassette *n.* 錄音帶 [luk9 yam1 daai2]

cast *v.* 掟 [deng3]; *n.* 演員陣容 [yin2 yun4 jan6 yung4]

cast iron *n.* 生鐵 [saang1 tit8]; ~ **stove** 生鐵爐

castle *n.* 城堡 [sing4 bou2]

Castries *n.* 卡斯特里 [ka1 si1 dak9 lei5]; ~, **capital of Saint Lucia** 聖盧西亞島嘅首都

casual *adj.* 求其 [kau4 kei4]

cat *n.* 貓 [maau1]

catalog(ue) *n.* 目錄 [muk9 luk9]

catch *v.* 捉 [juk7]

category *n.* 類型 [leui6 ying4]

cater *v.* 迎合 [ying4 hap9]

catering *n.* 承辦酒席 [sing4 baan6 jau2 jik9]; ~ **service** 餐飲服務

cathedral *n.* 大教堂 [daai6 gaau3 tong4]

Catholic *adj.* 天主教 [tin1 jyu2 gaau3]

catmint *n.* 樟腦草 [jeung1 nou5 chou2]

cattle *n.* 牛 [ngau4]

cauliflower *n.* 椰菜花 [ye4 choi3 fa1]

cause *n.* 原因 [yun4 yan1]; *v.* 引起 [yan5 hei2]

caution *n.* 謹慎 [gan2 san6]

cavalry *n.* 騎兵 [ke4 bing1]

cave *n.* 山窿 [saan1 lung1]

caviar *n.* 魚子醬 [yu4 ji2 jeung3]

cavity *n.* 蛀牙 [jyu3 nga4]

cayenne pepper *n.* 紅椒 [hung4 jiu1]

CD *n.* 唱片 [cheung3 pin2], ~ **burner** 錄唱片機, **rewritable** ~ 可重覆讀寫光碟

CD player *n.* 唱碟機 [cheung3 dip9 gei1]

cease *v.* 結束 [git8 chuk7]

ceiling *n.* 天花板 [tin1 fa1 baan2]

celebrate *v.* 慶祝 [hing3 juk7]

celebration *n.* 慶祝 [hing3 juk7]

celery *n.* 芹菜 [kan4 choi3], **Chinese** ~ 香芹, ~ **root** 芹菜根, ~ **sticks** 芹菜條

cell *n.* 細胞 [sai3 baau1]

cello *n.* 大提琴 [daai6 tai4 kam4]

cellphone *n.* 手機 [sau2 gei1]

cells *n.* 監倉 [gaam1 chong1]; **spreadsheet** ~ 數據表嘅挌

cellulose *n.* 纖維素 [chim1 wai4 sou3]

celsius *n.* 攝氏 [sip8 si6]

cement *n.* 水泥 [seui2 nai4]

cemetery *n.* 墳場 [fan4 cheung4]

censorship *n.* 審查 [sam2 cha4]

census *n.* 人口普查 [yan4 hau2 pou2 cha4]

cent *n.* 一分錢 [yat7 fan1 chin4] (*abbr.* **c., ct.**)

centenary *n.* 一百週年 [yat7 baak8 jau1 nin4]

center *n.* 中心 [jung1 sam1]

center of town *n.* 市中心 [si5 jung1 sam1]

centigrade *n.* 攝氏 [sip8 si6]

centimeter *n.* 厘米 [lei4 mai5] (*abbr.* **cm.**)

centipede *n.* 百足 [baak8 juk7]

central *adj.* 正中 [jing1 jung1]

Central African Republic *n.* 中非共和國 [jung1 fei1 gung6 wo4 gwok8]

Central American *adj.* 中美洲 [jung1 mei5 jau1]; ~ **food** 中美洲菜

central heating *n.* 中央暖氣系統 [jung1 yeung1 nyun5 hei3 hai6 tung2]

century *n.* 世紀 [sai3 gei2]

ceramic *adj.* 瓷器 [chi4 hei3]

ceramics *n.* 瓷器 [chi4 hei3]

cereal *n.* 麥片 [mak9 pin2], **whole grain** ~ 全糧麥片, **sweet** ~ 甜麥片, **oat** ~ 燕麥麥片, **morning** ~ 早餐麥片

ceremony *n.* 典禮 [din2 lai5], **wedding** ~ 結婚典禮, **graduation** ~ 畢業典禮

certain *adj.* 肯定 [hang2 ding6]; *pron.* 一啲 [yat7 di1]

certainly *adv.* 當然 [dong1 yin4]

certificate *n.* 證書 [jing3 syu1], **birth** ~ 出生紙, ~ **of deposit** 存款單

Chad *n.* 乍得 [ja3 dak7]

Chadian *adj.* 乍得 [ja3 dak7]

chain *n.* 鎖鏈 [so2 lin2]; *v.* 監禁 [gaam1 gam1]

chain guard *n.* 鍊罩 [lin6 jaau3]

chair *n.* 凳 [dang3]; ~ **lift** 纜車吊椅; **wheelchair** 輪椅

chairman, chairwoman *n.* 主席 [jyu2 jik9]

chalet *n.* 細木屋 [sai3 muk9 uk7]

challenge *n./v.* 挑戰 [tiu5 jin3]

chamber *n.* 議事廳 [yi5 si6 teng1]; **judge's** ~s 法官辦公室

chamomile *n.* 甘菊 [gam1 guk7]

champagne *n.* 香檳 [heung1 ban1]

champignons *n.* 食用香草 [sik9 yung6 heung1 chou2]

championship *n.* 錦標賽 [gam2 biu1 choi3]

chancellor *n.* 總理 [jung2 lei5]

chance *n.* 機會 [gei1 wui6]

change *v.* 改 [goi2], ~ **trains** 換車, ~ **baby** 換尿片; *n.* 變化 [bin3 fa3]

changing room *n.* 更衣室 [gang1 yi1 sat9]

channel *n.* 海峽 [hoi2 haap9]

chapel *n.* 教堂仔 [gaau3 tong2 jai2]

chapter *n.* 章 [jeung1]

char *v.* 燒燶 [siu1 nung1]

character *n.* 人物 [yan4 mat9]

characteristic *adj.* 獨特 [duk9 dak9]; *n.* 特徵 [dak9 jing1]

char-broiled *v.* 用炭燒 [yung6 taan3 siu1]

charcoal *n.* 木炭 [muk9 taan3]

charcoal-grilled *adj.* 用炭燒 [yung6 taan3 siu1]

charcuterie *n.* 熟食店 [suk9 sik9 dim3]

chard *n.* 甜菜 [tim4 choi3]

charge *n.* 收費 [sau1 fai3]; *v.* 指控 [ji2 hung3]; **to bring** ~s **against** 起訴

charged with *phr.* 被指控 [bei6 ji2 hung3]

charity *n.* 慈善 [chi4 sin6]

charm *v.* 魅力 [mei6 lik9]; *n.* 誘惑 [yau5 waak9]

charming *adj.* 有魅力 [yau5 mei6 lik9]

chart *n.* 圖 [tou4]; *v.* 紀錄 [gei2 luk9]

charter flight *n.* 包機 [baau1 gei1]

chase *v.* 追 [jeui1]; *n.* 打獵 [da2 lip9]

chat *v./n.* 傾計 [king1 gai2]

chauffeur *n.* 司機 [si1 gei1]

chayote *n.* 佛手瓜 [fat9 sau2 gwai1]

cheap *adj.* 平 [peng4]

cheaper *adj.* 仲平 [jung6 peng4]

cheapest *adj.* 最平

cheaply *adv.* 平 [peng4]

cheat *v.* 呃 [ngaak7]; *n.* 呃人 [ngaak7 yan4]

check *v.* 檢查 [gim2 cha4]; *n.* 檢查 [gim2 cha4]; **coat ~** 放褸處

checkbook *n.* 支票簿 [ji1 piu3 bou6]

checkers *n.* 西洋跳棋 [sai1 yeung4 tiu3 kei4]

check-in *n./v.* 報到 [bou3 dou3]; **~ desk** 登記處

check-out *n./v.* 退房 [teui3 fong2]

checkpoint *n.* 檢查站 [gim2 cha4 jaam6]

cheek *n.* 面珠墩 [min6 jyu1 deun1]

cheer *v.* 喝彩 [hot8 choi2]

cheerful *adj.* 興高采烈 [hing3 gou1 choi2 lit9]

cheerfully *adv.* 興高采烈 [hing3 gou1 choi2 lit9]

Cheers! *exclam.* 乾杯 [gon1 bui1]

cheese *n.* 芝士 [ji1 si2], **~ sauce** 芝士醬, **goat ~** 羊奶芝士, **cow ~** 牛奶芝士, **blue ~** 藍紋芝士, **muenster ~** 明斯特芝士, **cheddar ~** 車打芝士, **yellow ~** 黃色芝士, **american ~** 美式芝士, **monterey jack ~** 蒙特雷傑克芝士, **swiss ~** 瑞士芝士, **brie ~** 法國芝士

cheese fondue *n.* 芝士火鍋 [ji1 si2 fo2 wo1]

cheesecake *n.* 芝士蛋糕 [ji1 si2 daan6 gou1]

chef *n.* 廚師 [chyu4 si1]

chemical *adj.* 化學嘅 [fa3 hok9 ge3]; *n.* 化學藥品 [fa3 hok9 yeuk9 ban2]

chemist *n.* 化學家 [fa3 hok9 ga1]

chemistry *n.* 化學 [fa3 hok9]

cherry *n.* 車厘子 [che1 lei4 ji2], **~ pie** 車厘子批, **~ liqueur** 車厘子酒, **~ sauce** 車厘子醬

cherry tomatoes *n.* 蕃茄仔 [faan1 ke2 jai2]

chervil *n.* 山蘿蔔 [saan1 lo4 baak9]

chess *n.* 象棋 [jeung6 kei2]

chess set *n.* 一副象棋 [yat7 fu3 jeung6 kei2]

chessboard *n.* 棋盤 [kei4 pun2]

chest *n.* 心口 [sam1 hau2]

chestnut *n.* 栗子 [leut9 ji2]

chew *v.* 嚼 [jeuk8]

chewable *adj.* 爽口 [song2 hau2], **~ tablet** 可以咬嘅藥, **~ supplements** 可以咬嘅補品

chewing gum *n.* 香口膠 [heung1 hau2 gaau1]

chicken *n.* 雞肉 [gai1 yuk9], **~ breast** 雞胸肉, **~ soup** 雞湯, **~ wings** 雞翼, **~ wrap** 雞肉卷, **~ salad** 雞肉沙律

chickpea *n.* 鷹嘴豆 [ying1 jeui2 dau2]

chicory *n.* 紫色苦白菜 [ji2 sik7 fu2 baak9 choi3]

chief *adj.* 首席 [sau2 jik9]; *n.* 首領 [sau2 ling5]

child *n.* 細路 [sai3 lou6]; **~'s seat** 細路凳; **~'s bed** 細路床

childcare *n.* 兒童保育 [yi4 tung4 bou2 yuk9]

childhood *n.* 童年 [tung4 nin4]

childproof cap *n.* 兒童保護 [yi4 tung4 bou2 wu6]

children *n.* 細路仔 [sai3 lou6 jai2]; **~'s discount** 兒童折扣, **~'s menu** 兒童餐牌, **~'s pool** 小童泳池, **~'s game** 兒童遊戲, **~ portions** 細路仔份量

children's wear *n.* 童裝衫 [tung4 jong1 saam1]

Chile *n.* 智利 [ji3 lei6]

Chilean *adj.* 智利 [ji3 lei6]

chili *n.* 紅辣椒 [hung4 laat9 jiu1]; **~ pepper** 紅辣椒, **~ powder** 紅辣椒粉, **~ sauce** 紅辣椒醬, **~ soup** 紅辣椒湯

chill *v.* 凍 [dung3]

chilled *v.* 整凍 [jing2 dung3]; *adj.* 凍咗 [dung3 jo2]

chills *n.* 冷漠 [laang5 mok9]

chimney *n.* 煙筒 [yin1 tung2]

chin *n.* 下扒 [ha6 pa4]

China *n.* 中國 [jung1 gwok8]

Chinese *adj.* 中國 [jung1 gwok8]

Chinese food *n.* 中國菜 [jung1 gwok8 choi3]

Chinese pancake *n.* 大餅 [daai6 beng2]

chip *n.* 籌碼 [chau4 ma5]

chipotle *n.* 干紅辣椒 [gon1 hung4 laat9 jiu1]

chips *n.* 薯條 [syu4 tiu2], **potato ~** 薯條, **tortilla ~** 粟米片

chiropractor *n.* 按摩師 [on1 mo1 si1]

Chisinau *n.* 基希那烏 [gei1 hei1 na5 wu1]; **~, capital of Moldova** 摩爾多瓦嘅首都

chives *n.* 韭黃 [gau2 wong4]

chlorine *n.* 氯氣 [luk9 hei3]

chocolate *n.* 朱古力 [jyu1 gu1 lik7], **box of ~s** 一箱朱古力, **milk ~** 牛奶朱古力, **dark ~** 黑朱古力, **white ~** 白朱古力

chocolate bar *n.* 朱古力條 [jyu1 gu1 lik7 tiu2]

chocolate cake *n.* 朱古力蛋糕 [jyu1 gu1 lik7 daan6 gou1]

chocolate ice cream *n.* 朱古力雪糕 [jyu1 gu1 lik7 syut8 gou1]

chocolate syrup *n.* 朱古力漿 [jyu1 gu1 lik7 jeung2]

choice *n.* 選擇 [syun2 jaak9]

choir *n.* 唱詩班 [cheung3 si1 baan1]

choke *n.* 窒息 [jat9 sik7]

choose *v.* 揀 [gaan2]

chop *v.* 斬 [jaam2]

chopped *adj.* 斬好 [jaam2 hau2]

chopsticks *n.* 筷子 [faai3 ji2]

chord *n.* 弦 [yin4]

choreographer *n.* 排舞師 [paai4 mou5 si1]

choreography *n.* 排舞 [paai4 mou5]

chorizo *n.* 西班牙香腸 [sai1 baan1 nga4 heung1 cheung4]

chorus *n.* 合唱隊 [hap9 cheung3 deui2]

Christian *adj.* 基督徒 [gei1 duk7 tou4]

Christmas *n.* 聖誕節 [sing3 daan3 jit8]; **~ decorations** 聖誕節裝飾

Christmas Day *n.* 聖誕節當日 [sing3 daan3 jit8 dong3 yat9]

Christmas Eve *n.* 平安夜 [ping4 on1 ye6]

chromosome n. 染色體 [yim5 sik7 tai2]

chronic adj. 慢性 [maan6 sing3]

chuck steak n. 牛肩扒 [ngau4 gin1 pa4]

chunky adj. 肥矮 [fei4 ai2], ~ **pieces** 好大塊

church n. 教堂 [gaau3 tong4]; ~ **service** 禮拜

chutney n. 酸辣醬 [syun1 laat9 jeung3], **pineapple** ~ 菠蘿醬, **apple** ~ 蘋果醬, **date** ~ 海棗醬, **spicy** ~ 辣醬, **mango** ~ 芒果醬

cider (apple) n. 蘋果酒 [ping4 gwo2 jau2]

cigarette n. 煙 [yin1]; ~ **paper** 煙紙

cigars n. 雪茄 [syut8 ga1]

cilantro n. 芫茜 [yun4 sai1]; ~ **flakes** 芫茜碎; ~ **sauce** 芫茜醬

cinema n. 戲院 [hei3 yun2]

cinnamon n. 肉桂皮 [yuk9 gwai3 pei4], ~ **roll** 肉桂皮卷, ~ **stick** 肉桂皮條, ~ **powder** 肉桂皮粉, ~ **doughnut** 肉桂皮炸面圈, ~ **cake** 肉桂皮蛋糕

circle n. 圓圈 [yun4 hyun1]

circuit n. 電路 [din6 lou6]; **short** ~ 短路

circulation n. 血液循環 [hyut8 yik9 cheun4 waan4]

circulatory system n. 循環系統 [cheun4 waan4 hai6 tung2]

circumstance n. 環境 [waan4 ging2]

circumstantial adj. 有充分細節卻無法證實 [yau5 chung1 fan6 sai3 jit8 keuk8 mou4 faat8 jing3 sat9]

circumstantial evidence n. 旁證 [pong4 jing3]

citizen n. 市民 [si5 man4]

citizenship n. 公民 [gung1 man4]

citron n. 香櫞 [heung1 yun4]

citrus n. 柑 [gam1]; ~ **flavored** 柑味, ~ **fruit** 柑果, ~ **juice** 柑汁

city n. 城市 [sing4 si5]; ~ **center** 市中心, ~ **wall** 城牆, ~ **limits** 城市邊緣

civil adj. 文明 [man4 ming4]

civil rights n. 公民權利 [gung1 man4 kyun4 lei6]

civilian n. 平民 [ping4 man4]

claim v. 聲稱 [sing1 ching1]; n. 索賠 [sok8 pui4]

claim check (baggage) n. 收據 [sau1 geui3]

clam n. 蜆 [hin2]; ~ **bisque** 蜆肉濃湯, ~ **chowder** 蜆肉雜燴

clamor n. 吵雜聲 [chaau2 jaap9 seng1]

clap v./n. 鼓掌 [gu2 jeung2]

clarified adj. 澄清 [ching4 ching1]

clarify v. 澄清 [ching4 ching1]

class n. 班 [baan1]

classic adj. 古典 [gu2 din2]; n. 文學名著 [man4 hok9 ming4 juek8]

classical adj. 古典 [gu2 din2]

classical music n. 古典音樂 [gu2 din2 yam1 ngok9]

Classicism n. 古典主義 [gu2 din2 jyu2 yi6]

classics n. 文學名著 [man4 hok9 ming4 juek8]

classification n. 分類 [fan1 leui6]

classify v. 分類 [fan1 leui6]

classroom n. 課室 [fo3 sat7]

classy adj. 上等 [seung6 dang2]

clause n. 子句 [ji2 geui3]

clay n. 黏土 [nim1 tou2]

clean v. 清潔 [ching1 git8], ~ **up** 清潔好; adj. 乾淨 [gon1 jeng6]

cleaning n. 清潔 [ching1 git8]; **dry ~** 乾洗

clear v. 清楚 [ching1 cho2], ~ **the table** 抹台, ~ **through customs** 清關

clearance sale n. 清倉大減價 [ching1 chong1 daai6 gaam2 ga3]

clearly adv. 清楚 [ching1 cho2]

clementine n. 柑 [gam1]

clerk n. 夥計 [fo2 gai3]

clever adj. 醒目 [sing2 muk9]

click v. 合得來 [hap9 dak7 loi4], ~ **with mouse** 用鼠標點擊; n. 爪 [jaau2]

client n. 顧客 [gu3 haak8]; **(law)** 當事人 [dong1 si6 yan4]

cliff n. 懸崖 [yun4 ngaai4]

climate n. 氣候 [hei3 hau6]

climax n. 高潮 [gou1 chiu4]

climb n. 爬 [pa4]; v. 爬 [pa4]

climbing n. 爬山 [pa4 saan1]

clinic n. 診所 [jan2 so2]

clinical adj. 臨床 [lam4 chong4]

cloakroom n. 衣帽間 [yi1 mou2 gaan1]

clock n. 鐘 [jung1]

clog n. 塞 [sak7], **wear ~s** 著木屐; v. 塞住 [sak7 jyu6], ~**ged drain** 排水管塞咗

clone n./v. 克隆 [hak7 lung4]

cloning n. 克隆 [hak7 lung4]

close v. 閂 [saan1]; adj. 接近 [jip8 gan6]

close to prep. 接近 [jip8 gan6]

closed adj. 閂咗 [saan1 jo2], ~ **for renovations** 裝修停業, ~ **for vacation** 假期停業, ~ **to traffic** 唔准通行

closely adv. 親密 [chan1 mat9]

closet n. 衣櫃 [yi1 gwai6]

clot n. 結塊 [git8 faai3]; **blood ~** 血塊

cloth n. 布 [bou3]

clothes n. 衫 [saam1]

clothespins n. 衫夾 [saam1 gaap8]

clothing n. 衫 [saam1]; ~ **store** 成衣店

clotted adj. 結住 [git8 jyu6], ~ **cream** 凝結咗嘅奶油, ~ **sauce** 凝結咗嘅醬

cloud n. 雲 [wan4]

cloudberry n. 野生黃莓 [ye5 sang1 wong4 mui2]

cloudy adj. 多雲 [do1 wan4]

clove n. 丁香 [ding1 heung1]

clove of garlic n. 一瓣蒜 [yat7 faan6 syun3]

clover n. 三葉草 [saam1 yip9 chou2]

clown n. 小丑 [siu2 chau2]

club n. 社團 [se5 tyun4]; **golf ~** 高爾夫球俱樂部

clubhouse n. 俱樂部 [keui1 lok9 bou6]

cluster n. 群 [kwan4]; v. 生埋一齊 [saang1 maai4 yat7 chai4]

clutch n. 離合器 [lei4 hap9 hei3]; v. 捉住 [juk7 jyu6]

clutch pedal n. 離合器踏板 [lei4 hap9 hei3 daap9 baan2]

coach *n.* 教練 [gaau3 lin6]; *v.* 指導 [ji2 dou6]

coal *n.* 炭 [taan3]

coarse *adj.* 嘥 [haai4]

coast *n.* 海岸 [hoi2 ngon6]; *v.* 滑行 [waat9 hang4]

coat *v.* 塗 [tou4], **to ~** 塗一層; *n.* 褸 [lau1] **~ check** 放褸處, **~ hanger** 掛褸衣架

coated *adj.* 塗一層 [tou4 yat7 chang4]; **sugar~** 塗一層糖, **glaze ~** 上一層釉

coating *adj.* 糖衣 [tong4 yi1]

cobbler *n.* 酥皮水果餡餅 [sou1 pei2 seui2 gwo2 haam6 beng2], **peach ~** 酥皮桃仔餡餅, **cherry ~** 酥皮車厘子餡餅, **apple ~** 酥皮蘋果餡餅

cocaine *n.* 可卡因 [ho2 ka1 yan1]

cochineal seeds *n.* 胭脂蟲籽 [yin1 ji1 chung4 ji2]

cockles *n.* 海扇殼 [hoi2 sin3 hok8]

cockroach *n.* 甲由 [gaat9 jaat9]

cocktail *n.* 雞尾酒 [gai1 mei5 jau2]

cocoa *n.* 可可 [ho2 ho2], **~ powder** 可可粉, **~ milk** 可可奶, **~ cream** 可可忌廉

coconut *n.* 椰子 [ye4 ji2], **~ powder** 椰子粉, **~ milk** 椰子奶, **~ cream** 椰子忌廉

cod *n.* 鱈魚 [syut8 yu2]

code *n.* 密碼 [mat9 ma5]; **area ~** 區号

coffee *n.* 咖啡 [ga3 fe1]; **~ with milk** 加牛奶咖啡, **sugared ~** 甜咖啡, **dark ~** 黑咖啡, **mocca ~** 摩卡咖啡, **vanilla ~** 香草味咖啡, **cappucino ~** 卡布奇諾

coffee mug *n.* 咖啡杯 [ga3 fe1 bui1]

coffee shop *n.* 咖啡店 [ga3 fe1 dim3]

coffeemaker *n.* 磨咖啡機 [mo4 ga3 fe1 gei1]

coffeepot *n.* 咖啡罐 [ga3 fe1 gun3]

coin *n.* 銀仔 [ngan2 jai2]; **~ collection** 集幣

coincide *v.* 啱啱 [gam3 ngaam1]

coke *n.* 可樂 [ho2 lok9]

cold *adj.* 凍 [dung3], **feel ~** 覺得凍, **~ drink** 凍飲, **~ meal** 凍肉, **~ soup** 凍湯; *n. (illness)* 感冒 [gam2 mou6], **have a ~** 感冒

cold chocolate *n.* 凍朱古力奶 [dung3 jyu1 gu1 lik7 naai5]

cold cuts *n.* 冷盤 [laang5 pun2], **~ bologne** 冷盤大紅腸, **~ ham** 冷盤火腿, **~ turkey** 冷盤火雞

cold pack *n.* 冰袋 [bing1 doi2]

coldly *adv.* 冷漠 [laang5 mok9]

coleslaw *n.* 涼拌捲心菜 [leung4 pun6 gyun2 sam1 choi3]

collapse *v.* 冧 [lam3]; *n.* 冧 [lam3]

collard greens *n.* 羽衣甘藍葉 [yu5 yi1 gam1 laam4 yip9]

colleague *n.* 同事 [tung4 si6]

collect *v.* 收集 [sau1 jaap9]

collect call *n.* 對方付費電話 [deui3 fong1 fu6 fai3 din6 wa2]

collection *n.* 收藏 [sau1 chong4]

collector *n.* 收藏家 [sau1 chong4 ga1]

college *n.* 學院 [hok9 yun2]; **electoral ~** 選舉團

Colombia *n.* 哥倫比亞 [go1 leun4 bei2 a3]

Colombian *adj.* 哥倫比亞 [go1 leun4 bei2 a3]

Colombo *n.* 科倫坡 [fo1 leun4 po1]; **~, capital of Sri Lanka** 斯里蘭卡嘅首都

colon *n.* 結腸 [git8 cheung2]

color *n.* 顏色 [ngaan4 sik7]; *v.* 上顏色 [ ]

color film *n.* 彩色膠卷 [choi2 sik7 gaau1 gyun2]

colored *adj.* 彩色 [choi2 sik7] **multi-~** 彩色

colorfast *adj.* 唔甩色 [m4 lat7 sik7]

coloring *n.* 顏色 [ngaan4 sik7] **food ~** 色素

column *n.* 豎行 [syu6 hong4] **spreadsheet ~** 數據表嘅豎行

coma *n.* 昏迷 [fan1 mai4]

comb *n.* 梳 [so1] **v** 梳 [so1]

combination *n.* 配合 [pui3 hap9]

combine *v.* 加埋 [ga1 maai4]

come *v.* 嚟 [lei4]

come back *v.* 番嚟 [faan1 lei4]

comedy *n.* 喜劇 [hei2 kek9]

comfort *n.* 舒服 [syu1 fuk9]; *v.* 安慰 [on1 wai3]

comfort food *n.* 家常菜 [ga1 seung4 choi3]

comfortable *adj.* 舒服 [syu1 fuk9]

comfortably *adv.* 舒服 [syu1 fuk9]

comic *adj.* 搞笑 [gaau2 siu3]; *n.* 漫畫 [maan6 wa2] **stand-up ~** 棟篤笑, **~ book** 漫畫書

comics *n.* 漫畫 [maan6 wa2]

comma *n.* 逗號 [dau6 hou6]

command *v.* 指揮 [ji2 fai1]; *n.* 司令部 [si1 ling4 bou6]

commemoration *n.* 紀念儀式 [gei2 nim6 yi4 sik7]

comment *n.* 評論 [ping4 leun6]; *v.* 評論 [ping4 leun6]

commercial *adj.* 商業 [seung1 yip9]

commercial zone *n.* 商業區 [seung1 yip9 keui1]

commission *n.* 佣金 [yung2 gam1]; *v.* 委任 [wai1 yam6]

commissioned by *adj.* 委託 [wai1 tok8]

commit *v.* 犯法 [faan6 faat8]

commitment *n.* 承諾 [sing4 nok9]

committee *n.* 委員會 [wai2 yun4 wui2]

commodity *n.* 商品 [seung1 ban2]

common *adj.* 成日見 [sing4 yat9 gin3]

commonly *adv.* 一般 [yat7 bun1]

communicate *v.* 交流 [gaau1 lau4]

communication *n.* 交流 [gaau1 lau4]

communion *n.* 聖餐 [sing3 chaan1]

communist *adj.* 共產主義 [gung6 chaan2 jyu2 yi6]

community *n.* 社區 [se5 keui1]

commute *v.* 通勤 [tung1 kan4]; **~r train** 通勤車

Comoros *n.* 科摩羅 [fo1 mo1 lo4]

compact *adj.* 輕便 [hing1 bin4]

compact disc (CD) *n.* 光碟 [gwong1 dip2]

companion *n.* 同伴 [tung4 bun6]

company *n.* 公司 [gung1 si1]

comparative *adj.* 相對而言 [seung1 deui3 yi4 yin4]; *n.* 比較級 [bei2 gaau3 kap7]

compare *v.* 比較 [bei2 gaau3]

comparison *n.* 比較 [bei2 gaau3]

compass *n.* 指南針 [ji2 naam4 jam1]; **moral ~** 道德準則

compensation *n.* 報酬 [bou3 chau4]

compete *v.* 競爭 [ging3 jaang1]

competition *n.* 競爭 [ging3 jaang1]

competitive *adj.* 爭強好勝 [jaang1 keung6 hou3 sing3]

competitor *n.* 對手 [deui3 sau2]

complain *v.* 呻苦 [san1 fu2]

complainant (*legal*) *n.* 原告 [yun4 gou3]

complaint *n.* 投訴 [tau4 sou3]; (*legal*) **file a ~** 投訴

complete *adj.* 做完咗 [jou6 yun4 jo2], **~ meal** 一個大餐; *v.* 做完 [jou6 yun4], **to ~** 做完咗

completely *adv.* 全部 [cyun4 bou6]

completion *n.* 完工 [yun4 gung1]

complex *adj.* 複雜 [fuk7 jaap9]

complexion *n.* 面色 [min6 sik7]

complexity *n.* 錯綜複雜 [cho3 jung1 fuk7 jaap9]

complicate *v.* 搞複雜 [gaau2 fuk7 jaap9], **~ matters** 複雜嘅野

complicated *adj.* 複雜 [fuk7 jaap9]

comply *v.* 遵守 [jeun1 sau2]

component *n.* 零件 [ling4 gin2]; *adj.* 構成 [kau3 sing4]

compose *v.* 作曲 [jok8 kuk7]

composed *adj.* 鎮定 [jan3 ding6]

composer *n.* 作曲家 [jok8 kuk7 ga1]

composition *n.* 作曲 [jok8 kuk7]

composure *n.* 鎮定 [jan3 ding6]

compost *n.* 肥料 [fei4 liu2]

compote *n.* 果盤 [gwo2 pun2], **fruit ~** 水果盤, **apple ~** 蘋果盤

compound *n.* 場地 [cheung4 dei6]; *adj.* 複合 [fuk1 hap9]

comprise *v.* 包含 [baau1 ham4]

compromise *v./n.* 妥協 [to5 hip8]

compute *v.* 計 [gai3]

computer *n.* 電腦 [din6 nou5]; **~ art** 計算機技術; **~ games** 電腦遊戲

computing *n.* 計算 [gei3 syun3]

Conakry *n.* 科納克里 [fo1 naap9 hak7 lei5]; **~, capital of Guinea** 幾內亞嘅首都

conceal *v.* 隱藏 [yan2 chong4]

conceive *v.* 諗 [nam2]

concentrate *n.* 濃縮 [nung4 suk7], **juice ~** 濃縮水果汁, **fruit ~** 濃縮水果汁; *v.* 專心 [jyun1 sam1], **to ~** 專心做

concentration *n.* 專心 [jyun1 sam1]

concept *n.* 諗法 [nam2 faat8]

conception *n.* 競賽 [ging3 choi3]

conceptual *adj.* 概念 [koi3 nim6]

concern *v.* 關… 事 [gwaan1 … si6]; *n.* 關心 [gwaan1 sam1]

concerned *adj.* 關心 [gwaan1 sam1]

concerning *prep.* 關於 [gwaan1 yu1]

concert *n.* 音樂會 [yam1 ngok9 wui2], **live ~** 現場演奏; **~ hall** 音樂廳

concerto *n.* 協奏曲 [hip8 jau3 kuk7]

concession *n.* 遷就 [chin1 jau6]

conclude *v.* 做結論 [jou6 git8 leun6]

conclusion *n.* 結論 [git8 leun6]

concrete *adj.* 具體 [geui6 tai2]; *n.* 石屎 [sek9 si2]

concussion *n.* 腦震盪 [nou5 jan3 dong6], **he has a** ~ 佢有 腦震蕩

condensed *adj.* 濃縮 [nung4 suk7], ~ **milk** 濃牛奶, ~ **juice** 濃縮水果汁, ~ **soup** 濃湯

condiments *n.* 調味料 [tiu4 mei6 liu2]

condition *n.* 狀況 [jong6 fong3]

conditional *adj.* 有條件 [yau5 tiu4 gin6]

conditioner *n.* 調節器 [tiu4 jit8 hei3]; **hair** ~ 護髮素

condolence *n.* 哀悼 [oi1 dou6]

condom *n.* 避孕套 [bei6 yan6 tou3]

conduct *v.* 帶領 [daai3 ling5]; *n.* 指揮 [ji2 fai1]

conductor (*train*) *n.* 售票員 [sau6 piu3 yun4]

confection *n.* 甜品 [tim4 ban2], **cherry** ~ 車厘子甜品, **sweet** ~ 甜品

conference *n.* 會議 [wui6 yi5]

conference call *n.* 電話會議 [din6 wa2 wui6 yi5]

conference room *n.* 會議室 [wui6 yi5 sat7]

confess *v.* 懺悔 [chaam3 fui3]

confession *n.* 懺悔 [chaam3 fui3]

confidence *n.* 自信 [ji6 seun3]

confident *adj.* 自信 [ji6 seun3]

confidential *adj.* 絕密 [jyut9 mat9]

confidently *adv.* 自信 [ji6 seun3]

confine *v.* 困住 [kwan3 jyu6]

confined *adj.* 困住 [kwan3 jyu6]

confirm *v.* 證實 [jing3 sat9]

conflict *n.* 衝突 [chung1 dat9]; *v.* 發生衝突 [faat8 sang1 chung1 dat9]

confront *v.* 質問 [jat7 man6]

confuse *v.* 搞唔清楚 [gaau2 m4 ching1 cho2]

confused *adj.* 好亂 [hou2 lyun6]

confusing *adj.* 好亂 [hou2 lyun6]

confusion *n.* 混亂 [wan6 lyun6]

congealed *adj.* 凝結 [ying4 git8], ~ **fat** 凝固脂, ~ **sauce** 凝結醬, ~ **liquid** 冷凝液

Congo, Democratic Republic of the *n.* 剛果民主共和國 [gong1 gwo2 man4 jyu2 gung6 wo4 gwok8]

Congo, Republic of the *n.* 剛果 共和國 [gong1 gwo2 gung6 wo4 gwok8]

Congolese *adj.* 剛果人 [gong1 gwo2 yan4]

congratulate *n.* 恭喜 [gung1 hei2]

congratulations *n.* 恭喜 [gung1 hei2]; **Congratulations!** *phr.* 恭 喜晒！ [gung1 hei2 saai3]

congress *n.* 國會 [gwok8 wui2]

conjunction *n.* 連詞 [lin4 chi4]

connect *v.* 連接 [lin4 jip8]

connected *adj.* 連接 [lin4 jip8]

connection *n.* 連接 [lin4 jip8]

conscious *adj.* 清醒 [ching1 sing2]; **be** ~ 意識到

consciousness *n.* 神智 [san4 ji3]

consequence *n.* 後果 [hau6 gwo2]

consequently *adv.* 結果 [git8 gwo2]

conservation *n.* 傾計 [king1 gai2]

conservation area *n.* 保護區 [bou2 wu6 keui1]

conservative *adj.* 保守 [bou2 sau2]

conserve *v.* 保留 [bou2 lau4]

consider *v.* 考慮 [haau2 leui6]

considerable *adj.* 真係好 [jan1 hai6 hou2], ~ **odds** 可能性好大

considerably *adv.* 真係好 [jan1 hai6 hou2]

consideration *n.* 考慮 [haau2 leui6]

**consist of … ** *v.* 由…組成 [yau4 … jou2 sing4]

consistent *adj.* 一貫 [yat7 gun3]

consistently *adv.* 一貫 [yat7 gun3]

consommé *n.* 清湯 [ching1 tong1]

consonant *n.* 輔音 [fu6 yam1]

constant *adj.* 唔停 [m4 ting4]

constantly *adv.* 唔停 [m4 ting4]

constellation *n.* 星座 [sing1 jo6]

constipated *adj.* 便秘 [bin6 bei3]

constipation *n.* 便秘 [bin6 bei3]

constitute *v.* 構成 [kau3 sing4]

constitution *n.* 憲法 [hin3 faat8]

constitutional *adj.* 憲法 [hin3 faat8]; ~ **law** 憲法

constraint *n.* 約束 [yeuk8 chuk7]

construct *v.* 起 [hei2]

construction *n.* 建造 [gin3 jou6], **under** ~ 整緊

consulate *n.* 領事館 [ling5 si6 gun2]

consult *v.* 請教 [ching2 gaau3]

consultant *n.* 顧問 [gu3 man6]

consultation *n.* 請教 [ching2 gaau3]; ~ **room (doctor)** 診察室

consumer *n.* 消費者 [siu1 fai3 je2]

consumption *n.* 消費 [siu1 fai3]

contact *n./v.* 聯繫 [lyun4 hai6]; **be in ~ with** 聯繫

contact lens *n.* 隱形眼鏡 [yan2 ying4 ngaan5 geng3]; **eye drops for ~** 隱形眼鏡液

contagious *adj.* 會傳染嘅 [wui5 chyun4 yim5 ge3]

contain *v.* 包含 [baau1 ham4]

container *n.* 容器 [yung4 hei3]

contemporary *adj.* 一陣 [yat7 jan6], ~ **style** 現代風格, ~ **art** 現代藝術

content *n.* 內容 [noi6 yung4], **dietary ~** 飲食結構, **protein ~** 蛋白質含量, **fat ~** 脂肪含量, **fiber ~** 纖維素含量, **sugar ~** 糖含量

contest *n.* 比賽 [bei2 choi3]

context *n.* 上下文 [seung6 ha6 man4]

continent *n.* 大陸 [daai6 luk9]

continental *adj.* 大陸 [daai6 luk9]; ~ **United States** 美國大陸

continuance *n.* 持續時間 [chi4 juk9 si4 gaan3]

continue *v.* 繼續 [gai3 juk9]

continuous *adj.* 繼續 [gai3 juk9]

continuously *adv.* 繼續 [gai3 juk9]

contraception *n.* 避孕 [bei6 yan6]

contraceptive *adj.* 避孕嘅 [bei6 yan6 ge3]; *n.* 避孕藥 [bei6 yan6 yeuk9]; ~ **pill** 避孕藥

contract *n.* 合同 [hap9 tung4]; *v.* 訂約 [ding3 yeuk8]

contraction *n.* 收縮 [sau1 suk7]

contractor *n.* 承包人 [sing4 baau1 yan4]

contrast *n.* 差異 [cha1 yi6]; *v.* 對比 [deui3 bei2]

contrasting *adj.* 對比鮮明 [deui3 bei2 sin1 ming4]

contribute *v.* 貢獻 [gung3 hin3]

contribution *n.* 貢獻 [gung3 hin3]

control *n./v.* 控制 [hung3 jai3]

controlled *adj.* 控制住 [hung3 jai3 jyu6], ~ **substance** 管制藥

contusion *n.* 撞傷 [jong6 seung1]

convenience store *n.* 便利店 [bin6 lei6 dim3]

convenient *adj.* 方便 [fong1 bin6]

convent *n.* 修道院 [sau1 dou6 yun2]

convention *n.* 慣例 [gwaan3 lai6]; ~ **hall** 會議廳

conventional *adj.* 傳統 [chyun4 tung2]

conversation *n.* 傾計 [king1 gai2]

convert *v.* 皈依 [gwai1 yi1]

convey *v.* 傳達 [chyun1 daat9]

convince *v.* 講得聽 [gong2 dak7 teng1]

cook *v.* 煮 [jyu2]; *n.* 廚師 [chyu4 si1]; ~**ed** *adj.* 煮熟

cookbook *n.* 菜譜 [choi3 pou2]

cooker *n.* 廚具 [chyu4 geui6]

cookie *n.* 餅乾 [beng2 gon1]; **baked** ~ 焗餅; *tech.* **Internet** ~**s** 訪問網站數據

cooking *n.* 煮野 [jyu2 ye5]; ~ **facilities** 廚具; ~ **instructions** 烹飪方法

cool *adj.* 有型 [yau5 ying4], ~ **temperature** 溫度低; *v.* 整凍 [jing2 dung3]

cooperation *n.* 合作 [hap9 jok8]

cooperative *adj.* 合作 [hap9 jok8]

coordinate *v.* 協調 [hip8 tiu4]; *n.* 坐標 [jo6 biu1]

cope (~ with) *v.* 對付 [deui3 fu6]

Copenhagen *n.* 哥本哈根 [go1 bun2 ha1 gan1]; ~, **capital of Denmark** 丹麥嘅首都

copper *n.* 銅 [tung4]

copy *n./v.* 複製 [fuk7 jai3]; **make a** ~ 影印

copyright *n.* 版權 [baan2 kyun4]

cord *n.* 繩 [sing2]

core *n.* 核心 [hat9 sam1]

coriander *n.* 荒茜 [yun4 sai1]

cork *n.* 木塞 [muk9 sak7]

corkscrew *n.* 開塞鑽 [hoi1 sak7 jyun3]

corn *n.* 粟米 [suk7 mai5]; **creamed** ~ 牛油粟米

corn dog *n.* 麻鷹 [ma4 ying1]

corn oil *n.* 粟米油 [suk7 mai5 yau4]

corn syrup *n.* 粟米糖漿 [suk7 mai5 tong4 jeung1]

cornbread *n.* 粟米麵包 [suk7 mai5 min6 baau1]

corned beef *n.* 鹹牛肉 [haam4 ngau4 yuk9]

corner *n.* 街口 [gaai1 hau2]

cornerstone *n.* 奠基石 [din6 gei1 sek9]

cornflakes *n.* 脆粟米片 [cheui3 suk7 mai5 pin2]

cornmeal *n.* 燕麥 [yin3 mak9]

cornstarch *n.* 粟米澱粉 [suk7 mai5 din6 fan2]

corporate *adj.* 法人 [faat8 yan4]

corporation (*abbr.* **Corp.**) *n.* 公司 [gung1 si1]

correct *adj.* 啱 [ngaam1]; *v.* 改正 [goi2 jing3]

correctly *adv.* 啱 [ngaam1]

correlation *n.* 相關 [seung1 gwaan1]

correspond *v.* 通訊 [tung1 seun3]

corresponding *adj.* 對應 [deui3 ying3]

corrupt *adj.* 腐敗 [fu6 baai6]

corrupted *adj.* 腐敗 [fu6 baai6]

corruption *n.* 腐敗 [fu6 baai6]

cosmetics *n.* 化妝品 [fa3 jong1 ban2]; ~ **counter** 化妝品專櫃; ~ **department** 化妝品部

cosmos *n.* 宇宙 [yu5 jau6]

cost *n.* 成本 [sing4 bun2]

Costa Rica *n.* 哥斯達黎加 [go1 si1 daat9 lai4 ga1]

Costa Rican *adj.* 哥斯達黎加 [go1 si1 daat9 lai4 ga1]

costume *n.* 戲服 [hei3 fuk9]

cot *n.* 床仔 [chong4 jai2]

Cote d'Ivoire *n.* 科特迪瓦 [fo1 dak9 dik9 nga5]

cottage *n.* 屋仔 [uk7 jai2]

cottage cheese *n.* 鄉村芝士 [heung1 chyun1 ji1 si6]

cotton *n.* 棉花 [min4 fa1]; ~ **plant** 棉花廠

cottonseed oil *n.* 棉花籽油 [min4 fa1 ji2 yau4]

cough *v.* 咳 [kat7]; *n.* 咳 **[kat7]**; ~ **syrup** 止咳糖漿, ~ **medicine** 藥水

could *v.* 可以 [ho2 yi5]

coulis *n.* 泥 [nai4]

council *n.* 委員會 [wai1 yun4 wui2]

counsel *n.* 法律顧問 [faat8 leut9 gu3 man6], **legal** ~ 法律顧問

counselor *n.* 法律顧問 [faat8 leut9 gu3 man6]

count *v.* 計數 [gai3 sou3]; *n.* 計數 [gai3 sou3], **head** ~ 計人數

countable *adj.* 可數 [ho2 sou2]

counter *n.* 櫃台 [gwai6 toi4]; *adj.* 背道而馳 [bui6 dou6 yi4 chi4], ~ **strike** 反恐怖襲擊

counteroffer *n.* 還價 [waan4 ga3]

counting *n.* 計數 [gai3 sou3]

country *n.* 國家 [gwok8 ga1]; *adj.* 鄉村嘅 [heung1 chyun1 ge3], ~ **inn** 鄉村旅館, ~ **music** 鄉村音樂

country code *n.* 國家區號 [gwok8 ga1 keui1 hou6]

countryside *n.* 鄉村 [heung1 chyun1]

county *n.* 郡 [gwan6]

couple *n.* 兩夫婦 [leung5 fu1 fu5]

coupon *n.* 優惠券 [yau1 wai6 gyun3]

courage *n.* 膽量 [daam2 leung6]

course *n.* 課程 [fo3 ching4] **meal**, **direction**, **classes**; *adv.* **of** ~ 當然 [dong1 yin4]

court (*legal*) *n.* 法庭 [faat8 ting4]

courthouse *n.* 法院 [faat8 yun2]

courtesy *n.* 禮貌 [lai5 maau6]

courtyard *n.* 天井 [tin1 jeng2]

couscous *n.* 蒸粗麥粉 [jing1 chou1 mak9 fan2]

cousin *n.* 表 / 堂兄弟姊妹 [biu2/tong4 hing1 dai6 ji2 mui6]

cover v. 遮住 [je1 jyu6]; n. 蓋 [goi3]

cover charge n. 小費 [siu2 fai3]

covered adj. 遮住 [je1 jyu6]

covering n. 遮住嘅野 [je1 jyu6 ge3 ye5]

coward n. 冇膽匪類 [mou5 daam2 fei2 leui2]

cow n. 牛 [ngau4]

CPU n. 中央處理器 [jung1 yeung1 chyu2 lei5 hei3]; **computer** ~ 電腦中央處理器

crab n. 蟹 [haai5], ~**cakes** 蟹餅, ~**meat** 蟹肉, **artificial** ~ 素蟹

crack n. 罅 [la3]; v. 整開 [jing2 hoi1]

cracked adj. 有條罅 [yau5 tiu4 la3]

crackers n. 爆竹 [baau3 juk7], **graham** ~ 全麥餅乾, **salted** ~ 鹹餅乾

craft n. 手工 [sau2 gung1]; v. 手工整 [sau2 gung1 jing2]

craft store n. 工藝店 [gung1 ngai6 dim3]

crafts n. 飛機 [fei1 gei1]

cramp n. 抽筋 [chau1 gan1]

cranberry n. 細紅莓 [sai3 hung4 mui2]; ~ **juice** 細紅莓汁; ~ **sauce** 細紅莓醬

crash n. 撞車 [jong6 che1], **car** ~ 撞車; v. 猛撞 [maang5 jong6]; ~ **helmet** 頭盔, ~ **test dummy** 碰撞測試假人

crayfish n. 小龍蝦 [siu2 lung4 ha1]

crazy adj. 癡線 [chi1 sin3]

cream n. 忌廉 [gei6 lim1]; ~ **sauce** 忌廉汁, ~ **soup** 忌廉湯, ~ **cheese** 忌廉芝士, ~ **cake** 忌廉蛋糕, ~ **of chicken** 忌廉雞, ~ **of wheat** 忌廉小麥, ~ **of tomato** 忌廉番茄

cream puff n. 泡芙 [paau3 fu4]

creamed adj. 忌廉 [gei6 lim1], ~ **corn** 忌廉粟米, ~ **green beans** 忌廉青豆

create v. 創造 [chong1 jou6]

creation n. 產物 [chaan2 mat9]

creative adj. 有創意 [yau5 chong1 yi3]

creativity n. 創意 [chong1 yi3]

creature n. 生物 [sang1 mat9]

credit n. 信用 [seun3 yung6]

credit card n. 信用卡 [seun3 yung6 kat7]; ~ **number** 信用卡號碼

creditor n. 債主 [jaai3 jyu2]

creep v. 爬 [pa4]; n. (slang) 爬 [pa4]

crepe n. 薄煎餅 [bok9 jin1 beng2], **French** ~ 法國薄煎餅, **fruit** ~ 水果薄煎餅

crew n. 工作人員 [gung1 jok8 yan4 yun4]

crib n. 嬰兒床 [ying1 yi4 chong4]

crime n. 犯罪 [faan6 jeui6]

criminal adj. 犯罪 [faan6 jeui6], ~ **investigation** 刑事偵察; n. 罪犯 [jeui6 faan2]

crimp v. 捲髮 [gyun2 faat8], ~ **pastry** 蛋糕卷

crisis n. 危機 [ngai4 gei1]

crisp adj. 脆 [cheui3]

criterion n. 標準 [biu1 jeun2]

critic n. 批評家 [pai1 ping2 ga1], **film** ~ 影評家, **literary** ~ 文學評論家

critical adj. 關鍵 [gwaan1 gin6]

criticism n. 批評 [pai1 ping2]

criticize *v.* 批評 [pai1 ping2]

critique *n.* 評論 [ping4 leun6]

Croatia *n.* 克羅地亞 [hak7 lo4 dei6 a3]

Croatian *adj.* 克羅地亞 [hak7 lo4 dei6 a3]

crop *n.* 農作物 [nung4 jok8 mat9]

croquettes *n.* 炸肉丸 [ja3 yuk9 yun2]

cross *n.* 十字架 [sap9 ji6 ga2]; *v.* 行過 [haang4 gwo3]; *adj.* 對過 [deui3 gwo3]

cross-country *adj.* 越野 [yut9 ye5], ~ **running/team** 越野賽跑, ~ **skiing** 越野滑雪, ~ **skis** 越野滑雪

cross-examination *n.* 盤問 [pun4 man6]

crossing *n.* 人行道 [yan4 hang4 dou6]; ~ **guard** 交通協助員

crouton *n.* 多士粒 [do1 si2 nap7]

crowd *n.* 群眾 [kwan4 jung3]

crowded *adj.* 逼 [bik7]

crown *n.* 王冠 [wong4 gun1]; *v.* 加冕 [ga1 min5]

crucial *adj.* 緊要 [gan2 yiu3]

cruel *adj.* 殘忍 [chaan4 yan2]

cruelty *n.* 殘暴 [chaan4 bou6]; ~ **to animals** 瘧待動物

cruise *n.* 搭郵輪 [daap8 yau4 leun4]; *v.* 巡航 [cheun4 hong4]

crumb *n.* 碎 [seui3]; **bread ~** 麵包碎

crumble *v.* 整成碎 [jing2 sing4 seui3]

crunch *v.* 嚼得好大聲 [jeuk8 dak7 hou2 daai6 seng1]; *n.* 經濟緊縮 [ging1 jai3 gan2 suk7]

crunchy *adj.* 脆口 [cheui3 hau2]

crush *v.* 壓碎 [aat8 seui3]

crushed *v.* 壓碎 [aat8 seui3]; *adj.* 壓爛 [aat8 laan6], ~ **powder** 粉, ~ **ice** 米碎, ~ **almonds** 杏仁碎

crust *n.* 麵包皮 [min6 baau1 pei4]; **pie ~** 派邊

crustacean *n.* 甲殼類動物 [gaap8 hok8 leui6 dung6 mat9]

crusted *adj.* 古老 [gu2 lou5]

crutches *n.* 拐杖 [gwaai2 jeung2]

cry *v.* 喊 [haam3]; *n.* 大叫 [daai6 giu3]

crypt *n.* 地牢 [dei6 lou4]

crystal *n.* 水晶 [seui2 jing1]

crystallized *adj.* 結晶 [git8 jing1], ~ **sugar** 結晶糖

Cuba *n.* 古巴 [gu2 ba1]

Cuban *adj.* 古巴 [gu2 ba1]

cube *n.* 立方體 [laap9 fong1 tai2]

cubed *v.* 切成小塊 [chit8 sing4 siu2 faai3]; *adj.* 立方體形狀 [laap9 fong1 tai2 ying4 jong6], ~ **chicken** 雞塊, ~ **ice** 飯團, ~ **avocado** 牛油果塊

cucumber *n.* 黃瓜 [wong4 gwa1]; ~ **soup** 黃瓜湯

cuisine *n.* 菜 [choi3]

culinary *n.* 烹飪 [paang1 yam6]

cultivated *adj.* 耕種 [gaang1 jung3]

cultural *adj.* 文化 [man4 fa3]

culture *n.* 文化 [man4 fa3]

cumin *n.* 孜然 [ji1 yin4], ~ **powder** 孜然粉, ~ **seeds** 孜然籽

cunning *adj.* 狡猾 [gaau2 waat9]

cup *n.* 杯 [bui1]; *v.* 托住 [tok8 jyu6]

cupboard *n.* 櫥櫃 [chyu4 gwai6]

cupcake *n.* 紙杯蛋糕 [ji2 bui1 daan6 gou1]

Cupid *n.* 丘比特 [yau1 bei2 dak9]

curator *n.* 監護人 [gaam1 wu6 yan4]

curb *v.* 制止 [jai3 ji2]

curdle *v.* 凝結 [ying4 git8]; **~d milk** 凝結乳

curds *n.* 凝乳 [ying4 yu5]

cure *v.* 醫好 [yi1 hou2]; *n.* 治療 [ji6 liu4]

cured *adj.* 醫好咗 [yi1 hou2]

cured meat *n.* 臘肉 [laap9 yuk9]

curfew *n.* 宵禁 [siu1 gam3]

curing *n.* 醫好 [yi1 hou2]; **~ of meat** 凍肉

curious *adj.* 好奇 [hou3 kei4]

curiously *adv.* 好奇 [hou3 kei4]

curl *v.* 捲 [gyun2]; *n.* 捲髮 [gyun2 faat8]

curly *adj.* 捲[gyun2]; **~ fries** 捲薯條

curly lettuce *n.* 捲生菜 [gyun2 saang1 choi3]

currants *n.* 細葡萄乾 [sai3 pou4 tou4 gon1], **red ~** 紅細葡萄乾, **black ~** 黑細葡萄乾

currency *n.* 貨幣 [fo3 bai6]

currency exchange *n.* 換錢 [wun6 chin2], **~ office** 外匯兌換處, **~ rate** 匯率

current *adj.* 現時 [yin6 si4]; *n.* 趨勢 [cheui1 sai3]

current affairs *n.* 時事 [si4 si6]

currently *adv.* 現時 [yin6 si4]

curry *n.* 咖哩 [ga3 le1], **Indian ~** 印度咖哩, **chicken ~** 咖哩雞, **~ powder** 咖哩粉, **~ sauce** 咖哩醬

cursor (*computer*) *n.* 光標 [gwong1 biu1]

curtain *n.* 窗簾 [cheung1 lim4], **window ~** 窗簾, **theater ~** 幕布

curve *n.* 曲線 [kuk7 sin3]; *v.* 整彎 [jing2 waan1]

curved *adj.* 弧形 [wu4 ying4]

custard *n.* 蛋羹 [daan2 gang1], **egg ~** 蛋羹, **chocolate ~** 朱古力蛋羹

custody 監護 [gaam1 wu6]

custom *n.* 慣例 [gwaan3 lai6]

customer *n.* 顧客 [gu3 haak8]; **~ information/service** 顧客信息 / 客服, **~ parking** 顧客專用停車場

customize *v.* 訂做 [deng6 jou6]

customs *n.* 海關 [hoi2 gwaan1], **~ forms** 海關申報表, **~ official** 海關官員

customs declaration *n.* 海關申報表 [hoi2 gwaan1 san1 bou3 biu2]

cut *v.* 割 [got8]; *n.* 切口 [chit8 hau2], **~ of meat** 割紋

cutlery *n.* 刀叉 [dou1 cha1]

cutlet *n.* 肉餅 [yuk9 beng2], **lamb ~** 羊肉餅, **mutton ~** 羊肉餅, **chicken ~** 雞肉餅

cuttlefish *n.* 墨魚 [mak9 yu4]

cycle *n.* 週期 [jau1 kei4]; *v.* 循環 [cheun4 waan4]

cycling *n.* 踩單車 [chaai2 daan1 che1]; **~ path** 單車道, **~ enthusiast** 單車發燒友

cylindrical *adj.* 圓柱 [yun4 chyu5]

cyprinoid *n.* 鯉魚 [lei5 yu2]

Cypriot *n.* 塞浦路斯人 [choi3 pou2 lou6 si1 yan4]

Cyprus *n.* 塞浦路斯 [choi3 pou2 lou6 si1]

cyst *n.* 囊腫 [nong4 jung2]

cystitis *n.* 膀胱炎 [pong4 gwong1 yim4]

Czech *n.* 捷克人 [jit9 hak7 yan4]

Czech Republic *n.* 捷克共和國 [jit9 hak7 gung6 wo4 gwok8]

D

dad *n.* 爹咇 [de1 di3]

daikon *n.* 蘿蔔 [lo4 baak9]

daily *adj.* 日常 [yat9 seung4]; *adv.* 每日 [mui5 yat9]

dairy *n.* 乳製品 [yu5 jai3 ban2]; ~ **product** 奶製品, ~ **cream** 牛奶忌廉, **non**~不含乳製品

Dakar *n.* 達喀爾 [daat9 ka1 yi5]; ~, **capital of Senegal** 塞內加爾嘅首都

damage *n./v.* 損壞 [syun2 waai6]

damaged *adj.* 爛咗 [laan6 jo2]

damages *n.* 損壞 [syun2 waai6]

Damascus *n.* 大馬士革 [daai6 ma5 si6 gaak8]; ~, **capital of Syria** 敘利亞首都

damp *adj.* 潮濕 [chiu4 sap7]

dance *n./v.* 跳舞 [tiu3 mou5]

dancer *n.* 舞蹈家 [mou5 dou6 ga1]

dancing *n.* 跳舞 [tiu3 mou5]; **go** ~ 去跳舞

dandelion *n.* 蒲公英 [pou4 gung1 ying1], ~ **greens** 蒲公英嫩葉, ~ **leaves** 蒲公英葉

danger *n.* 危險 [ngai4 him2]

dangerous *adj.* 危險 [ngai4 him2]

Danish *n.* 丹麥人 [daan1 mak9 yan4]

Danish pastry *n.* 丹麥酥皮餅 [daan1 mak9 sou1 pei2 beng2]

Dar es Salaam *n.* 達累斯薩拉姆 [daat9 leui5 si1 saat8 laai1 mou5]; ~, **capital of Tanzania** 坦桑尼亞首都

dare *v.* 敢 [gam2]

dark *adj.* 深色嘅 [sam1 sik7 ge3]; *n.* 黑 [hak7], **grow** ~ 天黑

darker *adj.* 深色 [sam1 sik7]

dash *v.* 沖 [chung1]; *n.* 楂 [ja1], ~ **of salt** 一楂鹽, ~ **of pepper** 一楂辣椒

data *n.* 數據 [sou3 geui3]

database *n.* 數據庫 [sou3 geui3 fu3]; **computer** ~ 電腦數據庫

date *n.* 日期 [yat9 kei4]; *v.* 拍拖 [paak8 to1] // *n.* (*fruit*) **Mediterranean** ~ 地中海海棗

date of birth *n.* 出生日期 [cheut7 saang1 yat9 kei4]

daughter *n.* 女 [neui2]

dawn *n.* 黎明 [lai4 ming4]

day *n.* 日 [yat9]; *adj.* 日頭 [yat9 tau2]; ~ **after tomorrow** 後日, ~ **trip** 一日遊, ~ **pass/ticket** 日票

daycare *n.* 托兒所 [tok8 yi4 so2]

daytime *n.* 日頭 [yat9 tau2]

dead *adj.* 死咗 [sei2 jo2]; ~ **battery** 電池沒電

dead end *n.* 倔頭路 [gwat9 tau4 lou6]

deadline *n.* 截止日期 [jit9 ji2 yat9 kei4]

deaf *adj.* 聾 [lung4]

deal *v.* 發牌 [faat8 paai4], ~ **with smth/smne** 處理; *n.* 交易 [gaau1 yik9]

dealer *n.* 經銷商 [ging1 siu1 seung1], **drug** ~ 毒販, **car** ~ 汽車代理

dealings *n.* 買賣 [maai5 maai6]

dear *adj.* 親愛嘅 [chan1 oi3 ge3]

death *n.* 死 [sei2]

debate *n.* 辯論 [bin6 leun6]; *v.* 爭 [jang1]

debt *n.* 債 [jaai3]

debtor *n.* 借錢嘅人 [je3 chin2 ge3 yan4]

debut *n.* 第一次登台表演 [dai6 yat7 chi3 dang1 toi4 biu2 yin2]

decade *n.* 十年 [sap9 nin4]

decaffeinated *adj.* 冇咖啡因 [mou5 ga3 fe1 yan1]

decant *v.* 倒出來 [dou2 cheut7 loi4]

decanter *n.* 玻璃瓶 [bo1 lei1 ping4]

decay *n./v.* 腐爛 [fu6 laan6]

December (*abbr.* **Dec.**) *n.* 十二月 [sap9 yi6 yut9]

decide *v.* 決定 [kyut8 ding6]

decision *n.* 決定 [kyut8 ding6]; ~ **making** 做決定

deck *n.* 甲板 [gaap8 baan2], **ship ~** 輪船甲板, ~ **of cards** 一疊牌

declare *v.* 宣佈 [syun1 bou3]

decline *n.* 下降 [ha6 gong3]; *v.* 謝絕 [je6 jyut9]

decorate *v.* 裝修 [jong1 sau1]

decoration *n.* 裝修 [jong1 sau1]

decorative *adj.* 裝飾 [jong1 sik7]

decrease *v./n.* 減少 [gaam2 siu2]

decree *n.* 法令 [faat8 ling4]

dedicate *v.* 獻畀 [hin3 bei2]

dedicated *adj.* 投入 [tau4 yap9]

deduct *v.* 減 [gaam2]

deep *adj./adv.* 深 [sam1], ~ **end of pool** 泳池深水區

deep-fried *adj.* 油炸 [yau4 ja3]

deeply *adv.* 強烈 [keung4 lit9]

deer *n.* 鹿 [luk9]

defeat *v.* 擊敗 [gik7 baai6]; *n.* 失敗 [sat7 baai6]

defend *v.* 辯護 [bin6 wu6]

defendant *n.* 被告 [bei6 gou3]

defense *n.* 國防部 [gwok8 fong4 bou6]

deficiency *n.* 缺陷 [kyut8 haam6]

deficit *n.* 赤字 [chek8 ji6]

define *v.* 定義 [ding6 yi6]

definite *adj.* 確定 [kok8 ding6]

definitely *adv.* 確定 [kok8 ding6]

definition *n.* 定義 [ding6 yi6]

deforestation *n.* 砍伐森林 [ham2 fat9 sam1 lam4]

defrost *v.* 解凍 [gaai2 dung3]

degrease *v.* 除油污 [cheui4 yau4 wu1]

degree *n.* 學位 [hok9 wai6]

delay *n./v.* 延遲 [yin4 chi4]

delayed *adj.* 遲咗 [chi4 jo2]

delegate *n.* 代表 [doi6 biu2]; *v.* 授權 [sau6 kyun4]

delete *v.* 刪除 [saan1 cheui4], ~ **a file** 刪除文件; ~ **key** 消除鍵

deli *n.* 熟食店 [suk9 sik9 dim3]

deliberate *adj.* 故意 [gu3 yi3]

deliberately *adv.* 故意 [gu3 yi3]

delicacies *n.* 精緻 [jing1 ji3]

delicate *adj.* 精緻 [jing1 ji3]

delicatessen (deli) *n.* 熟食店 [suk9 sik9 dim3]

delicious *adj.* 好味 [hou2 mei6]

deity *n.* 神 [san4]

delight *n.* 開心 [hoi1 sam1]; *v.* 令人開心 [ling4 yan4 hoi1 sam1]

delighted *adj.* 開心 [hoi1 sam1]

delirious *adj.* 精神混亂 [jing1 san4 wan6 lyun6]

deliver *v.* 送貨 [sung3 fo3]

delivery *n.* 送貨上門 [sung3 fo3 seung5 mun2]; ~ **room** 傳達室

demand *n./v.* 要求 [yiu1 kau4]

democracy *n.* 民主 [man4 jyu2]

demonstrate *v.* 顯示 [hin2 si6]

demonstration *n.* 示威 [si6 wai1]

denim *n.* 牛仔布 [ngau4 jai2 bou3]

Denmark *n.* 丹麥 [daan1 mak9]

density *n.* 密度 [mat9 dou6]

dental *n.* 牙科 [nga4 fo1]

dental floss *n.* 牙線 [nga4 sin3]

dentist *n.* 牙醫 [nga4 yi1]

dentures *n.* 補牙 [bou2 nga4]

deny *v.* 否認 [fau2 ying6]

deodorant *n.* 清新劑 [ching1 san1 jai1]

depart *v.* 出發 [cheut7 faat8]

department store *n.* 百貨公司 [baak8 fo3 gung1 si1]

departure *n.* 出發 [cheut7 faat8]

depend (~ on) *v.* 依賴 [yi1 laai6]

dependent *adj.* 被撫養人 [bei6 fu2 yeung5 yan4]

depending on *prep.* 睇 [tai2]

depict *v.* 描述 [miu4 seut9]

deposit *n.* 存款 [chyun4 fun2]; *v.* 存款 [chyun4 fun2], ~ **money** 存錢

deposition *n.* 證供 [jing3 gung1]

depot *n.* 倉庫 [chong1 fu3]

depreciation *n.* 貶值 [bin2 jik9]

depress *v.* 令… 抑鬱 [ling4 … yik7 wat7]

depressed *adj.* 抑鬱 [yik7 wat7]

depressing *adj.* 令人好抑鬱 [ling yan4 hou2 yik7 wat7]

depression *n.* 抑鬱 [yik7 wat7]

depth *n.* 深度 [sam1 dou6]

derivative *n.* 導數 [dou6 sou3]

derive *v.* 來自 [loi4 ji6]

de-scale (~ a fish) *v.* 去鱗 [heui3 leun4]

describe *v.* 描述 [miu4 seut9]

description *n.* 描述 [miu4 seut9]

desert *n.* 沙漠 [sa1 mok9]; *v.* 拋棄 [paau1 hei3]

deserted *adj.* 拋棄咗 [paau1 hei3 jo2]

deserve *v.* 應得 [ying1 dak7]

design *n./v.* 設計 [chit8 gai3]

designed *adj.* 有計劃 [yau5 gai3 waak9]

designer *n.* 設計師 [chit8 gai3 si1]

desire *n.* 渴望 [hot8 mong6]; *v.* 好想要 [hou2 seung2 yiu3]

desk *n.* 書枱 [syu1 toi2]

desperate *adj.* 迫切 [bik7 chit8]

desperately *adv.* 迫切 [bik7 chit8]

despicable *adj.* 卑鄙 [bei1 pei2]

despite *prep.* 就算 [jau6 syun3]

dessert *n.* 甜品 [tim4 ban2]; ~ **course** 甜品, ~ **wine** 甜酒

destination *n.* 目的地 [muk9 dik7 dei6]

destroy *v.* 破壞 [po3 waai6]

destroyed *adj.* 破壞咗 [po3 waai6 jo2]

destruction *n.* 破壞 [po3 waai6]

detach *v.* 拆開 [chaak8 hoi1]

detail *n.* 細節 [sai3 jit8]

detailed *adj.* 詳細 [cheung4 sai3]

detect *v.* 察覺 [chaat8 gok8]

detective *n.* 偵探 [jing1 taam3]; ~ **novels** 偵探小說

detergent *n.* 洗碗液 [sai2 wun2 yik9]

determination *n.* 決心 [kyut8 sam1]

determine *v.* 下定決心 [ha6 ding6 kyut8 sam1]

determined *adj.* 堅決 [gin1 kyut8]

detour *n.* 繞路 [yiu2 lou6]

develop *v.* 發展 [faat8 jin2], ~ **film** 沖膠卷

development *n.* 發展 [faat8 jin2]

device *n.* 儀器 [yi4 hei3]

devil *n.* 魔鬼 [mo1 gwai2]

deviled eggs *n.* 芥末蛋 [gaai3 mut9 daan2]

devote *v.* 獻畀 [hin3 bei2]

devoted *adj.* 忠誠 [jung1 sing4]

devour *v.* 狼吞虎嚥 [long4 tan1 fu2 yin3]

Dhaka *n.* 達卡 [daat9 ka1]; ~, **capital of Bangladesh** 孟加拉首都

diabetes *n.* 糖尿病 [tong4 niu6 beng6]

diabetic *adj.* 糖尿病 [tong4 niu6 beng6]; *n.* 糖尿病患者 [tong4 niu6 beng6 waan6 je2]

diagnose *v.* 診斷 [chan2 dyun6]

diagnosis *n.* 診斷 [chan2 dyun6]

diagram *n.* 圖表 [tou4 biu2]

dial *v.* 撥 [but9]

dial tone *n.* 撥號音 [but9 hou6 yam1]

dialing code *n.* 區號 [keui1 hou6]

dialect *n.* 方言 [fong1 yin4]

dialogue *n.* 對話 [deui3 wa2], **memorize** ~ 記住對話

diameter *n.* 直徑 [jik9 ging3]

diamond *n.* 鑽石 [jyun3 sek9]

diaper *n.* 尿片 [niu6 pin2], ~ **rash** 尿布疹, **change a** ~ 換尿布

diaphragm *n.* 快門 [faai3 mun4]

diarrhea *n.* 肚屙 [tou5 ngo1]; **have** ~ 肚屙

diary *n.* 日記 [yat9 gei3]

dice *n.* 骰 [sik7], **roll the** ~ 掟骰仔 // *v.* 玩骰 [waan2 sik7]; ~**d** 切成丁

dictate *v.* 指定 [ji2 ding6]

dictionary *n.* 字典 [ji6 din2]

die *v.* 死 [sei2]

diesel *n.* 柴油 [chaai4 yau4]

diesel motor *n.* 柴油發動機 [chaai4 yau4 faat8 dung6 gei1]

diet *n.* 日常飲食 [yat9 seung4 yam2 sik9]; *v.* 減肥 [gaam2 fei4], **be on a** ~ 減肥; ~ **menu** 減肥餐

dietary *adj.* 飲食 [yam2 sik9] ~ **fiber** 食用纖維, ~ **supplements** 飲食補品, ~ **restrictions** 飲食限制

dieter *n.* 減肥嘅人 [gaam2 fei4 ge3 yan4]

differ *v.* 唔同 [m4 tung4]

difference *n.* 分別 [fan1 bit9]

different *adj.* 唔同 [m4 tung4]

differently *adv.* 唔同 [m4 tung4]

difficult *adj.* 難 [naan4]

difficulty *n.* 困難 [kwan3 naan4]

dig *v.* 掘 [gwat9]

digest *v.* 消化 [siu1 fa3]

digestive system *n.* 消化系統 [siu1 fa3 hai6 tung2]

digital *adj.* 數碼 [sou3 ma5]

Dili *n.* 帝力 [dai3 lik9]; ~, **capital of East Timor (Timor-Leste)** 東帝汶首都

dill *n.* 小茴香 [siu1 wui4 heung1], ~ **pickles** 小茴香酸果, ~ **seasoning** 小茴香調味品

dilute *v.* 沖淡 [chung1 taam5]; ~**d** *adj.* 稀釋咗

dim sum *n.* 點心 [dim2 sam1]

dimension *n.* 尺寸 [chek8 chyun3]

dine *v.* 食飯 [sik9 faan6]

diner *n.* 餐館仔 [chaan1 gun2 jai2]

dining *n.* 食飯 [sik9 faan6]; ~ **car** 餐車, ~ **out** 出去食飯

dining room *n.* 飯廳 [faan6 teng1]

dinner *n.* 正餐 [jing3 chaan1]; ~ **plate** 大盤, ~ **set** 晚餐套餐

dip *v.* 浸 [jam3]; *n.* 汁 [jap7]; (*sauce*) 點醬, **french** ~ 法國點肉汁

diplomat *n.* 外交官 [ngoi6 gaau1 gun1]

direct *adj.* 直接 [jik9 jip8]; *v.* 指路 [ji2 lou6], ~ **traffic** 指揮交通, ~ **a movie** 導演電影

direct flight *n.* 直飛 [jik9 fei1]

direction *n.* 方向 [fong1 heung3]; **in the** ~ **of** 沿著...方向

directions *n.* 方位 [fong1 wai2]

directive *n.* 指令 [ji2 ling4]

directly *adv.* 直接 [jik9 hip8]

director *n.* 董事 [dung2 si6]; ~ **of a company/university/film** 公司董事 / 大學主任 / 電影導演

directory *n.* 電話簿 [din6 wa2 bou6], **telephone** ~ 電話簿

directory assistance *n.* 查詢服務 [cha4 seun1 fuk9 mou6]

dirt *n.* 塵 [chan4]

dirty *adj.* 邋遢 [laat9 taat8]

disabled *adj.* 殘疾 [chaan4 jat9]

disabled person *n.* 殘疾人士 [chaan4 jat9 yan4 si6]

disability *n.* 冇能力 [mou4 nang4 lik9]

disadvantage *n.* 唔好 [m4 hou2]

disagree *v.* 唔同意 [m4 tung4 yi3]

disagreement *n.* 唔認同 [m4 ying6 tung4]

disappear *v.* 唔見咗 [m4 gin3 jo2]

disappoint *v.* 令...失望 [ling4 ... sat7 mong6]

disappointed *adj.* 失望 [sat7 mong6]

disappointing *adj.* 令人失望 [ling4 yan4 sat7 mong6]

disappointment *n.* 失望 [sat7 mong6]

disapprove (of) *v.* 唔批准 [m4 pai1 jeun2]

disapproving *adj.* 不滿 [bat7 mun5]

disaster *n.* 災難 [joi1 naan6]

disbarment (*legal*) *n.* 取消律師資格 [cheui2 siu1 leut9 si1 ji1 gaak8]

disc *n.* 唱片 [cheung3 pin2]

discharge *n.* 排出嘅野 [paai4 cheut7 ge3 ye5]; *v.* 排放 [paai4 fong3]

discharged *adj.* 卸貨 [se3 fo3]

discipline *n.* 紀律 [gei2 leut9]

disclose *v.* 披露 [pei1 lou6]

disclosure *n.* 披露 [pei1 lou6]

disco / discotheque *n.* 舞廳 [mou5 teng1]

discount *n.* 打折 [da2 jit8], **youth/children's ~** 兒童折扣, **senior ~** 老年折扣, **~ store** 打折店, **percent ~** 幾折

discourse *n.* 討論 [tou2 leun6]

discover *v.* 發現 [faat8 yin6]

discovered *adj.* 撞見 [jong6 gin3]

discovery *n.* 發現 [faat8 yin6]

discrimination *n.* 歧視 [kei4 si6]

discuss *v.* 討論 [tou2 leun6]

discussion *n.* 討論 [tou2 leun6]

disease *n.* 病 [beng6]

disgust *v./n.* 反感 [faan2 gam2]

disgusted *adj.* 覺得反感 [gok8 dak7 faan2 gam2]

disgusting *adj.* 令人反感 [ling4 yan4 faan2 gam2]

dish *n.* (*plate*) 碟 [dip9], (*meal*) 餐碟; **~ cover** 碟蓋, **~ rack** 碗架

dish towel *n.* 洗碗布 [sai2 wun2 bou3]

dishes *n.* 菜 [choi3] **wash the ~** 洗碗

dishonest *adj.* 唔老實 [m4 lou5 sat9]

dishonestly *adv.* 唔老實 [m4 lou5 sat9]

dishwasher *n.* 洗碗機 [sai2 wun2 gei1] **~ proof** 可放入洗碗機

dishwashing liquid/soap *n.* 洗碗機用洗碗液 [sai2 wun2 gei1 yung6 sai2 wun2 yik9]

disinfect *n.* 消毒 [siu1 duk9]

disk *n.* 唱片 [cheung3 pin2]

dislike *v.* 憎 [jang1]; *n.* 討厭 [tou2 yim3]

dislocated *adj.* 脫位 [tyut8 wai2]

dismiss *v.* 炒魷魚 [chaau2 yau4 yu2]

dismissal *n.* 炒魷魚 [chaau2 yau4 yu2]

disorder *n.* 亂 [lyun6]

display *v.* 顯示 [hin2 si6]; *n.* 展覽 [jin2 laam5]; **~ case** 展覽箱

disposable *adj.* 一次性 [yat7 chi3 sing3], **~ camera** 一次性相機, **~ diapers** 一次性尿片

disposal *n.* 處理 [chyu3 lei5]

dispute *n./v.* 討論 [tou2 leun6]

dissolve *v.* 溶解 [yung4 gaai2]; **~ in water** 可水中溶解

distance *n.* 距離 [keui5 lei4]; **keep your ~** 唔好再行近

distant *adj.* 好遠 [hou2 yun5]

distill *v.* 蒸餾 [jing1 lau6]

distillation *n.* 蒸餾 [jing1 lau6]

distilled *adj.* 蒸餾 [jing1 lau6], **~ water** 蒸餾水, **~ vinegar** 蒸醋

distinct *adj.* 明顯 [ming4 hin2]

distinction *n.* 榮譽 [wing4 yu6]

distinctive *adj.* 與眾不同 [yu5 jung3 bat7 tung4]

distinguish *v.* 區分 [keui1 fan1]

distribute *v.* 分發 [fan1 faat8]

distribution *n.* 分布 [fan1 bou3]

distributor *n.* 批發商 [pai1 faat8 seung1]

district *n.* 行政區 [hang4 jing3 keui1]

disturb *v.* 騷擾 [sou1 yiu2], **do not ~** 請勿打擾, **~ the peace** 破壞平靜

disturbing *adj.* 煩 [faan4]

diuretic *n.* 利尿 [lei6 niu6]; **~ supplement** 利尿劑

dive *n./v.* 潛水 [chim4 seui2]

divide *v.* 分 [fan1]

dividend *n.* 紅利 [hung4 lei6]

diving *n.* 潛水 [chim4 seui2]; **no ~** 禁止潛水, **~ equipment** 潛水設備

diving board *n.* 跳板 [tiu3 baan2]

division *n.* 隔開 [gaak8 hoi1]

divorce *n./v.* 離婚 [lei4 fan1]

divorced *adj.* 離婚 [lei4 fan1]

dizzy *adj.* 頭暈 [tau4 wan4]; **feel ~** 覺得好暈

Djibouti *n.* 吉布提 [gat7 bou3 tai4]; **~, capital of Djibouti** 吉布提首都

DNA (deoxyribonucleic acid) *n.* 基因 [gei1 yan1]

do *aux v.* 做 [jou6]

dock *n.* 碼頭 [ma5 tau4]; *v.* 停靠碼頭 **[ting4 kaau3 ma5 tau4]**

docket *n.* 記事表 [gei3 si6 biu2]

doctor (*abbr.* Dr.) *n.* 醫生 [yi1 sang1]

doctor's office *n.* 診所 [chan2 so2]

document (.doc file) *n.* 文件 [man4 gin2]

documentary film *n.* 紀錄片 [gei2 luk9 pin2]

dog *n.* 狗 [gau2]

dogfish *n.* 角鯊 [gok8 sa1]

Doha *n.* 多哈 [do1 ha1]; **~, capital of Qatar** 卡塔爾首都

do-it-yourself (*abbr.* DIY) *adj.* 自己哪手 [ji6 gei2 yuk7 sau2]

doll *n.* 木偶 [muk9 ngau5]

dollar *n.* 美金 [mei5 gam1]

domain *n.* 領土 [ling5 tou2]

dome *n.* 圓頂 [yun4 deng2]

domestic *adj.* 國內 [gwok8 noi6]

dominant *adj.* 佔支配地位 [jim3 ji1 pui3 dei6 wai6]

dominate *v.* 話事 [wa6 si6]

Dominica *n.* 多米尼加 [do1 mai5 nei4 ga1]

Dominican *adj.* 多米尼加 [do1 mai5 nei4 ga1]

Dominican Republic *n.* 多米尼加共和國 [do1 mai5 nei4 ga1 gung6 wo4 gwok8]

dominoes *n.* 多米諾骨牌 [do1 mai5 nok9 gwat7 paai2]

donate *v.* 捐 [gyun1]; **~d by** 由…捐贈, **~ blood** 捐血, **~ bone marrow** 捐骨髓, **~ an organ** 捐贈器官

donation *n.* 捐 [gyun1]

donkey *n.* 驢 [leui4]

door *n.* 門 [mun4]

doorway *n.* 門口 [mun4 hau2]

dormitory *n.* 宿舍 [suk7 se3]

dosage *n.* 劑量 [jai1 leung6]

dose *n.* 劑量 [jai1 leung6], **recommended ~** 建議用量

dot *v.* 點綴 [sim2 jeui6], **to ~** 用小圓點標出; *n.* 圓點 [yun4 dim2], **a ~** 一個小圓點

dot-com *n.* 網絡公司 [mong5 lok8 gung1 si1]

double *adj./det./n.* 兩倍 [leung5 pui5], **~ bed** 雙人床, **~ room** 雙人房; *v.* 加倍 [ga1 pui5]

doubt *n./v.* 懷疑 [waai4 yi4]

dough *n.* 麵團 [min6 tyun4]; **cookie ~** 曲奇麵團

doughnut *n.* 冬甩 [dung1 lat7], **sprinkled ~** 糖粉冬甩, **glazed ~** 糖衣冬甩, **chocolate ~** 朱古力冬甩, **frosted ~** 糖霜冬甩, **plain ~** 原味冬甩

dove *n.* 鴿 [gap8]

down *adv.* 下面 [ha6 min6]; *prep.* 喺…下面 [hai2 … ha6 min6]

downhill skiing *n.* 高山滑雪 [gou1 saan1 waat9 syut8]

download *comp. v./n.* 下載 [ha6 joi3], **free ~** 免費下載, **~ a file** 下載文件

downloadable *comp. adj.* 可以下載 [ho2 yi5 ha6 joi3], **~ content** 可下載內容

downstairs *adv.* 落樓 [lok9 lau2]; *adj./n.* 樓下 [lau4 ha6]

downtown *adv.* 鬧市 [naau6 si5]

downward *adj./adv.* 向下 [heung3 ha6]

dowry *n.* 嫁妝 [ga3 jong1]

doze *v.* 瞌眼瞓 [hap9 ngaan5 fan3]

dozen *n./det.* 一打 [yat7 da1]

Dr. (*abbr. of* **doctor**) *n.* 醫生 [yi1 sang1]

draft *n./adj.* 草稿 [chou2 gou2], **~ beer** 生啤酒; *v.* 打草稿 [da2 chou2 gou2]; **get ~ed** 徵兵

drag *v.* 拖 [to1] *n.* 拖 [to1]

drag queen *n.* 男扮女裝 [naam4 baan3 neui5 jong1]

dragon fruit *n.* 火龍果 [fo2 lung4 gwo2]

drain *v.* 排水 [paai4 seui2]; *n.* 排水渠 [paai4 seui2 keui4]

drama *n.* 戲劇 [hei3 kek9]; **~ class** 戲劇課, **~ teacher** 戲劇老師

dramatic *adj.* 劇烈 [kek9 lit9]

dramatically *adv.* 劇烈 [kek9 lit9]

draw *v.* 畫畫 [waak9 wa2], **~ an object** 畫靜物, **~ a crowd** 引起圍觀

drawbridge *n.* 吊橋 [diu3 kiu4]

drawer *n.* 櫃桶 [gwai6 tung2]

drawing *n.* 畫畫 [waak9 wa2]

dream *n.* 夢 [mung6]; *v.* 發夢 [faat8 mung6]

dredge *v.* 挖泥 [waait8 nai4]

dredging *n.* 挖泥 [waait8 nai4]

dress *n.* 連身裙 [lin4 san1 kwan4]; *v.* 着衫 [jeuk8 saam1]; **~ code** 穿衣要求

dressed *adj.* 打扮好 [da2 baan3 hou2]; **~ in formal attire** 穿著正式

dressing *n.* 調味料 [tiu4 mei6 liu2], **Italian ~** 意式沙律醬, **French ~** 法式沙律醬, **honey mustard ~** 蜜糖芥末沙律醬, **balsamic ~** 香醋沙律醬, **ranch ~** 牧場沙律醬

dried *adj.* 乾 [gon1] **~ sausage** 乾腸, **~ fruit** 乾果, **~ meat** 肉乾

drink *v.* 飲 [yam2]; *n.* 飲品 [yam2 ban2]

drinkable water *n.* 食用水 [sik9 yung6 seui2]

drip *v.* 滴水 [dik7 seui2]

drip pan *n.* 油滴盤 [yau4 dik7 pun2]

drippings *n.* 油汁 [yau4 jap7]

drive *v.* 揸 [ja1]; *n.* 動力 [dung6 lik9]

driver *n.* 司機 [si1 gei1]

driver's license *n.* 駕駛執照 [ga3 sai2 jap7 jiu3]

driving *n.* 揸車 [ja1 che1]

drizzle *v.* 落毛毛雨 [lok9 mou4 mou4 yu5]

drop *v.* 落 [lok9], **~ someone off** 放低; *n.* 空投 [hung1 tau4]

drought *n.* 乾旱 [gon1 hon5]

drown *v.* 浸死 [jam3 sei2]; **be drowning** 沈緊

drowsy *adj.* 眼瞓 [ngaan5 fan3]

drug *n.* 毒品 [duk9 ban2], **take ~s** 吸食毒品, **pharmaceutical ~** 藥

drug dealer *n.* 毒販 [duk9 faan3]

drugstore *n.* 藥店 [yeuk9 dim3]

drum *n.* 鼓 [gu2] **play; the ~s** 打鼓

drunk *adj.* 醉咗 [jeui3 jo2]; **be ~** 飲醉

dry *adj.* 乾 [gon1]; *v.* 整乾 [jing2 gon1]

dry cleaner *n.* 乾洗店 [gon1 sai2 dim3] **dry-cleaning**

dryer *n.* 乾衣機 [gon1 yi1 gei1]

dubbed *adj.* 配音 [pui3 yam1]

Dublin *n.* 都柏林 [dou1 paak8 lam4]; **~, capital of Ireland** 愛爾蘭首都

duck *n.* 鴨 [aap8]; **wild ~** 野鴨

duck in orange *n.* 鴨橙 [aap8 chaang2]

due *adj.* 要交 [yiu3 gaau1]; **~ to** 因為

due process (*legal*) 法定訴訟程序 [faat8 ding6 sou3 jung6 ching4 jeui6]

dulce de leche *n.* 甜牛奶 [tim4 ngau4 naai5]

dull *adj.* 蠢 [cheun2]

dump *v.* 掟 [deng3]; *n.* 垃圾場 [laap9 saap8 cheung4]

dumpling *n.* 餃子 [gaau2 ji2]; **Chinese ~** 餃子, **meat ~** 肉餃, **vegetable ~** 素餃, **cheese ~** 芝士餃

durian *n.* 榴蓮 [lau4 lin4]

during *prep.* 期間 [kei4 gaan1]

Dushanbe *n.* 杜尚別 [dou6 seung6 bit9]; **~, capital of Tajikistan** 塔吉克斯坦首都

dust *v.* 抹塵 [maat8 chan4]; *n.* 塵 [chan4]; **~ing** 掃塵, **~ed** 掃過塵

Dutch *adj.* 荷蘭 [ho4 laan1]

duty *n.* 責任 [jaak8 yam6]

duty-free *adj.* 免稅 [min5 seui3], **~ goods** 免稅品, **~ shop** 免稅店

duvet *n.* 羽絨被 [yu5 yung2 pei5]

DVD *n.* 光碟 [gwong1 dip9]

dye *v.* 染 [yim5]; *n.* 染料 [yim5 liu2]

dying *adj.* 就快死 [jau6 faai3 sei2]

dynamic *adj.* 成日變 [sing4 yat9 bin3]

dynamite *n.* 炸藥 [ja3 yeuk9]

dynasty *n.* 朝代 [chiu4 doi6]

E

e.g. 例如 [lai6 yu4]

each *det./pron./adj.* 每個 [mui5 go3]

each other *pron.* 互相 [wu6 seung1]

ear *n.* 耳仔 [yi5 jai2]; **~ drops** 耳藥水

earache *n.* 耳仔痛 [yi5 jai2 tung3]; **have an ~** 耳仔痛

earlier *adj./adv.* 早啲 [jou2 di1]

early *adj./adv.* 早 [jou2]; **too ~** 太早

earn *v.* 賺 [jaan6]

earnings *n.* 收入 [sau1 yap9], **YTD ~** 今年到現在為止收入, **quarterly ~** 季度收入

earring *n.* 耳環 [yi5 waan4]

Earth (*planet*) *n.* 地球 [dei6 kau4]

earth (*soil*) *n.* 地 [dei6]

earthenware pot *n.* 沙鍋 [sa1 wo1]

earthquake *n.* 地震 [dei6 jan3]

ease *n.* 自由自在 [ji6 yau4 ji6 joi6]; *v.* 緩解 [wun6 gaai2]

easily *adv.* 容易 [yung4 yi6]

east *n./adj./adv.* 東面 [dung1 min6]

East Timor (Timor-Leste) *n.* 東帝汶 [dung1 dai3 man6]

Easter *n.* 復活節 [fuk9 wut9 jit8]; **Happy ~** 復活節快樂

eastern *adj./adv.* 東面 [dung1 min6]

easy *adj.* 容易 [yung4 yi6]

eat *v.* 食 [sik9]

echo *n.* 回音 [wui4 yam1]; *v.* 重複 [chung4 fuk7]

éclair *n.* 閃電 [sim2 din6]

eclipse *n.* 日蝕 [yat9 sik9]

economic *adj.* 抵 [dai2]

economics *n.* 經濟學 [ging1 jai3 hok9]

economist *n.* 經濟學家 [ging1 jai3 hok9 ga1]

economy *n.* 經濟 [ging1 jai3]; **~ class** 經濟艙

ecosystem *n.* 生態系統 [sang1 taai3 hai6 tung2]

Ecuador *n.* 厄瓜多爾 [ak7 gwa1 do1 yi5]

Ecuadorian *adj.* 厄瓜多爾 [ak7 gwa1 do1 yi5]

Edam cheese *n.* 伊頓芝士 [yi1 deun6 ji1 si6]

edamame *n.* 青豆 [cheng1 dau2]

edge *n.* 邊邊 [bin1 bin1]

edible *adj.* 食得 [sik9 dak7]; **non-~** 唔食得

edit *v.* 編輯 [pin1 chap7]

edition *n.* 版本 [baan2 bun2]

editor *n.* 編輯 [pin1 chap7]

educate *v.* 教育 [gaau3 yuk9]

educated *adj.* 有良好教育 [yau5 leung4 hou2 gaau3 yuk9]

education *n.* 教育 [gaau3 yuk9]

eel *n.* 鰻魚 [maan4 yu2], **smoked ~** 煙薰鰻魚, **live ~** 生鰻魚

effect *n.* 效果 [haau6 gwo2]

effective *adj.* 有效 [yau5 haau6]

effectively *adv.* 有效 [yau5 haau6]

effectiveness *n.* 有效 [yau5 haau6]

efficiency *n.* 效率 [haau6 leut9]

efficient *adj.* 有效率 [yau5 haau6 leut9]

efficiently *adv.* 有效率 [yau5 haau6 leut9]

effort *n.* 努力 [nou5 lik9]

egg *n.* 雞蛋 [gai1 daan2]; ~ **white** 蛋白, ~ **yolk** 蛋黃, ~ **beater** 打蛋器

eggplant *n.* 茄子 [ke2 ji2]

eglantine fruit *n.* 玫瑰果 [mui4 gwai3 gwo2]

ego *n.* 自我 [ji6 ngo5]

egotism *n.* 自負 [ji6 fu6]

Egypt *n.* 埃及 [oi1 kap9]

Egyptian *adj.* 埃及 [oi1 kap9]

eight *num.* 八 [baat8]

eighteen *num.* 十八 [sap9 baat8]

eighteenth *adj.* 第十八個 [dai6 sap9 baat8 go3]

eighth *adj.* 第八個 [dai6 baat8 go3]

eightieth *adj.* 第八十個 [dai6 baat8 sap9 go3]

eighty *num.* 八十 [baat8 sap9]

either *det./pron./adv.* 邊一個 [bin1 yat7 go3]

El Salvador *n.* 薩爾瓦多 [saat8 yi5 nga5 do1]

elaborate *adj.* 詳細講 [cheung4 sai3 gong2]

elastic *adj.* 有彈力 [yau5 daan6 lik9]

elbow *n.* 手踭 [sau2 jaang1]

elderberry *n.* 接骨木莓 [jip8 gwat7 muk9 mui2]

elderly *adj.* 上咗年紀 [seung5 jo2 nin4 gei2]

elect *v.* 選 [syun2]

election *n.* 選舉 [syun2 geui2]

elective *adj.* 選修 [syun2 sau1]

electorate *n.* 選民 [syun2 man4]

electric *adj.* 電動嘅 [din6 dung6 ge3], ~ **toothbrush** 電動牙刷, ~ **razor/shaver** 電動鬚刨

electrical *adj.* 電動嘅 [din6 dung6 ge3]

electrical outlet *n.* 插座 [chaap8 jo2]

electricity *n.* 電 [din6]

electrolytes *n.* 電解質 [din6 gaai2 jat7]

electron *n.* 電子 [din6 ji2]

electronic *adj.* 電子 [din6 ji2]

electronics *n.* 電子元件 [din6 ji2 yun4 gin2]

elegant *adj.* 優雅 [yau1 nga5]

element *n.* 元素 [yun4 sou3]

elevator *n.* 升降機 [sing1 gong3 gei1]

eleven *num.* 十一 [sap9 yat7]

eleventh *adj.* 第十一個 [dai6 sap9 yat7 go3]

elf *n.* 精靈 [jing1 ling4]

eliminate *v.* 懟冧 [deui2 lam3]

elixer *n.* 仙丹 [sin1 daan1]

elk *n.* 麋鹿 [mei4 luk2]

eloquence *n.* 口才 [hau2 choi4]

eloquent *adj.* 有口才 [yau5 hau2 choi4]

else *adv.* 其他 [kei4 ta1]

elsewhere *adv.* 喺其他地方 [hai2 kei4 ta1 dei6 fong1]

e-mail *n.* 電子郵件 [din6 ji2 yau4 gin2]; *v.* 發電子郵件 [faat8 din6 ji2 yau4 gin2]

emancipation *n.* 解放 [gaai2 fong3]

embarrass v. 令…尷尬 [ling4 … gaam1 gaai3]

embarrassed adj. 覺得尷尬 [gok8 dak7 gaam1 gaai3]

embarrassing adj. 令人尷尬 [ling4 yan4 gaam1 gaai3]

embarrassment n. 尷尬 [gaam1 gaai3]

embassy n. 大使館 [daai6 si3 gun2]

embed v. 整入 [jing2 yap9]

embrace v. 接受 [jip8 sau6]; n. 擁抱 [yung2 pou5]

embroidery n. 刺繡 [chi3 sau3]

embryo n. 胚胎 [pui1 toi1]

emerald n. 翡翠 [fei2 cheui3]

emerge v. 顯露 [hin2 lou6]

emergency n. 緊急情況 [gan2 gap7 ching4 fong3]; adj. 緊急情況 [gan2 gap7 ching4 fong3], ~ **medical services** 緊急醫療服務, ~ **brake** 緊急煞制, ~ **exit** 逃生出口

emergency room n. 急症室 [gap7 jing3 sat7]

emigration n. 搬去國外 [bun1 heui3 gwok8 ngoi6]

emissary n. 特使 [dak9 si3]

emission n. 排放 [paai4 fong3]

emotion n. 情緒 [ching4 seui5]

emotional adj. 情緒化 [ching4 seui5 fa3]

emotionally adv. 情緒化 [ching4 seui5 fa3]

emphasis n. 重點 [jung6 dim2]

emphasize v. 強調 [keung4 diu6]

empire n. 帝國 [dai3 gwok8]

employ v. 請 [cheng2]

employee n. 伙記 [fo2 gei3]

employer n. 老細 [lou5 sai3]; **equal opportunity** ~ 平等機會僱主

employment n. 份工 [fan6 gung1]; ~ **office** 職業介紹所

empress n. 皇后 [wong4 hau6]

empty adj. 空嘅 [hung1 ge3]; v. 清空 [ching1 hung1]

emptying n. 倒晒 [dou2 saai3]

emulsion n. 乳液 [yu5 yik9]

enable v. 令…可以 [ling4 … ho2 yi5]

enamel n. 琺琅 [faat8 long4]

encased v. 包住 [baau1 jyu6]

enchilada n. 肉餡粟米卷 [yuk9 haam6 suk7 mai5 gyun2]

encounter v. 撞見 [jong6 gin3]; n. 衝突 [chung1 dat9]

encourage v. 鼓勵 [gu2 lai6]

encouragement n. 鼓勵 [gu2 lai6]

end n. 結局 [git8 guk9], **at the** ~ 最後, ~ **of construction** 建築完成; v. 結束 [git8 chuk7]

endangered species n. 瀕臨滅絕物種 [pan4 lam4 mit9 jyut9 mat9 jung2]; ~ **list** 瀕臨滅絕物種列表, ~ **rank** 瀕臨滅絕物種種類

ending n. 結局 [git8 guk9]

endive n. 苦苣 [fu2 geui6]

enemy n. 敵人 [dik9 yan4]

energy n. 活力 [wut9 lik9]

engage v. 從事 [chung4 si6]

engaged adj. 訂婚 [ding3 fan1]

engagement n. 訂婚 [ding3 fan1]

engine n. 發動機 [faat8 dung6 gei1]

engineer n. 工程師 [gung1 ching4 si1]

engineering *n.* 土木工程 [tou2 muk9 gung1 ching4]

England *n.* 英國 [ying1 gwok8]

English *adj.* 英文 [ying1 man2]

English language *n.* 英文 [ying1 man2]; ~ **spoken** 講英文, **in ~** 用英語

English-speaking *adj.* 講英文 [gong2 ying1 man2]

engraving *n.* 雕刻 [diu1 haak7]

engross *v.* 全神貫注 [cyun4 san4 gun3 jyu3]

engulf *v.* 吞沒 [tan1 mut9]

enhance *v.* 提高 [tai4 gou1]

enhanced *adj.* 放大 [fong3 daai6]

enjoy *v.* 享受 [heung2 sau6], ~ **oneself** 開心; **Enjoy your meal!** *phr.* 食得開心！ [sik9 dak7 hoi1 sam1]

enjoyable *adj.* 玩得開心 [waan2 dak7 hoi1 sam1]

enjoyment *n.* 開心 [hoi1 sam1]

enlarge *v.* 放大 [fong3 daai6]

enmity *n.* 敵意 [dik9 yi3]

enormous *adj.* 超大 [chiu1 daai6]

enough *det./pron./adv.* 夠 [gau3]

ensure *v.* 擔保 [daam1 bou2]

enter *v.* 入 [yap9]; *comp.* **hit ~** 按回車鍵

enterprise *n.* 企業 [kei5 yip9]

entertain *v.* 招待 [jiu1 doi6]

entertainer *n.* 藝人 [ngai6 yan4]

entertaining *adj.* 好玩 [hou2 waan2]

entertainment *n.* 娛樂 [yu4 lok9]

enthusiasm *n.* 熱情 [yit9 ching4]

enthusiastic *adj.* 熱情 [yit9 ching4]

enticing *adj.* 吸引 [kap7 yan5]

entire *adj.* 成個 [sing4 go3]

entirely *adv.* 徹底 [chit8 dai2]

entitle *v.* 俾 [bei2]

entrance *n.* 入口 [yap9 hau2]

entrapment *n.* 誘捕 [yau5 bou6]

entree *n.* 主菜 [jyu2 choi3]

entomology *n.* 昆蟲學 [kwan1 chung4 hok9]

entry *n.* 進入 [jeun3 yap9]

entry visa *n.* 入境簽證 [yap9 ging2 chim1 jing3]

envelope *n.* 信封 [seun3 fung1]

environment *n.* 環境 [waan4 ging2]

environmental *adj.* 周圍 [jau1 wai4]

environs *n.* 郊區 [gaau1 keui1]

enzymes *n.* 酵 [haau1]

epicure *n.* 美食家 [mei5 sik9 ga1]

epidemic *n.* 流行病 [lau4 hang4 beng6]

epileptic *adj.* 癲癇症患者 [din1 gaan4 jing3 waan6 je2]

episode *n.* 一集 [yat7 jaap9]

epoch *n.* 時代 [si4 doi6]

equal *adj./n.* 公平 [gung1 ping4]; *v.* 等於 [dang2 yu1]

equal rights *n.* 權利平等 [kyun4 lei6 ping4 dang2]

equality *n.* 平等 [ping4 dang2]

equally *adv.* 平等 [ping4 dang2]

equation *n.* 等式 [dang2 sik7]

Equatorial Guinea *n.* 赤道幾內亞 [chek8 dou6 gei1 noi6 a3]

equilibrium *n.* 均衡 [gwan1 hang4]

equipment *n.* 器材 [hei3 choi4]

equity *n.* 公平 [gung1 ping4]

equivalent *adj.* 相等 [seung1 dang2]; *n.* 對等物 [deui3 dang2 mat9]

era *n.* 時代 [si4 doi6]

eradicate *v.* 鏟除 [chaan2 cheui4]

erected *adj.* 豎起 [syu6 hei2]

Eritrea *n.* 厄立特里亞 [ak7 laap9 dak9 lei5 a3]

erotic *adj.* 色情 [sik7 ching4]

error *n.* 錯誤 [cho3 ng6]

escalator *n.* 扶手電梯 [fu4 sau2 din6 tai1]

escallope *n.* 魚片 [yu4 pin2]

escape *v./n.* 走甩 [jau2 lat7]; ~ **key** (*on computer*) 退出鍵

escrow *n.* 保管 [bou2 gun2]

especially *adv.* 特別 [dak9 bit9]

espresso *n.* 濃縮咖啡 [nung4 suk7 ga3 fe1]

essay *n.* 文章 [man4 jeung1]

essence *n.* 精華 [jing1 wa4], **almond** ~ 杏仁精華素, **tomato** ~ 番茄精華素, **vanilla** ~ 香草精華素, **citrus** ~ 西柚精華素

essential *adj.* 必要 [bit7 yiu3]; *n.* 必需品 [bit7 seui1 ban2]

essentially *adv.* 根本上 [gan1 bun2 seung6]

establish *v.* 建立 [gin3 laap9]

establishment *n.* 建立 [gin3 laap9]

estate *n.* 財產 [choi4 chaan2]

estimate *n.* 估價 [gu2 ga3]; *v.* 估計 [gu2 gai3]

Estonia *n.* 愛沙尼亞 [oi3 sa1 nei4 a3]

Estonian *adj.* 愛沙尼亞 [oi3 sa1 nei4 a3]

et al. *abbr.* 等等 [dang2 dang2]

etc. (*abbr.* of et cetera) 等等 [dang2 dang2]

etching *n.* 蝕刻版畫 [sik9 hak7 baan2 wa2]

ethical *adj.* 道德 [dou6 dak7], ~ **practices** 道德實踐, ~ **treatment** 有道德的對待

ethics *n.* 道德 [dou6 dak7]

ethnic *adj.* 民族嘅 [man4 juk9 ge3]

Ethiopia *n.* 埃塞俄比亞 [aai1 choi3 ngo4 bei2 a3]

Ethiopian *adj.* 埃塞俄比亞 [aai1 choi3 ngo4 bei2 a3]

etiquette *n.* 禮數 [lai5 sou3]

EU *abbr.*, *see* **European Union**

eunuch *n.* 太監 [taai3 gaam3]

euro *n.* 歐元 [au1 yun4]

Europe *n.* 歐洲 [au1 jau1]

European *adj.* 歐洲人 [au1 jau1 yan4]

European Union *n.* 歐盟 [au1 mang4], ~ **country** 歐盟國家, ~ **citizen** 歐盟公民

evacuate *v.* 疏散 [so1 saan3]

evaluate *v.* 評估 [ping4 gu2]

evaluation *n.* 評估 [ping4 gu2]

evaporated *adj.* 蒸發 [jing1 faat8] ~ **milk** 煉奶, ~ **alchohol** 蒸酒

even *adv.* 甚至 [sam6 ji3]; *adj.* 平均 [ping4 gwan1]

evening *n.* 黃昏 [wong4 fan1], **good** ~ 晚安, **this** ~ 今晚, ~ **service** 晚上禮拜服務

event *n.* 事情 [si6 ching4]

eventually *adv.* 終於 [jung1 yu1]

ever *adv.* 從來 [chung4 loi4]

evergreen *n.* 常青樹 [seung4 ching1 syu6]

everlasting *adj.* 永恆 [wing5 hang4]

every *adj./det.* 個個 [go3 go3], ~ **day** 每日, ~ **hour** 每個鐘, ~ **week** 每個星期, ~ **year** 每年

everybody *pron.* 個個人 [go3 go3 yan4]

everyday *adj.* 每日 [mui5 yat9]

everyone *pron.* 個個人 [go3 go3 yan4]

everything *pron.* 所有 [so2 yau5]

everywhere *adv.* 處處 [chyu3 chyu3]

evidence *n.* 證據 [jing3 geui3]

evident *adj.* 明顯 [ming4 hin2]

evil *adj.* 罪惡 [jeui6 ok8]; *n.* 魔鬼 [mo1 gwai2]

evict *v.* 趕走 [gon2 jau2]

eviction *n.* 趕走 [gon2 jau2]

evolution *n.* 進化 [jeun3 fa3]

evolutionary *adj.* 進化 [jeun3 fa3]

evolve *v.* 進化 [jeun3 fa3]

ex- *prefix* 前任 [chin4 yam4]

exact *adj.* 準確 [jeun2 kok8], ~ **amount** 準確用量, ~ **change** 準確找錢

exactly *adv.* 完全 [yun4 chyun4]

exaggerate *v.* 誇大 [kwa1 daai6]

exaggerated *adj.* 誇大 [kwa1 daai6]

exam *n.* 考試 [haau2 si3]

examination *n.* 考試 [haau2 si3]

examine *v.* 仔細檢查 [ji2 sai3 gim2 cha4]

example *n.* 例子 [lai6 ji2]; **for** ~ 例如

exceed *v.* 超過 [chiu1 gwo3]

excellent *adj.* 厲害 [lai6 hoi6]

except *prep./conj.* 除咗 [cheui4 jo2]

exception *n.* 例外 [lai6 ngoi6]

excess *n./adj.* 過量 [gwo3 leung6], ~ **baggage** 行李過重

exchange *v./n.* 交換 [gaau1 wun6], ~ **a purchase** 替換

exchange office *n.* 外匯局 [ngoi6 wui6 guk9]

exchange rate *n.* 匯率 [wui6 leut9]

excite *v.* 刺激 [chi3 gik7]

excited *adj.* 興奮 [hing1 fan5]

excitement *n.* 興奮 [hing1 fan5]

exciting *adj.* 令人興奮 [ling4 yan4 hing1 fan5]

exclamation *n.* 大叫 [daai6 giu3]

exclamation point *n.* 感歎號 [gam3 taan3 hou6]

exclude *v.* 排除 [paai4 cheui4]

excluding *prep.* 排除 [paai4 cheui4]

exclusive *adj.* 專用 [jyun1 yung6]

exclusively *adv.* 獨家 [duk9 ga1]

excursion *n.* 遠足 [yun5 juk7]

excuse *v.* 原諒 [yun4 leung6]; *n.* 藉口 [jik9 hau2]; ~ **me** 唔好意思

executive *n.* 總經理 [jung2 ging1 lei5]; *adj.* 執行 [jap7 hang4]

exemption *n.* 免除 [min5 cheui4]

exercise *n./v.* 練習 [lin6 jaap9]

exhaust *v.* 耗盡 [hou3 jeun6]

exhaust pipe *n.* 排氣管 [paai4 hei3 gun2]

exhausted *adj.* 好攰 [hou2 gui6]

exhibit *v./n.* 展覽 [jin2 laam5]

exhibition *n.* 展覽 [jin2 laam5]

exist *v.* 存在 [chyun4 joi6]

existence *n.* 存在 [chyun4 joi6]

exit (*from a highway/truck/vehicles*) *n.* 出口 [cheut7 hau2]

exonerate v. 宣佈無罪 [syun1 bou3 mou4 jeui6]

exotic adj. 外來 [ngoi6 loi4]

expand v. 擴展 [kong3 jin2]

expansion n. 膨脹 [paang4 jeung3]

expect v. 想 [seung2]

expectation n. 期望 [kei4 mong6]

expected adj. 估到 [gu2 dou2]

expenditure n. 費用 [fai3 yung6]

expense n. 費用 [fai3 yung6]

expensive adj. 貴 [gwai3]

experience n. 經驗 [ging1 yim6]; v. 經歷 [ging1 lik9]

experienced adj. 有經驗 [yau5 ging1 yim6]

experiment n./v. 試驗 [si3 yim6]

experimental adj. 試驗 [si3 yim6]

expert n. 專家 [jyun1 ga1]; adj. 老手 [lou5 sau2]

expertise n. 專業技能 [jyun1 yip9 gei6 nang4]

expiration date n. 有效日期 [yau5 haau6 yat9 kei4]

expire v. 過期 [gwo3 kei4]

explain v. 解釋 [gaai2 sik7]

explanation n. 解釋 [gaai2 sik7]

explode v. 爆炸 [baau3 ja3]

exploit n. 功勞 [gung1 lou4], **~s of smne** 事跡; v. 剝削 [mok7 seuk8]

exploitation n. 剝削 [mok7 seuk8]

exploration n. 探險 [taam3 him2]

explore v. 探索 [taam3 sok8]

explosion n. 爆炸 [baau3 ja3]

export v./n. 出口 [cheut7 hau2]; comp. **~ a file** 輸出

expose v. 公開 [gung1 hoi1]

exposure n. 公開 [gung1 hoi1]

express v. 表示 [biu2 si6]; adj. 快車 [faai3 che1], **~ checkout** 快速退房

express mail n. 快件 [faai3 gin6]

express train n. 快車 [faai3 che1]

expression n. 表達 [biu2 daat9]

expressway n. 高速路 [gou1 chuk7 lou6]

expressway entrance n. 高速路入口 [gou1 chuk7 lou6 yap9 hau2]

expunge v. 擦 [chaat8]

extend v. 延伸 [yin4 san1]

extension n. 分機 [fan1 gei1]; **~ cord** 延長電線

extensive adj. 全面 [chyun4 min6]

extent n. 程度 [ching4 dou6]

external adj. 外面 [ngoi6 min6]

extra adj./adv. 額外 [ngaak9 ngoi6]; n. 臨記 [lam4 gei3]

extract n. 濃縮 [nung4 suk7], **orange ~** 濃縮橙汁, **vanilla ~** 濃縮香草汁, **fruit ~** 濃縮果汁; v. 提取 [tai4 cheui2]

extraordinary adj. 厲害 [lai6 hoi6]

extreme adj. 極端 [gik9 dyun1]; n. 困境 [kwan3 ging2]

extremely adv. 極端 [gik9 dyun1]

eye n. 眼 [ngaan5]; **~ test** 視力測試

eyeball n. 眼球 [ngaan5 kau4]

eyeglasses n. 眼鏡 [ngaan5 geng3]

eyelash n. 眼睫毛 [ngaan5 jit9 mou4]

eyelet n. 針眼 [jam1 ngaan5]

eyewash n. 洗眼水 [sai2 ngaan5 seui2]

F

fabric *n.* 布料 [bou3 liu2]

fabricate *v.* 偽造 [ngai6 jou6]

face *n.* 面 [min2]; *v.* 面對 [min2 deui3]

facial *n.* (*beauty treatment*) 面部 [min6 bou6]; **~ features** 面部特徵

facilities *n.* 設施 [chit8 si1]

facility *n.* 設備 [chit8 bei6]

fact *n.* 事實 [si6 sat9]

factor *n.* 因素 [yan1 sou3]

factory *n.* 工廠 [gung1 chong2]

fahrenheit *n.* 華氏 [wa4 si6]

fail *v.* 衰咗 [seui1 jo2]

failure *n.* 失敗 [sat7 baai6]

faint *adj.* 模糊 [mou4 wu4]; *v.* 暈低 [wan4 dai1]; **feel ~** 暈

faintly *adv.* 有啲 [yau5 di1]

fair *adj.* 公平 [gung1 ping4]

fairground *n.* 露天市場 [lou6 tin1 si5 cheung4]

fairly *adv.* 幾 [gei2]

faith (*religion*) *n.* 信念 [seun3 nim6]

faithful *adj.* 忠誠 [jung1 sing4]

faithfully *adv.* 忠誠 [jung1 sing4]

falafel *n.* 法拉非 [faat8 laai1 fei1]

falcon *n.* 獵鷹 [lip9 ying1]

fall 1. *v.* 跌落嚟 [dit8 lok9 lei4], **~ over/down** 跌落嚟, **~ apart** 散咗 // **2.** (*season*) *n.* 秋天 [chau1 tin1]

fallacy *n.* 謬論 [mau6 leun6]

false *adj.* 假嘅 [ga2 ge3]

fame *n.* 出名 [cheut7 meng2]

familiar *adj.* 熟 [suk9]

family *n.* 家庭 [ga1 ting4]; *adj.* 全家人嘅 [chyun4 ga1 yan4 ge3]

famous *adj.* 出名 [cheut7 meng2]

fan (*admirer*) *n.* 迷 [mai4]

fan belt *n.* 風扇皮帶 [fung1 sin3 pei4 daai2]

fancy *v.* 幻想 [waan6 seung2]; *adj.* 奢侈 [che1 chi2]

fantastic *adj.* 十分之好 [sap9 fan1 ji1 hou2]

fantasy *n.* 幻想 [waan6 seung2]

far *adv./adj.* 遠 [yun5]; **how ~?** 有幾遠?

fare *n.* 票價 [piu3 ga3]

farm *n.* 農場 [nung4 cheung4]

farm-fresh *adj.* 生鮮 [saang1 sin1]

farm-grown *adj.* 農場大嘅 [nung4 cheung4 daai6 ge3]

farmer *n.* 農民 [nung4 man4]

farming *n.* 耕田 [gaang1 tin4]

far-sighted *adj.* 有遠見 [yau5 yun5 gin3]

farther, farthest *adj.* 遠啲 [yun5 di1]

fascinate *v.* 神魂顛倒 [san4 wan4 din1 dou2]

fascinated *adj.* 神魂顛倒 [san4 wan4 din1 dou2]

fascinating *adj.* 吸引人 [kap7 yan5 yan4]

fascination *n.* 神魂顛倒 [san4 wan4 din1 dou2]

fashion *n.* 時尚 [si4 seung6]

fashionable *adj.* 時尚 [si4 seung6]

fast *adj./adv.* 快 [faai3], **to be ~** 快

fast food *n.* 快餐 [faai3 chaan1]

fasten *v.* 扣好 [kau3 hou2]

fat *adj.* 肥 [fei4], **non~** 脫脂; *n.* 脂肪 [ji1 fong1], **~ content** 脂肪含量, **percent body ~** 身體脂肪百分比

fate *n.* 命 [meng6]

fat-free *n.* 脫脂 [tyut8 ji1]

father *n.* 爹哋 [de1 di3]

father-in-law *n.* 外父 [ngoi6 fu2]

fattened *adj.* 養肥 [yeung5 fei4] **~ chicken** 肥雞, **~ pig** 肥豬, **~ goose** 肥鵝, **~ duck** 肥鴨

fatty *adj.* 肥 [fei4]

faucet *n.* 水喉 [seui2 hau4]

fault *n.* 唔啱 [m4 ngaam1]

faulty *adj.* 有問題 [yau5 man6 tai4]

fava beans *n.* 一大片荒地 [yat7 daai6 pin3 fong1 dei6]

favor *n.* 忙 [mong4]

favorite *adj./n.* 最鍾意 [jeui3 jung1 yi3]; *comp.* **add to ~s** 加入收藏夾

fax *n./v.* 傳真 [chyun4 jan1]

fax machine *n.* 傳真機 [chyun4 jan1 gei1]

FBI (U.S. Federal Bureau of Investigation) *n.* 聯邦調查局 [lyun4 bong1 diu6 cha4 guk9]

fear *n.* 恐懼 [hung2 geui6]; *v.* 驚 [geng1]

feasible *adj.* 可行 [ho2 hang4]

feast *n.* 大食會 [daai6 sik9 wui2]

feather *n.* 羽毛 [yu5 mou4]

feature *n.* 特徵 [dak9 jing1]; *v.* 描寫 [miu4 se2]

February (*abbr.* Feb.) *n.* 二月份 [yi6 yut9 fan6]

federal *adj.* 聯邦 [lyun4 bong1]

fee *n.* 費 [fai3]

feed *n.* 飼料 [ji6 liu6], **chicken ~** 雞飼料, **pig ~** 豬飼料; *v.* 餵 [wai3]

feeding bottle *n.* 奶樽 [naai5 jeun1]

feel *v.* 覺得 [gok8 dak7], **~ sick** 病咗, **~ hot** 覺得熱, **~ cold** 覺得凍

feeling *n.* 感受 [gam2 sau6]

feet *n.* 腳 [geuk8], **chicken ~** 雞腳, **pig's ~** 豬腳

fellow *n.* 老友 [lou5 yau5]; *adj.* 同類 [tung4 leui6]

felony *n.* 重罪 [chung5 jeui6]

female *adj./n.* 女性 [neui5 sing3]

feminine *adj.* 女性 [neui5 sing3]

feminism *n.* 女權主義 [neui5 kyun4 jyu2 yi6]

feminist *n.* 女權主義者 [neui5 kyun4 jyu2 yi6 je2]

fence *n.* 圍欄 [wai4 laan4]

fencing (*sport*) *n.* 劍擊 [gim3 gik7]

fender *n.* 擋泥板 [dong2 nai4 baan2]

fennel *n.* 茴香 [wui4 heung1]

fenugreek *n.* 葫蘆巴 [wu4 lou4 ba1]

ferment *v.* 發酵 [faat8 haau1]

fermented fruits *n.* 罐頭水果 [gun3 tau4 seui2 gwo2]

ferry *n.* 渡輪 [dou6 leun4]

fervent *adj.* 狂熱 [kwong4 yit9]

fervor *n.* 熱情 [yit9 ching4]

festival *n.* 節日 [jit8 yat9]

fetch *v.* 接 [jip8]

fettuccini *n.* 意大利闊條麵 [yi3 daai6 lei6 fut8 tiu2 min6]

feud *n.* 世仇 [sai3 sau4]

feudal *adj.* 封建 [fung1 gin3]

fever *n.* 發燒 [faat8 siu1]

few *det./adj./pron.* 好少 [hou2 siu2]

fiancé *n.* 未婚夫 [mei6 fan1 fu1]

fiancée *n.* 未婚妻 [mei6 fan1 chai1]

fiasco *n.* 慘敗 [chaam2 baai6]

fiber *n.* 纖維 [chim1 wai4]

fiction *n.* 小說 [siu2 syut8]

fictional *adj.* 虛構 [heui1 kau3]

fiduciary *n.* 受託人 [sau6 tok8 yan4]

field *n.* 田 [tin4]; **soccer/football/ rugby** ~足球場; ~ **hockey** 草地曲棍球

fiery *adj.* 容易起火 [yung4 yi6 hei2 fo2]

fifteen *num.* 十五 [sap9 ng5]

fifteenth *adj.* 第十五個 [dai6 sap9 ng5 go3]

fifth *adj.* 第五個 [dai6 ng5 go3]

fiftieth *adj.* 第五十個 [dai6 ng5 sap9 go3]

fifty *num.* 五十 [ng5 sap9]

fig *n.* 無花果 [mou4 fa1 gwo2]

figment *n.* 虛構 [heui1 kau3]

fight *v./n.* 打交 [da2 gaau1]

fighting *n.* 打交 [da2 gaau1]

figurative *adj.* 比喻 [bei2 yu6]

figure *n.* 數字 [sou2 ji6]; *v.* 計 [gai3]

figures *n.* 身形 [san1 ying4]

figurines *n.* 雕像仔 [diu1 jeung6 jai2]

Fiji *n.* 斐濟 [fei2 jai3]

Fijian *adj.* 斐濟 [fei2 jai3]

file *n.* 文件 [man4 gin6]; *v.* 存檔 [chyun4 dong3]

filet mignon *n.* 菲力牛扒 [fei1 lik9 ngau4 pa2]

Filipino *adj.* 菲律賓人 [fei1 leut9 ban1 yan4]

fill *v.* 裝滿 [jong1 mun5], ~ **up/ out a form** 填寫表格

fillet *n.* 魚片 [yu4 pin2], **chicken** ~ 雞片, **fish** ~ 魚片

filling *n.* 填充物 [tin4 chung1 mat9], **fruit** ~ 水果餡, **pastry** ~ 糕點餡, **meat** ~ 肉餡, **jam** ~ 醬, **dental** ~ 補牙

film *n.* 電影 [din6 ying2], ~ **speed** 膠片速度; *v.* 拍攝 [paak8 sip8]

filter *v.* 過濾 [gwo3 leui6]; *n.* 過濾器 [gwo3 leui6 hei3], **coffee** ~ 咖啡過濾紙, **without** ~ 冇過濾

filtered *adj.* 過濾咗 [gwo3 leui6 jo2]; ~ **water** 過濾咗嘅水

filth *n.* 邋遢嘢 [laat9 taat8 ye5]

filthy *adj.* 邋遢 [laat9 taat8]

final *adj.* 最後 [jeui3 hau6]; *n.* 決賽 [kyut8 choi3]

finally *adv.* 終於 [jung1 yu1]

finance *n.* 金融 [gam1 yung4]; *v.* 資助 [ji1 jo6]

financial *adj.* 財政 [choi4 jing3]

find *v.* 搵 [wan2], ~ **out smth.** 搵到,; *n.* 發現 [faat8 yin6], **a real** ~ 好野

finding *n.* 研究結果 [yin4 gau3 git8 gwo2]

fine 1. *adj.* 上等 [seung6 dang2], ~ **cut** 細切煙草, ~ **powder** 細粉// **2.** *n.* 罰款 [fat9 fun2], **pay a** ~ 交罰款 // **3.** *adv.* 好好 [hou2 hou2]

fine arts *n.* 藝術品 [ngai6 seut9 ban2]

fine food *n.* 美食 [mei5 sik9]

finely *adv.* 精美 [jing1 mei5]

finger *n.* 手指 [sau2 ji2]

finish *v.* 完成 [yun4 sing4]; *n.* 結束 [git8 chuk7]

finished *adj.* 完成 [yun4 sing4]

Finland *n.* 芬蘭 [fan1 laan4]

Finnish *adj.* 芬蘭 [fan1 laan4]

fir *n.* 杉木 [chaam3 muk9]

fire *n.* 火 [fo2], **~pit** 火堆; *v. (~ someone from a job)* 炒魷魚 [chaau2 yau4 yu2]

fire alarm *n.* 火警 [fo2 ging2]

fire department *n.* 消防 [siu1 fong4]

fire escape *n.* 走火通道 [jau2 fo2 tung1 dou6]

fire extinguisher *n.* 滅火器 [mit9 fo2 hei3]

fire truck *n.* 消防車 [siu1 fong4 che1]

firewood *n.* 柴 [chaai4]

fireworks *n.* 煙花 [yin1 fa1]

firm 1. *n.* 公司 [gung1 si1] // **2.** *adj.* 硬 [ngaang6]; *adv.* 實淨 [sat9 jeng6]

firmly *adv.* 堅決 [gin1 kyut8]

first *det./num./adv./adj.* 第一 [dai6 yat7], **~ floor** 一樓, **~ gear** 一檔, **~ name** 名

first aid *n.* 急救 [gap7 gau3]

first-aid kit *n.* 急救箱 [gap7 gau3 seung1]

first class *n.* 一流 [yat7 lau4]

first course *n.* 頭盤 [tau4 pun4]

fiscal *adj.* 財政 [choi4 jing3]

fish *n.* 魚 [yu2]; **~ sauce** 魚露, **~**

allergy 對魚敏感, **~ stall** 魚檔, **~ sticks** 魚串

fish jelly *n.* 魚肉凍 [yu4 yuk9 dung3]

fish stock *n.* 魚群 [yu4 kwan4]

fish store *n.* 魚店 [yu4 dim3]

fishballs *n.* 魚蛋 [yu4 daan2]

fisherman *n.* 漁民 [yu4 man4]

fishing *n.* 釣魚 [diu3 yu2]; **no ~** 嚴禁釣魚

fishing license *n.* 釣魚証 [diu3 yu2 jing3]

fishing permitted *phr.* 允許釣魚 [wan5 heui2 diu3 yu4]

fishing rod *n.* 魚竿 [yu4 gon1]

fist *n.* 拳頭 [kyun4 tau4]

fit 1. *v.* 襯 [chan3] // **2.** *adj.* 啱身嘅 [ngaam1 san1 ge3]

fitness *n.* 健康 [gin6 hong1]; **~ room** 健身房, **~ test** 體檢

fitting *n.* 設備 [chit8 bei6]

fitting room *n.* 更衣室 [gang1 yi1 sat7]

five *num.* 五 [ng5]

fix *v.* 整 [jing2]

fixative *n.* 固定劑 [gu3 ding6 jai1]; **spray with ~** 噴摩絲

fixed *adj.* 固定 [gu3 ding6]

fixed price *n.* 定價 [ding6 ga3]

flag *n.* 旗 [kei4]

flakes *n.* 薄片 [bok9 pin2], **potato ~** 薯片, **corn~** 粟米片

flaky *adj.* 薄片 [bok9 pin2], **~ pastry** 千層餅

flambé *n.* 浸喺燒著嘅酒裡面嘅嘢 [jam3 hai6 siu1 joi6 ge3 jau2 leui5 min6 ge3 ye5]

flame *n.* 火焰 [fo2 yim6]

flamed *v.* 燒著 [siu1 jeuk9]

flan *n.* 餡餅[haam2 beng2]

flank *n.* 側面 [jak7 min6]; ~ **steak** 牛後腹牛扒

flare *v.* 閃 [sim2]

flash *v./n.* 閃光 [sim2 gwong1]

flash photography *n.* 閃光燈攝影 [sim2 gwong1 dang1 sip8 ying2]

flashlight *n.* 手電筒 [sau2 din6 tung2]

flat *adj.* 平 [ping4]; *n. (apartment/condo)* 套間 [tou3 gaan1]

flat bread *n.* 薄餅 [bok9 beng2]

flat cake *n.* 扁蛋糕 [bin2 daan6 gou1]

flat tire *n.* 漏氣嘅車軚 [lau6 hei3 ge3 che1 taai1]

flatter *v.* 奉承 [fung6 sing4]

flattery *n.* 奉承 [fung6 sing4]

flavor *n.* 味 [mei6]; **what ~s do you have?** 你點咗乜野味

flavored *adj.* 加味 [ga1 mei6], ~ **water** 有味水, **chocolate ~** 朱古力味, **vanilla ~** 香草味, **strawberry ~** 草莓味

flavoring *n.* 調味料 [tiu4 mei6 liu6]

flax *n.* 亞麻 [a3 ma4], ~**seed** 亞麻籽, ~ **powder** 亞麻粉

flea *n.* 狗虱 [gau2 sat7]

flea market *n.* 跳蚤市場 [tiu3 jou2 si5 cheung4]

flesh *n.* 肉 [yuk9]

flexibility *n.* 靈活性 [ling4 wut9 sing3]

flexible *adj.* 靈活 [ling4 wut9]

flicker *n.* 閃 [sim2]

flight *n.* 航班 [hong4 baan1]

flight attendant *n.* 空姐 [hung1 je2]

flight number *n.* 航班編號 [hong4 baan1 pin1 hou6]

flight of stairs *n.* 樓梯級 [lau4 tai1 kap7]

flimsy *adj.* 質地差 [jat7 dei2 cha1]

flip *v.* 彈走 [daan6 jau2]

flip-flops *n.* 人字拖 [yan4 ji6 to1]

float *v.* 浮 [fau4]

flood *n.* 洪水 [hung4 seui2]; *v.* 浸 [jam3]

floor *n.* 地板 [dei6 baan2]

florist *n.* 花店 [fa1 dim3]

flounder *n.* 扑嚇扑嚇 [pok8 haak8 pok8 haak8]

flour *n.* 麵粉 [min6 fan2]

floured *v.* 塗咗麵粉 [tou4 jo2 min6 fan2]

flourish *v.* 繁榮 [faan4 wing4]

flow *n.* 流 [lau4] *v.* 流 [lau4]

flower *n.* 花 [fa1]

flu *n.* 流感 [lau4 gam2]

fluent *adj.* 流利 [lau4 lei6]

fluid *n./adj.* 液體 [yik9 tai2]

flush *v.* 沖 [chung1]

flute *adj.* 長笛 [cheung4 dek9]

fly 1. *v.* 飛 [fei1] // **2.** *n.* 烏蠅 [wu1 ying1]

flying *adj.* 會飛 [wui5 fei1]; *n.* 飛 [fei1]

focus *v.* 集中 [jaap9 jung1]; *n.* 焦點 [jiu1 dim2]

fog *n.* 霧 [mou6]

fog light *n.* 霧燈 [mou6 dang1]

foggy *adj.* 有霧 [yau5 mou6]

foie gras *n.* 鵝肝醬 [ngo4 gon1 jeung3]

fold *v.* 疊 [dip9]; *n.* 摺痕 [jip8 han4]

foliage *n.* 樹葉 [syu6 yip9]

folk *n./adj.* 民間 [man4 gaan1]

folk art *n.* 民間藝術 [man4 gaan1 ngai6 seut9]

folk handicrafts *n.* 工藝品 [gung1 ngai6 ban2]

folk music *n.* 民俗音樂 [man4 juk9 yam1 ngok9]

follow *v.* 跟住 [gan1 jyu6]

following *adj./prep.* 跟住 [gan1 jyu6]; *n.* 以下 [yi5 ha6]

font *comp.* 字體 [ji6 tai2]; **large/small ~** 大 / 細字體,

food *n.* 食物 [sik9 mat9]

food additives *n.* 食物添加劑 [sik9 mat9 tim1 ga1 jai1]

food coloring *n.* 食用色素 [sik9 yung6 sik7 sou3]

food festival *n.* 美食節 [mei5 sik9 jit8]

food poisoning *n.* 食物中毒 [sik9 mat9 jung3 duk9]

food preservatives *n.* 食物防腐劑 [sik9 mat9 fong4 fu6 jai1]

food pyramid *n.* 食物金字塔 [sik9 mat9 gam1 ji6 taap8]

fool *n.* 蠢才[cheun2 choi4]; *v.* 整蠱 [jing2 gu2]

foosball (table soccer) *n.* 足球 [juk7 kau4]

foot *n.* 腳 [geuk8]; **on ~** 行路

football *n.* 足球 [juk7 kau4]

footer *n.* 頁尾 [yip9 mei5]; **add ~ to document** 文件加頁尾

footpath *n.* 行人路 [hang4 yan4 lou6]

for *prep.* 為咗 [wai6 jo2]

for instance *adv.* 例如 [lai6 yu4]

for now *adv.* 而家 [yi4 ga1]

for rent *phr.* 出租 [cheut7 jou1]

forbidden *adj.* 唔准 [m4 jeun2]

force *n.* 力 [lik9]; *v.* 強迫 [keung4 bik7]

forcemeat *n.* 調好味肉碎 [tiu4 hou2 mei6 yuk9 seui3]

forearm *n.* 前臂 [chin4 bei3]

forecast *n.* 預報 [yu6 bou3]; *v.* 預測 [yu6 chak7]

forefinger *n.* 食指 [sik9 ji2]

forehead *n.* 額頭 [ngaak9 tau4]

foreign *adj.* 外國 [ngoi6 gwok8]

foreign currency *n.* 外幣 [ngoi6 bai6]

foreign language *n.* 外語 [ngoi6 yu5]

foreign-language *adj.* 外語 [ngoi6 yu5]

foreigner *n.* 外國人 [ngoi6 gwok8 yan4]

foreleg *n.* 前腳 [chin4 geuk8]

foreman *n.* 工頭 [gung1 tau2]

foremost *adj.* 最重要 [jeui3 jung6 yiu3]

forerunner *n.* 先驅 [sin1 keui1]

foresight *n.* 先見之明 [sin1 gin3 ji1 ming4]

forest *n.* 森林 [sam1 lam4]

forestry *n.* 林業 [lam4 yip9]

forever *adv.* 永遠 [wing5 yun5]

forge 1. *(fake a signature)* *v.* 偽造 [ngai6 jou6] // **2.** *(fireplace)* *n.* 鐵工廠 [tit3 gung1 chong2]

forgery *n.* 贗品 [ngaan6 ban2]

forget *v.* 忘記 [mong4 gei3], **don't ~ to** 記得, **~ it** 算啦

forgive *v.* 原諒 [yun4 leung6]

fork *n.* 叉 [cha1]

form *n.* 外形 [ngoi6 ying4];
v. 形成 [ying4 sing4]

formal *adj.* 正式 [jing3 sik7]

formal dress *n.* 禮服 [lai5 fuk9]

formal wear *n.* 禮服 [lai5 fuk9]

formally *adv.* 正式 [jing3 sik7]

format *n.* 格式 [gaak8 sik7]; *v.*
設計格式 [chit8 gai3 gaak8
sik7], **~ a document** 文件統一
格式

formation *n.* 形成 [ying4 sing4]

former *adj.* 之前 [ji1 chin4]

formerly *adv.* 之前 [ji1 chin4]

formula *n.* 公式 [gung1 sik7];
spreadsheet ~ 數據表公式

formulate *v.* 用公式表達
[yung6 gung1 sik7 biu2 daat9]

formulated *adj.* 構思好 [kau3
si1 hou2]

forsake *v.* 捨棄 [se2 hei3]

fortieth *adj.* 第四十個 [dai6 sei3
sap9 go3]

fortified *adj.* 加強 [ga1 keung4]

fortnight *n.* 兩個星期 [leung5
go3 sing1 kei4]

fortress *n.* 城堡 [sing4 bou2]

fortunately *adv.* 好彩 [hou2
choi2]

fortune *n.* 運氣 [wan6 hei3]

fortuneteller *n.* 算命佬 [syun3
meng6 lou2]

forty *num.* 四十 [sei3 sap9]

forum *n.* 論壇 [leun6 taan4]

forward *adj./adv.* 向前 [heung3
chin4]; *v.* 前進 [chin4 jeun3],
move ~ 前進

fossil *n.* 化石 [fa3 sek9]

foster *v.* 收養 [sau1 yeung5]

foul (*sports*) *n.* 犯規 [faan6 kwai1];
v. 整邋遢 [jing2 laat9 taat8]

found *v.* 建立 [gin3 laap9]; *adj.*
搵到 [wan3 dou2]

foundation *n.* 基礎 [gei1 cho2]

fountain *n.* 噴水池 [pan3 seui2
chi4]

four *num.* 四 [sei3]

four-door car *n.* 四門汽車 [sei3
mun4 hei3 che1]

fourteen *num.* 十四 [sap9 sei3]

fourteenth *adj.* 第十四個 [dai6
sap9 sei3 go3]

fourth *adj.* 第四個 [dai6 sei3 go3]

four-wheel drive *n.* 四輪驅動
[sei3 leun4 keui1 dung6]

fowl *n.* 家禽 [ga1 kam4]; *v.* 打雀
仔 [da2 jeuk8 jai2]

foyer *n.* 休息室 [yau1 sik7 sat7]

fraction (*math term*) *n.* 分數
[fan6 sou3]

fracture *n.* 骨折 [gwat7 jit8]; *v.*
整斷 [jing2 tyun6]

fragment *n.* 碎片 [seui3 pin2]

fragrant *n.* 香味 [heung1 mei6]

frame *n.* 架 [ga2]; *v.* 陷害 [haam6
hoi6]

framework *n.* 框架 [kwaang1 ga2]

France *n.* 法國 [faat8 gwok8]

franchise *n.* 專賣 [jyun1 maai6];
v. 賣專賣權 [maai6 jyun1
maai6 kyun4]

frangipane *n.* 雞蛋花 [gai1
daan6 fa1]

frankfurter *n.* 法蘭克福香腸
[faat8 laan4 hak7 fuk7 heung1
cheung2]

frantic *adj.* 發癲 [faat8 din1]

fraud *n.* 詐騙 [ja3 pin3]

fraudulent *adj.* 呃人嘅 [aak7
yan4 ge3]

free *adj.* 自由 [ji6 yau4]; *v.* 解放 [gaai2 fong3]; *adv.* 免費 [min5 fai3]

free admission *n.* 免費 [min5 fai3]

free gift *n.* 贈品 [jang6 ban2]

free of charge *adj.* 免費 [min5 fai3]

free time *n.* 得閒 [dak7 haan4]

freedom *n.* 自由 [ji6 yau4]

freely *adv.* 隨心所欲 [cheui4 sam1 so2 yuk9]

Freetown *n.* 弗里敦 [fat7 lei5 deun1]; ~,**capital of Sierra Leone** 塞拉利昂首都

freeze *v.* 結冰 [jit8 bing1]

freeze-dried *adj.* 凍乾 [dung3 gon1]

freezer *n.* 冷藏櫃 [laang5 chong4 gwai6]

French *adj.* 法國 [faat8 gwok8], ~ **food** 法國菜

french fries *n.* 薯條 [syu4 tiu2]

french toast *n.* 法式土司 [faat8 sik7 tou2 si1]

frequency *n.* 頻率 [pan4 leut9]

frequent *adj.* 頻繁 [pan4 faan4]; **how ~?** 幾經常?

frequently *adv.* 頻繁 [pan4 faan4]

fresco *n.* 壁畫 [bik7 wa2]

fresh *adj.* 新鮮 [san1 sin1], ~ **fish** 新鮮魚, ~ **fruit** 新鮮水果, ~ **produce** 新鮮蔬果, ~ **meat** 新鮮肉, ~ **water** 淡水 [taam5 seui2]

freshly *adv.* 近排先 [gan6 paai2 sin1]

Friday (*abbr.* **Fri.**) *n.* 禮拜五 [lai5 baai3 ng5]

fridge *n.* 冰箱 [bing1 seung1]

fried *adj.* 油炸 [yau4 ja3]; ~ **calamari** 炸魷魚圈 [ja3 yau4 yu4 hyun1]

friend *n.* 朋友 [pang4 yau5]

friendly *adj.* 友好 [yau5 hou2]

friendship *n.* 友誼 [yau5 yi4]

fries *n.* 薯條 [syu4 tiu2]

frighten *v.* 嚇 [haak8]

frightened *adj.* 驚 [geng1]; **be ~** 驚

frightening *adj.* 得人驚 [dak7 yan4 geng1]

fritter *n.* 油炸餡餅 [yau4 ja3 haam2 beng2]

frog *n.* 田雞 [tin4 gai1]

frog's legs *n.* 田雞腳 [tin4 gai1 geuk8]

front *n./adj.* 前面 [chin4 min6], **in ~ of** 喺…前面

front desk *n.* 前枱 [chin4 toi2]

front door *n.* 前門 [chin4 mun2]

front light *n.* 前燈 [chin4 dang1]

front wheel *n.* 前輪 [chin4 leun2]

frost *n.* 霜 [seung1]; *v.* 結霜 [git8 seung1]

frosted *adj.* 霜凍 [seung1 dung3]

frosting *n.* 糖霜 [tong4 seung1]

frozen *adj.* 冷藏 [laang5 chong4], ~ **food** 冷藏食品, ~ **ice** 結冰, ~ **vegetables** 冷藏蔬菜, ~ **meat** 冷藏肉, ~ **pastry** 冷藏糕點

fructose *n.* 果糖 [gwo2 tong4]

frugal *adj.* 慳錢 [han1 chin2]

fruit *n.* 生果 [saang1 gwo2]; ~ **syrup** 水果糖漿, ~ **salad** 水果沙律, ~ **picking** 摘水果

fruit brandy *n.* 水果白蘭地 [seui2 gwo2 baak9 laan1 dei6]

fruit juice *n.* 果汁 [gwo2 jap7]

fry v. 油炸 [yau4 ja3]; n. 魚苗 [yu4 miu4]

frying pan n. 平底鍋 [ping4 dai2 wo1]

fudge n. 軟糖 [yun5 tong2]; ~ **pops** 軟糖汽水, ~ **brownie** 軟糖朱古力布朗尼

fuel n. 燃料 [yin4 liu6]; v. 加油 [ga1 yau2]

fuel gauge n. 油表 [yau4 biu1]

fuel tank n. 油箱 [yau4 seung1]

full adj. 滿嘅 [mun5 ge3] be ~ 食飽, ~ **flavor** 味道十足, ~ **amount** 足量

full board (with all meals) adv. 包食宿 [baau1 sik9 suk7]

full-fat adj. 全脂 [chyun4 ji1]

full stop n. 句號 [geui3 hou6]

full-time work n. 全職 [chyun4 jik7]

fully adv. 完全 [yun4 chyun4]

fully booked adj. 賣晒 [maai6 saai3]

fumble v. 亂摸 [lyun6 mo2]

fumes n. 煙 [yin1]

fun n. 樂趣 [lok9 cheui3]; adj. 好玩 [hou2 waan2]; **for ~** 玩玩, **have ~** 玩得開心

Funafuti province n. 福納省 [fuk1 naap9 saang2]; ~, **capital of Tuvalu** 圖瓦盧首都

function n. 功能 [gung1 nang4]; v. 起作用 [hei2 jok8 yung6]

functional adj. 用得 [yung6 dak7]

fund n. 基金 [gei1 gam1]; v. 提供資金 [tai4 gung1 ji1 gam1]

fundamental adj. 根本 [gan1 bun2]

funeral n. 葬禮 [jong3 lai5]

fungus n. 真菌 [jan1 kwan2]

funny adj. 搞笑 [gaau2 siu3]

fur n. 皮毛 [pei4 mou4]

furnace n. 火爐 [fo2 lou4]

furnished adj. 帶傢俬嘅 [daai3 ga1 si1 ge3]

furniture n. 傢俬 [ga1 si1]

further adj. 進一步 [jeun3 yat7 bou6]

further, furthest adv./adj. 遠啲 [yun5 di1]

furthermore adj. 仲有 [jung6 yau5]

fuse n. 保險絲 [bou2 him2 si1]

fuse box n. 保險絲盒 [bou2 him2 si1 hap9]

fusion n. 融合 [yung4 hap9]; ~ **cuisine** 混合美食

fuss n. 大驚小怪 [daai6 geng1 siu2 gwaai3]

future n./adj. 未來 [mei6 loi4]

G

g. (*abbr. for* **gram**) 克 [hak7]

Gabon *n.* 加蓬 [ga1 pung4]

Gaborone *n.* 哈博羅內 [ha1 bok8 lo4 noi6]; ~,**capital of Botswana** 博茨瓦納首都

gain *v.* 得到 [dak7 dou2]; *n.* 得益 [dak7 yik7]

galaxy *n.* 銀河系 [ngan4 ho4 hai6]

gale warning *n.* 大風警報 [daai6 fung1 ging2 bou3]

gallery *n.* 畫廊 [wa2 long4]

gallon *n.* 加侖 [ga1 leun4]

gamble *v./n.* 賭錢 [dou2 chin2]

gambling *n.* 賭錢 [dou2 chin2]

gambling machine *n.* 賭博機 [dou2 bok8 gei1]

game (*sport*) *n.* 遊戲 [yau4 hei3]

game room *n.* 遊戲室 [yau4 hei3 sat7]

game show *n.* 遊戲節目 [yau4 hei3 jit8 muk9]

games arcade *n.* 電子遊戲 [din6 ji2 yau4 hei3]

gap *n.* 罅 [la3]

garage *n.* 車房 [che1 fong4]

garbage *n.* 垃圾 [laap9 saap8]

garbage bags *n.* 垃圾袋 [laap9 saap8 doi2]

garbage can *n.* 垃圾桶 [laap9 saap8 tung2]

garden *n.* 花園 [fa1 yun2]

garden apartment *n.* 帶花園嘅公寓 [daai3 fa1 yun2 ge3 gung1 yu6]

garden center *n.* 園藝中心 [yun4 ngai6 jung1 sam1]

garden salad *n.* 田園沙律 [tin4 yun4 sa1 leut9]

gardening *n.* 園藝 [yun4 ngai6]

gargoyle *n.* 滴水獸 [dik7 seui2 sau3]

garlic *n.* 蒜 [syun3], ~ **sauce** 蒜茸醬, ~ **powder** 蒜粉

garlic mayonnaise (aioli) *n.* 蒜泥蛋黃醬 [syun3 nai4 daan6 wong4 jeung3]

garnet *n.* 石榴色 [sek9 lau4 sik7]

garnish *n.* 裝飾 [jong1 sik7]

gas (*gasoline / methane*) *n.* 汽油 [hei3 yau4]

gas bottle *n.* 氣瓶 [hei3 ping4]

gas cylinder *n.* 氣瓶 [hei3 ping4]

gas gauge *n.* 氣壓計 [hei3 aat8 gai3]

gas station *n.* 加油站 [ga1 yau2 jaam6]

gas tank *n.* 油箱 [yau4 seung1]

gasoline *n.* 汽油 [hei3 yau4]

gastritis *n.* 胃炎 [wai6 yim4]

gastroenteritis *n.* 腸胃炎 [cheung4 wai6 yim4]

gastronomy *n.* 烹調 [paang1 tiu4]

gastropod *n.* 腹足動物 [fuk7 juk7 dung6 mat9]

gate (*fence / airport*) *n.* 門 [mun4]

gather *v.* 收集 [sau1 jaap9]

gathering place *n.* 聚會地方 [jeui6 wui6 dei6 fong1]

gauge *n.* 測量範圍 [chak7 leung4 faan6 wai4]

gauze *n.* 紗布 [sa1 bou3]

gay 1. (*homosexual*) *n./adj.* 同
性戀 [tung4 sing3 lyun2] // **2.**
(*merry*) *adj.* 開心 [hoi1 sam1]

gay club *n.* 同性戀酒吧 [tung4
sing3 lyun2 jau2 ba1]

gazpacho *n.* 西班牙凍湯 [sai1
baan1 nga4 dung3 tong1]

GDP (Gross Domestic Product)
n. 國民生產總值 [gwok8
man4 sang1 chaan2 jung2 jik9]

gear *n.* 齒輪 [chi2 leun4]; *v.* 裝
上齒輪 [jong1 seung5 chi2
leun4]

gearbox *n.* 變速器 [bin3 chuk7
hei3]

gearshift lever *n.* 變速杆 [bin3
chuk7 gon1]

gel *n.* 啫喱 [je1 lei4]

gelatin *n.* 白乳膠 [baak9 yu5
gaau1]

gem *n.* 寶石 [bou2 sek9]

Gemini *n.* 雙子座 [seung1 ji2
jo6]

gemstone *n.* 寶石 [bou2 sek9]

gender *n.* 性別 [sing3 bit9]

gene *n.* 基因 [gei1 yan1]

general *adj.* 整體的 [jing2 tai2
dik7]

general delivery *n.* 郵件待領
[yau4 gin6 doi6 ling5]

general store *n.* 雜貨鋪 [jaap9
fo3 pou2]

generally *adv.* 通常 [tung1 seung4]

generate *v.* 產生 [chaan2 sang1]

generation *n.* 代 [doi6]

generator *n.* 發電機 [faat8 din6
gei1]

generous *adj.* 大方 [daai6 fong1]

generously *adv.* 大方 [daai6
fong1]

genetic *adj.* 遺傳 [wai4 chyun4]

genetically *adv.* 遺傳 [wai4
chyun4]

genetically modified food *n.*
基因改造食品 [gei1 yan1
goi2 jou6 sik9 ban2]

genetics *n.* 遺傳學 [wai4 chyun4
hok9]

genitals *n.* 生殖器 [sang1 jik9
hei3]

genius *n.* 天才 [tin1 choi4]

genre *n.* 類型 [leui6 ying4]

gentle *adj.* 溫柔 [wan1 yau4]

gentleman *n.* 紳士 [san1 si2]

gently *adv.* 溫柔 [wan1 yau4]

genuine *adj.* 坦誠 [taan2 sing4]

genuinely *adv.* 坦誠 [taan2 sing4]

geography *n.* 地理 [dei6 lei5]

geological *adj.* 地理 [dei6 lei5]

geologist *n.* 地質學家 [dei6 jat7
hok9 ga1]

geology *n.* 地質學 [dei6 jat7 hok9]

Georgetown *n.* 佐治敦 [jo3 ji6
deun1]; ~, **capital of Guyana**
圭亞那首都

Georgia *n.* 格魯吉亞 [gaak8
lou5 gat7 a3]

Georgian *adj.* 格魯吉亞 [gaak8
lou5 gat7 a3]

germ *n.* 細菌 [sai3 kwan2]

German *adj.* 德國 [dak7 gwok8]

Germany *n.* 德國 [dak7 gwok8]

germicide *n.* 消毒水 [siu1 duk9
seui2]

gerund *n.* 動名詞 [dung6 ming4
chi4]

gesture *v.* 姿勢 [ji1 sai3]

get *v.* 得到 [dak7 dou2]; **go ~** 去攞 [heui3 lo2]; **how do I ~ to …?** 請問我點去 [ching2 man6 ngo5 dim2 heui3]

get back *v.* 攞番 [lo2 faan1]

get lost *v.* 蕩失路 [dong6 sat7 lou6]

get off *v.* 落車 [lok9 che1]

get on *v.* 上車 [seung5 che1]

get on well *v.* 相處好 [seung1 chyu3 hou2]

get rid of *v.* 掉咗 [diu6 jo2]

get to *v.* 去 [heui3]

Ghana *n.* 加納 [ga1 naap9]

Ghanaian *adj.* 加納 [ga1 naap9]

gherkins *n.* 酸黃瓜 [syun1 wong4 gwa1]

giant *n.* 巨人 [geui6 yan4]; *adj.* 超大 [chiu1 daai6]

giblets *n.* 殘餘 [chaan4 yu4], **chicken ~** 雞雜碎, **turkey ~** 火雞雜碎

gift *n.* 禮物 [lai5 mat9]

gift shop/store *n.* 禮品店 [lai5 ban2 dim3]

gig *n.* 演唱會 [yin2 cheung3 wui2]

gilded *adj.* 鍍金 [dou6 gam1]

gin *n.* 杜松子酒 [dou6 chung4 ji2 jau2]

ginger *n.* 薑 [geung1], **~ powder** 薑粉, **~ ale** 薑汁無酒精飲料, **~ beer** 薑汁啤酒, **~ snap** 薑汁小食

ginger cake *n.* 薑餅蛋糕 [geung1 beng2 daan6 gou1]

gingerbread *n.* 薑餅 [geung1 beng2], **~ house** 薑餅屋

ginkgo *n.* 銀杏樹 [ngan4 hang6 syu6], **~ bilobo** 銀杏, **~ powder** 銀杏粉, **~ seeds** 銀杏籽

gin-tonic *n.* 金湯力 [gam1 tong1 lik6]

giraffe *n.* 長頸鹿 [cheung4 geng2 luk9]

girl *n.* 女仔 [neui5 jai2]; **little ~** 細路女 [sai3 lou6 neui5]

girlfriend *n.* 女朋友 [neui5 pang4 yau5]

give *v.* 俾 [bei2]; **please ~ me** 麻煩俾我

give birth (to) *v.* 生 [saang1]

give smth away *v.* 送走 [sung3 jau2]

give smth. out *v.* 排放 [paai4 fong3]

give (smth.) up *v.* 放棄 [fong3 hei3]

gizzard *n.* 喉嚨 [hau4 lung4], **turkey ~** 火雞砂囊

glacier *n.* 冰川 [bing1 chyun1]

glad *adj.* 開心 [hoi1 sam1]

gladly *adv.* 開心 [hoi1 sam1]

glamour *n.* 魅力 [mei6 lik9]

gland *n.* 腺 [sin3]

glass (*material / container*) *n.* 玻璃 [bo1 lei1]

glasses (eye) *n.* 眼鏡 [ngaan5 geng3]

glassware *n.* 玻璃器皿 [bo1 lei1 hei3 ming5]

glaze *n.* 上釉 [seung5 yau6], **barbecue ~** 燒烤釉, **sweet ~** 甜霜, **sugar ~** 糖霜, **honey ~** 蜜糖霜

glider *n.* 滑翔機 [waat9 cheung4 gei1]

glimpse *n.* 望一眼 [mong6 yat7 ngaan5]

global *adj.* 全球 [chyun4 kau4]

globalization *n.* 全球化 [chyun4 kau4 fa3]

glory *n.* 榮譽 [wing4 yu6]

gloss *n.* 光澤 [gwong1 jaak9]

glossary *n.* 詞彙表 [chi4 wui6 biu2]

glossy finish (*for photos*) *n.* 拋光 [paau1 gwong1]

glove *n.* 手套 [sau2 tou3]

glucose *n.* 葡萄糖 [pou4 tou4 tong4]

glue *n.* 膠水 [gaau1 seui2]; *v.* 黐埋一笪 [chi1 maai4 yat7 daat8]

gluten *n.* 麵筋 [min6 gan1]; **~free** 冇麵筋, ~ **extract** 麵筋濃縮物

glycerin *n.* 甘油 [gam1 yau4]

gnocchi *n.* 湯丸 [tong1 yun2]

go *v.* 走 [jau2]; **how is it ~ing?** *phr.* 最近點樣？ [jeui3 gan6 dim2 yeung2]; **let's ~!** *phr.* 走囉 [jau2 lo1]; **where does this bus ~?** 呢部巴士去邊架？ [ne1 bou6 ba1 si6 heui3 bin1 ga3] **Go away!** *phr.* 行開！ [haang4 hoi1]

go bad *v.* 粟咗 [suk7 jo2]

go by *v.* 經過 [ging1 gwo3]

go down *v.* 跌 [dit8]

go for a walk *v.* 散步 [saan3 bou6]

go on *v.* 繼續 [gai3 juk9]

go out for a meal *v.* 出去食 [cheut7 heui3 sik9]

go shopping *v.* 行街 [haang4 gaai1]

go skiing *v.* 滑雪 [waat9 syut8]

go to *v.* 去 [heui3]

go up *v.* 升 [sing1]

go wrong *v.* 出咗問題 [cheut7 jo2 man6 tai4]

goal (*objective / sports*) *n.* 目標 [muk9 biu1]

goalkeeper *n.* 守門員 [sau2 mun4 yun4]

goat *n.* 山羊 [saan1 yeung4], **kid** ~ 山羊仔

goat cheese *n.* 羊奶芝士 [yeung4 naai5 ji1 si6]

goat meat *n.* 山羊肉 [saan1 yeung4 yuk9]

goblet *n.* 高腳酒杯 [gou1 geuk8 jau2 bui1]

God *n.* 上帝 [seung6 dai3]

god *n.* 神 [san4]

goggles *n.* 防水鏡 [fong4 seui2 geng3]

going-out-of-business sale *n.* 清倉大減價 [ching1 chong1 daai6 gaam2 ga3]

gold *n.* 黃金 [wong4 gam1]; *adj.* 金色 [gam1 sik7]

gold plate *n.* 金器 [gam1 hei3]

golden *adj.* 金色 [gam1 sik7]

golf *n.* 高爾夫球 [gou1 yi5 fu1 kau4]

golf course *n.* 高爾夫球場 [gou1 yi5 fu1 kau4 cheung4]

gondola *n.* 貨架 [fo3 ga2]

gone *adj.* 走咗 [jau2 jo2]

good *adj.* 好 [hou2]; *n.* 好事 [hou2 si6]; **not very ~** 唔係幾好 [m4 hai6 gei2 hou2]; **very ~** 十分之好 [sap9 fan1 ji1 hou2] ~ **at** 叻 [lek7]

good afternoon *phr.* 午安 [ng5 on1]

good evening *phr.* 晚安 [maan5 on1]

good for *adj.* 對…好 [deui3 … hou2]

Good Friday *n.* 耶穌受難日 [ye4 sou1 sau6 naan6 yat9]

Good health! *phr.* 身體健康 [san1 tai2 gin6 hong1]

Good luck! *phr.* 好運！ [hou2 wan6]

good morning *phr.* 早晨 [jou2 san4]

good night *phr.* 晚安 [maan5 on1]

goodbye *phr.* 拜拜 [baai1 baai3]; *n.* 再見 [joi3 gin3]

goods *n.* 商品 [seung1 ban2]

goose *n.* 鵝 [ngo4]

goose liver *n.* 鵝肝 [ngo4 gon1]

gooseberries *n.* 醋栗 [chou3 leut9]

gorgonzola cheese *n.* 哥根蘇拿芝士 [go1 gan1 sou1 na4 ji1 si2]

gospel *n.* 福音 [fuk7 yam1]

Gothic style *n.* 哥德式 [go1 dak1 sik7]

gouda cheese *n.* 高達芝士 [gou1 daat9 ji1 si2]

goulash *n.* 菜燉牛肉 [choi3 dan6 ngau4 yuk9], **Hungarian ~** 奧地利菜燉牛肉, **Polish ~** 波蘭菜燉牛肉

gourd *n.* 葫蘆 [wu4 lou2], **vegetable ~** 菜葫蘆

govern *v.* 管理 [gun2 lei5]

government *n.* 政府 [jing3 fu2]

governor *n.* 州長 [jau1 jeung2]

grab *v.* 攞住 [lo2 jyu6]

grade *n.* 年級 [nin4 kap7]; *v.* 俾分 [bei2 fan1]

gradient *n.* 坡度 [bo1 dou6]

gradual *adj.* 逐啲 [juk9 di1]

gradually *adv.* 逐啲 [juk9 di1]

graduate *n.* 畢業生 [bat7 yip9 sang1]; *v.* 畢業 [bat7 yip9]

grain *n.* 糧食 [leung4 sik9]

gram (*abbr.* **g., gm.**) *n.* 克 [hak7]

grammar *n.* 語法 [yu5 faat8]

grand *adj.* 宏偉 [wang4 wai5]

grand jury *n.* 大陪審團 [daai6 pui4 sam2 tyun4]

grandchild(ren) *n.* 孫 [syun1]

granddaughter *n.* 孫女 [syun1 neui5]

grandfather *n.* 爺爺 [ye4 ye4], 公公 [gung1 gung1]

grandmother *n.* 麻麻 [ma4 ma4], 婆婆 [po4 po2]

grandparent *n.* 祖輩 [jou2 bui3]

grandson *n.* 孫仔 [syun1 jai2]

granny smith apple *n.* 青蘋果 [cheng1 ping4 gwo2]

granola *n.* 麥片 [mak9 pin2]; **~ bars** 麥片吧, **~ cereal** 麥片, **~ mix** 混合麥片

grant *v.* 俾 [bei2]; *n.* 經費 [ging1 fai3]

granulated *adj.* 一粒粒 [yat7 nap7 nap7]; **~ sugar** 糖粒

granules *n.* 細粒 [sai3 nap7]

grape *n.* 提子 [tai4 ji2]

grape juice *n.* 提子汁 [tai4 ji2 jap7]

grape spirit *n.* 提子烈酒 [tai4 ji2 klit6 jau2]

grapefruit *n.* 西柚 [sai1 yau2]

grapeseed oil *n.* 提子油 [tai4 ji2 yau4]

graph 286 grind

graph *n.* 圖表 [tou4 biu2]

graphic *adj.* 圖解 [tou4 gaai2]

graphic art *n.* 平面視覺藝術 [ping4 min2 si6 gok8 ngai6 seut9]; **~ist** 平面視覺藝術家

graphic design *n.* 平面設計 [ping4 min2 chit8 gai3]

graphics *n.* 製圖學 [jai3 tou4 hok9]; **computer ~** 電腦製圖, **~ card** 顯示卡

grass *n.* 草 [chou2]

grate *v.* 壓碎 [aat8 seui3]

grated *adj.* 壓碎咗 [aat8 seui3 jo2], **~ cheese** 芝士碎, **~ pepper** 辣椒粉, **~ spice** 辣椒粉

grateful *adj.* 感激 [gam2 gik7]

grater *n.* 砧板 [jam1 baan2], **cheese ~** 芝士刨絲器

gratuity *n.* 貼士 [tip1 si2]

grave *n.* 墳 [fan4] / *adj.* 嚴重 [yim4 jung6]

gravestone *n.* 墓碑 [mou6 bei1]

gravitational *adj.* 重力 [chung5 lik9]

gravity *n.* 重力 [chung5 lik9]

gravy *n.* 肉汁 [yuk9 jap7], **turkey ~** 火雞汁, **beef ~** 牛肉汁

gray *adj.* 灰色 [fui1 sik7]

gray-haired *adj.* 白頭髮 [baak9 tau4 faat8]

graze *v.* 放羊 [fong3 yeung4]

grease *n.* 油脂 [yau4 ji1], **cooking ~** 食用油脂

greasy hair *n.* 油性頭髮 [yau4 sing3 tau4 faat8]

great *adj.* 太好 [taai3 hou2]; **Great!** *phr.* 太好啦！ [taai3 hou2 la1]

Great Britain *n.* 英國 [ying1 gwok8]

greatly *adv.* 十分 [sap9 fan1]

Greece *n.* 希臘 [hei1 laap9]

Greek *adj.* 希臘 [hei1 laap9]

green *adj.* 綠色 [luk9 sik7] *n.* 綠色 [luk9 sik7]

green banana *n.* 青香蕉 [cheng1 heung1 jiu1]

green beans *n.* 青豆 [cheng1 dau2]

green pepper *n.* 青椒 [cheng1 jiu1]

green tea *n.* 綠茶 [luk9 cha4]

greengrocer *n.* 賣菜嘅 [maai6 choi3 ge3]

greens *n.* 綠色蔬菜 [luk9 sik7 so1 choi3], **mixed/assorted ~** 雜菜

greet *v.* 問候 [man6 hau6]

greeting *n.* 問候 [man6 hau6]

Grenada *n.* 格拉那達 [gaak8 laai1 na5 daat9]

Grenadian *adj.* 格拉那達 [gaak8 laai1 na5 daat9]

grey *adj.* 灰色 [fui1 sik7]; *n.* 灰色 [fui1 sik7]

grievance *n.* 牢騷 [lou4 sou1]

grief *n.* 傷心 [seung1 sam1]

grill *v./n.* 燒烤 [siu1 haau1]

grilled *v.* 燒烤 [siu1 haau1]; *adj.* 燒過 [siu1 gwo3]

grilled cheese *n.* 燒芝士 [siu1 ji1 si2]

grilled fish *n.* 燒魚 [siu1 yu2]

grilled sausage *n.* 燒香腸 [siu1 heung1 cheung1]

grillstones *n.* 膽結石 [daam2 git8 sek9]

grind *v.* 磨碎 [mo4 seui3]

grits *n.* 粗麵粉 [chou1 min6 fan2]

grocer *n.* 雜貨店 [jaap9 fo3 dim3]

groceries *n.* 雜貨 [jaap9 fo3]

grocery *n.* 雜貨店 [jaap9 fo3 dim3]

grocery store *n.* 小賣部 [siu2 maai6 bou6]

gross *adj.* 總 [jung2]; *v.* 總收入 [jung2 sau1 yap9]; *n.* 總數 [jung2 sou3]

ground 1. *adj.* 地下 [dei6 ha2], ~ **coffee** 咖啡粉, ~ **pepper** 辣椒粉, ~ **nuts** 乾果粉; *v.* 降落 [gong3 lok9] // **2.** *n.* (*earth / reason*) 地面 [dei6 min2]

ground floor *n.* 地下 [dei6 ha2]

groundcloth *n.* 防潮布 [fong4 chiu4 bou3]

group *n.* 組 [jou2]; *v.* 歸類 [gwai1 leui6]

grouse *n.* 牢騷 [lou4 sou1]

grow *v.* 種 [jung3]

grow up *v.* 長大 [jeung2 daai6]

growth *n.* 生長 [sang1 jeung2]

gruel *n.* 粥 [juk7]

gruyere cheese *n.* 格魯耶爾芝士 [gaak3 lou5 ye4 yi5 ji1 si2]

guacamole *n.* 鱷梨醬 [ngok9 lei4 jeung3]

guarantee *n./v.* 保證 [bou2 jing3]

guard *n.* 看更 [hon1 gaang1]; *v.* 看守 [hon1 sau2]

guardian *n.* 監護人 [gaam1 wu6 yan4]; **legal** ~ 法定監護人

guardianship *n.* 監護 [gaam1 wu6]

Guatemala *n.* 危地馬拉 [ngai4 dei6 ma5 laai1]

Guatemala City *n.* 危地馬拉城 [ngai4 dei6 ma5 laai1 sing4]; ~, **capital of Guatemala** 危地馬拉首都

Guatemalan *adj.* 危地馬拉 [ngai4 dei6 ma5 laai1]

guava *n.* 番石榴 [faan1 sek9 lau2]; ~ **nectar** 番石榴果茶

guess *v.* 估 [gu2]; *n.* 推測 [teui1 chak7]

guest *n.* 人客 [yan4 haak8]; **dinner** ~ 晚飯客人

guesthouse *n.* 賓館 [ban1 gun2]

guidance *n.* 指導 [ji2 dou6]

guide *n.* 導遊 [dou6 yau4]; *v.* 帶路 [daai3 lou6]

guidebook *n.* 旅遊指南 [leui5 yau4 ji2 naam4]

guided tour *n.* 有導遊嘅遊覽 [yau5 dou6 yau4 ge3 yau4 laam5], **museum** ~ 博物館有導遊嘅遊覽, ~ **walk** 有導遊嘅步行遊覽

guidedog *n.* 導盲犬 [dou6 maang4 hyun2]

guidelines *n.* 參考 [chaam1 haau2]

guilt *n.* 有罪 [yau5 jeui6]

guilty *adj.* 有罪 [yau5 jeui6]

Guinea *n.* 幾內亞 [gei1 noi6 a3]

guinea fowl *n.* 珍珠雞 [jan1 jyu1 gai1]

guinea pig *n.* 實驗品 [sat9 yim6 ban2]

Guinea-Bissau *n.* 幾內亞比紹共和國 [gei1 noi6 a3 bei2 siu6 gung6 wo4 gwok8]

guitar *n.* 吉他 [git8 ta1]

guitarist *n.* 吉他手 [git8 ta1 sau2]

gum (chewing ~) *n.* 香口膠 [heung1 hau2 gaau1]

gumdrop *n.* 橡皮糖 [jeung6 pei4 tong2]

gun *n.* 槍 [cheung1]

guy *n.* 人 [yan4]

guy rope *n.* 纜索 [laam6 sok8]

Guyana *n.* 圭亞那 [gwai1 a3 na5]

Guyananese *adj.* 圭亞那 [gwai1 a3 na5]

gym *n.* 健身房 [gin6 san1 fong2]

gymnasium *n.* 健身房 [gin6 san1 fong2]

gymnastics *n.* 體操 [tai2 chou1]

gynecologist *n.* 婦科醫生 [fu5 fo1 yi1 sang1]

gyro *n.* 陀螺 [to4 lo2]

H

habanero chilies *n.* 紅辣椒 [hung4 laat9 jiu1]

habeas corpus 人身保護令 [yan4 san1 bou2 wu6 ling6]; **writ of ~** 人身保護令

habit *n.* 習慣 [jaap9 gwaan3]; **be in the ~ of** 習慣 [jaap9 gwaan3]

habitat *n.* 棲息地 [chai1 sik7 dei6]

haddock *n.* 鱈魚 [syut8 yu2]

haggis *n.* 羊雜碎 [yeung4 jaap9 seui3]

hair *n.* 頭髮 [tau4 faat8]

hair conditioner *n.* 護髮素 [wu6 faat8 sou3]

hair dryer *n.* 風筒 [fung1 tung2]

hair mousse *n.* 慕絲 [mou6 si1]

hair spray *n.* 噴髮霧 [pan3 faat8 mou6]

hairbrush *n.* 梳 [so1]

haircare product *n.* 護髮產品 [wu6 faat8 chaan2 ban2]

haircut *n.* 剪頭髮 [jin2 tau4 faat8]; **have a ~** 剪頭髮

hairdo *n.* 髮型 [faat8 ying4]

hairdresser *n.* 髮型師 [faat8 ying4 si1]

hairdresser salon *n.* 髮廊 [faat8 long4]

Haiti *n.* 海地 [hoi2 dei6]

Haitian *adj.* 海地 [hoi2 dei6]

hake *n.* 鱈魚 [syut8 yu4]

half *n./det./pron./adv.* 一半 [yat7 bun3]

half a kilo (1.1 lb.) *quant.* 半公斤 [bun3 gung1 gan1]

half a liter (0.5 qt.) *quant.* 半公升 [bun3 gung1 sing1]

half board (*room with some meals*) *n.* 半食宿 [gun3 sik9 suk7]

half bottle *n.* 半瓶 [bun3 ping4]

half past (*time*) 點半 [dim2 bun3]

half price *n.* 半價 [bun3 ga3]

half-timbered *adj.* 半木式 [bun3 muk9 sik7]

halibut *n.* 大比目魚 [daai6 bei2 muk9 yu2]

hall *n.* 大堂 [daai6 tong4]

Halt! *phr.* 停 [ting4]

halva *n.* 哈爾瓦糕 [ha1 yi5 nga5 gou1]

ham *n.* 火腿 [fo2 teui2]

ham sandwich *n.* 火腿三文治 [fo2 teui2 saam1 man4 ji6]

hamburger *n.* 漢堡包 [hon3 bou2 baau1], **~ meat** 漢堡包肉, **~ roll** 漢堡包皮, **~ steak** 漢堡包牛肉

hammer *n.* 錘 [cheui4]

hammock *n.* 吊床 [diu3 chong4]

hamster *n.* 倉鼠 [chong1 syu2]

hand *n.* 手 [sau2]; *v.* 遞 [dai6]

hand baggage *n.* 手提行李 [sau2 tai4 hang4 lei5]

hand washable *adj.* 手洗 [sau2 sai2]

handbag *n.* 手袋 [sau2 doi2]

handbrake *n.* 手制 [sau2 jai3]

handcuff *n.* 手銬 [sau2 kaau3]

handicap *n.* 殘疾 [chaan4 jat9]

handicapped *adj.* 殘疾 [chaan4 jat9]

handicrafts *n.* 手工藝品 [sau2 gung1 ngai6 ban2]

handkerchief *n.* 手巾仔 [sau2 gan1 jai2]

handle *v.* 處理 [chyu2 lei5]; *n.* 手把 [sau2 ba2]

handlebars *n.* 手把 [sau2 ba2]

handmade *adj.* 手製 [sau2 jai3]

handsewn *adj.* 手縫 [sau2 fung4]

handsome *adj.* 靚仔 [leng3 jai2]

hang *v.* 掛 [gwa3]

hanger *n.* 衣架 [yi1 ga2]

hangglider *n.* 懸掛式滑翔機 [yun4 gwa3 sik7 waat9 cheung4 gei1]

hangover *n.* 宿醉 [suk7 jeui3]

Hanoi *n.* 河內 [ho4 noi6]; ~, **capital of Vietnam** 越南首都

happen *v.* 發生 [faat8 sang1]; **What ~ed?** *phr.* 發生乜野事? [faat8 sang1 mat7 ye5 si6]; ~ **to (do)** *v.* 啱啱好 [ngaam1 ngaam1 hou2]

happily *adv.* 開心 [hoi1 sam1]

happiness *n.* 開心 [hoi1 sam1]

happy *adj.* 開心 [hoi1 sam1]; *v.* **be happy** 開心 [hoi1 sam1]

Happy birthday! *phr.* 生日快樂 [sang1 yat9 faai3 lok9]

Happy Easter! *phr.* 復活節快樂 [fuk9 wut9 jit8 faai3 lok9]

Happy New Year! *phr.* 新年快樂 [san1 nin4 faai3 lok9]

Harare *n.* 哈拉雷 [ha1 laai1 leui4] ~, **capital of Zimbabwe** 津巴布韋首都

harass *v.* 騷擾 [sou1 yiu2]

harassment *n.* 騷擾 [sou1 yiu2]

harbor *n.* 港口 [gong2 hau2]; ~ **area** 港口區

hard *adj.* 硬 [ngaang6]; *adv.* 勤力 [kan4 lik9]

hard liquor *n.* 烈酒 [lit9 jau2]

hard-baked *n.* 烤硬咗 [haau1 ngaang6 jo2]; ~ **crust** 烤硬咗麵包皮

hard-boiled egg *n.* 水煮蛋 [seui2 jyu2 daan2]

hardly *adv.* 幾乎冇 [gei1 fu4 mou5]

hardware store *n.* 五金舖 [ng5 gam1 pou2]

hare *n.* 野兔 [ye5 tou3]

harm *n./v.* 傷害 [seung1 hoi6]

harmful *adj.* 有害 [yau5 hoi6]

harmless *adj.* 冇害 [mou5 hoi6]

harmony *n.* 和諧 [wo4 haai4]

harness *n.* 馬具 [ma5 geui6]

harp *n.* 豎琴 [syu6 kam4]

harvest *n.* 豐收 [fung1 sau1]

hash *n.* 大雜燴 [daai6 jaap9 wui6]

hash browns *n.* 薯餅 [syu4 beng2]

hashish *n.* 大麻 [daai6 ma4]

hat *n.* 帽 [mou2]

hate *v./n.* 憎 [jang1]

hatred *n.* 憎恨 [jang1 han6]

haunch of venison *n.* 鹿腰畫廊 [luk9 yiu1 wa2 long4]

haunt *v.* 陰魂不散 [yam1 wan4 bat7 saan3]

Havana *n.* 哈瓦那 [ha1 nga5 na5]; ~, **capital of Cuba** 古巴首都

have *v. aux.* 有 [yau5]; *v.* ~ **to** 有 [yau5]

Hawaiian *adj.* 夏威夷 [ha6 wai1 yi4], ~ **food** 夏威夷菜

hay fever *n.* 花粉過敏 [fa1 fan2 gwo3 man5]

hazard *n.* 危險 [ngai4 him2]

hazelnut *n.* 榛子 [jeun1 ji2]

he *pron.* 佢 [keui5]

head *n.* 頭 [tau4]; *v.* 出發 [cheut7 faat8]; *adj.* 首要 [sau2 yiu3]

head cheese *n.* 豬頭肉凍 [jyu1 tau4 yuk9 dung3]

head waiter *n.* 領班 [ling5 baan1]

headache *n.* 頭痛 [tau4 tung3]; **have a** ~ 頭痛

header *n.* 頁首 [yip9 sau2]; **add** ~ **to a document** 文件加頁首

heading *n.* 標題 [biu1 tai4]

headlight *n.* 車頭燈 [che1 tau4 dang1]

headroom *n.* 通行高度 [tung1 hang4 gou1 dou6]

headstrong *adj.* 硬頸 [ngaang6 geng2]

heal *v.* 醫好 [yi1 hou2]

health *n.* 健康 [gin6 hong1]

health center *n.* 診所 [chan2 so2]

health food *n.* 保健食品 [bou2 gin6 sik9 ban2]

health food store *n.* 保健食品店 [bou2 gin6 sik9 ban2 dim3]

health insurance *n.* 醫療保險 [yi1 liu4 bou2 him2]

healthy *adj.* 健康 [gin6 hong1]

hear *v.* 聽 [teng1]; ~ **about/of** 聽講 [teng1 gong2]

hearing *n.* 聽力 [ting1 lik9]

hearing aid *n.* 助聽器 [jo6 ting1 hei3]

hearing test *n.* 聽力測試 [ting1 lik9 chak7 si3]

hearsay *n.* 謠言 [yiu4 yin4]

heart *n.* 心臟 [sam1 jong6]; **turkey** ~ 火雞心, **chicken** ~ 雞心

heart attack *n.* 心臟病發 [sam1 jong6 beng6 faat8]

heart condition *n.* 心臟病 [sam1 jong6 beng6]

heart of palm *n.* 棕櫚心 [jung1 leui4 sam1]

heartbeat *n.* 心跳 [sam1 tiu3]

heat *n.* 高溫 [gou1 wan1]; *v.* 整熱 [jing2 yit9], **pre~** 先加熱, ~ **stove** 加熱爐頭, ~ **oven** 加熱焗爐, **to ~** 加熱

heater *n.* 暖爐 [nyun5 lou4]

heating *n.* 暖氣 [nyun5 hei3]

heaven *n.* 極樂 [gik9 lok9]

heavily *adv.* 重 [chung5]

heavy *adj.* 重 [chung5]

heavy cream *n.* 高脂濃忌廉 [gou1 ji1 nung4 gei6 lim4]

heel *n.* 腳踭 [geuk8 jaang1]

heifer *n.* 小母牛 [siu2 mou5 ngau4]

height *n.* 高度 [gou1 dou6]; ~ **above sea level** 海拔 [hoi2 bat9]

helicopter *n.* 直升機 [jik9 sing1 gei1]

hell *n.* 地獄 [dei6 yuk9]

hello *exclam.* 喂 [wai3]; *n./phr.* 你好 [nei5 hou2]

helmet *n.* 頭盔 [tau4 kwai1]

help *v./n.* 幫手 [bong1 sau2]; **can you ~ me?** 你可以幫幫我嗎?, **I need ~** 我需要幫忙, ~! *exclam.* 救命啊!, ~ **line** 求助行

helpful *adj.* 有用 [yau5 yung6]

Helsinki *n.* 赫爾辛基 [haak7 yi5 san1 gei1]; ~, **capital of Finland** 芬蘭首都

hemorrhoids *n.* 痔瘡 [ji6 chong1]

hen *n.* 母雞 [mou5 gai1]

hence *adv.* 所以 [so2 yi5]

her(s) *pron./det./adj.* 佢嘅 [keui5 ge3]

herb *n.* 草本植物 [chou2 bun2 jik9 mat9]

herbaceous *adj.* 草本 [chou2 bun2]

herbal *adj.* 草藥 [chou2 yeuk9], ~ **seasoning** 香草調味料

herbal tea *n.* 涼茶 [leung4 cha4]

herbivore *n.* 食草動物 [sik9 chou2 dung6 mat9]

here *adv.* 呢度 [ni1 dou6]; ~ **you are** *phr.* 俾你 [bei2 nei5]; **from ~** *adv.* 由呢度 [yau4 ni1 dou6]; **to ~** *adv.* 黎呢度 [lai4 ni1 dou6]

heritage *n.* 遺產 [wai4 chaan2]

hernia *n.* 疝氣 [saan3 hei3]

hero *n.* 英雄 [ying1 hung4]

heroin *n.* 海洛英 [hoi2 lok8 ying1]

herring *n.* 青魚 [cheng1 yu2]; **pickled ~** 醃青魚

hers *pron.* 佢嘅 [keui5 ge3]

herself *pron.* 佢自己 [keui5 ji6 gei2]

hesitate *v.* 猶豫 [yau4 yu6]

heterosexual *adj.* 異性戀 [yi6 sing3 lyun2]

hey *exclam.* 喂 [wai3], ~ **there** 喂，你啊！

heyday *n.* 鼎盛時期 [ding2 sing6 si4 kei4]

hi *exclam.* 喂 [wai3]; *phr.* 你好 [nei5 hou2]

hibernation *n.* 冬眠 [dung1 min4]

hiccup *n.* 打嗝 [da2 gaak8]

hide *v.* 匿埋 [nik7 maai4]

high *adj./adv.* 高 [gou1]

high quality *adj.* 高質量 [gou1 jat7 leung4]

high school *n.* 高中 [gou1 jung1]

high voltage line *n.* 高壓線 [gou1 aat8 sin3]

high-beam lights *n.* 遠光燈 [yun5 gwong1 dang1]

highlight *v.* 強調 [keung4 diu6]; *n.* 重點 [jung6 dim2]

highlight hair *v.* 挑染 [tiu1 yim5]

highly *adv.* 極之 [gik9 ji1]

high-rise apartment building *n.* 高層住宅 [gou1 chang4 jyu6 jaak9]

high-tech (*also* **hi-tech**) *adj.* 高科技 [gou1 fo1 gei6]

highway *n.* 高速公路 [gou1 chuk7 gung1 lou6]

highway interchange *n.* 高速公路交匯處 [gou1 chuk7 gung1 lou6 gaau1 wui6 chyu3]

highway police *n.* 高速公路警察 [gou1 chuk7 gung1 lou6 ging2 chaat8]

hike *v.* 遠足 [yun5 juk7]

hiking boots *n.* 登山靴 [dang1 saan1 heu1]

hiking gear *n.* 登山裝備 [dang1 saan1 jong1 bei6]

hiking route *n.* 登山路線 [dang1 saan1 lou6 sin3]

hilarious *adj.* 搞笑 [gaau2 siu3]

hill *n.* 山 [saan1]

him *pron.* 佢 [keui5]

himself *pron.* 佢自己 [keui5 ji6 gei2]

hint *n.* 貼士 [tip1 si2]; *v.* 俾貼士 [bei2 tip1 si2]

hip *n.* 屁股 [pei3 gu2]

hire *v.* 請 [cheng2]

his *det./pron./adj.* 佢嘅 [keui5 ge3]

historian *n.* 歷史學家 [lik9 si2 hok9 ga1]

historic *adj.* 有歷史價值 [yau5 lik9 si2 ga3 jik9]

historic building *n.* 古建築 [gu2 gin3 juk7]

historic site *n.* 古跡 [gu2 jik7]

historical *adj.* 歷史上 [lik9 si2 seung6]

history *n.* 歷史 [lik9 si2]

hit *v.* 撞 [jong6]; *n.* 碰撞 [pung3 jong6]

hitchhike *v.* 搭順風車 [daap8 seun6 fung1 che1]

hither *adv.* 去呢度 [heui3 ni1 dou6]

hits *n.* 打擊 [da2 gik7]; **website ~** 網站點擊率

HIV *n.* 愛滋病病毒 [oi3 ji1 beng6 beng6 duk9]

HIV-positive *adj.* 有愛滋病 [yau5 oi3 ji1 beng6]

hobby *n.* 愛好 [oi3 hou3]

hockey *n.* 曲棍球 [kuk7 gwan3 kau4]; **ice ~** 冰上曲棍球

hold *v.* 攞住 [lo2 jyu6]; *n.* 保留 [bou2 lau4]

holder *n.* 持有人 [chi4 yau5 yan4]

holding *n.* 持有股份 [chi4 yau5 gu2 fan2]

hole *n.* 窿 [lung1]

holiday *n.* 假期 [ga3 kei4]; **on ~** 休假

holiday discount *n.* 節日折扣 [jit8 yat9 jit8 kau3]

holiday resort *n.* 度假區 [dou6 ga3 keui1]

holiday schedule *n.* 節日安排 [jit8 yat9 on1 paai4]

hollow *adj.* 空心 [hung1 sam1]

holocaust *n.* 大屠殺 [daai6 tou4 saat8]

holy *adj.* 神聖 [san4 sing3]

Holy See (Vatican City) *n.* 梵蒂岡 [faan6 dai3 gong1]

Holy Week *n.* 受難週 [sau6 naan6 jau1]

home *n.* 屋企 [nguk7 kei2], **at ~** 喺屋企, **go ~** 返屋企; *adv.* 家用 [ga1 yung6]

home furnishings *n.* 家居裝修 [ga1 geui1 jong1 sau1]

homeland *n.* 祖國 [jou2 gwok8]

homeless *adj.* 無家可歸 [mou4 ga1 ho2 gwai1]

homeless person *n.* 乞兒 [hat7 yi1]

homemade *adj.* 自己整嘅 [ji6 gei2 jing2 ge3], **~ meal** 自己煮菜, **~ pie** 自製批

homeopathy *n.* 順勢療法 [seun6 sai3 liu4 faat8]

homepage *n.* 主頁 [jyu2 yip9]; **Internet ~** 互聯網主頁; **set ~ to** 設置主頁

home-style cooking *n.* 家常菜 [ga1 seung4 choi3]

homework *n.* 功課 [gung1 fo3]

homicide *n.* 謀殺 [mau4 saat8]

homogenize *v.* 整均勻 [jing2 gwan1 wan4]

homogenized *adj.* 均勻 [gwan1 wan4], ~ **meat** 均質肉, ~ **product** 均質產品

homosexual *adj./n.* 同性戀 [tung4 sing3 lyun2]

Honduran *adj.* 洪都拉斯 [hung4 dou1 laai1 si1]

Honduras *n.* 洪都拉斯 [hung4 dou1 laai1 si1]

honest *adj.* 老實 [lou5 sat9]

honestly *adv.* 老實 [lou5 sat9]

honey *n.* 蜜糖 [mat9 tong4]

honey mustard *n.* 蜂蜜芥末 [fung1 mat9 gaai3 mut9]

honeycomb *n.* 蜂巢 [fung1 chau4]

honeydew (melon) *n.* 蜜汁 [mat9 jap7]

honeymoon *n.* 蜜月 [mat9 yut9]; **on a ~** 度蜜月

Honiara *n.* 霍尼亞拉 [fok8 nei4 a3 laai1]; **~, capital of Solomon Islands** 所羅門群島首都

honk *v.* 響喇叭 [heung2 la1 ba1]

honor *n.* 榮譽 [wing4 yu6]; *v.* 授予榮譽 [sau6 yu5 wing4 yu6]

hood *(of a car)* *n.* 頭巾 [tau4 gan1]

hook *n.* 鉤 [ngau1]; *v.* 鉤住 [ngau1 jyu6]

hookah *n.* 水煙筒 [seui2 yin1 tung2]

hooray *interj.* 好嘢 [hou2 ye5]

hope *v./n.* 希望 [hei1 mong6]

hopefully *adj.* 希望 [hei1 mong6]

hops *n.* 單腳跳 [daan1 geuk8 tiu3]

horizontal *adj.* 水平 [seui2 ping4]

horn *(animal/instrument/car)* *n.* 角 [gok8]

horrible *adj.* 得人驚 [dak7 yan4 geng1]

horror *n.* 恐怖 [hung2 bou3]

horror film *n.* 恐怖片 [hung2 bou3 pin2]

horse *n.* 馬 [ma5]

horse races *n.* 跑馬 [paau2 ma5]

horse racing *n.* 跑馬 [paau2 ma5]

horseback riding *n.* 騎馬 [ke4 ma5]

horseradish *n.* 山葵 [saan1 kwai4]

horse-riding school *n.* 馬術學校 [ma5 seut9 hok9 haau6]

horseshoe crab *n.* 馬蹄蟹 [ma5 tai4 haai5]

hospital *n.* 醫院 [yi1 yun6]

hospitality *n.* 好客 [hou3 haak8]

host *n.* 主人 [jyu2 yan4], **a ~** 主持人; *v.* 做東 [jou6 dung1]

hostage *n.* 人質 [yan4 ji3]

hostel *n.* 旅館 [leui5 gun2]

hostile *adj.* 唔友善 [m4 yau5 sin6]

hot *adj.* 熱 [yit9]; **~ temperature** 氣溫高; **~ spicy** 好辣

hot chocolate *n.* 熱朱古力 [yit9 jyu1 gu1 lik7]

hot dog *n.* 熱狗 [yit9 gau2]

hot sauce *n.* 辣椒醬 [laat9 jiu1 jeung3]

hot spring *n.* 溫泉 [wan1 chyun4]

hot tea *n.* 熱茶 [yit9 cha4]

hot water *n.* 熱水 [yit9 seui2]

hot-dog stand *n.* 熱狗檔 [yit9 gau2 dong3]

hotel *n.* 酒店 [jau2 dim3]

hour *n.* 鐘頭 [jung1 tau4]

house *n.* 屋 [uk7], **~ for rent** *n.*

有屋出租 [yau5 uk7 cheut7 hou1]

house salad *n.* 田園沙律 [tin4 yun4 sa1 leut9]

house wine *n.* 招牌酒 [jiu1 paai4 jau2]

household *n.* 一家人 [yat1 ga1 yan4]; *adj.* 屋企 [uk7 kei2]

household goods *n.* 日用品 [yat9 yung6 ban2]

household linen *n.* 床上用品 [chong4 seung6 yung6 ban2]

housekeeping *n.* 家務 [ga1 mou6]; ~ **by tenant** *phr.* 租客自己做家務 [jou1 haak8 ji6 gei2 jou6 ga1 mou6]

housewife *n.* 家庭主婦 [ga1 ting4 jyu2 fu5]

housework *n.* 家務 [ga1 mou6]

housing *n.* 住宅 [jyu6 jaak9]

housing district *n.* 住宅區 [jyu6 jaak9 keui1]

how *conj./adv.* 點樣 [dim2 yeung2]
　how are things? *phr.* 最近點啊 [jeui3 gan6 dim2 a3]
　how are you? *phr.* 最近點啊？
　how long? *phr.* 要幾耐？
　how many? *phr.* 有幾多 [yau5 gei2 do1]
　how many times? *phr.* 幾多次 [gei2 do1 chi3]
　how much? *phr.* 幾多錢 [gei2 do1 chin2]
　how often? *phr.* 有幾經常 [yau5 gei2 ging1 seung4]
　how old? *phr.* 幾大年紀 [gei2 daai6 nin4 gei2]

however *adv.* 但係 [daan6 hai6]

hubcap *n.* 輪蓋 [leun4 goi3]

hug *n.* 擁抱 [yung2 pou5]; *v.* 攬 [laam2]; **give a ~** 擁抱

huge *adj.* 超大 [chiu1 daai6]

human *adj.* 有人性 [yau5 yan4 sing3]; *n.* 人類 [yan4 leui6]

human rights *n.* 人權 [yan4 kyun4]

humble *adj.* 謙虛 [him1 heui1]

humidity *n.* 濕度 [sap7 dou6]

humiliate *n.* 侮辱 [mou5 yuk9]

humiliation *n.* 侮辱 [mou5 yuk9]

humility *n.* 謙虛 [him1 heui1]

hummus *n.* 鷹嘴豆泥 [ying1 jeui2 dau6 nai4], **spicy ~** 辣鷹嘴豆泥

humorous *adj.* 風趣 [fung1 cheui3]

hundred *n.* 百 [baak8]

hundredth *adj.* 第一百個 [dai6 yat7 baak8 go3]

hung jury 做唔到決定嘅陪審團 [jou6 m4 dou2 kyut8 ding6 ge3 pui4 sam2 tyun4]

Hungarian *adj.* 匈牙利 [hung1 nga4 lei6]

Hungary *n.* 匈牙利 [hung1 nga4 lei6]

hunger *n.* 肚餓 [tou5 ngo6]

hungry *adj.* 肚餓 [tou5 ngo6]

hunt *v.* 打獵 [da2 lip9]

hunter *n.* 獵人 [lip9 yan4]

hunting *n.* 打獵 [da2 lip9]

hurry *v./n.* 匆忙 [chung1 mong4]; **be in a ~** 匆忙

hurt *v.* 受傷 [sau6 seung1], **be ~** 受傷; *adj.* 受咗傷 [sau6 jo2 seung1]; **where does it ~?** 邊度痛？

husband *n.* 老公 [lou5 gung1]

husk *n.* 殼 [hok8]; **corn** ~ 粟米殼; *v.* 去咗殼 [heui3 jo2 hok8], ~ **corn** 去咗殼粟米

hut *n.* 棚 [paang4]

hybrid *n.* 雜種 [jaap9 jung2]

hydrogen *n.* 氫 [hing1]

hydrogenized *adj.* 氫化 [hing1 fa3]

hygienist *n.* 牙醫助手 [nga4 yi1 jo6 sau2]

hyphen *n.* 連號 [lin4 hou6]

hypnotism *n.* 催眠 [cheui1 min4]

hypnotize *v.* 催眠 [cheui1 min4]

hypodermic needle *n.* 注射器針頭 [jyu3 se6 hei3 jam1 tau4]

hypothesis *n.* 前提 [chin4 tai4]

hysteria *n.* 歇斯底里 [hit8 si1 dai2 lei5]

hysterical *adj.* 歇斯底里 [hit8 si1 dai2 lei5]

I

I *pron.* 我 [ngo5]

i.e. *abbr.* 即係 [jik7 hai6]

ice *n.* 冰 [bing1], **with ~** 加冰, **without ~** 唔加冰, **no ~** 唔加冰; *v.* 結冰 [git8 bing1]; *adj.* 冰嘅 [bing1 ge3]

ice cream *n.* 雪糕 [syut8 gou1]

ice cream cone *n.* 甜筒 [tim4 tung2]

ice cream parlor *n.* 雪糕店 [syut8 gou1 dim3]

ice hockey *n.* 冰上曲棍球 [bing1 seung6 kuk7 gwan3 kau4]

ice pops *n.* 雪條 [syut8 tiu2]

ice skate *n./v.* 溜冰 [lau4 bing1]

iceberg *n.* 冰山 [bing1 saan1]

iceberg lettuce *n.* 西生菜 [sai1 saang1 choi3]

iced *adj.* 冰凍 [bing1 dung3], **~ tea** 冰茶, **~ bun** 冰皮包, **~ pastry** 冰皮糕點; *v.* 結冰 [git8 bing1]

Iceland *n.* 冰島 [bing1 dou2]

Icelandic *adj.* 冰島 [bing1 dou2]

icing *n.* 糖衣 [tong4 yi1], **flavored ~** 加味糖衣, **chocolate ~** 朱古力糖衣, **sweet ~** 糖衣, **sugar ~** 糖衣

icy *adj.* 凍 [dung3]

ID card (*abbr* **identification card**) *n.* 身份證 [san1 fan2 jing3]

idea *n.* 計仔 [gai2 jai2]

ideal *adj.n.* 理想 [lei5 seung2]

idealism *n.* 理想主義 [lei5 seung2 jyu2 yi6]

idealist *n.* 理想主義者 [lei5 seung2 jyu2 yi6 je2]

idealistic *adj.* 理想主義嘅 [lei5 seung2 jyu2 yi6 ge3]

ideally *adv.* 理想 [lei5 seung2]

identical *adj.* 完全一樣 [yun4 cyun4 yat7 yeung6]

identification *n.* 身份 [san1 fan2]

identify *v.* 認出 [ying6 cheut7]

identity card *n.* 身份證 [san1 fan2 jing3]

identity document *n.* 身份證明文件 [san1 fan2 jing3 ming4 man4 gin6]

ideological *adj.* 意識形態 [yi3 sik7 ying4 taai3]

idiom *n.* 成語 [sing4 yu5]

idle *adj.* 冇嘢做 [mou5 ye5 jou6]

if *conj.* 如果 [yu4 gwo2]

ignition *n.* 點火裝置 [dim2 fo2 jong1 ji3]

ignition key *n.* 點火開關 [dim2 fo2 hoi1 gwaan1]

ignorance *n.* 無知 [mou4 ji1]

ignorant *adj.* 無知 [mou4 ji1]

ignore *v.* 無視 [mou4 si6]

ill *adj.* 病咗 [beng6 jo2]

illegal *adj.* 犯法 [faan6 faat8]; **it is ~** 呢個係犯法, **is it ~?** 咁樣犯唔犯法？

illegal entry *n.* 非法入境 [fei1 faat8 yap9 ging2]

illegally *adv.* 犯法 [faan6 faat8]

illegibility *n.* 唔清楚 [m4 ching1 cho2]

illegible *adj.* 睇唔清楚 [tai2 m4 ching1 cho2]

illegitimate *adj.* 私生 [si1 sang1]

illiteracy *n.* 文盲 [man4 maang4]

illiterate *n.* 文盲 [man4 maang4]

illness *n.* 病 [beng6]

illuminate *v.* 照光 [jiu3 gwong1]

illumination *n.* 照明 [jiu3 ming4]

illustrate *v.* 說明 [syut8 ming4]

illustration *n.* 圖解 [tou4 gaai2]

image *n.* 圖像 [tou4 jeung6]

imagery *n.* 形象 [ying4 jeung6]

imaginary *adj.* 虛構 [heui1 kau3]

imagination *n.* 想像 [seung2 jeung6]

imaginative *adj.* 好有想像力 [hou2 yau5 seung2 jeung6 lik9]

imagine *v.* 想像 [seung2 jeung6]

imitation *n.* 模仿 [mou4 fong2]

immediate *adj.* 直接 [jik9 jip8]

immediately *adv.* 即刻 [jik7 hak7]

immigrant *n.* 移民 [yi4 man4]

immigration *n.* 移民 [yi4 man4]

immoral *adj.* 唔道德 [m4 dou6 dak7]

immune *n.* 免疫 [min5 yik9]

immune system *n.* 免疫系統 [min5 yik9 hai6 tung2]

immunity *n.* 免疫力 [min5 yik9 lik9]

immunization *n.* 免疫 [min5 yik9]

impact *n.* 影響 [ying2 heung2]

impatient *adj.* 唔耐煩 [m4 noi6 faan4]

impatiently *adv.* 唔耐煩 [m4 noi6 faan4]

imperative *adj.* 必要 [bit7 yiu3]; *n.* 命令 [ming6 ling6]

impersonate *v.* 模仿 [mou4 fong2]

impersonation *n.* 模仿 [mou4 fong2]

implement *v.* 實施 [sat9 si1]

implementation *n.* 實施 [sat9 si1]

implication *n.* 言外之意 [yin4 ngoi6 ji1 yi3]

imply *v.* 暗示 [am3 si6]

impolite *adj.* 冇禮貌 [mou5 lai5 maau6]

import *n.* 進口 [jeun3 hau2]; *v.* 進口 [jeun3 hau2]; *comp.* ~ **files** 輸入文件

importance *n.* 重要性 [jung6 yiu1 sing3]

important *adj.* 重要 [jung6 yiu1]; **it is ~** 呢個好重要

importantly *adv.* 重要嘅係 [jung6 yiu1 ge3 hai6]

impose *v.* 強加 [keung5 ga1]

impostor *n.* 騙子 [pin3 ji2]

imposture *n.* 詐騙 [ja3 pin3]

impossible *adj.* 冇可能 [mou5 ho2 nang4]

impress *v.* 留低印象 [lau4 dai1 yan3 jeung6]

impressed *adj.* 感動 [gam2 dung6]

impression *n.* 印象 [yan3 jeung6]

impressive *adj.* 令人印象深刻 [ling6 yan4 yan3 jeung6 sam1 hak7]

improve *v.* 改進 [goi2 jeun3]

improved *adj.* 改進咗 [goi2 jeun3 jo2]

improvement *n.* 進步 [jeun3 bou6]

in *adv.* 入 [yap9]; *prep.* 喺…入面 [hai2 … yap9 min6]

in a hurry 匆匆忙忙 [chung1 chung1 mong4 mong4]

in addition (to) 除咗 [cheui4 jo2]

in advance 事先 [si6 sin1]

in case (of) 萬一 [maan6 yat7]

in charge of 負責 [fu6 jaak8]

in common 共同 [gung6 tung4]

in control (of) 控制 [hung3 jai3]

in detail 詳細 [cheung4 sai3]

in excess of 超過 [chiu1 gwo3]

in exchange (for) 換 [wun6]

in favor (of) 鍾意 [jung1 yi3]

in front (of) *prep.* 喺…前面 [hai2 … chin4 min6]

in general 一般 [yat7 bun1]

in honor of 紀念 [gei3 nim6]

in memory of 懷念 [waai4 nim6]

in order to 為咗 [wai6 jo2]

in public 喺公眾場合 [hai2 gung1 jung3 cheung4 hap9]

in season 當季 [dong1 gwai3]; **fruit ~** 時令水果, **produce ~** 時令蔬果

in the end *prep.* 最後 [jeui3 hau6]

inability *n.* 冇能力 [mou5 nang4 lik9]

inaccessible *adj.* 難以得到 [naan4 yi5 dak7 dou2]

Inc. (*abbr.* for **incorporated**) 公司 [gung1 si1]

incarceration *n.* 監禁 [gaam1 gam1]

incentive *n.* 激勵 [gik7 lai6]

inch *n.* 英吋 [ying1 chyun3]

incidence *n.* 影響 [ying2 heung2]

incident *n.* 事件 [si6 gin6]

incise *v.* 刻 [haak7]

incline *n.* 傾斜 [king1 che4]

include *v.* 包括 [baau1 kut8]

included *adj.* 包括在內 [baau1 kut8 joi6 noi6]; **be ~ 包埋, is X ~? 包唔包埋X?**

including *prep.* 包括 [baau1 kut8]

inclusive *adj.* 包括在內 [baau1 kut8 joi6 noi6]

income *n.* 收入 [sau1 yap9]

income tax *n.* 入息稅 [yap9 sik7 seui3]

incompetent *adj.* 做唔好 [jou6 m4 hou2]

incomprehensible *adj.* 好難理解 [hou2 naan4 lei5 gaai2]

incorporate *v.* 成立公司 [sing4 laap6 gung1 si1]

incorporated (*abbr.* **Inc.**) *adj.* 公司 [gung1 si1]

incorrect *adj.* 唔啱 [m4 ngaam1]

increase *v.* 增加 [jang1 ga1]; *n.* 提高 [tai4 gou1]

increasingly *adv.* 愈來愈多 [yu6 loi6 yu6 do1]

incredible *adj.* 好犀利 [hou2 sai1 lei6]

incriminate *v.* 牽連 [hin1 lin4]

incubate *v.* 孵 [fu1]

incumbent *n.* 現任 [yin6 yam6]

incrusted *adj.* 有硬殼 [yau5 ngaang6 hok8]

incur *v.* 引起 [yan5 hei2]

indeed *adv.* 的確 [dik7 kok8]

independence *n.* 獨立 [duk9 laap9]

independent *adj.* 獨立 [duk9 laap9]

independently *adv.* 獨立 [duk9 laap9]

index *n.* 索引 [sok8 yan5]

India *n.* 印度 [yan3 dou6]

Indian *adj.* 印度 [yan3 dou6]; *n.* 印度人 [yan3 dou6 yan4]; **~ food** 印度菜, **~ tea** 印度茶, **~ seasoning** 印度菜調味料

indicate v. 顯示 [hin2 si6]

indication n. 跡象 [jik7 jeung6]

indict v. 控告 [hung3 gou3]

indictment n. 控告 [hung3 gou3]

indigestion n. 消化不良 [siu1 fa3 bat7 leung4]

indirect adj. 間接 [gaan3 jip8]

indirect speech n. 間接引語 [gaan3 jip8 yan5 yu5]

indirectly adv. 間接 [gaan3 jip8]

individual adj. 單獨 [daan1 duk9]; n. 個人 [go3 yan4]

Indonesia n. 印度尼西亞 [yan3 dou6 nei4 sai1 a3]

Indonesian adj. 印度尼西亞 [yan3 dou6 nei4 sai1 a3]

indoor adj. 室內 [sat7 noi6]

indoor pool n. 室內泳池 [sat7 noi6 wing6 chi4]

indoors adv. 室內 [sat7 noi6]

induce v. 引起 [yan5 hei2]

industrial adj. 工業 [gung1 yip9]

industrial district n. 工業區 [gung1 yip9 keui1]

industry n. 產業 [chaan2 yip9]

inequality n. 不平等 [bat7 ping4 dang2]

inevitable adj. 不可避免 [bat7 ho2 bei6 min5]

inevitably adv. 不可避免 [bat7 ho2 bei6 min5]

inexpensive adj. 唔貴 [m4 gwai3]

infant n. 嬰兒[ying1 yi4]; adj. 嬰兒嘅 [ying1 yi4 ge3]

infant formula n.嬰兒配方奶粉 [ying1 yi4 pui3 fong1 naai5 fan2]

infantry n. 步兵 [bou6 bing1]

infect v. 感染 [gam2 yim5]

infection n. 感染 [gam2 yim5]

infected adj. 感染咗 [gam2 yam5 jo2]; be ~ 感染咗

infectious adj. 傳染 [chyun4 yim5]

infectious mononucleosis n. 傳染性單核細胞增多症 [chyun4 yim5 sing3 daan1 hat9 sai3 baau1 jang1 do1 jing3]

infinitive n. 不定式 [bat7 ding6 sik7]

infirmary n. 醫院 [yi1 yun6]

inflammation n. 發炎 [faat8 yim4]

inflammatory adj. 發炎 [faat8 yim4]

inflation n. 通貨膨脹 [tung1 fo3 paang4 jeung3]

influence n. 影響力 [ying2 heung2 lik9]; v. 影響 [ying2 heung2]

influenza n. 流行性感冒 [lau4 hang4 sing3 gam2 mou6]

inform v. 通知 [tung1 ji1]

informal adj. 隨便 [cheui4 bin6]

information n. 資料 [ji1 liu2]

information counter/office n. 詢問處 [seun1 man6 chyu3]

information desk n. 服務台 [fuk9 mou6 toi4]

infraction n. 違犯 [wai4 faan2]

infrastructure n. 基礎設施 [gei1 cho2 chit8 si1]

infusion n. 灌輸 [gun3 syu1]

ingredient n. 原料 [yun4 liu2]

initial adj. 最初 [jeui3 cho1]; n. 第一個字母 [dai6 yat7 go3 ji6 mou5]

initially adv. 最初 [jeui3 cho1]

initiative n. 主動 [jyu2 dung6]

inject v. 注射 [jyu3 se6]

injection *n.* 注射 [jyu3 se6]

injunction *n.* 禁制令 [gam3 jai3 ling6]

injure *v.* 整傷 [jing2 seung1]

injured *adj.* 受傷 [sau6 seung1]

injury *n.* 受傷 [sau6 seung1]

ink *n.* 墨水 [mak9 seui2]

inn *n.* 旅館 [leui5 gun2]

innate *adj.* 天生 [tin1 sang1]

inner *adj.* 入面 [yap9 min6]

inner tube *n.* 內胎 [noi6 toi1]

innocent *adj.* 無辜 [mou4 gu1]

innovate *v.* 創新 [chong3 san1]

innovation *n.* 創新 [chong3 san1]

inoculation *n.* 打預防針 [da2 yu6 fong4 jam1]

input *n./v.* 輸入 [syu1 yap9]

inquiry *n.* 調查 [diu6 cha4]

inquiry *n.* 調查 [diu6 cha4]

insect *n.* 蟲 [chung4]

insect bite *n.* 蚊叮蟲咬 [man1 ding1 chung4 ngaau5]

insect repellant *n.* 殺蟲水 [saat8 chung4 seui2]

insert *v.* 插入 [chaap8 yap9]

inside *prep.* 喺…入面 [hai2 ... yap9 min6]; *adv./n./adj.* 入面 [yap9 min6]

insight *n.* 眼光 [ngaan5 gwong1]

insist (on) *v.* 堅持 [gin1 chi4]

insomnia *n.* 失眠 [sat7 min4]

inspect *v.* 審查 [sam2 cha4]

inspection *n.* 審查 [sam2 cha4]

inspiration *n.* 靈感 [ling4 gam2]

inspire *v.* 啓發 [kai2 faat8]

install *v.* 安裝 [on1 jong1]

installation *n.* 安裝 [on1 jong1]

instance *n.* 例子 [lai6 ji2]

instant *adj.* 即刻 [jik1 hak7], ~ **coffee** 即沖咖啡, ~ **rice** 即食米飯, ~ **meal** 微波爐餐

instead *adv.* 而唔係 [yi4 m4 hai6]; ~ **of** *prep.* 而唔係 [yi4 m4 hai6]

instigate *v.* 煽動 [sin3 dung6]

instigation *n.* 煽動 [sin3 dung6]

instinct *n.* 直覺 [jik9 gok8]

institute *n.* 協會 [hip8 wui2]

institution *n.* 機構 [gei1 kau3]

institutional *adj.* 機構 [gei1 kau3]

instruction *n.* 指示 [ji2 si6]

instructions *n.* 指令 [ji2 ling6]; ~ **for use** 使用說明

instructor *n.* 教練 [gaau3 lin6]

instrument *n.* 工具 [gung1 geui6]

instrumental *adj.* 有幫助 [yau5 bong1 jo6]

insufficient *adj.* 唔夠 [m4 gau3]

insulin *n.* 胰島素 [yi4 dou2 sou3]

insult *v./n.* 侮辱 [mou5 yuk9]

insulting *adj.* 冇禮貌 [mou5 lai5 maau6]

insurance *n.* 保險 [bou2 him2]; **comprehensive ~** *n.* 綜合保險 [jung3 hap9 bou2 him2]

insurance card *n.* 保險卡 [bou2 him2 kaat7]

insurance claim *n.* 保險索償 [bou2 him2 saak8 seung4]

insurance company *n.* 保險公司 [bou2 him2 gung1 si1]

integrate *v.* 融合 [yung4 hap9]

integrated *adj.* 和諧 [wo4 haai4]

intellectual *adj.* 智力 [ji3 lik9]; *n.* 知識份子 [ji1 sik7 fan6 ji2]

intelligence *n.* 智商 [ji3 seung1]

intelligent *adj.* 醒目 [sing2 muk9]

intend *v.* 意圖 [yi3 tou4]

intense *adj.* 激烈 [gik7 lit9]

intensity *n.* 激烈程度 [gik7 lit9 ching4 dou6]

intensive care *n.* 深切治療 [sam1 chit8 ji6 liu4]

intention *n.* 意圖 [yi3 tou4]

interaction *n.* 互動 [wu6 dung6]

interactive 互動 [wu6 dung6], ~ **program** 互動遊戲

intercity train *n.* 城際列車 [sing4 jai3 lit9 che1]

interest *n.* 興趣 [hing3 cheui3]; *v.* 引起興趣 [yan5 hei2 hing3 cheui3]

interested (in) *adj.* 有興趣 [yau5 hing3 cheui3]

interesting *adj.* 得意 [dak7 yi3]

interference *n.* 介入 [gaai3 yap9]

interim *adj.* 臨時 [lam4 si4]

interior *n.* 內部 [noi6 bou6]; *adj.* 室內 [sat7 noi6]

intermediate *adj.* 中間 [jung1 gaan1]

intermission *n.* 中場休息 [jung1 cheung4 yau1 sik7]

internal *adj.* 內部 [noi6 bou6]

international *adj.* 國際 [gwok8 jai3]

international call *n.* 國際長途 [gwok8 jai3 cheung4 tou4]

international student card *n.* 國際學生證 [gwok8 jai3 hok9 sang1 saang1 jing3]

Internet *n.* 互聯網 [wu6 lyun4 mong5]

Internet café *n.* 網吧 [mong5 ba1]

interpret *v.* 翻譯 [faan1 yik9]

interpretation *n.* 翻譯 [faan1 yik9]

interpreter *n.* 翻譯 [faan1 yik9]

interrupt *v.* 打攪 [da2 gaau2]

interruption *n.* 打攪 [da2 gaau2]; **without ~** 順利

intersection *n.* 交叉點 [gaau1 cha1 dim2]

interval *n.* 區間 [keui1 gaan1]

intervene *v.* 干涉 [gon1 sip8]

intervention *n.* 干涉 [gon1 sip8]

interview *n./v.* 面試 [min6 si3]

intimacy *n.* 親密 [chan1 mat9]

intimate *adj.* 親密 [chan1 mat9]

into *prep.* 入去 [yap9 heui3]

intrinsic *adj.* 本質 [bun2 jat7]

introduce *v.* 介紹 [gaai3 siu6]; **may I ~ X?** 不如我介紹X俾你識啊？

introduce oneself *v.* 自我介紹 [ji6 ngo5 gaai3 siu6]

introduction *n.* 介紹 [gaai3 siu6]

introspect *v.* 反省 [faan2 sing2]

introspection *n.* 反省 [faan2 sing2]

intrude *v.* 擅闖 [sin6 chong2]

intruder *n.* 擅闖者 [sin6 chong2 je2]

invent *v.* 發明 [faat8 ming4]

invention *n.* 發明 [faat8 ming4]

invest *v.* 投資 [tau4 ji1]

investigate *v.* 調查 [diu6 cha4]

investigation *n.* 調查 [diu6 cha4]

investment *n.* 投資 [tau4 ji1]

investor *n.* 投資者 [tau4 ji1 je2]

invigilate *v.* 監考 [gaam1 haau2]

invigilation *n.* 監考 [gaam1 haau2]

invigilator *n.* 監考 [gaam1 haau2]

invitation *n.* 邀請 [yiu1 ching2]

invite *v.* 邀請 [yiu1 ching2]; ~ **for** *v.* 邀請黎 [yiu1 ching2 lai4]

invoice *n.* 單 [daan1]; *v.* 開單 [hoi1 daan1]

involved in 參與 [chaam1 yu5]

involvement *n.* 加入 [ga1 yap9]

inwards *adv.* 向中心 [heung3 jung1 sam1]

iodine *n.* 碘 [din2]

ion *n.* 離子 [lei4 ji2]

Iran *n.* 伊朗 [yi1 long5]

Iranian *adj.* 伊朗 [yi1 long5]

Iraq *n.* 伊拉克 [yi1 laai1 hak7]

Iraqi *adj.* 伊拉克 [yi1 laai1 hak7]

Ireland *n.* 愛爾蘭 [oi3 yi5 laan4]

Ireland, Northern *n.* 北愛爾蘭 [bak7 oi3 yi5 laan4]

Irish *n.* 愛爾蘭人 [oi3 yi5 laan4 yan4]

iron *n./adj.* 鐵 [tit8]; *v.* 燙 [tong3]

ironic *adj.* 諷刺 [fung3 chi3]

ironwork *n.* 鐵製品 [tit8 jai3 ban2]

irony *n.* 諷刺 [fung3 chi3]

irregular *adj.* 冇規律 [mou5 kwai1 leut9]

irrigation *n.* 水利 [seui2 lei6]

irritate *v.* 激嬲 [gik7 nau1]

irritated *adj.* 激嬲咗 [gik7 nau1 jo2]

irritating *adj.* 乞人憎 [hat7 yan4 jang1]

-ish *suffix* 後綴 [hau6 jeui3]

Islamabad *n.* 伊斯蘭堡 [yi1 si1 laan4 bou2]; ~, **capital of Pakistan** 巴基斯坦首都

Islamic *adj.* 清真 [ching1 jan1]

island *n.* 島 [dou2]

isolate *v.* 孤立 [gu1 laap9]

isolated *adj.* 孤立 [gu1 laap9]

Israel *n.* 以色列 [yi5 sik7 lit9]

Israeli *adj.* 以色列 [yi5 sik7 lit9]

issue *n.* 問題 [man6 tai4]; *v.* 發表 [faat8 biu2]

it *pron./det.* 佢 [keui5]

Italian *adj.* 意大利 [yi3 daai6 lei6]

Italy *n.* 意大利 [yi3 daai6 lei6]

itch *v./n.* 痕 [han4]; **have an ~** 好痕

item *n.* 項目 [hong6 muk9]

itemized *adj.* 列清單 [lit9 ching1 daan1]

itemized bill *n.* 賬目 [jeung3 muk9]

itinerary *n.* 行程表 [hang4 ching4 biu2]

its *det.* 佢嘅 [keui5 ge3]

itself *pron.* 佢自己 [keui5 ji6 gei2]

Ivoirian *adj.* 象牙海岸 [jeung6 nga4 hoi2 ngon6]

J

jacket *n.* 皮褸 [pei1 lau1]

jackfruit *n.* 菠蘿蜜 [bo1 lo4 mat9]

jail *n.* 監獄 [gaam1 yuk9]

Jakarta *n.* 雅加達 [nga5 ga1 daat9]; ~,**capital of Indonesia** 印度尼西亞首都

jalapeno (peppers) *n.* 墨西哥辣椒 [mak9 sai1 go1 laat9 jiu1]

jam 1. *n.* 果醬 [gwo2 jeung3], fruit ~ 果醬,honey ~ 蜂蜜醬 // 2. *v.* 塞 [sak7], to be ~med 塞住

Jamaica *n.* 牙買加 [nga4 maai5 ga1]

Jamaican *adj.* 牙買加 [nga4 maai5 ga1]

January (*abbr.* Jan.) *n.* 一月 [yat7 yut9]

Japan *n.* 日本 [yat9 bun2]

Japanese *adj.* 日本 [yat9 bun2], ~ tea 日本茶

jar *n.* 罐 [gun3]

jasmine *n.* 茉莉 [mut9 lei2], ~ tea 茉莉花茶, ~ flower 茉莉花, ~ extract 茉莉花濃縮

jaundice *n.* 黃疸 [wong4 taan2]

jaw *n.* 下扒 [ha6 pa4]

jazz *n.* 爵士樂 [jeuk8 si6 ngok9]

jealous *adj.* 妒忌 [dou3 gei6]

jeans *n.* 牛仔褲 [ngau4 jai2 fu3]

jeep *n.* 吉普車 [gat7 pou2 che1]

jello *n.* 啫喱 [je1 lei2], ~ mix 雜啫喱, ~ powder 啫喱粉, ~ mold 啫喱模具

jelly *n.* 啫喱 [je1 lei2]

jelly roll *n.* 瑞士卷 [seui6 si6 gyun2]

jellybeans *n.* 啫喱糖 [je1 lei2 tong2]

jellyfish *n.* 水母 [seui2 mou5]

jerk *n.* 衰人 [seui1 yan4]

jerk seasoning *n.* 醃牛肉 [yip8 ngau4 yuk9]

jeroboam *n.* 大酒杯 [daai6 jau2 bui1]

Jerusalem *n.* 耶路撒冷 [ye4 lou6 saat8 laang5]; ~,**capital of Israel** 以色列首都

Jerusalem artichoke *n.* 洋薑 [yeung4 geung1]

jet *n.* 噴射機 [pan3 se6 gei1]

jet lag *n.* 時差 [si4 cha1]; be ~ged 有時差

jet-ski *n.* 水上電單車 [seui2 seung6 din6 daan1 che]

jetty *n.* 防波堤 [fong4 bo1 tai4]

Jew *n.* 猶太人 [yau4 taai3 yan4]

jewel *n.* 珠寶 [jyu1 bou2]

jeweler *n.* 珠寶商 [jyu1 bou2 seung1]

jewelry *n.* 珠寶 [jyu1 bou2]

Jewish *adj.* 猶太人 [yau4 taai3 yan4]

jicama *n.* 沙葛 [sa1 got8]

jimmies *n.* 朱古力粉 [jyu1 gu2 lik9 fan2]

job *n.* 工 [gung1]; what's your ~? 你做乜野嘎？

job advertisement (want ad) *n.* 招聘廣告 [jiu1 ping3 gwong2 guo3]

job center *n.* 就業中心 [jau6 yip9 fuk9 mou6 jung1 sam1]

job description *n.* 工作簡介 [gung1 jok8 gaan2 gaai3]

jockey *n.* 騎師 [ke4 si1]

jogging *n.* 慢跑 [maan6 paau2]

join (in) *v.* 加入 [ga1 yap9]; **join (someone)** *v.* 同某人見面 [tung4 mau5 yan4 gin3 min6], **may I ~ you?** 我同你一齊好唔好？

joint *adj.* 共同 [gung6 tung4]; *n.* 關節 [gwaan1 jit8]

joint passport *n.* 聯合護照 [lyun4 hap9 wu6 jiu3]

jointly *adv.* 一齊 [yat7 chai4]

joke *v./n.* 講笑 [gong2 siu3]; **are you joking?** 唔係講笑嘛？

Jordan *n.* 約旦 [yeuk8 daan3]

Jordan almonds *n.* 約旦杏仁 [yeuk8 daan3 hang6 yan4]

Jordan dates *n.* 約旦紅棗 [yeuk8 daan3 hung4 jou2]

Jordanian *adj.* 約旦 [yeuk8 daan3]

journal *n.* 日報 [yat9 bou3]

journalism *n.* 新聞業 [san1 man4 yip9]

journalist *n.* 新聞記者 [san1 man4 gei3 je2]

journey *n.* 旅行 [leui5 hang4]

joy *n.* 開心 [hoi1 sam1]

Juba *n.* 久巴 [gau2 ba1]; ~, **capital of South Sudan** 南蘇丹首都

judge *n.* 法官 [faat8 gun1]; *v.* 判斷 [pun3 dyun6]

judgement *n.* 判斷 [pun3 dyun6]

judiciary *n.* 司法部 [si1 faat8 bou6]

jug *n.* 壺 [wu2]

juice *n.* 果汁 [gwo2 jap7], **grape** ~ 葡萄汁, **grapefruit** ~ 柚子汁, **lemon** ~ 檸檬汁, **orange** ~ 橙汁, **cherry** ~ 車厘子汁, **apple** ~ 蘋果汁, **pear** ~ 梨汁, **tomato** ~ 番茄汁

jujube *n.* 棗 [jou2]

julienne *adj./v.* 切絲 [chit8 si1]; **vegetables** ~ 蔬菜絲

July (*abbr.* Jul.) *n.* 七月 [chat7 yut9]

jump *v./n.* 跳 [tiu3]

jumper *n.* 跳高運動員 [tiu3 gou1 wan6 dung6 yun4]

jumper cables *n.* 充電電線 [chung1 din6 din6 sin3]

junction *n.* 交叉點 [gaau1 cha1 dim2]

June (*abbr.* Jun.) *n.* 六月 [luk9 yut9]

jungle *n.* 叢林 [chung4 lam4]

junior *adj.* 資歷淺 [ji1 lik9 chin2]; *n.* 青少年 [ching1 siu3 nin4]

junior high school *n.* 初中 [cho1 jung1]

juniper berries *n.* 杜松子 [dou6 chung4 ji2]; ~ **liqueur** 杜松子酒

jurisdiction *n.* 司法權 [si1 faat8 kyun4]

jurisprudence *n.* 法理學 [faat8 lei5 hok9]

jury *n.* 陪審團 [pui4 sam2 tyun4]

just *adv.* 淨係 [jing6 hai6]

justice *n.* 公正 [gung1 jing3]

justified *adj.* 合理 [hap9 lei5]

justify *v.* 證明有理 [jing3 ming4 yau5 lei5]

K

k. (*abbr. of* **kilometer**) *n.* 公里 [gung1 lei5]

Kabul *n.* 喀布爾 [hak3 bou3 yi5]; ~, **capital of Afghanistan** 阿富汗首都

kale *n.* 甘藍菜 [gam1 laam4 choi3]

Kampala *n.* 坎柏拉 [ham2 paak8 laai1]; ~, **capital of Uganda** 烏干達首都

kasha *n.* 麥粥 [mak9 juk7]

Kathmandu *n.* 加德滿都 [ga1 dak7 mun5 dou1]; ~, **capital of Nepal** 尼泊爾首都

Kazakhstan *n.* 哈薩克斯坦 [ha1 saat8 hak7 si1 taan2]

Kazakhstani *adj.* 哈薩克斯坦 [ha1 saat8 hak7 si1 taan2]

kebab *n.* 烤羊肉串 [haau1 yeung4 yuk9 chyun3], **lamb** ~ 烤羊肉串, **chicken** ~ 烤雞肉串

keen *adj.* 熱心 [yit9 sam1]

keen on 熱衷 [yit9 chung1]

keep *v.* 保持 [bou2 chi4]; ~ **the change!** 唔使找

keep out *v.* 唔俾入黎 [m4 bei2 yap9 lai4]

kefir *n.* 酸奶酒 [syun1 naai5 jau2], **strawberry** ~ 草莓酸奶酒, **vanilla** ~ 香草酸奶酒

kennel *n.* 狗場 [gau2 cheung4]

Kenya *n.* 肯尼亞 [hang2 nei4 a3]

Kenyan *adj.* 肯尼亞 [hang2 nei4 a3]

kernel *n.* 仁 [yan4], **corn** ~ 粟米粒, **grain** ~ 糧粒

kerosene *n.* 火水 [fo2 seui2]

kerosene stove *n.* 火水爐 [fo2 seui2 lou4]

ketchup *n.* 茄汁 [ke2 jap7]

kettle *n.* 水壺 [seui2 wu2]

key *n.* 鎖匙 [so2 si4]; *adj.* 關鍵 [gwaan1 gin6]; *v.* 打字 [da2 ji6]

key ring *n.* 鎖匙扣 [so2 si4 kau3]

keyboard (*piano / computer*) *n.* 鍵盤 [gin6 pun2]

keyword *n.* 關鍵字 [gwaan1 gin6 ji6], ~ **search** 關鍵字搜索

Khartoum *n.* 喀土穆 [hak3 tou2 muk9]; ~, **capital of Sudan** 蘇丹首都

kick *v./n.* 踢 [tek8]

kick-off *n.* 開波 [hoi1 bo1]

kid (*child / goat*) *n.* 細路仔 [sai3 lou6 jai2]

kiddie pool *n.* 小童池 [siu2 tung4 chi4]

kidnap *v.* 綁架 [bong2 ga3]

kidney *n.* 腎 [san5]

kidney beans *n.* 雲豆 [wan4 dau2]

kidney stew *n.* 燉腎 [dan6 san5]

Kigali *n.* 基加利 [gei1 ga1 lei6]; ~, **capital of Rwanda** 盧旺達首都

kill *v.* 殺 [saat8]

killing *n.* 謀殺 [mau4 saat8]

kilobyte (*abbr.* **K.**) *comp. n.* 千位元組 [chin1 wai2 yun4 jou2], **file size in** ~**s** 文件大小系數千位元組

kilogram (**2.2 lbs.**) *n.* 公斤 [gung1 gan1]

kilometer (0.6 miles) *n.* 公里 [gung1 lei5]

kind *n.* 種類 [jung2 leui6], **what ~ of** 乜嘢種類; *adj.* 好人 [hou2 yan4]

kindergarten *n.* 幼稚園 [yau3 ji6 yun2]

kindly *adv.* 好心 [hou2 sam1]

kindness *n.* 好心 [hou2 sam1]

king *n.* 國王 [gwok8 wong4]

Kingston *n.* 金斯敦 [gam1 si1 seun1]; **~, capital of Jamaica** 牙買加首都

Kingstown *n.* 金斯敦 [gam1 si1 seun1]; **~, capital of Saint Vincent and the Grenadines** 聖文森特和格林納丁斯首都

Kinshasa *n.* 金沙薩 [gam1 sa1 saat8]; **~, capital of Congo** 剛果首都

kinship *n.* 親屬關係 [chan1 suk9 gwaan1 hai6]

Kiribati *n.* 基里巴斯 [gei1 lei5 ba1 si1]

kiss *v./n.* 錫 [sek8]

kit *n.* 工具箱 [gung1 geui6 seung1]

kitchen *n.* 廚房 [chyu4 fong2]; **~ counter** 廚房櫃台

kitchen set *n.* 廚具 [chyu4 geui6]

kitten *n.* 貓仔 [maau1 jai2]

kiwi *n.* 奇異果 [kei4 yi6 gwo2]

km. (*abbr. of* **kilometer**) *n.* 公里 [gung1 lei5]

knapsack *n.* 背囊 [bui3 nong4]

knead *v.* 搓 [cho1]; **~ed** 搓完, **~ing** 搓緊

knee *n.* 膝頭 [sat7 tau4]

knife *n.* 刀仔 [dou1 jai2]

knit *v.* 織 [jik7]; *n.* 編織物 [pin1 jik7 mat9]

knock *v./n.* 敲 [haau1]

knot *n.* 結 [git8]

know *v.* 知 [ji1]; **~ smth. or smn.** 知道 / 識, **how to ~** 點知

knowledge *n.* 知識 [ji1 sik7]

kohlrabi *n.* 大頭菜 [daai6 tau4 choi3]

Korea, North *n.* 北韓 [bak7 hon4]

Korea, South *n.* 南韓 [naam4 hon4]

Korean *adj.* 韓國 [hon4 gwok8]

kosher *adj.* 符合猶太教規嘅 [fu4 hap9 yau4 taai3 gaau3 kwai1 ge3]; **non-~** 唔符合猶太教規嘅, **~ meal** 符合猶太教規嘅食物

Kosovar *adj.* 科索沃 [fo1 sok8 yuk7]

Kosovo *n.* 科索沃 [fo1 sok8 yuk7]

Kuala Lumpur *n.* 吉隆坡 [gat7 lung4 po1]; **~, capital of Malaysia** 馬來西亞首都

kumquat *n.* 金桔 [gam1 gat7]

Kuwait *n.* 科威特 [fo1 wai1 dak9]

Kuwait City *n.* 科威特城 [fo1 wai1 dak9 sing4]; **~, capital of Kuwait** 科威特首都

Kuwaiti *adj.* 科威特 [fo1 wai1 dak9]

Kyiv *n.* 基輔 [gei1 fu6]; **~, capital of Ukraine** 烏克蘭首都

Kyrgyzstan *n.* 吉爾吉斯斯坦 [gat7 yi5 gat7 si1 si1 taan2]

Kyrgyzstani (*also* **Kyrgyz**) *adj.* 吉爾吉斯斯坦 [gat7 yi5 gat7 si1 si1 taan2]

L

La Paz *n.* 拉巴斯 [laai1 ba1 si1];
~,**administrative capital of**
Bolivia 玻利維亞行政首都

label *n.* 標簽 [biu1 chim1]; *v.* 貼
標簽 [tip8 biu1 chim1]

labor *n.* 勞動 [lou4 dung6]

Labor Day *n.* 勞動節 [lou4
dung6 jit8]

laboratory,lab *n.* 實驗室 [sat9
yim6 sat7]

lace *n.* 花邊 [fa1 bin1]

lack *n./v.* 缺少 [kyut8 siu2]**; be**
~**ing** 缺少

lacquered *v.* 油漆 [yau4 chat7]

lactose *n.* 乳糖 [yu5 tong4];~
intolerant 可以消化乳糖

lad *n.* 年輕人 [nin4 hing1 yan4]

ladder *n.* 梯 [tai1]

ladies restroom/toilet *n.* 女廁
[neui5 chi3]

ladieswear *n.* 女裝 [neui5 jong1]

ladle *n.* 長柄杓 [cheung4 beng3
hok8]

lady *n.* 女士 [neui5 si6]

lag *v.* 落後 [lok9 hau6]

laggard *n.* 落後嘅人 [lok9 hau6
ge3 yan4]

lake *n.* 湖 [wu4]

lamb *n.* 羊肉 [yeung4 yuk9],
breast of ~ 羊胸肉, **leg of ~** 羊
腿肉, **loin of ~** 羊腰肉

lamb trotter *n.* 羊蹄 [yeung4
tai4]

lambaste *v.* 猛打 [maang5 da2]

lame *adj.* 跛 [bai1]

lament *v.* 哀嘆 [oi1 taan3]

lamentable *adj.* 可憐 [ho2 lin4]

lamentation *n.* 哀嘆 [oi1 taan3]

lamp *n.* 燈 [dang1]

lamprey *n.* 七腮鰻 [chat7 soi1
maan4]

lance *n.* 長矛 [cheung4 maau4]

land *n.* 土地 [tou2 dei6]; *v.* 降落
[gong3 lok9]; **airplane ~ing** 飛
機降落

landlord *n.* 房東 [fong4 dung1]

landmark *n.* 地標 [dei6 biu1]

landscape *n.* 地形 [dei6 ying4]

lane *n.* 路 [lou6]

language *n.* 語言 [yu5 yin4]

language course *n.* 語言課程
[yu5 yin4 fo3 ching4]

languish *v.* 受苦 [sau6 fu2]

Laos *n.* 老撾 [lou5 wo1]

Laotian *adj.* 老撾 [lou5 wo1]

laparoscope *n.* 腹腔鏡 [fuk7
hong1 geng3]

lapse *n.* 疏忽 [so1 fat7]

laptop (computer) *n.* 手提電腦
[sau2 tai4 din6 nou5]

larceny *n.* 偷野 [tau1 ye5]

lard *n.* 豬油 [jyu1 yau4]

large *adj.* 大 [daai6], **~ prawn**
大蝦 [daai6 ha1]

largely *adv.* 主要 [jyu2 yiu3]

larger *adj.* 大過 [daai6 gwo3]

lark *n.* 雲雀 [wan4 jeuk8]

laryngitis *n.* 喉嚨發炎 [hau4
lung4 faat8 yim4]

lasagna *n.* 千層麵 [chin1
chang4 min6]

laser *n.* 激光 [gik7 gwong1]

last *adj./adv./n.* 最後 [jeui3 hau6];
adv. at ~ 終於 [jung1 yu1]

last call *n.* 收市價 [sau1 si5 ga3]

last month *adv.* 上個月 [seung6
go3 yut9]

last name *n.* 姓 [sing3]

last night *adv.* 琴晚 [kam4
maan5]

last stop *n.* 終點站 [jung1
dim2 jaam6]

last week *adv.* 上個星期
[seung6 go3 sing1 kei4]

last year *adv.* 舊年 [gau6 nin2]

late *adj.* 遲 [chi4] *adv.* 遲咗 [chi4
jo2] be ~ 遲到

lateness *n.* 遲 [chi4]

later *adv.* 遲啲 [chi4 di1] *adj.* 後
來嘅 [hau6 loi4 ge3]

latest *adj.* 最近 [jeui3 gan6]; *n.*
最近 [jeui3 gan6]

latitude *n.* 緯度 [wai5 dou6]

latter *adj.* 後者 [hau6 je2]

Latvia *n.* 拉脫維亞 [laai1 tyut8
wai4 a3]

Latvian *adj.* 拉脫維亞 [laai1
tyut8 wai4 a3]

laudable *adj.* 值得嘉獎 [jik9
dak7 ga1 jeung2]

laugh *v./n.* 笑 [siu3]

laugh(ter) *n.* 笑聲 [siu3 seng1]

launch *v./n.* 發射 [faat8 se6]

launderette *n.* 自動洗衣店 [ji6
dung6 sai2 yi1 dim3]

laundromat *n.* 洗衣店 [sai2 yi1
dim3]

laundry *n.* 洗衣店 [sai1 yi1 dim3]

laundry facilities *n.* 洗衫設備
[sai2 saam1 chit8 bei6]

laundry service *n.* 洗衫服務
[sai2 saam1 fuk9 mou6]

laureate *n.* 獲獎者 [wok9 jeung2
je2]

laurel *n.* 勝利 [sing3 lei6], ~
leaves 月桂葉

lava *n.* 熔岩 [yung4 ngaam4]

lavatory *n.* 廁所 [chi3 so2]

lavender *n.* 薰衣草 [fan1 yi1
chou2]

law *n.* 法律 [faat8 leut9]

lawsuit *n.* 官司 [gun1 si1]

lawyer *n.* 律師 [leut9 si1]

laxative *n.* 瀉藥 [se3 yeuk9],
~ **supplement** 瀉藥

lay *v.* 放 [fong3]

layer *n.* 層 [chang4]; ~**ed** 分層,
~**s** 好多層

layover *n.* 臨時滯留 [lam4 si4
jai6 lau4]

lazy *adj.* 懶 [laan5]

lead 1. *guide v.* 領導 [ling5 dou6]
// **2.** *metal n.* 領先 [ling5 sin1]

leaded *adj.* 加鉛 [ga1 yun4]

leaded gasoline *n.* 含鉛汽油
[ham4 yun4 hei3 yau4]

leader *n.* 領導人 [ling5 dou6
yan4]

leadership *n.* 領導能力 [ling5
dou6nang4 lik9]

lead-free *adj.* 無鉛 [mou4 yun4]

leading *adj.* 主要 [jyu2 yiu3]

leaf *n.* 葉 [yip9]

league *n.* 同盟 [tung4 mang4]

leak *n.* 泄露 [sit8 lou6]; *v.* 漏 [lau6]

lean 1. *adj.* 瘦 [sau3], ~ **meat** 瘦
肉, ~ **cuisine** 清淡飲食 //
2. *v.* 靠 [kaau3]; **to** ~ 依賴, ~
out 探出 [taam3 cheut7]

leap *v./n.* 跳 [tiu3]

learn *v.* 學 [hok9]

lease *n.* 租約 [jou1 yeuk8]; *v.* 出租 [cheut7 jou1]

leasing *n.* 大話 [daai6 wa6]

least *det./pron./adv.* 最少 [jeui3 siu2]

leather *n.* 皮 [pei2]

leather goods *n.* 皮革製品 [pei4 gaak8 jai3 ban2]

leave *v.* 離開 [lei4 hoi1], ~ **in peace** 和平分手, ~ **me alone** 唔好理我

leave out *v.* 漏咗 [lau6 jo2]

leaven *v.* 酵母 [haau1 mou5]

Lebanese *adj.* 黎巴嫩 [lai4 ba1 nyun6]

Lebanon *n.* 黎巴嫩 [lai4 ba1 nyun6]

lecture *n.* 演講 [yin2 gong2]

lecturer *n.* 講師 [gong2 si1]

ledge *n.* 暗礁 [am3 jiu1]

leech *n.* 螞蟥 [ma5 wong4]

leek *n.* 韭菜 [gau2 choi3], ~ **soup** 韭菜湯

left *adj./adv./n.* 左邊 [jo2 bin1], **on the ~** 左邊, **to the ~** 喺左邊

leftist *n.* 左翼分子 [jo2 yik9 fan6 ji2]

leftover *adj.* 剩菜 [sing6 choi3]

left-wing *adj.* 左翼 [jo2 yik9]

leg *n.* 腳 [geuk8]

legal *adj.* 合法 [hap9 faat8], **is it ~?** 合唔合法架？

legalization *n.* 合法化 [hap9 faat8 fa3]

legally *adv.* 合法 [hap9 faat8]

legend *n.* 傳奇 [zyun6 kei4]

leggings *n.* 緊身褲 [gan2 san1 fu3]

legislation *n.* 立法 [laap9 faat8]

legislature *n.* 立法機關 [laap9 faat8 gei1 gwaan1]

legumes *n.* 豆類 [dau2 leui6]

leguminous seeds *n.* 豆類植物嘅種子 [dau2 leui6 jik9 mat9 ge3 jung2 ji2]

leisure *n.* 得閒 [dak7 haan4]

lemon *n.* 檸檬 [ning4 mung4], ~ **extract** 檸檬濃縮, ~ **blossom** 檸檬花, ~ **peel** 檸檬皮, ~ **zest** 檸檬香味, ~ **sole** (*fish*) 檬鰈 [mung4 dip9]

lemonade *n.* 檸檬水 [ning4 mung1 seui2]

lemongrass *n.* 檸檬草 [ning4 mung1 chou2]

lend *v.* 借 [je3], **could you ~ me X?** 你可唔可以借X俾我？

lender *n.* 債主 [jaai3 jyu2]

length *n.* 長度 [cheung4 dou6]

leniency *n.* 寬容 [fun1 yung4]

lenient *adj.* 寬容 [fun1 yung4]

lens (*camera / eyeglasses*) *n.* 鏡片 [geng3 pin2]

lens cap *n.* 鏡頭蓋 [geng3 tau4 goi3]

Lent *n.* 四旬期 [sei3 cheun4 kei4]

lentil *n.* 扁豆 [bin2 dau2], ~ **soup** 扁豆湯, **black ~s** 黑豆, **green ~s** 青豆, **yellow ~s** 黃豆

Leo *n.* 獅子座 [si1 ji2 jo6]

leopard *n.* 豹 [paau3]

lesbian *adj./n.* 女同性戀 [neui5 tung4 sing3 lyun2]

Lesotho *n.* 萊索托 [loi4 sok8 tok8]

less *det./pron./adv.* 少啲 [siu2 di1]

lesson *n.* 教訓 [gaau3 fan3]

let v. 俾 [bei2], ~ **me take your coat** 遞你件褸俾我啦, ~ **me know** 話俾我知

lethargy n. 冇精神 [mou5 jing1 san4]

letter n. 信 [seun3]

lettuce n. 生菜 [saang1 choi3]

level n. 層次 [chang4 chi3]; adj. 水平 [seui2 ping4]

level area n. 水平面積 [seui2 ping4 min6 jik7]

level crossing n. 交叉路口 [gaau1 cha1 lou6 hau2]

levy v. 收稅 [sau1 seui3]

liability n. 責任 [jaak8 yam6]

liable adj. 要負責任 [yiu3 fu6 jaak8 yam6]

liar n. 大話精 [daai6 wa6 jing1]

libel n. 誹謗 [fei2 pong3]

liberal arts n. 文科 [man4 fo1]

Liberia n. 利比里亞 [lei6 bei2 lei5 a3]

Libra n. 天秤座 [tin1 ping4 jo6]

librarian n. 圖書管理員 [tou4 syu1 gun2 lei5 yun4]

library n. 圖書館 [tou4 syu1 gun2]

Libreville n. 利伯維爾 [lei6 baak8 wai4 yi5]; ~, **capital of Gabon** 加蓬首都

Libya n. 利比亞 [lei6 bei2 a3]

Libyan adj. 利比亞 [lei6 bei2 a3]

lice n. 虱 [sat7]

license n. 執照 [jap7 jiu3]

license plate n. 車牌 [che1 paai4]

license plate number n. 車牌號碼 [che1 paai4 hou6 ma5]

licorice n. 甘草精 [gam1 chou2 jing1], **red** ~ 紅甘草精, **black** ~ 黑甘草精

lid n. 蓋 [goi3]

lie 1. (falsehood) v. 講大話 [gong2 daai6 wa6]; n. 大話 [daai6 wa6] // **2.** ~ **on bed** 瞓喺張床度, ~ **down** 瞓低 [fan3 dai1]

Liechtenstein n. 列支敦士登 [lit9 ji1 deun1 si6 dang1]

Liechtensteiner adj. 列支敦士登 [lit9 ji1 deun1 si6 dang1]

lien n. 優先權 [yau1 sin1 kyun4]

lieutenant n. 陸軍中尉 [luk9 gwan1 jung1 wai3]

life n. 生命 [sang1 ming6]

life jacket n. 救生衣 [gau3 sang1 yi1]

life preserver n. 救生圈 [gau3 sang1 hyun1]

lifeboat n. 救生艇 [gau3 sang1 teng5]

lifeguard n. 救生員 [gau3 sang1 yun4]

lift v. 拎起 [ling1 hei2]; n. (ski / car ride) 升降機 [sing1 gong3 gei1]

lift pass n. 空中傳球 [hung1 jung1 chyun4 kau4]

light 1. adj. (color / weight) 輕 [heng1], ~ **beer** 淡啤酒, ~ **cake** 鬆軟蛋糕, ~ **meal** 食少少 // **2.** n. 光 [gwong1]; v. (~ a fire) 點著 [dim2 jeuk9]

light meter n. 測光表 [chak7 gwong1 bui1]

lightbulb n. 燈膽 [dang1 daam2]

lightening n. 閃電 [sim2 din6]

lighter n. 火機 [da2 fo2 gei1]

lighting n. 照明 [jiu3 ming4]

lightly adv./adj. 輕易 [hing1 yi6], ~ **salted** 稍微醃一下 [saau2 mei4 yip8 yat7 ha5]

like *prep./conj./adv.* 好似 [hou2 chi5]; *v.* 鍾意 [jung1 yi3]
likely *adj./adv.* 可能 [ho2 nang4]
lilac *n.* 丁香 [ding1 heung1]
Lilongwe *n.* 利隆圭 [lei6 lung4 gwai1]; ~, **capital of Malawi** 馬拉維首都
lily *n.* 百合花 [baak8 hap9 fa1]
Lima *n.* 利馬 [lei6 ma5]; ~, **capital of Peru** 秘魯首都
lima beans *n.* 利馬豆 [lei6 ma5 dau2]
limber *adj.* 靈活 [ling4 wut9]
lime *n.* 石灰 [sek9 fui1], ~ **extract** 青檸檬濃縮, ~ **juice** 青檸檬汁
limit *n./v.* 限制 [haan6 jai3]
limitation *n.* 局限 [guk9 haan6]
limited *adj.* 有限 [yau5 haan6]
limousine *n.* 豪華房車 [hou4 wa4 fong2 che1]
linden tree *n.* 菩提樹 [pou4 tai4 syu6]
line (*geom. / subway / queue*) *n.* 線 [sin3]
lineage *n.* 血統 [hyut8 tung2]
linear *adj.* 直線 [jik9 sin3]
lined *v.* 排隊 [paai4 deui2]
linen *n.* 亞麻 [a3 ma4]
lingerie *n.* 睡衣 [seui6 yi1]
linguist *n.* 語言學家 [yu5 yin4 hok9 ga1]
linguistics *n.* 語言學 [yu5 yin4 hok9]
link *n.* 關聯 [gwaan1 lyun4], **website** ~ 網站鏈結; *v.* 連 [lin4]
lion *n.* 獅子 [si1 ji2]
lip *n.* 嘴唇 [jeui2 seun4]
lipstick *n.* 唇膏 [seun4 gou1]
liquefy *v.* 液化 [yik9 fa3]
liqueur *n.* 白酒 [baak9 jau2]
liquid *n.* 液體 [yik9 tai2]; *adj.* 液體 [yik9 tai2]
liquidate *v.* 清盤 [ching1 pun2]
liquidation *n.* 清盤 [ching1 pun2]
liquidity *n.* 流動資金 [lau4 dung6 ji1 gam1]
liquor *n.* 含酒精飲品 [ham4 jau2 jing1 yam2 ban2]
liquor store *n.* 酒舖 [jau2 pou2]
Lisbon *n.* 里斯本 [lei5 si1 bun2]; ~, **capital of Portugal** 葡萄牙首都
list *n.* 清單 [ching1 daan1]; *v.* 列出黎 [lit9 cheut7 lai4]
listed building *n.* 受保護建築 [sau6 bou2 wu6 gin3 juk7]
listen *v.*聽 [teng1]
listener *n.* 聽眾 [teng1 jung3]
liter *n.* 升 [sing1]
literal *adj.* 字面上 [ji6 min2 seung6]
literary *adj.* 書面 [syu1 min2]
literature *n.* 文學 [man4 hok9]
Lithuania *n.* 立陶宛 [laap9 tou4 yun2]
Lithuanian *adj.* 立陶宛 [laap9 tou4 yun2]
litigant *n.* 訴訟當事人 [sou3 jung6 dong1 si6 yan4]
litigation *n.* 打官司 [da2 gun1 si1]
litter *n.* 垃圾 [laap9 saap8]
littering: no ~ *phr.* 唔好亂抌垃圾 [m4 hou2 lyun6 dam2 laap9 saap8]
little *adj./det.* 細/少 [sai3/siu2]; *pron.* 冇幾多 [mou5 gei2 do1]; *adv.* 好少 [hou2 siu2]; **a** ~ *det./pron.* 一啲 [yat7 di1]

live v. 生存 [sang1 chyun4]; adj. 生嘅 [saang1 ge3]; adv. 現場 [yin6 cheung4]

live together v. 一齊住 [yat7 chai4 jyu6]

livelihood n. 搵食 [wan2 sik9]

lively adj. 活潑 [wut9 put8]

liver n. 肝 [gon1]

liverwurst n. 肝泥香腸 [gon1 nai4 heung1 cheung2]

living adj. 仲生 [jung6 saang1]; n. 生計 [saang1 gai3], **do for a ~** 以…為生 [yi5 … wai4 sang1]

living room n. 客廳 [haak8 teng1]

living standard n. 生活水平 [sang1 wut9 seui2 ping4]

lizard n. 蜥蜴 [sik7 yik9]

Ljubljana n. 盧布爾雅那 [lou4 bou3 yi5 nga5 na5]; **~, capital of Slovenia** 斯洛文尼亞首都

llama n. 喇嘛 [la1 ma3]

load n. 裝貨 [jong1 fo3]; v. 裝 [jong1]

load limit n. 限載 [haan6 joi3]

loaf 1. v. 遊蕩 [yau4 dong6] // **2. ~ of bread** n. 一條麵包 [yat7 tiu4 min6 baau1]

loan n. 貸款 [taai3 fun2]

loath v. 唔情願 [m4 ching4 yun6]

loathsome adj. 乞人憎 [hat7 yan4 jang1]

lobby n. 大堂 [daai6 tong4]

lobster n. 龍蝦 [lung4 ha1]

lobster bisque n. 龍蝦湯 [lung4 ha1 tong1]

local adj. 當地 [dong1 dei6]; n. 當地人 [dong1 dei6 yan4]

local council n. 地方委員會 [dei6 fong1 wai2 yun4 wui2]

local speciality n. 特產 [dak9 chaan2]

local train n. 慢車 [maan6 che1]

locally adv. 當地 [dong1 dei6]

locate v. 定位 [ding6 wai2]

located adj. 搵到 [wan3 dou2]

location n. 位置 [wai6 ji3]

lock v./n. 鎖 [so2]

lock out v. 趕出屋企 [gon2 cheut7 uk7 kei2]

locker n. 儲物櫃 [chyu5 mat9 gwai6]; **~ for baggage** 行李櫃 [hang4 lei5 gwai6]

locomotive n. 火車頭 [fo2 che1 tau4]

locust n. 蝗蟲 [wong4 chung4]

lodestar n. 北極星 [bak7 gik9 sing1]

log in/on comp. v. 登陸 [dang1 luk9], **~ to your account** 登陸你嘅帳戶

log out/off comp. v. 退出 [teui3 cheut7]

logic n. 邏輯 [lo4 chap7]

logical adj. 符合邏輯 [fu4 hap9 lo4 chap7]

login comp. n. 登入 [dang1 yap9], **~ ID** 登入用戶名

lollipop n. 波板糖 [bo1 baan2 tong4]

Lome n. 洛美 [lok8 mei5]; **~, capital of Togo** 多哥首都

London n. 倫敦 [leun4 deun1]; **~, capital of United Kingdom** 英國首都

lonely adj. 孤獨 [gu1 duk9]

lonesome adj. 孤獨 [gu1 duk9]

long adj. 長 [cheung4]

long-distance adj. 長途 [cheung4 tou4]; **~ call** n. 長途電話

[cheung4 tou4 din6 wa2]; ~ **bus** n. 長途巴士 [cheung4 tou4 ba1 si6]; ~ **express train** n. 長途特快車 [cheung4 tou4 dak9 faai3 che1]

long grain n. 長穀 [cheung4 guk7]; ~ **rice** 長穀米

longer adj. 仲長 [jung6 cheung4]

longevity n. 長命 [cheung4 meng6]

longitude n. 經度 [ging1 dou6]

long-sighted n. 遠視 [yun5 si6]

long-term adj. 長期 [cheung4 kei4]

long-term parking n. 長期泊車 [cheung4 kei4 paak8 che1]

long-time adv. 長時間 [cheung4 si4 gaan3]

look v. 睇 [tai2], **I'm just ~ing** 睇睇 [tai2 tai2]; n. 樣 [yeung2]

    look after v. 照顧 [jiu3 gu3]

    look around v. 四圍望 [sei3 wai4 mong6]

    look for v. 搵 [wan2]

    look forward to v. 盼著 [paan3 jyu3]

    look like v. 似 [chi5]

loose adj. 鬆 [sung1]

loose-fitting adj. 鬆身 [sung1 san1]

loosely adv. 鬆 [sung1]

loquat n. 枇杷 [pei4 pa4]

lord n. 主公 [jyu2 gung1]

lorry n. 貨車 [fo3 che1]

lose v. 輸 [syu1]

    lose blood v. 失血 [sat7 hyut8]

    lose one's way v. 蕩失路 [dong6 sat7 lou6]

loser n. 輸家 [syu1 ga1]

loss n. 損失 [syun2 sat7]

lost adj. 唔見咗 [m4 gin3 jo2]; **be ~** 蕩失路, **get ~** 蕩失路

lost and found office n. 失物認領處 [sat7 mat9 ying6 ling5 chyu3]

lot: a ~ (of), also **lots (of)** pron./det./adv./quant. 好多 [hou2 do1]

lotion n. 乳液 [yu5 yik9]

lottery n. 六合彩 [luk9 hap9 choi2]

lotus seeds n. 蓮子 [lin4 ji2]

loud adj./adv. 大聲 [daai6 seng1]

louder adv. 仲大聲 [jung6 daai6 seng1]

loudly adv. 好大聲 [hou2 daai6 seng1]

loudness n. 大聲 [daai6 seng1]

lounge n. 休息室 [yau1 sik7 sat7]

love n./v. 愛 [oi3]

lovely adj. 得意 [dak7 yi3]

lover n. 愛人 [oi3 yan4]

low adj./adv. 低 [dai1]

low-alcohol beer n. 低醇度啤酒 [dai1 seun4 dou6 be1 jau2]

low-beam adj. 短距光 [dyun2 keui5 gwong1]

low-calorie adj. 低卡路里 [dai1 ka1 lou6 lei5]

lower adj. 放低 [fong3 dai1]; ~ **abdomen** 小腹 [siu2 fuk7]; ~ **berth** 下鋪 [ha6 pou1]

low-fat adj. 低脂 [dai1 ji1]

lowland n. 低地 [dai1 dei6]

lox n. 液態氧氣 [yik9 taai3 yeung5 hei3]

loyal adj. 忠誠 [jung1 sing4]

loyalty n. 忠臣 [jung1 san4]

lozenge *n.* 潤喉糖 [yeun6 hau4 tong2], **cough ~** 潤喉糖,**throat ~** 潤喉糖

Ltd. (*abbr. for* **Limited**) *n.* 有限公司 [yau5 haan6 gung1 si1]

Luanda *n.* 羅安達 [lo4 on1 daat9]; **~, capital of Angola** 安哥拉首都

lubricant *n.* 潤滑油 [yeun6 waat9 yau2]

lubricate *v.* 上油 [seung5 yau2]

lubrication *n.* 潤滑 [yeun6 waat9]

lucent *adj.* 發光 [faat8 gwong1]

luck *n.* 好運 [hou2 wan6]; **Good ~!** *phr.* 好運 [hou2 wan6]

lucky *adj.* 好彩 [hou2 choi2]

lucrative *adj.* 賺大錢 [jaan6 daai6 chin2]

luggage *n.* 行李 [hang4 lei5], **piece of ~** 一件行李, **~ cart** 行李車, **~ locker** 行李櫃

luggage allowance *n.* 行李限額 [hang4 lei5 haan6 ngaak9]

lukewarm *adj.* 冷淡 [laang5 daam6]

lullaby *n.* 搖籃曲 [yiu4 laam4 kuk7]

luminous *adj.* 發光 [faat8 gwong1]

lump *n.* 嚿 [gau6]

lunatic *n.* 癲佬 [din1 lou2]

lunch *n.* 午飯 [ng5 faan6]

lunchbox *n.* 飯盒 [faan6 hap9]

lunchmeat *n.* 午餐肉 [ng5 chaan1 yuk9]

lunchtime *n.* 食晏時間 [sik9 aan3 si4 gaan3]

lungs *n.* 肺 [fai3]

Lusaka *n.* 盧薩卡 [lou4 saat8 ka1]; **~, capital of Zambia** 尚比亞首都

lush *adj.* 豪華 [hou4 wa4]

lust *n.* 鹹濕 [haam4 sap7]

Luxembourg *adj./n.* 盧森堡 [lou4 sam1 bou2]

luxury *n.* 奢侈 [che1 chi2]

luxury goods *n.* 奢侈品 [che1 chi2 ban2]

lychee *n.* 荔枝 [lai6 ji1]

lyric *n.* 歌詞 [go1 chi4]

lyrical *adj.* 抒情 [syu1 ching4]

M

macaroni *n.* 通心粉 [tung1 sam1 fan2]; ~ **salad** 通心粉沙律, ~ **and cheese** 芝士通心粉

macaroon *n.* 蛋白杏仁餅 [daan2 baak6 hang6 yan4 beng2], **cocount** ~ 椰子蛋白杏仁餅, **nut** ~ 蛋白杏仁餅, **chocolate** ~ 朱古力蛋白杏仁餅, **vanilla** ~ 香草蛋白杏仁餅

Macedonia *n.* 馬其頓王國 [ma5 kei4 deun6 wong4 gwok8]

Macedonian *adj.* 馬其頓 [ma5 kei4 deun6]

macerate *v.* 浸脸 [jam3 nam4]

machine *n.* 機械 [gei1 haai6]

machine washable *adj.* 機洗 [gei1 sai2]

machinery *n.* 機器 [gei1 hei3]

mackerel *n.* 馬鮫魚 [ma5 gaau1 yu4]

mad *adj.* 發神經 [faat8 san4 ging1]

Madagascar *n.* 馬達加斯加 [ma5 daat9 ga1 si1 ga1]

madam *n.* 女士 [neui5 si6]

made *adj.* 人造 [yan4 jou6]; *v.* 整 [jing2]

Madrid *n.* 馬德里 [ma5 dak7 lei5]; ~, **capital of Spain** 西班牙首都

magazine *n.* 雜誌 [jaap9 ji3]

magic *n.* 魔術 [mo1 seut9]; *adj.* 不可思議 [bat7 ho2 si1 yi5]

magician *n.* 魔術師 [mo1 seut9 si1]

magnesium *n.* 鎂 [mei5]

magnet *n.* 磁石 [chi4 sek9]

magnetic *adj.* 磁性 [chi4 sing3]

magnetism *n.* 磁性 [chi4 sing3]

magnificent *adj.* 太靚 [taai3 leng3]

magnitude *n.* 震級 [jan3 kap7]

magpie *n.* 喜鵲 [hei2 cheuk8]

maid *n.* 工人 [gung1 yan4]

maiden name *n.* 娘家姓 [neung4 ga1 sing3]

mail *n.* 郵件 [yau4 gin6]; *v.* 寄 [gei3]

mailbox *n.* 信箱 [seun3 seung1]

main *adj.* 主要 [jyu2 yiu3]

main course *n.* 主菜 [jyu2 choi3]

main road *n.* 主要道路 [jyu2 yiu3 dou6 lou6]

main square *n.* 廣場 [gwong2 cheung4]

main street *n.* 大街 [daai6 gaai1]

mainly *adv.* 主要 [jyu2 yiu3]

mainstream *n./adj.* 主流 [jyu2 lau4]

maintain *v.* 維持 [wai4 chi4]

maintenance *n.* 維修 [wai4 sau1]

maize *n.* 粟米 [suk7 mai5]

major *adj.* 主要 [jyu2 yiu3]

majority *n.* 大多數 [daai6 do1 sou3]

Majuro *n.* 馬朱羅 [ma5 jyu1 lo4]; ~, **capital of Marshall Islands** 馬紹爾群島首都

make *v.* 整 [jing2]; *n.* 形狀 [ying4 jong6]

  make a phone call 打電話 [da2 din6 wa2]

  make friends (with) 交朋友 [gaau1 pang4 yau5]

  make fun of 笑 [siu3]

  make smth. up 作野 [jok8 ye5]

  make sure 確定 [kok8 ding6]

  make up (*do over*) 作 [jok8]

maker *n.* 製造商 [jai3 jou6 seung1]

make-up (*cosmetics*) *n.* 化妝 [fa3 jong1]

Malabo *n.* 馬拉博 [ma5 laai1 bok8]; ~, **capital of Equatorial Guinea** 赤道幾内亞首都

malady *n.* 弊病 [bai6 beng6]

malaria *n.* 瘧疾 [yeuk9 jat9]

Malawi *n.* 馬拉維 [ma5 laai1 wai4]

Malaysia *n.* 馬來西亞 [ma5 loi4 sai1 a3]

Malaysian *adj.* 馬來西亞 [ma5 loi4 sai1 a3]

Maldives *n.* 馬爾代夫 [ma5 yi5 doi6 fu1]

Male *n.* 馬累 [ma5 leui5]; ~, **capital of Maldives** 馬爾代夫首都

male *adj.* 男性 [naam4 sing3]; *n.* 男 [naam4]

Mali *n.* 馬里 [ma5 lei5]

malice *n.* 惡意 [ok8 yi3]

malicious *adj.* 居心不良 [geui1 sam1 bat7 leung4]

malign *v.* 誹謗 [fei2 pong3]

malignant *adj.* 惡意 [ok8 yi3]

mall *n.* 購物中心 [gau3 mat9 jung1 sam1]

mallet *n.* 大錘 [daai6 cheui4]

malnutrition *n.* 營養不良 [ying4 yeung5 bat7 leung4]

malpractice *n.* 醫療不當 [yi1 liu4 bat7 dong3]

Malta *n.* 馬耳他 [ma5 yi5 ta1]

malted *adj.* 整成麥芽 [jing2 seng4 mak9 nga4], ~ **beer** 麥芽啤酒, ~ **liquor** 麥芽酒

mammal *n.* 哺乳類動物 [bou6 yu5 leui6 dung6 mat9]

mammoth *n.* 毛象 [mou4 jeung6]

man *n.* 男人 [naam4 yan2]

manage *v.* 經營 [ging1 ying4]

management *n.* 管理層 [gun2 lei5 chang4]

manager *n.* 經理 [ging1 lei5]

managerial *adj.* 經營上嘅 [ging1 ying4 seung6 ge3]

Managua *n.* 馬那瓜湖 [ma5 na5 gwa1 wu4]; ~, **capital of Nicaragua** 尼加拉瓜首都

Manama *n.* 麥納麥 [mak9 naap9 mak9]; ~, **capital of Bahrain** 巴林首都

mandarin orange *n.* 蜜柑 [mat9 gam1]

mandatory *adj.* 強制 [keung5 jai3]

mango *n.* 芒果 [mong1 gwo2], ~ **jam** 芒果醬, ~ **chutney** 芒果酸辣醬, ~ **pickle** 酸芒果, ~ **juice** 芒果汁

mania *n.* 狂熱 [kwong4 yit9]

manicure *n.* 修甲 [sau1 gaap8]

manifesto *n.* 宣言 [syun1 yin4]

Manila *n.* 馬尼拉 [ma5 nei4 laai1]; ~, **capital of Philippines** 菲律賓首都

manner *n.* 態度 [taai3 dou6]

mannequin *n.* 人體模型 [yan4 tai2 mou4 ying4]

manslaughter *n.* 殺人 [saat8 yan4]

mansion *n.* 別墅 [bit9 seui5]

manual 1. *adj.* 手動 [sau2 dung6] // **2.** *n.* 指南 [ji2 naam4]

manual transmission *n.* 手動變速箱 [sau2 dung6 bin3 chuk7 seung1]

manufacture *v./n.* 生產 [sang1 chaan2]

manufacturing *n.* 生產 [sang1 chaan2]

manure *n.* 肥料 [fei4 liu2]

manuscript *n.* 手稿 [sau2 gou2]

many *det./pron./quant.* 好多 [hou2 do1]

map *n.* 地圖 [dei6 tou4]

Maputo *n.* 馬普托 [ma5 pou2 tok8]; ~, **capital of Mozambique** 莫桑比克首都

maraschino cherry *n.* 酒浸車厘子 [jau2 jam3 che1 lei4 ji2]

marathon *n.* 馬拉松 [ma5 laai1 chung4]

marble *n.* 大理石 [daai6 lei5 sek9]

marbled *adj.* 大理石花紋 [daai6 lei5 sek9 fa1 man4], ~ **meat** 五花肉

march *v./n.* 行軍 [hang4 gwan1]

March (*abbr*. **Mar.**) *n.* 三月 [saam1 yut9]

margarine *n.* 人造奶油 [yan4 jou6 naai5 yau4]

margin *n.* 邊緣 [bin1 yun4]; ~ **of error** 誤差範圍

marijuana *n.* 大麻 [daai6 ma4]

marinade *n.* 醃汁 [yim1 jap7]

marinated *adj.* 醃好 [yim1 hou2]; ~ **salmon** 醃三文魚 [yim1 saam1 man4 yu2]

marine *adj.* 海軍 [hoi2 gwan1]

marionberry *n.* 馬里恩莓 [ma5 lei5 yan1 mui4]

marital status *n.* 婚姻狀況 [fan1 yan1 jong6 fong3]

mark *n.* 記號 [gei3 hou6]; *v.* 做記號 [jou6 gei3 hou6]

marked *adj.* 有記號 [yau5 gei3 hou6]

marker *n.* 標記 [biu1 gei3]

market *n.* 市場 [si5 cheung4]

market price *n.* 市場價 [si5 cheung4 ga3]

marketing *n.* 經銷 [ging1 siu1]

marketplace *n.* 市場 [si5 cheung4]

marmalade *n.* 果醬 [gwo2 jeung3]

marriage *n.* 婚姻 [fan1 yan1]

married *adj.* 結咗婚嘅 [git8 jo2 fan1 ge3]

marrow *n.* 骨髓 [gwat7 seui5]

marry *v.* 結婚 [git8 fan1]

Mars *n.* 火星 [fo2 sing1]

marsh *n.* 沼澤 [jiu2 jaak9]

marshal *n.* 執法官 [jap7 faat8 gun1]

Marshall Islands *n.* 馬紹爾群島 [ma5 siu6 yi5 kwan4 dou2]

marshmallow *n.* 棉花糖 [min4 fa1 tong2]

martyr *n.* 烈士 [lit9 si6]

marvelous *adj.* 不可思議 [bat7 ho2 si1 yi5]

marzipan *n.* 杏仁蛋白軟糖 [hang6 yan4 daan2 baak9 yun5 tong2]

mascara n. 睫毛膏 [jit9 mou4 gou1]

mascot n. 吉祥物 [gat7 cheung4 mat9]

masculine adj. 男子漢 [naam4 ji2 hon3]

Maseru n. 馬塞盧 [ma5 sak7 lou4]; ~, **capital of Lesotho** 萊索托首都

mashed v./adj. 攪爛 [gaau2 laan6]

mashed potatoes n. 薯蓉 [syu4 yung4]

mashed turnips n. 蘿蔔蓉 [lo4 baak9 yung4]

mask n. 面具 [min6 geui6]; v. 掩飾 [yim2 sik7]; **diving** ~ 潛水面罩

mass 1. (*Catholic service*) 彌撒 [nei4 saat8] // **2.** (*solid*) n. 大量 [daai6 leung6] // **3.** (*amount*) v. 聚集 [jeui6 jaap9]

massacre n. 大屠殺 [daai6 tou4 saat8]

massage n. 按摩 [on3 mo1]

masseur n. 按摩師 [on3 mo1 si1]

massive adj. 大量 [daai6 leung6]

master n. 碩士 [sek9 si6]

masterpiece n. 傑作 [git9 jok8]

masturbate v. 自慰 [ji6 wai3]

mat n. 蓆[jek9]

match 1. (*game*) n. 比賽 [bei2 choi3] // **2.** (*for fire*) 火柴 [fo2 chaai4] // **3.** (*same*) v. 配上 [pui3 seung5]

matching adj. 匹配 [pat7 pui3]

mate n. 配偶 [pui3 ngau5]; v. 交配 [gaau1 pui3]

material n. 材料 [choi4 liu6]; adj. 物質 [mat9 jat7]

mathematics n. 數學 [sou3 hok9]

matinée n. 日場 [yat9 cheung4]

matriculate v. 大學錄取 [daai6 hok9 luk9 cheui2]

matriculation n. 大學錄取 [daai6 hok9 luk9 cheui2]

matrix n. 矩陣 [geui2 jan6]

matron n. 女護士長 [neui5 wu6 si6 jeung2]

matte finish n. 無光飾面 [mou4 gwong1 sik7 min6]

matter 1. n. 事 [si6] // **2.** v. 緊要 [gan2 yiu3], **it doesn't** ~ 有所謂, **what's the** ~? 乜野事

mattress n. 床墊 [chong4 din6]

matured v. 成熟 [sing4 suk9]

maturity n. 成熟 [sing4 suk9]

Mauritania n. 毛利塔尼亞 [mou4 lei6 taap8 nei4 a3]

Mauritius n. 毛里裘斯 [mou4 lei5 kau4 si1]

mausoleum n. 陵墓 [ling4 mou6]

maxim n. 座右銘 [jo6 yau6 ming2]

maximize (~ **profit)** v. 最大化 [jeui3 daai6 fa3]

maximum adj./n. 最多 [jeui3 do1]

may v. modal 可以 [ho2 yi5]

May n. 五月 [ng5 yut9]

May Day (May 1) n. 勞動節 [lou4 dung6 jit8]

maybe adv. 或者 [waak9 je2]

mayonnaise n. 蛋黃醬 [daan6 wong2 jeung3]

mayor n. 市長 [si5 jeung2]

maze n. 迷宮 [mai4 gung1]

Mbabane n. 姆巴巴納 [mou5 ba1 ba1 naap9]; ~, **capital of Swaziland** 斯威士蘭首都

me *pron.* 我 [ngo5]

mead *n.* 蜂蜜酒 [fung1 mat9 jau2]

meadow *n.* 草地 [chou2 dei6]

meager *adj.* 貧乏 [pan4 fat9]

meal *n.* 餐 [chaan1]

mean *v.* 意思 [yi3 si1], **what does this ~?** 呢個係乜野意思？

meaning *n.* 意思 [yi3 si1]

means *n.* 手段 [sau2 dyun6]

meanwhile *adv.* 同時 [tung4 si4]

measles *n.* 痲疹 [ma4 jan2]

measure *v.* 度 [dok9]; *n.* 尺寸 [chek8 chyun3]

measurement *n.* 尺寸 [chek8 chyun3]

measuring cup *n.* 量杯 [leung4 bui1]

meat *n.* 肉 [yuk9]

meat stock *n.* 肉汁 [yuk9 jap7]

meatballs *n.* 肉丸 [yuk9 yun2]

meatless dishes *n.* 素菜 [sou3 choi3]

meatloaf *n.* 大塊肉 [daai6 faai3 yuk9]

mechanic *n.* 技工 [gei6 gung1]

mechanical *adj.* 機械 [gei1 haai6]

mechanics *n.* 力學 [lik9 hok9]

mechanism *n.* 機械裝置 [gei1 haai6 jong1 ji3]

medal *n.* 獎牌 [jeung2 paai4]

media *n.* 媒體 [mui4 tai2]

mediate *v.* 調解 [tiu4 gaai2]

mediation *n.* 調解 [tiu4 gaai2]

mediator *n.* 調解員 [tiu4 gaai2 yun4]

medic *n.* 醫生 [yi1 sang1]

medical *adj.* 醫藥 [yi1 yeuk9]

medication *n.* 藥物 [yeuk9 mat9]

medicine (*drug / study*) *n.* 藥 [yeuk9]

medieval *adj.* 中世紀 [jung1 sai3 gei3]

mediocre *adj.* 麻麻地 [ma4 ma4 dei2]

mediocrity *n.* 普通 [pou2 tung1]

meditation *n.* 冥想 [ming2 seung2]

Mediterranean *adj.* 地中海 [dei6 jung1 hoi2], **~ food** 地中海菜

medium 1. (*size*) *adj.* 中等 [jung1 dang2] // **2.** (*mystic*) *n.* 媒介 [mui4 gaai3]

meet *v.* 遇見 [yu6 gin3], **pleased to ~ you** 好高興認識你

meeting *n.* 開會 [hoi1 wui2]

meeting place *n.* 見面地方 [gin3 min6 dei6 fong1]

megabyte (MB) *comp. n.* 百萬位元組 [baak8 maan6 wai2 yun4 jou2], **file size in ~s** 文件大小為數百萬位元組

melancholia *n.* 抑鬱症 [yik7 wat7 jing3]

melancholy *n.* 憂傷 [yau1 seung1]

melba *n.* 脆麵包片 [cheui3 min6 baau1 pin2], **~ sauce** 脆麵包碎醬, **~ toast** 脆麵包多士

meld *v.* 融合 [yung4 hap9]

Melekeok *n.* 梅萊凱奧克 [mui4 loi4 hoi2 ou3 hak7]; **~, capital of Palau** 帛琉群島首都

melody *n.* 旋律 [syun4 leut9]

melon *n.* 瓜 [gwa1]

melt *v.* 溶 [yung4]

melted *v.* 溶咗 [yung4 jo2]; ~
cheese 芝士泥, ~ **butter** 牛油
水, ~ **chocolate** 朱古力泥

member (*in/of a group*) *n.* 會員
[wui2 yun4]

membership *n.* 會員身分 [wui6
yun2 san1 fan6]

membrane *n.* 薄膜 [bok9 mok9]

memo *n.* 備忘錄 [bei6 mong4
luk9]

memoir *n.* 回憶錄 [wui4 yik7
luk9]

memorandum *n.* 備忘錄 [bei6
mong4 luk9]

memorial *n.* 紀念碑 [gei3 nim6
bei1]

memory *n.* 回憶 [wui4 yik7]

menace *n.* 威脅 [wai1 hip8]

meningitis *n.* 腦膜炎 [nou5 mok9
yim4]

menopause *n.* 更年期 [gang1
nin4 kei4]

men's restroom/toilet *n.* 男廁
[naam4 chi3]

menstruation *n.* 月經 [yut9
ging1]

menswear *n.* 男裝 [naam4 jong1]

mental *adj.* 精神 [jing1 san4]

mentally *adv.* 精神上 [jing1
san4 seung6]

menthol *n.* 薄荷醇[bok9 ho4
seun4]

mention *v.* 提到 [tai4 dou3],
Don't ~ it 唔好客氣

menu *n.* 餐牌 [chaan1 paai2],
~ **of the day** 例牌

merchandise *n.* 商品 [seung1
ban2]

merchant *n.* 商人 [seung1 yan4]

mercury *n.* 水銀 [seui2 ngan4]

mere *adj.* 只不過 [ji2 bat7 gwo3]

merge *v.* 合併 [hap9 bing3]

meridian *n.* 子午線 [ji2 ng5 sin3]

meringue *n.* 蛋白酥 [daan2
baak9 sou1], **lemon ~** 檸檬蛋
白酥, **lime ~** 青檸檬蛋白酥,
~ **pie** 蛋白酥派

Merry Christmas *phr.* 聖誕節快
樂 [sing3 daan3 jit8 faai3 lok9]

mess *n.* 亂 [lyun6]

message *n.* 口信 [hau2 seun3]

message board *n.* 留言板 [lau4
yin4 baan2]

messenger *n.* 郵遞員 [yau4 dai6
yun4]

metabolic *adj.* 新陳代謝 [san1
chan4 doi6 je6]

metabolism *n.* 新陳代謝 [san1
chan4 doi6 je6]

metal *n.* 金屬 [gam1 suk9]

metaphor *n.* 比喻 [bei2 yu6]

meteor *n.* 流星 [lau4 sing1]

meteorologist *n.* 氣象學家 [hei3
jeung6 hok9 ga1]

meteorology *n.* 氣象學 [hei3
jeung6 hok9]

meter *n.* 米 [mai5]

method *n.* 方法 [fong1 faat8]

metro *n.* 地鐵 [dei6 tit8]

metro station *n.* 地鐵站 [dei6
tit8 jaam6]

metropolis *n.* 首都 [sau2 dou1]

metropolitan *n.* 大城市 [daai6
sing4 si5]

Mexican *adj.* 墨西哥 [mak9 sai1
go1]

Mexico *n.* 墨西哥 [mak9 sai1
go1]

Mexico City *n.* 墨西哥城 [mak9 sai1 go1 sing4]; ~, **capital of Mexico** 墨西哥首都

mg. (*abbr.* **of milligram**) *n.* 毫克 [hou4 hak7]

Micronesia, Federated States of *n.* 密克羅尼西亞聯邦 [mat9 hak7 lo4 nei4 sai1 a3 lyun4 bong1]

microwave oven *n.* 微波爐 [mei4 bo1 lou4]; *v.* 用微波爐 整熱 [yung6 mei4 bo1 lou4 jing2 yit9]; **microwaveable** *adj.* 可以微波爐加熱, ~ **dinner** 微波爐餐, ~ **meal** 微波爐餐

mid- *prefix* 正中 [jing1 jung1]

midday *n.* 正午 [jing3 ng5]

middle *n.* 中間 [jung1 gaan1]

Middle Eastern *adj.* 中東 [jung1 dung1], ~ **food** 中東菜

midnight *n.* 午夜 [ng5 ye6]

midwife *n.* 接生婆 [jip8 sang1 po4]

might *v. modal* 可能 [ho2 nang4]

migraine *n.* 偏頭痛 [pin1 tau4 tung3]

mild *adj.* 温柔 [wan1 yau4]

mileage *n.* 里程 [lei5 ching4]

mile *n.* 英里 [ying1 lei5]

milestone *n.* 里程碑 [lei5 ching4 bei1]

military *adj.* 軍隊 [gwan1 deui2]

military service *n.* 兵役 [bing1 yik9]

milk *n.* 牛奶 [ngau4 naai5], ~ **subsitute** 牛奶替代品, **nonfat** ~ 脫脂牛奶, **skim** ~ 低脂 牛奶, **light** ~ 淡奶, **whole** ~ 全 脂牛奶, **soy** ~ 豆漿, **chocolate** ~ 朱古力奶, **vanilla** ~ 雲呢拿 味奶

milk bar *n.* 牛奶點心 [ngau4 naai5 dim2 sam1]

milkshake *n.* 奶昔 [naai5 sik7], **strawberry** ~ 草莓奶昔, **chocolate** ~ 朱古力奶昔, **vanilla** ~ 香草味奶昔

millet *n.* 小米 [siu2 mai5]

milligram (*abbr.* **mg.**) *n.* 毫克 [hou4 hak7]

millimeter (*abbr.* **mm.**) *n.* 毫米 [hou4 mai5]

million *num.* 百萬 [baak8 maan6]

millionaire *n.* 百萬富翁 [baak8 maan6 fu3 yung1]

mime *n.* 啞劇 [a2 kek9]

mince *v.* 切碎 [chit8 seui3]; *n.* 肉碎 [yuk9 seui3]; ~**d** 切碎咗

minced meat *n.* 肉碎 [yuk9 seui3]

mind *n.* 精神 [jing1 san4]; *v.* 介 意 [gaai3 yi3], **do you ~?** 你介 唔介意?, **never ~** 唔緊要

mine 1. *pron.* 我嘅 [ngo5 ge3], **that's ~** 我㗎! // **2.** (*ore deposit*) *n.* 礦 [kwong3]

mineral *n.* 礦物質 [kwong3 mat9 jat7]; *adj.* 礦物 [kwong3 mat9]

mineral water *n.* 礦泉水 [kwong3 chyun4 seui2]

minerals *n.* 礦物 [kwong3 mat9]

miniature *n.* 微型 [mei4 ying4]

minibar *n.* 冰箱仔 [bing1 seung1 jai2]

minimart *n.* 雜貨店 [jaap9 fo3 dim3]

minimize *v.* 最小化 [jeui3 siu2 fa3]; ~ **screen** *comp.* 屏幕最小化

minimum *adj./n.* 最少 [jeui3 siu2]

 minimum charge *n.* 最低收費 [jeui3 dai1 sau1 fai3]

minister *n.* 部長 [bou6 jeung2]

ministry *n.* 部門 [bou6 mun4]

minnow *n.* 米諾魚 [mai5 nok9 yu4]

minor *n.* 未成年人 [mei6 sing4 nin4 yan4], **he/she is a ~** 佢係未成年嘎; *adj.* 次要 [chi3 yiu1], **it's a ~ problem** 小問題嘅

minority *n.* 少數民族 [siu2 sou3 man4 juk9]

Minsk *n.* 明斯克 [ming4 si1 hak7]; **~, capital of Belarus** 白俄羅斯首都

mint *n.* 薄荷 [bok9 ho4], **breath ~** 香口糖, **~ chocolate** 薄荷朱古力, **~ tea** 薄荷茶, **~ leaves** 薄荷葉

minuscule *n.* 超細 [chiu1 sai3]

minute *n.* 分鐘 [fan1 jung1], **just a ~** 好快, **one ~** 好快

mirror *n.* 鏡 [geng3]

miscalculate *v.* 計錯 [gai3 cho3]

miscarriage *n.* 流產 [lau4 chaan2]

mischief *n.* 搞鬼 [gaau2 gwai2]

mischievous *adj.* 搞鬼 [gaau2 gwai2]

misconception *n.* 誤解 [ng6 gaai2]

misconduct *n.* 處理不當 [chyu5 lei5 bat7 dong3]

misdemeanor *n.* 輕罪 [hing1 jeui6]

misgiving *n.* 擔心 [daam1 sam1]

mishap *n.* 晦氣 [fui3 hei3]

Miss *(title)* 小姐 [siu2 je2]

miss *v.* 掛住 [gwa3 jyu6]

missile *n.* 導彈 [dou6 daan2]

missing *adj.* 唔見咗 [m4 gin3 jo2]; *v.* 錯過 [cho3 gwo3]

missionary *n.* 傳教士 [chyun4 gaau3 si6]

mistake *n.* 錯誤 [cho3 ng6]; *v.* 誤解 [ng6 gaai2]

mistaken *adj.* 搞錯咗 [gaau2 cho3 jo2]

mistress *n.* 二奶 [yi6 naai1]

mistrial *n.* 無效審判 [mou4 haau6 sam2 pun3]

misunderstanding *n.* 會錯意 [wui6 cho3 yi3], **there's been a ~** 有誤會

mix *v.* 攪 [gaau2]; *n.* 混合物 [wan6 hap9 mat9], **baking ~** 烘培粉

mixed *adj.* 混合 [wan6 hap9]

 mixed herbs *n.* 雜草藥 [jaap9 chou2 yeuk9]

 mixed nuts *n.* 雜果仁 [jaap9 gwo2 yan4]

 mixed rice *n.* 雜米 [jaap9 mai5]

 mixed salad *n.* 雜沙律 [jaap9 sa1 leut9]

mixture *n.* 混合 [wan6 hap9]

mm. *(abbr. for millimeter)* *n.* 毫米 [hou4 mai5]

moat *n.* 護城河 [wu6 sing4 ho4]

mobile *adj.* 移動 [yi4 dung6]

mobile phone *(also **mobile**)* *n.* 手機 [sau2 gei1]

mobility *n.* 流動性 [lau4 dung6 sing3]

mockery *n.* 笑柄 [siu3 beng3]

modal *n.* 情態動詞 [ching4 taai3 dung6 chi4]

mode n. 狀態 [jong6 taai3]

model n. 模特 [mou4 dak9]

modem n. comp. 數據機 [sou3 geui3 gei1]; **Internet ~** 上網數據機

modern adj. 現代 [yin6 doi6]

modest adj. 謙虛 [him1 heui1]

modification n. 修改 [sau1 goi2]

modify v. 修改 [sau1 goi2]

Mogadishu n. 摩加迪沙 [mo1 ga1 dik9 sa1]; **~, capital of Somalia** 索馬里首都

moisten v. 整濕 [jing2 sap7], **~ed** 整濕咗

moisturizing cream n. 潤膚霜 [yeun6 fu1 seung1]

molar n. 臼齒 [kau3 chi2]

molasses n. 糖漿 [tong4 jeung1]

mold (form) n. 模 [mou2]; v. 燒模 [siu1 mou2]

moldy adj. 發霉 [faat8 mui4]

Moldova n. 摩爾多瓦 [mo1 yi5 do1 nga5]

mole n. 鼴鼠 [yin2 syu2]

molecular adj. 由分子組成 [yau4 fan6 ji2 jou2 sing4]

molecule n. 分子 [fan6 ji2]

molest v. 性騷擾 [sing3 sou1 yiu2]

molestation n. 性騷擾 [sing3 sou1 yiu2]

molt v. 甩皮 [lat7 pei4]

molten adj. 熔咗 [yung4 jo2]

mom n. 媽咪 [ma1 mi3]

moment n. 瞬間 [seun3 gaan1]

momentary adj. 一陣間 [yat7 jan6 gaan1]

momentous adj. 重要 [jung6 yiu3]

momentum n. 動力 [dung6 lik9]

Monaco n. 摩納哥 [mo1 naap9 go1]; **~, capital of Monaco** 摩納哥首都

monarch n. 君主 [gwan1 jyu2]

monarchy n. 君主制 [gwan1 jyu2 jai3]

monastery n. 寺院 [ji6 yun2]

Monday (abbr. **Mon.**) n. 禮拜一 [lai5 baai3 yat7]

Monegasque (person from Monaco) adj. 摩納哥人 [mo1 naap9 go1 yan4]

monetary adj. 貨幣 [fo3 bai6]

money n. 錢 [chin2]

money order n. 匯票 [wui6 piu3]

Mongolia n. 蒙古 [mung4 gu2]

Mongolian adj. 蒙古 [mung4 gu2]

monitor n. 顯示屏 [hin2 si6 ping4], **computer ~** 電腦顯示屏; v. 監視 [gaam1 si6]

monkfish n. 僧鯊 [jang1 sa1]

monogamy n. 一夫一妻 [yat7 fu1 yat7 chai1]

monologue n. 長篇大論 [cheung4 pin1 daai6 leun6]

monopoly n. 壟斷 [lung5 dyun6]

Monrovia n. 蒙羅維亞 [mung4 lo4 wai4 a3]; **~, capital of Liberia** 利比里亞首都

monsoon n. 雨季 [yu5 gwai3]

Montenegro n. 蒙特內格羅 [mung4 dak9 noi6 gaak8 lo4]

Montevideo n. 蒙得維的亞 [mung4 dak7 wai4 dik7 a3]; **~, capital of Uruguay** 烏拉圭首都

monkey n. 馬騮 [ma5 lau1]

month *n.* 月 [yut9], **this ~** 呢個月

monthly *adj./adv.* 每個月 [mui5 go3 yut9]

monument *n.* 紀念碑 [gei3 nim6 bei1]

monumental *adj.* 巨大 [geui6 daai6]

mood *n.* 情緒 [ching4 seui5]

moody *adj.* 情緒化 [ching4 seui5 fa3]

moon *n.* 月亮 [yut9 leung6]

moor *n.* 荒野 [fong1 ye5]

moose *n.* 麋鹿 [mei4 luk9]

moot *adj.* 無實際意義 [mou4 sat9 jai3 yi3 yi6]

mop *v.* 抹 [maat8]; *n.* 地拖 [dei6 to1]

mope *v.* 悶悶不樂 [mun6 mun6 bat7 lok9]

moped *n.* 電動單車 [din6 dung6 daan1 che1]

moral *adj.* 道德上 [dou6 dak7 seung6]

moralist *n.* 道德家 [dou6 dak7 ga1]

morally *adv.* 道德 [dou6 dak7]

moray eel *n.* 海鱔 [hoi2 sin5]

morbid *adj.* 病態 [beng6 taai3]

morbidity *n.* 病態 [beng6 taai3]

more *det./pron./adv.* 多啲 [do1 di1], **some ~** 再多啲, **no ~** 唔要啦, **~ slowly** 再慢啲

morel mushroom *n.* 羊肚菇 [yeung4 tou5 gu1]

morello cherries *n.* 酸車厘子 [syun1 che1 lei4 ji2]

moreover *adv.* 仲有 [jung6 yau5]

morning *n.* 早晨 [jou2 san4]; **good ~** 早晨 [jou2 san4], **in the ~** 早上 [jou2 seung6], **this ~** 今朝 [gam1 jiu1]

morning-after pill *n.* 緊急避孕藥 [gan2 gap7 bei6 yan6 yeuk9]

Moroccan *adj.* 摩洛哥 [mo1 lok8 go1]

Morocco *n.* 摩洛哥 [mo1 lok8 go1]

Moroni *n.* 莫羅尼 [mok9 lo4 nei4]; **~, capital of Comoros** 科摩羅首都

morphia *n.* 嗎啡 [ma1 fe1]

morsel *n.* 一啖 [yat7 daam6]

mortal *adj.* 會死嘅 [wui5 sei2 ge3]

mortadella *n.* 燻香腸 [fan1 heung1 cheung4]

mortality *n.* 死亡率 [sei2 mong4 leut9]

mortar *n.* 追擊炮 [jeui1 gik7 paau3]

mortgage *n./v.* 按揭 [on3 kit8]

mortify *v.* 侮辱 [mou5 yuk9]

mosaic *n.* 馬賽克 [ma5 choi3 hak7]

Moscow *n.* 莫斯科 [mok9 si1 fo1]; **~, capital of Russia** 俄羅斯首都

mosque *n.* 清真寺 [ching1 jan1 ji6]

mosquito *n.* 蚊 [man1]

mosquito bite *n.* 蚊咬 [man1 ngaau5]

mosquito coil *n.* 蚊香 [man1 heung1]

mosquito net *n.* 蚊帳 [man1 jeung3]

moss *n.* 苔蘚 [toi4 sin2]

most *det./adv.* 最 [jeui3]

mostly *adv.* 多半 [do1 bun3]

mote *n.* 微粒 [mei4 nap7]

motel *n.* 汽車旅館 [hei3 che1 leui5 gun2]

moth *n.* 飛蛾 [fei1 ngo4]

mother *n.* 媽咪 [ma1 mi3]

motherhood *n.* 母性 [mou5 sing3]

mother-in-law *n.* 外母 [ngoi6 mou2]

motif *n.* 主題 [jyu2 tai4]

motion *n.* 運動 [wan6 dung6]

motion sickness *n.* 暈浪 [wan4 long6]

motivate *v.* 激勵 [gik7 lai6]

motivation *n.* 動機 [dung6 gei1]

motive *n.* 動機 [dung6 gei1]

motor *n.* 馬達 [ma5 daat9]

motorbike *n.* 電單車 [din6 daan1 che1]

motorboat *n.* 電動船 [din6 dung6 syun4]

motorcycle *n.* 電單車 [din6 daan1 che1]

motorway *n.* 機動車道 [gei1 dung6 che1 dou6]

mottle *n.* 斑點 [baan1 dim2]

motto *n.* 格言 [gaak8 yin4]

mound *n.* 土堆 [tou2 deui1]

mount *v.* 爬 [pa4]; *n.* 山 [saan1]

mountain *n.* 山 [saan1]

    mountain bike *n.* 爬山單車 [pa4 saan1 daan1 che1]

    mountain chain *n.* 山脈 [saan1 mak9]

    mountain climbing *n.* 爬山 [pa4 saan1]

    mountain pass *n.* 山口 [saan1 hau2]

    mountain path *n.* 山間小路 [saan1 gaan1 siu2 lou6]

    mountain range *n.* 山脈 [saan1 mak9]

mountaineer *n.* 登山家 [dang1 saan1 ga1]

mountainous *adj.* 多山 [do1 saan1]

mourn *v.* 哀悼 [oi1 dou6]

mourner *n.* 哀悼者 [oi1 dou6 je2]

mournful *adj.* 傷心 [seung1 sam1]

mourning *n.* 哀悼 [oi1 dou6]

mouse *n.* **1.** (*rodent*) 老鼠 [lou5 syu2] // **2.** (*computer*) 鼠標 [syu2 biu1]

mousse *n.* 慕斯 [mou6 si1], **chocolate ~** 朱古力慕斯

moustache *n.* 鬍鬚 [wu4 sou1]

mouth *n.* 口 [hau2]

mouth ulcer *n.* 口腔潰瘍 [hau2 hong1 kui2 yeung2]

mouthful *adj.* 成口 [seng4 hau2]

movable *adj.* 喐得 [yuk7 dak7]

move *v.* 搬 [bun1], **don't ~ him!** 唔好喐佢!; *n.* 移動 [yi4 dung6]

mover *n.* 搬運工人 [bun1 wan6 gung1 yan4]

movement *n.* 運動 [wan6 dung6]

movie(s) *n.* 電影 [din6 ying2]

movie theater *n.* 電影院 [din6 ying2 yun2]

moving *adj.* 感人 [gam2 yan4]

Mozambique *adj./n.* 莫桑比克 [mok9 song1 bei2 hak7]

mozzarella *n.* 馬蘇里拉芝士 [ma5 sou1 lei5 laai1 ji1 si6], **~ sticks** 馬蘇里拉芝士條

Mr. (*title*) 先生 [sin1 saang1]

Mrs. (*tite*) 太太 [taai3 taai2]

Ms (*title*) 小姐 [siu2 je2]

much *det./pron./adv.* 好多 [hou2 do1]

mucus *n.* 黏液 [nim1 yik9]

mud *n.* 泥 [nai4]

muddle *v.* 整亂 [jing2 lyun6]; *n.* 混亂 [wan6 lyun6]

muesli *n.* 果仁燕麥 [gwo2 yan4 yin3 mak9]

muffin *n.* 鬆餅 [sung1 beng2], **bran** ~ 麩皮鬆餅, **blueberry** ~ 藍莓鬆餅, **cherry** ~ 車厘子鬆餅, **banana nut** ~ 香蕉果仁鬆餅, **whole grain** ~ 全麥鬆餅

muffle *v.* 包住 [baau1 jyu6]

muffler *n.* 消聲器 [siu1 sing1 hei3]

mug 1. (*cup*) *n.* 杯 [bui1], **coffee** ~ 咖啡杯 // **2.** (*rob*) *v.* 搶劫 [cheung2 gip8]

muggy *adj.* 又悶又熱 [yau6 mun6 yau6 yit9]

mulberry *n.* 桑莓 [song1 mui4], **wild** ~ 野桑莓

mule *n.* 騾仔 [leui4 jai2]

mull *v.* 深思熟慮 [sam1 si1 suk9 leui6]

mulled wine *n.* 熱葡萄酒 [yit9 pou4 tou4 jau2]

mullet *n.* 胭脂魚 [yin1 ji1 yu2]

mullion *n.* 豎框 [syu6 kwaang1]

multiform *adj.* 多種形式 [do1 jung2 ying4 sik7]

multilateral *adj.* 多邊 [do1 bin1]

multimedia *n.* 多媒體 [do1 mui4 tai2]

multinational *adj.* 跨國 [kwa3 gwok8]; *n.* 跨國公司 [kwa3 gwok8 gung1 si1]

multipack *n.* 萬用箱 [maan6 yung6 seung1]

multiparous *adj.* 多胎 [do1 toi1]

multiped *n.* 多足動物 [do1 juk7 dung6 mat9]

multiple *adj.* 多個 [do1 go3]; *n.* 倍數 [pui5 sou3]

multiplex cinema *n.* 多功能電影院 [do1 gung1 nang4 din6 ying2 yun2]

multiplication *n.* 乘法 [sing4 faat8]

multiplicity *n.* 多樣性 [do1 yeung6 sing3]

multiply *v.* 乘 [sing4]

multi-tiered cake *n.* 多層蛋糕 [do1 chang4 daan6 gou1]

multitude *n.* 大量 [daai6 leung6]

mumble *v.* 講話唔清唔楚 [gong2 wa6 m4 ching1 m4 cho2]

mummy *n.* 木乃伊 [muk9 naai5 yi1]

mumps *n.* 腮腺炎 [soi1 sin3 yim4]

munch *v.* 大力咬 [daai6 lik9 ngaau5]

mundane *adj.* 普通 [pou2 tung1]

mung beans *n.* 綠豆 [luk9 dau2]

municipal *adv.* 市政 [si5 jing3]

municipality *n.* 自治區 [ji6 ji6 keui1]

munificent *adj.* 大方 [daai6 fong1]

muniment *n.* 證書 [jing3 syu1]

munitions *n.* 軍火 [gwan1 fo2]

mural *n.* 壁畫 [bik7 wa2]

murder *n./v.* 謀殺 [mau4 saat8]

murderer *n.* 殺人兇手 [saat8 yan4 hung1 sau2]

murderous *adj.* 兇殘 [hung1 chaan4]

murmur *v.* 細聲講 [sai3 seng1 gong2]

Muscat *n.* 馬斯喀特 [ma5 si1 kak1 dak9]; ~, **capital of Oman** 阿曼首都

muscle *n.* 肌肉 [gei1 yuk9]

muscular *adj.* 肌肉發達 [gei1 yuk9 faat8 daat9]

muse *n.* 靈感 [ling4 gam2]

museum *n.* 博物館 [bok8 mat9 gun2]

mush *n.* 糊 [wu2]

mushroom *n.* 蘑菇 [mo4 gu1] **mushroom sauce** *n.* 蘑菇汁 [mo1 gu1 jap7]

music *n.* 音樂 [yam1 ngok9]

music store *n.* 樂器店 [ngok9 hei3 dim3]

musical *adj.* 音樂 [yam1 ngok9]

musical instrument *n.* 樂器 [ngok9 hei3]

musician *n.* 音樂家 [yam1 ngok9 ga1]

musk *n.* 麝香 [se6 heung1]

musket *n.* 火槍 [fo2 cheung1]

musketeer *n.* 火槍手 [fo2 cheung1 sau2]

Muslim *adj.* 回教徒 [wui4 gaau3 tou4]

muslin *n.* 平紋細布 [ping4 man4 sai3 bou3]

mussels *n.* 蜆 [hin2]

must *v. modal* 一定 [yat7 ding6]

mustard *n.* 芥辣 [gaai3 laat9]

mustard greens *n.* 芥菜 [gaai3 choi3]

muster *v.* 聚集 [jeui6 jaap9]

musty *adj.* 發霉 [faat8 mui4]

mutant *adj.* 變異 [bin3 yi6]; *n.* 變種生物 [bin3 jung2 sang1 mat9]

mutation *n.* 變異 [bin3 yi6]

mutative *adj.* 變異 [bin3 yi6]

mute *adj.* 啞 [a2]

mutilate *v.* 嚴重毀壞 [yim4 jung6 wai2 waai6]

mutilation *n.* 嚴重毀壞 [yim4 jung6 wai2 waai6]

mutinous *adj.* 叛變 [bun6 bin3]

mutiny *n.* 叛變 [bun6 bin3]

mutter *v.* 細聲投訴 [sai3 seng1 tau4 sou3]

mutton *n.* 羊肉 [yeung4 yuk9]

mutual *adj.* 彼此 [bei2 chi2]

muzzle *n.* 口套 [hau2 tou3]

my *adj./pron./det.* 我嘅 [ngo5 ge3]

myalgia *n.* 肌肉痛 [gei1 yuk9 tung3]

myopia *n.* 近視 [gan6 si6]

Myanma (Burmese) *adj.* 緬甸 [min5 din6]

Myanmar (Burma) *n.* 緬甸 [min5 din6]

myrrh *n.* 沒藥 [mut9 yeuk9]

myself *pron.* 我自己 [ngo5 ji6 gei2], **I'll do it ~** 我自己黎啦

mysterious *adj.* 不可思議 [bat7 ho2 si1 yi5]

mystery *n.* 不可思議 [bat7 ho2 si1 yi5]

mystic *adj.* 神祕 [san4 bei3]

mysticism *n.* 神秘主義 [san4 bei3 jyu2 yi6]

mystify *v.* 搞神祕 [gaau2 san4 bei3]

myth *n.* 神話 [san4 wa2]

mythical *adj.* 虛構 [heui1 kau3]

mythology *n.* 神話故事 [san4 wa2 gu3 si6]

N

nachos *n.* 粟米片 [suk7 mai5 pin2]

nail *n.* 指甲 [ji2 gaap8]

Nairobi *n.* 奈洛比 [noi6 lok8 bei2]; ~, **capital of Kenya** 肯尼亞首都

naive *adj.* 幼稚 [yau3 ji6]

naked *adj.* 裸體 [lo2 tai2]

name *n.* 名 [meng2], **first ~** 名, **last ~** 姓, **what's your ~?** 你叫乜野名?, **my ~ is** 我叫; *v.* 改名 [goi2 meng2]

Namibia *n.* 納米比亞 [naap9 mai5 bei2 a3]

Namibian *adj.* 納米比亞 [naap9 mai5 bei2 a3]

napkin *n.* 餐巾 [chaan1 gan1], **paper ~** 紙巾

narcissism *n.* 自戀 [ji6 lyun2]

narcissus *n.* 水仙 [seui2 sin1]

narcosis *n.* 昏迷狀態 [fan1 mai4 jong6 taai3]

narcotic *n.* 麻醉藥 [ma4 jeui3 yeuk9]

narrative *adj.* 敘事 [jeui6 si6]; *n.* 敘述 [jeui6 seut9]

narrator *n.* 旁白 [pong4 baak9]

narrow *adj.* 窄 [jaak8]; **~ road** 窄路 [jaak8 lou6]

nascent *adj.* 初期 [cho1 kei4]

Nassau *n.* 拿騷 [na4 sou1]; **~, capital of The Bahamas** 巴哈馬首都

nasty *adj.* 衰格 [seui1 gaak8]

nation *n.* 民族 [man4 juk9]

national *adj.* 國有 [gwok8 yau5]

national holiday *n.* 法定假日 [faat8 ding6 ga3 yat9]

nationalism *n.* 愛國主義 [oi3 gwok8 jyu2 yi6]

nationality *n.* 國籍 [gwok8 jik9]

nationalization *n.* 國有化 [gwok8 yau5 fa3]

nationalize *v.* 國有化 [gwok8 yau5 fa3]

native *adj.* 土生土長 [tou2 sang1 tou2 jeung2]; *n.* 土著 [tou2 jyu3]

natural *adj.* 自然 [ji6 yin4], **~ ingredients** 天然原料, **~ flavors** 自然風味

natural sciences *n.* 自然科學 [ji6 yin4 fo1 hok9]

natualize *v.* 入籍 [yap9 jik9]

naturally *adv.* 自然 [ji6 yin4]

nature *n.* 大自然 [daai6 ji6 yin4]

nature reserve *n.* 自然保護區 [ji6 yin4 bou2 wu6 keui1]

nature trail *n.* 觀景小路 [gun1 ging2 siu2 lou6]

naughty *adj.* 調皮 [tiu4 pei4]

Nauru *n.* 瑙魯島 [nou5 lou5 dou2]

nausea *n.* 作嘔 [jok8 au2]

nauseous *adj.* 令人作嘔 [ling4 yan4 jok8 au2]

naval *adj.* 海軍 [hoi2 gwan1]

nave *n.* 教堂中殿 [gaau3 tong4 jung1 din6]

navigate *v.* 導航 [dou6 hong4]

navigation *n.* 航海 [hong4 hoi2]

navigator *n.* 導航員 [dou6 hong4 yun4]

navy *n.* 海軍 [hoi2 gwan1]

Naypyidaw (*or* **Nay Pyi Taw**) *n.* 內比都 [noi6 bei2 dou1]; ~, **administrative capital of Myanmar (Burma)** 緬甸行政首都

N'Djamena *n.* 恩賈梅納 [yan1 ga2 mui4 naap9]; ~, **capital of Chad** 乍得首都

near(by) *adj./adv.* 附近 [fu6 gan6]; *prep.* 喺…附近 [hai6 … fu6 gan6]

nearest *adj.* 最近 [jeui3 kan5]

nearly *adv.* 差啲 [cha1 di1]

near-sighted *adj.* 近視 [gan6 si6]

neat *adj.* 企里 [kei5 lei5]

neatly *adv.* 企里 [kei5 lei5]

nebula *n.* 星雲 [sing1 wan4]

necessarily *adv.* 有必要 [yau5 bit7 yiu3]

necessary *adj.* 有必要 [yau5 bit7 yiu3]

neck *n.* 頸 [geng2]

necklace *n.* 頸鏈 [geng2 lin2]

nectar *n.* 花蜜 [fa1 mat9]

nectarine *n.* 油桃 [yau4 tou2]

need *modal v./n.* 需要 [seui1 yiu3]

needle *n.* 針 [jam1]

negative *adj.* 負面 [fu6 min2]

neglect *v./n.* 疏忽 [so1 fat7]

negligence *n.* 疏忽 [so1 fat7]

negotiate *v.* 講數 [gong2 sou3]

negotiation *n.* 講數 [gong2 sou3]

neighbor *n.* 隔離鄰舍 [gaak8 lei4 leun4 se3]

neighborhood *n.* 附近地區 [fu6 gan6 dei6 keui1]

neighboring *adj.* 隔離 [gaak8 lei4]

neither *det./pron./adv.* 冇一個 [mou5 yat7 go3]

neolithic *adj.* 新石器時代 [san1 sek9 hei3 si4 doi6]

Nepal *n.* 尼泊爾 [nei4 bok9 yi5]

Nepali *adj.* 尼泊爾 [nei4 bok9 yi5]

nephew *n.* 侄仔 [jat9 jai2]

nepotism *n.* 裙帶關係 [kwan4 daai3 gwaan1 hai6]

Neptune *n.* 海王星 [hoi2 wong4 sing1]

nerve *n.* 神經 [san4 ging1]

nerveless *adj.* 鎮定 [jan3 ding6]

nervous *adj.* 緊張 [gan2 jeung1]

nervous system *n.* 神經系統 [san4 ging1 hai6 tung2]

nervously *adv.* 緊張 [gan2 jeung1]

nescience *n.* 無知 [mou4 ji1]

nest *n.* 巢 [chaau4]; *v.* 築巢 [juk7 chaau4]

net *n.* *(fishing)* 網 [mong5]; *adj.* 純 [seun4]

net weight *n.* 淨重 [jing6 chung5]

Netherlands,The (*aka* **Holland**) *n.* 荷蘭 [ho4 laan1]

nettle *n.* 蕁麻 [cham4 ma4]

network *n.* 網絡 [mong5 lok8], **computer ~** 電腦網絡; *v.* 溝通 [kau1 tung1], **~ through contacts** 關係網

neurologist *n.* 神經科專家 [san4 ging1 fo1 jyun1 ga1]

neurology *n.* 神經病學 [san4 ging1 beng6 hok9]

neurosis *n.* 神經衰弱 [san4 ging1 seui1 yeuk9]

neuter *n.* 閹割 [yim1 got8]

neutral *adj.* 中立 [jung1 laap9]

neutralize *v.* 中和 [jung1 wo4]

neutron *n.* 中子 [jung1 ji2]

never *adv.* 從來都唔會 [chung4 loi4 dou1 m4 wui5]

never mind *phr.* 唔緊要 [m4 gan2 yiu3]

nevertheless *adv.* 就算 [jau6 syun3]

new *adj.* 新嘅 [san1 ge3]

New Delhi *n.* 新德里 [san1 dak7 lei5]; **~, capital of India** 印度首都

new potatoes *n.* 新鮮薯仔 [san1 sin1 syu4 jai2]

new releases *n.* 新版本 [san1 baan2 bun2]

New Year *n.* 新年 [san1 nin4]

New Year's Day *n.* 元旦 [yun4 daan3]

New Year's Eve *n.* 新年前夕 [san1 nin4 chin4 jik9]

New Zealand *n.* 新西蘭 [san1 sai1 laan4]

New Zealander *adj.* 新西蘭 [san1 sai1 laan4]

newly *adv.* 新近 [san1 gan6]

news *n.* 新聞 [san1 man2]

newspaper *n.* 報紙 [bou3 ji2]

newsstand *n.* 報紙攤 [bou3 ji2 taan1]

next *adj.* 下一個 [ha6 yat7 go3]; *adv.* 跟住 [gan1 jyu6]; *n.* 下一個 [ha6 yat7 go3]

next month *adv.* 下個月 [ha6 go3 yut9]

next stop! *phr.* 下一站有落！ [ha6 yat7 jaam6 yau5 lok9]

next to *prep.* 僅次於 [gan2 chi3 yu1]

next week *n.* 下個星期 [ha6 go3 sing1 kei4]

next year *n.* 下年 [ha6 nin2]

Niamey *n.* 尼亞美 [nei4 a3 mei5]; **~, capital of Niger** 尼日爾首都

nib *n.* 筆尖 [bat7 jim1]

nibble *n.* 慢慢咬 [maan6 maan6 ngaau5]

Nicaragua *n.* 尼加拉瓜 [nei4 ga1 laai1 gwa1]

Nicaraguan *adj.* 尼加拉瓜 [nei4 ga1 laai1 gwa1]

nice *adj.* 心地好 [sam1 dei2 hou2]

nicely *adv.* 好靚 [hou2 leng3]

nickname *n.* 花名 [fa1 meng4]

Nicosia *n.* 尼科西亞 [nei4 fo1 sai1 a3]; **~, capital of Cyprus** 塞浦路斯首都

nicotine *n.* 尼古丁 [nei4 gu2 ding1]

niece *n.* 侄女 [jat9 neui5]

Niger *n.* 尼日爾 [nei4 yat9 yi5]

Nigeria *n.* 尼日利亞 [nei4 yat9 lei6 a3]

Nigerian *adj.* 尼日利亞 [nei4 yat9 lei6 a3]

night *adv./n.* 夜晚 [ye6 maan5], **at ~** 夜晚, **good~** 晚安, **spend the ~** 過夜

night bell *n.* 門鈴 [mun4 ling4]

night club *n.* 夜總會 [ye6 jung2 wui2]

night porter *n.* 看更 [hon1 gaang1]

nightlife *n.* 夜生活 [ye6 sang1 wut9]

nightmare *n.* 惡夢 [ok8 mung6]

nihilism *n.* 虛無主義 [heui1 mou4 jyu2 yi6]

nimble *n.* 靈活 [ling4 wut9]

nimbus *n.* 雨雲 [yu5 wan4]

nine *num.* 九 [gau2]

nineteen *num.* 十九 [sap9 gau2]

nineteenth *adj.* 第十九個 [dai6 sap9 gau2 go3]

ninetieth *adj.* 第九十個 [dai6 gau2 sap9 go3]

ninety *num.* 九十 [gau2 sap9]

ninth *adj.* 第九個 [dai6 gau2 go3]

nitrogen *n.* 氮氣 [daam6 hei3]

no *adv./exclam./det.*; ~ **way!** 唔使諗 [m4 sai2 nam2]

no one *pron.* 冇人 [mou5 yan4]

nobility *n.* 貴族階級 [gwai3 juk9 gaai1 kap7]

noble *adj.* 高貴 [gou1 gwai3]

nobleman *n.* 貴族 [gwai3 juk9]

nobody *pron.* 冇人 [mou5 yan4]

node *n.* 結 [git8]

noise *n.* 噪音 [chou3 yam1]

nominal *adj.* 名義上 [ming4 yi6 seung6]

nomination *n.* 提名 [tai4 ming4]

nominee *n.* 候選人 [hau6 syun2 yan4]

non-alcoholic *adj.* 冇酒精 [mou5 jau2 jing1], ~ **beverage** 無酒精飲料, ~ **beer** 無酒精啤酒

nonchalance *n.* 冷淡 [laang5 daam6]

nonchalant *adj.* 冷淡 [laang5 daam6]

none *pron.* 一個都冇 [yat7 go3 dou1 mou5]

non-EU citizens *n.* 非歐盟公民 [fei1 au1 mang4 gung1 man4]

non-fiction *n.* 非小說類 [fei1 siu2 seui3 leui6]

nonlinear *adj.* 非線性 [fei1 sin3 sing3]

non-prefix *n.* 非前綴 [fei1 chin4 jeui6]

nonreturnable *adj.* 冇得退 [mou5 dak7 teui3]

nonsense *n.* 亂噏 [lyun6 ap7]

non-smoker *n.* 唔食煙 [m4 sik9 yin1]

non-smoking *adj.* 非吸煙 [fei1 kap7 yin1]

non-stick *adj.* 唔黐 [m4 chi1], ~ **pan** 唔黐底鍋, ~ **cooking utensil** 唔黐底廚具

nonstop *adv.* 直達 [jik9 daat9]

noodles *n.* 麵 [min6]

noon *adv.* 晏晝 [ngaan3 jau3]

nor *conj./adv.* 亦唔係 [yik9 m4 hai6]

norm *n.* 標準 [biu1 jeun2]

normal *adj.* 正常 [jing3 seung4]; *n.* 常態 [seung4 taai3]
  normal skin *n.* 正常皮膚 [jing3 seung4 pei4 fu1]

normalize *v.* 正常化 [jing3 seung4 fa3]

normally *adv.* 正常黎講 [jing3 seung4 lai4 gong2]

north *n.* 北面 [bak7 min6]; *adj.* 北面嘅 [bak7 min6 ge3]; *adv.* 從北面 [chung4 bak7 min6]

North American *adj.* 北美 [bak7 mei5]

northeast *adj./n.* 東北 [dung1 bak7]

northern *adj.* 北面 [bak7 min6]

northwest *adj./n.* 西北 [sai1 bak7]

Norway *n.* 挪威 [no4 wai1]

Norwegian *adj.* 挪威 [no4 wai1]

nose *n.* 鼻 [bei6]

nostalgia *n.* 懷舊 [waai4 gau6]

nostrum *n.* 靈丹妙藥 [ling4 daan1 miu6 yeuk9]

nosy *adj.* 八卦 [baat8 gwa3]

not *adv.* 唔 [m4]; ~ **bad** 唔錯 [m4 cho3]

not at all *adv.* 冇所謂 [mou5 so2 wai6]

notability *n.* 名人 [ming4 yan4]

notable *adj.* 顯著 [hin2 jyu3]

notably *adv.* 尤其 [yau4 kei4]

notary *n.* 公證員 [gung1 jing3 yun4]

notation *n.* 標記 [biu1 gei3]

note *n.* 筆記 [bat7 gei3]; *v.* 指出 [ji2 cheut7]

notebook *n.* 筆記簿 [bat7 gei3 bou2]

noteworthy *adj.* 顯著 [hin2 jyu3]

nothing *pron./n.* 冇嘢 [mou5 ye5]

nothing else *pron.* 冇其他嘢 [mou5 kei4 ta1 ye5]

notice *n.* 通告 [tung1 gou3]; *v.* 注意 [jyu3 yi3]

noticeable *adj.* 睇得見 [tai2 dak7 gin3]

notify *v.* 通知 [tung1 ji1]

notion *n.* 意見 [yi3 gin3]

notoriety *n.* 臭名 [chau3 ming4]

notorious *adj.* 臭名遠播 [chau3 ming4 yun5 bo3]

Nouakchott *n.* 努瓦克肖特 [nou5 nga5 hak7 chiu3 dak9]; ~, **capital of Mauritania** 毛利塔尼亞首都

nougat *n.* 鳥結糖 [niu5 git8 tong2]

noun *n.* 名詞 [ming4 chi4]

nourish *v.* 施肥 [si1 fei4]

nourishment *n.* 營養 [ying4 yeung5]

novel *n.* 小說 [siu2 syut8]

novelist *n.* 作家 [jok8 ga1]

novelty *n.* 新穎 [san1 wing6]

November (*abbr.* Nov.) *n.* 十一月份 [sap9 yat7 yut9 fan6]

now *adv.* 而家 [yi4 ga1]

nowhere *adv.* 度度都冇 [dou6 dou6 dou1 mou5]

nuclear *adj.* 核心嘅 [hat9 sam1 ge3]

nuclear bomb *n.* 核彈 [hat9 daan2]

nuclear energy *n.* 核能 [hat9 nang4]

nuclear physics *n.* 核物理 [hat9 mat9 lei5]

nuclear power station *n.* 核電站 [hat9 din6 jaam6]

nuclear testing *n.* 核測試 [hat9 chak7 si3]

nuclear tests *n.* 核測試 [hat9 chak7 si3]

nuclear weapons *n.* 核武 [hat9 mou5]

nucleus *n.* 原子核 [yun4 ji2 hat9]

nudist beach *n.* 天體沙灘 [tin1 tai2 sa1 taan1]

nuisance *n.* 麻煩嘢 [ma4 faan4 ye5]

Nuku'alofa *n.* 努庫阿洛法 [nou5 fu3 a3 lok8 faat8]; ~, **capital of Tonga** 湯加首都

number *n.* 數字 [sou3 ji6]; *v.* 數 [sou2]

numerator *n.* 分子 [fan6 ji2]

numerous *adj.* 好多 [hou2 do1]

nun *n.* 修女 [sau1 neui5]

nunnery *n.* 尼姑庵 [nei4 gu1 am1]

nurse *n.* 護士 [wu6 si6]
nursery *n.* 幼兒園 [yau3 yi4 yun2]
nursery room *n.* 嬰兒房 [ying1 yi4 fong4]
nut *n.* 果仁 [gwo2 yan4]
nutmeg *n.* 肉豆蔻 [yuk9 dau6 kau3]

nutrient *n.* 養料 [yeung5 liu2]
nutrition *n.* 營養 [ying4 yeung5]
nutritious *adj.* 有營養 [yau5 ying4 yeung5]
nutty *adj.* 癡線 [chi1 sin3]
nylon *adj.* 尼龍 [nei4 lung4]

O

o'clock *adv.* 點鐘 [dim2 jung1]

oak *n.* 橡木 [jeung6 muk9]

oasis *n.* 綠洲 [luk9 jau1]

oath *n.* 誓言 [sai6 yin4]

oatmeal *n.* 燕麥 [yin3 mak9]

oats *n.* 燕麥 [yin3 mak9]

obese *adj.* 肥胖 [fei4 bun6]

obesity *n.* 肥胖症 [fei4 bun6 jing3]

obey *v.* 遵守 [jeun1 sau2]

obituary *n.* 訃聞 [fu6 man4]

object *n.* 物體 [mat9 tai2]; *v.* 唔贊成 [m4 jaan3 sing4]

objection *n.* 反對 [faan2 deui3]

objectionable *adj.* 令人反感 [ling4 yan4 faan2 gam2]

objective *n.* 目標 [muk9 biu1]; *adj.* 客觀 [haak8 gun1]

oblation *n.* 祭品 [jai3 ban2]

obligation *n.* 義務 [yi6 mou6]

obligatory *adj.* 義務 [yi6 mou6]

oblige *v.* 強制 [keung5 jai3]

oblique *adj.* 斜 [che4]

obliterate *v.* 毀滅 [wai2 mit9]

obliteration *n.* 毀滅 [wai2 mit9]

oblivion *n.* 冇意識 [mou5 yi3 sik7]

oblivious *adj.* 冇覺察到 [mou5 gok8 chaat8 dou2]

obnoxious *adj.* 乞人憎 [hat7 yan4 jang1]

obscene *adj.* 下流 [ha6 lau4]

obscenity *n.* 下流 [ha6 lau4]

obscure *adj.* 唔清楚 [m4 ching1 cho2]; *v.* 掩蓋 [yim2 koi3]

obscurity *n.* 默默無聞 [mak9 mak9 mou4 man4]

observance *n.* 遵守 [jeun1 sau2]

observation *n.* 觀察 [gun1 chaat8]

observatory *n.* 天文台 [tin1 man4 toi4]

observe *v.* 觀察 [gun1 chaat8]

observer *n.* 觀察員 [gun1 chaat8 yun4]

obsess *v.* 迷戀 [mai4 lyun2]

obsession *n.* 迷戀 [mai4 lyun2]

obsolete *adj.* 過咗時 [gwo3 jo2 si4]

obstacle *n.* 阻礙 [jo2 ngoi6]

obstinacy *n.* 硬頸 [ngaang6 geng2]

obstinate *adj.* 硬頸 [ngaang6 geng2]

obstruct *v.* 阻撓 [jo2 naau4]

obstruction *n.* 阻礙 [jo2 ngoi6]

obstructive *adj.* 故意刁難 [gu3 yi3 diu1 naan4]

obtain *v.* 攞到 [lo2 dou2]

obtainable *adj.* 可以攞到 [ho2 yi5 lo2 dou2]

obtuse *adj.* 遲鈍 [chi4 deun6]

obvious *adj.* 明顯 [ming4 hin2]

obviously *adv.* 明顯 [ming4 hin2]

occasion *n.* 機會 [gei1 wui6]; *v.* 引起 [yan5 hei2]

occupant *n.* 住客 [jyu6 haak8]

occupation *n.* 職業 [jik7 yip9]

occult *adj.* 神祕 [san4 bei3]

occupancy *n.* 佔用 [jim3 yung6]

occupant *n.* 住客 [jyu6 haak8]

occupation *n.* 職業 [jik7 yip9]

occupied *adj.* 用緊嘅 [yung6 gan2 ge3]

occupy *v.* 佔領 [jim3 ling5]

occur *v.* 發生 [faat8 sang1]

occurrence *n.* 發生 [faat8 sang1]

ocean *n.* 大海 [daai6 hoi2]

o'clock *n.* 點鐘 [dim2 jung1], **it's 5 ~** 宜家五點鐘啦

octagon *n.* 八邊形 [baat8 bin1 ying4]

October (*abbr.* Oct.) *n.* 十月份 [sap9 yut9 fan6]

octopus *n.* 八爪魚 [baat8 jaau2 yu4], **~ legs** 八爪魚腳, **~ soup** 八爪魚湯

ocular *adj.* 眼嘅 [ngaan5 ge3]

oculist *n.* 眼科醫生 [ngaan5 fo1 yi1 sang1]

odd *adj.* 奇怪 [kei4 gwaai3]

oddly *adv.* 奇怪 [kei4 gwaai3]

odds *n.* 可能性 [ho2 nang4 sing3]

ode *n.* 頌歌 [jung6 go1]

odious *adj.* 乞人憎 [hat7 yan4 jang1]

odium *n.* 反感 [faan2 gam2]

odometer *n.* 計程表 [gai3 ching4 biu1]

odorous *adj.* 有味 [yau5 mei6]

odor *n.* 味 [mei6]

of *prep.* 嘅 [ge3]

of course *adv.* 當然 [dong1 yin4]

off *adj.* 休息 [yau1 sik7]; *prep.* 從...離開 [chung4 ... lei4 hoi1]

offal *n.* 殘渣 [chaan4 ja1]

offend *v.* 得罪 [dak7 jeui6]

offense *n.* 進攻 [jeun3 gung1]

offensive *adj.* 得罪人 [dak7 jeui6 yan4]

offer *v.* 提出 [tai4 cheut7]; *n.* 開價 [hoi1 ga3]

offering *n.* 供品 [gung1 ban2]

office *n.* 寫字樓 [se2 ji6 lau4]

office work *n.* 文職 [man4 jik7]

office worker *n.* 白領 [baak9 leng5]

officer *n.* 軍官 [gwan1 gun1]

official *adj.* 官方 [gun1 fong1]; *n.* 官員 [gun1 yun4]

officially *adv.* 正式 [jing3 sik7]

officious *adj.* 多管閒事 [do1 gun2 haan4 si6]

offline *adj.* 離線 [lei4 sin3], **webpage is ~** 呢個網頁離咗線

off-peak *adj.* 淡季 [daam6 gwai3]

offset *v.* 抵消 [dai2 siu1]

offside *adj.* 越位 [yut9 wai6]

offspring *n.* 仔女 [jai2 neui2]

often *adv.* 周不時 [jau1 bat1 si4]

ogle *v.* 眼甘甘 [ngaan5 gam1 gam1]

oh! *exclam.* 啊 [a1]

oil *n.* 油 [yau4], **sesame ~** 芝麻油, **olive ~** 橄欖油, **canola ~** 油菜籽油

oil filter *n.* 機油濾清器 [gei1 yau2 leui6 ching1 hei3]

oil gauge *n.* 油表 [yau2 biu1]

oil painting *n.* 油畫 [yau4 wa2]

oily *adj.* 油性 [yau4 sing3]

oily skin *n.* 油性皮膚 [yau4 sing3 pei4 fu1]

ointment *n.* 藥膏 [yeuk9 gou1]

OK / okay *exclam./adj./adv.* 好呀 [hou2 a1]

okra *n.* 秋葵 [chau1 kwai4]

old *adj.* 老 [lou5], **~ town** *n.* 老鎮 [lou5 jan3]

old-fashioned *adj.* 老式 [lou5 sik7]

oleo *n.* 人造奶油 [yan4 jou6 naai5 yau4]

oligarchy *n.* 寡頭政治 [gwa2 tau4 jing3 ji6]

olive *n.* 橄欖 [gam2 laam2], **black ~** 黑橄欖, **green ~** 青橄欖, **pitted ~** 去核橄欖, **unpitted ~** 有核橄欖, **Greek ~** 希臘橄欖

olive oil *n.* 橄欖油 [gam2 laam2 yau4]

Olympic Games *n.* 奧運會 [ou3 wan6 wui2]

Oman *n.* 阿曼 [a3 maan6]

omelet *n.* 庵列 [am1 lit9], **breakfast ~** 早餐庵列

omen *n.* 兆頭 [siu6 tau4]

ominous *adj.* 唔吉利 [m4 gat7 lei6]

omission *n.* 省略 [saang2 leuk9]

omit *v.* 漏咗 [lau6 jo2]

omnipotence *n.* 萬能 [maan6 nang4]

omnipotent *adj.* 萬能 [maan6 nang4]

omnipresence *n.* 無處不在 [mou4 chyu3 bat7 joi6]

omnipresent *adj.* 無處不在 [mou4 chyu3 bat7 joi6]

omniscience *n.* 無所不知 [mou4 so2 bat7 ji1]

omniscient *adj.* 無所不知 [mou4 so2 bat7 ji1]

omnivore *n.* 雜食動物 [jaap9 sik9 dung6 mat9]

on *prep.* 喺…上 [hai2 … seung6]; *adv.* 上 [seung6]

on board 喺船上 [hai2 syun4 seung6]

on purpose 故意 [gu3 yi3]

on tap 錄起 [luk9 hei2]

on the house 免費 [min5 fai3]

on the rocks 就快唔掂 [jau6 faai3 m4 dim6]

once *adv.* 一次 [yat7 chi3]; *conj.* 一旦 [yat7 daan3]

one *num.* 一 [yat7]

one another *n.* 互相 [wu6 seung1]

one number *det.* 一個號碼 [yat7 go3 hou6 ma5]

one time *n.* 一次 [yat7 chi3]

one-story house *n.* 平房 [ping4 fong4]

one-way *adj.* 單行道 [daan1 hang4 dou6]

one-way street *n.* 單行道 [daan1 hang4 dou6]

one-way ticket *n.* 單程票 [daan1 ching4 piu3]

onerous *adj.* 繁重 [faan4 jung6]

onion *n.* 洋蔥 [yeung4 chung1], **red ~** 紅洋蔥, **green ~** 青洋蔥, **white ~** 白洋蔥, **sweet ~** 甜洋蔥

onion rings *n.* 洋蔥圈 [yeung4 chung1 hyun1]

onion soup *n.* 洋蔥湯 [yeung4 chung1 tong1]

online *adj./adv.* 網上 [mong5 seung6], **to go ~** 上網, **search ~** 網上搜尋

only *adj./adv.* 得 [dak7]

onto *prep.* 到…上 [dou3 … seung6]

opacity *n.* 唔透明 [m4 tau3 ming4]

opal *n.* 貓眼石 [maau1 ngaan5 sek9]

opaque *adj.* 唔透明 [m4 tau3 ming4]

open *adj.* 開 [hoi1] *v.* 開 [hoi1]

open air *n.* 空地 [hung1 dei6]

open all night *phr.* 二十四小時營業 [yi6 sap9 sei3 siu2 si4 ying4 yip9]

open here *phr.* 打開呢度 [da2 hoi1 ne1 dou6]

open hours *n.* 營業時間 [ying4 yip9 si4 gaan3]

open-faced sandwiches *n.* 露餡三文治 [lou6 haam6 saam1 man4 ji6]

opening *n.* 開幕 [hoi1 mok9]

openly *adv.* 開心見誠 [hoi1 sam1 gin3 sing4]

opera *n.* 歌劇 [go1 kek9]

opera house *n.* 歌劇院 [go1 kek9 yun2]

operate *n.* 操作 [chou1 jok8]

operation *n.* 運作 [wan6 jok8]

operational *adj.* 運作上 [wan6 jok8 seung6]

operator *n.* 操作員 [chou1 jok8 yun4]

opinion *n.* 意見 [yi3 gin3]

opium *n.* 鴉片 [a1 pin3]

opponent *n.* 對手 [deui3 sau2]

opportunism *n.* 機會主義 [gei1 wui6 jyu2 yi6]

opportunity *n.* 機會 [gei1 wui6]

oppose *v.* 反對 [faan2 deui3]

opposite *adj./adv./prep.* 對面 [deui3 min6]; *n.* 對立面 [deui3 laap9 min2]

opposition *n.* 反對黨 [faan2 deui3 dong2]

oppress *v.* 壓迫 [aat8 bik7]

oppression *n.* 壓迫 [aat8 bik7]

oppressor *n.* 暴君 [bou6 gwan1]

opthalmologist *n.* 眼科醫生 [ngaan5 fo1 yi1 sang1]

optical *adj.* 視力 [si6 lik9]

optician *n.* 眼鏡店 [ngaan5 geng3 dim3]

optimism *n.* 樂觀 [lok9 gun1]

optimist *n.* 樂天派 [lok9 tin1 paai3]

optimistic *adj.* 樂觀 [lok9 gun1]

optimum *adj.* 最好 [jeui3 hou2]

option *n.* 選擇 [syun2 jaak9]

optional *adj.* 選修 [syun2 sau1]

optometrist *n.* 驗光師 [yim6 gwong1 si1]

opulence *n.* 豪華 [hou4 wa4]

opulent *adj.* 豪華 [hou4 wa4]

or *conj.* 定 [ding6]

oral *adj.* 口述 [hau2 seut9]

oracle *n.* 先知 [sin1 ji1]

oracular *n.* 玄妙 [yun4 miu6]

orally *adv.* 口頭 [hau2 tau4]

orange *n.* 橙 [chaang2]; *adj.* 橙色嘅 [chaang2 sik7 ge3]

orange blossom *n.* 橙花 [chaang2 fa1]

orange juice *n.* 橙汁 [chaang2 jap7]

orange peel *n.* 橙皮 [chaang2 pei4]

oration *n.* 演講 [yin2 gong2]

orator *n.* 演講家 [yin2 gong2 ga1]

oratory *n.* 演講術 [yin2 gong2 seut9]

orbit *v.* 圍著...轉 [wai4 jyu3 ... jyun3]; *n.* 軌道 [gwai2 dou6]

orchard *n.* 果園 [gwo2 yun4]

orchestra *n.* 管弦樂隊 [gun2 yin4 ngok9 deui6]

orchestral *adj.* 管弦樂 [gun2 yin4 ngok9]

ordeal *n.* 磨難 [mo4 naan6]

order *n.* 次序 [chi3 jeui6], **numerical** ~ 數字順序, **out of** ~ 壞咗; *v.* 點 [dim2], **what did you** ~? 你點咗乜野？

orderly *n.* 整齊 [jing2 chai4]

ordinal *n.* 序數 [jeui6 sou3]

ordinance *n.* 條例 [tiu4 lai6]

ordinary *adj.* 普通 [pou2 tung1]

odor *n.* 味 [mei6]

ore *n.* 礦石 [kwong3 sek9]

oregano *n.* 牛至 [ngau4 ji3]

organ *n.* 器官 [hei3 gun1]

organic *adj.* 有機 [yau5 gei1], ~ **milk** 有機牛奶, ~ **chicken** 有機雞肉, ~ **produce** 有機蔬果, ~ **grown** 有機種植

organism *n.* 有機體 [yau5 gei1 tai2]

organization *n.* 組織 [jou2 jik7]

organizational *adj.* 組織上 [jou2 jik7 seung6]

organize *v.* 組織 [jou2 jik7]

orgasm *n.* 性高潮 [sing3 gou1 chiu4]

oriental *adj.* 東方 [dung1 fong1]

orientate *v.* 對著 [deui3 jyu3]

origin *n.* 起源 [hei2 yun4]

original *adj.* 原來 [yun4 loi4]; *n.* 原型 [yun4 ying4] **original version** *n.* 原版 [yun4 baan2]

originally *adv.* 原來 [yun4 loi4]

originator *n.* 創始人 [chong3 chi2 yan4]

ornament *n.* 裝飾物 [jong1 sik7 mat9]

orphan *n.* 孤兒 [gu1 yi4]

orphanage *n.* 孤兒院 [gu1 yi4 yun2]

orthodox *adj.* 正統 [jing1 tung2]

oscillate *v.* 波動 [bo1 dung6]

oscillation *n.* 波動 [bo1 dung6]

Oslo *n.* 奧斯陸 [ou3 si1 luk9]; ~, **capital of Norway** 挪威首都

ossify *v.* 硬化 [ngaang6 fa3]

ostracize *v.* 流放 [lau4 fong3]

ostrich *n.* 鴕鳥 [to4 niu5]

other *adj./pron.* 其他 [kei4 ta1]

otherwise *adv.* 如果唔係 [yu4 gwo2 m4 hai6]

Ottawa *n.* 渥太華 [ak7 taai3 wa4]; ~, **capital of Canada** 加拿大首都

otter *n.* 水獺 [seui2 chaat8]

Ouagadougou *n.* 瓦加杜古 [nga5 ga1 dou6 gu2]; ~, **capital of Burkina Faso** 布基納發索首都

ought 應該 [ying1 goi1]

ought to *modal v.* 應該 [ying1 goi1]

ounce *n.* 安士 [on1 si2]

our *adj.* 我哋嘅 [ngo5 dei6 ge3]

ours *pron.* 我哋嘅 [ngo5 dei6 ge3]

ourselves *pron.* 我哋自己 [ngo5 dei6 ji6 gei2]

oust *v.* 罷免 [ba6 min5]

out (of) *adv.* 出面 [cheut7 min6]; *prep.* 喺…出面 [hai2 … cheut7 min6]

outbreak *n.* 爆發 [baau3 faat8]

outburst *n.* 突發 [dat9 faat8]

outcast *n.* 被流放嘅人 [bei6 lau4 fong3 ge3 yan4]

outcome *n.* 結果 [git8 gwo2]

outcry *n.* 強烈抗議 [keung4 lit9 kong3 yi5]

outdated *adj.* 過時 [gwo3 si4]

outdo *v.* 叻過 [lek7 gwo3]

outdoor(s) *adj./adv.* 室外 [sat7 ngoi6]

outdoor swimming pool *n.* 室外泳池 [sat7 ngoi6 wing6 chi4]

outer *adj.* 外面 [ngoi6 min6]

outfit *n.* 一套衫 [yat7 tou3 saam1]

outgoing *adj.* 外向 [ngoi6 heung3]

outlet: factory ~ *n.* 工廠直銷店 [gung1 chong2 jik9 siu1 dim3]

outing *n.* 郊遊 [gaau1 yau4]

outlandish *adj.* 古怪 [gu2 gwaai3]

outlaw *n.* 逃犯 [tou4 faan2]

outlive *v.* 長命過 [cheung4 meng6 gwo3]

outlook *n.* 前景 [chin4 ging2]

outline *v.* 畫輪廓 [waak9 leun4 gwok8]; *n.* 大綱 [daai6 gong1]

outnumber *v.* 多過 [do1 gwo3]

out-patient department *n.* 門診部 [mun4 chan2 bou6]

outpost *n.* 前哨 [chin4 saau3]

output (*tech.*) *n.* 輸出 [syu1 cheut7]

outrage *n.* 憤怒 [fan5 nou6]

outrageous *adj.* 無禮 [mou4 lai5]

outrun *v.* 超過 [chiu1 gwo3]

outset *n.* 開始 [hoi1 chi2]

outshine *n.* 叻過 [lek7 gwo3]

outside *n./adj./adv.* 外面 [ngoi6 min6]; *prep.* 喺…外面 [hai2 … ngoi6 min6]

outsider *n.* 局外人 [guk9 ngoi6 yan4]

outskirts *n.* 郊區 [gaau1 keui1]

outspoken *adj.* 直腸直肚 [jik9 cheung4 jik9 tou5]

outstanding *adj.* 出色 [cheut7 sik7]

oval *adj.* 橢圓形 [to2 yun4 ying4]

ovary *n.* 卵巢 [leun2 chaau4]

ovation *n.* 熱烈歡迎 [yit9 lit9 fun1 ying4]

oven *n.* 焗爐 [guk9 lou4]; **~-browned** 焗燶; **~-roasted** 用焗爐焗

oven mitts *n.* 焗爐手套 [guk9 lou4 sau2 tou3]

over *adj.* 上面 [seung6 min6]; *prep.* 喺…上面 [hai2 … seung6 min6]

over here *adv.* 喺呢度 [hai2 ne1 dou6]

over there *adv.* 個度 [go3 dou6]

overall *adj.* 總體黎講 [jung2 tai2 lai4 gong2]; *adv.* 總體 [jung2 tai2]

overcast *adj.* 多雲 [do1 wan4]

overcharge *v.* 收多咗錢 [sau1 do1 jo2 chin4]

overcoat *n.* 褸 [lau1]

overcome *v.* 克服 [hak7 fuk9]

overdone *adj.* 煮得太熟 [jyu2 dak7 taai3 suk9]

overdose *n./v.* 用藥過量 [yung6 yeuk9 gwo3 leung6]

overdraft *n.* 透支 [tau3 ji1]

overdraw *v.* 透支 [tau3 ji1]

overdue *adj.* 過期 [gwo3 kei4]

overhanging *adj.* 掛住 [gwa3 jyu6]

overhear *v.* 無意中聽到 [mou4 yi3 jung1 teng1 dou2]

overheat *v.* 太熱 [taai3 yit9]

overlap *v.* 重疊 [chung4 dip9]

overload *v.* 超載 [chiu1 joi3]

overlook *v.* 忽略 [fat7 leuk9]

overnight *adv.* 過夜 [gwo3 ye6]

overrule *v.* 駁回 [bok8 wui4]

overrun *v.* 超時 [chiu1 si4]

overseas *adj./adv.* 國外 [gwok8 ngoi6]

oversight *n.* 疏忽 [so1 fat7]

overtake *v.* 超過 [chiu1 gwo3]

overtime *n.* 加班 [ga1 baan1]

overweight *adj.* 超重 [chiu1 chung5]

owe *v.* 欠 [him3], **how much do I ~?** 我爭幾多錢?

owl *n.* 貓頭鷹 [maau1 tau4 ying1]

own *adj.* 自己 [ji6 gei2]; *pron.* 自己人 [ji6 gei2 yan4]; *v.* 擁有 [yung2 yau5]

owner *n.* 主人 [jyu2 yan4]

ownership *n.* 所有權 [so2 yau5 kyun4]

oxidised *adj.* 氧化 [yeung5 fa3]

oxtail *n.* 牛尾 [ngau4 mei5]

oxtail soup *n.* 牛尾湯 [ngau4 mei5 tong1]

oxygen *n.* 氧氣 [yeung5 hei3]

oyster *n.* 蠔 [hou4], **~ soup** 生蠔湯, **~ shell** 蠔殼

ozone *n.* 臭氧 [chau3 yeung5] **ozone layer** *n.* 臭氧層 [chau3 yeung5 chang4]

P

pace n. 速度 [chuk7 dou6

pacemaker n. 帶頭人 [daai3 tau4 yan4]

pacific adj. 和平 [wo4 ping4]

pacifier n. 奶嘴 [naai5 jeui2]

pacify v. 平息 [ping4 sik7]

pack v. 打包 [da2 baau1], ~ a suitcase 打包行李; n. 包 [baau1], ~ of cigarettes 一包煙

package n. 包 [baau1]

packed adj. 塞滿 [sak7 mun5]; v. 包裝 [baau1 jong1]
packed lunch n. 自備午飯 [ji6 bei6 ng5 faan6]

packet n. 細包仔 [sai3 baau1 jai2]

pad n. 墊 [din3]

paddle n. 船槳 [syun4 jeung2]

paddy n. 水田 [seui2 tin4]

padlock n. 掛鎖 [gwa3 so2]

paella n. 西班牙什錦飯 [sai1 baan1 nga4 jaap9 gam2 faan6]

pageant n. 盛會 [sing6 wui6]

pageantry n. 盛況 [sing6 fong3]

page n. 頁 [yip9]

pageview n. 點擊量 [dim2 gik7 leung6]; website ~s 網站點擊量

pagoda n. 寶塔 [bou2 taap8]

paid adj. 有人工 [yau5 yan4 gung1]

pail n. 桶 [tung2]

pain n. 痛苦 [tung3 fu2], be in ~ 痛苦

painful adj. 痛 [tung3]

painkiller n. 止痛藥 [ji2 tung3 yeuk9]

painstaking adj. 辛苦 [san1 fu2]

paint n. 顏料 [ngaan4 liu2]; v. 畫畫 [waak9 wa2]

painter n. 畫家 [wa2 ga1]

painting n. (art) 畫 [waak9]; (activity) 塗色 [tou4 sik7]

pair n. 孖 [ma1]

pajamas n. 睡褲 [seui6 fu3]

Pakistan n. 巴基斯坦 [ba1 gei1 si1 taan2]

Pakistani adj. 巴基斯坦 [ba1 gei1 si1 taan2]

palace n. 皇宮 [wong4 gung1]

palanquin n. 轎 [giu6]

palatable adj. 好好食 [hou2 hou2 sik9]

Palau n. 帕勞群島 [paak8 lou6 kwan4 dou2]

pale adj. 面青青 [min6 cheng1 cheng1]

palette n. 調色板 [tiu4 sik7 baan2]

Palikir n. 帕利萊爾 [paak8 lei6 gei1 yi5]; ~, capital of Micronesia 密克羅尼西亞聯邦首都

palm n. 手板 [sau2 baan2]

palm oil n. 棕櫚油 [jung1 leui4 yau4]

Palm Sunday n. 棕櫚主日 [jung1 leui4 jyu2 yat9]

palmist n. 睇手相嘅人 [tai2 sau2 seung3 ge3 yan4]

palmistry *n.* 手相術 [sau2 seung3 seut9]

palpable *adj.* 明顯 [ming4 hin2]

palpitate *v.* 撲撲跳 [pok8 pok8 tiu3]

palpitations *n.* 心悸 [sam1 gwai3]

palsy *n.* 中風 [jung3 fung1]

pamper *v.* 縱容 [jung3 yung4]

pamphlet *n.* 小冊子 [siu2 chaak8 ji2]

pan *n.* 平底鑊 [ping4 dai2 wok9], **~fried** *adj.* 鍋煎, **~broiled** *adj.* 鍋煮

panacea *n.* 萬能之計 [maan6 nang4 ji1 gai3]

Panama *n.* 巴拿馬 [ba1 na4 ma5]

Panama City *n.* 巴拿馬城 [ba1 na4 ma5 sing4]; **~, capital of Panama** 巴拿馬首都

Panamanian *adj.* 巴拿馬 [ba1 na4 ma5]

pancake *n.* 班戟 [baan1 gik7]

pane *n.* 窗框 [cheung1 kwaang1]

panegyric *n.* 頌文 [jung6 man4]

panel *n.* 小組 [siu2 jou2]

panorama *n.* 全景 [chyun4 ging2]

pant *v.* 喘氣 [sok8 hei3]

panther *n.* 豹 [paau3]

pantomime *n.* 啞劇 [a2 kek9]

pantry *n.* 食品儲藏櫃 [sik9 ban2 chyu5 chong4 gwai6]

pants *n.* 褲 [fu3]

pantyhose *n.* 絲襪 [si1 mat9]

pap smear *n.* 抹片試驗 [mut9 pin2 si3 yim6]

papaya *n.* 木瓜 [muk9 gwa1]

paper *n.* 紙 [ji2]

paprika *n.* 辣椒粉 [laat9 jiu1 fan2]

Papua New Guinea *n.* 巴布亞新幾內亞 [ba1 bou3 a3 san1 gei1 noi6 a3]

parable *n.* 寓言 [yu6 yin4]

parachute *n.* 降落傘 [gong3 lok9 saan3]

parade *n.* 遊行 [yau4 hang4]

paradise *n.* 天堂 [tin1 tong4]

paradox *n.* 自相矛盾 [ji6 seung1 maau4 teun5]

paraffin *n.* 石蠟 [sek9 laap9]

paragon *n.* 模範 [mou4 faan6]

paragraph *n.* 段 [dyun6]

Paraguay *n.* 巴拉圭 [ba1 laai1 gwai1]

Paraguayan *adj.* 巴拉圭 [ba1 laai1 gwai1]

paralegal *n.* 律師助手 [leut9 si1 jo6 sau2]

parallel *adj.* 平行 [ping4 hang4]

paralyse *v.* 令…癱瘓 [ling6 … tann2 wun6]

paralysis *n.* 癱瘓 [tann2 wun6]

Paramaribo *n.* 帕拉馬里博 [paak8 laai1 ma5 lei5 bok8]; **~, capital of Suriname** 蘇里南首都

parameter *n.* 參數 [chaam1 sou3]

paramount *adj.* 最重要 [jeui3 jung6 yiu3]

paraplegic *adj.* 下身癱瘓 [ha6 san1 taan2 wun6]

parasite *n.* 寄生蟲 [gei3 sang1 chung4]

parasol *n.* 太陽遮 [taai3 yeung4 je1]

parcel *n.* 包裹 [baau1 gwo2]

parchment paper *n.* 假羊皮紙 [ga2 yeung4 pei4 ji2]

pardon *v./n.* 寬恕 [fun1 syu3]
pardon me? *phr.* 請再講一次 [ching2 joi3 gong2 yat7 chi3]

parent *n.* 父母 [fu6 mou5]

parenthesis *n.* 圓括號 [yun4 kut8 hou6]

parfait *n.* 凍奶糕 [dung3 naai5 gou1]

Paris *n.* 巴黎 [ba1 lai4]; ~, **capital of France** 法國首都

parish *n.* 教區 [gaau3 keui1]

parity *n.* 平等 [ping4 dang2]

park 1. *n.* 公園 [gung1 yun2], **city ~** 城市公園, // **2.** *v.* 泊車 [paak8 che1]; *n.* **car ~** 停車場 [ting4 che1 cheung4]

parking *n.* 泊車 [paak8 che1]; ~ **fines/ticket** 停車罰單, ~ **lot** 停車場, ~ **space** 車位
parking garage *n.* 停車場 [ting4 che1 cheung4]
parking meter *n.* 咪表 [mai1 biu1]

parlance *n.* 術語 [seut9 yu5]

parliament *n.* 國會 [gwok8 wui2]; ~ **building** 國會大廈

parlor *n.* 客廳 [haak8 teng1]

Parmesan cheese *n.* 巴馬臣芝士 [ba1 ma5 san4 ji1 si6]

parody *n.* 惡搞 [ok8 gaau2]

parole *n.* 假釋 [ga2 sik7]

parrot *n.* 鸚鵡 [ying1 mou5]; *v.* 死背 [sei2 bui6]

parsley *n.* 西芹 [sai1 kan5], ~ **flakes** 西芹碎, ~ **seasoning** 西芹調味料

parsnip *n.* 防風草 [fong4 fung1 chou2]

parson *n.* 牧師 [muk9 si1]

part *n.* 部份 [bou6 fan6]; *v.* 分開 [fan1 hoi1]

part of speech *n.* 詞類 [chi4 leui6]

partially *adv.* 偏袒 [pin1 taan2]

participant *n.* 參與者 [chaam1 yu5 je2]

participate *v.* 參加 [chaam1 ga1]

participle *n.* 分詞 [fan1 chi4]

particle *n.* 粒子 [lap7 ji2]

particular *adj.* 特定 [dak9 ding6]

partisan *n.* 游擊隊員 [yau4 gik7 deui2 yun4]

partition *n.* 隔牆 [gaak8 cheung4]

partly *adv.* 有部份 [yau5 bou6 fan6]

partner *n.* 拍檔 [paak8 dong3]

partnership *n.* 合營公司 [hap9 ying4 gung1 si1]

partridge *n.* 鵪鶉 [am1 cheun1]

part-time *n.* 兼職 [gim1 jik7]; ~ **job/work** 兼職

party *n.* 聚會 [jeui6 wui6], **social ~** 社交聚會, **political ~** 政黨

party politics *n.* 黨派政治 [dong2 paai3 jing3 ji6]

pass *n.* 通行證 [tung1 hang4 jing3]; *v.* 行過 [haang4 gwo3]
pass an exam *n.* 通過考試 [tung1 gwo3 haau2 si3]

passage *n.* 通道 [tung1 dou6]

passenger *n.* 乘客 [sing4 haak8]

passion *n.* 熱情 [yit9 ching4]

passion fruit *n.* 雞蛋果 [gai1 daan6 gwo2]

passionate *adj.* 熱情 [yit9 ching4]

passive *adj.* 消極 [siu1 gik9]; *n.* 被動語態 [bei6 dung6 yu5 taai3]

passport *n.* 護照 [wu6 jiu3], ~ **control** 護照管理, ~ **number** 護照號碼

passport-size photo *n.* 護照相 [wu6 jiu3 seung2]

password *n.* 密碼 [mat9 ma5], **account** ~ 帳戶密碼, **login with** ~ 登陸帳戶

past *adj./n.* 過去 [gwo3 heui3]; *prep./adv.* 行過 [haang4 gwo3]

pasta *n.* 意大利粉 [yi3 daai6 lei6 fan2], **angel hair** ~ 天使麵

paste *n.* 面糊 [min6 wu4]; *v.* 貼 [tip8], **copy and** ~ (*on computer*) 複製再貼上

pastel *n.* 蠟筆 [laap9 bat7]; *adj.* 蠟筆畫嘅 [laap9 bat7 waak9 ge3]

pasteurized *adj.* 巴氏消毒 [ba1 si6 siu1 duk9]; **non-**~ 冇巴氏 消毒

pastime *n.* 娛樂 [yu4 lok9]

pastry *n.* 糕點 [gou1 dim2]; **low carb** ~ 低碳水化合物糕點, **no sugar** ~ 無糖糕點

pastry shop *n.* 蛋糕店 [daan6 gou1 dim3]

pasture *n.* 牧場 [muk9 cheung4]

pat *n.* 輕輕拍 [heng1 heng1 paak8]

patch *n.* 補釘 [bou2 deng1]; *v.* 修補 [sau1 bou2]

paté *n.* 肉泥 [yuk9 nai4]

path *n.* 路線 [lou6 sin3]

patent *n.* 專利 [jyun1 lei6]

pathetic *adj.* 可憐 [ho2 lin4]

pathos *n.* 傷感 [seung1 gam2]

patience *n.* 耐心 [noi6 sam1], **have** ~ 有耐性

patient *n.* 病人 [beng6 yan4], **doctor's** ~ 醫生嘅病人; *adj.* 耐心 [noi6 sam1], **be** ~ 耐心啲

patriot *n.* 愛國者 [oi3 gwok8 je2]

patriotic *adj.* 愛國 [oi3 gwok8]

patriotism *n.* 愛國主義 [oi3 gwok8 jyu2 yi6]

patrol *v.* 巡邏 [cheun4 lo4]

patron *n.* 贊助人 [jaan3 jo6 yan4]

patronage *n.* 贊助 [jaan3 jo6]

patronize *v.* 贊助 [jaan3 jo6]

pattern *n.* 花紋 [fa1 man4]

patty *n.* 肉餅仔 [yuk9 beng2 jai2], **chicken** ~ 雞肉餅仔, **fish** ~ 魚肉餅仔

pattypan squash *n.* 扁南瓜 [bin2 naam4 gwa1]

pauper *n.* 窮鬼 [kung4 gwai2]

pause *v./n.* 停頓 [ting4 deun6]

pavement *n.* 行人路 [haang4 yan4 lou6]

pavilion *n.* 亭 [ting2]

paving stone *n.* 鋪路石 [pou1 lou6 sek9]

paw *n.* 爪 [jaau2]

pay *v.* 俾錢 [bei2 chin2]; *n.* 人工 [yan4 gung1] **pay attention** *adv.* 注意 [jyu3 yi3]

pay phone *n.* 付費電話 [fu6 fai3 din6 wa2]

payable *adj.* 要俾錢嘅 [yiu1 bei2 chin2 ge3]

payable to *adj.* 支票抬頭寫 [ji1 piu3 toi4 tau4 se2]

payment *n.* 付款 [fu6 fun2]

pea(s) *n.* 豌豆 [wun2 dau2], **green** ~ 青豌豆, **sugar snap** ~ 蜜豆

pea soup *n.* 濃豌豆湯 [nung4 wun2 dau2 tong1], **split ~ with ham** 濃火腿豌豆湯

peace *n.* 和平 [wo4 ping4]

peaceful *adj.* 和平 [wo4 ping4]

peach *n.* 桃 [tou2]

peacock *n.* 孔雀 [hung2 jeuk8]

peak *n.* 山頂 [saan1 deng2]

peanut *n.* 花生 [fa1 sang1], **~ butter** 花生奶油, **~ oil** 花生油, **~ spread** 花生醬

peapod *n.* 豆殼 [dau2 hok8]

pear *n.* 梨 [lei2]

pearl *n.* 珍珠 [jan1 jyu1]

pebble *n.* 鵝卵石 [ngo4 leun2 sek9]

pebbly *adj.* 有好多鵝卵石 [yau5 hou2 do1 ngo4 leun2 sek9]

pecan *n.* 山核桃 [saan1 hat9 tou4]; **~ pie** 山核桃批

peculiar *adj.* 奇怪 [kei4 gwaai3]; *n.* 專有財產 [jyun1 yau5 choi4 chaan2]

pedagogy *n.* 教學法 [gaau3 hok9 faat8]

pedal *n.* 腳踏 [geuk8 daap9]

pedant *n.* 書呆子 [syu1 daai1 ji2]

pedantic *adj.* 迂腐 [yu1 fu6]

pedantry *n.* 迂腐 [yu1 fu6]

pedestal *n.* 底座 [dai2 jo6]

pedestrian *n.* 路人 [lou6 yan4]; **~ crossing** 行人道, **~ zone** 行人區

pediatrician *n.* 兒科醫生 [yi4 fo1 yi1 sang1]

pedigree *n.* 血統 [hyut8 tung2]

peel *v.* 剝皮 [mok7 pei4]; *n.* 皮 [pei4], **orange ~** 橙皮

peeled *v.* 剝咗皮 [mok7 jo2 pei4]

peep *v.* 偷睇 [tau1 tai2]

peer *n.* 同輩 [tung4 bui3]

peg *n.* 釘 [deng2]

Peking duck *n.* 北京烤鴨 [bak7 ging1 haau1 aap8]

pen *n.* 筆 [bat7]

penalize *v.* 懲罰 [ching4 fat9]

penalty *n.* 懲罰 [ching4 fat9]

pencil *n.* 鉛筆 [yun4 bat7]

pending *adj.* 未定 [mei6 ding6]

pendulum *n.* 鐘擺 [jung1 baai2]

penetrate *v.* 滲入 [sam3 yap9]

penetration *n.* 滲入 [sam3 yap9]

peninsula *n.* 半島 [bun3 dou2]

penis *n.* 陽具 [yeung4 geui6]

penknife *n.* 折疊式小刀 [jit8 dip9 sik7 siu2 dou1]

penny *n.* 一分錢 [yat7 fan1 chin4]

pension *n.* 退休金 [teui3 yau1 gam1]

pensioner *n.* 領退休金嘅人 [ling5 teui3 yau1 gam1 ge3 yan4]

pentagon *n.* 五角大樓 [ng5 gok8 daai6 lau4]

people *n.* 人 [yan4]

pepper *n.* 胡椒粉 [wu4 jiu1 fan2], **green ~** 青胡椒粉, **red ~** 紅胡椒粉, **yellow ~** 黃胡椒粉, **orange ~** 橙色胡椒粉

pepper sauce *n.* 辣椒醬 [laat9 jiu1 jeung3]

pepper steak *n.* 黑椒牛扒 [hak7 jiu1 ngau4 pa2]

peppermint *n.* 薄荷 [bok9 ho6]

pepperoni *n.* 意大利辣香腸 [yi3 daai6 lei6 laat9 heung1 cheung2]

per *prep.* 每 [mui5], **~ hour** 每個鐘, **~ night** 每晚, **~ week** 每個星期, **~ day** 每日, **~ round** *adv.* 每場

perceive *v.* 察覺 [chaat8 gok8]

perceptible *adj.* 睇得出 [tai2 dak7 cheut7]

percent *n.* 百分之 [baak8 fan6 ji1]

percentage *n.* 百分比 [baak8 fan6 ji1]

perception *n.* 察覺 [chaat8 gok8]

perceptive *adj.* 觀察敏銳 [gun1 chaat8 man5 yeui6]

perch *n.* **1.** (*seat*) 棲息地 [chai1 sik7 dei6] // **2.** (*fish*) 鱸魚 [lou4 yu4]

perfect *adj.* 完美 [yun4 mei5]

perfection *n.* 完美 [yun4 mei5]

perfectly *adv.* 十分 [sap9 fan1]

perfidy *n.* 背信棄義 [bui6 seun3 hei3 yi6]

perform *v.* 表演 [biu2 yin2]

performance *n.* 表演 [biu2 yin2]

performer *n.* 表演嘅人 [biu2 yin2 ge3 yan4]

perfume *n.* 香水 [heung1 seui2]

perhaps *adv.* 或者 [waak9 je2]

peril *n.* 危險 [ngai4 him2]

perilous *adj.* 危險 [ngai4 him2]

period *n.* **1.** (*of time*) 時期 [si4 kei4] // **2.** (*punctuation*) 句號 [geui3 hou6]

period cramps (*menstruation*) *n.* 經期肚痛 [ging1 kei4 tou5 tung3]

periodic *adj.* 週期 [jau1 kei4]

periodical *adj.* 定期 [ding6 kei4]; *n.* 期刊 [kei4 hon2]

perish *v.* 死 [sei2]

perishable *adj.* 易變質 [yi6 bin3 jat7]

perjury *n.* 偽證 [ngai6 jing3]

perm *n.* 燙頭髮 [tong3 tau4 faat8]

permanent *adj.* 固定 [gu3 ding6]; *n.* (*hairdo*) 燙頭髮 [tong3 tau4 faat8]

permanent collection *n.* 永久收藏 [wing5 gau2 sau1 chong4]

permanently *adv.* 長期 [cheung4 kei4]

permission *n.* 批准 [pai1 jeun2]

permit *v.* 許可 [heui2 ho2]; *n.* 許可証 [heui2 ho2 jing3], **driver's ~** 駕駛執照

permit required *phr.* 需要許可證 [seui1 yiu3 heui2 ho2 jing3]

permit-holders only *phr.* 僅獲許可證者停放 [gan2 wok9 heui2 ho2 jing3 ke2 ting4 fong3]

permitted *adj.* 批准 [pai1 jeun2]

permutation *n.* 排列 [paai4 lit9]

pernicious *adj.* 害人 [hoi6 yan4]

perpendicular *adj.* 垂直 [seui4 jik9]; *n.* 垂直面 [seui4 jik9 min2]

perpetual *adj.* 永久 [wing5 gau2]

perpetuate *v.* 延續 [yin4 juk9]

perplex *v.* 困擾 [kwan3 yiu2]

perplexity *n.* 困擾 [kwan3 yiu2]

persecute *v.* 迫害 [bik7 hoi6]

persecution *n.* 迫害 [bik7 hoi6]

perseverance *n.* 毅力 [ngai6 lik9]

persevere *v.* 堅持 [gin1 chi4]

Persian *adj.* 波斯 [bo1 si1], **~ food** 波斯菜

persimmon *n.* 柿 [chi2]

persist *v.* 堅持 [gin1 chi4]

persistence *n.* 毅力 [ngai6 lik9]

persistent *adj.* 執著 [jap7 jeuk9]

person *n.* 人 [yan4]

personage *n.* 名人 [ming4 yan4]

personal *adj.* 個人 [go3 yan4]

personal computer (*abbr.* PC) *n.* 個人電腦 [go3 yan4 din6 nou5]

personality *n.* 個性 [go3 sing3]

personally *adv.* 親自 [chan1 ji6]

personification *n.* 人格化 [yan4 gaak8 fa3]

personnel *n.* 員工 [yun4 gung1]

perspective *n.* 睇法 [tai2 faat8]

perspiration *n.* 汗 [hon6]

perspire *v.* 出汗 [cheut7 hon6]

persuade *v.* 講得聽 [gong2 dak7 teng1]

persuasion *n.* 勸說 [hyun3 syut8]

pertain *v.* 關於 [gwaan1 yu1]

pertinent *adj.* 相關 [seung1 gwaan1]

perusal *n.* 讀 [duk9]

peruse *v.* 讀 [duk9]

pervade *v.* 滲透 [sam3 tau3]

perverse *adj.* 任性 [yam6 sing3]

perversion *n.* 變態 [bin3 taai3]

perversity *n.* 任性 [yam6 sing3]

pervert *n.* 色狼 [sik7 long4]

Peru *n.* 秘魯 [bei3 lou5]

Peruvian *adj.* 秘魯 [bei3 lou5]

pessimism *n.* 悲觀主義 [bei1 gun1 jyu2 yi6]

pessimist *n.* 悲觀者 [bei1 gun1 je2]

pessimistic *adj.* 悲觀 [bei1 gun1]

pest *n.* 害蟲 [hoi6 chung4]

pesticide *n.* 農藥 [nung4 yeuk9]

pestilence *n.* 瘟疫 [wan1 yik9]

pet *n.* 寵物 [chung2 mat9]

petal *n.* 花瓣 [fa1 faan2]

petition *n.* 請求 [ching2 kau4]

petrol *n.* 機油 [gei1 yau2]

petticoat *n.* 襯裙 [chan3 kwan4]

petulance *n.* 小題大做 [siu2 tai4 daai6 jou6]

pewter *n.* 白鑞 [baak9 laap9]

pH *n.* 酸鹼值 [syun1 gaan2 jik9]

pharmacy *n.* 藥房 [yeuk9 fong4]

phantom *n.* 幽靈 [yau1 ling4]

phase *n.* 階段 [gaai1 dyun6]

pheasant *n.* 野雞 [ye5 gai1]

phenomenal *adj.* 顯著 [hin2 jyu3]

phenomenon *n.* 現象 [yin6 jeung6]

philanthropic *adj.* 慈善 [chi4 sin6]

philanthropist *n.* 慈善家 [chi4 sin6 ga1]

philanthropy *n.* 慈善事業 [chi4 sin6 si6 yip9]

Philippines *n.* 菲律賓 [fei1 leut9 ban1]

philological *adj.* 語言學 [yu5 yin4 hok9]

philologist *n.* 語言學家 [yu5 yin4 hok9 ga1]

philology *n.* 語言學 [yu5 yin4 hok9]

philosopher *n.* 哲學家 [jit8 hok9 ga1]

philosophy *n.* 哲學 [jit8 hok9]

Phnom Penh *n.* 金邊 [gam1 bin1]; ~, **capital of Cambodia** 柬埔寨首都

phone *n.* 電話 [din6 wa2]; *v.* 打電話 [da2 din6 wa2]

   phone book *n.* 電話簿 [din6 wa2 bou6]

   phone booth *n.* 電話亭 [din6 wa2 ting4]

   phone call *n.* 電話 [din6 wa2] **make a ~** 打電話

phone card *n.* 電話卡 [din6 wa2 kat7]

phone number *n.* 電話號碼 [din6 wa2 hou6 ma5]

phonetics *n.* 語音 [yu5 yam1]

phosphorous *n.* 含磷 [ham4 leun4]

photo *n.* 相 [seung2] **take a ~** 影相

photocopier *n.* 影印機 [ying2 yan3 gei1]

photocopy *n.* 副本 [fu3 bun2]; *v.* 影印 [ying2 yan3]

photograph *n.* 相 [seung2]; *v.* (**take a ~**) 影相 [ying2 seung2]

photographer *n.* 攝影師 [sip8 ying2 si1]

photography *n.* 攝影 [sip8 ying2]

phrasal verb *n.* 動詞詞組 [dung6 chi4 chi4 jou2]

phrase *n.* 短語 [dyun2 yu5]

phrasebook *n.* 常用語手冊 [seung4 yung6 yu5 sau2 chaak8]

phraseology *n.* 措辭[chou3 chi4]

physical *adj.* 身體 [san1 tai2]; *n.* 身體檢查 [san1 tai2 gim2 cha4]

physical therapy *n.* 物理治療 [mat9 lei5 ji6 liu4]

physically *adv.* 身體上 [san1 tai2 seung6]

physician *n.* 醫師 [yi1 si1]

physicist *n.* 物理學家 [mat9 lei5 hok9 ga1]

physics *n.* 物理 [mat9 lei5]

physiognomy *n.* 面相 [min6 seung3]

piano *n.* 鋼琴 [gong3 kam4]

picarel *n.* 鱸魚 [lou4 yu2]

pick *v.* 摘 [jaak9]

pick smth. up *v.* 擺起 [lo2 hei2]

pick smb. up *v.* 接埋 [jip8 maai4]

pickaxe *n.* 鋤頭 [cho4 tau2]

picket *n.* 哨兵 [saau3 bing1]

pickle *v.* 醃 [yip8]; *n.* 泡菜 [paau1 choi3], **sandwich ~** 三文治泡菜

pickled *adj.* 醃 [yip8], **~ meat** 醃肉, **~ vegetables** 鹹菜

pick-up *n.* 接人 [jip8 yan4]

picnic *n.* 野餐 [ye5 chaan1], **~ lunch** 野餐

picnic area *n.* 野餐地方 [ye5 chaan1 dei6 fong1]

picnic basket *n.* 野餐籃 [ye5 chaan1 laam4]

pico de gallo *n.* 墨西哥辣蕃茄沙律 [mak9 sai1 go1 laat9 faan1 ke2 sa1 leut9]

picture *n.* 畫 [wa2]

picturesque *adj.* 好靚 [hou2 leng3]

pie *n.* 批 [pai1], **apple ~** 蘋果批, **blueberry ~** 藍莓批, **cherry ~** 車厘子批

piece *n.* 塊 [faai3]

piece of furniture *n.* 傢俬 [ga1 si1]

piece of land *n.* 一塊地 [yat7 faai3 dei6]

pier *n.* 碼頭 [ma5 tau4]

pig *n.* 豬 [jyu1], **~ ears** 豬耳, **~ feet** 豬腳, **~ knuckles** 豬肘

pigeon *n.* 白鴿 [baak9 gaap8]

pigmy *n.* 小矮人 [siu2 ai2 yan4]

pike *n.* 矛 [maau4]

pilaf *n.* 煲仔飯 [bou1 jai2 faan6]

Pilates *n.* 普拉提 [pou2 laai1 tai4]

pile *n.* 一堆 [yat7 deui1]; *v.* 堆起 [deui1 hei2]

pilfer *v.* 偷 [tau1]

pilgrim *n.* 朝聖者 [chiu4 sing3 je2]

pilgrimage *n.* 朝聖之旅 [chiu4 sing3 ji1 leui5]

pill *n.* 藥丸 [yeuk9 yun2]

pillar *n.* 柱 [chyu5]

pillow *n.* 枕頭 [jam2 tau4]

pillowcase *n.* 枕頭套 [jam2 tau4 tou3]

pilot *n.* 飛機師 [fei1 gei1 si1]

pilot light *n.* 指示燈 [ji2 si6 dang1]

pimiento *n.* 辣椒 [laat9 jiu1]

pimple *n.* 酒米 [jau2 mai5]

pin *n.* 大頭針 [daai6 tau4 jam1]; *v.* 釘住 [deng1 jyu6]

pinball machine *n.* 彈珠機 [daan6 jyu1 gei1]

pinch *n.* 撮 [chyut8], ~ **of salt** 一小撮鹽

pine *n.* 松樹 [chung4 syu6]

pine kernel *n.* 松仁 [chung4 yan4]

pineapple *n.* 菠蘿 [bo1 lo4]

ping-pong *n.* 乒乓波 [bing1 bam1 bo1]

pink *adj./n.* 粉紅色 [fan2 hung4 sik7]

pinnacle *n.* 尖塔 [jim1 taap8]

pint (*abbr.* **pt.**) *n.* 品脫 [ban2 tyut8]

pioneer *n.* 先驅 [sin1 keui1]

pious *adj.* 虔誠 [kin4 sing4]

pipe *n.* 管 [gun2]; **smoking** ~ 排煙管

piquant *adj.* 開胃 [hoi1 wai6]

piracy *n.* 盜版 [dou6 baan2]

piranha *n.* 食人魚 [sik9 yan4 yu2]

pirate *n.* 海盜 [hoi2 dou6]

Pisces *n.* 雙魚座 [seung1 yu4 jo6]

pistachios *n.* 開心果 [hoi1 sam1 gwo2]

pistol *n.* 手槍 [sau2 cheung1]

piston *n.* 活塞 [wut9 sak7]

pita bread *n.* 皮塔餅 [pei4 taap8 beng2]

pitch *n.* 瀝青 [laap9 cheng1]; *v.* 塗瀝青 [tou4 laap9 cheng1]

pitcher *n.* **1.** 水罐 [seui2 gun3], ~ **of water** 一罐水 // **2. baseball** ~ 棒球棒 [paang5 kau4 paang5]

piteous *adj.* 可憐 [ho2 lin4]

pitfall *n.* 圈套 [hyun1 tou3]

pitiable *adj.* 可憐 [ho2 lin4]

pitiful *adj.* 可憐 [ho2 lin4]

pitiless *adj.* 無情 [mou4 ching4]

pitman *n.* 礦工 [kong3 gung1]

pittance *n.* 雞碎 [gai1 seui2]

pitted *adj.* 去核 [heui3 wat9], ~ **cherries** 去核車厘子, ~ **prunes** 去核西梅, ~ **olives** 去核橄欖, ~ **dates** 去核海棗

pity *n.* 同情 [tung4 ching4]

pivot *n.* 中心 [jung1 sam1]

pizza *n.* 薄餅 [bok9 beng2], **cheese** ~ 芝士薄餅, **vegetable** ~ 青菜薄餅, **meat** ~ 有肉薄餅

pizza parlor *n.* 薄餅店 [bok9 beng2 dim3]

pizzeria *n.* 薄餅店 [bok9 beng2 dim3]

placard *n.* 海報 [hoi2 bou3]

place *n.* 地方 [dei6 fong1]; *v.* 放 [fong3]

place of birth *n.* 出世地方 [cheut7 sai3 dei6 fong1]

placebo *n.* 安慰劑 [on1 wai3 jai1]

placid *adj.* 溫和 [wan1 wo4]

plague *n.* 瘟疫 [wan1 yik9]

plaice *n.* 比目魚 [bei2 muk9 yu2]

plain *adj.* 樸素 [pok8 sou3], ~ **milk** 原味牛奶, ~ **yogurt** 原味酸奶, ~ **flavor** 原味

plaintiff *n.* 原告 [yun4 gou3]

plan *n./v.* 計劃 [gai3 waak9]

plane *n.* 飛機 [fei1 gei1]

planet *n.* 星球 [sing1 kau4]

plank *n.* 木板 [muk9 baan2]

planning *n.* 計劃 [gai3 waak9]

plant *n.* 植物 [jik9 mat9]; *v.* 種 [jung3]

plantain *n.* 大蕉 [daai6 jiu1]

plantation *n.* 種植園 [jung3 jik9 yun4]

planting *n.* 種 [jung3]

plasma *n.* 血漿 [hyut8 jeung1]

plaster *n.* 灰泥 [fui1 nai4]

plastic *n./adj.* 塑料 [sok8 liu2]

plastic bag *n.* 膠袋 [gaau1 doi2]

plastic wrap *n.* 保鮮膜 [bou2 sin1 mok9]

plate *n.* 碟 [dip9]

plateau *n.* 高原 [gou1 yun4]

platform *n.* 平台 [ping4 toi4]

platinum *n.* 白金 [baak9 gam1], ~ **card** 白金卡

platonic *adj.* 柏拉圖式 [paak8 laai1 tou4 sik7]

platoon *n.* 排 [paai4]

platter *n.* 唱片 [cheung3 pin2], **meat** ~ 肉類拼盤, **seafood** ~ 海鮮拼盤, **appetizer** ~ 前菜拼盤

play *v.* 玩 [waan2]; *n.* 劇本 [kek9 bun2]

play cards *v.* 玩啤牌 [waan2 pe1 paai2]

play group *n.* 遊戲小組 [yau4 hei3 siu2 jou2]

player *n.* 運動員 [wan6 dung6 yun4]

playground *n.* 操場 [chou1 cheung4]

playing cards *n.* 玩啤牌 [waan2 pe1 paai2]

playing field *n.* 操場 [chou1 cheung4]

plea *n.* 申訴 [san1 sou3]

plea bargain *n.* 認罪協議 [ying jeui6 hip8 yi5]

plead *v.* 辯護 [bin6 wu6]

pleader *n.* 答辯人 [daap8 bin6 yan4]

pleasant *adj.* 愉快 [yu4 faai3]

pleasantly *adv.* 愉快 [yu4 faai3]

pleasantry *n.* 客氣說話 [haak8 hei3 syut3 wa2]

please *exclam./v./phr.* 唔該 [m4 goi1], ~ **have a seat** 請坐

pleasing *adj.* 令人愉快 [ling4 yan4 yu6 faai3]

pleasure *n.* 快樂 [faai3 lok9]

plebiscite *n.* 全民投票 [chyun4 man4 tau4 piu3]

pledge *n.* 抵押權 [dai2 aat8 kyun4]; *v.* 抵押 [dai2 aat8]

plenty *pron./adv./n./det.* 好多 [hou2 do1]

plight *n.* 困境 [kwan3 ging2]

plod *v.* 行得好艱難 [haang4 dak7 hou2 gaan1 naan4]

plot *n.* 情節 [ching4 jit8]; *v.* 密謀 [mat9 mau4]

plow *v.* 耕田 [gaang1 tin4]

plowman *n.* 農民 [nung4 man4]

pluck *v.* 摘 [jaak9]

plug *n.* 插頭 [chaap8 tau2], **pull the ~** 搖插頭, **electric ~** 電插頭

plum *n.* 布冧 [bou3 lam1], **~ brandy** 布冧白蘭地, **~ pudding** 布冧布甸, **~ jam** 布冧果醬

plumber *n.* 水喉工 [seui2 hau4 gung1]

plunder *v.* 搶 [cheung2]

plump *v.* 突然跌低 [dat9 yin4 dit8 dai1]; *adj.* 豐富 [fung1 fu3], **~ chicken** 肥雞

plunge *v.* 俯衝 [fu2 chung1]

plural *n.* 複數形式 [fuk7 sou3 ying4 sik7]; *adj.* 複數 [fuk7 sou3]

plus *prep.* 加 [ga1]; *n.* 加號 [ga1 hou2]; *adj.* 正數 [jing3 sou3]

ply *v.* 唔停咁俾 [m4 ting4 gam3 bei2]

PM *adv.* 晚黑 [maan5 hak7]

pneumonia *n.* 肺炎 [fai3 yim4]

poached *v.* 侵佔 [cham1 jim4]; *adj.* 水煮 [seui2 jyu2], **~ egg** 水煮蛋

pocket *n.* 袋 [doi2]

pod *n.* 豆殼 [dau2 hok8]

Podgorica *n.* 波德戈里察 [bo1 dak7 gwo1 lei5 chaat8]; **~, capital of Montenegro** 蒙特內格羅首都

poem *n.* 詩 [si1]

poet *n.* 詩人 [si1 yan4]

poetic *adj.* 詩意 [si1 yi3]

poetics *n.* 詩學 [si1 hok9]

poetry *n.* 詩 [si1]

poignancy *n.* 辛酸 [san1 syun1]

poignant *adj.* 辛酸 [san1 syun1]

point *n.* 觀點 [gun1 dim2]; *v.* 指出 [ji2 cheut7], *comp.* **~ with a mouse** 用鼠標指 **point of interest** *n.* 名勝 [ming4 sing3] **point to** *v.* 指向 [ji2 heung3]

pointed *adj.* 尖銳 [jim1 yeui6]

poise *n.* 姿態 [ji1 taai3]

poison *n.* 毒藥 [duk9 yeuk9]; *v.* 落毒 [lok9 duk9]

poisonous *adj.* 有毒 [yau5 duk9]

poke *v.* 篤 [duk7]

poker (game) *n.* 啤牌 [pe1 paai2]

Poland *n.* 波蘭 [bo1 laan4]

polar *adj.* 兩極 [leung5 gik9]

pole *n.* 極點 [gik9 dim2]; **north ~** 北極, **south ~** 南極

polenta *n.* 粟米粥 [suk7 mai5 juk7]

police *n.* 警察 [ging2 chaat3]; **~ report** 警訊

police station *n.* 差館 [chaai1 gun2]

policeman *n.* 警察 [ging2 chaat3]

policy *n.* 政策 [jing3 chaak8]

Polish *adj.* 波蘭 [bo1 laan4], **~ food** 波蘭菜

polish *n.* 光澤 [gwong1 jaak9]; *v.* 拋光 [paau1 gwong1], **~ shoes** 刷鞋, **~ wood** 刨木

polite *adj.* 有禮貌 [yau5 lai5 maau6]

politely *adv.* 有禮貌 [yau5 lai5 maau6]

political *adj.* 政治上 [jing3 ji6 seung6]

politically *adv.* 政治上 [jing3 ji6 seung6]

politician *n.* 政客 [jing3 haak8]

politics *n.* 政治 [jing3 ji6]

pollen *n.* 花粉 [fa1 fan2]

pollen count *n.* 花粉量 [fa1 fan2 leung6]

polls *n.* 民意調查 [man4 yi3 diu6 cha4]

pollute *v.* 污染 [wu1 yim5]

pollution *n.* 污染 [wu1 yim5]

polo *n.* 馬球 [ma5 kau4]

polygamous *adj.* 一夫多妻 [yat7 fu1 do1 chai1]

polygamy *n.* 一夫多妻 [yat7 fu1 do1 chai1]

polyglot *n.* 識好多語言嘅人 [sik7 hou2 do1 yu5 yin4 ge3 yan4]

polyester *adj.* 聚脂嘅 [jeui6 ji2 gei3]

pomegranate *n.* 石榴 [sek9 lau4]; ~ **seeds** 石榴籽

pomelo *n.* 沙田柚 [sa1 tin4 yau2]

pomp *n.* 盛況 [sing6 fong3]

pomposity *adj.* 自負 [ji6 fu6]

pompous *adj.* 自負 [ji6 fu6]

pond *n.* 池塘 [chi4 tong4]

ponder *v.* 諗 [nam2]

pony *n.* 馬仔 [ma5 jai2]

pool *n.* 水池 [seui2 chi4]; **swimming** ~ 游泳池

poor *adj.* 窮 [kung4]

pop *v.* 爆開 [baau3 hoi1]; *n.* 流行音樂 [lau4 hang4 yam1 ngok9]

pop music *n.* 流行音樂 [lau4 hang4 yam1 ngok9]

popcorn *n.* 爆谷 [baau3 guk7]

pope *n.* 羅馬教皇 [lo4 ma5 gaau3 wong4]

popovers *n.* 酥餅 [sou1 beng2]

poppy *n.* 罌粟 [ang1 suk7]

poppy seed *n.* 罌粟籽 [ang1 suk7 ji2]; ~ **cake** 罌粟蛋糕

popsicle *n.* 雪條 [syut8 tiu2]

popular *adj.* 受歡迎 [sau6 fun1 ying4]

popularity *n.* 名氣 [ming4 hei3]

population *n.* 人口 [yan4 hau2]

populous *adj.* 人口多 [yan4 hau2 do1]

porcelain *n.* 瓷器 [chi4 hei3]

porch *n.* 門廊 [mun4 long4]

pore *n.* 毛孔 [mou4 hung2]

pork *n.* 豬肉 [jyu1 yuk9], ~ **fat** 豬油,

　　pork and beans *n.* 豬肉豆 [jyu1 yuk9 dau6]

　　pork chop *n.* 豬扒 [jyu1 pa2]

　　pork fillet *n.* 豬柳 [jyu1 lau5]

　　pork knuckle *n.* 豬手 [jyu1 sau2]

　　pork loin *n.* 豬柳肉 [jyu1 lau5 yuk9]

　　pork roast *n.* 燒豬肉 [siu1 jyu1 yuk9]

　　pork sausage *n.* 豬肉腸 [jyu1 yuk9 cheung2]

　　pork stew 燉豬肉 [dan6 jyu1 yuk9]

porridge *n.* 粥 [juk7]

port *n.* 港口 [gong2 hau2]

Port Louis *n.* 路易港 [lou6 yik9 gong2]; ~, **capital of Mauritius** 毛里裘斯首都

Port Moresby *n.* 莫爾茲比港 [mok9 yi5 ji1 bei2 gong2];

~, **capital of Papua New Guinea** 巴布亞新幾内亞首都

portable *adj.* 方便攜帶 [fong1 bin6 kwai4 daai3]

portable crib *n.* 輕便嬰兒床 [hing1 bin6 ying1 yi4 chong4]

portage *n.* 陸上運輸 [luk9 seung6 wan6 syu1]

portal *n.* 正門 [jing3 mun4]

Port-au-Prince *n.* 太子港 [taai3 ji2 gong2]; ~, **capital of Haiti** 海地首都

portend *v.* 預示 [yu6 si6]

porter *n.* 搬運工人 [bun1 wan6 gung1 yan4]

portfolio *n.* 投資組合 [tau4 ji1 jou2 hap9]

portico *n.* 柱廊 [chyu5 long4]

portion *n.* 份量 [fan6 leung6]

Port-of-Spain *n.* 西班牙港 [sai1 baan1 nga4 gong2]; ~, **capital of Trinidad and Tobago** 特立尼達和多巴哥首都

Porto-Novo *n.* 波多諾伏 [bo1 do1 nok9 fuk9]; ~, **capital of Benin** 貝寧彎首都

portrait *n.* 肖像 [chiu3 jeung6]

portrait artist *n.* 人物肖像畫家 [yan4 mat9 chiu3 jeung6 wa2 ga1]

portray *v.* 描寫 [miu4 se2]

Portugal *n.* 葡萄牙 [pou4 tou4 nga4]

Portuguese *adj.* 葡萄牙 [pou4 tou4 nga4]

Port-Vila *n.* 維拉港 [wai4 laai1 gong2]; ~, **capital of Vanuatu** 瓦努阿圖首都

pose *v.* 擺姿勢 [baai2 ji1 sai3];

n. 姿勢 [ji1 sai3], **photography** ~ 影相姿勢

position *n.* 位置 [wai6 ji3]

positive *adj.* 正面 [jing3 min6]

possess *v.* 掌握 [jeung2 ak7]

possession *n.* 財產 [choi4 chaan2]

possessive *adj.* 所屬 [so2 suk9] *n.* 佔有 [jim3 yau5]

possibility *n.* 可能性 [ho2 nang4 sing3]

possible *adv./adj.* 可能 [ho2 nang4]; **as soon as** ~ 盡快

possibly *adv.* 可能 [ho2 nang4]

post *n.* 郵件 [yau4 gin6]; *v.* 貼 [tip8]

post office *n.* 郵局 [yau4 guk9]

postage *n.* 郵費 [yau4 fai3]

postage paid *adv.* 已付郵資 [yi5 fu6 yau4 ji1]

postal code *n.* 郵政编碼 [yau4 jing3 pin1 ma5]

postbox *n.* 信箱 [seun3 seung1]

postcard *n.* 明信片 [ming4 seun3 pin2]

poster *n.* 海報 [hoi2 bou3]

posterity *n.* 後代 [hau6 doi6]

postman *n.* 郵差 [yau4 chaai1]

postmaster *n.* 郵政局長 [yau4 jing3 guk9 jeung2]

postpone *v.* 押後 [aat8 hau6]

postponement *n.* 押後 [aat8 hau6]

postscript *n.* 補充說明 [bou2 chung1 syut8 ming4]

posture *n.* 姿勢 [ji1 sai3]

pot *n.* 煲 [bou1], **cooking** ~ 煲, **flower** ~ 花盆

pot roast *n.* 燉肉 [dan6 yuk9]

potato *n.* 薯仔 [syu4 jai2], **baked** ~ 焗薯仔, **roasted** ~ 烤薯仔, **red** ~ 紅薯

potato chips *n.* 薯條 [syu4 tiu2], **barbecue ~** 燒烤味薯條, **sour cream and onion ~** 酸奶洋蔥味薯條, **salted ~** 加鹽薯條

potato soup *n.* 薯仔湯 [syu4 jai2 tong1]

potatoes au gratin *n.* 焗薯仔 [guk9 syu4 jai2]

potency *n.* 權勢 [kyun4 sai3]

potential *adj.* 有可能 [yau5 ho2 nang4]; *n.* 潛力 [chim4 lik9]

potholes *n.* 窿 [lung1]

potter *n.* 製陶工人 [jai3 tou4 gung1 yan4]

pottery *n.* 陶瓷品 [tou4 chi4 ban2]

pouch *n.* 細袋 [sai3 doi2]

poultry *n.* 家禽 [ga1 kam4]

pounce *v.* 猛撲 [maang5 pok8]

pound 1. (*hit*) *v.* 大力撞 [daai6 lik9 jong6] // **2.** (*weight*) *n.* 英鎊 [ying1 bong2]

pour *v.* 倒 [dou2]

poverty *n.* 詩歌 [si1 go1]

powder *n.* 粉末 [fan2 mut9]

powdered *adj.* 整成粉狀 [jing2 sing4 fan2 jong6], **~ sugar** 糖粉

powdery *adj.* 粉狀 [fan2 jong6]

power *n.* 勢力 [sai3 lik9]; *v.* 靠…發動 [kaau3 … faat8 dung6]

power of attorney (*legal*) *n.* 授權書 [sau6 kyun4 syu1]

power outage *n.* 停電 [ting4 din6]

power points *n.* 插蘇 [chaap8 sou1]

powerful *adj.* 強大 [keung4 daai6]

practicability *n.* 實用性 [sat9 yung6 sing3]

practical *adj.* 實際 [sat9 jai3]

practically *adv.* 實際 [sat9 jai3]

practice *n./v.* 練習 [lin6 jaap9]

practitioner *n.* 從業人員 [chung4 yip9 yan4 yun4]

pragmatic *adj.* 務實 [mou6 sat9]

pragmatism *n.* 實用主義 [sat9 yung6 jyu2 yi6]

Prague *n.* 布拉格 [bou3 laai1 gaak8]; **~, capital of Czech Republic** 捷克共和國首都

Praia *n.* 普拉亞 [pou2 laai1 a3]; **~, capital of Cape Verde** 佛得角首都

praise *n.* 稱讚 [ching1 jaan3]; *v.* 讚 [jaan3]

praiseworthy *adj.* 值得讚 [jik9 dak7 jaan3]

praline *n.* 果仁糖 [gwo2 yan4 tong2]

prank *n.* 開玩笑 [hoi1 wun6 siu3]

prattle *v.* 哦 [ngo4]

prawn *n.* 蝦 [ha1]

pray *v.* 祈禱 [kei4 tou2]

prayer *n.* 祈禱 [kei4 tou2]

preach *v.* 傳教 [chyun4 gaau3]

preacher *n.* 牧師 [muk9 si1]

preamble *n.* 開場白 [hoi1 cheung4 baak9]

precaution *n.* 預防 [yu6 fong4]

precautionary *adj.* 預防 [yu6 fong4]

precede *v.* 喺…之前 [hai2 … ji1 chin4]

precedence *n.* 領先 [ling5 sin1]

precedent *n.* 先例 [sin1 lai6]

precept *n.* 規範 [kwai1 faan6]

preceptor *n.* 導師 [dou6 si1]

precious *adj.* 珍貴 [jan1 gwai3]

precise *adj.* 精確 [jing1 kok8]

precisely *adv.* 正正 [jing3 jing3]

precision *adj.* 精確度 [jing1 kok8 dou6]

precook *v.* 預先煮好 [yu6 sin1 jyu2 hou2]

precursor *n.* 前輩 [chin4 bui3]

predator *n.* 食肉動物 [sik9 yuk9 dung6 mat9]

predecessor *n.* 前任 [chin4 yam4]

predestination *n.* 宿命論 [suk7 ming6 leun6]

predetermine *v.* 注定 [jyu3 ding6]

predicament *n.* 困境 [kwan3 ging2]

predict *v.* 預測 [yu6 chak7]

prediction *n.* 預測 [yu6 chak7]

predominance *n.* 優勢 [yau1 sai3]

predominant *adj.* 主要 [jyu2 yiu3]

predominate *v.* 佔優勢 [jim3 yau1 sai3]

preeminence *n.* 傑出 [git9 cheut7]

preeminent *adj.* 傑出 [git9 cheut7]

preface *n.* 前言 [chin4 yin4]

prefect *n.* 風紀 [fung1 gei2]

prefer *v.* 比較鍾意 [bei2 gaau3 jung1 yi3]

preference *n.* 偏愛 [pin1 oi3]

prefix *n.* 前綴 [chin4 jeui6]

pregnancy *n.* 懷孕 [waai4 yan6]; ~ **test** 驗孕

pregnant *adj.* 有咗 [yau5 jo2]

prehistoric *adj.* 史前 [si2 chin4]

prehistoric art *n.* 史前藝術 [si2 chin4 ngai6 seut9]

prejudice *n.* 成見 [sing4 gin3]

prelate *n.* 高級教士 [gou1 kap7 gaau3 si6]

preliminary *adj.* 初步 [cho1 bou6], ~ **hearing** (*legal*) 初步聽證

prelude *n.* 前奏 [chin4 jau3]

premature *adj.* 早產 [jou2 chaan2]

premeditate *v.* 預謀 [yu6 mau4]

premeditation *n.* 預謀 [yu6 mau4]

premenstrual tension *n.* 月經前緊張 [yut9 ging1 chin4 gan2 jeung1]

premier *n.* 首相 [sau2 seung3]

premiere *n.* 首映 [sau2 ying2]

premises *n.* 前言 [chin4 yin4]

premium *n.* 保險費 [bou2 him2 fai3]; *adj.* 優質 [yau1 jat7]

premium gas *n.* 高級汽油 [gou1 kap7 hei3 yau4]

premonition *n.* 預感 [yu6 gam2]

preoccupation *n.* 執著 [jap7 jeuk9]

preoccupy *v.* 佔據 [jim3 geui3]

preparation *n.* 準備 [jeun2 bei6]

prepare *v.* 準備 [jeun2 bei6]

prepared *adj.* 準備好 [jeun2 bei6 hou2], ~ **dish** 煮好嘅菜

preponderance *n.* 優勢 [yau1 sai3]

preponderate *v.* 叻過 [lek7 gwo3]

preposition *n.* 介詞 [gaai3 chi4]

prerequisite *n.* 前提 [chin4 tai4]

prerogative *n.* 特權 [dak9 kyun4]

prescience *n.* 預知 [yu6 ji1]

prescribe *v.* 開處方 [hoi1 chyu5 fong1]

prescription *n.* 處方 [chyu5 fong1]

presence *n.* 在場 [joi6 cheung4]
present *adj.* 現在 [yin6 joi6]; *n.* 禮物 [lai5 mat9]; *v.* 送 [sung3]
presentation *n.* 陳述 [chan4 seut9]
preservatives *n.* 防腐劑 [fong4 fu6 jai1]
preserve *v.* 保護 [bou2 wu6]
preserved *adj.* 醃製 [yim1 jai3]
preserves *n.* 蜜餞 [mat9 jin3], **fruit ~** 水果蜜餞
president *n.* 總统 [jung2 tung2]
press *v.* 壓 [aat8]; **~ed** 壓好
pressure *n.* 壓力 [aat8 lik9]
pressurize *v.* 俾壓力 [bei2 aat8 lik9]
prestige *n.* 威望 [wai1 mong6]
prestigious *adj.* 有威望 [yau5 wai1 mong6]
presumably *adv.* 可能 [ho2 nang4]
presume *v.* 假設 [ga2 chit8]
presumption *n.* 假設 [ga2 chit8]
presuppose *v.* 假設 [ga2 chit8]
presupposition *n.* 假設 [ga2 chit8]
pretence *n.* 扮野 [baan3 ye5]
pretend *v.* 扮 [baan3]
pretension *n.* 扮野 [baan3 ye5]
pretentious *adj.* 自負 [ji6 fu6]
pretext *n.* 藉口 [jik9 hau2]
Pretoria *n.* 比勒陀利亞 [bei2 lak9 to4 lei6 a3]; **~, administrative capital of South Africa** 南非行政首都
pretty *adv.* 幾 [gei2]; *adj.* 好靚 [hou2 leng3]
pretzel *n.* 油炸面圈 [yau4 ja3 min6 hyun1], **salted ~** 加鹽油炸面圈, **unsalted ~** 無鹽油炸面圈

prevail *v.* 流行 [lau4 hang4]
prevalence *n.* 普遍 [pou2 pin3]
prevalent *adj.* 普遍 [pou2 pin3]
prevent *v.* 制止 [jai3 ji2]
prevention *n.* 預防 [yu6 fong4]
preventive *adj.* 預防 [yu6 fong4]
previous *adj.* 之前 [ji1 chin4]
previously *adv.* 之前 [ji1 chin4]
prey *n.* 受害者 [sau6 hoi6 je2]; *v.* 獵食 [lip9 sik9]
price *n.* 價錢 [ga3 chin4]
price per liter *n.* 每升嘅價錢 [mui5 sing1 ge3 ga3 chin4]
prick *v.* 拮 [gat7]
pride *n.* 驕傲 [giu1 ngou6]
priest *n.* 神父 [san4 fu6]
prima facie *n.* 表面上 [biu2 min6 seung6]
primarily *adv.* 主要 [jyu2 yiu3]
primary *adj.* 主要 [jyu2 yiu3]
prime *n.* 全盛時期 [chyun4 sing6 si4 kei4]
prime minister *n.* 總理 [jung2 lei5]
prime rib *n.* 上等牛扒 [seung6 dang2 ngau4 pa4]
primeval *adj.* 遠古 [yun5 gu2]
primitive *adj.* 原始 [yun4 chi2]
prince *n.* 王子 [wong4 ji2]
princess *n.* 公主 [gung1 jyu2]
principal *adj.* 主要 [jyu2 yiu3]
principally *adv.* 主要 [jyu2 yiu3]
principle *n.* 原則 [yun4 jak7]
print *v.* 打印 [da2 yan3]; *n.* (art) 印刷品 [yan3 chaat8 ban2]
printer *n.* 打印機 [da2 yan3 gei1]
printing *n.* 印刷術 [yan3 chaat8 seut9]
prior *adj.* 喺...之前 [hai2 ... ji1 chin4]

priority *n.* 優先 [yau1 sin1]

prison *n.* 監獄 [gaam1 yuk9]

prisoner *n.* 監犯 [gaam1 faan2]

Pristina *n.* 普里什蒂纳 [pou2 lei5 sam6 dai3 naap9]; ~, **capital of Kosovo** 科索沃首都

privacy *n.* 私隱 [si1 yan2]

private *adj.* 私人 [si1 yan4]

    private hospital *n.* 私人醫院 [si1 yan4 yi1 yun2]

    private property *n.* 私有財產 [si1 yau5 choi4 chaan2]

    private room *n.* 私人房間 [si1 yan4 fong4 gaan1]

privately *adv.* 私底下 [si1 dai2 ha6]

privation *n.* 貧困 [pan4 kwan3]

privatization *n.* 私有化 [si1 yau5 fa3]

privilege *n.* 特權 [dak9 kyun4]

prize *n.* 獎金 [jeung2 gam1]

probability *n.* 可能性 [ho2 nang4 sing3]

probable *adj.* 可能 [ho2 nang4], ~ **cause** (*legal*) 可能嘅原因

probably *adv.* 多數 [do1 sou3]

probate *v.* 遺囑認證 [wai4 juk7 ying6 jing3]

probation *n.* 試用期 [si3 yung6 kei4]

probationer *n.* 實習生 [sat9 jaap9 sang1]

probe *v.* 探測 [taam3 chak7]; *n.* 探測儀 [taam3 chak7 yi4]

problem *n.* 問題 [man6 tai4]

problematic *adj.* 有問題 [yau5 man6 tai4]

procedure *n.* 程序 [ching4 jeui6]

proceed *v.* 進行 [jeun3 hang4]

proceeding *n.* 進行 [jeun3 hang4]

proceeds *n.* 收入 [sau1 yap9]

process *v.* 處理 [chyu5 lei5], **to ~ food** 加工食物

processed *adj.* 加工過 [ga1 gung1 gwo3], ~ **food** 加工食品, **un~ food** 新鮮食品

procession *n.* 隊伍 [deui6 ng5]

processor *n.* 處理器 [chyu5 lei5 hei3]

proclaim *v.* 宣佈 [syun1 bou3]

proclamation *n.* 聲明 [sing1 ming4]

proclivity *n.* 嗜好 [si3 hou3]

procrastinate *v.* 拖延 [to1 yin4]

procrastination *n.* 拖延 [to1 yin4]

proctor *n.* 監考員 [gaam1 haau2 yun4]

procure *v.* 攞到 [lo2 dou2]

procurement *n.* 採購 [choi2 gau3]

prodigal *adj.* 敗家 [baai6 ga1]

prodigality *n.* 浪費 [long6 fai3]

produce *n.* 產品 [chaan2 ban2]; *v.* 生產 [sang1 chaan2]

produce market *n.* 農產品市場 [nung4 chaan2 ban2 si5 cheung4]

producer *n.* 生產商 [sang1 chaan2 seung1]

product *n.* 產品 [chaan2 ban2]

production *n.* 生產 [sang1 chaan2]

productivity *n.* 生產力 [sang1 chaan2 lik9]

profane *v.* 褻瀆 [sit8 duk9]

profess *v.* 自稱 [ji6 ching1]

profession *n.* 職業 [jik7 yip9]

professional *adj.* 專業 [jyun1 yip9]; *n.* 專業人士 [jyun1 yip9 yan4 si6]

professor *n.* 教授 [gaau3 sau6]

profile *n.* 簡介 [gaan2 gaai3]

profit *n.* 利潤 [lei6 yeun6]

profitability *n.* 盈利能力 [ying4 lei6 nang4 lik9]

profitable *adj.* 盈利 [ying4 lei6]

profiteer *n.* 奸商 [gaan1 seung1]

profiteroles *n.* 泡芙 [paau3 fu4]

profligacy *n.* 浪費 [long6 fai3]

profligate *adj.* 浪費 [long6 fai3]

profound *adj.* 深刻 [sam1 haak7]

profoundity *n.* 深奧 [sam1 ou3]

profuse *adj.* 過多 [gwo3 do1]

profusion *n.* 大方 [daai6 fong1]

progeny *n.* 後代 [hau6 doi6]

program *n.* 程序 [ching4 jeui6], ~ of events 事情進展; *v.* 寫程式 [se2 ching4 sik7]

progress *n.* 進展 [jeun3 jin2]; *v.* 進化 [jeun3 fa3], in ~ 進行中

progressive *n.* 改革論者 [goi2 gaak8 leun6 je2]; *adj.* 進步 [jeun3 bou6]

prohibit *v.* 阻止 [jo2 ji2]

prohibited *n.* 禁止 [gam3 ji2]

prohibition *n.* 禁止 [gam3 ji2]

project *n.* 工程 [gung1 ching4]; *v.* 發射 [faat8 se6]

projectile *n.* 拋射物 [paau1 se6 mat9]

projection *n.* 預計 [yu6 gai3]

projector *n.* 投影機 [tau4 ying2 gei1]

proliferate *v.* 激增 [gik7 jang1]

proliferation *n.* 激增 [gik7 jang1]

prolific *adj.* 多產 [do1 chaan2]

prologue *n.* 前言 [chin4 yin4]

prolong *v.* 延長 [yin4 cheung4]

prolongation *n.* 延長 [yin4 cheung4]

prominence *n.* 聲望 [sing1 mong6]

prominent *adj.* 傑出 [git9 cheut7]

promise *v.* 應承 [ying1 sing4]; *n.* 承諾 [sing4 nok9]

promising *adj.* 有希望 [yau5 hei1 mong6]

promissory *adj.* 約好 [yeuk8 hou2]

promote *v.* 促進 [chuk7 jeun3]

promotion *n.* 升職 [sing1 jik7]

prompt *adj.* 即刻 [jik7 hak7]; *v.* 促進 [chuk7 jeun3]

promptly *adv.* 即刻 [jik7 hak7]

prone *adj.* 有傾向 [yau5 king1 heung3]

pronoun *n.* 代詞 [doi6 chi4]

pronounce *v.* 發音 [faat8 yam1]

pronunciation *n.* 發音 [faat8 yam1]

proof *n.* 證據 [jing3 geui3]

prop *n.* 靠山 [kaau3 saan1]

propaganda *n.* 宣傳 [syun1 chyun4]

propagandist *n.* 宣傳人員 [syun1 chyun4 yan4 yun4]

propagate *v.* 繁殖 [faan4 jik9]

propagation *n.* 傳播 [chyun4 bo3]

propel *v.* 推動 [teui1 dung6]

proper *adj.* 適當 [sik7 dong3]

properly *adv.* 適當 [sik7 dong3]

property *n.* 財產 [choi4 chaan2]

prophecy *n.* 預言 [yu6 yin4]

prophesy *v.* 預言 [yu6 yin4]

prophet *n.* 預言家 [yu6 yin4 ga1]

proportion *n.* 比例 [bei2 lai6]

proportional *adj.* 成比例 [sing4 bei2 lai6]

proposal *n.* 建議 [gin3 yi5]

propose v. 建議 [gin3 yi5]

proposition n. 建議 [gin3 yi5]

propound v. 提出 [tai4 cheut7]

proprietary adj. 專利 [jyun1 lei6]

proprietor n. 業主 [yip9 jyu2]

propriety n. 得體 [dak7 tai2]

prorogue v. 休會 [yau1 wui2]

prosaic adj. 無聊 [mou4 liu4]

prose n. 散文 [saan2 man4]

prosecute v. 檢舉 [gim2 geui2]

prosecution n. 檢舉 [gim2 geui2]

prosecutor n. 檢察官 [gim2 chaat8 gun1]

prosody n. 韻律學 [wan5 leut9 hok9]

prospect n. 前景 [chin4 ging2]

prospective adj. 可能 [ho2 nang4]

prospectus n. 說明書 [syut8 ming4 syu1]

prosper v. 繁榮 [faan4 wing4]

prosperity n. 繁榮 [faan4 wing4]

prosperous adj. 繁榮 [faan4 wing4]

prostitute n. 妓女 [gei6 neui5]

prostitution n. 賣淫 [maai6 yam4]

prostrate v. 趴低 [pa1 dai1]

prostration n. 衰竭 [seui1 kit8]

protagonist n. 主人公 [jyu2 yan4 gung1]

protect v. 保護 [bou2 wu6]

protected adj. 受保護 [sau6 bou2 wu6], ~ **species** 受保護動物

protection n. 保護 [bou2 wu6]

protein n. 蛋白質 [daan2 baak9 jat7]

protest n./v. 抗議 [kong3 yi5]

Protestant n. 新教徒 [san1 gaau3 tou4]

protocol n. 禮儀 [lai5 yi4]

proton n. 質子 [jat7 ji2]

prototype n. 樣品 [yeung6 ban2]

proud adj. 驕傲 [giu1 ngou6]

proudly adv. 驕傲 [giu1 ngou6]

prove v. 證明 [jing3 ming4]

proverb n. 諺語 [yin6 yu5]

provide v. 提供 [tai4 gung1]

provided/providing conj. 假如 [ga2 yu4]

provident adj. 慳 [haan1]

providential adj. 咁好 [gam3 hou2]

provider n. 供應商 [gung1 ying3 seung1]

province n. 省 [saang2]

provincialism n. 地方主義 [dei6 fong1 jyu2 yi6]

provision n. 條款 [tiu4 fun2]

provisionality n. 暫時性 [jaam6 si4 sing3]

provisionally adv. 暫時 [jaam6 si4]

provocation n. 激嬲 [gik7 nau1]

provocative adj. 挑釁性 [tiu1 yan6 sing3]

provoke v. 激嬲 [gik7 nau1]

prowess n. 厲害 [lai6 hoi6]

proximate adj. 最近 [jeui3 gan6]

proximity n. 接近 [jip8 gan6]

proxy n. 代理人 [doi6 lei5 yan4]

prudence n. 謹慎 [gan2 san6]

prudent adj. 謹慎 [gan2 san6]

prune n. 西梅乾 [sai1 mui2 gon1]; ~ **juice** 西梅汁

pry v. 偷睇 [tau1 tai2]

psalm n. 聖詩 [sing3 si1]

pseudonym n. 筆名 [bat7 meng4]

psyche n. 心靈 [sam1 ling4]

psychiatrist *n.* 精神科醫生 [jing1 san4 fo1 yi1 sang1]

psychiatry *n.* 精神病學 [jing1 san4 beng6 hok9]

psychic *n.* 問米婆 [man6 mai5 po2]

psychological *adj.* 心理學 [sam1 lei5 hok9]

psychologist *n.* 心理學家 [sam1 lei5 hok9 ga1]

psychopath *n.* 精神病患者 [jing1 san4 beng6 waan6 je3]

psychotherapy *n.* 心理治療 [sam1 lei5 ji6 liu4]

pt. (*abbr. of* **pint**) 品脱 [ban2 tyut8]

pub *n.* 酒吧 [jau2 ba1]

puberty *n.* 青春期 [ching1 cheun1 kei4]

public *adj./n.* 公眾 [gung1 jung3]

   public building *n.* 公眾地方 [gung1 jung3 dei6 fong1]

   public telephone *n.* 公共電話 [gung1 gung6 din6 wa2]

   public toilet *n.* 公廁 [gung1 chi3]

   public transportation *n.* 公共交通工具 [gung1 gung6 gaau1 tung1 gung1 geui6]

publication *n.* 出版 [cheut7 baan2]

publicity *n.* 宣傳 [syun1 chyun4]

publicly *adv.* 公開 [gung1 hoi1]

publish *v.* 出版 [cheut7 baan2]

publisher *n.* 出版商 [cheut7 baan2 seung1]

publishing *n.* 出版業 [cheut7 baan2 yip9]

pudding *n.* 布甸 [bou3 din1]

puddle *n.* 水坑 [seui2 haang1]

puerile *adj.* 幼稚 [yau3 ji6]

puff *n.* 粉撲 [fan2 pok8]

puff-pastry *n.* 鬆餅 [sung1 beng2]

pull *v./n.* 拉 [laai1]; (*sign on a door*) ~ **out** 拉開

pulley *n.* 滑輪 [waat9 leun4]

pullover *n.* 笠頭衫 [lap7 tau4 saam1]

pulp *n.* 果肉 [gwo2 yuk9]

pulpit *n.* 神壇 [san4 taan4]

pulsate *v.* 跳動 [tiu3 dung6]

pulsation *n.* 跳動 [tiu3 dung6]

pulse *n.* 脈搏 [mak9 bok8]

pump *n./v.* 泵 [bam1]

pumpernickel *n.* 粗麥麵包 [chou1 mak9 min6 baau1]

pumpkin *n.* 南瓜 [naam4 gwa1], ~ **pie** 南瓜批, ~ **bread** 南瓜餅, ~ **seeds** 南瓜籽

pun *n.* 雙關語 [seung1 gwaan1 yu5]

punch 1. (*hit*) *n./v.* 打 [da2] // **2.** (*drink*) *n.* **fruit** ~ 雜果賓治

punctual *adj.* 守時 [sau2 si4]

punctuality *n.* 守時 [sau2 si4]

punctuation *n.* 標點 [biu1 dim2]

puncture *n.* 穿窿 [chyun1 lung1]

pungency *n.* 好辣 [hou2 laat9]

pungent *adj.* 好辣 [hou2 laat9]

punish *v.* 罰 [fat9]

punishment *n.* 懲罰 [ching4 fat9]

pupil *n.* (*student*) 學生 [hok9 saang1]

puppet *n.* 木偶 [muk9 ngau5], ~ **show** 木偶劇

puppy *n.* 狗仔 [gau2 jai2]

purchase *n./v.* 購買 [gau3 maai5]

purchaser *n.* 買家 [maai5 ga1]

pure *adj.* 純 [seun4]

puree *n.* 濃湯 [nung4 tong1], **pea** ~ 青豆濃湯, **corn** ~ 粟米濃湯

purely *adv.* 純粹 [seun4 seui6]

purgation *n.* 淨化 [jing6 fa3]

purgative *n.* 瀉藥 [se3 yeuk9]

purgatory *n.* 煉獄 [lin6 yuk9]

purge *v.* 消除 [siu1 cheui4]

purification *n.* 淨化 [jing6 fa3]

purify *v.* 淨化 [jing6 fa3]

purist *n.* 純粹主義者 [seun4 seui6 jyu2 yi6 je2]

puritan *n.* 清教徒 [ching1 gaau3 tou4]

purity *n.* 純潔 [seun4 git8]

purple *adj./n.* 紫色 [ji2 sik7]

purpose *n.* 目的 [muk9 dik7], ~ **of visit** 訪問嘅目的

purport *v.* 標榜 [biu1 bong2]

purse *n.* 銀包 [ngan2 baau1]

pursue *v.* 追求 [jeui1 kau4]

pursuit *n.* 追求 [jeui1 kau4]

pus *n.* 膿 [nung4]

push *v./n.* 推 [teui1]

put *v.* 放 [fong3], ~ **in** 放入, ~ **out** 攞出, ~ **smth. on** 著, ~ **smth. out** 放出去

puzzle *n.* 砌圖 [chai3 tou4]

pygmy *n.* 小矮人 [siu2 ai2 yan4]

Pyongyang *n.* 平壤 [ping4 yeung6]; ~, **capital of North Korea** 北韓首都

pyramid *n.* 金字塔 [gam1 ji6 taap8]

pyre *n.* 柴堆 [chaai4 deui1]

python *n.* 蟒蛇 [mong5 se4]

Q

Qatar *n.* 卡塔爾 [ka1 taap8 yi5]

Qatari *adj.* 卡塔爾 [ka1 taap8 yi5]

quack *n. (fake doctor)* 黃綠醫生 [wong4 luk9 yi1 sang1]

quadrangle *n.* 四合院 [sei3 hap9 yun2]

quadruple *n.* 四倍 [sei3 pui5]

quail *n.* 鵪鶉 [am1 cheun1]

quaint *adj.* 古色古香 [gu2 sik7 gu2 heung1]

quake *v.* 發震 [faat8 jan3]

qualification *n.* 資格 [ji1 gaak8]

qualified *adj.* 有資格 [yau5 ji1 gaak8]

qualify *v.* 有資格 [yau5 ji1 gaak8]

quality *n.* 質量 [jat7 leung6]

quandary *n.* 左右為難 [jo2 yau6 wai4 naan4]

quantity *n.* 數量 [sou3 leung6]

quarantine *n.* 檢疫 [gim2 yik9]

quarrel *n./v.* 嗌交 [aai3 gaau1]

quarry *n.* 採石場 [choi2 sek9 cheung4]

quarter *quant./n.* 四分之一 [sei3 fan6 ji1 yat7], **~ past eight (8:15)** 八點三, **~ to one (12:45)** 十二點九, **~ tank of gas** 四分一油箱油

quartered *adj.* 四開 [sei3 hoi1]

queen *n.* 王后 [wong4 hau6]

quell *v.* 鎮壓 [jan3 aat8]

quench *v.* 撲滅 [pok8 mit9]

query *n.* 疑問 [yi4 man6]

quest *n.* 探索 [taam3 sok8]

question *n.* 問題 [man6 tai4]; *v.* 問問題 [man6 man6 tai4]

question mark *n.* 問號 [man6 hou6]

questionable *adj.* 有問題 [yau5 man6 tai4]

questionnaire *n.* 調查問卷 [diu6 cha4 man6 gyun2]

queue *n.* 隊 [deui2]; *v.* 排隊 [paai4 deui2]

quibble *n.* 謬論[mau6 leun6]

quiche *n.* 雞蛋餅 [gai1 daan6 beng2]

quick *adj.* 快 [faai3]

quickest *adj.* 最快 [jeui3 faai3]

quickly *adv.* 即刻 [jik7 hak7]

quicksand *n.* 流沙 [lau4 sa1]

quicksilver *n.* 水銀 [seui2 ngan4]

quiet *adj.* 安靜嘅 [on1 jing6 ge3]; *n.* 安靜 [on1 jing6]

quieter *adj.* 靜啲 [jing6 di1]

quietly *adv.* 安靜 [on1 jing6]

quince *n.* 青木瓜 [cheng1 muk9 gwa1]

quinoa *n.* 藜麥 [lai4 mak9]

quit *v.* 辭職 [chi4 jik7]

quite *adv.* 幾 [gei2]

Quito *n.* 基多 [gei1 do1]; **~, capital of Ecuador** 厄瓜多爾首都

quiver *v.* 打冷震 [da2 laang5 jan3]

quixotic *adj.* 不切實際 [bat7 chit8 sat9 jai3]

quiz *n.* 小測驗 [siu2 chak7 yim6]

quorum *n.* 法定人數 [faat8 ding6 yan4 sou3]

quota *n.* 配額 [pui3 ngaak2]

quotation *n.* 引用 [yan5 yung6]

quotation marks *n.* 引號 [yan5 hou6]

quote *v.* 引用 [yan5 yung6]

R

Rabat *n.* 拉巴特 [laai1 ba1 dak9]; ~, **capital of Morocco** 摩洛哥首都

rabbi *n.* 猶太教教士 [yau4 taai3 gaau3 gaau3 si6]

rabbit *n.* 兔仔 [tou3 jai2]

race *n.* 種族 [jung2 juk9]; *v.* 賽跑 [choi3 paau2]

racial *adj.* 種族 [jung2 juk9]

racialism *n.* 種族歧視 [jung2 juk9 kei4 si6]

racing *n.* 賽馬 [choi3 ma5]

racism *n.* 種族歧視 [jung2 juk9 kei4 si6]

rack *n.* 架 [ga2], ~ **of lamb** 羊架, ~ **of ribs** 排骨架

racket (*sports*) *n.* 球拍 [kau4 paak2]

radiance *n.* 發光 [faat8 gwong1]

radiant *adj.* 容光煥發 [yung4 gwong1 wun6 faat8]

radiate *v.* 輻射 [fuk7 se6]

radiation *n.* 輻射 [fuk7 se6]

radiator *n.* 暖氣裝置 [nyun5 hei3 jong1 ji3]

radical *adj.* 激進 [gik7 jeun3]

radicchio *n.* 菊苣 [guk7 geui6]

radio *n.* 收音機 [sau1 yam1 gei1]

radish *n.* 蘿蔔 [lo4 baak9]

radius *n.* 半徑 [bun3 ging3]

rag *n.* 爛布 [laan6 bou3]

rage *n.* 憤怒 [fan5 nou6]

ragout *n.* 蔬菜燉肉 [so1 choi3 dan6 yuk9]

raid *n.* 突擊搜查 [dat9 gik7 sau4 cha4]

rail *n.* 鐵軌 [tit8 gwai2]

railing *n.* 欄杆 [laan4 gon1]

railery *n.* 講笑 [gong2 siu3]

railroad *n.* 鐵路 [tit8 lou6]; ~ **crossing** 鐵路道口

rain *n.* 雨 [yu5]; *v.* 落雨 [lok9 yu5], **it's ~ing** 落緊雨

raincoat *n.* 雨衣 [yu5 yi1]

rainy *adj.* 成日落雨 [sing4 yat9 lok9 yu5]

raise *v.* 提高 [tai4 gou1]

raisin *n.* 提子乾 [tai4 ji2 gon1]

rally *n.* 集合 [jaap9 hap9]

ram *n.* 白羊座 [baak9 yeung4 jo6]

RAM *n. comp.* 英國皇家音樂學院; **computer** ~ 電腦內存

ramble *n.* 漫步 [maan6 bou6]

ramp *n.* 斜坡 [che3 po1]

rampage *n.* 發狂 [faat8 kwong4]

rampant *adj.* 猖狂 [cheung1 kwong4]

rampart *n.* 堡壘 [bou2 leui5]

rancour *n.* 深仇 [sam1 sau4]

random *adj.* 隨機 [cheui4 gei1]; *n.* 任意 [yam6 yi3]

range *n.* 範圍 [faan6 wai4]

ranger *n.* 護林員 [wu6 lam4 yun4]

Rangoon (Yangon) *n.* 仰光 [yeung5 gwong1]; ~, **capital of Myanmar (Burma)** 緬甸首都

rank *n.* 等級 [dang2 kap7]; *v.* 評級 [ping4 kap7]

ransack *v.* 洗劫 [sai2 gip8]

ransom *n.* 贖金 [suk9 gam1]

rape *n./v.* 強姦 [keung4 gaan1]

raped *adj.* 強姦 [keung4 gaan1]

rapeseed oil *n.* 菜油 [choi3 yau4]

rapid *adj.* 快 [faai3]

rapidly *adv.* 即刻 [jik7 hak7]

rapids *n.* 急流 [gap7 lau4]

rappeling *n.* 綁住繩滑落 [bong2 jyu6 sing4 waat9 lok9]

rapport *n.* 和睦 [wo4 muk9]

rapt *adj.* 專心 [jyun1 sam1]

rapture *n.* 極度開心 [gik9 dou6 hoi1 sam1]

rare *adj.* 罕見 [hon2 gin3], ~ **steak** 半熟牛扒, ~ **meat** 生肉, ~ **coin** 珍稀硬幣

rarely *adv.* 罕有 [hon2 yau5]

rascal *n.* 無賴 [mou4 laai2]

rash 1. *n.* 皮疹 [pei4 jan2] // **2.** *adj.* 衝動 [chung1 dung6]

raspberry *n.* 紅桑子 [hung4 song1 ji2]

rat *n.* 老鼠 [lou5 syu2]

rate *n.* 比率 [bei2 leut9]; *v.* 評級 [ping4 kap7]

rather (~ than) *adv.* 情願 [ching2 yun2],

ratify *v.* 批准 [pai1 jeun2]

ratio *n.* 比例 [bei2 lai6]

ration *n.* 定量 [ding6 leung6]

rational *adj.* 理性 [lei5 sing3]

rationale *n.* 理論基礎 [lei5 leun6 gei1 cho2]

rationality *n.* 合理性 [hap9 lei5 sing3]

rationalize *v.* 合理化 [hap9 lei5 fa3]

rattle *n.* 撥浪鼓 [but9 long6 gu2]

ravage *v.* 破壞 [po3 waai6]

rave *v.* 亂講野 [lyun6 gong2 ye5]

raven 1. (*black*) *adj.* 烏黑 [wu1 hak7] // **2.** (*bird*) *n.* 渡鴉 [dou6 a1]

ravine *n.* 峽谷 [haap9 guk7]

ravioli *n.* 意大利餛飩 [yi3 daai6 lei6 wan4 tan1]

raw *adj.* 生 [saang1]

ray *n.* 射線 [se6 sin3]

razor *n.* 鬚刨 [sou1 paau2], ~ **blade** 鬚刨刀片

re- *prefix* 再 [joi3], **~-use** 再用

reach *v.* 行到 [haang4 dou3]

react *v.* 反應 [faan2 ying3]

reactionary *n.* 反動派 [faan2 dung6 paai3]

reaction *n.* 反應 [faan2 ying3]

reactor *n.* 反應堆 [faan2 ying3 deui1]

read *v.* 睇 [tai2]

reader *n.* 讀者 [duk9 je2]

readily *adv.* 樂意 [lok9 yi3]

reading *n.* 讀書 [duk9 syu1]

ready *adj.* 準備好 [jeun2 bei6 hou2], **~-made** 整好

real *adj.* 真 [jan1]

real estate *n.* 房地產 [fong4 dei6 chaan2], ~ **agent** 房地產經紀

realism *n.* 現實主義 [yin6 sat9 jyu2 yi6]

realist *n.* 現實主義者 [yin6 sat9 jyu2 yi6 je2]

realistic *adj.* 現實 [yin6 sat9]

reality *n.* 現實 [yin6 sat9]

realization *n.* 領悟 [ling5 ng6]

realize *v.* 意識 [yi3 sik7]

really *adv.* 真係 [jan1 hai6]

realm *n.* 領域 [ling5 wik9]

ream *n.* 好多 [hou2 do1]

reap *v.* 收割 [sau1 got8]

reaper *n.* 收割機 [sau1 got8 gei1]

rear *n./adj.* 後面 [hau6 min6], ~ **door** 後門, ~ **light** 尾燈

reason *n.* 理由 [lei5 yau4], ~ **for travel** 旅遊嘅理由

reasonable *adj.* 合理 [hap9 lei5], ~ **doubt** (*legal*) 合理疑點

reasonably *adv.* 合理 [hap9 lei5]

reassure *v.* 再三保證 [joi3 saam1 bou2 jing3]

rebate *n.* 折扣 [jit8 kau3]

rebel *v.* 造反 [jou6 faan2]

rebellion *n.* 叛亂 [bun6 lyun6]

rebellious *adj.* 反叛 [faan2 bun6]

rebirth *n.* 重生 [chung5 sang1]

rebound *v.* 反彈 [faan2 daan2]

rebuff *n.* 堅決拒絕 [gin1 kyut8 keui5 jyut9]

rebuild *v.* 重建 [chung4 gin3]

rebuilt *adj.* 重建嘅 [chung4 gin3 ge3]

rebuke *v.* 指責 [ji2 jaak8]

rebut *v.* 駁番 [bok8 faan1]

recall *v.* 記得 [gei3 dak7]

recede *v.* 後退 [hau6 teui3]

receipt *n.* 收據 [sau1 geui3]

receive *v.* 收到 [sau1 dou2]

receiver *n.* 接收器 [jip8 sau1 hei3]

recent *adj.* 近排 [gan6 paai2]

recently *adv.* 近排 [gan6 paai2]

reception *n.* 接待處 [jip8 doi6 chyu3]; ~ **desk** 接待處

receptionist *n.* 前台 [chin4 toi4]

receptor *n.* 接收器 [jip8 sau1 hei3]

recess *v.* 休庭 [yau1 ting4]

recession *n.* 經濟衰退 [ging1 jai3 seui1 teui3]

recipe *n.* 食譜 [sik9 pou2]

recipient *n.* 收件人 [sau1 gin2 yan4]

reciprocal *adj.* 互惠互利 [wu6 wai6 wu6 lei6]

reciprocate *v.* 回報 [wui4 bou3]

recital *n.* 獨奏會 [duk9 jau3 wui2]

recitation *n.* 朗誦 [long5 jung6]

recite *v.* 朗誦 [long5 jung6]

reckon *v.* 認為 [ying6 wai4]

reclaim *v.* 開荒 [hoi1 fong1]

reclamation *n.* 開荒 [hoi1 fong1]

recluse *n.* 隱士 [yan2 si6]

recognition *n.* 認可 [ying6 ho2]

recognize *v.* 認出 [ying6 cheut7]

recoil *v.* 後退 [hau6 teui3]

recollect *v.* 記得 [gei3 dak7]

recommend *v.* 推薦 [teui1 jin3]

recommendation *n.* 推薦 [teui1 jin3]

recommended *adj.* 推薦 [teui1 jin3]

recompense *n.* 報酬 [bou3 chau4]

reconcile *v.* 和解 [wo4 gaai2]

reconciliation *n.* 和解 [wo4 gaai2]

record *n./v.* 記錄 [gei2 luk9]

recorder *n.* 錄音機 [luk9 yam1 gei1]

recording *n.* 錄音 [luk9 yam1]

recount *v.* 描述 [miu4 seut9]

recoup *v.* 攞番 [lo2 faan1]

recourse *n.* 依賴 [yi1 laai6]

recover *v.* 康復 [hong1 fuk9]

recovery *n.* 康復 [hong1 fuk9]

recruit *v.* 招聘 [jiu1 ping3]; *n.* 新成員 [san1 sing4 yun4]

recruitment *n.* 招聘 [jiu1 ping3]

rectangle *n.* 長方形 [cheung4 fong1 ying4]

recyclable *adj.* 可回收 [ho2 wui4 sau1]

recycle *v.* 回收 [wui4 sau1]

recycling *n.* 廢物回收 [fai3 mat9 wui4 sau1]; ~ **bin** 廢物 回收站

rectification *n.* 糾正 [dau2 jing3]

rectify *v.* 糾正 [dau2 jing3]

rectum *n.* 直腸 [jik9 cheung2]

recur *v.* 重現 [chung4 yin6]

recurrence *n.* 重現 [chung4 yin6]

recurrent *adj.* 週期性 [jau1 kei4 sing3]

red *adj./n.* 紅色 [hung4 sik7], ~ **pepper** 紅椒, ~ **wine** 紅酒

redeem *v.* 贖番 [suk9 faan1]

redemption *n.* 救贖 [gau3 suk9]

redirect *v.* 改寄 [goi2 gei3]

redress *v.* 糾正 [dau2 jing3]

reduce *v.* 減少 [gaam2 siu2], ~ **weight** 減肥, ~ **prices** 減價

reduced *adj.* 減少 [gaam2 siu2]

reduction *n.* 減少 [gaam2 siu2]

redundance *n.* 冗員 [yung2 yun4]

redundant *adj.* 多餘 [do1 yu4]

redundancy *n.* 太多 [taai3 do1]

reel *n.* 卷軸 [gyun2 juk9]

refer to *v.* 參考 [cham1 haau2]

referee *n.* 裁判 [choi4 pun3]

reference *n.* 參考 [cham1 haau2]

referendum *n.* 全民投票 [chyun4 man4 tau4 piu3]

refine *v.* 提煉 [tai4 lin6]

refined *adj.* 高雅 [gou1 nga5]; ~ **sugar** 精糖

refinery *n.* 提煉廠 [tai4 lin6 chong2]

reflect *v.* 反思 [faan2 si1]

reflection (*thought /mirror*) *n.* 反 射 [faan2 se6]

reflector *n.* 反射器 [faan2 se6 hei3]

reflex *n.* 反射作用 [faan2 se6 jok8 yung6]

reflexive *adj.* 反射性 [faan2 se6 sing3]

reform *v./n.* 改革 [goi2 gaak8]

reformation *n.* 改革 [goi2 gaak8]

reformatory *n.* 感化院 [gam2 fa3 yun2]

reformer *n.* 改革者 [goi2 gaak8 je2]

refrain *v.* 克制 [hak7 jai3]

refresh *v.* 提神 [tai4 san4], ~ **a webpage** 刷新網頁

refreshing *adj.* 提神 [tai4 san4]; **to be** ~ 提神

refreshments *n.* 點心 [dim2 sam1]

refrigeration *n.* 冷凍 [laang5 dung3]

refrigerator *n.* 雪櫃 [syut8 gwai6]

refuge *n.* 避難 [bei6 naan6]

refugee *n.* 難民 [naan6 man4]

refulgence *n.* 輝煌 [fai1 wong4]

refulgent *adj.* 輝煌 [fai1 wong4]

refund *n.* 退錢 [teui3 chin2]

refusal *n.* 拒絕 [keui5 jyut9]

refuse 1. *n.* 垃圾 [laap9 saap8] // **2.** *v.* 拒絕 [keui5 jyut9]

refutation *n.* 反駁 [faan2 bok8]

refute *v.* 反駁 [faan2 bok8]

regal *adj.* 帝王 [dai3 wong4]

regard *v.* 關係 [gwaan1 hai6]; *n.* 問候 [man6 hau6], **Give my ~s to ...** 請幫我問候

regarding *prep.* 關係 [gwaan1 hai6]

regenerate v. 再生[joi3 sang1]

regeneration n. 再生 [joi3 sang1]

regime n. 政權 [jing3 kyun4]

regicide n. 弒君 [si3 gwan1]

regime n. 政權 [jing3 kyun4]

regiment n. 軍團 [gwan1 tyun4]

region n. 地區 [dei6 keui1]

regional adj. 區域性 [keui1 wik9 sing3], ~ **cooking/dish/recipe** 地方菜

register v./n. 登記 [dang1 gei3]

registered mail n. 掛號信 [gwa3 hou6 seun3]

registration n. 登記 [dang1 gei3], ~ **form** 登記表, **vehicle ~ documents** 車輛登記文件

registry n. 登記處 [dang1 gei3 chyu3]

regret v. 後悔 [hau6 fui3]; n. 可惜 [ho2 sik7]

regular adj. 定期 [ding6 kei4]

regularly adv. 有規律 [yau5 kwai1 leut9]

regulate v. 管制 [gun2 jai3]

regulation n. 管制 [gun2 jai3]

regulator n. 監管機構 [gaam1 gun2 gei1 kau3]

regulatory adj. 管制 [gun2 jai3]

rehabilitate v. 戒酒 [gaai3 jau2]

rehabilitation n. 康復 [hong1 fuk9]

rehearsal n. 綵排 [choi2 paai4]

rehearse v. 綵排 [choi2 paai4]

re-heat v. 重新加熱 [chung4 san1 ga1 yit9];~**ed** 重新加熱咗

reign n. 統治 [tung2 ji6]

reimburse v. 賠償 [pui4 seung4]

reimbursement n. 賠償 [pui4 seung4]

reindeer n. 馴鹿 [suen4 luk9]

reinforce v. 加固 [ga1 gu3]

reinforcement n. 援軍 [wun4 gwan1]

reinstate v. 復職 [fuk9 jik7]

reinstatement n. 復職 [fuk9 jik7]

reiterate v. 重申 [chung4 san1]

reiteration n. 重申 [chung4 san1]

reject v. 拒絕 [keui5 jyut9]

rejection n. 拒絕 [keui5 jyut9]

rejoice v. 開心 [hoi1 sam1]

rejoinder n. 反駁 [faan2 bok8]

rejuvenate v. 恢復青春 [fui1 fuk9 ching1 cheun1]

rejuvenation n. 返老還童 [faan2 lou5 waan4 tung4]

relapse v. 復發 [fuk9 faat8]

relate v. 聯繫 [faan2 bok8]

related (to) adj. 聯繫起身 [lyun4 hai6 hei2 san1]

relation n. 聯繫 [lyun4 hai6]

relations n. 關係 [gwaan1 hai6]

relationship n. 關係 [gwaan1 hai6]

relative 1. adj. 相對 [seung1 deui3] // **2.** (family) n. 親戚 [chan1 chik7]

relatively adv. 相對 [seung1 deui3]

relax v. 放鬆 [fong3 sung1]

relaxation n. 放鬆 [fong3 sung1]

relaxed adj. 放鬆 [fong3 sung1]

relaxing adj. 令人放鬆 [ling4 yan4 fong3 sung1]

relay n. 接力 [jip8 lik9]

release v. 釋放 [sik7 fong3] n. 釋放 [sik7 fong3]

relent v. 心軟 [sam1 yun5]

relentless adj. 狠心 [han2 sam1]

relevance *n.* 相關性 [seung1 gwaan1 sing3]

relevant *adj.* 相關 [seung1 gwaan1]

reliable *adj.* 可靠 [ho2 kaau3]

reliance *n.* 依賴 [yi1 laai6]

relic *n.* 遺跡 [wai4 jik7]

relief *n.* 安心 [on1 sam1]

relieve *v.* 減輕 [gaam2 heng1]

religion *n.* 宗教 [jung1 gaau3]

religious *adj.* 虔誠 [kin4 sing4], ~ service 宗教儀式

relinquish *v.* 出讓 [cheut7 yeung6]

relish *n.* 調味料 [tiu4 mei6 liu2], sweet ~ 甜調味料, spicy ~ 辣調味料

reluctance *n.* 勉強 [min5 keung5]

reluctant *adj.* 唔願意 [m4 yun6 yi3]

rely on *v.* 依賴 [yi1 laai6]

remain *v.* 保留 [bou2 lau4]

remainder *n.* 淨低嘅野 [jing6 dai1 ge3 ye5]

remaining *adj.* 淨低嘅 [jing6 dai1 ge3]

remains *n.* 遺址 [wai4 ji2]

remand *v.* 還押候審 [waan4 aat8 hau6 sam2]

remark *n./v.* 評論 [ping4 leun6]

remarkable *adj.* 好犀利 [hou2 sai1 lei6]

remedy *n.* 治療方法 [ji6 liu4 fong1 faat8]

remember *v.* 記住 [gei3 jyu6], ~ me 記住我

remembrance *n.* 紀念 [gei3 nim6]

remind *v.* 提醒 [tai4 seng2]

reminder *n.* 提醒 [tai4 seng2]

reminiscence *n.* 回憶 [wui4 yik7]

reminiscent *adj.* 懷舊 [waai4 gau6]

remission *n.* 減輕 [gaam2 heng1]

remit *v.* 匯錢 [wui6 chin2]

remittance *n.* 匯錢 [wui6 chin2]

remorse *n.* 悔恨 [fui3 han6]

remote *adj.* 遙遠 [yiu4 yun5]

remote control *n.* 遙控器 [yiu4 hung3 hei3]

removal *n.* 去除 [heui3 cheui4]

remove *v.* 移開 [yi4 hoi1]

remunerate *v.* 出糧 [cheut7 leung4]

remuneration *n.* 人工 [yan4 gung1]

renaissance *n.* 文藝復興 [man4 ngai4 fuk9 hing1]; the R~ 文藝復興

render *v.* 使到 [sai2 dou3]

rendezvous *n.* 約會 [yeuk8 wui6]

renew *v.* 重新開始 [chung4 san1 hoi1 chi2]

renewal *n.* 續約 [juk9 yeuk8]

renounce *v.* 放棄 [fong3 hei3]

renovate *v.* 翻新 [faan1 san1]

renovation *n.* 翻新 [faan1 san1]

renown *n.* 聲望 [sing1 mong6]

renowned *adj.* 有名 [yau5 meng4]

rent *n.* 租金 [jou1 gam1]; *v.* 租 [jou1], for ~ 出租, ~ out 租出, ~ed 租

rental *adj.* 租 [jou1], ~ car 租嘅車

renunciation *n.* 宣佈斷絕關係 [syun1 bou3 tyun5 jyut9 gwaan1 hai6]

repair *v.* 整 [jing2]; *n.* 修理 [sau1 lei5]

repair shop *n.* 修理舖 [sau1 lei5 pou2]

reparable *n.* 可以整番好 [ho2 yi5 jing2 faan1 hou2]

repartee *n.* 巧妙嘅應答 [haau2 miu6 ge3 ying3 daap8]

repatriate *v.* 遣返 [hin2 faan2]

repatriation *n.* 遣返 [hin2 faan2]

repay *v.* 還 [waan4]

repayment *n.* 報答 [bou3 daap8]

repeal *v.* 廢除 [fai3 cheui4]

repeat *v.* 重複 [chung4 fuk7], **please ~ that** 請再講一次

repeated *adj.* 重複 [chung4 fuk7]

repeatedly *adv.* 重複 [chung4 fuk7]

repel *v.* 擊退 [gik7 teui3]

repellent *n.* 驅蟲劑 [keui1 chung4 jai1]

repent *v.* 後悔 [hau6 fui3]

repentance *n.* 後悔 [hau6 fui3]

repercussion *n.* 壞影響 [waai6 ying2 heung2]

repetition *n.* 重複 [chung4 fuk7]

replace *v.* 代替 [doi6 tai3]

replacement *n.* 代替 [doi6 tai3]; **~ part** 替換零件

replenish *v.* 重新裝滿 [chung4 san1 jong1 mun5]

replete *n.* 充滿 [chung1 mun5]

replica *n.* 複製品 [fuk7 jai3 ban2]

reply *n./v.* 回覆 [wui4 fuk7]

report *v./n.* 報道 [bou3 dou6]

reporter *n.* 記者 [gei3 je2]

repose *n.* 休息 [yau1 sik7]

repository *n.* 倉庫 [chong1 fu3]

represent *v.* 代表 [doi6 biu2]

representation *n.* 代表 [doi6 biu2]

representative *n.* 代表 [doi6 biu2]; *adj.* 典型 [din2 ying4]

repress *v.* 鎮壓 [jan3 aat8]

repression *n.* 鎮壓 [jan3 aat8]

reprimand *v.* 譴責 [hin2 jaak8]

reprint *v.* 重印 [chung4 yan3]

reproach *v.* 指責 [ji2 jaak8]

reproduce *v.* 重現 [chung4 yin6]

reproduction *n.* 複製品 [fuk7 jai3 ban2]

reproductive *adj.* 生殖 [sang1 jik9]

reproof *n.* 指責 [ji2 jaak8]

reptile *n.* 爬行動物 [pa4 hang4 dung6 mat9]

republic *n.* 共和國 [gung6 wo4 gwok8]

republican *n.* 共和黨 [gung6 wo4 dong2]

repudiate *v.* 拒絕 [keui5 jyut9]

repudiation *n.* 斷絕關係 [tyun5 jyut9 gwaan1 hai6]

repugnance *n.* 反感 [faan2 gam2]

repugnant *adj.* 乞人憎 [hat7 yan4 jang1]

repulse *v.* 擊退 [gik7 teui3]

repulsion *n.* 反感 [faan2 gam2]

repulsive *adj.* 乞人憎 [hat7 yan4 jang1]

reputation *n.* 聲譽 [sing1 yu6]

repute *v.* 認為 [ying6 wai4]

request *n./v.* 請求 [ching2 kau4]

require *v.* 需要 [seui1 yiu3]

required *adj.* 要求 [yiu1 kau4]

requirement *n.* 要求 [yiu1 kau4]

requisite *n.* 必需品 [bit7 seui1 ban2]

requisition *n.* 徵用 [jing1 yung6]

requite *v.* 回報 [wui4 bou3]

rescue *v./n.* 救援 [gau3 wun4]

research *n.* 研究 [yin4 gau3]

researcher *n.* 研究員 [yin4 gau3 yun4]

resemblance *n.* 相似 [seung1 chi5]

resemble *v.* 類似 [leui6 chi5]

reservation *n.* 預訂 [yu6 deng6]; ~ **desk** 預訂處

reserve *v.* 保留 [bou2 lau4], ~ **a table** 訂枱; *n.* 儲備 [chyu5 bei6]

reserved *adj.* 預訂 [yu6 deng6], ~ **table** 訂咗嘅枱, ~ **lane** 訂咗嘅球道

reservoir *n.* 水庫 [seui2 fu3]

reside *v.* 住 [jyu6]

resident *n.* 居民 [geui1 man4]; *adj.* 定居 [ding6 geui1]

residue *n.* 殘渣 [chaan4 ja1]

resign *v.* 辭職 [chi4 jik7]

resignation *n.* 辭職 [chi4 jik7]

resist *v.* 抵制 [dai2 jai3]

resistance *n.* 抵抗 [dai2 kong3]

resolute *adj.* 堅決 [gin1 kyut8]

resolution *n.* 決心 [kyut8 sam1]

resolve *v.* 解決 [gaai2 kyut8]

resort *n.* 度假勝地 [dou6 ga3 sing3 dei6]

resound *v.* 回響 [wui4 heung2]

resource *n.* 資源 [ji1 yun4]

respect *n./v.* 尊重 [jyun1 jung6]

respectful *adj.* 有禮貌 [yau5 lai5 maau6]

respective *adj.* 各自 [gok8 ji6]

respectively *n.* 各自 [gok8 ji6]

respiration *n.* 呼吸 [fu1 kap7]

respiratory system *n.* 呼吸系統 [fu1 kap7 hai6 tung2]

respire *v.* 呼吸 [fu1 kap7]

respond *v.* 答 [daap8]

respondent *n.* 被告 [bei6 gou3]

response *n.* 回答 [wui4 daap8]

responsibility *n.* 責任 [jaak8 yam6], **take** ~ 負責任

responsible *adj.* 負責任 [fu6 jaak8 yam6]

rest *n.* 剩餘 [sing6 yu4]; *v.* 唞 [tau2]; ~ **area** 休息區, **allow to** ~ 可以休息

restaurant *n.* 餐廳 [chaan1 teng1], **formal** ~ 高級餐廳, **informal** ~ 大排擋

restoration *n.* 復原 [fuk9 yun4]

restore *v.* 復原 [fuk9 yun4]

restored *adj.* 復原咗 [fuk9 yun4 jo2]

restrain *v.* 壓抑 [aat8 yik7]

restraint *n.* 限制 [haan6 jai3]

restrict *v.* 限制 [haan6 jai3]

restricted *adj.* 受約束 [sau6 yeuk8 chuk7]

restriction *n.* 限制 [haan6 jai3]

restroom *n.* 廁所 [chi3 so2]

restructure *v.* 重組 [chung4 jou2]

restructuring *n.* 重組 [chung4 jou2]

result *n.* 結果 [git8 gwo2]; *v.* 導致 [dou6 ji3]

resumé *n.* 簡歷 [gaan2 lik9]

resume *v.* 重新開始 [chung4 san1 hoi1 chi2]

resumption *n.* 重新開始 [chung4 san1 hoi1 chi2]

resurgence *n.* 復活 [fuk9 wut9]

resurgent *adj.* 復興 [fuk9 hing1]

retail *n./adv./v.* 零售 [ling4 sau6], ~ **price** 零售價

retailer *n.* 零售商 [ling4 sau6 seung1]

retailing *n.* 零售業 [ling4 sau6 yip9]

retain *v.* 留有 [lau4 yau5]

retaliate *v.* 反擊 [faan2 gik7]

retaliation *n.* 反擊 [faan2 gik7]

retard *v.* 阻礙 [jo2 ngoi6]

retardation *n.* 留級 [lau4 kap7]

retention *n.* 扣留 [kau3 lau4]

retentive *adj.* 好記性 [hou2 gei3 sing3]

reticence *n.* 沈默寡言 [cham4 mak9 gwa2 yin4]

reticent *adj.* 含蓄 [ham4 chuk7]

retina *n.* 視網膜 [si6 mong5 mok9]

retinue *n.* 跟班 [gan1 baan1]

retire *v.* 退休 [teui3 yau1]

retired *adj.* 退咗休 [teui3 jo2 yau1]

retirement *n.* 退休 [teui3 yau1]

retrieve *v.* 搵翻 [wan2 faan1]; *comp.* ~ **a file** 檢索文件

retort *v.* 駁嘴 [bok8 jeui2]

retouch *v.* 修飾 [sau1 sik7]

retrace *v.* 原路行番 [yun4 lou6 haang4 faan1]

retread *v.* 翻新 [faan1 san1]

retreat *v.* 撤退 [chit8 teui3]

retrench *v.* 緊縮 [gan2 suk7]

retrenchment *n.* 緊縮 [gan2 suk7]

retrieve *v.* 攞番 [lo2 faan1]

retrospect *v.* 諗番 [nam2 faan1]

retrospection *n.* 回憶 [wui4 yik7]

return *v.* 俾翻 [bei2 faan1]; *n.* 番黎 [faan1 lai4], ~ **ticket** 回程票, **in ~** 作為回報

returnable *n.* 有得退嘅 [yau5 dak7 teui3 ge3]

reveal *v.* 話俾人知 [wa6 bei2 yan4 ji1]

revel *n.* 狂歡 [kwong4 fun1]

revelation *n.* 暴露 [bou6 lou6]

reveler *n.* 酒鬼 [jau2 gwai2]

revelry *n.* 狂歡 [kwong4 fun1]

revenge *n.* 報仇 [bou3 sau4]

revenue *n.* 收入 [sau1 yap9]

revere *v.* 尊敬 [jyun1 ging3]

reverence *n.* 尊敬 [jyun1 ging3]

reverential *adj.* 恭敬 [gung1 ging3]

reverie *n.* 白日夢 [baak9 yat9 mung6]

reversal *n.* 顛倒 [din1 dou2]

reverse *v.* 向後退 [heung3 hau6 teui3], **Please ~ the charges** 請撤回控訴; *n.* 倒退 [dou2 teui3], **drive in ~** 倒車

revert *v.* 恢復 [fui1 fuk9]

review *n./v.* 複習 [fuk7 jaap9]

revise *v.* 修改 [sau1 goi2]

revision *n.* 修改 [sau1 goi2]

revive *v.* 復活 [fuk9 wut9]

revival *n.* 復活 [fuk9 wut9]

revocable *adj.* 可以撤消 [ho2 yi5 chit8 siu1]

revocation *n.* 撤消 [chit8 siu1]

revoke *v.* 撤消 [chit8 siu1]

revolting *adj.* 令人作嘔 [ling4 yan4 jok8 au2]

revolution *n.* 革命 [gaak8 ming6]

revolutionary *adj.* 創新 [chong1 san1]

reward *n./v.* 獎勵 [jeung2 lai6]

Reykjavik *n.* 雷克雅末克 [leui4 hak7 nga5 mut9 hak7]; ~, **capital of Iceland** 冰島首都

rhetoric *n.* 花言巧語 [fa1 yin4 haau2 yu5]

rhetorical *adj.* 誇張 [kwa1 jeung1]

rheumatic *adj.* 風濕 [fung1 sap7]

rheumatism *n.* 風濕 [fung1 sap7]

rhinoceros *n.* 犀牛 [sai1 ngau4]

rhubarb *n.* 大黃 [daai6 wong4]

rhyme *n.* 押韻 [aat8 wan5]

rhythm *n.* 節奏 [jit8 jau3]

rhythmic *adj.* 有節奏 [yau5 jit8 jau3]

rib *n.* 肋骨 [laak9 gwat7]

ribbon *n.* 絲帶 [si1 daai2]

rib-eye steak *n.* 肉眼牛扒 [yuk9 ngaan5 ngau4 pa2]

rice *n.* 米 [mai5], ~ **pudding** 米布甸, ~ **pilaf** 米肉飯, ~ **cake** 年糕

ricepaper *n.* 宣紙 [syun1 ji2]

rich *adj.* 有錢 [yau5 chin2], ~ **flavor** 濃味, ~ **texture** 肉質細膩

rickets *n.* 駝背 [to4 bui3]

rickshaw *n.* 黃包車 [wong4 baau1 che1]

ricotta *n.* 意大利乳清芝士 [yi3 daai6 lei6 yu5 ching1 ji1 si6]

rid *v.* 擺脫 [baai2 tyut8]

riddle *n.* 謎語 [mai4 yu5]

ride *v.* 騎 [ke4], ~ **a horse** 騎馬, ~ **a bike** 騎車; *n.* 坐車 [cho5 che1], **take a** ~ 搭順風車, **give a** ~ **to smb.** 搭某人一程

rider *n.* 騎師 [ke4 si1]

ridge *n.* 山脊 [saan1 jek8]

ridicule *v.* 嘲笑 [jaau1 siu3]

ridiculous *adj.* 荒謬 [fong1 mau6]

riding *n.* 騎馬 [ke4 ma5]

rifle *n.* 步槍 [bou6 cheung1]

Riga *n.* 里加 [lei5 ga1]; ~, **capital of Latvia** 拉脫維亞首都

right *adj.* (*correct*) 啱 [ngaam1]; *adv.* 即刻 [jik7 hak7]; *n.* 權利 [kyun4 lei6], ~ **now** 即刻, **that's** ~ 冇錯, **to the** ~ 喺右邊, **on the** ~ 喺右邊, ~~**wing** 右翼

rightly *adv.* 理所當然 [lei5 so2 dong1 yin4]

righteous *adj.* 正直 [jing3 jik9]

rigid *adj.* 死板 [sei2 baan2]

rigorous *adj.* 嚴厲 [yim4 lai6]

rigor *n.* 嚴厲 [yim4 lai6]

rim *n.* 邊 [bin1]

rind *n.* 皮 [pei4]

ring *n.* (*jewelry*) 戒指 [gaai3 ji2]; *v.* 撳鐘 [gam6 chung1]

ringing *n.* 鈴聲 [ling4 sing1]

ringlet *n.* 捲髮 [gyun2 faat8]

ringworm *n.* 癬 [sin2]

rinse *v.* 沖 [chung1]

riot *n.* 動亂 [dung6 lyun6]

rip *v.* 搣爛 [mit7 laan6], ~ **off** 搶, **that's a** ~ **off** 佔便宜, **it is** ~**ped** 扯咗落黎

ripe *adj.* 熟 [suk9]; ~**ned** 熟咗, ~ **fruit** 熟生果, ~ **vegetables** 食得嘅青菜

ripple *n.* 波紋 [bo1 man4]

rippled *adj.* 起波紋 [hei2 bo1 man4]

rise *v.* 升起 [sing1 hei2]; *n.* 增加 [jang1 ga1]

risk *n.* 風險 [fung1 him2]; *v.* 冒險 [mou6 him2]

risotto *n.* 意大利肉汁燴飯 [yi3 daai6 lei6 yuk9 jap7 wui6 faan6]

ritual *n.* 儀式 [yi4 sik7]; *adj.* 例行公事 [lai6 hang4 gung1 si6]

rival *n.* 對手 [deui3 sau2]; *adj.* 競爭 [ging6 jang1]

rivalry *n.* 競爭 [ging6 jaang1]

river *n.* 河 [ho4], ~ **bank** 河邊, ~ **boat** 河船, ~ **cruise** 游船河

rivulet *n.* 小溪 [siu2 kai1]

Riyadh *n.* 利雅得 [lei6 nga5 dak7]; ~, **capital of Saudi Arabia** 沙特阿拉伯首都

roach *n.* 甲由 [gaat9 jaat9]

road *n.* 道路 [dou6 lou6], ~ **closed** 前路不通, ~ **conditions** 道路狀況, ~ **work** 整路

road map *n.* 路線圖 [lou6 sin3 tou4]

roam *v.* 漫步 [maan6 bou6]

roar *v.* 狂笑 [kwong4 siu3]

roast *adj.* 烤 [haau1]; *n.* 烤肉 [haau1 yuk9], ~ **beef** 烤牛肉

roasted *v.* 烤咗 [haau1 jo2]

rob *v.* 搶劫 [cheung2 gip8]

robbed *adj.* 俾人搶劫 [bei2 yan4 cheung2 gip8], **I was** ~ 我俾人搶劫！

robber *n.* 搶劫犯 [cheung2 gip8 faan2]

robbery *n.* 搶劫 [cheung2 gip8]

robe *n.* 睡袍 [seui6 pou4]

robot *n.* 機器人 [gei1 hei3 yan4]

rock (*stone / music*) *n.* 岩石 [ngaam4 sek9], ~ **band** 搖滾樂團, ~ **and roll** 搖滾; ~ **climbing** 攀岩

rocket *n.* 火箭 [fo2 jin3]

Rococo-style *n.* 落可可風格 [lok9 ho2 ho2 fung1 gaak8]

rod *n.* 杆 [gon1]

roe *n.* 魚籽 [yu4 ji2]

rogue *n.* 無賴 [mou4 laai2]

role *n.* 角色 [gok8 sik7]

roll *n.* 卷 [gyun2], **bread** ~ 麵包卷; *v.* 捲起 [gyun2 hei2], ~ **call** 點名

rolling pin *n.* 麵棍 [min6 gwan3]

romaine (lettuce) *n.* 油麥菜 [yau4 mak9 choi3]

romance *n.* 愛情小說 [oi3 ching4 siu2 syut8]

Romanesque style *n.* 羅馬式建築風格 [lo4 ma5 sik7 gin3 juk7 fung1 gaak8]

Romania *n.* 羅馬尼亞 [lo4 ma5 nei4 a3]

Romanian *adj.* 羅馬尼亞 [lo4 ma5 nei4 a3]

romantic *adj.* 浪漫 [long6 maan6]

Romanticism *n.* 浪漫主義 [long6 maan6 jyu2 yi6]

Rome *n.* 羅馬 [lo4 ma5]

romp *n.* 風流嘢 [fung1 lau4 ye5]

rood *n.* 十字架 [sap9 ji6 ga2]

roof *n.* 屋頂 [uk7 deng2] ~ **rack** 屋架

room *n.* 房 [fong2]; ~ **number** 房間號碼

room rate *n.* 房價 [fong4 ga3]

room service *n.* 房間服務 [fong4 gaan1 fuk9 mou6]

roommate *n.* 室友 [sat7 yau5]

rooster *n.* 公雞 [gung1 gai1]

root *n.* 根 [gan1]

roots (*cultural*) *n.* 祖籍 [jou2 jik9]

rope *n.* 繩 [sing2]

rose *n.* 玫瑰 [mui4 gwai3]

Roseau *n.* 羅索 [lo4 sok8]; ~, **capital of Dominica** 多米尼加首都

rosemary *n.* 迷迭香 [mai4 dit9 heung1]

rostrum *n.* 領獎台 [ling5 jeung2 toi4]

rot *v.* 腐爛 [fu6 laan6]

rotary *n.* 旋轉 [syun4 jyun2]

rotation *n.* 輪班 [leun4 baan1]

rotisserie *adj.* 烤肉架 [haau1 yuk9 ga2]

rotted *adj.* 變質 [bin3 jat7]

rotten *adj.* 腐爛咗 [fu6 laan6 jo2]

rough *adj.* 嚡 [haai4]

roughly *adv.* 大概 [daai6 koi3]

round *adj./n.* 圓形 [yun4 ying4]; *adv./prep.* 周圍 [jau1 wai4]

round-trip *adj.* 來回旅程嘅 [loi4 wui4 leui5 ching4 ge3]

round-trip ticket *n.* 來回票 [loi4 wui4 piu3]

rouse *v.* 叫醒 [giu3 seng2]

rout *v.* 徹底打敗 [chit8 dai2 da2 baai6]

route *n.* 路線 [lou6 sin3]

routine *n.* 常規 [seung4 kwai1]; *adj.* 例行 [lai6 hang4]

rove *v.* 流浪 [lau4 long6]

rover *n.* 傻佬 [so4 lou2]

row 1. *n.* 行 [hong4], **spreadsheet** ~ 數據表橫行 // **2.** *v.* 划艇 [wa4 teng5], ~ **a boat** 划船

rowing *n.* 划艇 [wa4 teng5]

royal *adj.* 王室 [wong4 sat7]

royalty *n.* 忠心 [jung1 sam1]

rub *v.* 磨 [mo4]

rubber *n.* 橡膠 [jeung6 gaau1]

rubbish *n.* 垃圾 [laap9 saap8]

rubble *n.* 碎石 [seui3 sek9]

ruby *n.* 紅寶石 [hung4 bou2 sek9]

rucksack *n.* 帆布包 [faan4 bou3 baau1]

rude *adj.* 冇禮貌 [mou5 lai5 maau6]

rudely *adv.* 冇禮貌 [mou5 lai5 maau6]

rudiment *n.* 雛形 [cho1 ying4]

rudimentary *adj.* 初步 [cho1 bou6]

ruffled *adj.* 唔平 [m4 ping4]

rue *v.* 悔恨 [fui3 han6]

rueful *adj.* 後悔 [hau6 fui3]

rug *n.* 地氈仔 [dei6 jin1 jai2]

rugby *n.* 欖球 [laam2 kau4]

ruffian *n.* 歹徒 [daai2 tou4]

ruffle *v.* 整巢 [jing2 chaau4]

ruin *v.* 破壞 [po3 waai6]; *n.* 遺跡 [wai4 jik7]

ruined *adj.* 荒廢 [fong1 fai3]

ruins *n.* 遺址 [wai4 ji2]

rule *n.* 規定 [kwai1 ding6]; *v.* 統治 [tung2 ji6]

ruler *n.* 統治者 [tung2 ji6 je2]

rules *n.* 規定 [kwai1 ding6]

rum *n.* 朗姆酒 [long5 mou5 jau2]

rumor *n.* 謠言 [yiu4 yin4]

rump *n.* 屁股 [pei3 gu2]

rumpsteak *n.* 牛後髀肉扒 [ngau4 hau6 bei2 yuk9 pa2]

run *v.* 跑 [paau2], ~ **into** (*crash*) 衝入, ~ **out of fuel** 冇油; *n.* 跑步 [paau2 bou6]

runner *n.* 跑步嘅人 [paau2 bou6 ge3 yan4]

running *n./adj.* 跑步 [paau2 bou6]; ~ **shoes** 跑鞋, ~ **water** 水喉水

runny nose *n.* 流鼻水 [lau4 bei6 seui2]

rural *adj.* 農村 [nung4 chyun1]

ruse *n.* 詭計 [gwai2 gai3]

rush v. 趕 [gon2]; n. 高峰 [gou1 fung1]

rush hour n. 高峰期 [gou1 fung1 kei4]

rusk n. 甜麵包乾[tim4 min6 baau1 gon1]

rust n. 鏽 [sau3]; v. 生鏽 [saang1 sau3]

rustic n. 鄉下佬 [heung1 ha5 lou2]

rusticity n. 田園生活 [tin4 yun4 sang1 wut9]

rusty adj. 生咗鏽 [saang1 jo2 sau3]

Russia n. 俄羅斯 [ngo4 lo4 si1]

Russian adj. 俄羅斯 [ngo4 lo4 si1]

Russian Federation n. 俄羅斯聯邦 [ngo4 lo4 si1 lyun4 bong1]

rustic adj. 鄉下 [heung1 ha5], ~ **flavor** 鄉村風味

rut n. 發情期 [faat8 ching4 kei4]

rutabaga n. 甘藍 [gam1 laam4]

Rwanda n. 盧旺達 [lou4 wong6 daat9]

Rwandan adj. 盧旺達 [lou4 wong6 daat9]

rye n. 黑麥 [hak7 mak9]; adj. 用黑麥整嘅 [yung6 hak7 mak9 jing2 ge3], ~ **bread** 黑麥麵包

S

Sabbath *n.* 安息日 [on1 sik7 yat9]

sabotage *n.* 破壞 [po3 waai6]

saccharin *n.* 糖精 [tong4 jing1]

sack 1. *n.* 麻包袋 [ma4 baau1 doi2] // **2.** *v.* 搶 [cheung2]

sacrament *n.* 聖禮 [sing3 lai5]

sacred *adj.* 神聖 [san4 sing3]

sacrilege *n.* 褻瀆 [sit8 duk9]

sad *adj.* 難過 [naan4 gwo3]

saddle *n.* 馬鞍 [ma5 on1]

saddle of lamb *n.* 羊鞍肉 [yeung4 on1 yuk9]

sadism *n.* 瘧待狂 [yeuk9 doi6 kwong4]

sadly *adv.* 難過 [naan4 gwo3]

sadness *n.* 難過 [naan4 gwo3]

safe 1. *adj.* 安全嘅 [on1 chyun4 ge3], ~ **sex** 安全性交, **feel ~** 覺得安全 // **2.** *n.* 保險箱 [bou2 him2 seung1]

safely *adv.* 安全 [on1 chyun4]

safety *n.* 安全 [on1 chyun4]; ~ **pins** 回形針

safflower oil *n.* 紅花油 [hung4 fa1 yau4]

saffron *n.* 藏紅花 [jong6 hung4 fa1]

sagacious *adj.* 精明 [jing1 ming4]

sagacity *n.* 精明 [jing1 ming4]

sage *n.* 聖人 [sing3 yan4]

Sagittarius *n.* 射手座 [se6 sau2 jo6]

sail *v./n.* 出海 [cheut7 hoi1]

sailing *n.* 出海 [cheut7 hoi1]; ~ **instructor** 帆船教練; ~ **club** 航海俱樂部

sailor *n.* 水手 [seui2 sau2]

saint *n.* 聖人 [sing3 yan4]

Saint George's *n.* 聖佐治 [sing3 jo3 ji6]; ~, **capital of Grenada** 格林納達首都

Saint John's *n.* 聖約翰 [sing3 yeuk8 hon6]; ~, **capital of Antigua and Barbuda** 安提瓜同巴布達首都

Saint Kitts and Nevis *n.* 聖克里斯托弗和尼維斯島 [sing3 hak7 lei5 si1 tok8 fat7 wo4 nei4 wai4 si1 dou2]

Saint Lucia *n.* 聖盧西亞島 [sing3 lou4 sai1 a3 dou2]

Saint Vincent and the Grenadines *n.* 聖文森特和格林納丁斯 [sing3 man4 sam1 dak9 wo4 gaak8 lam4 naap9 ding1 si1]

salad *n.* 沙律 [sa1 leut2]; ~ **bar** 沙律吧

salami *n.* 薩拉米香腸 [saat8 laai1 mai5 heung1 cheung2]

salary *n.* 人工 [yan4 gung1]

sale *n.* 大減價 [daai6 gaam2 ga3]

sales *n.* 銷路 [siu1 lou6]; ~ **clerk** 推銷員, ~ **department** 銷售部

sales receipt *n.* 收據 [sau1 geui3]

sales tax *n.* 銷售稅 [siu1 sau6 seui3]

saliva *n.* 口水 [hau2 seui2]

salmon *n.* 三文魚 [saam1 man4 yu2]

salmon mousse *n.* 三文魚慕斯 [saam1 man4 yu4 mou6 si1]

salon *n.* 美容院 [mei5 yung4 yun2]

salsa *n.* 辣蕃茄醬 [laat9 faan1 ke2 jeung3], **hot ~** 特辣蕃茄醬, **mild ~** 中辣蕃茄醬, **spicy ~** 辣蕃茄醬

salt *n.* 鹽 [yim4]

salt shaker *n.* 鹽瓶 [yim4 ping4]

salted *adj.* 鹽醃 [yim4 yip8]

salty *adj.* 鹹 [haam4]

salutation *n.* 致意 [ji3 yi3]

salute *v.* 敬禮 [ging3 lai5]

Salvadoran *n.* 薩爾瓦多 [saat8 yi5 nga5 do1]

salvage *v.* 搶救 [cheung2 gau3]

salvation *n.* 救世主 [gau3 sai3 jyu2]

same *adj./pron.* 一樣 [yat7 yeung6]; **if it's the ~ to you ...** 如果你情況都一樣, **the ~ thing** 同一樣野, **I'll have the ~** 我都點同一樣野

Samoa *n.* 薩摩亞群島 [saat8 mo1 a3 kwan4 dou2]

Samoan *adj.* 薩摩亞 [saat8 mo1 a3]

sample *n.* 樣板 [yeung6 baan2]

sanatorium *n.* 療養院 [liu4 yeung5 yun2]

sanctification *n.* 神聖化 [san4 sing3 fa3]

sanctify *v.* 清洗罪孽 [ching1 sai2 jeui6 yip9]

sanction *n.* 認可 [ying6 ho2]

sanctuary *n.* 聖地 [sing3 dei6]

sandal *n.* 涼鞋 [leung4 haai4]

sanitary napkin *n.* 衛生巾 [wai6 sang1 gan1]

San Jose *n.* 聖荷西 [sing3 ho4 sai1]; **~, capital of Costa Rica** 哥斯達黎加首都

San Marino *n.* 聖馬力諾 [sing3 ma5 lik9 nok9]

San Salvador *n.* 聖薩爾瓦多 [sing3 saat8 yi5 nga5 do1]; **~, capital of El Salvador** 薩爾瓦多首都

Sanaa *n.* 薩那 [saat8 na5]; **~, capital of Yemen** 也門首都

sand *n.* 沙 [sa1]

sandals *n.* 拖鞋 [to1 haai2]

sandwich *n.* 三文治 [saam1 man4 ji6], **ham and cheese ~** 火腿芝士三文治, **veggie ~** 素菜三文治, **turkey ~** 火雞三文治

sandy *adj.* 有沙 [yau5 sa1], **~ beach** 沙灘

sanitary napkin *n.* 衛生巾 [wai6 sang1 gan1]

Santiago *n.* 聖地牙哥 [sing3 dei6 nga4 go1]; **~, capital of Chile** 智利首都

Santo Domingo *n.* 聖多明各 [sing3 do1 ming4 gok8]; **~, capital of Dominican Republic** 多米尼加共和國首都

Sao Tome *n.* 聖多美 [sing3 do1 mei5]; **~, capital of Sao Tome and Principe** 聖多美和普林西比首都

Sao Tome and Principe *n.* 聖多美和普林西比 [sing3 do1 mei5 wo4 pou2 lam4 sai1 bei2]

sapling *n.* 樹仔 [syu6 jai2]

sapphire *n.* 藍寶石 [laam4 bou2 sek9]

Sarajevo *n.* 薩拉熱窩 [saat8 laai1 yit9 wo1]; ~, **capital of Bosnia and Herzegovina** 波黑首都

sarcasm *n.* 諷刺 [fung3 chi3]

sardine *n.* 沙甸魚 [sa1 din1 yu2]

Satan *n.* 撒旦 [saat8 daan3]

satellite *n.* 衛星 [wai6 sing1]; ~ **dish** 碟形衛星電視天線, ~ **TV** 衛星電視

satin *n.* 綢緞 [chau4 dyun6]

satire *n.* 諷刺 [fung3 chi3]

satisfaction *n.* 滿意 [mun5 yi3]

satisfied *adj.* 滿意 [mun5 yi3], **I'm not ~ with this** 我唔滿意

satisfy *v.* 令…滿意 [ling4 … mun5 yi3]; **to ~** 取悅

satisfying *adj.* 令人滿意 [ling4 yan4 mun5 yi3]

saturate *v.* 整濕 [jing2 sap7]

saturated *v.* 濕晒 [sap7 saai3]; ~ **fat** 飽和脂肪

saturation *n.* 飽和度 [baau2 wo4 dou6]

Saturday *n.* 禮拜六 [lai5 baai3 luk9]

sauce *n.* 汁 [jap7]

saucepan *n.* 平底鑊 [ping4 dai2 wok9]

saucer *n.* 杯托 [bui1 tok8]

Saudi Arabia *n.* 沙特阿拉伯 [sa1 dak9 a3 laai1 baak8]

sauerkraut *n.* 德國鹹酸菜 [dak7 gwok8 haam4 syun1 choi3]

sauna *n.* 桑拿 [song1 na4]

sausage *n.* 香腸 [heung1 cheung2]

sautéed *n.* 爆炒 [baau3 chaau2]

savage *adj.* 兇殘 [hung1 chaan4]; *n.* 野蠻人 [ye5 maan4 yan4]

save *v.* 救 [gau3] *n.* 救援 [gau3 wun4]

saving *n.* 存錢 [chyun4 chin2]; ~**s account** 儲蓄存款賬號, **life ~s** 成世嘅積蓄

savior *n.* 救星 [gau3 sing1]

savor *n.* 味 [mei6] **to ~** 欣賞

savory *adj.* 好食 [hou3 sik9]

saw 1. (*tool*) *n.* 鋸 [geu3] // **2.** *v. past tense of* "**see**"

say *v.* 講 [gong2], **Can you ~ it again?** 你可唔可以再講一次?, **How do you ~ …?** 你話點?, **Can you ~ it in English?** 請你用英文再講一次好嗎?

saying *n.* 話 [wa6]

scab *n.* 痂 [ga1]

scald *v.* 炳親 [naat8 chan1]

scalding *adj.* 好炳 [hou2 naat8]

scaffold *n.* 斷頭台 [dyun6 tau4 toi4]

scale 1. *v.* 秤 [ching3] // **2.** *n.* 規模 [kwai1 mou4]

scales *n.* 魚鱗 [yu4 leun4]

scallops *n.* 扇貝 [sin3 bui3]

scalp *n.* 頭皮 [tau4 pei4]

scalpel *n.* 手術刀 [sau2 seut9 dou1]

scandal *n.* 醜聞 [chau2 man4]

scan *v./n.* 掃描 [sou3 miu4]

scanner *n.* 掃描器 [sou3 miu4 hei3]

scapegoat *n.* 替死鬼 [tai3 sei2 gwai2]

scar *n.* 疤 [ba1]

scare *v.* 嚇 [haak8]; *n.* 恐懼 [hung2 geui6]

scared *adj.* 驚 [geng1]

scarf *n.* 頸巾 [geng2 gan1]

scary *adj.* 得人驚 [dak7 yan4 geng1]

scatter *v.* 散開 [saan3 hoi1]

scattered *adj.* 分散 [fan1 saan3]

scene *n.* 景色 [ging2 sik7]

scenery *n.* 風景 [fung1 ging2]

schedule *n.* 時間表 [si4 gaan1 biu2]; *v.* 安排 [on1 paai4]; **~d flight** *n.* 定期航班 [ding6 kei4 hong4 baan1]

scheme *n.* 密謀 [mat9 mau4]

schmear *n.* 事 [si6]

schnitzel *n.* 炸肉排 [ja3 yuk9 paai4]

scholar *n.* 學者 [hok9 je2]

school *n.* 學校 [hok9 haau6]

sciatica *n.* 坐骨神經痛 [jo6 gwat7 san4 ging1 tung3]

science *n.* 科學 [fo1 hok9]; **~ fiction** 科幻小說

scientific *adj.* 科學 [fo1 hok9]

scientist *n.* 科學家 [fo1 hok9 ga1]

scissors *n.* 鉸剪 [gaau3 jin2]

scone *n.* 英式鬆餅 [ying1 sik7 sung1 beng2]

scope *n.* 範圍 [faan6 wai4]

score *n.* 分數 [fan1 sou3]; *v.* 記分 [gei3 fan1]

scoreboard *n.* 記分板 [gei3 fan1 baan2]

Scorpio *n.* 天蠍座 [tin1 kit8 jo6]

scorpion *n.* 蠍子 [kit8 ji2]

scotch *n.* 威士忌 [wai1 si6 gei6]

Scotland *n.* 蘇格蘭 [sou1 gaak8 laan4]

Scottish *adj.* 蘇格蘭 [sou1 gaak8 laan4]

scramble *v.* 爬 [pa4]

scrambled *adj.* 混亂 [wan6 lyun6], **~ eggs** 炒蛋

scrape *v./n.* 刮 [gwaat8] *n.* 刮 [gwaat8], **a ~** 刮痕

scratch *v.* 睇 [ngaau1]; *n.* 睇痕 [ngaau1 han4]

scream *v./n.* 尖叫 [jim1 giu3]

screen *n.* 屏幕 [ping2 mok9], **~ door** 紗門, **computer ~** 電腦屏幕; *v.* 放映 [fong3 ying2], **~ phone calls** 睇來電決定接唔接電話

screw *n.* 螺絲 [lo4 si1]; *v.* 擰緊 [ning6 gan2]

screwdriver *n.* 螺絲批 [lo4 si1 pai1]

script *n.* 劇本 [kek9 bun2]

sculptor *n.* 雕刻家 [diu1 haak7 ga1]

sculpture *n.* 雕像 [diu1 jeung6]

sea *n.* 海 [hoi2], **~ level** 海平面, **inland ~** 地中海

sea bass *n.* 海鱸 [hoi2 lou4]

sea bream *n.* 海鯛 [hoi2 diu1]

sea kale *n.* 海甘藍 [hoi2 gam1 laam4]

sea perch *n.* 海鱸魚 [hoi2 lou4 yu4]

sea snails *n.* 海螺 [hoi2 lo2]

sea urchin *n.* 海膽 [hoi2 daam2]

seafood *n.* 海鮮 [hoi2 sin1]

seal *v.* 密封 [mat9 fung1]; **to ~ closed** 黏好

sear *v.* 燒燶 [siu1 nung1]

search *n./v.* 搜查 [sau2 cha4]

search engine *comp. n.* 搜索引擎 [sau2 sok8 yan5 king4]

search warrant (*legal*) *n.* 搜查令 [sau2 cha4 ling4]

seashore *n.* 海邊 [hoi2 bin1]

seasick *adj.* 暈船浪 [wan4 syun4 long6]

season v. 季節 [gwai3 jit8]

seasonal adj. 季節性 [gwai3 jit8 sing3]

seasoned adj. 調好味 [tiu4 hou2 mei6]

seasoning n. 調味料 [tiu4 mei6 liu6]

seat n. 位 [wai2]; ~ **reservation** 訂座, **Excuse me, you're in my** ~ 唔好意思，你坐咗我 嘅位

seat belt n. 安全帶 [on1 chyun4 daai2]

seat number n. 座號 [jo6 hou6]

seawater n. 海水 [hoi2 seui2]

seaweed n. 海帶 [hoi2 daai3]; ~ **wrap** 海帶卷

second 1. (*number*) n./adv. 第 二 [dai6 yi6] // **2.** (*time*) n. 秒 [miu5], **ten** ~**s** 好快

second opinion n. 第二意見 [dai6 yi6 yi3 gin3]

secondary adj. 中等 [jung1 dang2]

secondhand n. 二手 [yi6 sau2], ~ **bookstore** 二手書店, ~ **goods** 二手嘢, ~ **store** n. 二手店

secret adj./n. 秘密 [bei3 mat9]

secretary n. 秘書 [bei3 syu1]

secretly adv. 秘密 [bei3 mat9]

section v. 切開 [chit8 hoi1], **to** ~ **parts of meat** 切一部分嘅 肉; n. 節 [jit8] **a** ~ 一部分, **vegetables** ~ 蔬菜部

sector n. 部門 [bou6 mun4]

secular adj. 世俗 [sai3 juk9]

secure adj. 安全 [on1 chyun4]; v. 獲得 [wok9 dak7]

security n. 安全 [on1 chyun4]

sedative n. 鎮定劑 [jan3 ding6 jai1]

sediment n. 沈澱 [cham4 din6]

see v. 見 [gin3], ~ **you later!** 拜 拜, ~ **you soon!** 拜拜, **Can you** ~ **it?** 你睇唔睇到?

seeds n. 種子 [jung2 ji2]

seek v. 搵 [wan2]

seem v. 好似 [hou2 chi5]

segment n. 部分 [bou6 fan6]; v. 劃分 [waak9 fan1]

seizure n. 沒收 [mut9 sau1]

select v. 揀 [gaan2]; adj. 揀擇 [gaan2 jaak9]

selection n. 選擇 [syun2 jaak9]

self n. 自己 [ji6 gei2]

self-defense n. 自衛 [ji6 wai6]

self-employed 自己做生意 [ji6 gei2 jou6 sang1 yi3]

selfish adj. 自私 [ji6 si1]

self-service n. 自助 [ji6 jo6]

sell v. 賣 [maai6]; ~**by date** 保 質期

seller n. 賣家 [maai6 ga1]

semicolon n. 分號 [fan1 hou6]

seminar n. 研討會 [yin4 tou2 wui2]

semi-sweet adj. 半甜 [bun3 tim4]

semolina pudding n. 小麥布甸 [siu2 mak9 bou3 din1]

senate n. 參議院 [chaam1 yi5 yun2]

senator n. 參議員 [chaam1 yi5 yun4]

send v. 發 [faat8]

sender n. 寄信人 [gei3 seun3 yan4]

Senegal n. 塞內加爾 [choi3 noi6 ga1 yi5]

Senegalese adj. 塞內加爾 [choi3 noi6 ga1 yi5]

senior *n.* 長者 [jeung2 je2]; *adj.* 年長嘅 [nin4 jeung2 ge3], ~ **citizen** 老年人, ~ **discount** 老年人折扣

sense *n.* 理性 [lei5 sing3]

sensible *adj.* 明智 [ming4 ji3]

sensitive *adj.* 敏感 [man5 gam2]

sensitivity *n.* 敏感 [man5 gam2]

sentence *n.* 句子 [geui3 ji2]

Seoul *n.* 首爾 [sau2 yi5]; ~, **capital of Korea** 南韓首都

separate *adj.* 分開咗 [fan1 hoi1 jo2]; *v.* 分開 [fan1 hoi1]

separated *adj.* 分居 [fan1 geui1]

separately *adv.* 一個個 [yat7 go3 go3], **wash** ~ 分開洗

separation *n.* 分開 [fan1 hoi1]

September (*abbr.* **Sept.**) *n.* 九月份 [gau2 yut9 fan6]

sequence *n.* 一連串 [yat7 lin4 chyun3]; *v.* 按順序排列 [on3 seun6 jeui6 paai4 lit9]

sequential *adj.* 按順序 [on3 seun6 jeui6]

sequester *v.* 隔離 [gaak8 lei4]

Serbia *n.* 塞爾維亞 [choi3 yi5 wai4 a3]

Serbian *adj.* 塞爾維亞 [choi3 yi5 wai4 a3]

series *n.* 一連串 [yat7 lin4 chyun3]

serious *adj.* 嚴重 [yim4 jung6]

seriously *adv.* 認真 [ying6 jan1]

serum *n.* 血清 [hyut8 ching1]

servant *n.* 傭人 [yung4 yan4]

serve *v.* 服務 [fuk9 mou6]

server (*tech.*) *n.* 服務器 [fuk9 mou6 hei3]

service *n.* 服務 [fuk9 mou6], **car** ~ 接送服務, ~ **charge** 服務費

serving tray *n.* 托盤 [tok8 pun2]

sesame *n.* 芝麻 [ji1 ma4], ~ **seeds** 芝麻, ~ **powder** 芝麻粉, ~ **seed bun** 芝麻包

session *n.* 開庭 [hoi1 ting4]

set 1. *v.* 設定 [chit8 ding6], ~ **fire to** 放火 // **2.** *n.* 一系列 [yat7 hai6 lit9], **dinner** ~ 晚飯整好咗 // **3.** *adj.* 固定 [gu3 ding6]

setting *n.* 背景 [bui3 ging2], **place** ~ 餐位餐具, **dinner** ~ 晚飯餐位

settle *v.* 解決 [gaai2 kyut8]

settlement *n.* 協議 [hip8 yi5]

setup *n.* 設立 [chit8 laap9]

seven *num.* 七 [chat7]

seventeen *num.* 十七 [sap9 chat7]

seventeenth *adj.* 第十七個 [dai6 sap9 chat7 go3]

seventh *adj.* 第七個 [dai6 chat7 go3]

seventieth *adj.* 第七十個 [dai6 chat7 sap9 go3]

seventy *num.* 七十 [chat7 sap9]

several *det./pron.* 好幾個 [hou2 gei2 go3]

severe *adj.* 十分嚴重 [sap9 fan1 yim4 jung6]

severely *adv.* 十分嚴重 [sap9 fan1 yim4 jung6]

sew *v.* 車 [che1]

sewing *n.* 車衫 [che1 saam1]

sewing machine *n.* 衣車 [yi1 che1]

sex *n.* 性別 [sing3 bit9]; **have** ~ 性交

sexism *n.* 性別歧視 [sing3 bit9 kei4 si6]

sexual *adj.* 性別 [sing3 bit9], ~ **relations** 性關係

sexuality *n.* 性取向 [sing3 cheui2 heung3]

sexually *adv.* 性別上 [sing3 bit9 seung6]

sexy *adj.* 性感 [sing3 gam2]

Seychelles *n.* 塞舌爾 [choi3 sit8 yi5]

shade *n.* 陰涼 [yam1 leung4]

shadow *n.* 影 [ying2]; **cast a ~** 蒙上陰影

shady *adj.* 陰涼 [yam1 leung4]

shake *v.* 搖 [yiu4]; *n.* 震 [jan3]

shakes (*malaise*) *n.* 奶昔 [naai5 sik7]

shall *v.* 就快 [jau6 faai3]

shallots *n.* 蔥 [chung1]

shallow *adj.* 淺 [chin2], **~ end** 淺水區, **a ~ person** 膚淺嘅人

shame *n.* 丟架 [diu1 ga2]

shampoo *n.* 洗頭水 [sai2 tau4 seui2]

shank (*top of leg*) *n.* 腳瓜囊 [geuk8 gwa1 nong1]

shape *v.* 塑造 [sou3 jou6]; *n.* 形狀 [ying4 jong6]

shaped *adj.* 啱身嘅 [ngaam1 san1 ge3]

share *v.* 分享 [fan1 heung2]; *n.* 股份 [gu2 fan2]

shareholder *n.* 股東 [gu2 dung1]

shark *n.* 鯊魚 [sa1 yu2], **~ steak** 鯊魚扒, **~ fin** 魚翅, **~ tail** 鯊魚尾

sharp *adj.* 利 [lei6]; **~-edged** 利

sharply *adv.* 急 [gap7]

shave *v.* 剃鬚 [tai3 sou1], **~ one's face** 剃鬚

shaver *n.* 剃刀 [tai3 dou1]

shaving brush *n.* 剃鬚刷 [tai3 sou1 chaat2]

shaving cream *n.* 剃鬚膏 [tai3 sou1 gou1]

she *pron.* 佢 [keui5]

sheep *n.* 綿羊 [min4 yeung2]; **~'s milk cheese** 羊奶芝士

sheer *adj.* 純粹 [seun4 seui6]

sheet *n.* 床單 [chong4 daan1]

shelf *n.* 架 [ga2]

shell *v.* 剝殼 [mok7 hok8]; *n.* 殼 [hok8], **oyster ~** 龍蝦殼, **clam ~** 蜆殼

shellfish *n.* 貝殼類動物 [bui3 hok3 leui6 dung6 mat9]

shelter *n.* 收容所 [sau1 yung4 so2] *v.* 收容 [sau1 yung4]

shepherd's pie *n.* 牧羊人批 [muk9 yeung4 yan4 pai1]

sherbet *n.* 冰凍果汁 [bing1 dung3 gwo2 jap7], **lemon ~** 檸檬冰凍果汁, **orange ~** 冰凍橙汁

sheriff *n.* 警長 [ging2 jeung2]

sherry *n.* 雪梨酒 [syut8 lei4 jau2], **~ glass** 高腳酒杯

shield *n.* 盾 [teun5]; *v.* 保護 [bou2 wu6]

shift *v.* 換 [wun6], **~ gears** 換檔; *n.* 輪班 [leun4 baan1]; *comp.* **~ key** 換檔鍵

shiitake mushroom *n.* 香菇 [heung1 gu1]

shine *v.* 發光 [faat8 gwong1]

shiny *adj.* 發光 [faat8 gwong1]

ship *n.* 船 [syun4]; *v.* 用船運 [yung6 syun4 wan6]

shipping charge *n.* 運費 [wan6 fai3]

shirt *n.* 恤衫 [seut7 saam1]

shish kebab *n.* 羊肉串 [yeung4 yuk9 chyun3], **chicken ~** 雞肉串, **lamb ~** 羊肉串

shivers *n.* 打冷震 [da2 laang5 jan3]

shock *n.* 打擊 [da2 gik7]; *v.* 嚇 [haak8]

shock absorber *n.* 緩衝器 [wun6 chung1 hei3]

shocked *adj.* 震驚 [jan3 ging1]

shocking *adj.* 得人驚 [dak7 yan4 geng1]

shockproof *adj.* 抗震 [kong3 jan3]

shoe *n.* 鞋 [haai4]; **~ repair shop** 繡鞋鋪; **~ store** 鞋店; **~ polisher** 刷鞋佬

shoestring *adj.* 小本經營 [siu2 bun2 ging1 ying4]

shoot *v.* 開槍 [hoi1 cheung1]; **~ing** 槍戰; **bamboo ~** 竹筍

shop *n.* 店 [dim3]; *v.* 行街 [haang4 gaai1]

shopkeeper *n.* 店主 [dim3 jyu2]

shoplifting *n.* 偷嘢 [tau1 ye5]

shopping *n.* 行街 [haang4 gaai1]; **~ cart** 購物車, **go ~** 行街

shopping basket *n.* 購物籃 [kau3 mat9 laam5]

shopping center/mall *n.* 購物中心 [kau3 mat9 jung1 sam1]

shore *n.* 海岸 [hoi2 ngon6]

short *adj.* 短 [dyun2], **~ story** 短篇小說

shortage *n.* 缺點 [kyut8 dim2]

shortcake *n.* 脆餅 [cheui3 beng2] **strawberry ~** 草莓脆餅

shortly *adv.* 好快 [hou2 faai3]

shorts *n.* 短褲 [dyun2 fu3]

short-sighted *adj.* 短視 [dyun2 si6]

short-term parking *n.* 暫時停車 [jaam6 si4 ting4 che1]

shot (*gun/injection*) *n.* 射擊 [se6 gik7]

should *v.* 應該 [ying1 goi1]

shoulder *n.* 膊頭 [bok8 tau4]

shout *v.* 叫 [giu3]; *n.* 大叫 [daai6 giu3]

shovel *n.* 鏟 [chaan2]

show *v.* 表明 [biu2 ming4], **Can you ~ me?** 你示範俾我睇, 好唔好?; *n.* 演出 [yin2 cheut7]

shower *n.* 沖涼 [chung1 leung4] **~ room** 沖涼房, **rain ~** 陣雨, **baby ~** 迎嬰派對, **bridal ~** 新娘送禮會

shred *v.* 撕爛 [si1 laan6]

shrimp *n.* 蝦 [ha1]; **butterfly ~** 蝴蝶蝦, **~ scampi** *n.* 蒜蓉忌廉大蝦 [syun3 yung4 gei6 lim1 daai6 ha1]

shrine *n.* 神龕 [san4 ham1]

shut *v.* 關 [gwaan1]; *adj.* 關咗嘅 [gwaan1 jo2 ge3]

shutoff valve *n.* 截流閥 [jit9 lau4 fat9]

shutter (*window/camera*) *n.* 百葉窗 [baak8 yip9 cheung1]

shuttle (**~ service**) *n.* 快線 [faai3 sin3]

shy *adj.* 怕丑 [pa3 chau2]

siblings *n.* 兄弟姊妹 [hing1 dai6 ji2 mui6]

sick *adj.* 病咗 [beng6 jo2], **I feel ~** 我病咗, **car ~** 暈車, **~ to one's stomach** 兀突到死, **~ in the head** 有精神病

sickness *n.* 病 [beng6]

side *n.* 邊 [bin1], **~ effects** 副作用, **~ mirror** 側鏡, **~ order** 配菜, **~ street** 小路, **back~** 後面, **~ dish** *n.* 配菜

sidebar 工具欄 [gung1 geui6 laan4]

sidewalk *n.* 人行道 [yan4 hang4 dou6]

sideways *adj./adv.* 斜埋一邊 [che3 maai4 yat7 bin1]

Sierra Leone *n.* 塞拉利昂 [choi3 laai1 lei6 ngong4]

Sierra Leonean *adj.* 塞拉利昂 [choi3 laai1 lei6 ngong4]

sieve *n.* 篩 [sai1]; *v.* 篩選 [sai1 syun2]

sift *v.* 篩 [sai1]

sight *n.* 視力 [si6 lik9]

sights *n.* 視力 [si6 lik9]

sightseeing *n.* 觀光 [gun1 gwong1]; **go ~** 旅遊

sightseeing tour *n.* 觀光旅遊 [gun1 gwong1 leui5 yau4]

sign *n.* 標記 [biu1 gei3]; *v.* 做標記 [jou6 biu1 gei3]

signal *n.* 信號 [seun3 hou6]; *v.* 發信號 [faat8 seun3 hou6]

signature *n.* 簽名 [chim1 meng4]

significance *n.* 重要性 [jung6 yiu3 sing3]

significant *adj.* 重要 [jung6 yiu3]

significantly *adv.* 顯著 [hin2 jyu3]

signpost *n.* 路標 [lou6 biu1]

silence *n.* 唔出聲 [m4 cheut7 seng1]

silent *adj.* 唔出聲 [m4 cheut7 seng1]

silk *n.* 絲綢 [si1 chau4]

silly *adj.* 傻 [so4]

silver *n./adj.* 銀 [ngan2], **~plate** 銀碟, **~ware** 銀器

similar *adj.* 相似 [seung1 chi5]

similarly *adv.* 相似 [seung1 chi5]

simmer *v.* 燉 [dan6]

simple *adj.* 簡單 [gaan2 daan1]

simply *adv.* 直情 [jik9 ching4]

sin *n.* 罪孽 [jeui6 yip9]

since *prep./conj.* 自從 [ji6 chung4]; *adv.* 以後 [yi5 hau6]

sincere *adj.* 真誠 [jan1 sing4]

sincerely *adv.* 衷心 [chung1 sam1]

sing *v.* 唱 [cheung3]

Singapore *n.* 新加坡 [san1 ga3 bo1]; **~, capital of Singapore** 新加坡首都

Singaporean *adj.* 新加坡 [san1 ga3 bo1]

singe *v.* 燙傷 [tong3 seung1]

singer *n.* 歌星 [go1 sing1]

singing *n.* 唱歌 [cheung3 go1]

single *adj.* 單身 [daan1 san1]; *n.* 單程票 [daan1 ching4 piu3]

singular *n./adj.* 單數 [daan1 sou3]

sink *n.* 水池 [seui2 chi4]; *v.* 沉 [cham4]

sir *n.* 先生 [sin1 saang1]

siren *n.* 警笛聲 [ging2 dek9 seng1]

sirloin *n.* 牛腩 [ngau4 naam5], **~ steak** 西冷牛扒

sister *n.* 姊妹 [ji2 mui6]

sit *v.* 坐 [cho5]; **~ down, please** 請坐

site *n.* 場地 [cheung4 dei6]; **web~** 網站

situation *n.* 情況 [ching4 fong3]

six *num.* 六 [luk9]

sixteen *num.* 十六 [sap9 luk9]

sixteenth *adj.* 第十六個 [dai6 sap9 luk9 go3]

sixth *adj.* 第六個 [dai6 luk9 go3]

sixtieth *adj.* 第六十個 [dai6 luk9 sap9 go3]

sixty *num.* 六十 [luk9 sap9]

size *n.* 碼 [ma5]

skate *v.* 溜冰 [lau4 bing1]

skates *n.* 溜冰鞋 [lau4 bing1 haai4]

skeleton *n.* 骨架 [gwat7 ga3]

sketch *n.* 素描 [sou3 miu4]; *v.* 畫素描 [waat9 sou3 miu4]

skewer *v.* 串成一串 [chyun3 sing4 yat7 chyun3]

skewered *adj.* 串好 [chyun3 hou2], ~ **kebab** *n.* 肉串 [yuk9 chyun3]

ski *v.* 滑雪 [waat9 syut8], ~ **boots** 雪靴, ~ **lifts** 滑雪纜車, ~ **poles** 滑雪杆, ~ **school** 滑雪學校, ~ **trail** 滑雪道, ~**ing** 滑雪, ~**er** 滑雪者, ~**s** *n.* 滑雪 [waat9 syut8]

skill *n.* 技能 [gei6 nang4]

skilled *adj.* 熟練 [suk9 lin6]

skillet *n.* 長柄鑊 [cheung4 beng3 wok9]

skillful *adj.* 有技能 [yau5 gei6 nang4]

skillfully *adv.* 有技巧 [yau5 gei6 haau2]

skim milk *n.* 脫脂奶 [tyut8 ji1 naai5]

skin *n.* 皮膚 [pei4 fu1]

skinned *adj.* 剝咗皮 [mok7 jo2 pei4], ~ **almonds** 無皮杏仁

skirt *n.* 裙 [kwan4]

Skopje *n.* 斯科普里 [si1 fo1 pou2 lei5]; ~, **capital of Macedonia** 馬其頓王國首都

skull *n.* 頭骨 [tau4 gwat7]

sky *n.* 天 [tin1]

slang *n.* 俗語 [juk9 yu5]

slash *n.* 亂劈 [lyun6 pek8]

slaw *n.* 捲心菜[gyun2 sam1 choi3], **cole ~** 捲心菜沙律, **apple ~** 蘋果絲沙律, **cabbage ~** 大白菜絲沙律

sleep *v.* 瞓 [fan3]; *n.* 瞓覺 [fan3 gaau3]

sleeper *n.* 臥鋪 [ngo6 pou1]

sleeping bag *n.* 睡袋 [seui6 doi2]

sleeping car *n.* 臥鋪 [ngo6 pou1]

sleeping pills *n.* 安眠藥 [on1 min4 yeuk9]

sleepy *adj.* 眼瞓 [ngaan5 fan3]

sleeve *n.* 手袖 [sau2 jau6]

slice *n.* 一塊 [yat7 faai3]; *v.* 切成塊 [chit8 sing4 faai3]; ~**s** 一塊塊; *adj.* 切塊 [chit8 faai3]; ~**d meats** *n.* 肉片 [yuk9 pin2]

slide *v.* 滑 [waat9]

slides (*photographic*) *n.* 幻燈片 [waan6 dang1 pin2]

slight *adj.* 微小 [mei4 siu2]

slightly *adv.* 略略 [leuk9 leuk9]

slim *adj.* 苗條 [miu4 tiu4]

sling *n.* 吊帶 [diu3 daai2]

slip *v.* 跌低 [dit8 dai1]

slippers *n.* 拖鞋 [to1 haai2]

slope *n.* 斜坡 [che3 bo1]; *v.* 傾斜 [king1 che4]

Slovak *adj.* 斯洛伐克 [si1 lok8 fat9 hak7]

Slovakia *n.* 斯洛伐克 [si1 lok8 fat9 hak7]

Slovakian *adj.* 斯洛伐克人 [si1 lok8 fat9 hak7 yan4]

Slovenia *n.* 斯洛文尼亞 [si1 lok8 man4 nei4 a3]

Slovenian *adj.* 斯洛文尼亞 [si1 lok8 man4 nei4 a3]

slow *adj.* 慢 [maan6], ~ **traffic** 車輛前進緩慢; *v.* 減速 [gaam2 chuk7], ~ **down!** *phr.* 慢啲！

slowly *adv.* 慢 [maan6]

SLR camera *n.* 單反相機 [daan1 faan2 seung1 gei1]

small *adj.* 細 [sai3], ~ **change** 小改變

smaller *adj.* 細啲 [sai3 di1]

smart *adj.* 醒目 [sing2 muk9]

smash *v./n.* 撞爛 [jong6 laan6]

smell *v.* 聞 [man4]; *n.* 氣味 [hei3 mei6], **What's that ~?** 咩嘢味？

smile *v.* 微笑 [mei4 siu3]; *n.* 笑容 [siu3 yung4]

smoke *n.* 煙 [yin1] *v.* 食煙 [sik9 yin1]

smoked *adj.* 煙薰 [yin1 fan1], ~ **meat** 煙肉, ~ **bacon** 煙肉, ~ **salmon** 煙三文魚

smoker *n.* 煙民 [yin1 man4]

smoking *n.* 食煙 [sik9 yin1], **No ~** *phr.* 禁止吸煙

smooth *adj.* 滑 [waat9]

smoothie *n.* 冰沙 [bing1 sa1], **fruit ~** 水果冰沙

smoothly *adv.* 順利 [seun6 lei6]

snack *n.* 零食 [ling4 sik9]

snack bar *n.* 小食店 [siu2 sik9 dim3]

snail *n.* 蝸牛 [wo1 ngau4]

snake *n.* 蛇 [se4]

sneakers *n.* 運動鞋 [wan6 dung6 haai4]

snipe *n. (rude person)* 卑鄙小人 [bei1 pei2 siu2 yan4]; *v.* 中傷 [jung3 seung1]

snorkel *n.* 潛水吸氣管 [chim4 seui2 kap7 hei3 gun2]

snow *n.* 雪 [syut8], **powdered ~** 粉狀雪, **fresh ~** 初雪, **wet ~** 雪水, ~**storm** 暴風雪; *v.* 落雪 [lok9 syut8]; ~ **tires** 雪地防滑輪胎,

so *adv.* 咁 [gam3]; *conj.* 所以, ~ **that** 所以

soap *n.* 番梘 [faan1 gaan2]

soap opera *n.* 電視連續劇 [din6 si6 lin4 juk9 kek9]

so-called *adj.* 人稱 [yan4 ching1]

soccer *n.* 足球 [juk7 kau4], ~ **game** 足球比賽

sociable *adj.* 合得人 [gaap8 dak7 yan4]

social *adj.* 社會 [se5 wui2], ~ **sciences** 社會科學, ~ **security** 社保金, ~ **welfare** 社會福利, ~ **democratic** 社會民主黨

socialist *adj.* 社會主義者 [se5 wui2 jyu2 yi6 je2]

socially *adv.* 社會上 [se5 wui2 seung6]

society *n.* 社會 [se5 wui2]

sock *n.* 襪 [mat9]

socket *n.* 插座 [chaap8 jo6]

socks *n.* 襪 [mat9]

soda *n.* 汽水 [hei3 seui2], ~ **pop** 汽水, **flavored ~** 有味汽水, ~ **water** 蘇打水,

sodium *n.* 鈉 [naap9]

Sofia *n.* 索非亞 [sok8 fei1 a3]; ~, **capital of Bulgaria** 保加利亞首都

soft *adj.* 軟熟 [yun5 suk9], ~ **cheese** 軟士, ~**boiled egg** 水煮蛋

soft drink (soda) *n.* 汽水 [hei3 seui2]

softly *adv.* 輕輕 [heng1 heng1]

software *n.* 軟件 [yun5 gin6]

soil *n.* 泥 [nai4]

sojourn *n.* 暫住 [jaam6 jyu6]

solar *adj.* 日光 [yat9 gwong1]

sold *adj.* 賣咗 [maai6 jo2]

sold out *adj.* 賣曬 [maai6 saai3]

soldier *n.* 軍人 [gwan1 yan4]

sole 1. (*of a shoe*) *n.* 鞋帶 [haai4 daai3] // **2.** (*fish*) 比目魚 [bei2 muk9 yu4] // **3.** (*only*) *adj.* 唯一 [wai4 yat7]

solid *adj.* 實心 [sat9 sam1]; *n.* 固體 [gu3 tai2]

solo *adj.* 單獨 [daan1 duk9]; *n.* 獨唱 [duk9 cheung3]

soloist *n.* 獨唱嘅人 [duk9 cheung3 ge3 yan4]

Solomon Islands *n.* 所羅門群島 [so2 lo4 mun4 kwan4 dou2]

solution *n.* 解決方法 [gaai2 kyut8 fong1 faat8]

solve *v.* 解決 [gaai2 kyut8]

solvent *n.* 溶劑 [yung4 jai1]

Somalia *n.* 索馬里 [sok8 ma5 lei5]

Somalian *adj.* 索馬里 [sok8 ma5 lei5]

some *det./pron./quant.* 啲 [di1], ~ **kind of** 某種, **You're ~ friend!** 你真是好朋友！

somebody *pron.* 有人 [yau5 yan4]

somehow *adv.* 唔知點解 [m4 ji1 dim2 gaai2]

someone *pron.* 有人 [yau5 yan4]

something *pron.* 啲野 [di1 ye5]

sometimes *adv.* 有時 [yau5 si4]

somewhat *adv.* 有啲 [yau5 di1]

somewhere *adv.* 某個地方 [mau5 go3 dei6 fong1]

son *n.* 仔 [jai2]

song *n.* 歌 [go1]

songwriter *n.* 作詞人 [jok8 chi4 yan4]

soon *adv.* 即刻 [jik7 hak7]

soothe *v.* 安撫 [on1 fu2]

sophisticated *adj.* 精明 [jing1 ming4]

sorbet *n.* 冰沙 [bing1 sa1]

sore *adj.* 酸痛 [syun1 tung3], **have a ~ throat** 喉嚨痛, **be ~** 覺得痛

sorghum *n.* 高粱 [gou1 leung4]

sorghum alcohol *n.* 高粱酒 [gou1 leung4 jau2]

sorrel *n.* 栗色 [leut9 sik7]

sorry *adj.* 對唔住 [deui3 m4 jyu6], **be ~** 覺得唔好意思, **feel ~** 覺得唔好意思, **I'm ~** 對唔住

sort *n.* 類 [leui6]; *v.* 分類 [fan1 leui6]

soufflé *n.* 蛋奶酥 [daan6 naai5 sou1]

soul *n.* 靈魂 [ling4 wan4], ~ **music** 靈魂音樂, ~ **food** 美國南方黑人傳統食物

sound *n.* 聲 [seng1]; *v.* 聽起身 [teng1 hei2 san1]

soup *n.* 湯 [tong1], **chicken ~** 雞湯, **vegetable ~** 菜湯, **cream ~** 奶油湯, **cabbage ~** 大白菜湯, **fish ~** 魚湯, **tomato ~** 蕃茄湯, **~ of the day** 例湯 [lai6 tong1]

soup bowl *n.* 湯碗 [tong1 wun2]

sour *adj.* 酸 [syun1], ~ **milk** 酸奶

sour cream *n.* 酸奶油 [syun1 naai5 yau4]

source *n.* 來源 [loi4 yun4]

south *n./adj./adv.* 南面 [naam4 min6]

South Africa *n.* 南非 [naam4 fei1]

South African *adj.* 南非 [naam4 fei1]

South America *n.* 南美洲 [naam4 mei5 jau1]

South American *adj.* 南美 [naam4 mei5], ~ **food** 南美菜

South Sudan *n.* 南蘇丹 [naam4 sou1 daan1]

southeast *n./adj.* 東南面 [dung1 naam4 min6]

southern *adj.* 南方 [naam4 fong1]

southwest *n./adj.* 西南面 [sai1 naam4 min6]

Southwest (American) *adj.* 美國西南部印地安人 [mei5 gwok8 sai1 naam4 bou6 yan3 dei6 on1 yan4], ~ **food** 美國西南部印地安人菜, ~ **spice** 美國西南部印地安人辣椒粉

souvenir *n.* 紀念品 [gei3 nim6 ban2]; ~ **shop** 紀念品店

sowing *n.* 播種 [bo3 jung2]

soy *n.* 黃豆 [wong4 dau2], ~ **sauce** 黃豆醬, ~ **milk** 豆漿

soya *n.* 黃豆 [wong4 dau2]

soybean *n.* 黃豆 [wong4 dau2]; ~ **oil** 大豆油

space *n.* 空間 [hung1 gaan1]

spacebar *comp. n.* 空格鍵 [hung1 gaak8 gin6]

spade *n.* 鏟 [chaan2]

spaghetti *n.* 意大利麵 [yi3 daai6 lei6 min6]

Spain *n.* 西班牙 [sai1 baan1 nga4]

Spanish *adj.* 西班牙 [sai1 baan1 nga4]

spare *adj.* 多餘 [do1 yu4], ~ **part** 後備零件, ~ **wheel** 後備胎; *n.* 備用 [bei6 yung6]

spareribs *n.* 排骨 [paai4 gwat7]

sparkling *adj.* 閃閃發光 [sim2 sim2 faat8 gwong1], ~ **wine** 汽酒

spatula *n.* 鏟 [chaan2]

speak *v.* 演講 [yin2 gong2], ~ **to** 同...講, **Do you ~ English?** 請問你講英文嗎?, ~ **up!** 大聲講!

speaker *n.* 揚聲器 [yeung4 sing1 hei3]

special *adj.* 特別 [dak9 bit9], ~ **delivery** 特別運送, ~ **needs** 特殊需要, **today's** ~ 今日特價

specialist *n.* 專家 [jyun1 ga1]

specialize *v.* 專攻 [jyun1 gung1]

specialized *adj.* 專科 [jyun1 fo1]

specially *adv.* 特別 [dak9 bit9]

specialty *n.* 特色 [dak9 sik7], ~ **of the day** 今日特色菜, **house** ~ 招牌菜

species *n.* 物種 [mat9 jung2]

specific *adj.* 特定 [dak9 ding6]

specifically *adv.* 指定 [ji2 ding6]

specification *n.* 規格 [kwai1 gaak8]

specify *v.* 詳細說明 [cheung4 sai3 syut8 ming4]

specimen *n.* 標本 [biu1 bun2]

spectacles *n.* 眼鏡 [ngaan5 geng2]

spectator *n.* 觀眾 [gun1 jung3]

spectrum *n.* 範圍 [faan6 wai4]

speech *n.* 演講 [yin2 gong2]

speed *n.* 速度 [chuk7 dou6], ~**ing** 超速

speed limit *n.* 限速 [haan6 chuk7]

speedometer *n.* 速度計 [chuk7 dou6 gai3]

spell 1. *v.* 串 [chyun3] // **2.** *n.* 咒語 [jau3 yu5]

spelling *n.* 拼寫 [ping1 se2]

spelt flour *n.* 斯佩爾特麵粉 [si1 pui3 yi5 dak9 min6 fan2]

spend *v.* 用 [yung6]

spherical *adj.* 球狀 [kau4 jong6]

spice *n.* 香料 [heung1 liu6], ~ **blend** 混合香料

spicy *adj.* 辣 [laat9], ~ **pepper** 辣椒, ~ **sauce** 辣醬, ~ **taste** 辣味

spider *n.* 蜘蛛 [ji1 jyu1]

spill *v.* 瀉出 [se3 cheut7]

spin *v.* 旋轉 [syun4 jyun2]

spinach *n.* 菠菜 [bo1 choi3], ~ **leaves** 菠菜葉, ~ **dip** 菠菜點醬

spinal column *n.* 脊骨 [jek8 gwat7]

spine *n.* 腰骨 [yiu1 gwat7]

spire *n.* 螺旋 [lo4 syun4]

spirit *n.* 精神 [jing1 san4]

spirits *n.* 興致 [hing3 ji3]

spiritual *adj.* 精神上 [jing1 san4 seung6]

spite *n.* (*in ~ of*) 怨恨 [yun3 han6]

spit-roast *v.* 叉住燒 [cha1 jyu6 siu1]

spit-roasted *adj.* 叉住燒 [cha1 jyu6 siu1]

spleen *n.* 脾臟 [pei4 jong6]

splinter *n.* 木刺 [muk9 chi3]

split *v.* 分 [fan1]

spoil *v.* 寵壞 [chung2 waai6]

spoiled *adj.* 變質 [bin3 jat7], ~ **goods** 變質嘅野

spoke (of a wheel) *n.* 輪輻 [leun4 fuk7]

spoken *adj.* 口頭 [hau2 tau4]

sponge *n.* 海綿 [hoi2 min4]

sponge cake *n.* 海綿蛋糕 [hoi2 min4 daan6 gou1]

sponsor *n.* 贊助商 [jaan3 jo6 seung1]; *v.* 贊助 [jaan3 jo6]

spoon *n.* 匙羹 [chi4 gang1]

spoonful *n.* 一匙羹 [yat7 chi4 gang1]

spork *n.* 匙羹連叉 [chi4 gang1 lin4 cha1]

sport *n.* 運動 [wan6 dung6]

sporting goods *n.* 體育用品 [tai2 yuk9 yung6 ban2]; ~ **store** 體育用品店

sporting ground *n.* 運動場 [wan6 dung6 cheung4]

sports *n.* 有關運動 [yau5 gwaan1 wan6 dung6]; ~ **club** 健身房, ~ **field** 運動場

spot (*place/stain*) *n.* 地方 [dei6 fong1]

spouse *m./f. n.* 配偶 [pui3 ngau5]

sprain *n./v.* 扭傷 [nau2 seung1]

sprained *adj.* 扭傷咗 [nau2 seung1 jo2], ~ **ankle** 扭傷腳

spray *n.* 噴霧 [pan3 mou6]; *v.* 噴 [pan3]

spread *v.* 散播 [saan3 bo3]; *n.* 範圍 [faan6 wai4]; ~ **ing** 散播緊

spreadsheet *n.* 電子表格 [din6 ji2 biu2 gaak8]

spring *n.* **1.** (*coil*) 彈簧 [daan6 wong4] // **2.** (*season*) 春天 [cheun1 tin1] // **3.** (*water source*) 泉水 [chyun4 seui2]

spring chicken *n.* 童子雞 [tung4 ji2 gai1]

spring onion *n.* 蔥 [chung1]

sprinkle v. 灑 [sa2]; n. 少量 [siu2 leung6]; **~d** 有汽

sprouts n. 豆芽 [dau6 nga4], **soy ~** 大豆芽, **bean ~** 綠豆芽

spuds n. 鋤頭仔 [cho4 tau4 jai2]

squab n. 乳鴿 [yu5 gap8] **fowl**

square v. 平方 [ping4 fong1]; adj./n. 正方形 [jing3 fong1 ying4], **geometric ~** 直角

squash 1. (vegetable) n. 濃縮果汁 [nung4 suk7 gwo2 jap7], **summer ~** 西葫蘆 // **2.** (game of~) n. 壁球比賽 // **3.** v. (crush) 壓扁 [aat8 bin2]

squeeze v. 揸 [ja1]; n. 財政困難 [choi4 jing3 kwan3 naan4]

squid n. 魷魚 [yau4 yu2]

squirrel n. 松鼠 [chung4 syu2]

Sri Lanka n. 斯里蘭卡 [si1 lei5 laan4 ka1]

Sri Lankan adj. 斯里蘭卡 [si1 lei5 laan4 ka1]

stable adj. 穩定 [wan2 ding6]; n. 馬棚 [ma5 paang4]

stables n. 馬棚 [ma5 paang4]

stadium n. 體育場 [tai2 yuk9 cheung4]

staff n. 員工 [yun4 gung1]

stage n. 舞台 [mou5 toi4]

stain v. 整邋遢 [jing2 laat9 taat8]; n. 邋遢 [laat9 taat8], **~ remover** 除污劑, **tea ~** 茶漬, **food ~** 菜漬

stained glass n. 彩色玻璃 [choi2 sik7 bo1 lei1]

stainless steel adj. 不鏽鋼 [bat7 sau3 gong3]

stair n. 樓梯 [lau4 tai1]

staircase n. 樓梯 [lau4 tai1]

stairs n. 樓梯 [lau4 tai1]

stairway n. 樓梯 [lau4 tai1]

stairwell n. 樓梯井 [lau4 tai1 jing2]

stake n. 股份 [gu2 fan2]

stale adj. 唔新鮮 [m4 san1 sin1]

stamp n. 郵票 [yau4 piu3]; v. 蓋 [koi3], **~ a ticket** 驗票, **to ~ a passport** 蓋印

stand v. 企 [kei5], **~ in line** 排隊, **~ up** 企起身; n. 台 [toi4]

standard n. 標準 [biu1 jeun2]; adj. 標準嘅 [biu1 jeun2 ge3], **~ charge** 標準收費

standby ticket n. 候補票 [hau6 bou2 piu3]

standing n. 地位 [dei6 wai6]

star 1. n. 星星 [sing1 sing1] // **2.** v. 主演 [jyu2 yin2]

star-shaped adj. 星星形狀 [sing1 sing1 ying4 jong6]

starch n. 澱粉 [din6 fan2]

stare v./n. 吼住 [hau3 jyu6]

starfish n. 海星 [hoi2 sing1]

stars n. 星象 [sing1 jeung6]

start v./n. 開始 [hoi1 chi2], **~ a car** 開車, **~~up company** 開公司

starter motor n. 啓動摩打 [kai2 dung6 mo1 da2]

state 1. n. 州 [jau1] // **2.** adj. 國家 [gwok8 ga1] // **3.** v. 聲稱 [sing1 ching1]

statement n. 聲明 [sing1 ming4]; **make a ~ (to the police)** 落證供

stateroom n. 大廳 [daai6 teng1]

station n. 車站 [che1 jaam6], **police ~** 警察局, **train ~** 火車站

statistic *n.* 統計上 [tung2 gai3 seung6]

statistical *adj.* 統計 [tung2 gai3]

statistics *n.* 統計學 [tung2 gai3 hok9]

statue *n.* 雕像 [diu1 jeung6]

status *n.* 地位 [dei6 wai6]

statute *n.* 法規 [faat8 kwai1]

statutory *adj.* 法定 [faat8 ding6]

stay *v.* 留低 [lau4 dai1]; *n.* 逗留 [dau6 lau4]

steadily *adv.* 平穩 [ping4 wan2]

steady *adj.* 平穩 [ping4 wan2]

steak *n.* 牛扒 [ngau4 pa2], **T'bone ~** T骨牛扒, **~ tartare** 韃靼牛扒

steal *v.* 偷 [tau1]

stealing *n.* 偷 [tau1]

steam *n.* 蒸氣 [jing1 hei3]; *v.* 蒸 [jing1]

steamed *adj.* 蒸熱 [jing1 yit9], **~ vegetables** 蒸熱青菜

steamer *n.* 輪船 [leun4 syun4]

steel *n.* 鋼 [gong3]

steep 1. *v.* (*brew tea*) 浸 [jam3] // 2. *adj.* (*high*) 好斜 [hou2 che3]

steeply *adv.* 好斜 [hou2 che3]

steer *v.* 開 [hoi1]

steering wheel *n.* 軑盤 [taai5 pun4]

stem *n.* 莖 [ging3], **word ~** 詞幹; *v.* 起源於 [hei2 yun4 yu1]

step *n.* 步 [bou6]

sterile *adj.* 不孕不育 [bat7 yan6 bat7 yuk9]

sterilize *v.* 消毒 [siu1 duk9]

sterilized *adj.* 消毒 [siu1 duk9]

sterilizing solution *n.* 消毒水 [siu1 duk9 seui2]

sterling *n.* 英鎊 [ying1 bong2]

stew *n.* 燉 [dan6], **beef ~** 燉牛肉, **vegetable ~** 燉青菜

stewed *adj.* 燉[dan6], **~ meat** 燉肉

stewing fowl *n.* 燜雞 [man1 gai1]

stick 1. *v.* 貼 [tip8], **~ out** 伸出 // 2. *n.* 棍 [gwan3]

sticky *adj.* 黏 [nim4]

stiff *adj.* 僵硬 [geung1 ngaang6], **~ neck** 頸硬硬

stiffly *adv.* 硬頸 [ngaang6 geng2]

still *adv.* 仲係 [jung6 hai6], **I'm ~ waiting** 仲等緊嘅; *adj.* 唔喐 [m4 yuk7], **~-life painting** 靜物繪畫

stimulate *v.* 刺激 [chi3 gik7]

stimulus *n.* 激勵 [gik7 lai6]

sting *n.* 毒刺 [duk9 chi3]; *v.* 針 [jam1]

stir *v.* 攪 [gaau2]

stir-fry *n.* 大火炒 [daai6 fo2 chaau2]; **~ chicken** 炒雞

stitch *n.* 針 [jam1]

stock 1. (*financial*) *n.* 股票 [gu2 piu3], **~ option** 期權 // 2. (*soup*) **chicken ~** 雞肉, **fish ~** 魚肉

stock exchange *n.* 股票交易所 [gu2 piu3 gaau1 yik9 so2]

Stockholm *n.* 斯德哥爾摩 [si1 dak7 go1 yi5 mo1]; **~, capital of Sweden** 瑞典首都

stockings *n.* 長筒襪 [cheung4 tung2 mat9]

stolen *adj.* 俾人偷咗 [bei2 yan4 tau1 jo2]

stomach *n.* 胃 [wai6]; **cow ~ (tripe)** 牛肚

stomachache *n.* 胃痛 [wai6 tung3], **have a ~** 胃痛

stone *n.* 石頭 [sek9 tau4]

stoned (*drugged*) *adj.* 飲醉酒 [yam2 jeui3 jau2]

stool *n.* **1.** (*chair*) 高凳 [gou1 dang3] // **2.** (*feces*) 糞便樣本 [fan3 bin6 yeung6 bun2]

stop *v.* 停止 [ting4 ji2], ~ **at ...** 停喺, ~!, 唔好喇！; *n.* 站 [jaam6], **bus ~** 巴士站, ~ **sign** 停止指示牌

stopcock (*plumbing*) *n.* 活塞 [wut9 sak7]

stopper *n.* 瓶塞 [ping4 sak7]

store *n.* 商店 [seung1 dim3], ~ **directory** 商店目錄, ~ **window** 商店櫥窗; *v.* 存放 [chyun4 fong3]

stork *n.* 鸛 [gun3]

storm *n.* 暴風雨 [bou6 fung1 yu5], ~ **warning** 暴風雨警告, **snow~** 暴風雪, **to brain~** 頭腦風暴

stormy *adj.* 激烈 [gik7 lit9]

story (*narrative / building level*) *n.* 故仔 [gu2 jai2]

storyboard *n.* 情節提要 [ching4 jit8 tai4 yiu1]; **film or cartoon ~** 電影或動畫情節提要

stove *n.* 火爐 [fo2 lou4]

straight *adv./adj.* 直 [jik9]; ~ **ahead** 直行

strain *v.* **1.** (*in cooking*) 拉傷 [laai1 seung1] // **2.** ~ **a muscle** 拉傷肌肉 [laai1 seung1 gei1 yuk9]

strange *adj.* 奇怪 [kei4 gwaai3]

strangely *adv.* 奇怪 [kei4 gwaai3]

stranger *n.* 陌生人 [mak9 sang1 yan4]

strategic *adj.* 戰略性 [jin3 leuk9 sing3]

strategically *adv.* 戰略上 [jin3 leuk9 seung6]

strategy *n.* 戰略 [jin3 leuk9]

straw *n.* 禾稈草 [wo4 gon2 chou2]

strawberry *n.* 士多啤梨 [si6 do1 be1 lei4]

stream *n.* 小溪 [siu2 kai1]

street *n.* 街 [gaai1]; ~ **children** 乞兒仔, ~ **light** 街燈, ~ **food** 大排擋

streetcar *n.* 有軌電車 [yau5 gwai2 din6 che1]

strength *n.* 力量 [lik9 leung6]

stress *n.* 壓力 [aat8 lik9]; *v.* 強調 [keung5 diu6]

stressed *adj.* 緊張 [gan2 jeung1]

stretch *v.* 伸 [san1]

stretcher *n.* 擔架 [daam1 ga2]

strict *adj.* 嚴格 [yim4 gaak8]

strictly *adv.* 完全 [yun4 chyun4]

strike *v.* (*hit*) 攻擊 [gung1 gik7]; *n.* 罷工 [ba6 gung1], **labor ~** 罷工

striking *adj.* 顯著 [hin2 jyu3]

string *n.* 繩 [sing2]

string bean *n.* 豆仔 [dau2 jai2]

stringy *adj.* 有筋 [yau5 gan1]

strip 1. *v.* 除 [cheui4] // **2.** *n.* 長條 [cheung4 tiu2]; ~**s** 條 [tiu2], **bacon ~** 煙肉條

stripe *n.* 條紋 [tiu4 man4]

striped *adj.* 有條紋 [yau5 tiu4 man4]

striploin *n.* 西冷牛扒 [sai1 laang1 ngau4 pa2]

stroke *n.* (*medical*) 中風 [jung3 fung1] *v.* 擊球 [gik7 kau4]

stroll v. 散步 [saan3 bou6]

strong adj. 強大 [keung4 daai6]

strongly adv. 強烈 [keung4 lit9]

structural adj. 結構上 [git8 kau3 seung6]

structurally adv. 結構上 [git8 kau3 seung6]

structure n. 結構 [git8 kau3]

strudel n. 批 [pai1], **apple ~** 蘋果批

struggle v. 努力 [nou5 lik9]; n. 奮鬥 [fan5 dau3]

stubborn adj. 硬頸 [ngaang6 geng2]

stuck adj. 郁唔到 [yuk7 m4 dou2], **be ~** 郁唔到

student n. 學生 [hok9 saang1]; **~ card** 學生證, **~ discount** 學生折扣

studio n. 工作室 [gung1 jok8 sat7]

study n. 書房 [syu1 fong2]; v. 學習 [hok9 jaap9]

stuff n. 野 [ye5]

stuffed adj. 塞滿 [sak7 mun5], **I'm ~** 食飽勒, **~ eggs** 釀蛋, **~ bell peppers** 釀燈籠椒, **~ tomatoes** 釀蕃茄

stuffing n. 餡 [haam6], **turkey ~** 火雞餡

stun v. 擊暈 [gik7 wan4]

stunning adj. 好靚 [hou2 leng3]

stupid adj. 蠢 [cheun2]

sturgeon n. 鱘魚 [cham4 yu2]

style n. 風格 [fung1 gaak8]

stylistic adj. 風格上 [fung1 gaak8 seung6]

subject n. 話題 [wa6 tai4], **change the ~** 轉話題; v. (**~ to**) 根據 [gan1 geui3]

submit v. 服從 [fuk9 chung4]

subpoena n. 傳票 [chyun4 piu3]

subscribe v. 訂 [deng6]

subscriber n. 用戶 [yung6 wu6]

subscription n. 訂閱 [deng6 yut9]

subsequent adj. 後來 [hau6 loi4]

subsequently adv. 跟住 [gan1 jyu6]

subsidiary adj. 附屬 [fu6 suk9]; n. 子公司 [ji2 gung1 si1]

substance n. 實質 [sat9 jat7]

substantial adj. 大量 [daai6 leung6]

substantially adv. 實質上 [sat9 jat7 seung6]

substitute n. 代替品 [doi6 tai3 ban2]; v. 代替 [doi6 tai3], **Can I ~ X for Y?** (*at a restaurant*) 我可唔可以用X換Y？

subtitles n. 字幕 [ji6 mok9]; **film with ~** 一部有字幕嘅電影

subtle adj. 微妙 [mei4 miu6]

suburb n. 郊區 [gaau1 keui1]

subway n. 地鐵 [dei6 tit8]; **~ map** 地鐵地圖

subway station n. 地鐵站 [dei6 tit8 jaam6]

succeed v. 成功 [sing4 gung1]

success n. 成功 [sing4 gung1]

successful adj. 成功 [sing4 gung1]

successfully adv. 成功 [sing4 gung1]

succotash n. 豆煮粟米 [dau2 jyu2 suk7 mai5]

such det. 咁 [gam2]; pron. 呢啲野 [ne1 di1 ye5], **~ as** 例如, **~ and ~** 等等, **~ a shame!** 真係可惜！

suck v. 吸 [kap7]

suckling pig n. 豬仔 [jyu1 jai2]

Sucre *n.* 蘇克雷 [sou1 hak7 leui4]; ~, **judicial capital of Bolivia** 玻利維亞司法首都

Sudan *n.* 蘇丹 [sou1 daan1]

Sudanese *adj.* 蘇丹 [sou1 daan1]

sudden *adj.* 突然 [dat9 yin4]

suddenly *adv.* 突然 [dat9 yin4]

suffer *v.* 受苦 [sau6 fu2]

suffering *n.* 痛苦 [tung3 fu2]

sufficient *adj.* 足夠 [juk7 gau3]

sufficiently *adv.* 足夠 [juk7 gau3]

suffix *n.* 後綴 [hau6 jeui6]

sugar *n.* 糖 [tong4], **brown** ~ 紅糖

sugarcane *n.* 甘蔗 [gam1 je3]

sugar-free *adj.* 無糖 [mou4 tong4]

suggest *v.* 提議 [tai4 yi5]

suggestion *n.* 提議 [tai4 yi5]

suit 1. (*clothing*) *n.* 一套衫 [yat7 tou3 saam1] // **2.** *v.* 適合 [sik7 hap9], ~ **yourself** 隨便你！

suitable *adj.* 適合 [sik7 hap9], ~ **for** 適合, ~ **with lunch** 午飯食, ~ **with dinner** 晚飯食, ~ **with dessert** 甜品食

suitcase *n.* 行李箱 [hang4 lei5 seung1]

suite *n.* 套 [tou3]

suited *adj.* 適合 [sik7 hap9]

sum *n.* 總數 [jung2 sou3]

summary *n.* 總結 [jung2 git8]

summary judgment (*legal*) *n.* 即決審判 [jik7 kyut8 sam2 pun3]

summer *n.* 夏天 [ha6 tin1]; ~ **schedule** 夏令時間, ~ **solstice** 夏至, ~ **vacation** 暑假

summer squash *n.* 西葫蘆 [sai1 wu4 lou2]

summon 召集 [jiu6 jaap9]

sun *n.* 太陽 [taai3 yeung4]

sunbathe *v.* 日光浴 [yat9 gwong1 yuk9]

sunblock *n.* 防曬霜 [fong4 saai3 seung1]

sunburn *n.* 曬傷 [saai3 seung1]

sundae *n.* 新地 [san1 dei2]

Sunday *n.* 星期日 [sing1 kei4 yat9]

sunflower *n.* 向日葵 [heung3 yat9 kwai4]

sunflower oil *n.* 葵花油 [kwai4 fa1 yau4]

sunflower seeds *n.* 葵花子 [kwai4 fa1 ji2]

sunglasses *n.* 墨鏡 [mak9 geng3]

sunlight *n.* 陽光 [yeung4 gwong1]

sunny *adj.* 大太陽 [daai6 taai3 yeung4]

sunrise *n.* 日出 [yat9 cheut7]

sunroof *n.* 天窗 [tin1 cheung1]

sunscreen (lotion) *n.* 防曬霜 [fong4 saai3 seung1]

sunset *n.* 日落 [yat9 lok9]

sunshade *n.* 天棚 [tin1 paang4]

sunstroke *n.* 中暑 [jung3 syu2]

suntan lotion *n.* 防曬霜 [fong4 saai3 seung1]

super *adj.* 超級 [chiu1 kap7]; (*premium gas*) 高級汽油 [gou1 kap7 hei3 yau4]

superb *adj.* 十分之好 [sap9 fan1 ji1 hou2]

superman *n.* 超人 [chiu1 yan4]

superior *adj.* 高竇 [gou1 dau3]

superlative *adj.* 上好 [seung6 hou2]; *n.* 最高級形式 [jeui3 gou1 kap7 ying4 sik7]

supermarket *n.* 超市 [chiu1 si5]

supervision *n.* 監督 [gaam1 duk7]

supper *n.* 晚飯 [maan5 faan6]

supplement *n.* 補充 [bou2 chung1], **calcium ~** 補鈣, **vitamin ~** 補維他命, **mineral ~** 補礦物質, **fiber ~** 補纖維素

supplier *n.* 供應商 [gung1 ying3 seung1]

supplies *n.* 日常用品 [yat9 seung4 yung6 ban2]

supply *n.* 供應 [gung1 ying3]; *v.* 提供 [tai4 gung1]

support *n./v.* 支持 [ji1 chi4]

supporter *n.* 支持者 [ji1 chi4 je2]

suppose *v.* 估 [gu2]

suppository *n.* 藥拴 [yeuk9 saan1]

suppress *v.* 鎮壓 [jan3 aat8]

supreme *adj.* 至高無上 [ji3 gou1 mou4 seung6]

sure *adj.* 肯定 [hang2 ding6]; *adv.* 當然 [dong1 yin4], **Are you ~?** 你肯唔肯定嘅？

surely *adv.* 必然 [bit7 yin4]

surf *v.* 衝浪 [chung1 long6], **~ waves** 滑浪, **~ the Internet** 上網

surf and turf *n.* 牛扒海鮮套餐 [ngau4 pa2 hoi2 sin1 tou3 chaan1]

surface *n.* 表面 [biu2 min6]; **~ mail** 水陸路信件

surfboard *n.* 衝浪板 [chung1 long6 baan2]

surfer *n.* 衝浪運動員 [chung1 long6 wan6 dung6 yun4]

surfing *n.* 衝浪 [chung1 long6]

surgeon *n.* 外科醫生 [ngoi6 fo1 yi1 sang1]

surgery *n.* 手術 [sau2 seut9]

Suriname *n.* 蘇里南 [sou1 lei5 naam4]

surname *n.* 姓 [sing3]

surplus *n.* 盈餘 [ying4 yu4]; *adj.* 多餘 [do1 yu4]

surprise *n.* 驚喜 [ging1 hei2]; *v.* 使…措手不及 [sai2 … chou3 sau2 bat7 kap9]

surprised *adj.* 驚訝 [ging1 nga6]

surprising *adj.* 出人意料 [cheut7 yan4 yi3 liu6]

surprisingly *adv.* 估唔到 [gu2 m4 dou2]

surrender *v.* 投降 [tau4 hong4]

surround *v.* 包圍 [baau1 wai4]

surrounding *adj.* 環境 [waan4 ging2]

surroundings *n.* 環境 [waan4 ging2]

surveillance *n.* 監視 [gaam1 si6]

survey *n./v.* 調查 [diu6 cha4]

survival *n.* 生存 [sang1 chyun4]

survive *v.* 生存 [sang1 chyun4]

sushi *n.* 壽司 [sau6 si1]; **~ roll** 壽司卷

suspect *v.* 懷疑 [waai4 yi4]; *n.* 疑犯 [yi4 faan2]

suspicion *n.* 疑心 [yi4 sam1]

suspicious *adj.* 覺得可疑 [gok8 dak7 ho2 yi4]

sustain *v.* 保持 [bou2 chi4]

sustainable *adj.* 可持續 [ho2 chi4 juk9]

Suva *n.* 蘇瓦 [sou1 nga5]; **~, capital of Fiji** 斐濟首都

swab *n.* 棉簽 [min4 chim1]

swallow *v.* 吞 [tan1]

swamp *n.* 濕地 [sap7 dei6]

Swaziland *n.* 斯威士蘭 [si1 wai1 si6 laan4]

swear *v.* 發誓 [faat8 sai6]; **~ words** 誓言

swearing n. 講粗口 [gong2 chou1 hau2]

sweat n. 汗 [hon6]; v. 流汗 [lau4 hon6]

sweater n. 冷衫 [laang1 saam1]

sweatshirt n. 運動衫 [wan6 dung6 saam1]

Sweden n. 瑞典 [seui6 din2]

Swedish adj. 瑞典 [seui6 din2]

sweep v. 掃 [sou3]

sweet adj. 甜 [tim4], ~ **and sour sauce** 甜酸醬, ~ **bread**, 甜麵包 ~ **pepper** 甜椒, ~ **potato** 蕃薯; **un~ened** 冇加甜; n. 糖果 [tong4 gwo2]

sweetener n. 甜味劑 [tim4 mei6 jai1], **no calorie** ~ 無熱量甜味劑, **artificial** ~ 人工甜味劑

swell v. 脹 [jeung3]

swelling n. 腫 [jung2]

swim n./v. 游水 [yau4 seui2], **go for a** ~ 游水

swimming n. 游水 [yau4 seui2]; **No** ~ 禁止游泳

swimming pool n. 游泳池 [yau4 wing6 chi4], **indoor** ~ 室內泳池, **outdoor** ~ 室外泳池

swimsuit n. 泳衣 [wing6 yi1]

swindler n. 騙子 [pin3 ji2]

swing n. 韆鞦 [chin1 chau1]; v. 搖來搖去 [yiu4 loi4 yiu4 heui3]

Swiss adj. 瑞士 [seui6 si6]

Swiss chard n. 牛皮菜 [ngau4 pei4 choi3]

Swiss cheese n. 瑞士芝士 [seui6 si6 ji1 si6]

switch n. 開關 [hoi1 gwaan1], **on** ~ 接通; v. 轉 [jyun2], ~ **smth. off** 關

Switzerland n. 瑞士 [seui6 si6]

swollen adj. 腫咗 [jung2 jo2]

sword n. 劍 [gim3]

swordfish n. 劍魚 [gim3 yu2]

syllable n. 音節 [yam1 jit8]

symbol n. 標誌 [biu1 ji3]

symmetry n. 對稱 [deui3 ching3]

sympathetic adj. 有同情心 [yau5 tung4 ching4 sam1]

sympathy n. 同情 [tung4 ching4]

symphony n. 交響樂 [gaau1 heung2 ngok9]

symptom (of an illness) n. 症狀 [jing3 jong6]

synagogue n. 猶太教堂 [yau4 taai3 gaau3 tong4]

syndrome n. 綜合症 [jung1 hap9 jing3]

synthesis n. 綜合 [jung1 hap9]

synthetic adj. 合成 [hap9 sing4], ~ **material** 合成材料

Syria n. 敘利亞 [jeui6 lei6 a3]

Syrian adj. 敘利亞 [jeui6 lei6 a3]

syringe n. 針筒 [jam1 tung2]

syrup n. 糖漿 [tong4 jeung1], **maple** ~ 楓葉糖漿, **fruit** ~ 水果糖漿

system n. 系統 [hai6 tung2]

T

tabasco sauce *n.* 辣椒油 [laat9 jiu1 yau4]

table *n.* 枱 [toi2], **dinner ~** 餐台, **~ cover** 台布

table tennis *n.* 乒乓波 [bing1 bam1 bo1]

tableau *n.* 舞台造型 [mou5 toi4 jou6 ying4]

tablecloth *n.* 枱布 [toi2 bou3]

tablespoon *n.* 大匙羹 [daai6 chi4 gang1]

tablet *n.* 牌 [paai2]

tableware *n.* 餐具 [chaan1 geui6]

taboo *adj.* 禁忌 [gam1 gei6]

tackle *v.* 解決 [gaai2 kyut8]; *n.* 器材 [hei3 choi4]

taco *n.* 粟米薄餅卷 [suk7 mai5 bok9 beng2 gyun2], **fish ~** 魚肉粟米薄餅卷, **~ sauce** 粟米薄餅卷醬, **~ shell** 粟米薄餅卷皮, **~ meat** 肉粟米薄餅卷

tag *n.* 標籤 [biu1 chim1], **price ~** 標價; **play a game of ~** 玩追拍遊戲

tail *n.* 尾 [mei5]

taillight *n.* 車尾燈 [che1 mei5 dang1]

tailor *n.* 裁縫 [choi4 fung2]

tailor-made *adj.* 度身訂做 [dok9 san1 ding6 jou6]

Taipei *n.* 台北 [toi4 bak7]; **~, capital of Taiwan** 台灣首都

Taiwan *n.* 台灣 [toi4 waan1]

Taiwanese *adj.* 台灣 [toi4 waan1]

Tajikistan *adj./n.* 塔吉克斯坦 [taap8 gat7 hak7 si1 taan2]

take *v.* 攞走 [lo2 jau2], **~ a taxi** 坐的士, **~ time** 慢慢, **~ a nap** 瞓一陣, **~ action** 行動, **~ advantage of** 佔便宜, **~ away** 攞走, **~ care (of)** 照顧, **~ in** 吸收, **~ me to** 帶我去, **~ off** 除衫, **~ out** 攞出去, **~ part (in)** 參加, **~ photographs** 影相, **~ place** 發生, **~ smth. off** 除衫, **~ offense** 俾激嬲

taken *adj.* 感興趣 [gam2 hing3 cheui3]

take-out food *n.* 外賣 [ngoi6 maai6], **Chinese ~** 中餐外賣

takeover *n.* 接管 [jip8 gun2], **hostile ~** 惡意收購

tale *n.* 傳說 [chyun4 syut8]

talent *n.* 天份 [tin1 fan6]

talented *adj.* 有天份 [yau5 tin1 fan6]

talk *v.* 傾計 [king1 gai2], **~ to** 同...講話, **~ it over** 接手; *n.* 傾計 [king1 gai2]

tall *adj.* 高 [gou1]

Tallinn *n.* 塔林 [taap8 lam4]; **~, capital of Estonia** 愛沙尼亞首都

tamale *n.* 粟米餡卷 [suk7 mai5 haam6 gyun2]

tamarind *n.* 羅望子 [lo4 mong6 ji2]

tampon *n.* 衛生棉棒 [wai6 saang1 min4 paang5]

tan *adj.* 小麥色 [siu2 mak9 sik7]

tangelo *n.* 蜜柚 [mat9 yau2]

tangerine *n.* 砂糖桔 [sa1 tong4 gat7]

tangy *adj.* 好大浸味 [hou2 daai6 jam3 mei6]

tank *n.* 坦克 [taan2 hak7]

Tanzania *n.* 坦桑尼亞 [taan2 song1 nei4 a3]

Tanzanian *adj.* 坦桑尼亞 [taan2 song1 nei4 a3]

tap *v.* 輕拍 [hing1 paak8]; *n.* 水龍頭 [seui2 lung4 tau4]

tape *n.* 帶 [daai2]

tapestry *n.* 掛氈 [gwa3 jin1]

tapioca *n.* 西米 [sai1 mai5]; ~ **pudding** 西米布甸

Tarawa Atoll *n.* 塔拉瓦環礁 [taap8 laai1 nga5 waan4 jiu1]; ~, **capital of Kiribati** 基里巴斯首都

target *n.* 目標 [muk9 biu1]

taro *n.* 香芋 [heung1 wu6]

tarragon *n.* 龍篙 [lung4 gou1]

tart 1. (*sour*) *adj.* 酸 [syun1], ~ **taste** 酸味 // **2.** (*pastry*) *n.* 蛋撻 [daan6 taat3], **fruit** ~ 水果撻

tartar sauce *n.* 他他醬 [ta1 ta1 jeung3]

tartlet *n.* 蛋撻仔 [daan6 taat3 jai2]

Tashkent *n.* 塔什干 [taap8 sam6 gon1]; ~, **capital of Uzbekistan** 烏茲別克斯坦首都

task *n.* 任務 [yam4 mou6]

taste *n.* 味道 [mei6 dou6]; *v.* 食 [sik9]

tasty *adj.* 好味 [hou2 mei6]

Taurus *n.* 金牛座 [gam1 ngau4 jo6]

tax *n.* 稅 [seui3]; *v.* 收稅 [sau1 seui3]

taxation *n.* 稅收 [seui3 sau1]

taxi *n.* 的士 [dik7 si2], ~ **stand** 的士站, **hail a** ~ 截的士

taxpayer *n.* 納稅人 [naap9 seui3 yan4]

Tbilisi *n.* 第比利斯 [dai6 bei2 lei6 si1]; ~, **capital of Georgia** 格魯吉亞首都

T-bone steak *n.* 丁字骨牛扒 [ding1 ji6 gwat7 ngau4 pa2]

tea *n.* 茶 [cha4], **a cup of** ~ 一杯茶, **green** ~ 綠茶, **black** ~ 紅茶, ~ **bag** *n.* 茶包 [cha4 baau1]

teach *v.* 教 [gaau3]

teacher *n.* 老師 [lou5 si1]

teaching *n.* 教學 [gaau3 hok9]

teakettle *n.* 茶壺 [cha4 wu4]

team *n.* 團隊 [tyun4 deui2]

teapot *n.* 茶煲 [cha4 bou1]

tear *n.* 眼淚 [ngaan5 leui6]; *v.* ~ **up** (*weep*) 流眼淚 [lau4 ngaan5 leui6]

teaspoon *n.* 茶匙 [cha4 chi4]

technical *adj.* 技術上 [gei6 seut9 seung6]

technique *n.* 技巧 [gei6 haau2]

technology *n.* 技術 [gei6 seut9], **cutting edge** ~ 尖端技術

teddy bear *n.* 泰迪熊 [taai3 dik9 hung4]

Tegucigalpa *n.* 特古西加爾巴 [dak9 gu2 sai1 ga1 yi5 ba1]; ~, **capital of Honduras** 洪都拉斯首都

Tehran *n.* 德黑蘭 [dak7 hak7 laan4]; ~, **capital of Iran** 伊朗首都

telecommunications *n.* 電訊 [din6 seun3]

telegram *n.* 電報 [din6 bou3]

telephone *n.* 電話 [din6 wa2], ~ **bill** 電話賬單, **public** ~ 公用電話, ~ **call** 電話, ~ **operator** 電話接線員, ~ **number** 電話號碼; *v.* 打電話 [da2 din6 wa2]

telescope *n.* 望遠鏡 [mong6 yun5 geng3]

television *n.* 電視 [din6 si6]

tell *v.* 話…知 [wa6 … ji1]

temperature *n.* 溫度 [wan1 dou6]

temple *n.* 廟 [miu2]

temporarily *adv.* 暫時 [jaam6 si4]

temporary *adj.* 暫時 [jaam6 si4], ~ **exhibit** 臨時展覽, ~ **worker** 臨時工, **a** ~ **situation** 暫時嘅情況

ten *num.* 十 [sap9]

tenant *n.* 租客 [jou1 haak8]

tend *v.* 照顧 [jiu3 gu3]

tendency *n.* 趨勢 [cheui1 sai3]

tender 1. (*payment*) *n.* 聯絡船 [lyun4 lok8 syun4], **legal** ~ 法定貨幣 // **2.** (*hand in*) *v.* 正式提出 [jing1 sik7 tai4 cheut7] // **3.** (*soft*) *adj.* 溫柔 [wan1 yau4]

tenderize *v.* 整嫩 [jing2 nyun6]

tenderloin *n.* 腰部嫩肉 [yiu1 bou6 nyun6 yuk9], **beef** ~ 牛腰部嫩肉

tendon *n.* 筋 [gan1]

tennis *n.* 網球 [mong5 kau4]; ~ **court** 網球場

tense *n.* 時態[si4 taai3]

tension *n.* 緊張 [gan2 jeung1]

tent *n.* 帳篷 [jeung3 pung4]; ~ **peg** 帳篷樁, ~ **pole** 帳篷柱, **pitch a** ~ 起帳篷

tenth *adj.* 第十個 [dai6 sap9 go3]

teriyaki *n.* 照燒 [jiu3 siu1], ~ **sauce** 照燒醬, ~ **paste** 照燒醬, ~ **chicken** 照燒雞肉

term *n.* 任期 [yam4 kei4]; ~ **of office** 任期

terminal 1. *n.* 終點站 [jung1 dim2 jaam6]; **computer** ~ 終端機 // **2.** *adj.* 晚期 [maan5 kei4]

terminus *n.* 終點站 [jung1 dim2 jaam6]

terrace *n.* 陽臺[yeung4 toi4]

terra-cotta *adj.* 赤陶 [chek8 tou4]

terrible *adj.* 得人驚 [dak7 yan4 geng1]

terribly *adv.* 十分 [sap9 fan1]

terrific *adj.* 十分之好 [sap9 fan1 ji1 hou2]

territory *n.* 地頭 [dei6 tau4]

terrorist *n.* 恐怖分子 [hung2 bou3 fan6 ji2]

test *n./v.* 測驗 [chak7 yim6]

testicles *n.* 睪丸 [gou1 yun2]

testimony *n.* 證供 [jing3 gung1]

tetanus *n.* 破傷風 [po3 seung1 fung1]

text *n.* 文字 [man4 ji6]

textiles *n.* 紡織品 [fong2 jik7 ban2]

texture *n.* 質地 [jat7 dei2]

Thai *adj.* 泰國 [taai3 gwok8]

Thailand *n.* 泰國 [taai3 gwok8]

than *prep./conj.* 比 [bei2]

thank *v.* 多謝 [do1 je6], **give ~s** 轉達謝意

thank you *phr.* 唔該曬 [m4 goi1 saai3]; *exclam.* 多謝!

that *det./pron./conj.* 嗰個 [go2 go3], ~ **one** 嗰個, ~**'s all** 係咁多, ~**'s fine** 冇問題, ~**'s true!** 冇錯, **Did you see ~?** 你有冇睇到?

the *det.* 嗰個 [go2 go3]

The Gambia *n.* 岡比亞 [gong1 bei2 a3]

The Hague (*seat of government of Netherlands*) *n.* 海牙 [hoi2 nga4]

theater *n.* 戲院 [hei3 yun2]

theft *n.* 偷嘢 [tau1 ye5]

their *adj.* 佢哋嘅 [keui5 dei6 ge3]

theirs *pron.* 佢哋嘅 [keui5 dei6 ge3]

them *pron.* 佢哋 [keui5 dei6]

theme *n.* 主題 [jyu2 tai4]

themselves *pron.* 佢哋自己 [keui5 dei6 ji6 gei2]

then *adv.* 當時 [dong1 si4]

theoretical *adj.* 理論上 [lei5 leun6 seung6]

theory *n.* 理論 [lei5 leun6]

therapeutic *n.* 令人放鬆 [ling4 yan4 fong3 sung1]

therapy *n.* 心理治療 [sam1 lei5 ji6 liu4]

there *adv.* 嗰度 [go2 dou6], ~ **are** 有, ~ **is** 有, **over** ~ 嗰度, **Please go** ~ 請去嗰度

therefore *adv.* 所以 [so2 yi5]

thermometer *n.* 溫度計 [wan1 dou6 gai3]

thermos *n.* 保溫瓶 [bou2 wan1 ping4]

these *adj./pron.* 呢啲 [ni1 di1]

they *pron.* 佢哋 [keui5 dei6]

thick *adj.* 厚 [hau5]

thickly *adv.* 密 [mat9]

thickness *n.* 厚度 [hau5 dou6]

thief *n.* 賊仔 [chaak9 jai2]

thigh *n.* 大髀 [daai6 bei2]; **turkey** ~ 火雞髀, **chicken** ~ 雞髀

Thimphu *n.* 廷布 [ting4 bou3]; ~, **capital of Bhutan** 不丹首都

thin *adj.* 瘦 [sau3]

thing *n.* 嘢 [ye5]

think *v.* 諗 [nam2]

thinking *n.* 思考 [si1 haau2]

third *adj.* 第三個 [dai6 saam1 go3], ~ **party** 第三方, **one-~** 三分之一

thirst *n.* 頸渴 [geng2 hot8]

thirsty *adj.* 頸渴 [geng2 hot8]

thirteen *num.* 十三 [sap9 saam1]

thirteenth *adj.* 第十三個 [dai6 sap9 saam1 go3]

thirtieth *adj.* 第三十個 [dai6 saam1 sap9 go3]

thirty *num.* 三十 [saam1 sap9]

this *adj./pron.* 呢個 [ni1 go3], ~ **afternoon** 今日晏晝, ~ **one** 呢個, ~ **is impossible!** 冇可能, ~ **time** 呢次, **I want** ~ 我想要呢個

thorough *adj.* 徹底 [chit8 dai2]

thoroughly *adv.* 徹底 [chit8 dai2]

those *adj./pron.* 嗰啲 [go3 di1]

though *conj./adv.* 即管 [jik7 gun2]

thought *n.* 諗法 [nam2 faat8]

thousand *num.* 千 [chin1]

thousandth *adj.* 第一千個 [dai6 yat7 chin1 go3]

thread *n.* 線 [sin3]

threat *n.* 威脅 [wai1 hip8]

threaten *v.* 威脅 [wai1 hip8]

threatening *adj.* 危險 [ngai4 him2]

three *num.* 三 [saam1]

thrill *n./v.* 激動 [gik7 dung6]

thrilled *adj.* 激動 [gik7 dung6]

thrilling *adj.* 毛骨悚然 [mou4 gwat7 sung2 yin4]

throat *n.* 喉嚨 [hau4 lung4]

thrombosis *n.* 血拴症 [hyut8 saan1 jing3]

through *prep./adv.* 經過 [ging1 gwo3]

throughout *prep.* 由始至終 [yau4 chi2 ji3 jung1]; *adv.* 度度 [dou6 dou6]

throw *v.* 掟 [deng3], **~ smth. away** 掟咗, **~ a party** 舉辦排隊, **~ a fit** 大發脾氣, **~ a ball** 掟球

thumb *n.* 手指公 [sau2 ji2 gung1]

thunder *n.* 行雷 [haang4 leui4]

Thursday *n.* 禮拜四 [lai5 baai3 sei3]

thus *adv.* 所以 [so2 yi5]

thyme *n.* 百里香 [baak8 lei5 heung1]

ticket *n.* 票 [piu3], **~ agency** 票務代理, **~ holder** 持票人, **~ collector** 收票員, **~ machine** 售票機, **~ office** 售票處, **Can I see your ~?** 麻煩票, **a one-way ~** 單程票

tide *n.* 潮汐 [chiu4 jik9]

tidy *adj.* 企里 [kei5 lei5]; *v.* 執 [jap7], **~ up** 整企里

tie *v.* 打吠 [da2 taai1], **~ smth. up** 綁埋一齊; *n.* 吠 [taai1], **to knot a ~** 打, **bow ~** 蝴蝶結; **~ game** 打成平手

tier *n.* 等級 [dang2 kap7]

tight *adj.* 緊 [gan2]; *adv.* 貼身 [tip8 san1]

tightly *adv.* 緊 [gan2]

tights *n.* 緊身褲 [gan2 san1 fu3]

tilapia *n.* 羅非魚 [lo4 fei1 yu2]

tile *n.* 瓷磚 [chi4 jyun1]

till (until) *prep.* 直到 [jik9 dou3]

time *n.* 時間 [si4 gaan3], **free ~** 得閒, **on ~** 準時, **What ~ is it?** 宜家幾點?, **short on ~** 唔夠時間

timer *n.* 計時器 [gai3 si4 hei3], **oven ~** 焗爐計時器

timetable *n.* 時間表 [si4 gaan3 biu2]

tin *n.* 罐頭 [gun3 tau2]

tiny *adj.* 超細 [chiu1 sai3]

tip *n.* 小費 [siu2 fai3]; *v.* 俾小費 [bei2 siu2 fai3]

Tirane *n.* 地拉那 [dei6 laai1 na5]; **~, capital of Albania** 阿爾巴尼亞首都

tire 1. (*wheel*) *n.* 軚 [taai1] // **2.** (*grow weary*) *v.* 边 [gui6]

tired *adj.* 好边 [hou2 gui6]

tiring *adj.* 好边 [hou2 gui6]

tissue *n.* 紙巾 [ji2 gan1]

title *n.* 頭銜 [tau4 haam4]

to *prep.* 去 [heui3]

toad *n.* 蛤蟆 [ha1 mo1]

toast 1. *n.* 多士 [do1 si6]; *v.* 烘 [hung3] // **2.** *v.* **to ~ with a drink** 祝酒

toaster *n.* 多士爐 [do1 si6 lou4]

toaster oven *n.* 烘爐 [hung3 lou4]

tobacco *n.* 煙草 [yin1 chou2], **~ shop** 煙草店, **chewing ~** 咬煙草, **~ plant** 煙草廠

today *adv./n.* 今日 [gam1 yat9]

toe *n.* 腳趾 [geuk8 ji2]

toffee *n.* 太妃糖 [taai3 fei1 tong2]

tofu *n.* 豆腐 [dau6 fu6]

together *adv.* 一齊 [yat7 chai4]; **~ with ...** 同...一齊

Togo *n.* 多哥 [do1 go1]

toilet *n.* 馬桶 [ma5 tung2], **public** ~ 公廁

toilet paper *n.* 廁紙 [chi3 ji2]

token *n.* 購物券 [gau3 mat9 gyun3]

Tokyo *n.* 東京 [dung1 ging1]; ~, **capital of Japan** 日本首都

toll *n.* 路費 [lou6 fai3]

tomato *n.* 蕃茄 [faan1 ke4], **green** ~ 青蕃茄, ~ **sauce** 蕃茄醬, ~ **paste** 蕃茄醬, ~ **juice** 蕃茄汁, ~ **puree** 蕃茄泥

tomorrow *adv./n.* 聽日 [ting1 yat9], ~ **morning** 聽日晏晝, **day after** ~ 後日, **See you** ~! 聽日見！

ton *n.* 噸[deun1]

tone *n.* 語氣 [yu5 hei3]

Tonga *n.* 湯加 [tong1 ga1]

tongue *n.* 脷 [lei6], **pig** ~ 豬脷, **cow** ~ 牛脷

tonic water *n.* 開胃水 [hoi1 wai6 seui2]

tonight *adv./n.* 今晚 [gam1 maan5]

tonsilitis *n.* 扁桃腺發炎 [bin2 tou4 sin3 faat8 yim4]

tonsils *n.* 扁桃腺 [bin2 tou4 sin3]

too *adv.* 都係 [dou1 hai6], ~ **expensive** 太貴, **I'll have one,** ~ 我都想買一件, ~ **much** 太多

tool *n.* 架撐 [ga3 chang1]

toolbar *n.* 工具欄 [gung1 geui6 laan4], **computer program** ~ 電腦工具欄

tooth *n.* 牙 [nga4]

toothache *n.* 牙痛 [nga4 tung3]

toothbrush *n.* 牙刷 [nga4 chaat8]

toothpaste *n.* 牙膏 [nga4 gou1]

toothpick *n.* 牙籤 [nga4 chim1]

top *n.* 頂 [deng2]; *adj.* 上面 [seung6 min6]

topic *n.* 題目 [tai4 muk9]

topping *n.* 上面一層 [seung6 min6 yat7 chang4], **salad** ~ 沙律配料, **meat** ~ 肉餡

topside *n.* 最上層 [jeui3 seung6 chang4]

torn *adj.* 撕爛 [si1 laan6]

torrent *n.* 激流 [gik7 lau4]

tort (*legal*) *n.* 侵權行為 [cham1 kyun4 hang4 wai4]

torte (*pastry*) *n.* 果仁蛋糕 [gwo2 yan4 daan6 gou1]

tortilla *n.* 墨西哥粟米薄餅 [mak9 sai1 go1 suk7 mai5 bok9 beng2], **flour** ~ 麵粉墨西哥粟米薄餅, **yellow** ~ 黃墨西哥粟米薄餅, **soft** ~ 軟墨西哥粟米薄餅, **hard** ~ 硬墨西哥粟米薄餅, **corn** ~ 墨西哥粟米薄餅, ~ **shell** 墨西哥粟米薄餅皮, ~ **chips** 墨西哥粟米薄餅薯條

tortoise *n.* 烏龜 [wu1 gwai1]

torture *v.* 折磨 [jit8 mo4]

toss *v.* 掟 [deng3]; ~**ed salad** 油拌沙律

total *adj.* 全部 [chyun4 bou6]; *n.* 全體員工 [chyun4 tai2 yun4 gung1]

totally *adv.* 百分百 [baak8 fan6 baak8]

touch *v./n.* 摸 [mo2], **keep in** ~ 保持聯繫

tough *adj.* 堅強 [gin1 keung4]

tour *n./v.* 巡迴演出 [cheun4 wui4 yin2 cheut7]; ~ **guide** 導遊, ~ **group** 旅遊團

tourist *n.* 遊客 [yau4 haak8]; ~ **attraction** 景點, ~ **office** 旅客諮詢處

tow *v.* 拖 [to1]; ~ **truck** 拖車

toward(s) *prep.* 向 [heung3]

towel *n.* 手巾 [sau2 gan1]

tower *n.* 塔 [taap8]

town *n.* 鎮 [jan3]; ~ **hall** 市政廳

toxic *adj.* 有毒 [yau5 duk9]; ~ **waste** 有毒廢物

toxin *n.* 毒素 [duk9 sou3]

toy *n.* 玩具 [wun6 geui6]; *adj.* 玩弄 [wun6 nung6], ~ **store** 玩具店

trace *v.* 追蹤 [jeui1 jung1]; *n.* 蹤跡 [jung1 jik7]

track *n.* 跑道 [paau2 dou6], ~ **race** 賽馬場, **running** ~ 跑道, **railroad** ~ 鐵路軌道; *v.* 跟蹤 [gan1 jung1]

trade *n./v.* 貿易 [mau6 yik9], ~ **union** 工會, **international** ~ 國際貿易, **a fair** ~ 公平交易

trader *n.* 商人 [seung1 yan4]

trading *n.* 買賣 [maai5 maai6]

tradition *n.* 傳統 [chyun2 tung2]

traditional *adj.* 傳統嘅 [chyun2 tung2 ge3]

traditionally *adv.* 傳統上 [chyun2 tung2 seung6]

traffic *n.* 交通 [gaau1 tung1], ~ **circle** 交通環島, ~ **jam** 塞車, ~ **accident** 交通事故, ~ **light** 紅綠燈, ~ **police** 交通警察, ~ **ticket** 交通罰單

trafficking (drug ~) *n.* 販毒 [faan3 duk9]

tragedy *n.* 悲劇 [bei1 kek9]

trail *n.* 足跡 [juk7 jik7]

trailer *n.* 拖車 [to1 che1]

train 1. *n.* 火車 [fo2 che1]; ~ **of thought** 思路 // **2.** (*teach*) *v.* 訓練 [fan3 lin6]

train station *n.* 火車站 [fo2 che1 jaam6]

trained *adj.* 受過訓練 [sau6 gwo3 fan3 lin6]

trainer *n.* 教練 [gaau3 lin6]

training *n.* 訓練 [fan3 lin6]; **sports** ~ 體育訓練

tramway *n.* 有軌電車 [yau5 gwai2 din6 che1]

transaction *n.* 業務 [yip9 mou6]

transcript *n.* 成績單 [sing4 jik7 daan1]

transfer *v.* 轉讓 [jyun2 yeung6]; *n.* 調動 [diu6 dung6]

transform *v.* 改造 [goi2 jou6]

transformation *n.* 改造 [goi2 jou6]

transfusion *n.* 輸血 [syu1 hyut8]

transit *n.* 運輸 [wan6 syu1]; **in** ~ 途中

transition *n.* 轉型 [jyun2 ying4]

translate *v.* 翻譯 [faan1 yik9]

translation *n.* 翻譯 [faan1 yik9]

translator *n.* 翻譯 [faan1 yik9]

transmission *n.* 傳播 [chyun4 bo3]; **auto** ~ 自動排擋

transmit *v.* 傳播 [chyun4 bo3]

transparent *adj.* 透明 [tau3 ming4]

transplant *v.* 移植 [yi4 jik9]

transport *v.* 運送 [wan6 sung3]

transportation *n.* 運輸 [wan6 syu1]

trap *n.* 圈套 [hyun1 tou3]; *v.* 陰 [yam1]

trash *n.* 垃圾 [laap9 saap8]; ~ **can** 垃圾桶

travel *v./n.* 旅遊 [leui5 yau4]; ~ **agency** 旅行社

traveler *n.* 遊客 [yau4 haak8]

traveler's check *n.* 旅行支票 [leui5 hang6 ji1 piu3]

traveling *n.* 旅遊 [leui5 yau4]

tray *n.* 托盤 [tok8 pun2]

treasure *n.* 珍寶 [jan1 bou2]; *v.* 珍惜 [jan1 sik7]

treasury *n.* 財政部 [choi4 jing3 bou6]

treat *n./v.* 請客 [cheng2 haak8]; **a** ~ 真係開心

treatment *n.* 治療 [ji6 liu4], ~ **room** 治療室, **alternative** ~ 替代治療

tree *n.* 樹 [syu6]

trek *n.* 長途跋涉 [cheung4 tou4 bat9 sip8]

tremendous *adj.* 巨大 [geui6 daai6]

trend *n.* 趨勢 [cheui1 sai3]

trespass *v.* 非法入侵 [fei1 faat8 yap9 cham1]

trespassing *n.* 非法入侵 [fei1 faat8 yap9 cham1], **No** ~ *phr.* 非請勿入

trial *n.* 審判 [sam2 pun3]

triangle *n.* 三角形 [saam1 gok8 ying4]

tribe *n.* 部落 [bou6 lok9]

tribute *n.* 進貢 [jeun3 gung3]

trick *n.* 詭計 [gwai2 gai3]; *v.* 欺騙 [hei1 pin3]

trim *v.* 修剪 [sau1 jin2]

trimming *n.* 修剪 [sau1 jin2]

Trinidad and Tobago *n.* 特立尼 達和多巴哥 [dak9 laap9 nei4 daat9 wo4 do1 ba1 go1]

Trinidadian *adj.* 特立尼達 [dak9 laap9 nei4 daat9]

trio *n.* 三人組合 [saam1 yan4 jou2 hap9]

trip *n./v.* 旅行 [leui5 hang4]

tripe *n.* 牛百葉 [ngau4 baak8 yip9]

Tripoli *n.* 的黎波里 [dik7 lai4 bo1 lei5 leui5]; ~, **capital of Libya** 利比亞首都

triumph *n.* 非凡嘅成就 [fei1 faan4 ge3 sing4 jau6]; *v.* 得勝 [dak7 sing3]

trolley *n.* 手推車 [sau2 teui1 che1]

tropical *adj.* 熱帶 [yit9 daai3], ~ **flavor** 熱帶風味, ~ **fruit** 熱 帶水果, ~ **juice** 熱帶水果汁

trouble *n.* 麻煩 [ma4 faan4]

trousers *n.* 褲 [fu3]

trout *n.* 鱒魚 [jyun1 yu2]

truck *n.* 貨車 [fo3 che1]

true *adj.* 真 [jan1], **That's not** ~ 唔係真嘅, ~ **or false** 真定假, **be** ~ 真嘅

truffle *n.* 松露 [chung4 lou6], **chocolate** ~ 朱古力松露

truly *adv.* 完全 [yun4 cyun4]

trunk (of a car) *n.* 樹身 [syu6 san1]

truss *v.* 綁緊 [bong2 gan2]

trust *n./v.* 信任 [seun3 yam6]

trustee *n.* 託管人 [tok8 gun2 yan4]

truth *n.* 真相 [jan1 seung3]

try *v.* 試 [si3], ~ **hard** 好努力, ~ **on** 試衫

T-shirt *n.* T恤 [ti1 seut7]

tube *n.* 管 [gun2]

tuber *n.* 球莖 [kau4 ging3]

Tuesday *n.* 禮拜二 [lai5 baai3 yi6]

tumor *n.* 瘤 [lau4], **benign ~** 良性腫瘤, **malignant ~** 惡性腫瘤

tuna (fish) *n.* 吞拿魚 [tan1 na4 yu2], **~ salad** 吞拿魚沙律

tune *n.* 旋律 [syun4 leut9]; *v.* 調整 [tiu4 jing2]

Tunis *n.* 突尼斯 [dat9 nei4 si1]; **~, capital of Tunisia** 突尼斯首都

Tunisia *n.* 突尼斯 [dat9 nei4 si1]

Tunisian *adj.* 突尼斯 [dat9 nei4 si1]

tunnel *n.* 隧道 [seui6 dou6]

turbot *n.* 大比目魚 [daai6 bei2 muk9 yu2]

Turkey (*country*) *n.* 土耳其 [tou2 yi5 kei4]

turkey (*bird*) *n.* 火雞 [fo2 gai1], **roasted ~** 烤火雞, **honey-glazed ~** 蜜烤火雞, **smoked ~** 煙薰火雞

Turkish *adj.* 土耳其 [tou2 yi5 kei4]; **~ bath** 土耳其浴

Turkmen (*citizen of Turkmenistan*) *adj.* 土庫曼斯坦 [tou2 fu3 maan6 si1 taan2]

Turkmenistan *n.* 土庫曼斯坦 [tou2 fu3 maan6 si1 taan2]

turmeric *n.* 黃薑粉 [wong4 geung1 fan2]

turn *v.* 轉 [jyun3], **~ down** 拒絕, **~ left!** 左轉, **~ on** 開, **~ signal** 轉彎指示, **~ up the volume** 大聲啲, **Where do I ~?** 我要

係邊度轉彎?; *n.* 輪 [leun4], **Whose ~ is it?** 輪到邊個?,

turnip *n.* 大頭菜 [daai6 tau4 choi3]

turnover *n.* 營業額 [ying4 yip9 ngaak2]

turret *n.* 角樓 [gok8 lau2]

turtle *n.* 海龜 [hoi2 gwai1]

turtle soup *n.* 甲魚湯 [gaap8 yu2 tong1]

tutor *n.* 家教 [ga1 gaau3]

tutorial *n.* 教程 [gaau3 ching4]; **online ~** 網上教程

Tuvalu *n.* 圖瓦盧 [tou4 nga5 lou4]

TV (television) *n.* 電視 [din6 si6] **~ set** 電視

tweezers *n.* 鉗仔 [kim2 jai2]

twelfth *adj.* 第十二個 [dai6 sap9 yi6 go3]

twelve *num.* 十二 [sap9 yi6]

twentieth *adj.* 第二十個 [dai6 yi6 sap9 go3]

twenty *num.* 二十 [yi6 sap9]; **~-four hour service** 全天候服務

twice *adv.* 兩次 [leung5 chi3], **~ a day** 一日兩次

twin *n./adj.* 孖生 [ma1 saang1]; **~ beds** 單人床

twins *n.* 孖胎 [ma1 toi1]

twist *v.* 扭 [nau2], **~ an ankle** 扭傷腳; *n.* 轉機 [jyun2 gei1]

twist bun (*fried bread*) *n.* 麻花 [ma4 fa1]

twisted *adj.* 變態 [bin3 taai3]

two *num.* 二 [yi6] **~-door car** 兩門車, **~-lane highway** 雙行高速公路

type 1. (*kind*) *n.* 類型 [leui6 ying4], **What ~ of ...?** 乜野種類...?, **She is not my ~** 我唔鍾意佢 // **2.** (*keystroke*) *v.* 打字 [da2 ji6]

typical *adj.* 典型 [din2 ying4]
typically *adv.* 一般 [yat7 bun1]

U

Uganda *n.* 烏干達 [wu1 gon1 daat9]

Ugandan *adj.* 烏干達 [wu1 gon1 daat9]

ugli fruit *n.* 牙買加丑橘 [nga4 maai5 ga1 chau2 gwat7]

ugly *adj.* 丑樣 [chau2 yeung2]

UK (United Kingdom) *n.* 英國 [ying1 gwok8]

Ukraine *n.* 烏克蘭 [wu1 hak7 laan4]

Ukrainian *adj.* 烏克蘭 [wu1 hak7 laan4]

Ulaanbaatar *n.* 烏蘭巴托 [wu1 laan4 ba1 tok8]; **~, capital of Mongolia** 蒙古首都

ulcer *n.* 潰瘍 [kui2 yeung4]

ultimate *adj.* 最終 [jeui3 jung1]

ultimately *adv.* 歸根究底 [gwai1 gan1 gau3 dai2]

ultrasound *adj.* 超聲波 [chiu1 sing1 bo1]

umbrella *n.* 遮 [je1]

unable *adj.* 冇能力 [mou5 nang4 lik9]

unacceptable *adj.* 唔可能接受 [m4 ho2 nang4 jip8 sau6]

unbearable *adj.* 唔可能忍受 [m4 ho2 nang4 yan2 sau6]

uncap *v.* 打開蓋 [da2 hoi1 goi3]; **~ped** 打開咗蓋

uncertain *adj.* 唔肯定 [m4 hang2 ding6]

uncertainty *n.* 唔確定 [m4 kok8 ding6]

uncle *n.* 阿叔 [a3 suk7]

uncomfortable *adj.* 唔舒服 [m4 syu1 fuk9]

unconscious *adj.* 昏迷 [fan1 mai4]

uncontrolled *adj.* 失控 [sat7 hung3]

uncooked *adj.* 未熟 [mei6 suk9]

uncork *v.* 打開蓋 [da2 hoi1 goi3]

uncountable *adj.* 數唔晒 [sou2 m4 saai3]

under *prep./adv.* 低於 [dai1 yu1], **~ control** 制服

underdone (*in cooking*) *adj.* 未熟晒 [mei6 suk9 saai3]

undergo *v.* 承受 [sing4 sau6]

underground *adj./adv.* 地下 [dei6 ha6]; **~ garage** 地下車庫

underlie *v.* 係...嘅基礎 [hai6 ... ge3 gei1 cho2]

underlying *adj.* 深層 [sam1 chang4]

underneath *prep.* 喺...下面 [hai2 ... ha6 min6]; *adv.* 底下 [dai2 ha6]

underpants *n.* 底褲 [dai2 fu3]

underpass *n.* 地下通道 [dei6 ha6 tung1 dou6]

understand *v.* 理解 [lei5 gaai2], **I don't ~** 我唔明白

understanding *n.* 理解 [lei5 gaai2], **to reach an ~** 達成共識

undertake *v.* 承擔 [sing4 daam1]

undertaking *n.* 任務 [yam6 mou6]

underwater *adj./adv.* 水下面 [seui2 ha6 min6]

underwear *n.* 底褲 [dai2 fu3]

undo *v.* 解開 [gaai2 hoi1]

undoubtedly *adv.* 毫無疑問 [hou4 mou4 yi4 man6]

undress *v.* 除衫 [cheui4 saam1]

unemployed *adj.* 失業 [sat7 yip9]

unemployment *n.* 失業 [sat7 yip9]; ~ **compensation** 失業救濟

uneven *adj.* 唔平 [m4 ping4]; ~ **road surface** 路面唔平

unexpected *adj.* 意料之外 [yi3 liu6 ji1 ngoi6]

unexpectedly *adv.* 意料之外 [yi3 liu6 ji1 ngoi6]

unfair *adj.* 唔公平 [m4 gung1 ping4]

unfairly *adv.* 唔公平 [m4 gung1 ping4]

unfamiliar *adj.* 陌生 [mak9 sang1]

unfortunate *adj.* 唔好彩 [m4 hou2 choi2]

unfortunately *adv.* 可惜 [ho2 sik7]

unfriendly *adj.* 唔友好 [m4 yau5 hou2]

unfurnished *adj.* 未裝修 [mei6 jong1 sau1]

unhappiness *n.* 唔開心 [m4 hoi1 sam1]

unhappy *adj.* 唔開心 [m4 hoi1 sam1]

uniform *n.* 制服 [jai3 fuk9]

unimportant *adj.* 唔重要 [m4 jung6 yiu3]

uninterrupted *adj.* 連續 [lin4 juk9]

union *n.* 聯盟 [lyun4 mang4]

unique *adj.* 獨特 [duk9 dak9]

unit *n.* 單位 [daan1 wai2]

unite *v.* 聯合 [lyun4 hap9]

united *adj.* 統一 [tung2 yat7]

United Arab Emirates (UAE) *n.* 阿聯酋 [a3 lyun4 yau4]

United Kingdom (UK) *n.* 英國 [ying1 gwok8]

United States of America (USA) *n.* 美國 [mei5 gwok8]

universe *n.* 宇宙 [yu5 jau6]

university *n.* 大學 [daai6 hok9]; ~ **degree** 大學學位

unkind *adj.* 惡 [ok8]

unknown *adj.* 未知 [mei6 ji1]

unleaded *adj.* 無鉛 [mou4 yun4], ~ **gasoline** 無鉛汽油

unleavened *adj.* 未發酵 [mei6 faat8 haau1], ~ **bread** 未發酵麵包

unless *conj.* 除非 [cheui4 fei1]

unlike *prep./adj.* 唔似 [m4 chi5]

unlikely *adj.* 可能性唔大 [ho2 nang4 sing3 m4 daai6]

unlimited *adj.* 無限 [mou4 haan6], ~ **mileage** 冇里程限制

unload *v.* 落貨 [lok9 fo3]

unlock *v.* 開 [hoi1]

unlucky *adj.* 唔好彩 [m4 hou2 choi2]

unmarried *adj.* 單身 [daan1 san1]

unmixed *adj.* 純 [seun4]

unmold *v.* 取模 [cheui2 mou2]

unnecessary *adj.* 冇必要 [mou5 bit7 yiu3]

unpleasant *adj.* 令人唔開心 [ling4 yan4 m4 hoi1 sam1]

unreasonable *adj.* 無理 [mou4 lei5]

unrefined *adj.* 粗俗 [chou1 juk9], ~ **sugar** 粗糖

unripe *adj.* 未熟 [mei6 suk9], ~ **fruit** 生水果, ~ **vegatable** 未熟嘅青菜

unsafe *adj.* 唔安全 [m4 on1 cyun4]

unsanitary *adj.* 唔衛生 [m4 wai6 sang1]

unsaturated *adj.* 不飽和 [bat7 baau2 wo4], ~ **fat** 不飽和脂肪

unscrew *v.* 扭開 [nau2 hoi1]

unstable *adj.* 唔穩定 [m4 wan2 ding6]

unsteady *adj.* 震震地 [jan3 jan3 dei2]

unsuccessful *adj.* 失敗咗 [sat7 baai6 jo2]

untidy *adj.* 亂七八糟 [lyun6 chat7 baat8 jou1]

until *prep.* 除非 [cheui4 fei1]

until *conj./prep.* 直到 [jik9 dou3]

unusual *adj.* 罕有 [hon2 yau5]

unusually *adv.* 出奇 [cheut7 kei4]

unwilling *adj.* 唔願意 [m4 yun6 yi3]

unwillingly *adv.* 勉強 [min5 keung5]

unzip *v.* 拉開 [laa1 hoi1], ~ **clothing** 拉鍊, ~ **a file** *comp.* 解壓縮文件

up *adv./prep.* 企起身 [kei5 hei2 san1], ~ **there** 上面個度, ~ **to** 由…決定, ~ **till now** 直到宜家, **going** ~ 上緊去, **look** ~ 抬頭

updated *adj.* 更新咗 [gang1 san1 jo2]

uphill *adj.* 上坡 [seung5 bo1]

upon *prep.* 喺…上面 [hai2 … seung6 min6]

upper *adj.* 上面 [seung6 min6], ~ **berth** 上鋪, ~ **body** 上身

upset *v.* 激嬲 [gik7 nau1]; *adj.* 唔開心 [m4 hoi1 sam1], ~ **stomach** 胃唔舒服

upsetting *adj.* 激氣 [gik7 hei3]

upside down *adv.* 上下顛倒 [seung6 ha6 din1 dou2]

upside-down cake *n.* 倒置蛋糕 [dou2 ji3 daan6 gou1]

upstairs *adv.* 上樓 [seung5 lau4]; *adj./n.* 樓上 [lau4 seung6]

upward *adj.* 向上 [heung3 seung6]

upwards *adv.* 向上 [heung3 seung6]

urban *adj.* 城市 [sing4 si5]

urge *v.* 主張 [jyu2 jeung1]; *n.* 衝動 [chung1 dung6]

urgent *adj.* 緊急 [gan2 gap7]

urinary tract infection *n.* 尿道感染 [niu6 dou6 gam2 yim5]

urine *n.* 尿 [niu6]

URL (Uniform Resource Locator) *n.* 網址 [mong5 ji2]

Uruguay *n.* 烏拉圭人 [wu1 laai1 gwai1 yan4]

Uruguayan *adj.* 烏拉圭 [wu1 laai1 gwai1]

us *pron.* 我哋 [ngo5 dei6]

USA (United States of America) *n.* 美國 [mei5 gwok8]

usage *n.* 使用 [sai2 yung6]

use *v.* 用 [yung6], ~ **before** 保質期係; *n.* 用途 [yung6 tou4], **for my personal** ~ 私用

used to: ~ **smth.** 習慣, ~ **do smth.** 以前成日做

useful *adj.* 有用 [yau5 yung6]

useless *adj.* 冇用 [mou5 yung6]

user *n.* 用戶 [yung6 wu6]

username *n.* 用戶名 [yung6 wu6 meng4]; **website** ~ 網站 用戶名

usual *adj.* 通常 [tung1 seung4]

usually *adv.* 通常 [tung1 seung4]

usury *n.* 大耳窿 [daai6 yi5 lung1]

utensils (eating ~) *n.* 餐具 [chaan1 geui6]

utility *n.* 效用 [haau6 yung6]

utterance *n.* 講話 [gong2 wa6]

Uzbek *adj.* 烏茲別克斯坦人 [wu1 ji1 bit9 hak7 si1 taan2 yan4]

Uzbekistan *n.* 烏茲別克斯坦 [wu1 ji1 bit9 hak7 si1 taan2]

V

vacancy *n.* 空缺 [hung1 kyut8];
~ **no** *phr.* 唔請人

vacant *adj.* 空 [hung1]

vacate *v.* 空出 [hung1 cheut7]

vacation *n.* 假期 [ga3 kei4]; **on ~**
度假

vaccinate *v.* 注射疫苗 [jyu3 se6
yik9 miu4]; **be ~d against** 防疫

vaccination *n.* 接種疫苗 [jip8
jung2 yik9 miu4]

vaccine *n.* 疫苗 [yik9 miu4]

Vaduz *n.* 瓦杜茲 [nga5 dou6
ji1]; ~, **capital of Liechtenstein**
列支敦士登首都

vagina *n.* 陰道 [yam1 dou6];
~l infection 陰道感染

valet *n.* 男僕人 [naam4 buk9
yan4]; ~ **service** 男僕人服伺

valid *adj.* 有效 [yau5 haau6]

validate *v.* 驗證 [yim6 jing3],
~ **tickets** 驗票

Valletta *n.* 瓦萊塔 [nga5 loi4
taap8]; ~, **capital of Malta** 馬
耳他首都

valley *n.* 山谷 [saan1 guk7]

valuable *adj.* 值錢 [jik9 chin2]; ~
article 貴重物品

valuables *n.* 貴重物品 [gwai3
jung6 mat9 ban2]

valuation *n.* 估價 [gu2 ga3]

value *n.* 價值 [ga3 jik9], **a good ~**
好抵; *v.* 重視 [jung6 si6]

value-added tax *n.* 增值稅
[jang1 jik9 seui3]

van *n.* 麵包車 [min6 baau1 che1]

vanilla *n.* 香草 [heung1 chou2];
~ **pod** 香草豆莢, ~ **bean** 香草
豆, ~ **extract** 香草濃縮,
~ **essence** 香草精華, ~ **milk**
香草味牛奶

Vanuatu *n.* 瓦努阿圖 [nga5
nou5 a3 tou4]

vapor *n.* 水蒸氣 [seui2 jing1 hei3]

vaporize *v.* 蒸發 [jing1 faat8]

variable *adj.* 變來變去 [bin3
loi4 bin3 heui3]; *n.* 變量 [bin3
leung6]

variation *n.* 變化 [bin3 fa3]

varied *adj.* 多種多樣 [do1 jung2
do1 yeung6]

variety *n.* 種類 [jung2 leui6]

various *adj.* 各種各樣 [gok8
jung2 gok8 yeung6]

vary *v.* 變化 [bin3 fa3]

vase *n.* 花瓶 [fa1 ping4]

vast *adj.* 大量 [daai6 leung6]

VAT *n.* 增值稅 [jang1 jik9
seui3]; ~ **receipt** 增值稅發票

Vatican City *n.* 梵蒂岡 [faan6
dai3 gong1]; ~, **capital of
Vatican City** 梵蒂岡首都

vault *n.* 地牢 [dei6 lou4]

veal *n.* 牛仔肉 [ngau4 jai2 yuk9];
~ **stew** 燉牛仔肉

vector *n.* 向量 [heung3 leung6]

vegan *adj./n.* 純素食者 [seun4
sou3 sik9 je2]

vegetable *n.* 蔬菜 [so1 choi3],
~ **stew** 燉青菜, ~ **broth** 菜湯

vegetarian *adj.* 素食者 [sou3 sik9 je2], ~ **dish** 素菜, ~ **soup** 素湯, ~ **menu** 素菜菜單

vegetation *n.* 植物 [jik9 mat9]

vehicle *n.* 車輛 [che1 leung6]

veil *n.* 面纱 [min6 sa1]

vein *n.* 静脈 [jing6 mak9]

velocity *n.* 速度 [chuk7 dou6]

vendor *n.* 小販 [siu2 faan2]

venereal *adj.* 性傳染 [sing3 chyun4 yim5], ~ **disease** 性傳染病

Venezuela *n.* 委內瑞拉 [wai1 noi6 seui6 laai1]

Venezuelan *adj.* 委內瑞拉 [wai1 noi6 seui6 laai1]

venison *n.* 鹿肉 [luk9 yuk9]

venom *n.* 惡意 [ok8 yi3]

ventilator *n.* 通風設備 [tung1 fung1 chit8 bei6]

venture *n./v.* 冒險 [mou6 him2]

venue *n.* 場地 [cheung4 dei6]

verb *n.* 動詞 [dung6 chi4]

verdict *n.* 裁定 [choi4 ding6]

verse *n.* 詩 [si1]

version *n.* 版本 [baan2 bun2]

vertical *adj.* 垂直 [seui4 jik9]

very *adv.* 好 [hou2], ~ **good** 十分之好, ~ **much** 非常

via *prep.* 經過 [ging1 gwo3]

victim *n.* 受害者 [sau6 hoi6 je2]

Victoria *n.* 維多利亞 [wai4 do1 lei6 a3]; ~, **capital of Seychelles** 塞舌爾首都

victorious *adj.* 勝利 [sing3 lei6]

victory *n.* 勝利 [sing3 lei6]

video *n.* 錄影帶 [luk9 ying2 daai2]; ~ **camera** 錄影機, ~ **card** 視頻卡, ~ **game** 電子遊戲,

~ **recorder** 錄影機, ~**cassette** 錄像帶

Vienna *n.* 維也納 [wai4 ya5 naap9]; ~, **capital of Austria** 奧地利首都

Vientiane *n.* 萬象 [maan6 jeung6]; ~, **capital of Laos** 老撾首都

Vietnam *n.* 越南 [yut9 naam4]

Vietnamese *adj.* 越南 [yut9 naam4]

view *n.* 意見 [yi3 gin3], **sea ~** 海景, **a nice ~** 風景唔錯, **political ~s** 政治觀點, ~**ing gallery** 觀景台; *v.* 睇 [tai2]

viewer *n.* 觀眾 [gun1 jung3]

viewpoint *n.* 觀點 [gun1 dim2]

village *n.* 村 [chyun1]; ~ **inn** 鄉村旅館

Vilnius *n.* 維爾紐斯 [wai4 yi5 nau2 si1]; ~, **capital of Lithuania** 立陶宛首都

vinaigrette *n.* 嗅鹽瓶 [chau3 yim4 ping4]

vine *n.* 藤蔓 [tang4 maan6]

vinegar *n.* 醋 [chou3], **white ~** 白醋, **red ~** 紅醋, **apple cider ~** 蘋果醋, ~ **dressing** 香醋沙律醬

vineyard *n.* 葡萄園 [pou4 tou4 yun4]

vintage *adj.* 古董 [gu2 dung2], ~ **wine** 佳釀

viola *n.* 中提琴 [jung1 tai4 kam4]

violence *n.* 暴力 [bou6 lik9]

violent *adj.* 暴力 [bou6 lik9]

violently *adv.* 暴力 [bou6 lik9]

violin *n.* 小提琴 [siu2 tai4 kam4]

virgin *n.* 處女 [chyu3 neui5]

Virgo *n.* 處女座 [chyu3 neui5 jo6]

virtually *adv.* 事實上 [si6 sat9 seung6]

virtue *n.* 美德 [mei5 dak7]

virus *n.* 病毒 [beng6 duk9]; **computer** ~ 電腦病毒

visa *n.* 簽證 [chim1 jing3]

visible *adj.* 明顯 [ming4 hin2]

vision *n.* 視力 [si6 lik9]

visit *v./n.* 參觀 [chaam1 gun1]; ~**ing hours** 探病時間

visitor *n.* 到訪者 [dou3 fong2 je2]

visor *n.* 面罩 [min6 jaau3]

visual *adj.* 視覺 [si6 gok8]; *n.* 畫面 [wa2 min6]

vital *adj.* 至關重要 [ji3 gwaan1 jung6 yiu3]

vitamin *n.* 維他命 [wai4 ta1 ming6]; ~ **tablet** 維他命丸, ~ **supplement** 維他命補品

vocabulary *n.* 詞彙 [chi4 wui6]

vocal *adj.* 大膽講 [daai6 daam2 gong2]

vodka *n.* 伏特加 [fuk9 dak9 ga1]

voice *n.* 聲 [seng1]

voir dire (*legal*) 一切照實陳述 [yat7 chai3 jiu3 sat9 chan4 seut9]

volcano *n.* 火山 [fo2 saan1]

volleyball *n.* 排球 [paai4 kau4]

voltage *n.* 電壓 [din6 aat8]

volume *n.* 冊 [chaak8]

voluntarily *adv.* 自願 [ji6 yun6]

voluntary *adj.* 自願 [ji6 yun6]

volunteer *n.* 義工 [yi6 gung1]

vomit *n.* 嘔吐物 [ngau2 tou3 mat9]; *v.* 嘔 [ngau2]

vote *n./v.* 投票 [tau4 piu3]

vowel *n.* 元音 [yun4 yam1]

W

wafer *n.* 威化餅 [wai1 fa3 beng2]

waffle *n.* 格仔餅 [gaak8 jai2 beng2]

wage *n.* 工資 [gung1 ji1]

waist *n.* 腰 [yiu1]

wait *n./v.* 等 [dang2], ~ **for** 等, ~ **for the tone** 等待音, ~**ing room** 候診室, ~! 等等!, ~ **time** 等候時間

waiter *n.* 男夥計 [naam4 fo2 gai3]

waitress *n.* 女夥計 [neui5 fo2 gai3]

waiver *n.* 棄權證書 [hei3 kyun4 jing3 syu1]

wake *v.* 叫醒 [giu3 seng2], ~ **someone** 叫醒某人, ~ **up** 叫醒, ~**up call** 叫醒服務

Wales *n.* 威爾士 [wai1 yi5 si6]

walk *v./n.* 散步 [saan3 bou6], ~ **on** 繼續行

walking *n.* 散步 [saan3 bou6]; ~ **shoes** 旅遊鞋, ~ **route** 步行路線

walkway *n.* 人行道 [yan4 hang4 dou6]

wall *n.* 牆 [cheung4]

wallet *n.* 銀包 [ngan2 baau1]

walnut *n.* 核桃 [hat9 tou4]

wander *v.* 周圍行下 [jau1 wai4 haang4 ha5]

wanderer *n.* 流浪漢 [lau4 long6 hon3]

want *v.* 想 [seung2]

war *n.* 戰爭 [jin3 jang1]; ~ **movies** 戰爭片, ~ **memorial** 戰爭紀念碑, **World W~ II** 二次大戰

ward (*hospital*) *n.* 病房 [beng6 fong2]

wardrobe *n.* 衣櫃 [yi1 gwai6]

warehouse *n.* 倉庫 [chong1 fu3]

warm *adj.* 暖 [nyun5], ~ **weather** 溫暖氣候, **It's too ~ in here** 尼度太熱啦; *v.* 整熱 [jing2 yit9]

warmer *adj.* 暖啲 [nyun5 di1]

warmth *n.* 溫暖 [wan1 nyun5]

warn *v.* 警告 [ging2 gou3]

warning *n.* 警告 [ging2 gou3], ~ **light** 警告信號燈, **health ~** 健康警告

warrant *n.* 許可證 [heui2 ho2 jing3]

warranty *n.* 擔保 [daam1 bou2]

Warsaw *n.* 華沙 [wa6 sa1]; ~, **capital of Poland** 波蘭首都

wart *n.* 疣 [yau4]

wasabi *n.* 芥辣 [gaai3 laat9]

wash *v.* 洗 [sai2], ~ **dishes** 洗碗, **hand ~** 手洗

washbasin *n.* 洗面盆 [sai2 min6 pun4]

washing *n.* 洗 [sai2], ~ **powder** 洗衣粉

washing machine *n.* 洗衣機 [sai2 yi1 gei1]

Washington, D.C. *n.* 華盛頓特區 [wa6 sing4 deun6 dak9 keui1]; ~, **capital of United States of America** 美國首都

washroom *n.* 廁所 [chi3 so2]

wasp *n.* 黃蜂 [wong4 fung1]

waste *v.* 浪費 [long6 fai3]; *n.* 廢物 [fai3 mat9]; *adj.* 有用 [mou5 yung6]

watch 1. (*look at*) *v.* 睇 [tai2], **~ out!** *exclam.* 睇住！ // **2.** (*timepiece*) *n.* 錶 [biu1], **an analog ~** 指針式電子錶

watchmaker *n.* 鐘錶商 [jung1 biu1 seung1]

water *n.* 水 [seui2]; **~ bottle** 水瓶, **~ faucet** 水喉, **~ heater** 熱水器, **~ supply** 水供應, **mineral ~** 礦泉水, **spring ~** 山泉水, **sparkling ~** 汽水, **soda ~** 汽水

water chestnut *n.* 菱角 [ling4 gok8]

watercolor *n.* 水彩 [seui2 choi2]

watercress *n.* 昂菜 [ngong4 choi3], **~ soup** 昂菜湯

waterfall *n.* 瀑布 [buk9 bou3]

watermelon *n.* 西瓜 [sai1 gwa1]

waterproof *adj.* 防水 [fong4 seui2], **~ shoes** 水鞋

water-ski *v.* 滑水 [waat9 seui2]; **~s** *n.* 滑水

water-skiing *n.* 滑水 [waat9 seui2]

wave *n.* 浪 [long6]; *v.* 擺 [baai2]

wax *v.* 打蠟 [da2 laap9]

waxing *n.* 打蠟 [da2 laap9]

waxwork *n.* 蠟像 [laap9 jeung6]

way *n.* 方法 [fong1 faat8], **it's on the ~ to …** 黎緊…, **I've lost my ~** 盪失路, **which ~?** 點行?, **that ~** 個邊

we *pron.* 我哋 [ngoo5 dei6]

weak *adj.* 軟弱 [yun5 yeuk9], **~ flavor** 冇乜味, **~ taste** 冇乜味

weakness *n.* 軟弱 [yun5 yeuk9]

wealth *n.* 財富 [choi4 fu3]

wealthy *adj.* 有錢 [yau5 chin2]

weapon *n.* 武器 [mou5 hei3]

wear *v.* 着 [jeuk8]

wearing *n.* 好劫 [hou2 gui6]

weather *n.* 天氣 [tin1 hei3]; **~ forecast** 天氣預報, **~ report** 天氣報告

web *n.* 鐵絲網 [tit8 si1 mong5]

webpage *n.* 網頁 [mong5 yip9]

website *n.* 網站 [mong5 jaam6]

wedding *n.* 婚禮 [fan1 lai5]; **~ anniversary** 結婚週年紀念, **~ cake** 結婚蛋糕, **~ present** 結婚禮物, **~ ring** 結婚戒指

Wednesday *n.* 禮拜三 [lai5 baai3 saam1]

week *n.* 禮拜 [lai5 baai3], **this ~** 呢個禮拜

weekday *n.* 工作日 [gung1 jok8 yat9]

weekend *n.* 周末 [jau1 mut9]

weekly *adv./adj.* 個個星期 [go3 go3 sing1 kei4]

weigh *v.* 秤重 [ching3 chung4], **he ~ed the apples** 佢秤咗個啲蘋果, **What do you ~?** 你有幾重?

weight *n.* 重量 [chung5 leung6], **My ~ is 112 kgs.** 我有112公斤重, **lose ~** 減肥

welcome *v./n.* 歡迎 [fun1 ying4], **~ to …** 歡迎來到…, **~!** *exclam.* 熱烈歡迎!, **you're ~** 唔使客氣; *adj.* 受歡迎 [sau6 fun1 ying4]

well 1. *adv./adj.* 好 [hou2]; *exclam.* 好呀 [hou2 a1] // **2.** (*water ~*) *n.* 井 [jing2]

well-behaved *adj.* 聽話 [ting1 wa2]

well-done *adj.* 做得非常好 [jou6 dak7 fei1 seung4 hou2]

well-known *adj.* 出名 [cheut7 meng4];

Wellington *n.* 威靈頓 [wai1 ling4 deun6]; **capital of New Zealand** 新西蘭首都

Welsh *adj.* 威爾士 [wai1 yi5 si6]

west *n./adj./adv.* 西面 [sai1 min6]

western *adj.* 歐美 [au1 mei5]

wet *adj.* 濕 [sap7]; **~ paint** 油漆未乾

wetsuit *n.* 潛水衫 [chim4 seui2 saam1]

what *pron./det.* 乜 [mat7], **~ is that?** 乜野黎嘎, **~ time is it?** 宜家幾點鐘？

whatever *det.* 乜都得 [mat7 dou1 dak7]; *pron.* 乜都 [mat7 dou1]

wheat *n.* 小麥 [siu2 mak9]; **~ bread** 小麥麵包, **~ pasta** 小麥糊

wheat germ *n.* 麥芽 [mak9 nga4]

wheel *n.* 轆 [luk7]

wheelchair *n.* 輪椅 [leun4 yi2]

wheezing *n.* 嗍氣 [sok8 hei3]

when *adv./pron./conj.* 幾時 [gei2 si4]

whenever *conj.* 幾時都得 [gei2 si4 dou1 dak7]

where *adv./conj.* 邊度 [bin1 dou6], **~ to** 去邊度, **~ were you born?** 你喺邊度出世？

whereas *conj.* 但係 [daan6 hai6]

wherever *conj.* 邊度都得 [bin1 dou6 dou1 dak7]

whether *conj.* 定係 [ding6 hai6]

whey *n.* 乳清 [yu5 ching1]

which *pron./det./adj.* 邊個 [bin1 go3]

while *conj.* 喺...期間 [hai2 ... kei4 gaan1]; *n.* 一陣 [yat7 jan6], **~ you wait** 喺你等嘅期間

whip *v.* 鞭打 [bin1 da2]

whipped *adj.* 攪好 [gaau2 hou2], **~ cream** 生奶油, **~ eggs** 打蛋, **~ up** 鞭打, **~ milk** 生奶, **~ cheese** 奶油芝士

whisk *v.* 掃 [sou3]

whiskey *n.* 威士忌 [wai1 si6 gei2]

whisper *v./n.* 細細聲講 [sai3 sai3 seng1 gong2]

whistle *n.* 口哨 [hau2 saau3]; *v.* 吹口哨 [cheui1 hau2 saau3]

white *adj.* 白色嘅 [baak9 sik7 ge3], **~ bread** 白麵包, **~ cabbage** 白菜, **~ sauce** 白汁, **~ wine** 葡萄白酒; *n.* 白色 [baak9 sik7]

whitebait (*fish*) *n.* 銀魚 [ngan4 yu2]

whitefish *n.* 白魚 [baak9 yu2]

whither *adv.* 邊度 [bin1 dou6]

whiting *n.* 鱈魚 [syut8 yu2]

who *pron.* 邊個 [bin1 go3]

whoever *pron.* 邊個都得 [bin1 go3 dou1 dak7]

whole *adj.* 成個 [seng4 go3]; *n.* 全部 [chyun4 bou6]

whole milk *n.* 全脂牛奶 [cyun4 ji1 ngau4 naai5]

whole wheat *n.* 全麥 [chyun4 mak9], **~ flour** 全麥粉, **~ bread** 全麥麵包, **~ pasta** 全麥意大利麵

whom *pron.* 邊個 [bin1 go3]

whose *det./pron.* 邊個嘅 [bin1 go3 ge3]

why *adv./conj.* 點解 [dim2 gaai2], **~ is that?** 點解?, **~ not?** 好啊

wide *adj.* 闊 [fut8]

widely *adv.* 廣泛 [gwong2 faan3]

widespread *adj.* 普遍 [pou2 pin3]

widow *n.* 寡婦 [gwa2 fu5]

widower *n.* 寡佬 [gwa2 lou2]

width *n.* 闊度 [fut8 dou6]

wife *n.* 老婆 [lou5 po4]

wild *adj.* 野生 [ye5 sang1], **~ animal** 野生動物, **~ duck** 野鴨, **~ berries** 野莓

wild boar *n.* 野豬 [ye5 jyu1]

wild cherry *n.* 野生車厘子 [ye5 saang1 che1 lei4 ji2]

wildlife *n.* 野生動物 [ye5 sang1 dung6 mat9]

wildly *adv.* 發顛咁 [faat8 din1 gam3]

will 1. *v. aux.* 會 [wui5] // **2.** *n.* (*legal document*) 遺囑 [wai4 juk7]

willing *adj.* 自願 [ji6 yun6]

willingly *adv.* 自願 [ji6 yun6]

willingness *n.* 意願 [yi3 yun6]

win *v.* 贏 [yeng4]

wind 1. (*weather*) *n.* 風 [fung1] // **2.** *v.* (*~ smth. up*) 上發條 [seung5 faat8 tiu4]

windbreaker *n.* 防風衣 [fong4 fung1 yi1]

Windhoek *n.* 溫得和克 [wan1 dak7 wo4 hak7]; **~, capital of Namibia** 納米比亞首都

windmill *n.* 風車 [fung1 che1]

window *n.* 窗 [cheung1]; **~ shopping** 隨便睇睇, **~ seat** 窗口位**, open the ~** 開窗, *comp.* **open a new ~** 再開一個窗口

windshield *n.* 擋風玻璃 [dong2 fung1 bo1 lei1]; **~ wiper** 雨刮

windsurf *v.* 滑浪風帆 [waat9 long6 fung1 faan4]

windy *adj.* 好大風 [hou2 daai6 fung1]

wine *n.* 紅酒 [hung4 jau2], **~ cellar** 酒窖, **~ list** 酒單, **rose ~** 淡紅葡萄酒, **merlot ~** 梅洛葡萄酒, **sparkling ~** 汽酒, **vintage ~** 佳釀, **sweet ~** 甜酒, **medium dry ~** 半乾葡萄酒, **medium sweet ~** 半甜葡萄酒, **frothy ~** 汽酒, **table ~** 餐酒

wineglass *n.* 酒杯 [jau2 bui1]

winery *n.* 酒莊 [jau2 jong1]

wing (*of a bird/building*) *n.* 翼 [yik9]

winner *n.* 贏家 [yeng4 ga1]

winning *adj.* 贏咗 [yeng4 jo2]

winter *n.* 冬天 [dung1 tin1]

wipe *v.* 抹 [maat8]

wire *n.* 電線 [din6 sin3]

wireless Internet *n.* 無線上網 [mou4 sin3 seung5 mong5]

wisdom *n.* 智慧 [ji3 wai6]

wise *adj.* 英明 [ying1 ming4]

wish *v.* 希望 [hei1 mong6]; *n.* 願望 [yun6 mong6]; **best ~es** *phr.* 僅致問候

wit *n.* 才智 [choi4 ji3]

with *prep.* 同 [tung4]

withdraw *v.* 攞出黎 [lo2 cheut7 lai4], **~ money** 取錢

withdrawal *n.* 撤離 [chit8 lei4]

within *prep.* 喺…範圍內 [hai2 … faan6 wai4 noi6]

without *prep.* 冇咗 [mou5 jo2]

witness *n.* 證人 [jing3 yan4]; *v.* 作證 [jok8 jing3]

wok *n.* 鑊 [wok9]

woman *n.* 女人 [neui5 yan2]

women *n.pl.* 女人 [neui5 yan2]; **~'s room** 女廁, **~'s clothing** 女裝

wonder *v.* 想知道 [seung2 ji1 dou6]

wonderful *adj.* 精彩 [jing1 choi2]

wood *n.* 木 [muk9]; **~ carving** 木雕刻

wood grouse *n.* 松雞 [chung4 gai1]

wooden *adj.* 木整 [muk9 jing2], **~ knife** 木刀, **~ spoon** 木羹

woods *n.* 樹林 [syu6 lam4]

wool *n.* 羊毛 [yeung4 mou4]

Worcestershire sauce *n.* 辣醬油 [laat9 jeung3 yau4]

word *n.* 字 [ji6]

word processing 文字處理 [man4 ji6 chyu5 lei5]

work *v.* 返工 [faan1 gung1], **it doesn't ~** 唔得, **I hope this ~s out** 我希望今次得啦; *n.* 工 [gung1], **~ permit** 工作證, **I'm late for ~** 我返工遲到

worker *n.* 工人 [gung1 yan4]

workforce *n.* 勞動力 [lou4 dung6 lik9]

working *adj.* 返工 [faan1 gung1]

workout *n.* 鍛鍊 [dyun3 lin6]

works *n.* 工廠 [gung1 chong2]

workshop *n.* 車間 [che1 gaan1]

world *n.* 世界 [sai3 gaai3]; **W~ Cup** 世界杯, **the New W~** 新大陸

worldwide *adj.* 全世界 [chyun4 sai3 gaai3]; *adv.* 世界各地 [sai3 gaai3 gok8 dei6]

worm *n.* 蟲 [chung4]

wormwood *n.* 艾草 [ngaai6 chou2]

worried *adj.* 擔心 [daam1 sam1]

worry *v./n.* 擔心 [daam1 sam1]

worrying *adj.* 令人擔心 [ling4 yan4 daam1 sam1]

worse *adj./adv.* 仲差 [jung6 cha1]

worship *n./v.* 崇拜 [sung4 baai3]

worst *adj./adv.* 最差 [jeui3 cha1]

worth *adj.* 值 [jik9], **~ seeing** 好值得一睇, **What is this ~?** 呢個值幾多錢?

worthy *adj.* 值得 [jik9 dak7]

would *v.* 會 [wui5]

wound *n.* 傷口 [seung1 hau2]; *v.* 整傷 [jing2 seung1]

wounded *adj.* 受咗傷 [sau6 jo2 seung1]

wrap *v.* 包 [baau1]; **chicken ~** 雞肉卷

wrapped *adj.* 包好 [baau1 hou2], **was ~** 包咗起身

wrapping *n.* 包裝紙 [baau1 jong1 ji2]

wrist *n.* 手腕 [sau2 wun2]

writ *n.* 文書 [man4 syu1]

write *v.* 寫 [se2], **~ down** 寫低

writer *n.* 作家 [jok8 ga1]

writing *n.* 文章 [man4 jeung1]

written *adj.* 書面 [syu1 min2]

wrong *adj./adv.* 錯 [cho3], **~ number** 打錯電話, **there's something ~** 有啲唔妥, **What's ~?** *phr.* 做乜野?

wrongly *adv.* 錯誤咁 [cho3 ng6 gam3]

www. (world wide web) *n.* 互聯網 [wu6 lyun4 mong5]

X-Y-Z

X-ray *n.* X光 [X gwong1];
v. 照X光 [jiu3 X gwong1];
~ **examination** X光檢查

yacht *n.* 遊艇 [yau4 teng5]

yam *n.* 蕃薯 [faan1 syu4];
candied ~ 甜薯

Yamoussoukro *n.* 亞穆蘇克羅
[a3 muk9 sou1 hak7 lo4];
~, **capital of Cote d'Ivoire**
科特迪瓦首都

Yaounde *n.* 雅溫得 [nga5 wan1
dak7]; ~, **capital of Cameroon**
喀麥隆首都

yard *n.* 後院 [hau6 yun2]

yarrow *n.* 蓍草 [si1 chou2]

yawn *v.* 打喊櫓 [da2 haam3
lou5]; *n.* 喊櫓 [haam3 lou5]

yeah *exclam.* 好野 [hou2 ye5]

year *n.* 年 [nin4]; **Happy New
~!** *phr.* 新年好!, **this** ~ 今年,
twenty-seven ~s old 二十七歲

yeast *n.* 酵母菌 [gaau3 mou5
kwan2]

yell *v.* 叫 [giu3]

yellow *adj./n.* 黃色 [wong4 sik7];
~ **pages** 黃頁

Yemen *n.* 也門 [ya5 mun4]

Yemeni *adj.* 也門 [ya5 mun4]

Yerevan *n.* 耶烈萬 [ye4 lit9 maan6];
~, **capital of Armenia** 亞美尼
亞首都

yes *exclam./n./adv.* 係 [hai6]

yesterday *adv./n.* 琴日 [kam4
yat9], **the day before** ~ 前晚

yet *adv.* 仲未 [jung6 mei6]; *conj.*
但係 [daan6 hai6], **not** ~ 未啊

yield *v.* 投降 [tau4 hong4]; *n.* 產
量 [chaan2 leung6]

yoga *n.* 瑜珈 [yu4 ga1]

yogurt *n.* 乳酪 [yu5 lok3]; **low-fat**
~ 低脂酸奶

yolk *n.* 蛋黃 [daan6 wong4]

you *pron.* 你 [nei5]

young *adj.* 後生 [hau6 saang1]

your *det.* 你嘅 [nei5 ge3]

yours *pron.* 你嘅 [nei5 ge3]; **Y~
Truly** 僅致問候, **Is this ~?** 系
唔系真嘎

yourself *pron.* 你自己 [nei5 ji6
gei2]

youth *n.* 青春 [ching1 cheun1]; ~
hostel 青年旅館

Zagreb *n.* 薩格勒布 [saat8
gaak8 lak9 bou3]; ~, **capital of
Croatia** 克羅地亞首都

Zambia *n.* 贊比亞 [jaan3 bei2 a3]

zander *n.* 鱘魚 [cham4 yu2]

zebra *n.* 斑馬 [baan1 ma5]

zero *num.* 零 [ling4]

zest *n.* 熱情 [yit9 ching4], **lemon**
~ 檸檬皮, **lime** ~ 青檸檬皮

zesty *adj.* 好熱情 [hou2 yit9
ching4]

Zimbabwe *n.* 津巴布韋 [jeun1
ba1 bou3 wai5]

zip *v.* 拉鍊 [laai1 lin2]; *comp.* ~ **a
file** 壓縮文件

zip drive *comp. n.* 磁盤驅動器
[chi4 pun4 keui1 dung6 hei3]

zipper *n.* 拉鏈 [laai1 lin2]

ziti *n.* 通心粉 [tung1 sam1 fan2]

zodiac *n.* 十二宮圖 [sap9 yi6 gung1 tou4]

zone *n.* 地區 [dei6 keui1]

zoning *adj.* 分區 [fan1 keui1]; ~ **laws** 城市區劃法

zoo *n.* 動物園 [dung6 mat9 yun4]

zucchini *n.* 西葫蘆 [sai1 wu4 lou4]; **fried** ~ 炒西葫蘆, ~ **chips** 西葫蘆薯條

Computer Terms

access *v.* 存取 [chyun4 cheui2]

access time *n.* 存取時間 [chyun4 cheui2 si4 gaan3]

alignment *n.* 對齊 [deui3 chai4]

architecture *n.* 架構 [ga3 kau3]

array *n.* 陣列 [jan6 lit9]

arrow *n.* 箭嘴 [jin3 jeui2]

artificial intelligence *n.* 人工智能 [yan4 gung1 ji3 nang4]

asynchrinous *adj.* 非同步 [fei1 tung4 bou6]

authorization code *n.* 授權碼 [sau6 kyun4 ma5]

availability *n.* 可用度 [ho2 yung6 dou6]

backspace *n.* 退格鍵 [teui3 gaak8 gin6]

backup *n.* 備份 [bei6 fan6]

bandwidth *n.* 頻寬 [pan4 fun1]

binary *n.* 二進制 [yi6 jeun3 jai3]

bluetooth *n.* 藍牙 [laam4 nga4]

bookmark *n.* 書籤 [syu1 chim1]

boot *v.* 啟動 [kai2 dung6]

brightness *n.* 亮度 [leung6 dou6]

browser *n.* 瀏覽器 [lau4 laam5 hei3]

buffer *n.* 緩衝器 [wun6 chung1 hei3]

cache *n.* 快取 [faai3 cheui2]

call center *n.* 客戶服務中心 [haak8 wu6 fuk9 mou6 jung1 sam1]

caps lock *n.* 大寫鎖定 [daai6 se2 so2 ding6]

cells *n.* 格 [gaak8]

chip *n.* 晶片 [jing1 pin2]

circuits *n.* 電路 [din6 lou6]

click *v.* 撳 [gam6]

column *n.* 行 [hong4]

compact disc *n.* 光碟 [gwong1 dip2]

computer *n.* 電腦 [din6 nou5]

control panel *n.* 控制台 [hung3 jai3 toi4]

copy *v.* 複製 [fuk7 jai3]

copyright *n.* 版權 [baan2 kyun4]

CPU *n.* 中央處理器 [jung1 yeung1 chyu5 lei5 hei3]

create *v.* 創建 [chong3 gin3]

criterion *n.* 標準 [biu1 jeun2]

cursor *n.* 游標 [yau4 biu1]

customize *n.* 自訂 [ji6 ding3]

cut *v.* 剪下 [jin2 ha6]

databases *n.* 數據庫 [sou3 geui3 fu3]

delete *v.* 刪除 [saan1 cheui4]

disk *n.* 光碟 [gwong1 dip2]

document *n.* 文件 [man4 gin6]

download *v.* 下載 [ha6 joi3]

edit *v.* 編輯 [pin1 chap7]

electronic *adj.* 電子 [din6 ji2]

e-mail *n.* 電子郵件 [din6 ji2 yau4 gin2]

enter *v.* 輸入 [syu1 yap9]

escape *v.* 退出 [teui3 cheut7]

export *v.* 輸出 [syu1 cheut7]

favorite *adj.* 收藏夾 [sau1 chong4 gaap8]

field *n.* 格 [gaak8]

files *n.* 文件 [man4 gin6]

firewall *n.* 防火牆 [fong4 fo2 cheung4]

flash memory n. 快閃記憶體 [faai3 sim2 gei3 yik7 tai2]

folder n. 文件夾 [man4 gin2 gaap8]

font n. 字體 [ji6 tai2]

footer n. 頁尾 [yip9 mei5]

format n. 格式 [gaak8 sik7]

formula n. 公式 [gung1 sik7]

functions n. 函數 [haam4 sou3]

graph n. 圖表 [tou4 biu2]

graphics n. 製圖法 [jai3 tou4 faat8]

hard disc n. 硬碟 [ngaang6 dip2]

header n. 頁首 [yip9 sau2]

hits n. 點擊 [dim2 gik7]

homepage n. 主頁 [jyu2 yip9]

hub n. 集線器 [jaap9 sin3 hei3]

hyperlink n. 超連結 [chiu1 lin4 git8]

import v. 輸入 [syu1 yap9]

information n. 信息 [seun3 sik7]

input n. 輸入嘅數據 [syu1 yap9 ge3 sou3 geui3]

interactive adj. 互動 [wu6 dung6]

interface n. 介面 [gaai3 min2]

Internet n. 互聯網 [wu6 lyun4 mong5]

keyboard n. 鍵盤 [gin6 pun2]

keyword n. 關鍵詞 [gwaan1 gin6 chi4]

kilobyte (abbr. **K.**) n. 千位元組 [chin1 wai2 yun4 jou2]

latency n. 延遲時間 [yin4 chi4 si4 gaan3]

LCD n. 液晶顯示器 [yik9 jing1 hin2 si6 hei3]

linear adj. 線性 [sin3 sing3]

link v. 連接 [lin4 jip8]

login ID n. 用戶名 [yung6 wu6 meng4]

machine language n. 機器語言 [gei1 hei3 yu5 yin4]

margin n. 頁邊 [yip9 bin1]

maximize v. 最大化 [jeui3 daai6 fa3]

megabyte (abbr. **MB**) n. 百萬位元組 [baak8 maan6 wai2 yun4 jou2]

menu n. 選單 [syun2 daan1]

microprocessor n. 微處理器 [mei4 chyu5 lei5 hei3]

minimize v. 最小化 [jeui3 siu2 fa3]

modem n. 數據機 [sou3 geui3 gei1]

modify v. 修改 [sau1 goi2]

monitor n. 顯示器 [hin2 si6 hei3]

motherboard n. 主板 [jyu2 baan2]

mouse n. 鼠標 [syu2 biu1]

multi-application adj. 多重應用 [do1 chung4 ying3 yung6]

multichannel adj. 多聲道 [do1 sing1 dou6]

multimedia n. 多媒體 [do1 mui4 tai2]

network n. 網絡 [mong5 lok8]

nonlinear adj. 非線性 [fei1 sin3 sing3]

offline adj. 離線 [lei4 sin3]

online adj. 線上 [sin3 seung6]

operating system n. 操作系統 [chou1 jok8 hai6 tung2]

option n. 選項 [syun2 hong6]

output n. 輸出嘅數據 [syu1 cheut7 ge3 sou3 geui3]

pageview n. 點擊量 [dim2 gik7 leung6]

password n. 密碼 [mat9 ma5]

paste v.貼上 [tip8 seung5]

point v. 指向 [ji2 heung3]

print *v.* 打印 [da2 yan3]

printer *n.* 打印機 [da2 yan3 gei1]

properties *n.* 屬性 [suk9 sing3]

protocol *n.* 協定 [hip8 ding6]

query *n.* 查詢 [cha4 seun1]

RAM *n.* 內存 [noi6 chyun4]

recognition *n.* 辨識 [bin6 sik7]

refresh *v.* 刷新 [chaat8 san1]

restore *v.* 修復 [sau1 fuk9]

retrieve *v.* 檢索 [gim2 sok8]

row *n.* 列 [lit9]

scanner *n.* 掃描器 [sou3 miu4 hei3]

scapebook *n.* 剪貼簿 [jin2 tip8 bou2]

save *v.* 儲存 [chyu5 chyun4]

screen *n.* 屏幕 [ping4 mok9]

search engine *n.* 搜索引擎 [sau2 sok8 yan5 king4]

security *n.* 安全 [on1 cyun4]

sector *n.* 扇區 [sin3 keui1]

select *v.* 選定 [syun2 ding6]

sequential/linear *adj.* 順序 [seun6 jeui6]

server *n.* 服務器 [fuk9 mou6 hei3]

setup *n.* 設置 [chit8 ji3]

shift *n.* 移位 [yi4 wai6]

site *n.* 網站 [mong5 jaam6]

software *n.* 軟件 [yun5 gin2]

spacebar *n.* 空格鍵 [hung1 gaak8 gin6]

spreadsheet *n.* 電子數據表 [din6 ji2 sou3 geui3 biu2]

surf *v.* 衝浪 [chung1 long6]

table *n.* 表 [biu2]

technology *n.* 技術 [gei6 seut9]

telecommunication *n.* 電訊 [din6 seun3]

terabyte (*abbr.* **TB**) *n.* 太位元組 [tai3 wai2 yun4 jou2]

terminal *n.* 終端機 [jung1 dyun1 gei1]

toolbar *n.* 工具欄 [gung1 geui6 laan4]

touchpad *n.* 觸控板 [chuk7 hung3 baan2]

track *n.* 磁軌 [chi4 gwai2]

traffic *n.* 流量 [lau4 leung6]

trash *n.* 資源回收筒 [ji1 yun4 wui4 sau1 tung4]

tutorial *n.* 使用說明 [sai2 yung6 syut8 ming4]

Unicode *n.* 萬國碼 [maan6 gwok8 ma5]

unzip *n.* 解壓縮 [gaai2 aat8 suk7]

URL *n.* 網址 [mong5 ji2]

user *n.* 用戶 [yung6 wu6]

viruses *n.* 病毒 [beng6 duk9]

webpage *n.* 網頁 [mong5 yip9]

wide band *n.* 寬帶 [fun1 daai3]

window *n.* 視窗 [si6 cheung1]

word processing *n.* 文字處理 [man4 ji6 chyu5 lei5]

www. *n.* 互聯網 [wu6 lyun4 mong5]

zip *v.* 壓縮 [aat8 suk7]

zip drive *n.* 光盤驅動器 [gwong1 pun4 keui1 dung6 hei3]

Legal Terms

acquit *v.* 宣佈無罪 [syun1 bou3 mou4 jeui6]

affidavit *n.* 宣誓書 [syun1 sai6 syu1]

aid and abet *v.* 同謀 [tung4 mau4]

allegation *n.* 指控 [ji2 hung3]

appeal *n/v.* 上訴 [seung6 sou3]

arrest *v.* 拘捕 [keui1 bou6]

assault *n.* 故意傷害 [gu3 yi3 seung1 hoi6]

attorney *n.* 律師 [leut9 si1]

bail *n.* 保釋 [bou2 sik7]

bail bond *n.* 保釋保證書 [bou2 sik7 bou2 jing3 syu1]

bailiff *n.* 庭警 [ting4 ging2]

bankrupt *v./adj.* 破產 [po3 chaan2]

bankruptcy *n.* 破產 [po3 chaan2]

bar *n.* 律師 [leut9 si1]

bar exam *n.* 律師資格考試 [leut9 si1 ji1 gaak8 haau2 si3]

bench warrant *n.* 法院拘票 [faat8 yun2 keui1 piu3]

bond *n.* 保證書 [bou2 jing3 syu1]

burden of proof *n.* 提供證據嘅責任 [tai4 gung1 jing3 geui3 ge3 jaak8 yam6]

capital crime *n.* 死罪 [sei2 jeui6]

case *n.* 案件 [on3 gin2]

case law *n.* 判例法 [pun3 lai6 faat8]

chambers *n.* 法官辦公室 [faat8 gun1 baan6 gung1 sat7]

claim *n.* 索賠 [sok8 pui4]

circumstantial evidence *n.* 旁證 [pong4 jing3]

complainant *n.* 原告 [yun4 gou3]

complaint *n.* 控告 [hung3 gou3]

confess *v.* 認罪 [ying6 jeui6]

confession *n.* 認罪 [ying6 jeui6]

constitution *n.* 憲法 [hin3 faat8]

constitutional law *n.* 憲法 [hin3 faat8]

contract *n.* 合同 [hap9 tung4]

continuance *n.* 延期審理 [yin4 kei4 sam2 lei5]

counsel *n.* 法律顧問 [faat8 leut9 gu3 man6]

court *n.* 法庭 [faat8 ting4]

crime *n.* 犯罪 [faan6 jeui6]

criminal law *n.* 刑法 [ying4 faat8]

cross-examination *n.* 交叉盤問 [gaau1 cha1 pun4 man6]

custody *n.* 監護權 [gaam1 wu6 kyun4]

damages *n.* 損害賠償 [syun2 hoi6 pui4 seung4]

decree *n.* 法令 [faat8 ling4]

defendant *n.* 被告人 [bei6 gou3 yan4]

defense *n.* 辯護 [bin6 wu6]

deposition *n.* 書面證詞 [syu1 min6 jing3 chi4]

disbarment *n.* 取消律師資格 [cheui2 siu1 leut9 si1 ji1 gaak8]

discovery *n.* 顯示證據 [hin2 si6 jing3 geui3]

docket *n.* 訴訟時間表 [sou3 jung6 si4 gaan3 biu2]

due process *n.* 法定訴訟程序 [faat8 ding6 sou3 jung6 ching4 jeui6]

entrapment *n.* 誘捕 [yau5 bou6]

equity *n.* 衡平法 [hang4 ping4 faat8]

escrow *n.* 第三者保管嘅資產 [dai6 saam1 je2 bou2 gun2 ge3 ji1 chaan2]

estate *n.* 不動產 [bat7 dung6 chaan2]

ethics *n.* 道德 [dou6 dak7]

evidence *n.* 證據 [jing3 geui3]

examination *n.* 盤問 [pun4 man6]

exonerate *v.* 宣佈無罪 [syun1 bou3 mou4 jeui6]

expunge *v.* 消除紀錄 [siu1 cheui4 gei3 luk9]

family law *n.* 家庭法 [ga1 ting4 faat8]

felony *n.* 重罪 [chung5 jeui6]

fiduciary *n.* 受託人 [sau6 tok8 yan4]

file *v.* 提出訴訟 [tai4 cheut7 sou3 jung6]

fraud *n.* 詐騙 [ja3 pin3]

grand jury *n.* 大陪審團 [daai6 pui4 sam2 tyun4]

grievance *n.* 冤情 [yun1 ching4]

guardian *n.* 監護人 [gaam1 wu6 yan4]

guardianship *n.* 監護權 [gaam1 wu6 kyun4]

guilty *adj.* 有罪 [yau5 jeui6]

habeas corpus *n.* 人身保護權 [yan4 san1 bou2 wu6 kyun4]

hearing *n.* 聆訊 [ling4 seun3]

hearsay *n.* 傳聞證據 [chyun4 man4 jing3 geui3]

hung jury *n.* 做唔到決定嘅 陪審團 [jou6 m4 dou3 kyut8 ding6 ge3 pui4 sam2 tyun4]

immunity *n.* 豁免 [kut8 min5]

incarceration *n.* 監禁 [gaam1 gam3]

incompetent *n.* 無行為能力 [mou4 hang4 wai4 nang4 lik9]

indictment *n.* 起訴書 [hei2 sou3 syu1]

infraction *n.* 違法 [wai4 faat8]

injunction *n.* 禁制令 [gam1 jai3 ling4]

innocent *n.* 無辜 [mou4 gu1]

jail *n.* 監獄 [gaam1 yuk9]

judge *n.* 法官 [faat8 gun1]

judiciary *n.* 司法部 [si1 faat8 bou6]

jurisdiction *n.* 司法權 [si1 faat8 kyun4]

jurisprudence *n.* 法理學 [faat8 lei5 hok9]

jury *n.* 陪審團 [pui4 sam2 tyun4]

justice *n.* 法律制裁 [faat8 leut9 jai3 choi4]

larceny *n.* 盜竊罪 [dou6 sit8 jeui6]

law *n.* 法律 [faat8 leut9]

lawsuit *n.* 官司 [gun1 si1]

lawyer *n.* 律師 [leut9 si1]

legal *adj.* 合法 [hap9 faat8]

legislation *n.* 立法 [laap9 faat8]

leniency *n.* 寬大處理 [fun1 daai6 chyu5 lei5]

liable *adj.* 負有法律責任 [fu6 yau5 faat8 leut9 jaak8 yam6]

lien *n.* 留置權 [lau4 ji3 kyun4]

litigant *n.* 訴訟當事人 [sou3 jung6 dong1 si6 yan4]

litigation *n.* 打官司 [da2 gun1 si1]

manslaughter *n.* 誤殺 [ng6 saat8]

marshal *n.* 執法官 [jap7 faat8 gun1]

mediation *n.* 調解 [tiu4 gaai2]

minor *n.* 未成年人 [mei6 sing4 nin4 yan4]

misdemeanor *n.* 輕罪 [heng1 jeui6]

mistrial *n.* 無效審判 [mou5 haau6 sam2 pun3]

moot *v.* 提出討論 [tai4 cheut7 tou2 leun6]

murder *n.* 謀殺 [mau4 saat8]

negligence *n.* 過失 [gwo3 sat7]

oath *n.* 宣誓 [syun1 sai6]

objection *n.* 反對 [faan2 deui3]

opinion *n.* 法律意見 [faat8 leut9 yi3 gin3]

order *n.* 頒令 [baan1 ling4]

ordinance *n.* 法令 [faat8 ling4]

overrule *n.* 宣佈無效 [syun1 bou3 mou4 haau6]

paralegal *n.* 律師助手 [leut9 si1 jo6 sau2]

pardon *n.* 赦免 [se3 min5]

parole *n.* 假釋 [ga2 sik7]

party *n.* 一方 [yat7 fong1]

perjury *n.* 偽證罪 [ngai6 jing3 jeui6]

petition *n.* 上訴書 [seung6 sou3 syu1]

plaintiff *n.* 原告 [yun4 gou3]

plea *n.* 抗辯 [kong3 bin6]

plea bargain *n.* 認罪協議 [ying6 jeui6 hip8 yi5]

power of attorney *n.* 授權書 [sau6 kyun4 syu1]

precedent *n.* 先例 [sin1 lai6]

preliminary hearing *n.* 預審 [yu6 sam2]

prison *n.* 監獄 [gaam1 yuk9]

probable cause *n.* 可能嘅原因 [ho2 nang4 ge3 yun4 yan1]

probate *v.* 遺囑認證 [wai4 juk7 ying6 jing3]

probation *n.* 緩刑 [wun6 ying4]

prosecute *v.* 控告 [hung3 gou3]

prosecutor *n.* 檢察官 [gim2 chaat8 gun1]

proxy *n.* 委託書 [wai2 tok8 syu1]

reasonable doubt *n.* 合理疑點 [hap9 lei5 yi4 dim2]

rebut *v.* 駁斥 [bok8 chik7]

record *n.* 紀錄 [gei3 luk9]

redress *n.* 賠償 [pui4 seung4]

rejoinder *n.* 答辯 [daap8 bin6]

resolution *n.* 決議 [kyut8 yi5]

reverse *n.* 撤消 [chit8 siu1]

revoke *n.* 撤消 [chit8 siu1]

robbery *n.* 搶劫罪 [cheung2 gip8 jeui6]

rules *n.* 規則 [kwai1 jak7]

search warrant *n.* 搜查令 [sau2 cha4 ling4]

self-defense *n.* 自衛 [ji6 wai6]

sentence *n.* 判決 [pun3 kyut8]

sequester *n.* 扣押 [kau3 aat8]

settlement *n.* 正式協議 [jing3 sik7 hip8 yi5]

sheriff *n.* 縣治安官 [yun6 ji6 on1 gun1]

standing *adj.* 常務 [seung4 mou6]

state *v.* 聲明 [sing1 ming4]

statute *n.* 法令 [faat8 ling4]

stay *v.* 暫緩執行 [jaam6 wun6 jap7 hang4]

subpoena *n.* 傳票 [chyun4 piu3]

summary judgment *n.* 即決審判 [jik7 kyut8 sam2 pun3]

suit *n.* 訴訟 [sou3 jung6]

suppress *v.* 排除 [paai4 cheui4]

sustain *v.* 維持 [wai4 chi4]

testimony *n.* 證詞 [jing3 chi4]

theft *n.* 偷竊罪 [tau1 sit8 jeui6]

title *n.* 所有權 [so2 yau5 kyun4]

tort *n.* 民事侵權行為 [man4 si6 cham1 kyun4 hang4 wai4]

transcript *n.* 審訊紀錄文本 [sam2 seun3 gei3 luk9 man4 bun2]

trial *n.* 審訊 [sam2 seun3]

trust *n.* 信託 [seun3 tok8]

trustee *n.* 受託人 [sau6 tok8 yan4]

usury *n.* 高利貸 [gou1 lei6 taai3]

venue *n.* 案發地點 [on3 faat8 dei6 dim2]

verdict *n.* 裁決 [choi4 kyut8]

voir dire *n.* 一切照實陳述 [yat7 chai3 jiu3 sat9 chan4 seut9]

waiver *n.* 棄權聲明書 [hei3 kyun4 sing1 ming4 syu1]

warrant *n.* 令 [ling4]

will *n.* 遺囑 [wai4 juk7]

witness *n.* 證人 [jing3 yan4]

writ *n.* 法院文書 [faat8 yun6 man4 syu1]

zoning *n.* 分區 [fan1 keui1]

Cantonese Foods

Chinese herbs

adenophora elata *n.* 沙蔘 [sa1 sam1]

black date *n.* 黑棗 [hak7 jou2]

candied jujube *n.* 蜜棗 [mat9 jou2]

Chinese angelica *n.* 當歸 [dong1 gwai1]

Chinese herbal tea *n.* 涼茶 [leung4 cha4]

Chinese yam *n.* 淮山 [waai4 saan1]

codonopsis *n.* 黨蔘 [dong2 sam1]

coptis chinensis *n.* 黃連 [wong4 lin4]

dandelion *n.* 蒲公英 [pou4 gung1 ying1]

dried longan *n.* 桂圓 [gwai3 yun4]

dried night blooming cereus *n.* 霸王花 [ba3 wong4 fa1]

gastrodia elata *n.* 天麻 [tin1 ma4]

ginseng *n.* 人蔘 [yan4 sam1]

hawthorn *n.* 山楂 [saan1 ja1]

honeysuckle flower *n.* 金銀花 [gam1 ngan4 fa1]

licorice root *n.* 甘草 [gam1 chou2]

polygonum multiflorum *n.* 何首烏 [ho4 sau2 wu1]

poria cocos *n.* 茯苓 [fuk9 ling4]

radix ophiopogonis *n.* 麥冬 [mak9 dung1]

red date *n.* 紅棗 [hung4 jou2]

rehmannia Glutinosa *n.* 熟地 [suk9 dei6]

star anise *n.* 八角 [baat8 gok8]

wolfberry *n.* 枸杞 [gau2 gei2]

Condiments

black bean sauce *n.* 蒜茸豆豉醬 [syun3 yung4 dau6 si6 jeung3]

black pepper sauce *n.* 黑椒汁 [hak7 jiu1 jap7]

chili powder *n.* 辣椒粉 [laat9 jiu1 fan2]

chili sauce *n.* 辣椒醬 [laat9 jiu1 jeung3]

corn oil *n.* 粟米油 [suk7 mai5 yau4]

cornstarch *n.* 生粉 [saang1 fan2]

dark soy sauce *n.* 老抽 [lou5 chau1]

fish sauce *n.* 魚露 [yu4 lou4]

garlic powder *n.* 蒜粉 [syun3 fan2]

ginger powder *n.* 薑粉 [geung1 fan2]

hau chu paste *n.* 柱侯醬 [chyu5 hau6 jeung3]

lard *n.* 豬油 [jyu1 yau4]

olive oil *n.* 橄欖油 [gaam3 laam2 yau4]

oyster sauce *n.* 蠔油 [hou4 yau4]

peanut oil *n.* 花生油 [fa1 sang1 yau4]

red vinegar *n.* 紅醋 [hung4 chou3]

satay paste *n.* 沙茶醬 [sa1 cha4 jeung3]

seafood sauce *n.* 海鮮醬 [hoi2 sin1 jeung3]

sesame oil *n.* 麻油 [ma4 yau4]

sesame paste *n.* 芝麻醬 [ji1 ma4 jeung3]

Shaoxing wine *n.* 花雕酒 [fa1 diu1 jau2]

shochu *n.* 燒酒 [siu1 jau2]

sweet and sour sauce *n.* 甜酸醬 [tim4 syun1 jeung3]

soy sauce *n.* 豉油 [si6 yau4]

white vinegar *n.* 白醋 [baak9 chou3]

Dessert/dim sum

almond cake *n.* 杏仁餅 [hang6 yan4 beng2]

black sesame paste *n.* 芝麻糊 [ji1 ma4 wu2]

char siu baau *n.* 叉燒包 [cha1 siu1 baau1]

chicken cake *n.* 雞仔餅 [gai1 jai2 beng2]

coconut bar *n.* 椰汁糕 [ye4 jap7 gou1]

crispy triangles *n.* 油角 [yau4 gok8]

dace fish balls *n.* 鯪魚球 [leng4 yu4 kau4]

double skin milk *n.* 雙皮奶 [seung1 pei4 naai5]

egg tart *n.* 蛋撻 [daan6 taat1]

fried dumplings *n.* 煎堆 [jin1 deui1]

ginger milk tart *n.* 薑汁撞奶 撻 [geung1 jap7 jong6 naai5 taat1]

green bean soup *n.* 綠豆沙 [luk9 dau2 sa1]

har gow *n.* 蝦餃 [ha1 gaau2]

lard cake *n.* 豬油糕 [jyu1 yau4 gou1]

lotus leaf rice *n.* 糯米雞 [no6 mai5 gai1]

mochi *n.* 麻糬 [ma4 syu4]

mooncake *n.* 月餅 [yut9 beng2]

phoenix claws *n.* 鳳爪 [fung6 jaau2]

piggy cake *n.* 豬仔餅 [jyu1 jai2 beng2]

red bean soup *n.* 紅豆沙 [hung4 dau2 sa1]

rice cake *n.* 年糕 [nin4 gou1]

sai mai lo *n.* 西米露 [sai1 mai5 lou6]

sesame balls *n.* 笑口棗 [siu3 hau2 jou2]

shaomai *n.* 燒賣 [siu1 maai6]

spring rolls *n.* 春卷 [cheun1 gyun2]

steamed frog on lotus leaf *n.* 荷葉蒸田雞 [ho4 yip9 jing1 tin4 gai1]

steamed meatballs *n.* 蒸牛肉球 [jing1 ngau4 yuk9 kau4]

sweet cream buns *n.* 奶皇包 [naai5 wong4 baau1]

sweet heart cake *n.* 老婆餅 [lou5 po4 beng2]

sweet potato soup *n.* 蕃薯糖水 [faan1 syu4 tong4 seui2]

sweet rice dumplings *n.* 湯圓 [tong1 yun2]

sweet-scented osmanthus cake *n.* 桂花糕 [gwai3 fa1 gou1]

sweet spoiled rice soup *n.* 甜糟 [tim4 jou1]

sweet tofu soup *n.* 豆腐花 [dau6 fu6 fa1]

taro cake *n.* 芋頭糕 [wu6 tau2 gou1]

taro dumplings *n.* 芋角酥 [wu6 gok8 sou1]

tortoise herb jelly *n.* 龜苓膏 [gwai1 ling4 gou1]

turnip cake *n.* 蘿蔔糕 [lo4 baak9 gou1]

water chestnut cake *n.* 馬蹄糕 [ma5 tai2 gou1]

wonton noodles *n.* 雲吞麵 [wan4 tan1 min6]

yau zaa gwai *n.* 油炸鬼 [yau4 ja3 gwai2]

zaa Leung *n.* 炸兩 [ja3 leung2]

Drinks

aged pu'er tea *n.* 陳年普洱 [chan4 nin4 pou2 nei2]

biluochun tea *n.* 碧螺春 [bik7 lo4 cheun1]

black tea *n.* 紅茶 [hung4 cha4]

boricha *n.* 大麥茶 [daai6 mak9 cha4]

Chinese herbal tea *(assorted)* *n.* 八寶茶 [baat8 bou2 cha4]

chrysanthemum tea *n.* 菊花茶 [guk7 fa1 cha4]

Coca Cola *n.* 可口可樂 [ho2 hau2 ho2 lok9]

coconut water *n.* 椰子汁 [ye4 ji2 jap7]

coffee and milk tea mix *n.* 鴛鴦 [yun1 yeung1]

earl grey tea *n.* 伯爵茶 [baak8 jeuk8 cha4]

Fanta *n.* 芬達 [fan1 daat9]

flower tea *n.* 花茶 [fa1 cha4]

green tea *n.* 綠茶 [luk9 cha4]

jasmine tea *n.* 茉莉花茶 [mut9 lei6 fa1 cha4]

junshan silver needle tea *n.* 君山銀針 [gwan1 saan1 ngan4 jam1]

keemun black tea *n.* 祁門紅茶 [kei4 mun4 hung4 cha4]

lavender tea *n.* 薰衣草茶 [fan1 yi1 chou2 cha4]

Lipton black tea *n.* 立頓紅茶 [laap9 deun6 hung4 cha4]

longjing tea *n.* 龍井 [lung4 jeng2]

maojian tea *n.* 毛尖 [mou4 jim1]

milk *n.* 牛奶 [ngau4 naai5]

milk tea *n.* 奶茶 [naai5 cha4]

mint tea *n.* 薄荷茶 [bok9 ho4 cha4]

oolong tea *n.* 烏龍茶 [wu1 lung4 cha4]

orange juice *n.* 橙汁 [chaang2 jap7]

papaya juice *n.* 木瓜汁 [muk9 gwa1 jap7]

Pepsi *n.* 百事可樂 [baak8 si6 ho2 lok9]

pu'er tea *n.* 普洱 [pou2 nei2]

Seven Up *n.* 七喜 [chat7 hei2]

Sprite *n.* 雪碧 [syut8 bik7]

tea *n.* 茶 [cha4]

tieguanyin tea *n.* 鐵觀音 [tit8 gun1 yam1]

water *n.* 水 [seui2]

    cold water *n.* 凍水 [dung3 seui2]

    distilled water *n.* 蒸餾水 [jing1 lau6 seui2]

    hot water *n.* 滾水 [gwan2 seui2]

    ice water *n.* 冰水 [bing1 seui2]

    mineral water *n.* 礦泉水 [kwong3 chyun4 seui2]

tap water *n.* 水喉水 [seui2 hau4 seui2]

white tea *n.* 白茶 [baak9 cha4]

Wuyi Mountain rock tea *n.* 大紅袍 [daai6 hung4 pou4]

Entrees

beef brisket noodles *n.* 牛腩麵 [ngau4 naam5 min6]

beef chow fun *n.* 干炒牛河 [gon1 chaau2 ngau4 ho2]

beef entrails *n.* 牛雜 [ngau4 jaap9]

boiled shrimp *n.* 白灼蝦 [baak9 jeuk8 ha1]

Cantonese seafood soup *n.* 海皇羹 [hoi2 wong4 gang1]

century egg *n.* 皮蛋 [pei4 daan2]

chicken braised with chestnuts *n.* 栗子炆雞 [leut9 ji2 man1 gai1]

chicken in soy sauce *n.* 豉油雞 [si6 yau4 gai1]

Chinese sausage *n.* 臘腸 [laap9 cheung2]

chow mein *n.* 炒麵 [chaau2 min6]

congee with pork and century egg *n.* 皮蛋瘦肉粥 [pei4 daan2 sau3 yuk9 juk7]

cooked rice *n.* 飯 [faan6]

crispy fried chicken *n.* 炸子雞 [ja3 ji2 gai1]

deep-fried pigeon *n.* 燒乳鴿 [siu1 yu5 gap8]

deep-fried tofu *n.* 油豆腐 [yau4 dau6 fu6]

dried cabbage *n.* 菜乾 [choi3 gon1]

dried fish bladder *n.* 魚肚 [yu4 tou5]

dried oyster *n.* 蠔豉 [hou4 si2]

dried scallops *n.* 乾瑤柱 [gon1 yiu4 chyu5]

dried small shrimp *n.* 蝦米 [ha1 mai5]

duck with taro *n.* 芋頭炆鴨 [wu6 tau2 man1 aap8]

fermented black beans *n.* 豆豉 [dau6 si6]

fermented tofu *n.* 腐乳 [fu6 yu2]

fish head *n.* 魚頭 [yu4 tau4]

frog porridge/congee *n.* 生滾田雞粥 [saang1 gwan2 tin4 gai1 juk7]

hand-pulled noodles *n.* 拉麵 [laai1 min6]

hotpot *n.* 火鍋 [fo2 wo1]

lo mein *n.* 撈麵 [lou1 min6]

lobster with ginger and scallions *n.* 薑蔥龍蝦 [geung1 chung1 lung4 ha1]

longevity noodles *n.* 長壽麵 [cheung4 sau6 min6]

mapo toufu *n.* 麻婆豆腐 [ma4 po4 dau6 fu6]

master stock *n.* 鹵水 [lou5 seui2]

mantis shrimp *n.* 瀨尿蝦 [laai6 niu6 ha1]

meat sticky rice dumplings *n.* 肉糭 [yuk9 jung3]

orange cuttlefish *n.* 鹵水墨魚 [lou5 seui2 mak9 yu4]

preserved salted duck *n.* 臘鴨 [laap9 aap8]

preserved salted pork *n.* 臘肉 [laap9 yuk9]

pickled cabbage *n.* 梅菜 [mui4 choi3]

plain porridge/congee *n.* 白粥 [baak9 juk7]

poached duck in master stock *n.* 鹵水鴨 [lou5 seui2 aap8]

pork giblet porridge/congee *n.* 及第粥 [kap9 dai6 juk7]

pork liver porridge/congee *n.* 豬膶粥 [jyu1 yeun2 juk7]

porridge/congee *n.* 粥 [juk7]

rice noodle roll *n.* 豬腸粉 [jyu1 cheung4 fan2]

rice noodles *n.* 河粉 [ho2 fan2]

river snail *n.* 田螺 [tin4 lo2]

roast duck *n.* 燒鴨 [siu1 aap8]

roast goose *n.* 燒鵝 [siu1 ngo4]

roast pork *n.* 叉燒 [cha1 siu1]

roast suckling pig *n.* 乳豬 [yu5 jyu1]

salt roasted chicken *n.* 鹽焗雞 [yim4 guk9 gai1]

salted duck egg *n.* 鹹蛋 [haam4 daan2]

salted fish *n.* 鹹魚 [haam4 yu2]

sampan porridge/congee *n.* 艇仔粥 [teng5 jai2 juk7]

sea cucumber *n.* 海蔘 [hoi2 sam1]

shark fin *n.* 魚翅 [yu4 chi3]

shrimp sauce *n.* 蝦醬 [ha1 jeung3]

silver needle noodles *n.* 銀針粉 [ngan4 jam1 fan2]

Singapore fried rice noodles *n.* 星洲炒米 [sing1 jau1 chaau2 mai5]

spare ribs with salt and pepper *n.* 椒鹽排骨 [jiu1 yim4 paai4 gwat7]

steamed egg *n.* 蒸水蛋 [jing1 seui2 daan2]

steamed fish *n.* 蒸魚 [jing1 yu2]

steamed ground pork with salted egg *n.* 鹹蛋蒸肉餅 [haam4 daan6 jing1 yuk9 beng2]

steamed scallops with ginger and garlic *n.* 蒜茸蒸扇貝 [syun3 yung4 jing1 sin3 bui3]

stewed beef brisket with radish *n.* 蘿蔔炆牛腩 [lo4 baak9 man1 ngau4 naam5]

sticky rice dumpling wrapped in lotus leaf *n.* 裹蒸糭 [gwo2 jing1jung2]

stokvis and peanut porridge/congee *n.* 柴魚花生粥 [chaai4 yu4 fa1 sang1 juk7]

sweet and sour pork *n.* 咕嚕肉 [gu1 lou1 yuk9]

tofu skin *n.* 腐竹 [fu6 juk7]

vegetable with minced garlic *n.* 蒜茸炒油菜 [syun3 yung4 chaau2 yau4 choi3]

white cut chicken *n.* 白切雞 [baak9 chit8 gai1]

yi mein *n.* 伊麵 [yi1 min6]

Fish

ballonfish *n.* 河豚 [ho4 tyun4]

bass *n.* 鱸魚 [lou4 yu2]

carp *n.* 鯉魚 [lei5 yu2]

catfish *n.* 鯰魚 [nim4 yu2]

cichild *n.* 慈鯛 [chi4 diu1]

cod *n.* 鱈魚 [syut8 yu4]

dogfish *n.* 狗鯊 [gau2 sa1]

dried seafood *n.* 海味 [hoi2 mei2]

eel *n.* 鰻魚 [maan6 yu2]

goldfish *n.* 金魚 [gam1 yu2]

grouper *n.* 石斑 [sek9 baan1]

herring *n.* 鯡魚 [fei1 yu2]

mackerel *n.* 鯖魚 [ching1 yu2]

monkfish *n.* 安康魚 [on1 hong1 yu2]

piranha *n.* 水虎魚 [seui2 fu2 yu2]

pomfret *n.* 鯧魚 [cheung1 yu2]

salmon *n.* 三文魚 [saam1 man4 yu2]

sardine *n.* 沙甸魚 [sa1 din1 yu2]

seabream *n.* 真鯛 [jan1 diu1]

shark *n.* 鯊魚 [sa1 yu2]

skate *n.* 鰩魚 [yiu4 yu2]

sturgeon *n.* 鱘魚 [cham4 yu2]

tilapia *n.* 羅非魚 [lo4 fei1 yu2]

trout *n.* 鱒魚 [jyun1 yu2]

tuna *n.* 吞拿魚 [tan1 na4 yu2]

Fruits

carambola *n.* 楊桃 [yeung4 tou2]

dragon fruit *n.* 火龍果 [fo2 lung4 gwo2]

durian *n.* 榴槤 [lau4 lin4] **fruit**

ginseng fruit *n.* 人蔘果 [yan4 sam1 gwo2]

gonggan/imperial citrus *n.* 貢柑 [gung3 gam1]

guava *n.* 番石榴 [faan1 sek9 lau2]

jackfruit *n.* 菠蘿蜜 [bo1 lo4 mat9]

kiwi *n.* 奇異果 [kei4 yi6 gwo2]

kumquat *n.* 金桔 [gam1 gat7]

litchi *n.* 荔枝 [lai6 ji1]

longan/dragon eye *n.* 龍眼 [lung4 ngaan5]

loquat *n.* 枇杷 [pei4 pa4]

mangosteen *n.* 山竹 [saan1 juk7]

plantain *n.* 芭蕉 [ba1 jiu1]

pomelo *n.* 沙田柚 [sa1 tin4 yau2]

rambutan *n.* 紅毛丹 [hung4 mou4 daan1]

red bayberry *n.* 楊梅 [yeung4 mui2]

tangerine *n.* 砂糖桔 [sa1 tong4 gat7]

water chestnut *n.* 菱角 [ling4 gok8]

Plants

aloe *n.* 蘆薈 [lou4 wui6]

azalea *n.* 杜鵑花 [dou6 gyun1 fa1]

bamboo *n.* 竹 [juk7]

banyan tree *n.* 榕樹 [yung4 syu6]

bauhinia *n.* 紫荊花 [ji2 ging1 fa1]

begonia *n.* 海棠花 [hoi2 tong4 fa1]

bonsai *n.* 盆栽 [pun4 joi1]

cactus *n.* 仙人掌 [sin1 yan4 jeung2]

calla lily *n.* 馬蹄蓮 [ma5 tai4 lin4]

camellia *n.* 山茶花 [saan1 cha4 fa1]

carnation *n.* 康乃馨 [hong1 naai5 hing1]

cherry blossom *n.* 櫻花 [ying1 fa1]

chrysanthemum *n.* 菊花 [guk7 fa1]

cockscomb *n.* 雞冠花 [gai1 gun1 fa1]

daffodil *n.* 水仙 [seui2 sin1]

daisy *n.* 雛菊 [cho1 guk7]

datura *n.* 牽牛花 [hin1 ngau4 fa1]

evergreen *n.* 萬年青 [maan6 nin4 ching1]

forget-me-not *n.* 勿忘我 [mat9 mong4 ngo5]

ginkgo tree *n.* 銀杏樹 [ngan4 hang6 syu6]

hyacinth *n.* 風信子 [fung1 seun3 ji2]

hydrangea *n.* 繡球花 [sau3 kau4 fa1]

jasmine *n.* 茉莉花 [mut9 lei6 fa1]

juniper tree *n.* 柏樹 [paak8 syu6]

kapok *n.* 木棉花 [muk9 min4 fa1]

lily *n.* 百合花 [baak8 hap9 fa1]

lotus *n.* 荷花 [ho4 fa1]

mulberry tree *n.* 桑樹 [song1 syu6]

orchid *n.* 蘭花 [laan4 fa1]

osmanthus *n.* 桂花 [gwai3 fa1]

pagoda tree *n.* 槐樹 [waai4 syu6]

passion flower *n.* 西番蓮 [sai1 faan1 lin4]

peach blossom *n.* 桃花 [tou4 fa1]

peony *n.* 牡丹花 [mau5 daan1 fa1]

pine tree *n.* 松樹 [chung4 syu6]

plumeria *n.* 雞蛋花 [gai1 daan6 fa1]

poplar tree *n.* 楊樹 [yeung4 syu6]

prunus *n.* 杏花 [hang6 fa1]

rose *n.* 玫瑰花 [mui4 gwai3 fa1]

tulip *n.* 鬱金香 [wat7 gam1 heung1]

violet *n.* 紫羅蘭 [ji2 lo4 laan4]

water lily *n.* 睡蓮 [seui6 lin4]

winter jasmine *n.* 迎春花 [ying4 cheun1 fa1]

Snacks

candied lotus roots *n.* 糖蓮藕 [tong4 lin4 ngau5]

candied lotus seeds *n.* 糖蓮子 [tong4 lin4 ji2]

candied winter melon *n.* 糖冬瓜 [tong4 dung1 gwa1]

sunflower seeds *n.* 葵花子 [kwai4 fa1 ji2]

Soups

spare ribs soup *n.* 豬骨湯 [jyu1 gwat7 tong1]

winter melon soup *n.* 冬瓜湯 [dung1 gwa1 tong1]

Teas. *See* Drinks

Vegetables

amaranth *n.* 莧菜 [yin6 choi3]

bitter melon *n.* 苦瓜 [fu2 gwa1]

cabbage *n.* 西生菜 [sai1 saang1 choi3]

cauliflower *n.* 椰菜花 [ye4 choi3 fa1]

Chinese broccoli *n.* 芥蘭 [gaai3 laan2]

Chinese celery *n.* 香芹 [heung1 kan4]

Chinese wolfberry *n.* 枸杞菜 [gau2 gei2 choi3]

green bean sprouts *n.* 豆芽 [dau6 nga4]

hairy melon *n.* 節瓜 [jit8 gwa1]

hotbed chives *n.* 韭黃 [gau2 wong4]

leek *n.* 韭菜 [gau2 choi3]

lettuce *n.* 生菜 [saang1 choi3]

luffa *n.* 絲瓜 [si1 gwa1]

mustard *n.* 芥菜 [gaai3 choi3]

okra *n.* 羊角豆 [yeung4 gok8 dau2]

snap bean *n.* 豆角 [dau6 gok8]

string bean *n.* 四季豆 [sei3 gwai3 dau2]

winter melon *n.* 冬瓜 [dung1 gwa1]

water chestnut *n.* 馬蹄 [ma5 tai4]

water spinach *n.* 通菜 [tung1 choi3]

watercress *n.* 西洋菜 [sai1 yeung4 choi3]

Geographical Names

Centrally Administered Municipality
直轄市 [jik9 hat9 si5]

Beijing 北京 [bak7 ging1]
Chongqing 重慶 [chung4 hing3]
Shanghai 上海 [seung6 hoi2]
Tianjin 天津 [tin1 jeun1]

Provinces and their Capitals
省及其省會
[saang2 kap9 kei4 saang2 wui6]

Anhui 安徽 [on1 fai1]
Changchun (capital of Jilin) 長春 [cheung4 cheun1]
Changsha (capital of Hunan) 長沙 [cheung4 sa1]
Chengdu (capital of Sichuan) 成都 [sing4 dou1]
Fujian 福建 [fuk7 gin3]
Fuzhou (capital of Fujian) 福州 [fuk7 jau1]
Gansu 甘肅 [gam1 suk7]
Guangdong 廣東 [gwong2 dung1]
Guangzhou (capital of Guangdong) 廣州 [gwong2 jau1]
Guiyang (capital of Guizhou) 貴陽 [gwai3 yeung4]
Guizhou 貴州 [gwai3 jau1]
Ha'erbin (capital of Heilongjiang) 哈爾濱 [ha1 yi5 ban1]
Haikou (capital of Hainan) 海口 [hoi2 hau2]
Hainan 海南 [hoi2 naam4]
Hangzhou (capital of Zhejiang) 杭州 [hong4 jau1]

Hebei 河北 [ho4 bak7]
Hefei (capital of Anhui) 合肥 [hap9 fei4]
Heilongjiang 黑龍江 [hak7 lung4 gong1]
Henan 河南 [ho4 naam4]
Hubei 湖北 [wu4 bak7]
Hunan 湖南 [wu4 naam4]
Jiangxi 江西 [gong1 sai1]
Jiangsu 江蘇 [gong1 sou1]
Jilin 吉林 [gat7 lam4]
Jinan (capital of Shandong) 濟南 [jai3 naam4]
Kunming (capital of Yunnan) 昆明 [kwan1 ming4]
Lanzhou (capital of Gansu) 蘭州 [laan4 jau1]
Liaoning 遼寧 [liu4 ning4]
Nanchang (capital of Jiangxi) 南昌 [naam4 cheung1]
Nanjing (capital of Jiangsu) 南京 [naam4 ging1]
Qinghai 青海 [ching1 hoi2]
Shandong 山東 [saan1 dung1]
Shaanxi 陝西 [sim2 sai1]
Shanxi 山西 [saan1 sai1]
Shenyang (capital of Liaoning) 瀋陽 [sam2 yeung4]
Shijiazhuang (capital of Hebei) 石家莊 [sek9 ga1 jong1]
Sichuan 四川 [sei3 chyun1]
Taiyuan (capital of Shanxi) 太原 [taai3 yun4]
Wuhan (capital of Hubei) 武漢 [mou5 hon3]

Xi'an *(capital of Shaanxi)* 西安 [sai1 on1]

Xining *(capital of Qinghai)* 西寧 [sai1 ning4]

Yunnan 雲南 [wan4 naam4]

Zhejiang 浙江 [jit8 gong1]

Zhengzhou *(capital of Henan)* 鄭州 [jeng6 jau1]

Autonomous Regions and their Capitals
自治區及其省會
[ji6 ji6 keui1 kap9 kei4 saang2 wui6]

Guangxi Zhuangzu 廣西壯族 [gwong2 sai1 jong3 juk9]

Huhehaote *(capital of Neimenggu)* 呼和浩特 [fu1 wo4 hou6 dak9]

Lhasa *(capital of Tibet)* 拉薩 [laai1 saat8]

Nanning *(capital of Guangxi)* 南寧 [naam4 ning4]

Neimenggu 內蒙古 [noi6 mung4 gu2]

Ningxia Huizu 寧夏回族 [ning4 ha6 wui4 juk9]

Tibet 西藏 [sai1 jong6]

Wulumuqi *(capital of Xinjiang)* 烏魯木齊 [wu1 lou5 muk9 chai4]

Xinjiang Weiwuer 新疆維吾爾 [san1 geung1 wai4 ng4 yi5]

Yinchuan *(capital of Ningxia)* 銀川 [ngan4 chyun1]

Special Administrative Regions
特別行政區
[dak9 bit9 hang4 jing3 keui1]

Hong Kong 香港 [heung1 gong2]
Macau 澳門 [ngou3 mun4]

Places in Hong Kong

Aberdeen 香港仔 [heung1 gong2 jai2]

Admiralty 金鐘 [gam1 jung1]

Avenue of Stars 星光大道 [sing1 gwong1 daai6 dou6]

Big Buddha 大佛 [daai6 fat9]

Causeway Bay 銅鑼灣 [tung4 lo4 waan1]

Central 中環 [jung1 waan4]

Chek Lap Kok 赤臘角 [chek8 laap8 gok8]

Cheung Chau 長洲 [cheung4 jau1]

Clear Water Bay 清水灣 [ching1 seui2 waan1]

Clock Tower 鐘樓 [jung1 lau4]

Disneyland 迪士尼 [dik9 si6 nei4]

Golden Bauhinia Square 金紫荊廣場 [gam1 ji2 ging1 gwong2 cheung4]

Happy Valley 跑馬地 [paau2 ma5 dei6]

Hong Kong Convention and Exhibition Centre 香港會議展覽中心 [heung1 gong2 wui6 yi5 jin2 laam5 jung1 sam1]

Hong Kong Islands 香港島 [heung1 gong2 dou2]

Hung Hom 紅磡 [hung4 ham3]

Kennedy Town 堅尼地城 [gin1 nei4 dei6 sing4]

Kowloon 九龍 [gau2 lung4]

Kowloon City 九龍城 [gau2 lung4 sing4]

Kowloon Tong 九龍塘 [gau2 lung4 tong4]

Kwun Tong 觀塘 [gun1 tong4]

Ladies' Market 女人街 [neui5 yan4 gaai1]

Lamma Island 南丫島 [naam4 a1 dou2]

Lan Kwai Fong 蘭桂坊 [laan4 gwai3 fong1]

Lantau Island 大嶼山 [daai6 yu4 saan1]

Mong Kok 旺角 [wong6 gok8]

New Territories 新界 [san1 gaai3]

North Point 北角 [bak7 gok8]

Ocean Park 海洋公園 [hoi2 yeung4 gung1 yun4]

Peng Chau 坪洲 [ping4 jau1]

Po Lin Monastery 寶蓮寺 [bou2 lin4 ji6]

Repulse Bay 淺水灣 [chin2 seui2 waan1]

Sai Kung 西貢 [sai1 gung3]

Sai Wan 西環 [sai1 waan4]

Sha Tin 沙田 [sa1 tin4]

Sham Shui Po 深水埗 [sam1 seui2 bou6]

Sheung Shui 上水 [seung6 seui2]

Soho 蘇豪 [sou1 hou4]

Stanley 赤柱 [chek8 chyu5]

Star Ferry 天星小輪 [tin1 sing1 siu2 leun4]

Statue Square 皇后像廣場 [wong4 hau6 jeung6 gwong2 cheung4]

Tai Po 大埔 [daai6 bou3]

Temple Street Night Market 廟街夜市 [miu6 gaai1 ye6 si5]

The Peak 山頂 [saan1 deng2]

Tsim Sha Tsui 尖沙咀 [jim1 sa1 jeui2]

Tsuen Wan 荃灣 [chyun4 waan1]

Tuen Mun 屯門 [tyun4 mun4]

Victoria Habor 維多利亞港 [wai4 do1 lei6 a3 gong2]

Wan Chai 灣仔 [waan1 jai2]

Wong Tai Sin 黃大仙 [wong4 daai6 sin1]

Yau Tsim Mong 油尖旺 [yau4 jim1 wong6]

Yuen Long 元朗 [yun4 long5]

Places in Macau

A-Ma Temple 媽閣廟 [ma1 gok8 miu6]

Camoes Garden 賈梅士花園 [ga2 mui4 si6 fa1 yun4]

Kun Iam Temple 普濟禪院 [pou2 jai2 sim4 yun6]

Lin Fung Temple 蓮峰廟 [lin4 fung1 miu6]

Lou Lim Lok Garden 盧九花園 [lou4 gau2 fa1 yun4]

Macau Tower 澳門旅遊塔 [ngou3 mun4 leui5 yau4 taap8]

Monte Fort 蒙特城堡 [mung4 dak9 sing4 bou2]

Museum of Macau 澳門博物館 [ngou3 mun4 bok8 mat9 gun2]

Senado Square 議事亭前地 [yi5 si6 ting4 chin4 dei6]

St. Domingo's Church 玫瑰聖母堂 [mui4 gwai3 sing3 mou5 tong4]

St. Paul's Church Facade 大三巴牌坊 [daai6 saam1 ba1 paai4 fong1]

Sun Yat-Sen Park 紀念孫中山市政公園 [gei3 nim6 syun1 jung1 saan1 si5 jing3 gung1 yun4]

Chinese Holidays & Festivals

Official Holidays in Mainland China
中國法定假期
[jung1 gwok8 faat8 ding6 ga3 kei4]

Chinese New Year *n.* 農曆新年 [nung4 lik9 san1 nin4]

Labor Day *n.* 勞動節 [lou4 dung6 jit8]

Mid-Autumn Festival *n.* 中秋節 [jung1 chau1 jit8]

National Day *n.* 國慶 [gwok8 hing3]

New Year *n.* 元旦 [yun4 daan3]

Qingming Festival *n.* 清明節 [ching1 ming4 jit8]

Tuen Ng Festival *n.* 端午節 [dyun1 ng5 jit8]

Lunar calendar holidays
農曆節日 [nung4 lik9 jit8 yat9]

Birth of Avalokitesvara Festival *(Lunar Calendar Feb. 19)* 觀音誕 [gun1 yam1 daan3]

Birth of Buddah Festival *(Lunar Calendar Apr. 8)* 佛誕 [fat7 daan3]

Che Kung Festival *(Lunar Calendar Jan. 2)* 車公誕 [che1 gung1 daan3]

Cold Clothing Festival *(Lunar Calendar Oct. 1)* 寒衣節 [hon4 yi1 jit8]

Cold Food Festival *(The day before Qingming Festival)* 寒食節 [hon4 sik9 jit8]

Double Ninth Festival *(Lunar Calendar Sept. 9)* 重陽節 [chung4 yeung4 jit8]

Ghost Festival *(Lunar Calendar July 14)* 鬼節 [gwai2 jit8]

Kitchen God Festival *(Lunar Calendar Dec. 24)* 祭灶節 [jai3 jou3 jit8]

Lantern Festival *(Lunar Calendar Jan. 15)* 元宵節 [yun4 siu1 jit8]

Magpie Festival *(Lunar Calendar July 7)* 七夕 [chat7 jik9]

Spring Festival *(also* **Chinese New Year***)* 農曆新年 [nung4 lik9 san1 nin4]

Spring Festival Eve *(also* **Chinese New Year's Eve***)* 除夕 [cheui4 jik9]

Welcome the God of Wealth *(Lunar Calendar Jan. 5)* 接財神 [jip8 choi4 san4]

The 24 Solar Phases
二十四節氣
[yi6 sap9 sei3 jit8 hei3]

Autumn Equinox 秋分 [chau1 fan1]

Autumn begins 立秋 [laap9 chau1]

Clear and bright 清明 [ching1 ming4]

Cold dews 寒露 [hon4 lou6]

Grain buds 小滿 [siu2 mun5]

Grain in ear 芒種 [mong4 jung3]

Grain rain 穀雨 [guk7 yu5]
Great cold 大寒 [daai6 hon4]
Great heat 大暑 [daai6 syu2]
Heavy snow 大雪 [daai6 syut8]
Hoar-frost falls 霜降 [seung1 gong3]
Insects awaken 驚蟄 [ging1 jat9]
Light snow 小雪 [siu2 syut8]
Slight cold 小寒 [siu2 hon4]
Slight heat 小暑 [siu2 syu2]
Spring begins 立春 [laap9 cheun1]
Stopping the heat 處暑 [chyu3 syu2]

Summer begins 立夏 [laap9 ha6]
Summer solstice 夏至 [ha6 ji3]
The rains 雨水 [yu5 seui2]
Vernal Equinox 春分 [cheun1 fan1]
White dews 白露 [baak9 lou6]
Winter begins 立冬 [laap9 dung1]
Winter Solstice 冬至 [dung1 ji3]

Special Occasion Traditions

Spring Festival Traditions

auspicious words *n.* 吉利說話 [gat7 lei6 syut8 wa2]

bow to the ancestors *v.* 拜祖先 [baai3 jou2 sin1]

buy a kumquat plant *v.* 買桔 [maai5 gat7]

clean the house *v.* 洗邋遢 [sai2 laat9 taat8]

close business for Spring Festival *v.* 農曆新年休市 [nung4 lik9 san1 nin4 yau1 si5]

couplet *n.* 揮春 [fai1 cheun1]

dragon dance *n.* 舞龍 [mou5 lung4]

dragon head *n.* 龍頭 [lung4 tau4]

festive lantern *n.* 花燈 [fa1 dang1]

firecrackers *n.* 炮仗 [paau3 jeung2]

flower fair *n.* 花市 [fa1 si5]

fortune comes *n.* 福到 [fuk1 dou3]

fry crispy dumplings *v.* 炸角仔 [ja3 gok8 jai2]

give red packets *v.* 派利是 [paai3 lei6 si6]

lion dance *n.* 舞獅 [mou5 si1]

make sticky rice dumpling wrapped in lotus leaf *v.* 包裹糭 [baau1 gwo2 jung2]

pair of scrolls containing a poetic couplet *n.* 對聯 [deui3 lyun4]

paper-cut for window decoration *n.* 窗花剪紙 [cheung1 fa1 jin2 ji2]

pray to the gods *v.* 拜神 [baai3 san4]

red packets containing money as a gift *v.* 利是 [lei6 si6]

reunion dinner *n.* 團年飯 [tyun4 nin4 faan6]

shoe-shaped gold ingot *n.* 元寶 [yun4 bou2]

shop at flower fair *v.* 行花市 [haang4 fa1 si5]

take a tour to collect good luck *v.* 行大運 [haang4 daai6 wan6]

touch off firecreckers *v.* 放炮仗 [fong3 paau3 jeung2]

visit friends and relatives *v.* 拜年 [baai3 nin4]

wait for midnight before Spring Festival to come *v.* 守歲 [sau2 seui3]

welcome the new year *v.* 開年 [hoi1 nin4]

Wedding Traditions

arrive at the groom's home *v.* 過門 [gwo3 mun4]

betrothal gift *n.* 聘禮 [ping3 lai5]

bridal chamber *n.* 新房 [san1 fong4]

bride's family *n.* 女家 [neui5 ga1]

bow to heaven and earth *v.* 拜天地 [baai3 tin1 dei6]

Cantonese bridal dress *n.* 裙褂 [kwan4 gwa3]

cast uncooked rice around v. 撒米 [saat8 mai5]

children and grandchildren everywhere phr. 兒孫滿堂 [yi4 syun1 mun5 tong4]

children and grandchildren ruler n. 子孫尺 [ji2 syun1 chek8]

Chinese long gown n. 長衫 [cheung4 saam1]

Chinese sugarcane n. 竹蔗 [juk7 je3]

cross-cupped wine n. 合卺酒 [haap9 gen2 jau2]

date v. 拍拖 [paak8 to1]

daughter-in-law n. 新抱 [san1 pou5]

dowry n. 嫁妝 [ga3 jong1]

dragon and pheonix blanket n. 龍鳳被 [lung4 fung6 pei5]

dragon and pheonix bowl and chopsticks n. 龍鳳碗筷 [lung4 fung6 wun2 faai3]

dragon and pheonix candle n. 龍鳳燭 [lung4 fung6 juk7]

fried pomelo skin n. 柚皮 [yau2 pei4]

gift box n. 禮盒 [lai5 hap9]

groom's family n. 男家 [naam4 ga1]

groom and bride bow to each other v. 拜堂 [baai3 tong4]

groom and bride walk into the bridal chamber v. 洞房 [dung6 fong4]

grow old together phr. 白頭到老 [baak9 tau4 dou3 lou5]

go to the bride's home and escort her to the wedding v. 迎親 [ying4 chan1]

hair combing on the day of wedding n. 上頭 [seung5 tau4]

hundreds of children and grandchildren phr. 百子千孫 [baak8 ji2 chin1 syun1]

leave the bride's home v. 出門 [cheut7 mun4]

Mandarin duck pillow n. 鴛鴦枕 [yun1 yeung1 jam2]

monetary gifts to the new couple n. 人情 [yan4 ching4]

older lady who holds the umbrella for the bride n. 大妗姐 [daai6 kam5 je2]

pine leaf n. 松柏 [chung4 paak8]

pomelo leaf n. 柚葉 [yau2 yip9]

propose a toast v. 敬酒 [ging3 jau2]

red string n. 紅繩 [hung4 sing4]

remain a devoted couple to the end of life phr. 白髮齊眉 [baak9 faat8 chai4 mei4]

return to the bride's home 3rd day after the wedding v. 回門 [wui4 mun4]

roasted pig's head n. 燒豬頭 [siu1 jyu1 tau4]

send a present in return n. 回禮 [wui4 lai5]

serve tea to seniors v. 斟茶俾長輩 [jam1 cha4 bei2 jeung2 bui3]

set the bridal bed v. 安床 [on1 chong4]

sewing kit n. 針線包 [jam1 sin3 baau1]

son-in-law n. 女婿 [neui5 sai3]

unfixed rooster n. 生雞 [saang1 gai1]

wedding banquet n. 擺酒 [baai2 jau2]

wedding cake n. 禮餅 [lai5 beng2]

wedding candies n. 喜糖 [hei2 tong2]

wedding dried fruits n. 喜果 [hei2 gwo2]

wedding invitation n. 喜帖 [hei2 tip8]

wedding net n. 喜帳 [hei2 jeung3]

wedding night n. 洞房花燭夜 [dung6 fong4 fa1 juk7 ye6]

welcome the guest v. 迎賓 [ying4 ban1]

women with both sons and daughters n. 好命婆 [hou2 meng6 po2]

Childbirth and Baby Traditions

abacus n. 算盤 [syun3 pun4]

bellybutton n. 肚臍 [tou5 chi4]

childbirth n. 生仔 [saang1 jai2]

delivery room n. 產房 [chaan2 fong4]

finding godparents for babies v. 上契 [seung5 kai3]

grabbing test for one year old baby n. 抓周 [ja1 jau1]

intermittent headache n. 頭風 [tau4 fung1]

jade pendant n. 玉佩 [yuk9 pui3]

labor pains n. 陣痛 [jan6 tung3]

little bracelet for babies n. 手鈪仔 [sau2 ngaak2 jai2]

little foot bracelets for babies n. 腳鈪仔 [geuk8 ngaak2 jai2]

name a baby v. 改名 [goi2 meng2]

new mother confined to indoors the first month after childbirth n. 坐月 [cho2 yut2]

no hair washing in the first month after childbirth v. 坐月唔可以洗頭 [cho2 yut2 m4 ho2 yi5 sai2 tau4]

no shower in the first month after childbirth v. 坐月唔可以沖涼 [cho2 yut2 m4 ho2 yi5 chung1 leung4]

one month old banquet n. 滿月酒 [mun5 yut9 jau2]

red hardboiled egg n. 紅雞蛋 [hung4 gai1 daan6]

rituals to comfort the baby from crying n. 收驚 [sau1 ging1]

shave head for new babies v. 剃頭 [tai3 tau4]

two months old n. 雙滿月 [seung1 mun5 yut9]

vinegar ginger soup n. 薑醋 [geung1 chou3]

Birthday Traditions

Beijing opera n. 京劇 [ging1 kek9]

birthday banquet n. 壽宴 [sau6 yin3]

birthday cake n. 生日蛋糕 [saang1 yat9 daan6 gou1]

birthday song n. 生日歌 [saang1 yat9 go1]

God of Longevity n. 壽星公 [sau6 sing1 gung1]

wish longevity v. 祝壽 [juk7 sau6]

Religious Terms

religion 宗教 [jung1 gaau3]

Buddhism
佛教 [fat7 gaau3]

abode of the gods *n.* 天宮 [tin1 gung1]

Amitabha *n.* 阿彌陀佛 [o1 mei4 to4 fat7]

Avalokitesvara *n.* 觀音 [gun1 yam1]

Avalokitesvara with thousand arms and thousand eyes *n.* 千手觀音 [chin1 sau2 gun1 yam1]

Bodhisattva *n.* 菩薩 [pou4 saat8]

burn incense for the Buddha *v.* 裝香 [jong1 heung1]

eighteen layers of hells *n.* 十八 層地獄 [sap9 baat8 chang4 dei6 yuk9]

enter into meditation *v.* 入定 [yap9 ding6]

four guardians of the universe *n.* 四大天王 [sei3 daai6 tin1 wong4]

great mercy and great pity *n.* 大 慈大悲 [daai6 chi4 daai6 bei1]

Hinayana *n.* 小乘佛教 [siu2 sing4 fat7 gaau3]

immortals *n.* 天仙 [tin1 sin1]

inside this world *v.* 入世 [yap9 sai3]

kowtow *v.* 叩頭 [kau3 tau4]

Mahayana *n.* 大乘佛教 [daai6 sing4 fat7 gaau3]

outside of this world *v.* 出世 [cheut7 sai3]

pubic region *n.* 丹田 [daan1 tin4]

pure land *n.* 淨土 [jing6 tou2]

queen of heaven *n.* 天后 [tin1 hau6]

six patriarchs of the Zen school *n.* 六祖 [luk9 jou2]

Tiantai or Heavenly Terrace mountain *n.* 天台山 [tin1 toi4 saan1]

vira, a strong or mighty man *n.* 力士 [lik9 si6]

Western heaven *n.* 西天 [sai1 tin1]

wooden fish *n.* 木魚 [muk9 yu2]

Taoism
道教 [dou6 gaau3]

chi/life force *n.* 氣 [hei3]

Daodejing *n.* 道德經 [dou6 dak7 ging1]

fengshui *n.* 風水 [fung1 seui2]

fortune telling *v.* 算命 [syun3 meng6]

place where Taoist rituals are performed *n.* 道場 [dou6 cheung4]

practice divination *v.* 占卜 [jim1 buk7]

Taoist divination tool *n.* 八卦 [baat8 gwa3]

Taoist monk *n.* 道士 [dou6 si2]

Taoist temple *n.* 道觀 [dou6 gun3]

robe for Taoist monks *n.* 道袍 [dou6 pou4]

Wutai Mountain *n.* 五台山 [ng5 toi4 saan1]

yang (*the masculine or positive principle in nature*) *n.* 陽 [yeung4]

Yi-ching/Book of Changes *n.* 易經 [yik9 ging1]

yin (*the feminine or negative principle in nature*) *n.* 陰 [yam1]

Confucianism
儒家 [yu4 ga1]

Analects of Confucius *n.* 論語 [leun4 yu5]

benevolent governance *n.* 仁政 [yan4 jing3]

Book of Documents *n.* 尚書 [syu1 ging1]

Book of Rites *n.* 禮記 [lai5 gei3]

burning of books and burying of scholars *n.* 焚書坑儒 [fan4 syu1 haang1 yu4]

cardinal guides and constant virtues *n.* 綱常 [gong1 seung4]

Classic of Poetry *n.* 詩經 [si1 ging1]

Confucius *n.* 孔子 [hung2 ji2]

contention of a hundred schools of thought *n.* 百家爭鳴 [baak8 ga1 jang1 ming4]

divine rights *n.* 君權神授 [gwan1 kyun4 san4 sau6]

Doctrine of the Mean *n.* 中庸 [jung1 yung4]

fathers behave paternally *v.* 父父 [fu6 fu6]

feudal princes *n.* 諸侯 [jyu1 hau4]

Five Classics *n.* 五經 [ng5 ging1]

Four Books *n.* 四書 [sei3 syu1]

Great Learning *n.* 大學 [daai6 hok9]

human desire *n.* 人慾 [yan4 yuk9]

human relations *n.* 人倫 [yan4 leun4]

kings behave royally *n.* 君君 [gwan1 gwan1]

Mencius *n.* 孟子 [maang6 ji2]

moral principles *n.* 倫理 [leun4 lei5]

old-style private school *n.* 私塾 [si1 suk9]

Period of Warring States *n.* 戰國 [jin3 gwok8]

show filial respect to 孝敬 [haau3 ging3]

Spring and Autumn Annals *n.* 春秋 [cheun1 chau1]

Spring and Autumn Period *n.* 春秋 [cheun1 chau1]

sons behave filially *v.* 子子 [ji2 ji2]

subjects behave loyally *v.* 臣臣 [san4 san4]

Xunzi *n.* 荀子 [seun1 ji2]

Zhou Li (*a classical book in ancient China*) *n.* 周禮 [jau1 lai5]

Miscellaneous Terms

bad luck *n.* 衰運 [seui1 wan6]

Cantonese opera *n.* 粵劇 [yut9 kek9]

complicated Chinese *n.* 繁體字 [faan4 tai2 ji6]

classical-style of Chinese writing *n.* 文言文 [man4 yin4 man2]

Danone *n.* 達能 [daat9 nang4]

double-decker bus *n.* 雙層巴士 [seung1 chang4 ba1 si2]

Evian *n.* 依雲 [yi1 wan4]

God of Door *n.* 門神 [mun4 san4]

God of Kitchen *n.* 灶君 [jou3 gwan1]

good luck *n.* 好彩 [hou2 choi2]

Huangmei drama *n.* 黃梅調 [wong4 mui4 diu6]

ink stone *n.* 墨硯 [mak9 yin6]

KFC *n.* 肯德基 [hang2 dak7 gei1]

luck *n.* 彩頭 [choi2 tau4]

lucky star *n.* 福星 [fuk7 sing1]

May 4th Movement *n.* 五四運動 [ng5 sei3 wan6 dung6]

McDonalds *(fast-food restaurant)* *n.* 麥當勞 [mak9 dong1 lou4]

Ming and Qing dynasty novels *n.* 明清小說 [ming4 ching1 siu2 syut3]

mini-bus *n.* 小巴 [siu2 ba1]

Nestle *n.* 雀巢 [jeuk8 chaau4]

Octopus card *n.* 八達通 [baat8 daat9 tung1]

open a business *v.* 開張 [hoi1 jeung1]

open after a cessation of business *v.* 開市 [hoi1 si5]

Tang Dynasty poetry *n.* 唐詩 [tong4 si1]

Seven Eleven *(convenience store)* *n.* 七十一便利店 [chat7 sap9 yat7 bin6 lei6 dim3]

shadow play *n.* 皮影戲 [pei4 ying2 hei3]

simplified Chinese *n.* 簡體字 [gaan2 tai2 ji6]

Song dynasty poetry *n.* 宋詞 [sung3 chi4]

walking on stilts *v.* 踩高蹺 [chaai2 gou1 kiu3]

Watsons *n.* 屈臣氏 [wat7 san4 si2]

Also available from Hippocrene Books

Cantonese-English/English-Cantonese Dictionary & Phrasebook
This convenient dictionary & phrasebook provides travelers to south
China with the tools they need to communicate effectively in Cantonese.
Includes:

- · 4,000 entries
- · Intuitive phonetic system and written Cantonese characters
- · Essential phrases for travelers
- · Concise grammar and pronunciation section

ISBN 978-0-7818-1279-5 · $13.95 pb

Other Chinese-interest titles

DICTIONARIES & LANGUAGE GUIDES

Beginner's Chinese with 2 Audio CDs, Second Edition
ISBN 978-0-7818-1257-3 · $32.00 pb

Intermediate Chinese with Audio CD, Second Edition
ISBN 978-0-7818-1311-2 · $29.95 pb

Chinese through Tone and Color
*A Unique Visual Method for Learning over 100 Basic Chinese
Characters*
2 Audio CDs · ISBN 978-0-7818-1204-7 · $24.95 pb

Hippocrene Children's Illustrated Chinese (Mandarin) Dictionary
ISBN 978-0-7818-0848-4 · $14.95 pb

**Chinese-English/English-Chinese Dictionary & Phrasebook
(Mandarin)**
4,000 entries · ISBN 0-7818-1135-X · $13.95 pb

Chinese-English/English-Chinese Pocket Legal Dictionary
ISBN 0-7818-1215-1 · $19.95 pb

Chinese-English/English-Chinese Practical Dictionary
15,000 entries · ISBN 978-0-7818-1236-8· $19.95 pb

Emergency Chinese Phrasebook
200 entries · ISBN 0-7818-0975-4 · $5.95 pb

Fujiannese-English/English-Fujianese Dictionary & Phrasebook
4,000 entries · ISBN 978-0-7818-1313-6 · $14.95 pb

Shanghainese-English/English-Shanghainese Dictionary & Phrasebook
4,000 entries · ISBN 978-0-7818-1261-0 · $13.95 pb

COOKBOOKS

COOKING FROM CHINA'S FUJIAN PROVINCE
Dr. Jacqueline M. Newman

"Through her insightful writing and well-researched recipes, Newman is casting much-deserved light on the wonderful cooking culture of Fujian province. Her scholarly approach and keen eye for details make this book a joy to read and a real keeper for any library and kitchen."
—**Martin Yan**, host of "Yan Can Cook,"
cookbook author and restaurateur

Fujian, a province in South-Eastern China, boasts a distinct culinary tradition that enjoys a thousand year-old recorded history but is barely known in the Western world. This collection of 200 easy to follow, authentic recipes provides the perfect introduction to this unique cuisine.

258 pages · ISBN: 978-0-7818-1183-5 · $29.95 hc

Other Asian Languages

LANGUAGE GUIDES

Cambodian-English/English-Cambodian Standard Dictionary
15,000 entries· ISBN: 0-87052-818-1 · $19.95 pb

Khmer-English/English-Khmer (Cambodian) Dictionary and Phrasebook
4,500 entries · ISBN: 978-0-7818-1318-1 · $14.95 pb

English-Ilocano Dictionary & Phrasebook
7,000 entries · ISBN: 0-7818-0642-9 · $16.95 pb

Modern Indonesian-English/English-Modern Indonesian Practical Dictionary
20,000 entries · ISBN: 978-0-7818-1235-1 · $19.95 pb

Speak Standard Indonesian
283 pages · ISBN: 0-7818-0186-9 · $11.95 pb

Japanese-English/English-Japanese Concise Dictionary, *Romanized*
8,000 entries · ISBN: 0-7818-0162-1 · $11.95 pb

Beginner's Japanese with 2 Audio CDs, Second Edition
ISBN: 978-0-7818-1327-3 · $32.00 pb

Korean-English/English Korean Standard Dictionary
20,000 entries · ISBN: 978-0-7818-1234-4 · $24.95 pb

Korean-English/English Korean Practical Dictionary
8,500 entries· ISBN: 0-87052-092-X · $19.95 pb

Korean-English/English-Korean Dictionary & Phrasebook
5,000 entries · ISBN: 0-7818-1029-9 · $14.95 pb

Lao-English/English-Lao Dictionary and Phrasebook
2,500 entries · ISBN: 0-7818-0858-8 · $12.95 pb

Pilipino-English/English-Pilipino (Tagalog) Concise Dictionary
5,000 entries · ISBN: 0-8705-2491-7 · $12.95 pb

Pilipino-English/English-Pilipino (Tagalog) Dictionary & Phrasebook
2,200 entries · ISBN: 0-7818-0451-5 · $11.95 pb

Tagalog-English/English-Tagalog (Pilipino) Standard Dictionary
Revised and Expanded Edition
20,000 entries · ISBN: 0-7818-0960-6 · $32.00 pb

Thai-English/English-Thai Dictionary & Phrasebook,
Revised Edition
2,500 entries · ISBN: 978-0-7818-1285-6 · $13.95 pb

Beginner's Vietnamese with 2 Audio CDs
262 pages · ISBN: 978-0-7818-1265-8 · $29.95 pb

Vietnamese-English/English-Vietnamese Practical Dictionary
15,000 entries · ISBN: 978-0-7818-1244-3 · $19.95 pb

Vietnamese-English/English-Vietnamese Dictionary & Phrasebook
3,000 entries · ISBN: 978-0-7818-0991-7 · $14.95 pb

Vietnamese Children's Picture Dictionary
625 entries · ISBN: 0-7818-1133-3 · $14.95 pb

Prices subject to change without prior notice. **To purchase Hippocrene Books**
contact your local bookstore, visit www.hippocrenebooks.com, call (212) 685-4373, or write to: HIPPOCRENE BOOKS, 171 Madison Avenue, New York, NY 10016.